eBook and Digital Learning Tools

for

By the People

Fourth Edition

JAMES A. MORONE
ROGAN KERSH

Carefully scratch off the silver coating with a coin to see your personal redemption code.

This code can be used only once and cannot be shared!

If the code has been scratched off when you receive it, the code may not be valid. Once the code has been scratched off, this access card cannot be returned to the publisher. You may buy access at **www.oup.com/us/morone**.

The code on this card is valid for 2 years from the date of first purchase. Complete terms and conditions are available at **https://oup-arc.com**.

Access length: 6 months from redemption of the code.

OXFORD
UNIVERSITY PRESS

P9-AGX-460

Directions for accessing your **eBook and Digital Learning Tools**

VIA THE OUP SITE

Visit **www.oup.com/us/morone**

⬇

Select the edition you are using and the student resources for that edition.

⬇

Click the link to upgrade your access to the student resources.

⬇

Follow the on-screen instructions.

⬇

Enter your personal redemption code when prompted on the checkout screen.

VIA YOUR SCHOOL'S LEARNING MANAGEMENT SYSTEM

Log in to your instructor's course.

⬇

When you click a link to a protected resource, you will be prompted to register for access.

⬇

Follow the on-screen instructions.

⬇

Enter your personal redemption code when prompted on the checkout screen.

For assistance with code redemption or registration, please contact customer support at **arc.support@oup.com**.

BY THE PEOPLE

DEBATING AMERICAN GOVERNMENT

BY THE PEOPLE

DEBATING AMERICAN GOVERNMENT | **FOURTH EDITION**

JAMES A. MORONE
Brown University

ROGAN KERSH
Wake Forest University

NEW YORK | OXFORD
OXFORD UNIVERSITY PRESS

Oxford University Press is a department of the University of Oxford. It furthers the University's objective of excellence in research, scholarship, and education by publishing worldwide. Oxford is a registered trade mark of Oxford University Press in the UK and certain other countries.

Published in the United States of America by Oxford University Press
198 Madison Avenue, New York, NY 10016, United States of America.

For titles covered by Section 112 of the US Higher Education Opportunity Act, please visit www.oup.com/us/he for the latest information about pricing and alternate formats.

Library of Congress Cataloging-in-Publication Data

Names: Morone, James A., 1951- author. | Kersh, Rogan, author.
Title: By the people: debating American government / James A. Morone, Brown
   University, Rogan Kersh, Wake Forest University.
Description: Fourth Edition. | New York: Oxford University Press, [2018] |
   Includes bibliographical references and index.
Identifiers: LCCN 2018049760 (print) | LCCN 2018050653 (ebook) | ISBN
   9780190928629 (ebook) | ISBN 9780190928711 (Paperback) | ISBN
   9780190928636 (Looseleaf)
Subjects: LCSH: United States—Politics and government—Textbooks. |
   United States. Constitution.
Classification: LCC JK276 (ebook) | LCC JK276 .M67 2019 (print) |
   DDC 320.473—dc23
LC record available at https://lccn.loc.gov/2018049760

9 8 7 6 5 4 3 2 1
Printed by LSC Communications, United States of America

Many teachers and colleagues inspired us. We dedicate this book to four who changed our lives. Their passion for learning and teaching set the standard we aim for every day—and on every page that follows.

Richard O'Donnell

Murray Dry

Jim Barefield

Rogers Smith

By the People comes from the Gettysburg Address. Standing on the battlefield at Gettysburg, President Abraham Lincoln delivered what may be the most memorable presidential address in American history—defining American government as a government "of the people, by the people, for the people." Here is the full address.

Four score and seven years ago our fathers brought forth on this continent, a new nation, conceived in liberty, and dedicated to the proposition that all men are created equal.

Now we are engaged in a great civil war, testing whether that nation, or any nation so conceived and so dedicated, can long endure. We are met on a great battle-field of that war. We have come to dedicate a portion of that field, as a final resting place for those who here gave their lives that that nation might live. It is altogether fitting and proper that we should do this.

But, in a larger sense, we can not dedicate—we can not consecrate—we can not hallow—this ground. The brave men, living and dead, who struggled here, have consecrated it, far above our poor power to add or detract. The world will little note, nor long remember what we say here, but it can never forget what they did here. It is for us the living, rather, to be dedicated here to the unfinished work which they who fought here have thus far so nobly advanced. It is rather for us to be here dedicated to the great task remaining before us—that from these honored dead we take increased devotion to that cause for which they gave the last full measure of devotion—that we here highly resolve that these dead shall not have died in vain—that this nation, under God, shall have a new birth of freedom—and that government of the people, by the people, for the people, shall not perish from the earth.

Brief Contents

Contents

About the Authors

JAMES MORONE (BA, Middlebury College, MA and PhD, University of Chicago) is the John Hazen White Professor of Political Science and Public Policy at Brown University and five-time winner of the Hazeltine Citation for outstanding teacher of the year. Dr. Morone, an award-winning author, has published ten books, including *The Heart of Power* (2009, a "New York Times Notable Book"), *Hellfire Nation* (2003, nominated for a Pulitzer Prize), and *The Democratic Wish* (1990, winner of the American Political Science Association's Kammerer Award for the best book on American politics). He has written over 150 articles and essays, and has commented on politics in the *New York Times*, the *London Review of Books*, and the *American Prospect*. Dr. Morone has been elected to the National Academy of Medicine and the National Academy of Social Insurance. He has served as president of the politics and history section of the American Political Science Association and the New England Political Science Association. He also has served on the board of editors for eight scholarly journals.

ROGAN KERSH (BA, Wake Forest University, MA and PhD, Yale University) is provost and professor of political science at Wake Forest University. A leading scholar in American political science, Dr. Kersh is best known for his work on health reform, obesity politics, and interest groups/lobbying. As a political science faculty member at Syracuse from 1996 to 2006, he won three different teaching awards; from 2006 to 2012, as associate dean of New York University's Wagner School of Public Service, he won both the Wagner and NYU's teaching awards, as well as the Martin Luther King, Jr. Award for scholarship, teaching, and university service. Dr. Kersh has published two books and more than 50 academic articles and has provided commentary on U.S. politics for dozens of different media outlets including CNN, *Newsweek*, and the *New York Times*. He was president of the American Political Science Association's organized section on health politics and policy in 2011–2012 and is an elected fellow of the National Academy of Public Administration.

Preface

At first, they came in small numbers: one child, two children, a few huddled together. Then a surge: In the spring and summer of 2014, more than 63,000 unaccompanied minors crossed the Mexican border into the United States. The exhausted children—mostly from Honduras, Guatemala, and El Salvador—faced poverty and violence at home. Their exodus was a humanitarian tragedy. But it was also a political problem.

Conservative critics of the Barack Obama administration slammed the White House for not acting sooner to stem the tide and for being "soft on immigration." Donald Trump launched his long-shot presidential bid, a year later, with a tough attack on undocumented migrants. From the left, another set of voices condemned the president for not providing services to children whose families were so desperate they would send them alone across dangerous ground to an uncertain destiny. Whatever course the administration took, it faced angry rebukes.

As partisans traded insults and pundits criticized the government's mistakes, something remarkable happened: Americans of all backgrounds—urban and rural, churched and secular, liberal and conservative—came together to help the children. College students and local residents joined to hand out medical kits and food packets. Lawyers flew in to offer free legal assistance in securing asylum. Church leaders created makeshift shelters and organized short-term housing among the congregants. One bishop in San Antonio, Texas, said the crisis had deepened his prayer life. This is a classic story that runs right through American history: People pull together in the face of troubled times.

Help or Clash?

That's the United States in a nutshell. People pitch in. This is a nation of joiners and helpers and activists. It always has been. Visitors in the nineteenth century were astonished by the nation's civic spirit. To this day Americans form book groups, organize car washes to raise money for good causes, stack sandbags during floods, send checks to the Red Cross, support the military, and insist that the government help those who need help. "We are inevitably our brother's keeper because we are our brother's brother," wrote Martin Luther King. "Whatever affects one directly affects all indirectly."[1]

But that's only one side of the story. Stream a news show and what do you see? Fights! A few years ago, one of us (Jim) was about to go on a news show to discuss the fallout after singer Janet Jackson inadvertently (and very briefly) went X-rated during the Super Bowl halftime show. Jim was scheduled alongside another commentator who was very agitated about Jackson's behavior and believed that it signaled the decline of America. Jim told the producer that, after exploring our different views, it would be great if we could find some common ground. No way, retorted the producer, who explained her ideal closing shot: You'll be shouting over each other on a split screen while the host coolly ends the segment by saying, "We'll have to leave it there for now, but feelings run high and we'll be hearing a lot more on this topic." Unfortunately, searching for common ground does not draw an audience like people screaming onscreen.

The producer was demonstrating another side of America: rugged individualists who push their own views and self-interests. Individualism is also an all-American story. Its origins lie in a frontier culture that expected everyone to watch out for themselves. This is the America that resents anyone—especially the government—telling people what to do.

Which is the real America? They both are. Sometimes this is a land of cooperation, sometimes a nation of competition. American politics, as you will see, reflects both views.

By the People?

We picked the book's title—*By the People*—because Lincoln's phrase raises the deepest question in American politics: Who has the power? Or to put it more pointedly, do the people rule in this day and age? Democracy is a constant struggle; it is an aspiration, a wish, a quest. In every chapter we'll ask how well Americans are living up to Lincoln's ideal. Does the new media (Chapter 9) or the contemporary Congress (Chapter 13) or the bureaucracy (Chapter 15) or state government (Chapter 4) support or subvert government by the people? We'll present the details—and let you decide whether we should press for reform or leave things alone.

We'll be straight with you: We won't pretend there was a golden age in some imaginary past. After all, the United States has been home to political machines that enthusiastically stole votes, maintains an Electoral College designed to distort the people's vote for president, and governs through an elaborate system of checks and balances that blunts the popular will. (Again, you'll soon see two sides to each of these features of American government.) At the same time, you'll read about bold popular movements and unexpected electoral surges that changed the face of the nation. In many ways, these are the most exciting moments in American history. They spring up at unexpected times, inspiring ordinary people to achieve great things. Does Donald Trump's election signify such a surge? Or are

---

[1] *Where Do We Go from Here: Chaos or Community?* (New York: Harper & Row, 1967) 181.

the protest movements that have sprung up the larger agent of change? Read on and you'll be able to answer those questions—and many more.

Who Are We?

Here's Jim's very first political memory: My parents were watching TV, and as soon as I walked into the room I could see that my mother was trying hard not to cry. "What's going on?" I asked my parents nervously. My dad—a proud Republican who had fought in World War II—said, "Well, the U.S. had a racial problem, but that man there, he's going to get us past it." "That man there" was Martin Luther King Jr., giving one of the most famous speeches in American history: "I have a dream," said King, that "my four little children will one day live in a country where they will not be judged by the color of their skin but by the content of their character." My mother had been born in Poland and her near tears reflected pride in her new nation—and the uplifting aspirations of that August day.

Both of us grew up thinking about the dream—and about the nation that dreams it. America is constantly changing, constantly new. In every chapter we'll ask the same question: Who are we? We'll explore a lot of different answers.

Four themes are especially important in this book. **Race** touches everything in the United States, from the Constitution (Chapter 3) to our political parties (Chapter 11). The nation rose up out of both freedom and slavery; race quickly became one of the great crucibles of American liberty. Likewise, **immigration** includes some of history's saddest passages involving the mistreatment of recent arrivals. And yet we are a nation of immigrants that continues to welcome the world's "huddled masses yearning to breathe free"—the famous words long associated with the Statue of Liberty. More than a fifth of all the emigrants around the globe come to the United States every year. Race and immigration are tied up in another powerful topic: **gender and sexuality**. From women in Congress to same-sex marriage, from teen pregnancy to abortion, we'll show how negotiating an answer to "Who are we?" always puts an emphasis on questions of gender and sexuality. Finally, we're especially interested in **American generations**, and more specifically the attitudes and contributions of today's young people, the millennial generation. If you're one of them, the future belongs to you. This book is an owner's manual for the government that you're going to inherit. We'll have much to say about you as we go along.

The most important thing about all these categories is not their history, or the ways they've influenced voting behavior, or how the courts treat them—although we'll cover all those topics. Rather, what matters most about American politics are the opportunities to get involved. As you'll see, groups and individuals can and do make a difference in a nation that is always evolving. We hope our book inspires you to actively participate in making the American future.

How Government Works

We won't oversell the role of individuals. People's ability to advance political change is always shaped by the way the government is organized and operates. From the very start, this book emphasizes the unusual structure of American government.

Begin with a Constitution full of checks and balances, add a multilayered federalism, develop a chaotic public administration (President Franklin Roosevelt cheerfully called the uproar a three-ring circus), spin off functions to the private sector (especially during wars), complexify Congress (thirty-one different committees and subcommittees tried to claim jurisdiction over just one national health insurance proposal), and inject state and federal courts into every cranny of the system. Then throw the entire apparatus open to any interest group that shows up. The twenty-first century adds a 24/7 news cycle with commentary all the time and from every angle.

Turn to foreign policy, where high principles contend with tough-minded realism in a fractious world. When the most formidable military in human history is mustered into action, watch presidential power expand so rapidly that it sets off international debates about whether the great republic is morphing into an empire.

In Short

As you read this book, you'll repeatedly encounter four questions:

- *Who governs?* This is the question of democracy and power—or, as we phrased it earlier: Is this government by the people? And if and where it falls short, how might we refresh our democracy?
- *How does American politics work?* Our job is to make you think like a political scientist. What does that involve? You'll learn in the next chapter—and throughout the book.
- *What does government do?* You can't answer the first two questions if you don't know what the courts or the White House or Congress or interest groups actually do—and how they do it.
- *Who are we?* Americans endlessly debate America's identity. We are students, businesspeople, Hispanics, seniors, Texans, environmentalists, gays, Republicans, Democrats, Christians, Muslims, military families—and the list goes on. Sometimes it adds up to one united people; at other times we're left to wonder how to get along. Either way, American politics rises up from—and shapes—a cacophony of identities and interests.

Changes to the Fourth Edition

In this new edition, we have,

- Analyzed recent seismic events, especially involving the Trump administration, that have shaken up U.S. institutions, ideas, and interests.
- Supplied new and updated statistics and figures in each chapter, tracking both long- and short-run political trends.
- Analyzed the mixed results of the 2018 midterm elections.
- Traced the erosion of civil discourse and expanding polarization within American society, made manifest in moments such as the controversial Supreme Court nomination of Justice Brett Kavanaugh and related #metoo movement.
- Directly encouraged readers to plunge into the great pageant of American government, in part through posing queries inviting them to take a side on vital issues.
- Tackled the issue of "fake news" and related charges of media bias.

- Included a new section to cover the rights of non-citizens in the United States and updated immigration coverage.

- Provided students with the background needed to understand contentious policies surrounding trade wars, free trade, and trade agreements.

- Called attention to the important role of the federal bureaucracy in under-served, rural areas in a new chapter opening vignette.

- Added a new evaluation of how federalism has evolved during the Obama and Trump administrations.

- Expanded coverage of the LGBTQ civil rights movement.

- Added a new What Do YOU Think? about appointing bureaucrats to address the issue and concern regarding a "deep state."

- Incorporated updated data on millennial trends regarding party affiliation, attitudes, and changing styles of participation.

- Revised By the Numbers features to focus on a theme within the chapter and ask a fundamental question related to that theme.

- Updated infodata features so that the first question always asks students to quantitatively analyze the visual and the second question asks students to apply that information to consider a related issue.

- Systematically balanced examples from left and right, to take into account new political sensitivities in our highly partisan age.

Getting Involved

By the People is a new approach to courses in American government. The book displays U.S. politics and government in all its glory, messiness, and power. Like every textbook, this one informs our readers. But, as we hope you can already see, we don't describe government (or ideas about government) as inert and fixed. What's exciting about American politics, like the nation itself, is how fast it changes. And the constant, endless arguments about what it is and what it should be next. Our aim is to get you engaged—whether you already love politics, are a complete newcomer to government, or whether you are a newcomer to the United States itself. In the pages that follow, we'll bring American government to life. Get ready to start a great debate . . . about your future.

One final word: We've been working out the story line for this book throughout our teaching careers. We've taught everything from very large lectures to small seminars. Like all teachers, we've learned through trial and error. We've worked hard to pack this book with the stories, questions, and features that all our students have found effective. That spirit—the lessons we've learned in the classroom—animates everything that follows.

Teaching and Learning Support

Oxford University Press (OUP) offers instructors and students a comprehensive teaching and learning package of support materials for adopters of ***By the People, 4e.***

Ancillary Resource Center

The Ancillary Resource Center (ARC) at www.oup.com/us/Morone is a convenient destination for all teaching and learning resources that accompany this book. Accessed online through individual user accounts, the ARC provides instructors with up-to-date ancillaries while guaranteeing the security of grade-significant resources. In addition, it allows OUP to keep users informed when new content becomes available. The ARC for *By the People: Debating American Government, 4e* contains a variety of materials to aid in teaching:

- **Instructor's Resource Manual with Test Item File**—The Instructor's Resource Manual includes chapter objectives, detailed chapter outlines, lecture suggestions and activities, discussion questions, video resources, and web resources. The Test Item File includes more than 2,500 test questions including multiple-choice, short-answer, and essay questions.
- **Computerized Test Bank**—The computerized test bank that accompanies this text is designed for both novice and advanced users. It enables instructors to create and edit questions, create randomized quizzes and tests with an easy-to-use drag-and-drop tool, publish quizzes and tests to online courses, and print quizzes and tests for paper-based assessments.
- **PowerPoint-Based Slides**—Each chapter has two slide decks to support your lectures. One deck includes the chapter outline and content; the other includes only the artwork included in the text.
- **CNN and other video resources**—Offering recent clips on timely topics, clips are approximately 5 to 10 minutes in length providing a great way to launch your lectures about key concepts with real-world issues and examples.

Digital Learning Tools

www.oup.com/us/Morone

By the People: Debating American Government, 4e comes with an extensive array of digital learning tools to ensure your students get the most out of your course. Approximately 45 homework assignments—totaling over 12 hours of assignable materials—organized by chapter, with autograded assessments have been developed exclusively to support OUP's ***By the People*** text. These activities have been extensively reviewed by users of similar digital content in their classrooms. Several assignment types provide your students with various activities that teach core concepts, allow students to develop data literacy around important contemporary topics and issues, and to role play as decision makers to engage with problems that simulate real-world political challenges. The activities are optimized to work on any mobile device or computer. For users of learning management systems, results can be recorded to the gradebooks in one of several currently supported systems. Access to these activities are provided free with purchase of a new print or electronic textbook. These and additional study tools are available at www.oup.com/us/Morone, through links embedded in the enhanced eBook, and within course cartridges. Each activity is described below:

Interactive Media Activities are simulations of real-world events, problems, and challenges developed to connect text and classroom topics to everyday life. Designed to be assigned as homework, each activity takes approximately 15 to 20 minutes to complete and produces unique results for each student. Students are placed into the role of a political actor or decision maker, get to experience how various aspects of politics works, and see the trade-offs required to produce meaningful policies and outcomes. Topics include the following:

- *Individualism versus Solidarity*
- *Passing Immigration Reform*
- *Electing Cheryl Martin*
- *Building the USS Relief*
- *Intervening in Bhutan*
- *The Fight Against Warrantless Wiretapping*
- *Balancing the Budget*
- *Redistricting in "Texachusetts"*
- *Saving the Electric Car*
- *Election Reform*
- *Fact Checking the Media*

- *Passing the Thirteenth Amendment*
- *Negotiating with China*
- *NEW—Healthcare and Federalism*
- *NEW—The Changing Face of Affirmative Action*
- *NEW—Surveys, Bias, and Fake News*
- *NEW—Free Speech on Campus*
- *NEW—The People Versus the Pipeline*

Media Tutorials: These animated videos are designed to teach key concepts taught in the course, as well as address important contemporary issues. Each tutorial runs 2 to 4 minutes in length and ends with an assessment for students to test what they know. Topics include the following:

- *The Constitution: A Brief Tour*
- *Civil Rights: How Does the Fourteenth Amendment Ensure Equal Rights for All Citizens?*
- *Federalism: What Does It Mean to Incorporate the Bill of Rights?*
- *Political Participation: What Affects Voter Turnout?*
- *Media: How Is the News Shaped by Agenda Setting, Framing, and Profit Bias?*
- *Interest Groups: What Is a Political Action Committee (PAC), and What Makes Some PACs Super PACs?*
- *Congress: Why Do We Hate Congress but Keep Electing the Same Representatives?*

- *The Judiciary: How Do Judges Interpret the Constitution?*
- *Polling: How Do We Know What People Know?*
- *Campaigns and Elections: How Does Gerrymandering Work?*
- *NEW—Democracy Versus Republic*
- *NEW—Freedom of Religion*
- *NEW—Executive Orders*
- *NEW—Political Culture Across States*
- *NEW—Party Organization*
- *NEW—Bureaucracies*
- *NEW—Discretionary and Mandatory Spending*

***NEW* Issue Navigators:** These *new* features offer students an interactive way to explore data related to major issues in American politics today, and allow students to reflect on the sources of their own views and opinions. Each activity will improve your students' abilities to think through their political opinions by using compelling and vetted information to raise the level of classroom debate. Students will analyze several data sources and positions for each topic. They'll then get to answer questions that indicate their own beliefs and values on these issues, and compare them to national polling data. The exercises include assessments around the data to ensure students can interpret the data presented and understand what it means. Issues include the following:

- *Climate Change*
- *Immigration*
- *Gerrymandering/Redistricting*
- *Gun Control*
- *Free Trade and Tariffs*
- *Healthcare Reform*
- *Social Security*
- *Tax Reform*

Enhanced eBook: The enhanced eBook provides students with a versatile, accessible, online version of the textbook, with all of the above resources integrated on the appropriate pages via clickable icons that connect to each study tool. The eBook reader also provides functionality that will help students be more effective in their study time—for instance, bookmarking, highlighting, note taking, and search tools. Every new copy of the print text includes access to the eBook. The eBook is also available for separate purchase, either online or through campus bookstores.

Online Study Tools: Many additional online study tools are available at www.oup.com/us/Morone for the student's self-paced learning and assessment. For each chapter, these include interactive flashcards, chapter review PowerPoint slides, key term quizzes, chapter quizzes, chapter exams, short-answer essay tests, videos, web activities, and web links.

Learning Management System Integration: OUP offers the ability to integrate OUP content into currently supported versions of Canvas, D2L, or Blackboard. Contact your local rep or visit oup-arc.com/integration for more information.

Format Choices

Oxford University Press offers cost-saving alternatives to meet the needs of all students. This text is offered in a loose-leaf format at a 30 percent discount off the list price of the text; and in an eBook format, through Redshelf for a 50 percent discount. You also can customize our textbooks to create the course material you want for your class. For more information, please contact your Oxford University Press representative, call 800.280.0280, or visit us online at www.oup.com/us/Morone.

Packaging Options

Adopters of *By the People* can package *any* Oxford University Press book with the text for a 20 percent savings off the total package price. See our many trade and scholarly offerings at www.oup.com, then contact your local OUP sales representative to request a package ISBN. Below are additional suggestions to package with the text:

STAY CURRENT

For an additional $10, package Emenaker and Morone's *Current Debates in American Government*, Second Edition!

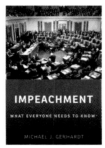

GET SPECIALIZED

Package with a *What Everyone Needs to Know* paperback **for only $5!** Written by leading experts, each volume in this acclaimed series offers a balanced and authoritative primer on complex issues and countries.

WRITE AND RESEARCH BETTER

Package with *Writing in Political Science* **for only $5** or *Research and Writing Guide for Political Science* for free!

KNOW YOUR RIGHTS

Package with *The United States Constitution: What It Says, What It Means* **for free!**

BECOME AN EXPERT IN NO TIME

Package one of Oxford's *Very Short Introductions* **for free!**

 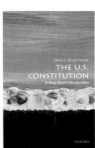

Acknowledgments

One particular goal we had with this edition was to ensure that our presentation of this subject was as balanced and unbiased as possible, given the political climate today. In order to achieve this, we sought the council and advice of David C. W. Parker from Montana State University. His expertise on Congress, and especially the Conservative Republican agenda, both before and after Trump was elected, helped us to present and celebrate the multiplicity of political perspectives in U.S. politics today. David read every word, and saved us from errors of fact and judgment alike. We are very thankful for his contributions which were thoughtful and considerable and which made the book all the better.

When he signed us up to write this book, publisher John Challice looked us each in the eye and said, "You know, this is going to be so much work—you're going to be married to us." He was right. Yes, it was a lot of work. And yes, the Oxford team has been like a family that carried us through the process.

There would be no book without Jennifer Carpenter, our extraordinary editor. She guided us through the process with enormous skill. Along the way, Jen earned the highest praise authors can give their editor: She cared about the book as much as we did. Our development editor, Naomi Friedman, helped us so much she ought to be considered a coauthor—she suggested, edited, cut, and cheered. Development manager Thom Holmes gracefully turned our messy manuscript into a tight narrative bursting with special features. Assistant editor Alison Ball guided the art program and tracked down every picture in the following pages. Senior production editor Barbara Mathieu and production manager Phil Scott coordinated an amazing production process; we broke the publishing record for the number of times two authors wrote, "Good point!" in the margins of an edited manuscript. Judy Ann Levine did a fine copy edit on an impossible schedule. Art director Michele Laseau did the beautiful design. We are especially grateful to marketing manager Tony Mathias for getting this book into your hands. To all of you in our immediate Oxford family: Thank you! Thank you!

We had an even more important team at our side—our families and our friends. Over the course of this book's initial conception and subsequent writing, Rogan moved from Syracuse University's Maxwell School to New York University's Wagner School, with a sabbatical leave at Yale along the way—and then, just as we were finishing the first edition, to Wake Forest University. Colleagues in all four places were unfailingly generous with ideas and comments; thanks especially to Suzanne Mettler, Jeff Stonecash, David Mayhew, Ellen Schall, Shanna Rose, and Shankar Prasad. Because we strive throughout to get both the political science and the practical politics right, a group of experienced and reflective inside-the-Beltway friends cheerfully and patiently provided insight into their world: Bill Antholis, Matt Bennett, Laura Schiller, Erik Fatemi, Tom Dobbins, Dan Maffei, Bob Shrum, Marylouise Oates, and Don and Darrel Jodrey. Grateful thanks to them as well as a wonderful set of current and former students, many now working in government and politics.

By the People's long journey to completion grew infinitely more enjoyable once Sara Pesek joined me for the trip—through this book and everywhere else, from Australia to Ze Café in midtown New York City. Sara's insights into public policy made for the liveliest newlyweds' conversations (if you're a politics junkie) imaginable; my biggest bouquet of thanks to her for that rarest of gifts: loving, fully joined partnership.

Jim offers warm thanks to my colleagues at Brown who form a wonderful community of scholars and teachers—always ready for coffee, lunch, or wine and a conversation about political science. Extra thanks to Peter Andreas, Mark Blyth, Corey Brettschneider, Ross Cheit, Elisabeth Fauquert, Alex Gourevitch, Rebecca Henderson, Bonnie Honig, Sharon Krause, Rick Locke, Susan Moffitt, Rich Snyder, Wendy Schiller, and Ashu Varshney. And my wonderful students sampled every idea in this book. They are my constant teachers. Grateful thanks to Ryan Emenaker, Dan Carrigg, Kevin McGravey, Ferris Lupino, Rachel Meade, Meghan Wilson, Aaron Weinstein, Brandon Welch, and Cadence Willse.

My brothers, Joe and Peter Morone—and their families—are lifelong companions always ready with a cheerful take on the state of politics and the world. Special thanks to Lindsay, Ann, Joe, James (now a rising political scientist at Penn), Noreen, and Maegan Morone. My mother, Stasia, kept reminding me to enjoy the journey—and that there might be more to life than *By the People*. And the memory of my dad was a constant visitor as I read, and thought, and wrote. The revisions for this edition were joyfully interrupted by Jim's wedding. If you detect a smile between the lines, it's because we were celebrating my new family. Rebecca Henderson leapt into my life filling it with talk and ideas and dreams (and much more). And Harry, my wonderful son, takes me hiking and talks me through high ridges that I couldn't imagine trying without him. If this edition reads happier than the last—it's the spirit of Harry and Rebecca on the pages.

Manuscript Reviewers

We have greatly benefited from the perceptive comments and suggestions of the many talented scholars and instructors who reviewed the manuscript of *By the People*. They went far beyond the call of duty in sharing thoughts and making corrections. Their insight and suggestions contributed immensely to the work.

Fourth Edition

Matthew Eshbaugh-Soha,
University of North Texas

Andra Gillespie,
Emory University

Lawrence L. Giventer,
California State University Stanislaus

Robert Porter,
Ventura College

Eric Schwartz,
Hagerstown Community College

Third Edition

Bryan T. Calvin
Tarrant County College, Northwest

John Carnes
Lone Star College–Kingwood

Rosalind Blanco Cook
Tulane University

Paul B. Davis
Truckee Meadows Community College

Michael Dichio
Fort Lewis College

Dawn Eaton
San Jacinto College South

Kathleen Ferraiolo
James Madison University

Ingrid Haas
University of Nebraska–Lincoln

James Hite
Portland State University

Jeneen Hobby
Cleveland State University

Michael Hoover
Seminole State College

Daniel Hummel
Idaho State University

Nina Kasniunas
Goucher College

Nicholas LaRowe
University of Southern Indiana

Brad Lockerbie
East Carolina University

A. Lanethea Mathews-Schultz
Muhlenberg College

Don Mirjanian
College of Southern Nevada

Carolyn Myers
Southwestern Illinois College

Hong Min Park
University of Wisconsin–Milwaukee

Marjorie K. Nanian
Schoolcraft College

Coyle Neal
Southwest Baptist University

Paul Parker
Truman State University

Jane Rainey
Eastern Kentucky University

Joseph Romance
Fort Hays State University

Michael Romano
Georgia Southern University

Jennifer Sacco
Quinnipiac University

Eric Schwartz
Hagerstown Community College

Daniel Lavon Spinks
Stephen F. Austin State University

Jeffrey M. Stonecash
Syracuse University

Kathleen Tipler
University of Oklahoma

Carl Wege
Social Sciences College of Coastal Georgia

Geoffrey Willbanks
Tyler Junior College

Second Edition

Nathan Blank
Casper College, University of Wyoming, Kentucky Community & Technical College System

Nichole Boutte-Heiniluoma
Jarvis Christian College

Blake Farrar
Texas State University

Jennifer Felmley

Santa Fe Community College

Paul Foote
Eastern Kentucky University

Jeneen Hobby
Cleveland State University

Gary Johnson
Weber State University

Steven Nawara
Valdosta State University

Geoffrey Peterson
University of Wisconsin–Eau Claire

Ronald C. Schurin
University of Connecticut

John Shively
Longview Community College

Toni-Michelle C. Travis
George Mason University

First Edition

Brian A. Bearry
University of Texas at Dallas

Emily Bentley
Savannah State University

R. M. Bittick
Sam Houston State University

Wendell S. Broadwell Jr.
Georgia Perimeter College

Allison Bunnell
Fitchburg State University

Frank P. Cannatelli
Southern Connecticut State University

Jason P. Casellas
University of Texas at Austin

Stefanie Chambers
Trinity College, Hartford, Connecticut

Suzanne Chod
Pennsylvania State University

Michael Cobb
North Carolina State University

McKinzie Craig
Texas A&M University

Michael Crespin
University of Georgia

Amanda DiPaolo
Middle Tennessee State University

Stewart Dippel
University of the Ozarks

Jasmine Farrier
University of Louisville

Michaela Fazecas
University of Central Florida

Joseph J. Foy
University of Wisconsin–Parkside

Megan Francis
Pepperdine University

Rodd Freitag
University of Wisconsin–Eau Claire

Joseph Gardner
Northern Arizona University

David Goldberg
College of DuPage

Frederick Gordon
Columbus State University

Jeff Harmon
University of Texas at San Antonio

Jeneen Hobby
Cleveland State University

Mark S. Jendrysik
University of North Dakota

Brian Kessel
Columbia College

Christopher L. Kukk
Western Connecticut State University

Sujith Kumar
University of Central Arkansas

Lisa Langenbach
Middle Tennessee State University

William W. Laverty
University of Michigan–Flint

Jeffrey Lazarus
Georgia State University

Angela K. Lewis
University of Alabama at Birmingham

Gregg Lindskog
Temple University

Brent A. Lucas
North Carolina State University

Thomas R. Marshall
University of Texas at Arlington

A. Lanethea Mathews
Muhlenberg College

Vaughn May
Belmont University

Lauri McNown
University of Colorado at Boulder

Christina A. Medina
New Mexico State University

Patrick R. Miller
University of Cincinnati

Michael K. Moore
University of Texas at Arlington

Roger Morton
California State University, Long Beach

Yamini Munipalli
Florida State College at Jacksonville

Gary Mucciaroni
Temple University

Jason Mycoff
University of Delaware

Steven Nawara
Valdosta State University

Anthony Neal
Buffalo State College

Mark Nicol
Saginaw Valley State University

Stephen A. Nuño
Northern Arizona University

Michael Parkin
Oberlin College

Richard Pious
Barnard College

Elizabeth A. Prough
Eastern Michigan University

Wesley B. Renfro
St. John Fisher College

John F. Roche, III
Palomar College

Amanda M. Rosen
Webster University

Anjali Sahay
Gannon University

Joanna Vecchiarelli Scott
Eastern Michigan University

Samuel Shelton
Troy University

Majid Shirali
University of Nevada, Las Vegas

Joyce Stickney Smith
Hillsborough Community College,
Ybor Campus

Mitchel A. Sollenberger
University of Michigan–Dearborn

Chris Soper
Pepperdine University

Barry L. Tadlock
Ohio University

Edwin A. Taylor, III
Missouri Western State University

Delaina Toothman
Texas State University

Jan P. Vermeer
Nebraska Wesleyan University

Jennifer E. Walsh
Azusa Pacific University

Donn Worgs
Towson University

Larry L. Wright
Florida A&M University

Shoua Yang
St. Cloud State University

Mike Yawn
Sam Houston State University

Melanie C. Young
University of Nevada, Las Vegas

Khodr M. Zaarour
Shaw University

Marketing Reviewers

Oxford University Press would also like to acknowledge the contribution of additional scholars and instructors who class tested and provided their assessment of the completed manuscript, using this work with hundreds of students in classrooms across the nation.

Second Edition

Ted Anagnoson
University of California, Santa Barbara

Steven Bayne
Century College

Joshua Berkenpas
Western Michigan University

Jeff Bloodworth
Gannon University

Theodore C. Brown
Virginia State University

Kim Casey
Northwest Missouri State University

Jay Cerrato
Bronx Community College

Ericka Christensen
Washington State University

Kevin Davis
North Central Texas College—Corinth

Dennis Driggers
California State University, Fresno

Paul Gottemoller
Del Mar College

Sara Gubala
Lamar University

Dan Guerrant
Middle Georgia College

Timothy Kersey
Kennesaw State University

Michael Latner
California Polytechnic State University

Maruice Mangum
Texas Southern University

Donna Merrell
Kennesaw State University

Patrick Moore
Richland College

Martha Musgrove
Tarrant County College—Southeast
Campus

Michael Petersen
Utah State University

Mikhail Rybalko
Texas Tech University

Joanna Sabo
Monroe County Community College

Hayden Smith
Washington State University

First Edition

Gayle Alberda
Owens Community College

Herrick Arnold
Orange Coast College

Alex L. Avila
Mesa Community College

John Barnes
University of Southern California

Charles Barrilleaux
Florida State University

Ronald Bee
Cuyamaca College

Michael Berkman
Pennsylvania State University

Angelina M. Cavallo
San Jacinto College

Adam Chamberlain
Coastal Carolina University

Matt Childers
University of Georgia

Benjamin Christ
Harrisburg Area Community College

Diana Cohen
Central Connecticut State University

Paul M. Collins
University of North Texas

William Corbett
New Mexico State University

Mark Ellickson
Missouri State University

Deborah Ferrell-Lynn
University of Central Oklahoma

Paul Foote
Eastern Kentucky University

Peter L. Francia
East Carolina University

Rodd Freitag
University of Wisconsin–Eau Claire

Fred Gordon
Columbus State University

John I. Hanley
Syracuse University

Jeff Hilmer
Northern Arizona University

Jeneen Hobby
Cleveland State University

Ronald J. Hrebenar
University of Utah

Mark Jendrysik
University of North Dakota

Aubrey Jewett
University of Central Florida

Gary Johnson
Weber State University

Michelle Keck
The University of Texas at Brownsville

William Kelly
Auburn University

John Klemanski
Oakland University

Richard Krupa
Harper College

Christine Lipsmeyer
Texas A&M University

Brent Lucas
North Carolina State University

Margaret MacKenzie
San Jacinto College

Jason McDaniel
San Francisco State University

John Mercurio
San Diego State University

Melissa Merry
University of Louisville

Roger Morton
California State University,
Long Beach

Gary Mucciaroni
Temple University

Adam J. Newmark
Appalachian State University

Randall Newnham
Pennsylvania State University

Roger Nichols
Southwestern College

Anthony J. Nownes
University of Tennessee, Knoxville

Anthony O'Regan
Los Angeles Valley College

Kenneth O'Reilly
Milwaukee Area Technical College

Sunday P. Obazuaye
Cerritos College

Amanda M. Olejarski
Shippensburg University

Kevin Parsneau
Minnesota State University

Michelle Pautz
University of Dayton

Martin J. Plax
Cleveland State University

Sherri Replogle
Illinois State University

Kim Rice
Western Illinois University

Ray Sandoval
Dallas County Community College
District

Laura Schneider
Grand Valley State University

Scot Schraufnagel
Northern Illinois University

Ronnee Schreiber
San Diego State University

Ronald Schurin
University of Connecticut

Jeffrey M. Stonecash
Syracuse University

Katrina Taylor
Northern Arizona University

Ryan Lee Teten
University of Louisiana

John P. Todsen
Drake University

Delaina Toothman
University of Maine

Dan Urman
Northeastern University

Ronald W. Vardy
University of Houston

Adam L. Warber
Clemson University

Gerald Watkins
Kentucky Community & Technical
College System

Patrick Wohlfarth
University of Maryland, College Park

Wayne L. Wolf
South Suburban College

Jeff Worsham
West Virginia University

Finally, thanks to you for picking up this book. We hope you enjoy reading it as much as we did writing.

Jim Morone and Rogan Kersh

BY THE PEOPLE

DEBATING AMERICAN GOVERNMENT

1 The Spirit of American Politics

INAUGURATION DAY, 2017 . . . 2021 . . . 2025 . . .

Every four years, the president stands in front of the U.S. Capitol and repeats the oath of office. The ceremony represents an American legacy that stretches back to President George Washington, who used the same words in 1789 that we hear today. The inaugural oath remains a solemn moment in the world's oldest **democracy**. Even George Washington was visibly nervous when he spoke the oath.

Members of Congress surround the president on the inaugural stage. Chief Justice John Roberts of the U.S. Supreme Court leads the president through the oath of office. The Supreme Court serves as a check on Congress and the executive branch. It decides whether government actions (both national and state) violate the U.S. Constitution. For example, the Court recently ruled that laws forbidding same-sex marriage violated the Constitution's Fourteenth Amendment.

What you cannot see on Inauguration Day is the sheer depth of this democracy. Americans elect more than five hundred thousand public officials—from the governors of their states to the mayors of their cities, from soil and water commissioners in Iowa City, Iowa, to cemetery trustees in Lempster, New Hampshire. No other country in the world comes close to voting on so many offices.

Yet this democracy faces a lot of paradoxes. Americans have inaugurated presidential candidates who lost the popular vote five times. Think about that: More than one in every ten presidents (and two out of the last three) was not the people's choice. Congress adds another peculiar twist to popular rule. Its approval rating averaged a dismal 19 percent on November 6, 2018, when Americans went to the polls.[1] Yet nearly 93 percent of the House of Representatives incumbents won reelection, most of them by large majorities. The public expressed sharp disapproval—then voted to return nearly all of them to Washington for another term.

The Supreme Court's nine members represent still another limit on American democracy. Justices are not elected but are appointed for life. At times, the Court has looked more like a bastion of privilege than a protector of rights. Back in 1857, the Court ruled that, according to the Constitution, black people "were so far inferior" that they had "no rights which the white man was bound

- Who governs?

- How does American politics work?

- What does government do?

- Who are we?

Democracy: A form of government in which the people hold power, either by acting directly or through elected representatives.

Opposite: President Trump and Vice President Pence greet supporters after winning the 2016 election.

● *The first inauguration: George Washington takes the oath of office in New York in 1789 while a crowd cheers from the street . . . and President Trump's inauguration in Washington, DC, 228 years later. America and Americans keep changing, but each new generation embraces this tradition.*

to respect."[2] More recently, the Court struck down popular laws that started the school day with a prayer, regulated pornography, banned burning the American flag, and many other measures passed by Congress or state governments.

As you can see, democracy is complicated. Yes, the United States is the world's oldest democratic country. Yet a candidate who loses the popular vote wins the White House; a terribly unpopular Congress is reelected in a landslide; and unelected judges, appointed for life, can strike down the will of the people's representatives. Over the course of this book, you will see why these limits to democracy were introduced, and judge whether they are still a good idea—or whether they are out of date and distort American democracy.

We address four questions throughout this book to help make sense of American politics and government. By the time you finish reading, you will understand the debates sparked by each question—and you will be ready (and, we hope, eager) to join the debates.

1. **Who governs?** Do the people rule? Some answer, "Yes, and today more than ever." Others are not so sure. What if the people are *not* in charge—then who is?

2. **How does American politics work?** This may be the most confusing, messy, and fascinating government on earth. We will guide you through the political maze, and help you understand what makes American politics and government tick.

3. **What does government do?** Many people view politics as dirty and see government as a problem, or irrelevant to their lives. We will show you how politics can be honorable, and why government is often important, even essential. By the time you finish this book, you will have the tools to judge whether government is a problem, a solution . . . or perhaps a mixture of both.

4. **Who are we?** In a rapidly changing, diverse, immigrant nation, this may be the deepest question of all. American politics helps define who we are—as a community, a people, and a nation.

Before we examine these four questions, we want to share our bias: We love politics. We think there is nothing more interesting—not the new Jay-Z and Beyoncé album, not the Oscars, not the Super Bowl. (Actually, all those involve politics too.) Yes, in recent years politics has gotten nasty and personal. We will not duck that issue. But we also aim to project the excitement that we see in politics and power and democracy. We brief you on basic facts, then ask you to ponder the key questions, and join in the debates. And we will suggest many ways that you can get involved in the pageant of American politics.

Now, let's turn to our four big questions.

Who Governs?

As Benjamin Franklin left the Constitutional Convention in 1787, a woman stopped him. "What kind of government have you given us?" she asked. According to legend, the wise old Franklin responded, "A republic, madam—if you can keep it." The Declaration of Independence began with a ringing proclamation of popular rule: Governments derive "their just powers from the consent of the governed." In a **republic**, the people are in charge. The Constitution drives home this point in its first three words: "We the People." Franklin knew, however, that popular governments were extremely difficult to "keep." All previous republics—such as Athens, Rome, and Florence—had collapsed. His point was that the people have to be vigilant and active if they are to maintain control. Every American generation faces new challenges in keeping the republic.

Popular rule in the United States was a bold breakthrough by eighteenth-century standards, but it certainly did not empower everyone. The Constitution protected slavery and gave slaveholders an extra three-fifths of a vote for every person they kept in chains. Women could not vote, nor could most poor men, white or black. American Indians were considered foreigners in their native land. At the heart of American history lies the long, hard struggle to actually live up to the republic's founding ideals, to genuinely empower "We the People."

Now that most adults finally have the right to vote (although, as we will see, some states make voting more difficult than others) does the public really rule? Or do the rich and powerful make most of the decisions? Americans have always worried that ordinary people will lose control. Back in 1961, for example, President Dwight Eisenhower, a Republican concerned about the size of government, warned that insiders wielded too much power. A juggernaut of big government, big business, and big contracts was creating a "military–industrial complex." Eisenhower's background gave him special credibility: He was a five-star general who had commanded U.S. forces during World War II.

Today, critics still charge that the very wealthy—the top 1 percent—have stripped the people of money and influence. Many of the 600 American billionaires pour money into political campaigns and fund their favorite causes. Do they dominate our common lives by the sheer force of their wealth?[3] At the same time, many conservative Americans feel that government bureaucrats and mainstream media elites have grabbed control; in response, they voted for Donald Trump in the hope that he would return power to the people. Different voices across the political spectrum—including the president's most ardent supporters and opponents—share the same opinion: The people's voice is not being properly heard.

Republic: A government in which citizens rule indirectly and make government decisions through their elected representatives.

See President Eisenhower's warning against the military-industrial complex.

● Students from Marjory Stoneman Douglas High School in Parkland, Florida, changed the national debate when they confronted political leaders about gun control and school safety—after a tragic shooting in their school.

Watch students challenge Florida Senator Marco Rubio.

Alongside these fears, we see many examples where ordinary American people have made enormous differences. Sometimes, individuals simply stand up and take a stand. After a gunman murdered seventeen people at Marjory Stoneman Douglas High School in Parkland, Florida, students confronted politicians about guns and school safety. Many observers predicted that they would achieve the usual result: nothing. But the students kept at it. Six weeks later Florida Governor Rick Scott signed bipartisan legislation introducing some gun controls. At other times, people create change by voting or joining political movements. Perhaps our government does still reflect the ideas and passions of the people.

Over the years, political scientists have developed different theories to answer the question of where power really lies in American politics. The following four theories (summarized in Table 1.1) are especially important:

- *Pluralist theory* suggests that people can influence government through the many interest groups that spring up to champion everything from fighting global warming to banning abortions. Pluralists suggest that interest groups give most people a voice.

- *Elite theory* counters that power actually rests in the hands of a small number of wealthy and powerful individuals—particularly the richest Americans, corporate executives, and the top government officials— especially in the executive branch.

- *Bureaucratic theory* argues that real control lies with the millions of men and women who carry out the day-to-day operations of modern government. Bureaucratic experts establish policy and sideline the influence of most Americans.

- *Social movement theory* emphasizes the power citizens can wield when they organize and rise up in protest—regardless of who is in control of day-to-day politics.

TABLE 1.1 Theories of Power

THEORY	LOCATION OF POLITICAL POWER	SOURCE OF INFLUENCE
Pluralist theory	Interest groups	A group's resources, political awareness, and connections
Elite theory	"Power elite" in corporations, government (especially the executive), the military, and an upper class of billionaires	Status based on economic influence and leadership positions
Bureaucratic theory	Government organizations	Organizational rules and day-to-day decisions
Social movement theory	Protest movements	The ability to persuade the rest of the country to support their cause

What Do YOU Think? **Who Governs?**

| Political scientists' two most popular theories of power are pluralism and elite theory. If you had to choose between them, which would you pick? | Pluralism! Power is spread out in America. Any group can have its say. | Elitism! A small circle of wealthy and powerful people hold most of the control in America. | Perhaps you would like to speak up for one of the other theories. Do you prefer the social movement theory, which places power in the hands of an active, engaged group of citizens? If you are not sure, don't worry: We're just getting started. |

These theories represent very different answers to the vital question: Who rules in America? Have we remained a republic, governed by the people? We will often return to this question—and ask you to consider which of these theories best describes power in the United States today. (And, yes, you'll be able to mix, match, and create your own theories.)

The Bottom Line

» In a republic, power rests with the people. However, this is a difficult form of government to maintain. The first question of American politics—raised in every generation—is whether the people hold the power. Is the United States a government by the people?

» Scholars have developed four approaches to political power in America: pluralism, elite theory, bureaucratic theory, and social movement theory.

» We return to this issue in every chapter of this book.

How Does American Politics Work?

Consider a classic definition of politics: *Who gets what, when, and how.*[4] Every society has limited amounts of money, prestige, power, and other desirables. Politics helps determine how we distribute them—to which people, in what amounts, under which rules. A second definition is even simpler: *Politics is how a society makes its collective decisions.* Every nation has its own way of deciding. In this book we explain how collective decisions are made in the United States by focusing on four "Is": ideas, institutions, interests, and individuals.

Ideas

Powerful ideas shape American politics. The nation began with what, at the time, was a stunning idea: "All men are created equal." In Chapter 2, we explore seven essential ideas: liberty, democracy (or self-rule), individualism, limited government, the American dream, equality, and faith in God. At first glance, these ideas all look simple, but as you will quickly learn, each has at least two very different sides. Each idea provokes long, loud controversies.

Take democracy as an example. It sounds simple—government by the people—but defining and achieving democracy in America has been a constant

How have our ideas about democracy and republics shaped our government?

Checks and balances: The principle that each branch of government has the authority to block the other branches, limiting the power of any one branch or individual. This system makes passing legislation far more difficult in the United States than in most other democracies.

struggle. The United States has seen a Constitution that limited the people's influence, an elaborate system of **checks and balances** that blunts the popular will, political machines that enthusiastically stole votes in the nineteenth century, a Jim Crow system that drove African Americans out of politics until the 1960s, and many other limits to popular rule. In fact, most people are shocked to learn that on the very first day of the Constitutional Convention in 1787, one delegate rose and said, to general approval, "the people should have as little to do as may be about the government. They lack information and are constantly liable to be misled."[5] Can checking the people's influence actually elevate popular rule? Most of the men at the Constitutional Convention thought so. Americans still debate this question.

Instead of embracing popular sovereignty, many American leaders preferred the rule of a few—the elite founders of the nation, expert bureaucrats trying to solve technical problems, big banks regulating themselves, or judges appointed for life. All have aimed to protect government from the tumult of the masses.

At the same time, bold popular movements and unforeseen electoral surges have changed the nation. In many ways, these are the most exciting moments in American history. They attract widespread attention, inspiring ordinary citizens to achieve great things. The chapters that follow highlight moments when the United States has reflected populist democracy, as well as periods when it has turned away from the people. We also explore the great contested zone between democracy and elitism. Ultimately, the struggle for power between the elite few and the democratic many goes back to our first question: Who governs?

The United States bursts with entrepreneurial energy. New ideas bubble up all the time. Ideas alone do not drive government decisions, but it is impossible to make sense of American politics without understanding ideas, big and small.

Institutions

Institutions: The organizations, norms, and rules that structure government and public action.

When most people talk about politics, they think about individuals: President Donald Trump, senators such as Kamala Harris (D-CA) or Tim Scott (R-SC), governors like Kate Brown (D-OR) and Greg Abbott (R-TX), or commentators such as Michael Savage and Samantha Bee. Political scientists, on the other hand, stress **institutions**—*the organizations, norms, and rules that structure political action.*

Congress, the Texas legislature, the Missoula (Montana) City Council, the Supreme Court, the Department of Homeland Security, and the news media are all institutions. If you want to understand why they do some things and not others, study the rules that govern their behavior.

Think about how institutions influence your own behavior. You may compete in a classroom by making arguments. If the debate gets heated and you shove someone, however, you are in trouble. But if you play basketball after class, things are quite the opposite. There, a little shoving is fine, but no one wants to play hoops with someone

● *Bold popular movements can change the nation. Gun rights activists rally outside the Wyoming Supreme Court.*

who is always arguing. Different institutions—the classroom, the gym—have different rules, and most people adopt them without a second thought. Notice how shifting institutional rules give some people advantages over others. Smart students who think quickly have an advantage in one institution (the classroom), while fast, athletic students with good post moves have an advantage in another (the gym). Political institutions work in the same way. The Department of Agriculture, the Chicago City Council, the Nevada legislature, the state courts in Florida, the governor's office in Wisconsin, the Marine Corps, and thousands of other institutions all have their own rules and procedures. Each institution organizes behavior. Each gives an advantage to some interests over others.

● *The U.S. Capitol, Washington, DC. Tourists see an impressive monument to democracy. Political scientists see an institution with complicated rules that give advantage to some individuals and groups.*

By the time you finish this book, you will know to ask the essential question every time you look at a political issue: Which institutions are involved?

Interests

For many social scientists, interests are often at the center of the story. Political action flows from individuals, groups, and nations pursuing their own self-interest.

The traditional view of interests focuses on groups. If you want to influence environmental politics, join a group such as Greenpeace, ConservAmerica, or the Audubon Society. Their lawyers, lobbyists, and members all play an active role in American politics and society. Remember that pluralists believe interest groups are the central actors in American government—in contrast to governments in England, Brazil, or Korea.

Other analyses focus on individual interests as the essential particles of politics. **Rational choice theory** suggests that people calculate the costs and benefits of any action to determine what will maximize their own self-interest. At an extreme, "rat-choice" models suggest that all political outcomes—elections, the passage of a law, even mass rallies—are an aggregate of the public's individual interests.

Rational choice theory: An approach to political behavior that views individuals as rational, decisive actors who know their political interests and seek to act on them.

Political theorists and politicians alike often seek (or claim to seek) the public interest, the shared good of the whole society. Idealists reject pandering to the interests of individuals or groups. Instead, they suggest that government ought to pursue "the greatest good for the greatest number." Well, who decides what is the "greatest good?" This returns us to our first question: Who governs? The real answer lies in who can most effectively get his or her voice heard.

In the chapters that follow, we explore all three types of interests: group interest, self-interest, and public interest. Behavioral scientists add one more twist. Although we may think of our own interests, including our political views, as perfectly rational, most people exhibit a large degree of self-deception and nonrational behavior. Experiments repeatedly show, for example, that people do not change their views when confronted with evidence that they are mistaken—on the contrary, it only strengthens their attitudes. Experts are often no wiser than anyone else for they overlook data that does not fit their expectations. For a dramatic

● *Individuals can make a difference. Marla Ruzicka in Kabul, Afghanistan.*

example, look no further than President Trump's election—something that surprised most public opinion experts.[6]

Individuals

Finally, individuals influence political outcomes. This book places special emphasis on how ordinary people change the world. Our hope is simple: We want to inspire you to get involved. Here we share one example.

Marla Ruzicka was a self-described "civics junkie" who visited Afghanistan and Iraq while U.S. forces were on the ground there. She was shaken when she saw the terrible toll that the wars took on civilians. With no particular foreign policy experience, the twenty-five-year-old established a public service organization in Iraq that she called the Campaign for Innocent Victims in Conflict, or CIVIC. Along with providing first aid, food, clothing, and comfort to ordinary Iraqis injured during the war, Marla formed survey teams of volunteers that kept a count of Iraqi civilians killed, regardless of who was responsible.

Marla's efforts attracted attention back in Washington, where Pentagon officials initially sought to dissuade her from publicizing her count. Eventually she received substantial support from Congress for her CIVIC efforts to aid civilian victims in both Iraq and Afghanistan.

There is a tragic note to Marla's story: As she traveled to an injured Iraqi's home, her car was targeted by an explosive device, and she was killed. We highlight Marla's example both to honor her memory (one of your authors was her friend) and to emphasize the importance of individual initiative in every operation of American government. Today, the organization she founded has programs not only in Iraq and Afghanistan, but also in Syria, Somalia, Mali, and other war-torn countries. She is an example of how individuals with a passion for political change can make a difference in politics—and in people's lives.

History

As the four "Is" reappear throughout this book, you will see that we pay special attention to the history of each. Why is an idea like freedom powerful? Why does an institution such as Congress behave as it does? To understand you have to know how they developed over time. You cannot understand where the nation is, or where it might be going, without knowing where it has been.

The Bottom Line

» American political decisions are shaped by four "I" factors: ideas, institutions, interests, and individuals.

» Mastering how the four "Is" shaped politics also requires an understanding of history.

What Does Government Do?

When Patrick Henry, one of the greatest orators in Virginia, read the newly written Constitution of the United States, he declared, "I smell a rat." This new government was too strong. President Ronald Reagan said the same thing, more politely, when he took the oath of office almost two hundred years later: "Government is not the solution to the problem. Government is the problem."[7] Americans have always been critical of their own government. And yet there are 2.8 million people working as "feds"—roughly the same count as during the Reagan administration. Is government still the problem? Before you can answer that, you have to know what government actually does.

Context: Government in Society

Let's start with the context. There are three sectors of society. *Private life* involves individuals, families, and friends connecting with one another. *Civil society* refers to people joining with others to do something—you might run for student government, form a Bible study circle, or volunteer at a recycling center. Finally, *government* is the set of institutions that make decisions for the whole society.

The lines separating these different sectors are blurry. Successful democracy requires a vibrant civic spirit. When people join groups—even if it's just a soccer club or knitting group, they get used to interacting with others and solving problems together. They develop what Alexis de Tocqueville, a French visitor to America in 1831–1832, called the "habits of the heart"—the relationships they develop and the shared goals they pursue lay the foundation for robust democracy. Private groups foster the skills and attitudes that make people effective citizens.[8]

In addition, the different sectors come together to undertake public projects. **Public–private partnerships** bring private actors such as businesses together with government officials to renovate parks, construct sports arenas, or launch innovative schools.

> **Public–private partnership:** A government program or service provided through the joint efforts of private sector actors (usually businesses) and public officials.

Posted by **Huntington Beach Police Department** 532,906 Views

● The three sectors of society. Individuals engage in all three sectors: personal life when they work or raise a family; civil society when they volunteer at a soup kitchen; and government when they get a driver's license or engage with a police officer.

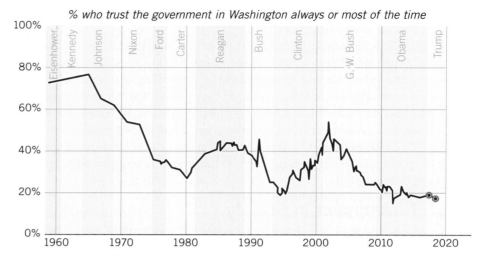

● **Figure 1.1** *Americans' trust in government remains at historic lows. (Pew Research Center)*

No Big Government!

Americans have a very active civil society. In the abstract, at least, they prefer voluntary groups to government action. Today, only 18 percent of Americans trust the national government "to do the right thing most of the time"[9] (see Figure 1.1).

If Americans dislike "Big Government," then how did we get such a thicket of over thirteen hundred federal agencies and fifteen Cabinet departments, populated by more than 2.8 million civilian employees? Include another nearly 2.5 million members of the active and reserve armed forces, and you get a sprawling national government. Add 19.4 million state and local government workers alongside the 500,000 elected officials, and you get an idea of the sheer size of the U.S. government—more than twenty-five million men and women who touch every aspect of our lives.

Americans have long told admiring stories about individual heroes who won greatness on their own—free of government meddling. But the details are often more nuanced. Take those famous inventors, the Wright brothers. Working out of their bicycle shop, Orville and Wilbur created the first viable airplanes. What you may not have heard is that the Wrights were able to develop their invention because of timely investments from their first client: the U.S. military.[10] Yes, government support was essential to launching the aviation industry—just as it was to exploring space; creating the Internet; and building the infrastructure we drive, walk, fly, run, and otherwise move around on every day. And despite the low trust in government generally, Americans give the government high marks for specific tasks such as keeping the country safe from terrorism (66% approval), responding to natural disasters (64%), and ensuring safe food and medicine (61%).[11]

Could we—and should we—shift some of the national government's functions to civil society and let volunteers do the work? To answer such questions, you first have to know what government does.

What Government Does

The Constitution begins with the basic functions of government, circa 1787: "Establish justice, ensure domestic tranquility, provide for the common defense, promote the general welfare, and secure the blessings of liberty." Their list—we'll

Test your knowledge
of civics.

get to the details in Chapter 3—still describes the functions of the government, even as its size has grown. We can get a more focused look at the federal government's priorities by looking at what it spends its money on. Figure 1.2 shows you the major budget categories in the $4.4 trillion annual budget.

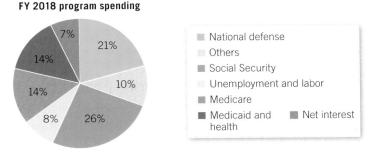

FY 2018 program spending

- National defense — 21%
- Others — 10%
- Social Security — 26%
- Unemployment and labor — 8%
- Medicare — 14%
- Medicaid and health — 14%
- Net interest — 7%

● **Figure 1.2** *The U.S. federal budget. What government spends. Notice the big four: Social Security, Medicare, Medicaid, and National Defense. (Christopher Chantrill)*

Many people are surprised when they examine the federal budget for the first time. More than 75 percent of all federal spending goes to just four categories: the military, Social Security (which provides a steady income for people over sixty-five, as well as payments for those with disabilities), Medicare (which provides healthcare for people over sixty-five), and Medicaid and related healthcare programs (which provides healthcare for children and lower income Americans; about half of Medicaid spending also goes to those over sixty-five). These four programs add up to more than $3 trillion. They are all very popular, so most politicians are careful about meddling with them. Tune into the budget debates and you'll hear lots of noise about budgets being out of control. But unless they are cutting one of these big four programs, budget cuts will not produce small government.

Notice how America's national government devotes a large share of its resources to the military and to seniors. Only one out of every 6.6 Americans is over sixty-five years old. What about the rest of us? We are mainly squeezed into the slice listed as "non-defense discretionary." That includes federal spending on education, housing, veterans, agriculture, infrastructure, food stamps and a long list of other programs, which all stack up to 14 percent of the budget or, roughly, $615 billion.[12]

Of course, government does a lot more than spend. It sets the rules for society: Drive on the right side of the street. Stop at red lights. No tobacco for children. No rat hairs or bug parts in restaurant food. No discrimination against women when hiring. No insider trading in stocks. Most people agree with these rules. Others are much more controversial.

Over 600,000 people were arrested in 2017 on marijuana related charges. At the same time, marijuana is legal in nine states and Washington, DC. In Oregon people with terminal illnesses can choose to end their lives with the assistance of a physician, but anyone who assisted euthanasia in Georgia or Florida would face murder charges. Abortions are much easier to obtain in New York than in North Dakota. Guns are easier to get in Texas than California. Government—national, state, and local—constantly sets the rules for society. Sometimes the rules make sense to most people; other times, they trigger fierce debates. Certain federal, state, and local rules are the same; in other cases, they clash. Governments affect what we do almost every minute of every day—from the moment you wake up and turn on the light

● *Americans often vote for budget cuts—but don't want their own favorite programs cut.*

(government is responsible for electricity), jump in the shower (local government provides water and makes sure it's clean), and eat breakfast (federal, state and local governments all regulate food safety). As we go through this book, we keep coming back to a vital question: Should government do fewer things? Or more?

A Chronic Problem

Although Americans dislike government in the abstract, by and large they support many of the things that government actually does. This paradox creates a chronic problem: How should we pay for government spending? Americans pay lower taxes compared to citizens of most other advanced industrial nations. Yes, you read that right. The U.S. tax burden (including federal, state, and local taxes) ranks thirty-first—right near the bottom—among the thirty-four wealthiest nations[13] (see Comparing Nations 1.1). Even so, many Americans think they are taxed too much. Americans like their federal programs but oppose paying taxes to support them. In 2017, Republicans in Congress passed major tax cuts—lowering the U.S. tax burden still further.

Partly as a result of our antitax spirit, the federal government usually spends more than it takes in. You can see one consequence in Figure 1.2. Notice the seventh-largest spending category: interest on the national debt. The United States borrows money to cover the difference between government spending and tax revenues. The resulting debt reflects a serious political problem. It is hard to raise taxes (people hate them), but it is also hard to cut programs (people like them), so the United States keeps borrowing to make up the difference.

COMPARING NATIONS 1.1	U.S. Taxpayers Less Burdened Than Other Advanced Countries

Citizens in the United States pay less in taxes than citizens in many other countries. In the countries near the top of the chart, roughly half of all economic activity goes into the government's coffers. In the United States, that figure is closer to one-quarter—and falling. Is this too little? Or still too much? These questions get back to the proper size of the government, and what the government should do. *(Organisation for Economic Co-operation and Development)*

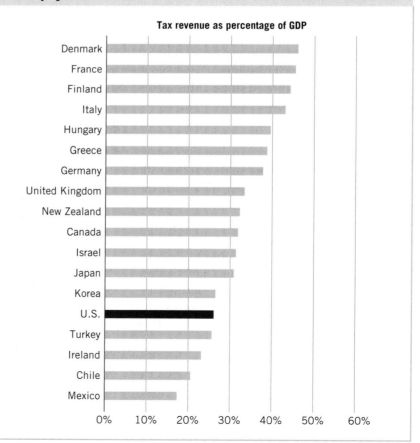

Tax revenue as percentage of GDP

The Hidden Government

Another peculiar aspect of modern American government is that it can be hard to see. Scholars identify a "hidden" or "submerged" central government, with many functions deliberately tucked out of sight. Why is it people do not see their government at work?[14]

Because of Americans' antipathy to "big government," many federal programs work *indirectly*: They operate through the private sector. Take healthcare as an example. Rather than administering a national health insurance program as in Canada or France, the American government provides employers a major tax deduction if they offer employees health insurance. Today, the tax deduction for employers amounts to $260 billion a year.[15] That makes it one of the largest government-funded healthcare programs in the world. The national government offers similar tax deductions that help people buy homes, buy health insurance, save for retirement, pay for schooling, or receive support if their income is low. However, the people who benefit do not see the government's hand at work.[16]

Political scientist Suzanne Mettler asked American citizens whether they receive federal benefits; more than half of the respondents incorrectly answered "no." They did not stop to think that the government had helped set up their retirement savings or their student loans by organizing the tax code to encourage their behavior. About a quarter of the people getting healthcare coverage through Medicaid or groceries through food stamps did not realize they were involved in government programs (see Figure 1.3).

Liberal scholars conclude that the government does not get enough credit for helping people and creating a stronger nation. Conservatives, on the other hand, are more likely to worry that a hidden government is more difficult to control and cut back. Our job is to make sure you see all the ways that government operates—then you can decide whether it should grow, shrink, or stay about the same size.

The Best of Government

Despite powerful antigovernment sentiment—or perhaps inspired by it to promote change—millions of Americans cheer what is best in our national government and seek to improve it. In this book, you will meet dozens of people who act to improve government. You will meet policy entrepreneurs from across the political spectrum who promote innovative new solutions to pressing problems; organizers who engage their neighbors and larger communities in collective action for change; inventive bureaucrats who conceive ways to deliver public services more effectively;

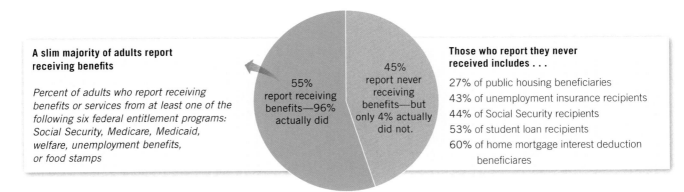

A slim majority of adults report receiving benefits

Percent of adults who report receiving benefits or services from at least one of the following six federal entitlement programs: Social Security, Medicare, Medicaid, welfare, unemployment benefits, or food stamps

55% report receiving benefits—96% actually did

45% report never receiving benefits—but only 4% actually did not.

Those who report they never received includes . . .

27% of public housing beneficiaries
43% of unemployment insurance recipients
44% of Social Security recipients
53% of student loan recipients
60% of home mortgage interest deduction beneficiares

● **Figure 1.3** *A recent poll found that 55 percent of Americans report receiving government benefits, but Suzanne Mettler calculated that the number is closer to 96 percent. Even beneficiaries of the biggest programs do not realize they are getting benefits from the government. (Pew Research Center and Washington Post)*

and tech wizards who devise faster, better connections between national policy-makers and the public.

We will return repeatedly to ways you can get involved, have a say, and enhance the workings of American government. You can engage within our political system: volunteer on a Senate campaign, attend a town meeting, intern at a federal agency, join the school board, or run for the state legislature. You also can get involved from outside: call media attention to a problem, serve in (or start) an advocacy group, or launch an online idea that might improve local education policy or spotlight fresh solutions in crime prevention. In addition, you can get involved in the life of your community. You are already enough of a social scientist to know that when you join a group or activity, you are participating in "civil society"—the basic building block of strong democracy.

The Bottom Line

» Every nation is made up of three primary sectors: private life; civil society, where people interact voluntarily; and government. Those sectors are increasingly blurred in the United States.

» Americans tend to dislike their national government—but like the benefits that government programs provide.

» Democratic government at its best involves popular involvement, either through direct engagement with public officials or through civil society activities that help develop "habits of the heart."

Who Are We?

The United States is a nation of immigrants, a country where individuals come to reinvent themselves. The nation is always changing. American politics constantly addresses the most fundamental question about a people: Who are we?

The United States grew as a nation of immigrants. Here a group from Ireland arrives during the 1870s.

This question goes back to the earliest European settlers. When the Puritans landed in Massachusetts in 1620, they suddenly had to define their community for themselves. The colonists came up with a remarkable response: We are a collection of saints, a "city on a hill," a model for the whole world to follow. That city on a hill immediately discovered threats: The Puritans defined or imagined enemies that included Indians, witches, and heretics. These settlers learned to answer the question "Who are we?" both by affirming who they were ("us!") and by sharply declaring who they were *not* ("them!"). They defined themselves by celebrating their values, but also by demonizing their foes—promoting their cohesion by opposing dangerous "others."

At the same time, different settlers were arriving chained in terrible slave ships. Slave drivers and traders tried to strip Africans of their families, their heritage, their names, and their very identities. Together, American slaves would have to remake their lives and redefine themselves. Through religion, close communities, great myths, secret gatherings, personal narratives, and an enduring struggle for freedom, this community too would help the nation face up to the great question, *Who are we*?

Every generation brings new Americans. They arrive from all corners of the world: Ireland and Germany in the 1840s; Poland and Italy in the 1900s; Mexico, China, India, and Korea (among a great many other places) today. The newcomers, each in their own turn, wrestle with their identity in a new land. Each generation helps remake American society, culture, and politics. Each tells us who we are. In 2017, approximately 44.5 million foreign born people were living in the United States, making up about 13.7 percent of the population.

We are also an aging nation (see Comparing Nations 1.2). As the baby boomers get older, Americans need a different mix of government services. Today, a larger proportion of Americans receive Social Security and Medicare than ever before. Younger generations also introduce new ideas, especially around social issues. Seventy percent of **millennials** (born after 1983) believe marijuana should be legalized, while only 35 percent of the generation born between 1928 and 1945 agrees.[17] Each generation of Americans embraces different values, engages in civic life to greater/lesser degrees, and accesses some but not other institutions.

Millennials: Americans born between 1983 and 2001. Though a very large (some 80 million people) and diverse group, millennials tend to share certain characteristics, including political outlook.

COMPARING NATIONS 1.2 | **Aging Populations**

The United States population is getting older. But not as fast as the populations in many other nations. By the year 2050, 40 percent of the Japanese population will be over sixty-five. In Germany, senior citizens will make up 30 percent of the population and in Canada, 27 percent. The United States is getting older less rapidly. By 2050 only one in five Americans will be over sixty-five. Why is this so? Partially because as nations get wealthier, families generally get smaller. And in most wealthy nations, people are living longer—though the United States lags behind the other nations listed here in life expectancy. *(U.S. Census Bureau)*

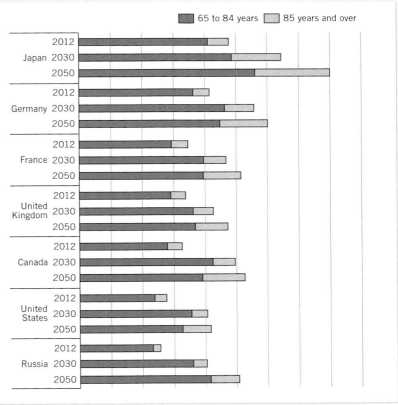

65 to 84 years   85 years and over

Demographics in America

HOW ARE RACE AND ETHNICITY CHANGING OVER TIME?

Answers to the age-old question "Who are we?" have been changing as long as there have been settlers on our shores, dating back to the Native American inhabitants. Looking back fifty years and forward a half-century, we may see dramatic changes in our population: Some demographic models used by the Census Bureau project that the nation's fastest growth will occur among Americans of Hispanic, Asian, and African descent.

THINK ABOUT IT

How does the projected growth of the Hispanic, Asian, and African American populations compare to that of whites? At what point will the white population become a minority?

Should the proportion of members of Congress, or Supreme Court justices, who are Hispanic also grow? Why or why not? We'll come back to this issue—what does proper representation look like—throughout the book.

Source: Pew Research Center

Changing Face of America

Percentage of total U.S. population by race and ethnicity, 1960–2060

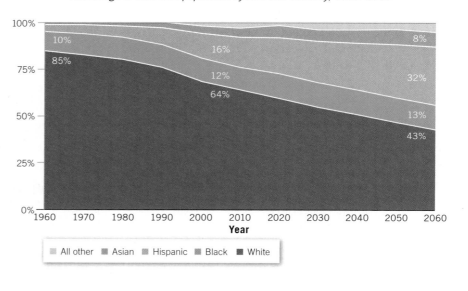

Legend: All other · Asian · Hispanic · Black · White

What Do YOU Think?   Getting Engaged in Politics—Or Not

	Disagree.	**Agree.**	**Unsure.**
Past public opinion data suggested that the younger generation has been less involved and interested in politics than were previous generations. Do you think this remains true today? What is your experience? Do you agree or disagree with this assertion?	Millennials engage as civic volunteers like never before. From "voluntour" travel involving service learning to social media-fueled protests to start-ups that disrupt traditional political forms, they are promoting new styles that more traditional observers have failed to appreciate. Describe the types of activities you have seen or engaged in.	I do see a lack of political engagement around me. This may well be a problem for American democracy, but I shun electoral politics that seems to be dominated by two sides screaming at one another without engaging in civil discourse. I see more value in volunteering for a private organization or giving my time and money directly to causes that interest me.	You may be new to the study of politics—or to the United States itself. If so, no worries. By the end of the book, we think you will have well-founded opinions on this and many other matters.

Every feature of American government—the ideas, the Constitution, the president, Congress, the media, the political parties, the bureaucrats, and more—are all part of the struggle to define and redefine the United States. We begin every chapter by showing you how the topic helps answer the same question: Who are we?

Who are we? The most important answer to that question is *you*. If you are part of the so-called millennial generation, individuals born between 1983 and 2001, you are the future of American politics. To us, that is a comforting thought. Millennials are, on average, more responsible, harder working, and more law-abiding than the generations that came before (including those of your authors). They tend to volunteer more, donate a higher share of their incomes to charity, and start more entrepreneurial organizations with social impact. They are also a generation at home in a rapidly changing and diverse world.[18]

As we will see throughout the book, American politics has become especially rough—full of raised voices and bitter name-calling. Yet democracy thrives on tolerance. Our hope is that a new generation will take up the challenge of "keeping the republic" by expressing their own voices loudly and clearly while respecting and listening carefully to those of all others.

 **The Bottom Line**

» American politics constantly addresses the most fundamental question about a people: Who are we?

» Because the nation is so diverse—and so rapidly changing—the answer to this question is constantly being rewritten.

» Each generation of Americans, including newly arriving immigrants, answers this question in its own way. Today we see millennials constructing their own version of a response.

Conclusion: Your Turn

The United States has solved many problems in the last two generations. It also has failed in some dramatic ways. The torch is now passing to you. We do not encourage you to get involved naively. This book details the many problems and frustrations of running for office, advocating passionately on issues, or working in government. But we also hope our book will inspire you—whatever your age, whatever your background—to join the great debate about how to forge a better society. We invite you to use what you learn about American politics and government to help build a good community around you.

CHAPTER SUMMARY

Check your understanding of Chapter 1.

● To understand America's—or any other nation's—government and politics, keep four central questions in mind.

● *Who governs?* This remains a deeply disputed topic, organized around four main theories. *Pluralist* thinkers claim that a wide array of interest groups, both private firms and public interest advocates, shapes government decisions and policy outcomes. *Elite theorists* view a handful of powerful people in prominent roles, and their wealthy supporters, as the central sources of political influence. *Bureaucratic theorists* look to millions of public officials in government organizations as the primary decision makers. Adherents of *social movement theory* argue that members of the public, when they join a protest movement, can have the ultimate say. Note that more than one of these theories can be true at the same time.

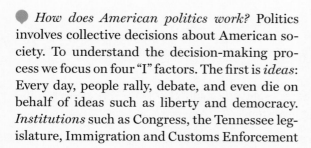

Need to review key ideas in greater depth? Click here.

● *How does American politics work?* Politics involves collective decisions about American society. To understand the decision-making process we focus on four "I" factors. The first is *ideas*: Every day, people rally, debate, and even die on behalf of ideas such as liberty and democracy. *Institutions* such as Congress, the Tennessee legislature, Immigration and Customs Enforcement (ICE), or regular elections provide the rules and procedures that shape political outcomes. *Interests* motivate people to act politically and come in different forms: individual self-interest, the goals of interest groups, and the overarching public interest we all share. *Individuals* can have surprising amounts of political influence, even in a nation as large as the United States.

● *What does government do?* Many Americans oppose a strong national government, yet the United States has a very large one. The majority of the public embraces programs such as Social Security, Medicare, and a strong military. We also depend on vigorous civic engagement by the American public. In addition, government regulates the rules of everyday life, from who can get married to where to place a stoplight.

● *Who are we?* American politics constantly addresses the most fundamental question about a people: Who are we? Because the nation is so diverse—and so rapidly changing—the answer to this question is constantly being rewritten. Every feature of American politics—the foundational ideas, the Constitution, the media, Congress, the courts, and now the millennial generation—engages in this constant debate over defining the nation and its people.

KEY TERMS

Checks and balances, p. 8
Democracy, p. 3
Institutions, p. 8

Millennials, p. 17
Public–private partnership, p. 11

Rational-choice theory, p. 9
Republic, p. 5

Flashcard review.

STUDY QUESTIONS

1. Why do we describe American democracy as "paradoxical" at the opening of this chapter?

2. Why did Franklin add "if you can keep it" to his description of the new American nation as a republic?

3. What are some of the ways that ideas are influential in national government and politics?

4. Think of a political issue you care about—cutting taxes, global warming, immigration, healthcare, and so forth. Which government institutions are involved in determining how that issue is addressed and resolved?

5. What are the three types of "interests" that political scientists pay attention to in assessing whether political outcomes are interest based?

6. How might an individual make an impact on the vast U.S. system of government and politics? How might *you* be meaningfully involved?

7. Think of the various groups that you belong to. How would you describe each group? In what ways is each group part of the larger American society?

Go to www.oup.com/us/Morone to find quizzes, flash cards, simulations, tutorials, videos, and other study tools.

2 The Ideas That Shape America

ARMY CAPTAIN RUSSELL BURGOS hunkered down in his bunker as mortars ripped through the night. A year ago he had been a political science professor; now he was a soldier in Iraq. Burgos's unit was operating in an area where the fighting was fierce. "A mortar attack in the middle of the night," he mused, "is an odd place to reconsider a course syllabus." But that is exactly what he found himself doing. Experiencing war made him see politics and societies in new ways.

As shells fell on the American base, Burgos thought about something that his classes had been missing: the study of ideas. All around him, men and women were fighting and dying over ideas—ideas such as freedom, democracy, equality, power, and faith in God. Strangely enough, Burgos wrote later, ideas had barely come up in his own political science classes. Yet ideas helped explain why the United States launched the war, how it fought the war, and how it explained the war to both friends and enemies.

Who are we? Our ideas tell us—and they tell the world. The United States is a nation built on ideas. You will see ideas at work in every chapter of this book, for they touch every feature of government and politics. As you read about these concepts—and as you continue through this book—think about other important ideas that should be added to the list alongside the seven we discuss in this chapter. If you come up with a compelling example, we may quote you in the next edition.

In this chapter, you will:

● Learn about the seven key American ideas.

● Review the arguments that surround each of them.

● Explore the essential question: How do ideas affect politics?

🗨 A Nation of Ideas

On July 4, 1776, American leaders issued a Declaration of Independence explaining their decision to break away from England. Its second paragraph describes the idea that animated them:

> *We hold these truths to be self-evident, that all men are created equal, that they are endowed by their Creator with certain unalienable rights, that among these are life, liberty and the pursuit of happiness.*

● *Army Captain Russell Burgos hands out supplies to Iraqi children in 2004.*

BY THE NUMBERS

American Ideas

Number of times the word *rights* appears in the Declaration of Independence	**10**
Number of times the word *rights* appears in the original Constitution	**0**
Number of times the word *rights* appears in amendments to the Constitution	**15**
Number of times the word *democracy* appears in the Constitution	**0**
Number of times the word *equality* appears in the original U.S. Constitution	**0**
Percentage of Americans who say a representative democracy, a direct democracy, rule by experts, and rule by military is a good way to govern the country	**86, 67, 40, 17**[1]
Percentage of total wealth in the United States owned by top 1%, top 10%, and bottom 90%, respectively	**40, 78, 22**
Percentage of Americans who say that government should act to reduce economic inequality	**65**
Percentage of Americans who think prayer should be allowed in public schools	**57**[2]

What expectations do you have of government? What ideas guide your political actions?

Most people have heard that line so often that it has lost its force, but it is one of the most powerful ideas in history. It explains the role of government—securing each individual's rights to life, liberty, and the pursuit of happiness. The Declaration states that people form governments for one purpose—*"to secure those rights."* And although the men and women who fought the revolution fell far short of this ideal, they left the nation an inspiring goal. Every American generation argues about how it can best achieve the Declaration's shimmering promise to "secure" the rights of every citizen.

American exceptionalism: The view that the United States is uniquely characterized by a distinct set of ideas such as equality, self-rule, and limited government.

Many people believe that the United States is a unique nation, different from every other. That view is known as **American exceptionalism**. Of course, every nation is distinctive in some way. The United States is exceptional in large part because of seven key ideas that guide our politics. Most of them can be traced back to the Declaration of Independence.

What are the seven big ideas? Liberty, self-rule (which is often called democracy), individualism, limited government, the American dream, equality, and faith in God. These ideas touch almost everything we do as a nation. They are the foundation of American politics and lie at the core of what makes America distinctive.

PUBLISHED BY CURRIER & IVES.
Robt. Morris.   Saml. Adams.   Benjamin Rush   Charles Carroll   John Adams   John Hancock   125 NASSAU ST. NEW YORK
Richard Henry Lee   Rev. John Witherspoon.   Edwd. Rutledge.

JOHN HANCOCK'S DEFIANCE.

JULY 4TH 1776.

The Declaration of Independence being fully adopted, John Hancock, President of the Continental Congress took up the pen and signed his name to it in a large bold hand; then rising he said, "There! John Bull can read my name without spectacles, and may double his reward for my head. That is my defiance!"

● *Ideas have consequences. John Hancock of Massachusetts defiantly signs the Declaration. According to legend, he signed it in big, bold letters so that King George III could read Hancock's name without his spectacles—and "double the reward for my head."*

There is an unusual twist to these ideas. Americans rarely agree on what they mean. Instead, we constantly debate them. The Declaration of Independence declares that all men are created equal, but many of the men who signed it owned slaves. Our stamps and coins say "In God We Trust," but Americans passionately disagree about whether the Constitution permits prayer in schools or menorahs in public parks. All our foundational ideas have (at least) two sides and spark ardent disputes. To reveal the real truth about American politics, we should post signs at all the airports that say: *Welcome to the great argument that is the USA.*

Now let's consider the first key idea.

 **The Bottom Line**

» Seven ideas guide our politics: liberty, self-rule, individualism, limited government, the American dream, equality and faith in God.

🔵 Liberty

As the Revolutionary War broke out, the royal governor of Virginia promised freedom to any slave who joined the British. Eighty thousand slaves ran for the British lines. Some of them fought in black units, with their motto—"liberty for the slaves"—sewn onto their uniforms.[3]

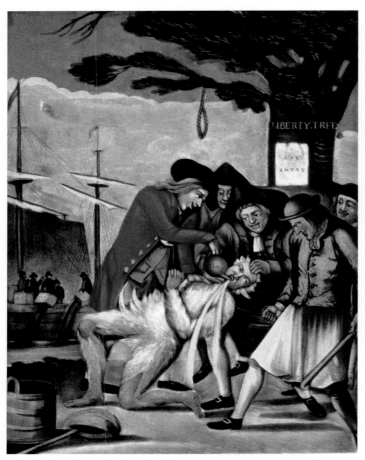

During the Revolutionary War, radicals met under trees they called "liberty trees" and erected poles they called "liberty poles." In this painting, Bostonians have dragged the British tax collector to the liberty tree where they have tarred and feathered him. The painting was British propaganda that mocked the liberty tree and the revolutionaries.

The enslaved men and women who fought for the British saw their hopes dashed when their side surrendered at the Battle of Yorktown in 1781—effectively ending the Revolutionary War. After the battle, the Redcoats, as the English soldiers were known, began to withdraw, rowing out to the warships bobbing in the harbor for their long retreat. One desperate group of slaves raced past the sentries on the wharf, dove into the sea, and swam toward the long rowboats that were ferrying the defeated British troops out to their naval vessels.

As the black men tried to clamber aboard the small boats, British troops pushed them away. Fearful that the swimmers would swamp the craft, the troops pulled out axes and hacked off the slaves' hands and fingers. And *still* they kept coming, trying to surge aboard, thrashing after their fading dream of liberty. The image is unforgettable: These men were so desperate for freedom that even as the Redcoats swung their bloody hatchets, they kept clutching for the boats that might carry them away from bondage.

"The Land of the Free"

No idea comes up more often in American history than *freedom* or *liberty* (we use the words interchangeably in this book). The national anthem declares America "the land of the free." During the civil rights movement of the 1950s and 1960s, high school students spilled out of Baptist churches and marched toward dogs and high-pressure fire hoses, singing, "Everyone shout freedom, freedom, freedom!" The Statue of Liberty is inscribed "Give me your huddled masses . . . yearning to breathe free." A group of conservative Republicans in Congress established the Freedom Caucus in 2015.

What is **freedom**? It means that the government will protect your life, your liberty, and your property from the coercion of others (including public officials) in order to permit you to pursue the goals you define for yourself.

Freedom: The ability to pursue one's own desires without interference from others.

The Two Sides of Liberty

Everyone agrees that freedom is a basic American value. But, in practice, Americans disagree about what it means—and what governments should do to ensure it. There are two different views: negative liberty and positive liberty.[4]

The more familiar view is **negative liberty**: *Freedom is the absence of constraints.* Society's responsibility, from this perspective, is to make sure that others (especially government officials) do not interfere with individuals. The government protects your right to believe what you wish, to say what you like, to declare any faith (or none), and to go into whatever profession you want—all without constraints or fear of punishment. Negative liberty firmly limits government action. Public officials violate your freedom when they collect taxes from you to feed the

Negative liberty: Freedom from constraints or the interference of others.

What Do YOU Think? Negative Versus Positive Liberty

Americans disagree about the meaning of "freedom." Is freedom the absence of constraints (negative liberty) or the freedom to pursue one's goals with equal opportunity (positive liberty)?

Do you believe in negative liberty?
Government should not interfere with individuals. Freedom means leaving every person alone to do what he or she wishes—without interference. As President Reagan famously said, "as government expands, liberty contracts."

Or do you believe in positive liberty?
Freedom simply is not a meaningful concept if you or your family are chronically hungry. A decent society has to lift everyone to a basic minimum. That is what living in a democracy should be about, said President Franklin D. Roosevelt: "True individual freedom cannot exist without economic security and independence."

Or do your beliefs fall somewhere in between?
Think about how you might combine these two concepts. You may find it easier to answer this question after reading about the other major ideas. If you are not ready to choose, read on—and then return to this question.

---

hungry or punish you for smoking tobacco or marijuana. Negative freedom is the right to act as you want.

The alternative is **positive liberty**: *the freedom to pursue one's goals*. From this perspective, individuals cannot really be free—they cannot pursue their desires—if they lack the basic necessities of life. Protecting liberty means ensuring that every citizen has food, shelter, healthcare, and educational opportunities. After all, how can people truly be free if they are hungry or homeless? This view justifies government action as a way to help give all people a legitimate chance to achieve their desires.

President Franklin D. Roosevelt forcefully expressed this view in 1941. As the United States prepared for World War II, he proclaimed that the nation was fighting for "four freedoms": freedom of speech, freedom of worship, freedom from want, and freedom from fear. The first two—freedom of speech and religion—were traditional negative liberties: No one could infringe on these individual rights. However, "freedom from want" was something new, a positive liberty that entails helping needy people who have fallen on hard times. Roosevelt was suggesting that social welfare policies such as unemployment insurance and Social Security were part of the all-American idea of freedom. Contemporary ideas of positive freedom include efforts to ensure that all people are well educated or do not ruin their health by smoking. The guiding notion is that a lack of education, or illness or addiction, makes it difficult for individuals to pursue their goals.

Which idea of freedom is right? That depends on your values. Beneath these two visions of liberty lie different accounts of the good society. The negative view emphasizes personal autonomy: Taxing me violates my freedom of property. The positive view follows Roosevelt: Membership in a free society means sharing enough wealth so that everyone enjoys freedom from want. The two perspectives reflect different values, different visions of society, and different definitions of liberty.

Positive liberty: The ability—and provision of basic necessities—to pursue one's goals.

Hear President
Roosevelt deliver his
1941 speech on the
four freedoms.

The Idea of Freedom Is Always Changing

Once upon a time, Americans permitted slavery and racial segregation. Women lost all their legal rights the day they were married; their possessions—even their very bodies—passed into the custody of their husbands. Immigrants from China, and later from India, were denied any hope of becoming Americans no matter how long they lived in the country. The ideal of freedom moved Americans to reverse each of these prejudices.

Scholars disagree about how to interpret the results. Some see American history as a steady march toward greater liberty. Yes, they admit, American history is full of oppression. However, our faith in freedom leads oppressed groups to fight for their rights. The American promise, wrote Samuel Huntington, is the "promise of disharmony," as a constant parade of groups—African Americans, women, immigrants, and many others—successfully challenge the nation to live up to its ideals.[5]

Other political thinkers, such as Rogers Smith, warned against viewing American history as a steady rise of freedom. The outcome in the fight is never inevitable, they argued. Instead, freedom is won and lost . . . and won and lost again. Americans fought their bloody civil war to end slavery, only to watch new forms of racial segregation and oppression take hold and last for another century. Native Americans have never had their place on the land or in society fully restored. Struggles to secure rights are still part of the long battle for freedom. No one can say how those conflicts will end. Nor should we ever take liberty for granted.[6]

 **The Bottom Line**

» Liberty—or the freedom to pursue your goals—is the most often-invoked American value.

» There are two different views of what liberty means. *Negative liberty* emphasizes a lack of constraints on individuals, even if those constraints are intended to help others. *Positive liberty* calls on the community to help everyone satisfy their basic needs.

» Freedom has expanded to new groups over time. Some scholars see the rise of freedom as inevitable, reflecting American ideals; others see it as a constant battle that can always go either way.

Self-Rule

As the American Revolution began, crowds gathered in the towns and cities. The people, they declared, would seize authority from their royal governors (appointed by the tyrannical king) and exercise power themselves. "The mob has begun to think for itself," complained one wealthy New Yorker. "Poor reptiles, before noon they will bite" (meaning *revolt*).[7]

Patriotic crowds ignored the skeptics. At mass meetings, the people voted for laws, enforced decrees, and even issued wedding licenses. Here is a powerful image of democracy: American people bypassing government officials and running the country themselves from the town commons. The people ruled.

That principle sounds simple. The United States is the world's longest running democracy—of course the people rule. But from the beginning, a great debate arose about how to achieve **self-rule**. The Constitution was meant to settle the issue—but we are still arguing about its meaning more than 230 years later.

How do we achieve self-rule? Americans have long vacillated between two very different paths—a *democracy* and a *republic*.

> **Self-rule:** The idea that legitimate government flows from the people.

One Side of Self-Rule: Democracy

Democracy involves citizen participation in making government decisions. (*Demos* is the Greek word for "the people," and *kratia* is the Greek word for "rule/power.") In early New England, citizens governed in town meetings—without relying on elected officials. To this day, some towns are still run this way. How high should taxes be? How much should the town pay its schoolteachers? Eligible voters all can have their say before voting to decide the matter.

Many states still reach for this democratic ideal—let the public make decisions without relying on elected officials. In 2018, voters in 26 states weighed in on over 160 ballot questions including legalizing recreational marijuana (in Michigan), permitting medical marijuana (three states), raising the minimum wage (in Arkansas and Missouri), expanding Medicaid to provide health care for more people (three states), supporting the rights of crime victims (six states), permitting same day voter registration and other measures to encourage voter turnout (four states), requiring voter IDs (two states), responding to climate change (seven states), and protecting the rights of transgender people (in Massachusetts). People vote directly on an issue through a **referendum**, allowed by twenty-seven states and the District of Columbia (see Figure 2.1). **Initiatives** permit the public in twenty-four states to circulate a petition that would propose a new law or amendment to its Constitution. And most city and state governments have **sunshine laws** that open their meetings to the public.

> **Referendum:** An election in which citizens vote directly on an issue.
>
> **Initiative:** A process in which citizens propose new laws or amendments to the state constitution.

Thomas Jefferson, who drafted the Declaration of Independence and served as the third U.S. president (1801–1809), was the most vocal proponent of maximizing democracy. "The will of the majority," wrote Jefferson, is a "sacred principle" and "the only sure guardian of the rights of man." If the people cannot govern themselves, asked Jefferson, how can they possibly be trusted with the government of others?[8]

> **Sunshine laws:** Laws that permit the public to watch policymakers in action and to access the records of the proceedings.

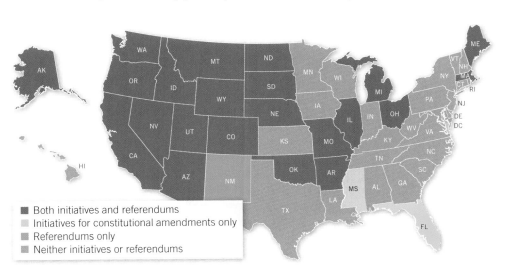

- ■ Both initiatives and referendums
- ▨ Initiatives for constitutional amendments only
- ▨ Referendums only
- ▨ Neither initiatives or referendums

● **Figure 2.1** *Most states in the Midwest and Pacific Northwest have both referendums and initiatives. These vehicles of direct democracy are less common along the East Coast. (NY Constitution.org)*

The result is a rich American legacy of taking to the streets to demonstrate, rally, and protest. Examples include demonstrations on behalf of young immigrant "Dreamers"; gun owners rallying in support of the Second Amendment; giant Earth Day demonstrations that launched the modern environmental movement; and the 1963 March on Washington, which was electrified by Martin Luther King's "I Have a Dream" speech. Some of these movements drew supporters from right across the political spectrum.

Thomas Jefferson's dream of direct democracy lives on. Idealists throughout American history have returned to his first principle: The people should exercise power as much as possible.

Another Side of Self-Rule: A Republic

Most of the men who drafted the Constitution did not agree with Jefferson about democracy. The states had tried to create direct democracy right after the American Revolution. George Washington thought the result was chaos. "We have probably had too good an opinion of human nature," he grumbled. James Madison put it most famously: "Democracies have [always] been spectacles of turbulence and contention . . . as short in their lives as violent in their deaths." The problem, said Madison, was that in direct democracy, the majority often gets carried away. They push their self-interest without paying attention to the rights of the minority. Direct democracy, he concluded, offers no barrier to lynch mobs crying for blood.[9]

Republic: A government in which citizens rule indirectly and make government decisions through their elected representatives.

The alternative is a **republic**. In this form of government, the people rule indirectly through their elected representatives. The constitutional framers made an important contribution to the theory of self-rule. Classical democratic theory suggested that popular government would only work if the people were virtuous. The founders realized that popular government would have to work with leaders and citizens who were often not very virtuous at all. "If men were angels," wrote Madison in *Federalist* No. 51, "no government would be necessary." The great challenge, he concluded, was to devise government institutions that would protect individual rights even if a majority of the people were selfish and corrupt. His solution: A republic.

Another form of democracy in action: Americans take to the streets to express their views. Here, students protest the Trump administration's attitudes toward race and immigration.

A Mixed System

Which view of self-rule holds in the United States? Both do. We can say that the United States is a democratic republic because it includes elements of a democracy *and* of a republic. There are plenty of opportunities for direct participation. At the same time, American government is organized to check the majority. The House, the Senate, the president, and the Supreme Court all put the brakes on one another. And all of them face fifty different state governments, each with its own politics, powers, and programs. The American government operates through elected and unelected officials who answer (sometimes indirectly) to the public.

The sheer number of U.S. elected officials—more than five hundred thousand—reveals our hybrid form of government. There is one elected government official for every six hundred people in the country. Few other nations come close to this ratio. We elect representatives, reflecting our origins as a republic, but the enormous number of opportunities to serve in elective office moves us closer to a democracy.

Although our government combines elements of both democracy and republic, the debate continues about which way we should tilt. Which stance do you prefer? Jefferson's faith in direct democracy? Or Madison's warning that people are not angels and that government is best pursued indirectly, with the people electing some representatives who in turn select others?

You may have noticed that these two principles—the democratic and the republican—are also the names of America's two major political parties. However, to complicate matters, the party labels do not really correspond to the party principles. Many Republican Party members are committed democrats and vice versa. We always capitalize the names of the parties—Democrats and Republicans—to avoid confusing them with the two pathways to self-rule.

The Bottom Line

» Self-rule is a powerful and enduring idea guiding American government. Lincoln put it best: "Government of the people, by the people, for the people."

» There are two chief pathways to government by the people: a *democracy* and a *republic*. Americans have always sought to balance these two ideals.

Limited Government

Back in 1691, while America was still part of Great Britain, King William III appointed Benjamin Fletcher to be governor of New York and gave him control over the New England colonies (which had been independent until then). The Connecticut legislature did not want to cede its power to Governor Fletcher and immediately selected a new commander for the local militia—a direct challenge to the new governor's authority. Fletcher could not ignore this intransigence, so on a beautiful October day he sailed to Hartford, the capital of Connecticut, with a small detachment of troops. He assembled the Connecticut militia and had an officer read aloud the royal proclamation declaring his authority over the state—and its militia.

As the officer spoke, the Connecticut militiamen began to beat their drums in defiance. Fletcher tried to restore order by commanding his soldiers to fire their muskets in the air; in the ensuing silence, he threatened to punish the militia members for their insolence. In response, the commander of the Connecticut militia stepped forward, put his hand on the hilt of his sword, and issued his own warning: "If my drummers are again interrupted, I'll make sunlight shine through you. We deny and defy your authority." Outnumbered and in no mood for bloodshed, Fletcher beat a quick retreat to his vessel and sailed ignominiously back to New York City. Because the king and his ministers were more than three thousand miles away, they never heard about this little rebellion against their authority.[10]

The Origins of Limited Government

The tale of Governor Fletcher illustrates an enduring idea: Americans distrust centralized leadership and have consistently sought to limit its power. Eighty years before the Revolutionary War, Connecticut had grown used to electing its own leaders and going its own way. The people saw the king as a distant figure with no right to interfere in their affairs. The image of central government as a remote, unfeeling, untrustworthy authority that threatens our freedoms runs through American history.

Why did Americans develop this distrust? The answer lies in how the people secured their rights in the first place. In most nations, the central government—made up of kings or aristocrats, or both—grudgingly granted their people rights such as the vote or jury trials. Sometimes the people rebelled (as in France), sometimes they negotiated with kings (England), and sometimes monarchs expanded rights to modernize their nations (Thailand). All these countries share a common experience: Kings or the central governments that replaced them were the source of rights and liberties. No wonder citizens in these nations instinctively look to the government for help in solving their problems.

The United States was dramatically different. Americans enjoyed political rights such as voting long before they even had a central government. As Governor Fletcher's humiliation illustrates, for most of colonial history the king was too far away to meddle in colonial affairs. Experience taught Americans to see the central government not as a potential source of rights, but as a threat to their life, liberty, and happiness.

This is one important reason why Americans are slow to trust their national government. Proposals such as national health insurance, a cap on carbon emissions to stop global warming, regulating the Internet, or a nationwide registry of gun sales all run up against a deep suspicion of government. The French aristocrat Alexis de Tocqueville was struck by this lack of trust. Any visitor from Europe, he wrote back in 1831, would be amazed that the American government is so "feeble and restricted." Fifty years later, the English ambassador to the United States summarized the American spirit: "The less of government the better."[11] Even today, Americans are less satisfied with how their government is working than citizens of many other nations (Comparing Nations 2.1).

And Yet . . . Americans Keep Demanding More Government

Here is the paradox lying at the heart of the limited-government idea. People across the political spectrum demand government action. Many **conservatives** seek to use federal authority to secure the border against undocumented immigration, crack down on illegal drugs, forbid abortions, or enhance homeland security. Many conservatives dream of restoring traditional morality through restrictions on obscenity in the media, regulation of video games, and a restoration of traditional marriages. Using government to restore moral values is not a new idea. Back in the 1920s, conservatives in both parties banded together with feminists and public health reformers to outlaw all sales of alcohol from coast to coast—a remarkably ambitious government effort to change people's everyday behavior. And many people still demand regulations of liquor and drugs; the United States is alone among advanced democracies in setting the drinking age at twenty-one, compared to Denmark (where it is 16), France (18), or Germany (14 for beer and wine if accompanied by an adult).

Most **liberals** reject the idea that public officials should interfere in people's private lives. You should be able to smoke marijuana, they say. But they are all for active government when it comes to economic policy or corporate regulation

Conservatives: Americans who believe in reduced government spending, personal responsibility, traditional moral values, secure borders, and a strong national defense. Also known as *right* or *right-wing*.

Liberals: Americans who value cultural diversity, government programs for the needy, public intervention in the economy, and individuals' right to a lifestyle based on their own social and moral positions. Also known as *left* or *left-wing*.

COMPARING NATIONS 2.1 | Satisfaction With How Democracies Are Working

Until the economic shock of 2008, citizens in wealthy democracies thought their system worked pretty well. Northern European nations still generally give their democracy high marks. Others do not agree. Notice how the U.S. public is right near the middle in their views of how the democracy is working—behind Canada and Sweden (and Russia) but well ahead of France, Italy, and Greece.

Notice where satisfaction is highest (in African and Asian nations) and where it is lowest (in South America and the Middle East). (*Pew Research Center*)

How satisfied are you with the way democracy is working in our country?

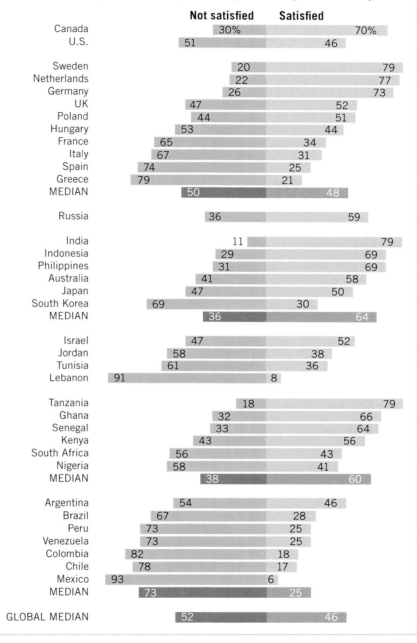

	Not satisfied	Satisfied
Canada	30%	70%
U.S.	51	46
Sweden	20	79
Netherlands	22	77
Germany	26	73
UK	47	52
Poland	44	51
Hungary	53	44
France	65	34
Italy	67	31
Spain	74	25
Greece	79	21
MEDIAN	50	48
Russia	36	59
India	11	79
Indonesia	29	69
Philippines	31	69
Australia	41	58
Japan	47	50
South Korea	69	30
MEDIAN	36	64
Israel	47	52
Jordan	58	38
Tunisia	61	36
Lebanon	91	8
Tanzania	18	79
Ghana	32	66
Senegal	33	64
Kenya	43	56
South Africa	56	43
Nigeria	58	41
MEDIAN	38	60
Argentina	54	46
Brazil	67	28
Peru	73	25
Venezuela	73	25
Colombia	82	18
Chile	78	17
Mexico	93	6
MEDIAN	73	25
GLOBAL MEDIAN	52	46

(Figure 2.2). They call on the government to sponsor fast trains, regulate Wall Street, protect the environment, and offer school lunch programs (there's the freedom from want, again). From this perspective, why shouldn't everyone have good access to healthcare? People over sixty-five like Medicare; why not extend it to all Americans? And the same for good education.

Libertarians break with both liberals and conservatives; they are strong proponents of negative liberty and aim to reduce all government to a minimum. Government, libertarians insist, should protect public safety, private property,

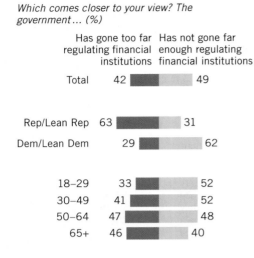

Which comes closer to your view? The government... (%)

	Has gone too far regulating financial institutions	Has not gone far enough regulating financial institutions
Total	42	49
Rep/Lean Rep	63	31
Dem/Lean Dem	29	62
18–29	33	52
30–49	41	52
50–64	47	48
65+	46	40
College grad+	34	56
Some college	37	52
HS or less	51	41

Figure 2.2 *Democrats, young people, and college graduates are more likely to say government has not gone far enough in regulating financial institutions. (Pew Research Center)*

and national borders—and do little else. No giant army or navy; no public schools; no regulating banks; no telling people which drugs they cannot use; no helping people who are hungry, or homeless, or need healthcare; no laws against discrimination. The popularity of this perspective rises and falls over time because every national crisis—from tainted food to bank failures to terrorist attacks—inspires widespread demands for government action. When a storm slams into a city, the vast majority demand a fast response from elected officials.

There's one more reason for the rising distrust of government. Stoking distrust is a good way to get voters to the polls. Republicans lashed the Obama administration as incompetent and socialistic; Democrats returned the favor by charging, for example, that Congressional Republicans were waging a war on women. President Trump has upped the ante with harsh criticism of rivals from across the political spectrum. The attacks erode basic levels of trust of and respect for our political institutions. A healthy democracy has to balance a lively clash about ideas with basic respect for the other side. That respect has been eroding for the last quarter century.[12]

Limits on Government Action

In short, Americans often say they do not like government and then demand that government address the problems they are concerned about. The Constitution itself often creates a limit to action.

When the framers designed our political system, they built suspicion of government right into the core. The federal Constitution includes an intricate system of checks and balances on power, which we explore in Chapter 3. The Constitution limits what Congress may do—but Americans vigorously debate exactly where those boundaries lie.

Although it is difficult for government officials to undertake new tasks, the barriers they face are not insurmountable. During times of crisis, people turn to the government and demand action. Skilled leadership can also negotiate sweeping changes. And once programs go into effect, they often prove popular.

Ironically, the limits on change make it difficult to repeal new programs once they make it past all the hurdles and are up and running. For example, Social Security was passed in 1935 during the economic crisis of the Great Depression; Medicare passed in part because of a great electoral landslide in 1964. Both are now extremely popular; in fact, they are so widely embraced that they are known in Washington as "the third rails" of American politics—touch them and die (politically, of course). Yes, Americans do not like government and it is difficult to win new programs. But that is only half the story. Americans also demand government action and fiercely defend the programs they like.

When Ideas Clash: Democracy and Limited Government

When President Trump was running for president, he promised to repeal and replace the Obama administration's healthcare legislation and to build a wall on the southern border. Despite months of trying, neither happened. The lack of action is no surprise. Election winners always face difficulties putting their policies into effect—a result of the many limits that Americans have placed on their own government.

Note the clash between two leading American ideas: Democracy and limited government. Democracy says that the winning party should be able to put their policies into place. In a democracy, the majority should rule. But another value, limited government, responds: Not so fast. We do not like government meddling in our private lives, so we make it very difficult for elected officials to follow through on their promises and to actually get things done. Even a president who wins a national election by a large margin must still convince the majority in the House of Representatives and 60 percent of the Senate to vote his way. (Why 60% of the Senate? You'll see in Chapter 13.) Even when Congress does pass

When people are suffering, even many critics of the government set their views aside to demand action. Here a Houston SWAT officer rescues Catherine Pham and her son Aiden from floodwaters.

Watch President Trump talking about a border wall.

What Do YOU Think?   Democracy Versus Limited Government

Some observers think we do not have a true government by the people because it is too difficult for elected officials to get things done, even with a large popular majority. These reformers seek an easier path to government action. However, that prospect raises fears of a more active government. Which should we emphasize, democratic self-rule or limited government? It's time to make your choice.

I'm with Thomas Jefferson.
It should be easier for elected officials to enact the programs they promised. If they cannot do so, elections become less meaningful. When the people vote for something and their representatives fail to deliver, it fosters cynicism about the entire political process. Democracy requires us to follow the people's mandate. If the majority does not like the results, it can express its displeasure in the next election.

I'm with James Madison.
The checks and balances that make large-scale reforms difficult protect the United States from overbearing government and from sudden changes—whether rapidly expanding or cutting programs. The barriers to government action *should* be high. If the public really wants something, it will probably happen over time. Limited government is more important. Don't change the process.

Not sure?
This is a formidable question. You may very well change your mind—maybe more than once—as you continue to read this book.

a law—which is no easy task—the program often faces challenges in the courts for violating constitutional limits on government power.

The result is an important question for political scientists—and for all Americans: How should we balance democracy and limited government? Erecting too many boundaries means that we undermine government by the majority. But remove the barriers and the winning party can pass all the programs it promised—until it loses in elections and the other party eliminates all those programs and pushes through the agenda that it promised.

The Bottom Line

» Americans distrust their government more than people in most wealthy democracies traditionally have—though new pressures are making many other nations more like the United States. The Constitution builds that distrust into our governing rules by providing for limited government. The result is a very durable status quo.

» In many countries, politicians can usually deliver the programs they promised on the campaign trail. In the United States, winners confront multiple barriers to fulfilling their pledges—the antigovernment idea is built into multiple checks and balances.

» However, once programs do go into effect, they often prove popular and difficult to change.

Individualism

Political scientist John Kingdon was visiting his niece in Norway. She was expecting a baby, and Professor Kingdon asked what she planned to do about her job. Casually, she replied that she would receive a full year's leave at 80 percent of her normal pay, and that her company was required to give her job back after the leave. "Who pays for all this?" asked Professor Kingdon. "The government, of course," his niece replied. She was surprised the question had even come up. "Is it any different in the United States?" she asked innocently.[13]

As Kingdon explained, it is completely different in the United States: Advocates fought for years to win the Family and Medical Leave Act (1993), which requires employers with more than fifty workers to allow up to twelve weeks of *unpaid* leave for pregnancy, adoption, illness, or military service.

Individualism: The idea that individuals, not the society, are responsible for their own well-being.

Americans generally value **individualism**: *The idea that individuals, not the society or the community or the government, are responsible for their own well-being.* We, as a society, do not pay for maternity leave. Instead, we expect private individuals and families to handle birth, or adoption, or caregiving. But that is only one part of the American story.

Community Versus Individualism

The idea of individualism is a source of controversy in every nation (see Comparing Nations 2.2). There are two ways to see any society: as a single *community* or as a collection of *individuals*. Every nation includes both, but government policies can

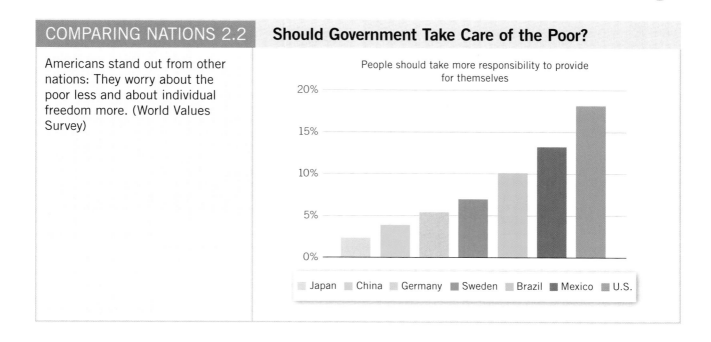

COMPARING NATIONS 2.2 | **Should Government Take Care of the Poor?**

Americans stand out from other nations: They worry about the poor less and about individual freedom more. (World Values Survey)

People should take more responsibility to provide for themselves

Japan China Germany Sweden Brazil Mexico U.S.

be designed to emphasize the community or to focus on individuals. Let us take a closer look at these two principles.

Countries that emphasize the community are called **social democracies**. Social democrats believe that members of a society are responsible for one another. They view government as a source of mutual assistance. The government provides citizens with the basics: good health insurance, retirement benefits, generous unemployment packages, and—as we saw in the Norwegian case—maternity benefits.

In exchange, people pay high taxes. Almost half of a Norwegian's income goes to taxes. One effect of high taxation is to make it difficult for most citizens to get very rich. At the same time, the extensive welfare state makes it far less likely that people will live in poverty. Communal societies are far more equal—not just in opportunity, but in outcome. Most Western European nations are social democracies.

Social democracies are based on *solidarity*, the idea that people have a tight bond and are responsible for one another. Some societies exhibit a very strong sense of solidarity. In general, solidarity increases during wars, economic depressions, or other crises that get everyone to pull together. Scholars have found that more homogeneous societies—those in which people look alike, share the same values, and practice the same religion—exhibit higher rates of solidarity than very diverse societies. They point out that even long-established social democracies in Europe (historically populated primarily by Christians) have seen their sense of solidarity falter with the arrival of Muslim immigrants. Growing diversity has challenged national solidarity.[14]

American politics includes a strong streak of solidarity that balances its individualism. Martin Luther King put it eloquently: "I am inevitably my brother's keeper because I am my brother's brother."[15] However, the commitment to solidarity rises and falls in the United States. Perhaps it will strengthen, again, with the rising generations?

Social democracy: the idea that government policy should ensure that all are comfortably cared for within the context of a capitalist economy.

● Images of individualism and solidarity. The Republican National Convention backdrop emphasizes self-reliance and individual achievement; Democrat Bernie Sanders emphasizes community and solidarity.

Now let us turn to individualism. In this view, people and their families are responsible for their own welfare. The economist Milton Friedman famously argued that the world runs on individuals pursuing their separate interests. Leave people free to choose their interests, Friedman continued, and the public interest of the whole society will emerge.[16] Rather than taxing people and using funds to aid the less well-off, proponents of this perspective opt for low taxes and a green light for private entrepreneurs. People who work hard will get ahead, they believe, and society will grow and prosper.

Individualists value the chance to get ahead more than they value a society in which everyone is equal. In social democracies, government regulations aim to protect workers. In contrast, individualists oppose government controls and believe that private companies should be able to expand or contract their workforce as they see fit (as long as they hire and fire without discriminating). People should take care of one another through churches, charities, or other private means. Individualism points toward limited government, faith in economic markets, and a strong emphasis on *negative liberty*.

The Roots of American Individualism: Opportunity and Discord

Americans lean toward individualism and away from social democracy. Why? Two famous explanations look to the past. One finds the answer in golden opportunities. A second emphasizes social and racial discord.

Golden Opportunity. For centuries, most Europeans and Asians lived as serfs or peasants working small plots of land. Powerful rulers kept them firmly in their place—there was little chance for individuals to get ahead by working hard. In early America, by contrast, there appeared to be endless land and opportunity. With hard work and a little luck, anyone (at least any white male) could earn a decent living and perhaps even a fortune. Stories about early settlers clearing their own land were later reinforced by images of rugged individuals on the western frontier. Hard workers relied on themselves—not the government.

There is a lot of myth in these stories. Frontier life was less about brave individualism and more about communities. Settlers could not build a barn, a church, or a meetinghouse without their neighbors' help. But the image of hardy individuals on the frontier remains a powerful ideal in American culture and politics. And there was an important truth at its core: Few societies have ever offered so many individuals as much opportunity to rise and prosper as early America did.[17]

Social Conflict. Another explanation for American individualism emphasizes the enormous differences within our society. The country is too big and the population too diverse to develop a sense of solidarity. What, after all, did Calvinist Yankees in New England have in common with

● *Individualism in historical memory: At high noon on April 22, 1889, bugles sounded and a great mob—lined up impatiently outside the territory—surged across the Oklahoma border and snatched up as much land as they could stake out. Although the government sponsored the land giveaway, the image that has stuck is of people grabbing the land for themselves. Oklahoma still honors the scalawags that snuck in early ("sooner") and staked the best land—which is where the motto "The Sooner State" comes from.*

Roman Catholics in Baltimore or Anglican planters in Virginia—much less Spanish speakers in Florida or Texas? Moreover, a nation that included four million black slaves by 1860 had a terrible divide running through its heart.

By the 1830s still another source of division had arisen. Immigrants speaking different languages and practicing what seemed like strange customs were arriving by the tens (and later hundreds) of thousands. Each generation of immigrants added to the American cacophony. For example, Irish Catholics (who arrived in the 1830s and 1840s) seemed strange to the English Protestants who had immigrated a century earlier. Could Catholics, with their allegiance to a foreign pope, really understand or uphold American values? Fifty years later, newly arriving Italians, Poles, and Chinese seemed just as threatening to the Irish, who by then had settled in.[18] All of these divisions made solidarity far more difficult to feel than in the more stable, homogeneous populations.

Which explanation is correct? Both are on target. Unprecedented economic opportunity and vast social divisions have reinforced individualism.

Who We Are? Individualism and Solidarity

Americans are not individualists pure and simple. Rather, the two themes—individualism and solidarity—always compete in American politics. Individualism is more robust and more often in evidence, but a sense of solidarity also unites the population. Americans often pull together as a nation. They take care of our neighbors and pass government programs to improve the lives of people they do not know. The United States may have deep divisions, but it is remarkable how quickly they can disappear. A substantial majority of Americans today are children, grandchildren, or great-grandchildren of immigrants—many of whom were once regarded as strange and different.

All this raises another question to ponder: Where would you draw the line between solidarity and individualism? The answer directly relates to one of this book's central questions: *Who are we?* Take the test in "What Do You Think?" to learn where you stand on the continuum between rugged individualism and strong solidarity.

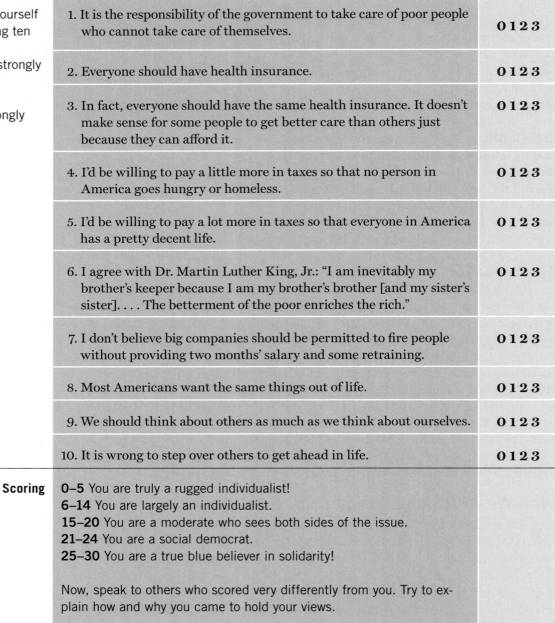

What Do YOU Think?

Individualism Versus Solidarity

Please score yourself on the following ten statements:

0 = Disagree strongly
1 = Disagree
2 = Agree
3 = Agree strongly

Take the test online and find out how you score.

1. It is the responsibility of the government to take care of poor people who cannot take care of themselves.	0 1 2 3
2. Everyone should have health insurance.	0 1 2 3
3. In fact, everyone should have the same health insurance. It doesn't make sense for some people to get better care than others just because they can afford it.	0 1 2 3
4. I'd be willing to pay a little more in taxes so that no person in America goes hungry or homeless.	0 1 2 3
5. I'd be willing to pay a lot more in taxes so that everyone in America has a pretty decent life.	0 1 2 3
6. I agree with Dr. Martin Luther King, Jr.: "I am inevitably my brother's keeper because I am my brother's brother [and my sister's sister]. . . . The betterment of the poor enriches the rich."	0 1 2 3
7. I don't believe big companies should be permitted to fire people without providing two months' salary and some retraining.	0 1 2 3
8. Most Americans want the same things out of life.	0 1 2 3
9. We should think about others as much as we think about ourselves.	0 1 2 3
10. It is wrong to step over others to get ahead in life.	0 1 2 3

Scoring

0–5 You are truly a rugged individualist!
6–14 You are largely an individualist.
15–20 You are a moderate who sees both sides of the issue.
21–24 You are a social democrat.
25–30 You are a true blue believer in solidarity!

Now, speak to others who scored very differently from you. Try to explain how and why you came to hold your views.

The Bottom Line

» American politics includes both individualism and solidarity.

» Different leaders, parties, groups, and individuals weigh the two values in different ways. However, compared to other nations, the United States is very much at the individualist end of the spectrum.

🎯 The American Dream

Benjamin Franklin perfected a classic American literary form—tips for getting rich. Anyone, he assured his readers, could be successful by following a formula: be frugal ("A penny saved is a penny earned"), hardworking ("No gains without pains"), steady ("Little strokes fell great oaks"), bold ("God helps those who help themselves"), and—most important—morally upright ("Leave your vices, though ever so dear").[19]

Franklin summarized what later became known as the American dream: *If you are talented and work hard, you can achieve personal (and especially financial) success.* A popular historian, James Truslow Adams, was the first to actually label it the American dream. The United States, he wrote, is "a land in which life should be better and richer and fuller for everyone, with opportunity for each according to ability or achievement."[20] The idea scarcely changes across generations. "The American dream that we were all raised on is a simple but powerful one," averred President Bill Clinton more than two centuries after Ben Franklin. "If you work hard and play by the rules, you should be given a chance to go as far as your God-given abilities will take you."[21]

Spreading the Dream

The legacy of the Revolutionary War, according to historian Gordon Wood, was the spread of the American dream to all classes. National leaders originally imagined that they were establishing a classical republic, such as Athens, in which a few outstanding men would govern the people. Instead, the Revolution established the common people (at the time, that meant white men) as the basis of government and gave them an unprecedented chance to make their fortunes. What did the mass of people care about? "Making money and getting ahead," wrote Wood. Yes, it was vulgar, material, and crass. But such opportunity had never been available on such a broad scale before.[22]

Enabling the dream of success remains an important part of any policy debate. Will a proposal help small business? Will it create jobs? Will it stifle entrepreneurs? Immigrants still come to the United States in large numbers—far more than to any other country—partly to pursue the dream of success.

Challenging the Dream

As with every important idea, the American dream generates conflict. Critics raise two questions: Has the system become rigged to favor the wealthy at the expense of giving everyone a fair shot at success? And is the pursuit of wealth an undesirable value because it crowds out other important values?

Is the System Tilted Toward the Wealthy?   Some critics question whether the American dream is still open to everyone or whether it has grown biased toward the rich and powerful. When Tocqueville wrote *Democracy in America* in the 1830s, the United States offered more opportunities to get ahead than perhaps any nation in history. Vast open lands (open, that is, once Native Americans had been driven away—see Chapter 6) offered a fresh start for the ambitious and the resourceful.

For much of U.S. history, including the boom years after World War II, middle class incomes rose faster than incomes at the top. Then, starting around 1979, this trend changed. Money began to flow to the wealthiest more than to the other classes. Figure 2.3A and 2.3B compare the two periods.

Today, the wealthiest three million Americans, the top 1 percent of households, enjoy a lot more of the nation's wealth (about 40%) than the 290 million people who make up the bottom 90 percent (and control 22% of the wealth). The sixty million

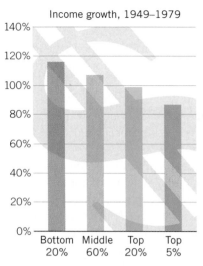

Income growth, 1949–1979

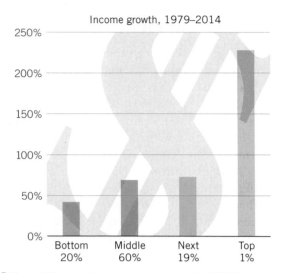

Income growth, 1979–2014

● **Figure 2.3A** *Between 1949 and 1979, those on the bottom saw their earnings grow faster than those on the top. (Robert Frank, Falling Behind)*

● **Figure 2.3B** *. . . but look how that changed after 1979. Now those on the bottom have very little income growth while the wealthy have very rapid growth. Is this a bad thing? Americans disagree. (Russell Sage Foundation, Chartbook of Inequality)*

Americans at the bottom of the charts own almost nothing—one-tenth of one percent of the national wealth. The median white family is ten times wealthier than the median black family. Inequality continues to rise, as the gap between richest and poorest widens.[23]

Many social scientists now argue that the chance of moving up from poverty to wealth is fading in the United States. Studies suggest that someone in the bottom fifth of the income distribution is twice as likely to move up at least one category (or quintile) in Canada, Denmark, or France as they are in the United States (see Comparing Nations 2.3). Critics worry that the system is tilted toward insiders with good connections (known as crony capitalism) or the children of the wealthy. Both conservatives and liberals challenge the United States to live up to its promise of equality of opportunity.[24]

Does the American Dream Promote the Wrong Values?   A second critique of the American dream questions the chase for wealth as a human value. Environmentalists criticize the damage caused by big houses, sprawling suburbs, gas-guzzling cars, and opulent lifestyles. Others cite the harm to old-fashioned communal ideals. "These dark days will be worth all they cost us," said President Franklin Roosevelt during the depths of the Great Depression, "if they teach us that our true destiny is . . . to minister . . . to our fellow man." Today, young American evangelicals are offering an even sharper challenge to greed and the race for success as a threat to the biblical call to service.[25]

President Lyndon Johnson put civil rights in the same larger context. "Should we double our wealth and conquer the stars, and still not be equal to this issue [racial equity], then we will have failed as a people and as a nation. For with a whole country as with a person, 'What is a man profited, if he should gain the whole world, and lose his own soul?'" Voices like these have questioned the pursuit of economic success to the exclusion of community and social justice. Fifteen million children—around 21 percent—live below the poverty line in the United States. Critics charge that

| COMPARING NATIONS 2.3 | **Social Mobility Around the World** |

Many nations—including Japan, New Zealand, and even Pakistan—have developed more social mobility than the United States. In 2015, China's president Xi Jinping began calling the aspirations of upward mobility the "Chinese dream," nudging the American dream aside—though China still has lower mobility rates than most Western democracies, including the United States. The chart displays the sharp increase in U.S. inequality over a thirty-year period, compared to other countries. (Organization for Economic Cooperation and Development)

How much does the top 1% earn?

Share of top 1% as percent of total pre-tax income
2012
1981

20%

15%

10%

5%

0%

United States | United Kingdom | Germany | Canada | Switzerland | Ireland | Portugal | Japan | Italy | Australia | Spain | France | Norway | Finland | New Zealand | Sweden | Denmark | Netherlands

something is amiss with the American dream if we let so many of our children live in poverty.[26]

The criticisms, however, rarely stick for long. Ralph Waldo Emerson, a nineteenth-century essayist and lecturer, summed up the usual view when he questioned the motives of his iconoclastic friend, Henry David Thoreau. "I cannot help counting it a fault in him that he had no ambition," said Emerson at Thoreau's funeral. "Instead of engineering for all America, he was the captain of a huckleberry party."[27]

Many people would rather go out in the woods like Thoreau and pick huckleberries than join the rat race for greater material benefits. The capitalists who celebrate wealth often have to wrestle with economic populists who would rather share it. In a 2017 poll, just 11 percent agreed that "becoming wealthy" is a key feature of the American dream; far more (77%) emphasized "freedom of choice in how to live one's life" (the idea of liberty, highlighted above), and 48 percent "making valuable contributions to my community" (the idea of solidarity).[28]

Despite critics and challenges, Americans usually celebrate the gospel of success. The nation's politics, economics, and culture accommodate dreams of wealth. In comparison with other wealthy nations, our taxes are relatively low, we regulate business less, we take fewer vacations, and we place more emphasis on getting ahead. One group that may be questioning these long-standing truths is younger Americans. In a series of Harvard University studies, nearly half (between 44–48%) of the eighteen- to twenty-nine-year-olds said that the American Dream did not apply to their generation—a trend worth watching closely in coming years.[29]

Compare liberties and poverty levels among nations.

The Bottom Line

» The American dream is the belief that anyone who works hard can get ahead and grow wealthy.

» Critics argue that hard work is no longer enough. They offer two criticisms: First, the poor and the middle class are falling farther behind the wealthy because of bias in the political economy; and second, other values are more important than wealth.

» Despite the critics, the dream remains a powerful American idea.

Equality

When Tocqueville arrived in the United States in 1831, he was amazed by the widespread equality. In one of his first letters home, he reported watching servers in a tavern sit down at the next table to eat and drink alongside the guests. Here was a society in which people from all ranks shook hands, discussed politics, and chased money. Everyone seemed to be equals.

Tocqueville distilled this thought into the first sentence of his great book *Democracy in America*: "No novelty in the United States struck me more vividly . . . than the equality of condition." In a world that was still full of aristocrats and inherited privilege, American society embodied the great idea at the heart of the Declaration of Independence: "All men [and women] are created equal."[30]

Equality means that *every citizen enjoys the same privileges, status, and rights before the law*. There are three different types of equality to consider when analyzing the concept: *social*, *political*, and *economic*.

Equality: All citizens enjoy the same privileges, status, and rights before the law.

Three Types of Equality

Social equality means that all individuals enjoy the same status in society. There are no American barons or archdukes who inherit special benefits when they are born. This aspect of American society has not changed since the nation's founding. Except for slavery, there have never been fixed social classes. Few American politicians boast of noble origins or good family lineage. On the contrary, for the past 150 years candidates have flaunted (or invented) their working-class roots. Even very wealthy politicians often claim to have humble origins (for many years, they boasted about the log cabins they supposedly grew up in). An old cliché in American politics, one with a lot of truth to it, is the saying that any little boy or girl could grow up to be the president—or a millionaire.

Social equality: All individuals enjoy the same status in society.

Political equality means that every citizen has the same political rights and opportunities. Americans enjoyed universal white, male *suffrage*—or the right to vote—much earlier than did citizens of most nations. Over time the opportunity to vote spread. Today there are lively debates about whether we still ensure everyone an equal opportunity to affect the political process. Some reformers suggest, for example, that if everyone is to have the same chance to influence the political process, we should remove money from elections. Otherwise, the wealthy will have outsized influence over the outcome. Others counter that individuals who are excited by candidates should be allowed to contribute to them (we discuss the issue in Chapter 10).

Political equality: All citizens have the same political rights and opportunities.

The quest for political equality raises many other issues: Does everyone enjoy an equal right to a fair trial—or have the costs of going to court elevated this basic value

Most Americans Believe

THERE IS "OPPORTUNITY TO GET AHEAD"

Although most people see the American dream as a viable goal, demographic groups differ in their perception of their chances of achieving it.

Most people say they have achieved the American dream – or are on their way to achieving it

Do you believe your family has achieved the American dream? (%)

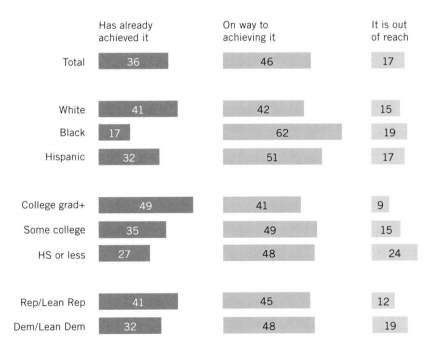

	Has already achieved it	On way to achieving it	It is out of reach
Total	36	46	17
White	41	42	15
Black	17	62	19
Hispanic	32	51	17
College grad+	49	41	9
Some college	35	49	15
HS or less	27	48	24
Rep/Lean Rep	41	45	12
Dem/Lean Dem	32	48	19

Note: Whites and blacks include only those who are not Hispanic; Hispanics are of any race. "Don't know" responses not shown.

THINK ABOUT IT

What percentage of whites, Hispanic, and African Americans believe that they have achieved or are achieving the American dream?

How does education affect a person's perception of whether the American dream is within reach?

Which of the groups do you belong to? Does your attitude align with the majority of others in your demographic group?

Source: Pew Research Center

Economic equality: A situation in which there are small differences in wealth among citizens.

beyond the reach of many people? Does the voting system make it too difficult for some people to register and cast their ballots? Does every citizen have an *equal opportunity* to influence the political process, and are they all treated the same way before the law?

Economic equality focuses on differences in wealth. When President Washington toured the country in 1790 he noticed that in some regions there were few very wealthy people and little poverty. For more than a century and a half, the nation truly was exceptional in its relative economic equality.[31]

Today the United States has changed dramatically—toward inequality. In 1970, the level of economic inequality in the United States was similar to that in most other wealthy democracies. On one measure of economic inequality, known as the Gini coefficient, the United States ranked between France and Japan on the equality tables. Today, in contrast, America has become far less equal than nations such as Japan, Sweden, and Germany. We are now closer to the most unequal country in the world (Lesotho) than we are to the most equal (Sweden). Should we adopt public policies that aim to limit economic inequality? Let us look more closely at this much contested issue.

How Much Economic Inequality Is Too Much?

Median: A statistical term for the number in the middle or the case that has an equal number of examples above and below it.

Inequality in America has reached levels not seen in almost a century. One illustration of national differences in economic inequality is the "salary gap." In 1965, the **median** (or typical) American chief executive officer (CEO) made twenty-six times more than a typical worker in his or her company. In Japan today the figure is roughly the same. But in the contemporary United States, the average CEO makes (depending on the study) between three hundred to five hundred times the salary of the average employee. Is this a problem for the idea that "all men are created equal"?

People in many countries would answer "yes." Too much inequality, they say, divides society. In Japan, cultural norms encourage individuals to avoid attracting attention through great wealth or ostentation. In fact, Tocqueville warned Americans that they might be vulnerable to economic inequality: "The friends of democracy should keep their eyes anxiously fixed in [the] direction [of] . . . the manufacturing aristocracy we see rising up."[32]

Our public policies (and public opinions) often endorse the race to wealth. People who have won great success—hedge fund managers, basketball stars, successful musicians, CEOs, and breakout entrepreneurs—should enjoy the wealth they accumulate. On the other side, critics charge that the richest 1 percent take

Alice Walton, daughter of Wal-Mart founder Sam Walton, inherited over $30 billion.

Should we worry about economic inequality? Should we change the rules so that the wealthy get less and poor people more?

advantage of everyone else. Tax laws and other rules are tilted in their favor. This debate stretches back over American history: Should our laws encourage or discourage the accumulation of terrific fortunes?

Opportunity or Outcome?

Many Americans accept high levels of economic inequality, contending that these are not fatal to our hopes for an egalitarian society. That is because of an important distinction between *equal opportunity* and *equal outcome.*

Equal opportunity is the idea that every American has a similar chance in life. In politics, this means that each person gets one vote and that the process is transparent and open to all. In economics, it means that every individual gets a fair shot at achieving the American dream. Whether you are white or black, Anglo or Latino, male or female, rich or poor, you have a similar opportunity to influence the political process and to win economic success.

Equal outcome, in contrast, is the idea that a society guarantees not just opportunity but also results. Some nations reserve a minimum number of seats in the national legislature for women or members of specific ethnic groups. And, as we have already seen, others keep their taxes high and offer extensive social benefits, knowing that this arrangement will keep successful people from getting too far ahead of everyone else.

Today, the United States aims for equal opportunity. The winners fly in private jets; the losers may end up with nothing. Questions—and hard political choices—about equal opportunity remain. How do we give people a real chance to affect the governing process? How much education is enough to help ensure that a graduate can make it in the marketplace? Do we need to provide early childhood reading programs? Offer English-language programs for everyone not fluent? And what should we do about past injustices? Does the long legacy of slavery, segregation, and repressive policies toward Native American Indians require our society to offer special forms of compensation to these groups? What about inheritance laws that permit some people to start life with billions and others with nothing?

These questions return us to the same policy debates we introduced during the discussion of positive and negative liberty. Should we guarantee the basics—or simply protect individual rights and let every person run the great race alone? As you can see, debates about equality lead back to debates about freedom (positive or negative) and individualism.

Concern has grown in recent years that the gap between rich and poor will grow so large that it undermines equality of opportunity. Americans have long pointed proudly to our prosperous middle class—and indeed, for most of the nation's history middle-class Americans had the highest average incomes in the world. Yet the percentage of Americans who are middle class shrunk from sixty-one in 1971 to fifty by 2015[33] (see Figure 2.4). As the gap continues to widen, liberals warn that growing disparities are creating a land of a few billionaires and many hungry children with grim prospects. Conservatives respond that the effort to redistribute wealth from rich to poor discourages entrepreneurs from innovating and generating

Equal opportunity: The idea that every American has the same chance to influence politics and achieve economic success.

Equal outcome: The idea that citizens should have roughly equal economic circumstances.

Assess current debates on tax reform.

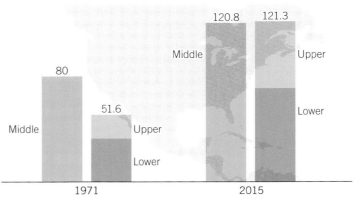

Middle-income Americans are no longer in the majority ...

Adult population by income tier (in millions)

● **Figure 2.4** *The middle class is losing ground in the United States.* *(Pew Social Research)*

new wealth. And they point out that today there are more wealthy people as well as more poor ones. Expanded wealth at the top, in their view, will help the many through job creation.

Over time, the United States has gone from the most equal society in the world to one that is considerably less equal than other wealthy nations. The past thirty-five years, in particular, have seen a very sharp spike in inequality. American politics has come to emphasize other ideas—negative liberty, individualism, the American dream of getting ahead—over equality. Still, we live in a dynamic and fluid society. Today, many Americans, both conservatives and liberals, call for renewed efforts to increase equality of opportunity. This may be one of the hottest political issues facing Americans today.

 **The Bottom Line**

» Equality means that every citizen enjoys the same privileges, status, and rights before the law.

» Equality applies to social status, political rights, and economic conditions.

» Today, America generally aims for *equal opportunity* rather than *equal outcome*, though heated discussions rage over what society must provide to ensure equal opportunity.

Religion

In the 1630s, a large contingent of Puritans escaped European persecution and sailed to New England with an ambitious aim: to establish a biblical commonwealth that would serve as a Christian model for the rest of the world. Governor John Winthrop called their settlement "a city upon a hill" and expected "the eyes of all people on us."[34] How did they fare? If people really were watching, they soon saw unexpected complications.

For example, Quakers from Pennsylvania—whom the Puritans despised for lacking discipline—began sailing north to convert the New Englanders. If the Quakers succeeded, they would subvert the whole idea of the model Puritan society. New England's women, the ministers worried, might be especially vulnerable to Quaker heresies. The authorities banned Quakers from Massachusetts under threat of having an ear cut off (one each for the first and second offense), having their tongues pierced by hot pokers (third offense), and finally death. Quaker martyrs piously and joyfully challenged the Puritan authorities. Four were hanged before English authorities ordered an end to the punishment.

This story illustrates the importance of religion, the intense competition between sects, and a missionary fervor to save the world. Even today, politicians of every stripe repeat the idea of a "city on a hill" (although few realize that Winthrop was quoting the Sermon on the Mount from the New Testament).

Still a Religious Country

Religion plays an enduring role in American politics and society. The centrality of religion in U.S. national life may not surprise you. But it is a powerful example of American exceptionalism. As most nations grow wealthier, their religious fervor wanes. Citizens in developed countries, from Britain and France to Japan and South Korea,

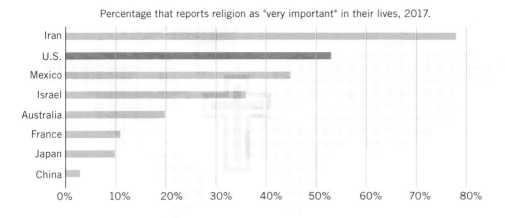

Percentage that reports religion as "very important" in their lives, 2017.

● **Figure 2.5** *Look how American religiosity stands out. As nations grow wealthy, religion nearly always loses its importance. The United States is the great exception. (Pew Research Center)*

tell pollsters that God is not very important in their lives. In contrast, Americans maintain high (and by some measures, rising) levels of religiosity (see Figure 2.5). Some 87 percent of Americans say they believe in God, 54 percent belong to a church (or synagogue, mosque, etc.), and 46 percent attend services at least once a month.[35] To find higher levels you have to go to poorer nations such as India, Egypt, and Indonesia. However, the percentage of Americans who are religiously unaffiliated—who describe themselves as atheist, agnostic, or "no religion"—appears to be growing. A recent survey found a little more than one in five (one in three for millennials) identified with these "nones."[36]

So Many Religions

Americans have a lot of religions to choose from (see Figure 2.6). One recent survey found sixteen different Christian denominations with more than a million members each.[37] That is just the beginning. Jews number over 6.7 million, Muslims some three million, and seven other non-Christian groups over 100,000 adherents each (two of the fastest growing are Wiccans and Pagans).[38] In contrast, many other nations have a single major faith, often supported by the government through tax dollars.

Why does the United States have so many religions? From the start, different colonies began with distinct religious affiliations. By forbidding the federal government from boosting any official faith, the Constitution has kept the field open for any new preacher with a religious idea that might attract a following. Because none can win official recognition, each religious institution is only as strong as the congregation it can muster.

This open market explains why new religions spring up all the time. It does not explain why Americans respond. Religious leaders and scholars continue to

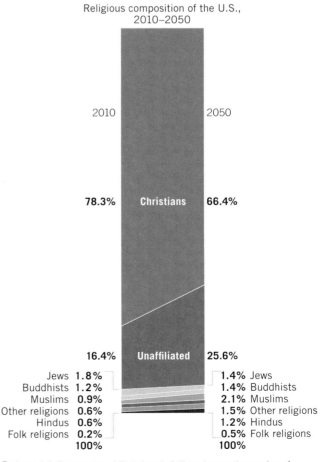

Religious composition of the U.S., 2010–2050

● **Figure 2.6** *The number of Christians is falling whereas the number of unaffiliated is rapidly rising. Muslims, Hindus, and folk religions are also rising. Even with these changes the U.S. population remains more churched than most wealthy nations. (Pew Forum)*

TABLE 2.1 **Changing American Religious Landscape**

	SILENT GENERATION (BORN 1928–1945)	BABY BOOMERS (BORN 1946–1964)	GENERATION X (BORN 1965–1980)	OLDER MILLENNIALS (BORN 1981–1989)	YOUNGER MILLENNIALS (BORN 1990–1996)
Christian	85	78	70	57	56
Other faiths	4	5	6	8	8
Unaffiliated	11	17	23	34	36
Source: Pew Research Center					

explore why Americans continue to worship, while citizens in other wealthy nations show a declining interest in religion.

Religious observance is not the same throughout the United States. Texas and Georgia (proud members of the "Bible Belt") have very high religiosity, Florida and Missouri are in the middle, Colorado and Wisconsin are not especially religious, and Maine is the least religious of all.

Generational change is also at work: Although younger cohorts continue to report high rates of religious faith, an unusual number do not affiliate with any denomination (see Table 2.1). Most believe in God, but not organized religion. In surveys asking about formal religious affiliation, nearly a quarter of all Americans, and four in ten millennials, responded "none." Still, a large majority continue to report a high level of religiosity.[39]

Politics of Religion

How is religion relevant to politics? The First Amendment declares, "Congress shall make no law respecting an establishment of religion or prohibiting the free exercise thereof." Thomas Jefferson described "a wall of separation between church and state."[40] And yet America's energetic religious life—marked through our history by great evangelical revivals—injects three different types of political issues into American politics.

First, there is the question of what exactly the Constitution forbids. Even the founders disagreed. Presidents George Washington and John Adams held national days of prayer; President Jefferson thought that this practice violated the First Amendment.

The argument about what is permissible continues to this day. May teachers lead prayers in public schools? May public school students in the bleachers organize prayers before football games? May judges post the Ten Commandments in a courthouse? Questions such as these spark intense debates about where to draw the line between church and state (see Chapter 5 for the answers).

Second, religious faith often inspires people to throw themselves into political issues. The civil rights movement spilled out from Baptist and Methodist churches across the South, with religious rhetoric, religious symbols, and religious zeal. The opponents of racial equality—arguing for slavery and segregation—also framed their response in religious terms. In American politics, both sides often invoke God. The controversies swirling around the politics of peace, abortion, the environment, equality, same-sex marriage, and many other issues have all, to varying extents, made the same leap from pulpit to politics. Today, conservatives are more likely to take their faith into the political arena, but this has not always been true.

Third, religious fervor sometimes fosters a missionary sense in American politics. As the nation expanded westward, Americans declared their "manifest destiny"—God had given an entire continent to his chosen people. During the Cold War, American leaders constantly invoked God as a way of contrasting the United States with communist nations. Congress added "under God" to the Pledge of Allegiance in 1954 and "In God We Trust" to paper money in 1955. A half-century later, President George W. Bush invoked "God's gift of freedom" to explain America's mission in Iraq. John Winthrop's idea—America as a model for the world—echoes from one generation to the next.

Political scientists often write about liberty, democracy, and equality. Religion usually flies below researchers' radar, but it is a constant element in American politics. Ignoring religion means regularly being surprised as intense religious feelings sweep past the separation between church and state.

● What constitutes religious teaching?

 **The Bottom Line**

» Religion plays an enduring role in American politics and society. This is unusual—almost unique—among wealthy countries.

» Americans have an unusually large number of faiths to choose from, although younger people are less likely than their elders to affiliate with an organized religion.

» Religious politics raise questions about the role and extent of religion in our national public life. They inspire political participation on a host of issues—from civil rights to abortion. And they foster a missionary sense in American foreign policy.

How Do Ideas Affect Politics?

Most political scientists agree that the seven ideas of this chapter are central to American society. But how do these ideas influence our politics? There are two familiar answers. Either ideas influence our culture, or they operate through our institutions. There is still another possibility to bear in mind: perhaps ideas have a life all their own.

Find out how political culture shapes government.

Ideas in American Culture

Each nation has a unique **political culture**, constructed over the years by a people and its leaders. Anthropologist Clifford Geertz described culture as the stories a group tells about itself. Ideas such as liberty, the fear of government, individualism, and the American dream together are the foundation of American political culture. They are the stories Americans tell about themselves.[41]

A culture shapes the way people think about politics and government. Culture develops over time, shaped by history and experience. Colonial Americans' shared beliefs, stories, and mental habits—their culture—inspired the founding generation to develop a Constitution that limits the power of government. Why did the framers add a bill of rights to the Constitution? Their faith in individualism. Why are there so many checks and balances in our national government? A fear of too much government, dating back to colonial times. Why do we regulate and tax less than other nations? The American dream's gospel of success. This shared culture leads men and women to fight for policies that reflect freedom or democracy; policies that reflect social-democratic solidarity are more difficult to win because they resonate more faintly in American culture. Americans' hopes and fears often seem peculiar to people in other nations—just as their hopes and fears may not make sense to us.

In short, the United States, like every other nation, has a rich national culture that should be read as a perpetual work in progress. Every era and each generation experience their own exuberant debate about what the nation has been, and what it should to be.[42]

Ideas in Political Institutions

A different perspective suggests that ideas operate through political institutions. The institutions are the key to political action. James Madison explained the *institutional perspective*. Past political theory expected republican citizens to virtuously seek the public interest. But, Madison wrote sardonically in the *Federalist Papers*, "enlightened statesmen will not always be at the helm."[43] The Constitution did not ask people to be virtuous; instead, it envisioned a government that could operate smoothly even if its citizens were greedy and their leaders corrupt. The institution—the rules and organizations built into the government—would shape political behavior.

Many political scientists continue to follow in Madison's footsteps. It is our governing institutions, starting with the Constitution, that shape American politics.

From an institutional perspective, the barriers to enacting new programs emerge not from a dislike of government but from the way the government is organized. The U.S. government is slow to act, according to this view, because we have *designed* it to be slow to act by building in multiple checks and balances on every level of government. When Americans criticize their policymakers for inaction,

● *Ideas move politics. A member of Americans for Prosperity, a conservative group, goes door to door to persuade voters about the benefits of tax cuts.*

perhaps they miss the point: Gridlock is a consequence of the institutions we have inherited.

Culture or Institutions?

Although historians and sociologists tend to emphasize political culture, many political scientists are skeptical about its explanatory power. How, they ask, can something as static as national culture explain the fluid, fast-changing American political scene?

For example, the cultural perspective suggests that the United States has never had national health insurance, supplied and paid for by the federal government, because Americans do not trust government. The institutional perspective counters that this lack of legislation is less a matter of popular belief and more the way we have designed the government. After all, they say, Harry Truman won the presidential election of 1948 in part by promising national health insurance. No deep-seated fear of government reared its head while Americans were voting. If we had been operating with a Canadian or English legislature, we would have put the program in place after Truman won the election. But Congress—and the checks and balances built into the legislature—buried the proposal.

Proponents of culture as the primary driver of politics respond that cultural values are not meant to explain every possible political action. Events, leaders, movements, and government agencies all introduce change. But culture forms the boundary of those changes. It limits the possibilities, shapes our perceptions, and influences our reactions. When terrorists launch an attack, for example, the American response is driven by the types of institutions we have built to provide for the common defense—but the debate about that response is deeply influenced by the values and ideas we share. Ideas, culture, and institutions all reinforce one another. Truly understanding a nation means understanding all three.

 **The Bottom Line**

» Political scientists point to three different ways in which foundational ideas influence politics.

» First, ideas shape American culture, which in turn affects our politics.

» Second—and the most popular argument among political scientists—ideas operate through political institutions. We have to study those institutions to appreciate how ideas shape politics and policies.

» Third, ideas may have their own independent power.

🔒 Conclusion: Culture and Institutions, Together

Do the ideas described in this chapter add up to a political culture that shapes the attitudes of American men and women? That cultural argument seems intuitive to many people. On balance, however, most political scientists underscore the importance of institutions.

As a political science student, you can decide for yourself on the relative power of ideas and institutions as you read this book. But you do not have to choose one or the other. We believe that culture and institutions together play a role in American politics. They reinforce each other. Yes, national institutions make it difficult to pass big national programs such as health insurance; and, yes again, opponents invoke powerful cultural norms—such as individualism and liberty—to persuade Americans that such legislation threatens their values. For us, the most interesting question is how ideas, culture, and institutions (along with interests and individuals—the four "Is" in the introductory chapter) all interact to shape American politics.

Finally, ideas have a power of their own—above and beyond the culture and institutions they have helped to shape. Ideas of liberty, democracy, and the American dream can move people to act. That is exactly what Captain (and Professor) Russell Burgos was thinking as the mortars slammed into his post in northern Iraq. As you read this book, you will constantly encounter the seven ideas we described in this chapter. Think about which seem most important and powerful to you. And pay attention to how they appear to operate—through the culture, through institutions, with a life of their own, or (as we believe) in all these ways at different times and in different circumstances.

CHAPTER SUMMARY

Check your understanding of Chapter 2.

● Seven important ideas influence American politics. Each idea has at least two different interpretations—differences that spur intense political debates. The seven key American ideas are freedom, self-rule, limited government, individualism, the American dream, equality, and religion.

● *Freedom* means that the government will protect your life, liberty, and property from the coercion of others (including government) so that you can pursue the goals you define for yourself. In one view, freedom requires *positive government action* to make sure that everyone has the basics to permit them to pursue their goals. In another view, the government guarantees only *negative freedom*—the freedom to pursue your goals. You are free to succeed or to fail on your own, but there are no government guarantees about food, or homes, or healthcare.

● *Self-rule* means that people govern themselves through clearly defined procedures such as elections. In a democracy, citizens participate directly in making government decisions. In a republic, the people rule indirectly through their elected representatives. The American system is a combination of the two, a democratic republic.

● Americans value *limited government*: They distrust government and place limits on the authority it can exercise.

● *Individualism* means that individuals—not society or the government—are responsible for their own well-being. For those who favor community or social democracy, the public interest is best served when members of a society use government to take care of one another. Americans take both an individual and a communal view, but in contrast to many other nations, the individualistic view is more powerful.

● The *American dream* holds that if you are talented and work hard, you will succeed and grow wealthy. Critics argue that the system is rigged and that the dream promotes the wrong values. However, the dream remains a powerful force in American politics.

● *Equality* allows each citizen to enjoy the same privileges, status, and rights before the law. Some define equality as a matter of *opportunity*—the idea that every American has an equal chance. Others promote equal *outcome*—a guarantee of results. There are three types of equality to consider: Social equality means that all individuals enjoy the same status in society. Political equality guarantees every citizen the same rights and opportunities to participate in politics. Economic equality minimizes the gap between citizens' wealth and earnings.

● *Religion* plays an enduring role in American politics and society. The great question is how we limit government interference without limiting religion itself.

● These seven ideas mark Americans' beliefs as a people. They shape politics through national culture, through political institutions, and through their direct public influence.

Need to review key ideas in greater depth? Click here.

KEY TERMS

American exceptionalism, p. 24
Conservatives, p. 32
Economic equality, p. 46
Equality, p. 44
Equal opportunity, p. 47
Equal outcome, p. 47
Freedom, p. 26

Individualism, p. 36
Initiative, p. 29
Liberals, p. 32
Median, p. 46
Negative liberty, p. 26
Political culture, p. 52
Political equality, p. 44

Positive liberty, p. 27
Referendum, p. 29
Republic, p. 30
Self-rule, p. 29
Social democracy, p. 37
Social equality, p. 44
Sunshine laws, p. 29

Flashcard review.

STUDY QUESTIONS

1. The second paragraph of the Declaration of Independence boldly explains why "governments are instituted among men." Why? Why are governments formed? Do you agree with that assertion about government's most basic function?

2. *Liberty* is often described as the most important American idea. Describe the two different views of liberty. Which do you think is more accurate?

3. Review the seven principal "American ideas" we have identified in this chapter. Are *new* foundational ideas bubbling up in American politics today? What examples can you imagine?

4. The Declaration of Independence asserts that all men are endowed by their creator with the inalienable rights to life, liberty, and the pursuit of happiness. Over time, Americans have extended that idea to more and more people, such as former slaves and women. Are there groups in our society today who are *not* getting the full benefits of this ideal? How might that change?

5. What is the difference between a democracy and a republic? Which principle does contemporary American government reflect, or does it reflect both? If you were a founder, which of these principles would you emphasize?

6. George Washington declared national days of prayer during his presidency. Thomas Jefferson rejected this practice, saying that it violated the First Amendment. Who was right, in your view—and what *does* the First Amendment say about this?

7. There are three forms of equality—social, political, and economic. Define each.

8. Describe the two approaches to economic equality: opportunity and outcome.

9. When it comes to religion, the United States is different from most wealthy societies. How? How do young people differ from previous generations in their approach to religion?

10. Ideas shape both culture and institutions. Explain.

Go to www.oup.com/us/Morone to find quizzes, flash cards, simulations, tutorials, videos, and other study tools.

3 The Constitution

THE R. R. MOTON HIGH SCHOOL, in Farmville, Virginia,

was a mess. The roof leaked, the heat barely worked, the classrooms were over-crowded, and the school bus kept breaking down. When it rained, students sat under umbrellas and shivered in their coats. Moton was a black school; across town, the white students were warm and dry. On April 23, 1951, a Moton junior named Barbara Johns decided to take action. She fooled the principal into leaving the school for the day and forged notes to the teachers calling an assembly. When the students had all filed into the auditorium, the sixteen-year-old stood on stage, called for a strike, and led a student march to the Prince Edward County Courthouse to protest the school's shabby state.

As you can imagine, Barbara Johns and her fellow student protesters landed in trouble. The students and their families called a leading civil rights group, the National Association for the Advancement of Colored People (NAACP), which dispatched a team of lawyers. The lawyers explained that local governments run American schools, and there was not much the NAACP could do about the conditions at Moton High. However, continued the lawyers, they could challenge the entire policy of racial segregation. The NAACP sued the school district, arguing that forcing African Americans into a separate school violated the United States Constitution. The Supreme Court took the case, *Davis v. School Board of Prince Edward County*, bundled it together with two similar cases, and three years after the student strike delivered one of the most famous court decisions in American history, a ruling known as *Brown v. Board of Education*.

A sixteen-year-old took a bold risk, the Supreme Court unanimously ruled that she was right, and hundreds of laws across many states were struck down for violating the Constitution. The Court ruled that segregated education facilities are inherently unequal and violated the Fourteenth Amendment of the United States Constitution, which declares, "No state shall . . . deny to any person . . . the equal protection of the laws."

Stop and think about the power Americans invest in this document written 230 years ago. The **Constitution** is the owner's manual and rulebook for American government. It specifies how the government operates. It tells us what the government may do and how it should do it. If you want to learn about any feature of American politics, always check the Constitution first.

● *Student strikers at Moton High School (Farmville, Virginia), led by Barbara Johns. The protestors had an enormous impact because civil rights lawyers found a way to place their grievance in the context of the U.S. Constitution.*

In this chapter, you will:

● Discover the roots of the Constitution.

● See why Americans declared independence from England and learn about their first constitution, the Articles of Confederation.

● Follow the arguments that shaped the Constitution and the debate over its adoption.

● Learn how Americans have changed the Constitution—and how the Constitution has changed America.

Constitution: A statement of fundamental principles that governs a nation or an organization.

Who are we? The answer to that question is always changing, but the Constitution provides the ground rules for those changes. It organizes our political life. The Declaration of Independence sets out the ideas behind America. The Constitution takes those ideas and turns them into laws. It *institutionalizes* American ideas.

This sounds simple: The Constitution guides the government. But there is a wrinkle. It is often unclear how the Constitution applies to modern questions. After all, it is just 4,400 words written on four pages of parchment a long time ago. Many provisions can be read in two (or more) different ways, and the document is silent on many topics. As a result, we always have to *interpret* how the Constitution applies to a case today.

Segregation is a prime example. The Constitution does not say anything about racial segregation. Back in 1896, the Supreme Court ruled that segregation did not violate the "equal protection" clause of the Fourteenth Amendment. In 1954, the Court ruled that it did (in the case that the Moton High students initiated). Different justices in different eras read the same words in changing ways. We constantly debate how to read the Constitution's words—and how to apply them to the questions we face.

BY THE NUMBERS
The Constitution

Number of the thirteen states that voted for the Constitution within six months	6
Number of states that initially voted against the Constitution	2
Number of delegates in New York, Virginia, and Massachusetts who could have defeated the entire Constitution by switching their votes	18 (3% of the delegates in those states)
Number of *proposed* amendments to the U.S. Constitution introduced in Congress since 1791	over 11,600
Number of *successful* amendments since 1791	17
Percentage of the U.S. population that can block a constitutional amendment	3

How easy is it to change the Constitution? How easy should it be?

The Colonial Roots of the Constitution

No nation in the eighteenth century had anything like the American Constitution. Most nations wrote their governing documents much later; some countries, such as England and Israel, never wrote one at all (see Comparing Nations 3.1). However, the American Constitution did not appear out of nowhere. Many features of colonial politics propelled the new nation toward its constitution.

Watch the commemoration of the Constitution's 200th birthday.

- First, the colonies were three thousand miles away from the king and his armies. Authorities back in England debated policies and issued orders; the American colonists frequently ignored them and did what they wished. No one back in London paid much attention. The English policy of ignoring colonies was known as *salutary neglect*; it permitted the colonies to develop their own political institutions. When England started interfering in colonial affairs, the Americans revolted.

- Second, beginning with the Virginia House of Burgesses in 1620, every colony elected its own legislature. As a result, the colonists had a great deal

COMPARING NATIONS 3.1	The U.S. Constitution in Comparative Context	
The United States has the oldest constitution still in use. Of the eighteen democratic countries listed here, only Canada and the Netherlands wrote a still-operating constitution within a century of the United States. Many political scientists believe the American document has lasted so long because it works well. Others, however, believe that it has grown out of date and that our form of government is not effective or fair enough for the twenty-first century. Keep this debate in mind as you read about how the American Constitution came into existence and how it operates today.	**NATION**	**YEAR THE CURRENT CONSTITUTION WAS WRITTEN**
	United States	1789
	Argentina	1853 (revised text, 1994)
	Austria	1920
	Brazil	1988
	Canada	1867 (revised text, 1982)
	Costa Rica	1949
	Denmark	1953
	France	1958
	Germany	1949
	Great Britain	No written constitution
	India	1950
	Ireland	1937
	Israel	No written constitution
	Italy	1948
	Japan	1947
	Netherlands	1814
	New Zealand	No written constitution
	Thailand	2017

of experience with representation. New settlements demanded seats in the assemblies. New immigrants wanted the right to vote (Polish workers went on strike in Virginia over the issue). In some places, such as New Jersey, women with property could vote. America grew up arguing about representation—and that prepared them for the debate over the Constitution.

- Third, plentiful land created opportunities for ordinary people. Early America was not an equal society by any means: There were aristocratic families and slaves, prosperous merchants and **indentured servants**. However, by the standards of the time, the New World was a land of extraordinary social mobility. When North Carolina tried to establish a system of titles and social classes, the effort collapsed, as ordinary people made their fortunes and soon were wealthier than the would-be lords and dukes. Economic conditions helped foster a republic.

- Fourth, some colonies began with mutual agreements between the settlers, known as **compacts** or **covenants**. The Pilgrims, who landed in Massachusetts in 1620, introduced the idea; before they went ashore all forty-one adult males signed a mutual agreement known as the Mayflower Compact (named after their vessel, the *Mayflower*). In most nations, the right to rule stretched back through history and was based on tradition and force. In contrast, the individuals on the *Mayflower* formed a new society based on their mutual agreement. Many New England communities began with such compacts or covenants—often religiously inspired forerunners of a constitution.

- Fifth, many colonists came to the New World to practice their religion in peace. Across the colonies, different religions flourished: Calvinists in Boston, Quakers in Philadelphia, Catholics in Baltimore, Anglicans in Virginia, and an unusually diverse mix of religions in Savannah, Georgia, which was home to Anglicans, Lutherans, and Jews, among others. All these different faiths did not always live in harmony; the Massachusetts Puritans hanged Quaker missionaries (discussed in Chapter 2). But beginning in Rhode Island in 1636, a revolutionary idea began to emerge: the individual's freedom to practice religion without government interference. In some colonies, this idea was followed by other rights, such as freedom of speech and freedom of the press. The rights of citizens would become the single greatest issue in the debate over whether to accept (ratify) the new constitution.

- Sixth, border areas in early America were violent and insecure, often erupting in brutal wars with the Native Americans. The French claimed land to the north and west, the Spanish to the south and west. Colonists also constantly fought one another over their own boundaries. After the break with England, insecure borders helped inspire the colonists to adopt a strong central government.

Each colony governed itself in its own way. However, the six features described here—distance from English authority, representation, social mobility, covenants, individual rights, and violent borders—all propelled Americans toward the Constitution of 1787.

Indentured servant: A colonial American settler contracted to work for a fixed period (usually three to seven years) in exchange for food, shelter, and transportation to the New World.

Compact: A mutual agreement that provides for joint action to achieve defined goals.

Covenant: A compact invoking religious or moral authority.

● *The Mayflower Compact. The settlers, who had begun to argue about who was in charge, agreed among themselves to enter into a "civic body politic"—a government. The authority of their government rose from their own agreement, which was signed only by men, including two indentured servants.*

The Bottom Line

» Colonists developed their own political institutions, including compacts, that became forerunners of the Constitution.

Why the Colonists Revolted

The roots of the American Revolution lie in a great English victory. Centuries of rivalry between England and France burst into war in 1754. Known as the French and Indian War in North America, the conflict spread through the colonies from Virginia all the way to Canada. Colonial American militias fought side by side with the British army and defeated the French in 1763. Thirteen years later the colonists declared independence and turned their muskets on the English.

Why did the Americans suddenly revolt? Because the victory over France introduced two fateful changes. First, ten thousand English troops remained in the colonies to protect the newly won land. The existence of those "Redcoats" meant that England could now enforce its policies: The days of salutary neglect were over. Second, the English had run up a crushing debt during the ten years of war and thought that the colonists should help pay it. The Americans' reaction was explosive.

The Colonial Complaint: Representation

It was not just Britain's demand for money that provoked the colonists. Americans had grown used to making their own decisions through their elected assemblies. When the English imposed new taxes, without the approval of the thirteen colonial assemblies, they violated the idea of self-rule. The result was an unusual revolution. Most revolutionaries rise up against regimes that have long repressed them. In contrast, the Americans fought to preserve rights that they had been exercising during the many years of happy neglect.

Delegate representation: Representatives follow the expressed wishes of the voters.

Beneath the conflict lay a deep philosophical difference about representative democracy. The colonists considered their assemblies the legitimate voice of the people; if taxes had to be raised, they were the ones to do it. Colonial assemblies were very responsive to the voters and their daily concerns—they worried about things such as building roads and surveying new lands. Political theorists call the colonial view **delegate representation**: Do what the voters want.

The British never understood this view of representation because they operated under an entirely different one. Unlike the colonists, the English did not change their electoral districts every time the population shifted. English elected officials were expected to pursue the good of the whole nation. Your representative is

The colonial borders were the site of considerable fighting, with both the French and the Native Americans.

Trustee representation:
Representatives do what they regard as being in the best interest of their constituents—even if constituents do not agree.

not an "agent" or an "advocate," argued English statesman Edmund Burke, but must be guided by "the general good." This view is known as **trustee representation**—do what is best for the voters regardless of what they wish.[1] The debate would spur an innovative provision in the U.S. Constitution: The United States would conduct a census every ten years to ensure that congressional districts matched up to the changing population—a direct reaction to Britain's trustee theory of representation.

The Conflict Begins with Blood on the Frontier

After the French and Indian War, settlers poured westward (Figures 3.1 and 3.2). Native Americans fought back; they rallied around Chief Pontiac and overran colonial settlements and English forts in Virginia, Maryland, and Pennsylvania. To end the fighting, England closed the border and prohibited settlers from moving westward past the crests of the lengthy Appalachian Mountain chain. The colonists were stunned. The arbitrary boundary, announced in the Proclamation of 1763, had been drawn amid lobbying by land speculators, who could make or lose fortunes depending on whether their own land was open to settlement. The proclamation threatened the westward thrust that spelled opportunity to the restless colonists. American settlers did not care about Native American rights to the land. As they saw it, a corrupt English monarchy was blocking American pioneers from settling the wide-open spaces that they had helped win from France.[2]

The colonists responded in their traditional way—they ignored regulations that did not suit them. But now there was a British army in America to enforce

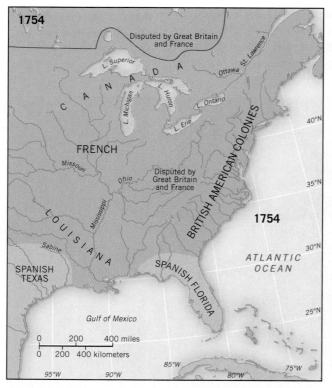
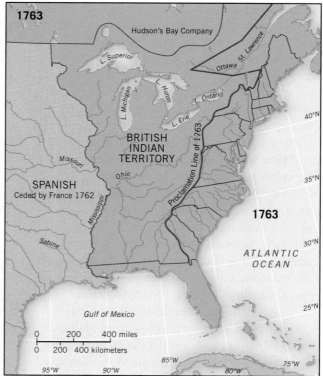

● **Figure 3.1 and Figure 3.2** *The colonies before (left) and after (right) the French and Indian War. Spain lost Florida but gained the land west of the Mississippi in compensation for backing France. Napoleon would later seize this land back from Spain; in 1803, his armies were defeated by rebelling former slaves in Haiti and he soured on expanding into the New World, so he sold the land to the United States. Note the line formed by the Proclamation of 1763 on the map on the right. England tried to forbid settlers from crossing that line.*

the English policies. The Proclamation of 1763 was followed by the Quartering Act (1765), which required colonial assemblies to billet British troops in empty barns and warehouses. Suddenly, the Redcoats seemed like an occupying army.

Britain also began to enforce its **mercantilist** trade policies, which meant American ships had to bypass their traditional (and lucrative) partners and do business only with English colonies at higher prices. Colonists who ignored the decree were charged with smuggling—wealthy merchants now faced imprisonment or fines for trading with French colonies. To make matters even worse, the English introduced taxes to help support their army of Redcoats. These widely reviled duties culminated in the Stamp Act of 1765.

Mercantilism: An economic theory according to which government controls foreign trade to maintain prosperity and security.

The Stamp Tax and the First Hints of Independence

Stamp taxes were a common way to raise money in England, but the effort to impose one on the colonies set off a firestorm. Parliament ignored the colonial assemblies (violating colonial ideas of representation) and simply announced the new tax. Colonists responded by convening a Stamp Act Congress that met in October 1765. Delegates from nine colonies sent a protest to the king and to Parliament. The English policies were pushing the colonists into working together.

Protests against the stamp tax spread throughout the colonies. Mobs hung, burned, and beheaded tax collectors in effigy. They attacked tax collectors' offices and homes. Across the sea, English authorities were incredulous. All they could see were ungrateful colonists who refused to pay for their own protection.[3]

The Townshend Acts Worsen the Conflict

After Parliament reluctantly lifted the stamp taxes, colonists celebrated the repeal and tensions eased—until Parliament followed up with the Townshend Acts in 1767. These acts instituted another round of new taxes; revenues were earmarked to pay a new colonial authority, the American Board of Customs, which would collect taxes independently of the colonial assemblies. Now an imperial bureaucracy was explicitly denying the colonists self-governance. The Townshend Acts also suspended the New York State Assembly for refusing to house and supply British troops.

Once again, American colonists responded with meetings, petitions, and mobs. New Yorkers and, later, Bostonians seethed with anger over having their legislatures dissolved. Mobs harassed the customs officials, who found it impossible to carry out their duties and called for help. A British warship arrived in Boston, discharging officials who seized a vessel owned by John Hancock, one of the resistance leaders, and charged him with smuggling. That move set off riots, bringing British troops into the city to restore order. Before long, there were almost four thousand Redcoats in a city of fifteen thousand people. The Boston mobs harassed the soldiers with taunts, rocks, and snowballs until, on March 5, 1770, one detachment of Redcoats panicked and fired point-blank on the crowd.

The Boston Massacre, as the event quickly became known, left five civilians dead. The first to fall was a sailor named Crispus Attucks, the son of an African slave and a Natick Indian who had escaped slavery some twenty years earlier. Ironically, the son of two groups who would not be liberated by the Revolution—an African slave and an American Indian—was the first to bleed for the cause. Paul Revere memorialized the massacre in an engraving that transformed the panicky soldiers threatened by a mob into a line of killers firing into a heroic cluster of civilians. Historian Gordon Wood described the engraving as "perhaps the most famous piece of antimilitary propaganda in American history."[4]

At the start of the crisis, six years earlier, colonial leaders had respectfully petitioned the king to rescind his policies. Now, blood had been shed and the colonists began to talk about rebellion.

The Boston Tea Party

The British repealed all the Townshend duties except a tariff on tea. Tea was a global industry in 1773; think of it as the must-have product of the eighteenth century. But the East India Tea Company, which had a monopoly in England, was on the verge of bankruptcy. In 1773, Parliament tried to rescue the company by granting it a monopoly over the tea trade in the New World. The colonial shippers who had long been trading tea would be shut out by this rival trading network.

When ships with East India tea arrived, mobs in Philadelphia and New York forced them to sail away without unloading their cargo. In Boston, however, Governor Thomas Hutchinson would not permit such nonsense. He insisted that the three ships in Boston Harbor not leave until their tea was safely delivered. On a dark December night, about fifty men, some "dressed in the Indian manner," blackened their faces and boarded one of the ships. They hefted 342 chests of tea onto the deck, bashed them open with hatchets, and dumped the contents—worth about £9,600 (between $1.5 and $2.5 million today)—into Boston Harbor.[5]

● An engraving of the Boston Massacre done by Paul Revere. This version of the event makes the British look like cold-blooded killers—not historically accurate, but powerful propaganda for independence.

Revolution!

British leaders were furious. Past insubordination paled next to this direct economic hit on a struggling British company. The English introduced what colonists dubbed the Intolerable Acts. The laws closed Boston Harbor until the tea was paid for, abolished town meetings, authorized the quartering of troops in any home in Massachusetts, and essentially put the state under military control. King George III himself put it bluntly: "The colonists must either triumph or submit."

First Continental Congress: A convention of delegates from twelve of the thirteen colonies that met in 1774.

Americans refused to submit. Instead, twelve colonies sent representatives to the **First Continental Congress** in September 1774. The Congress petitioned for an end to the Intolerable Acts, called for a boycott on British goods, and asserted colonial rights to "life, liberty, and property." They agreed to meet again in May 1775.

Before the Continental Congress reconvened, fighting had begun. In April 1775, the British commander in Boston, General Thomas Gage, sent one thousand troops from Boston to seize guns and ammunition stored at Concord, Massachusetts. Armed colonists who called themselves "minutemen" blocked the way and came under British fire at Lexington and Concord. Eight were shot dead. The British found and destroyed the weapons, but their march back to Boston was horrific. Minutemen hid behind rocks and trees and sniped at them all along the way. By the time the English army limped back into the city, they had lost three hundred men.

A Long Legacy

Revolutionary images and slogans still resonate in American politics today. The Tea Party holds rallies around the nation. Civilians anxious about immigration call themselves "minutemen" and patrol the border with Mexico. "Militias" organize and train to defend their personal rights. And Americans from across the political spectrum aspire to live up to the Revolution's dreams of equality. The Revolution left the new United States with symbols, slogans, and an enduring political concern: arbitrary government that threatens the people's liberties. But it also raises a provocative question: Are Americans too quick to exaggerate routine disagreements by making analogies to the revolutionaries?

 **The Bottom Line**

» For over a century, England largely ignored its American colonies and elected assemblies governed the colonists. After the French and Indian War, the English bypassed the colonial legislatures and imposed new rules and taxes.

» These actions violated traditional colonial rights and exposed two different ideas of representation—the American concept of *delegate representation* (representatives respond to their constituents' desires) and the English concept of *trustee representation* (representatives do what they consider best for all, regardless of constituent demands).

» English action also harmed colonial economic interests.

» Americans fought an unusual revolution: Rather than demanding new rights, they were trying to preserve existing rights and economic interests.

The Declaration of Independence

The **Second Continental Congress**, which met in May 1775, faced the job of declaring independence, mobilizing an army, organizing a government, and rallying thirteen colonies very different from one another around a single cause. A year later, on July 4, 1776, the Congress voted to adopt a Declaration of Independence as a statement to the world of America's purpose. The document has two parts: a statement of principles and a list of grievances. (The full Declaration is reprinted in Appendix I to this book.)

Second Continental Congress: A convention of delegates from the thirteen colonies that became the acting national government for the duration of the Revolutionary War.

The Principle: "We Hold These Truths . . ."

In one elegant paragraph, the Declaration of Independence distills America's political philosophy (see Table 3.1 for how the Declaration reflects the ideas discussed in Chapter 2):

- All people are equal.
- Their creator endowed them with rights that cannot be taken away.
- These rights include life, liberty, and the pursuit of happiness.
- People form governments to protect those rights.
- Governments derive their just powers from the consent of the governed.

TABLE 3.1 **The Declaration of Independence and America's Enduring Ideas**

HOW DOES THE DECLARATION REFLECT THE KEY AMERICAN IDEAS DISCUSSED IN CHAPTER 2?
Liberty. The Declaration asserts that liberty is an "unalienable right" (meaning that no one can take it away), endowed to all people by their creator.
Self-rule. The right of representation is one of the Declaration's central themes: It contends that governments derive "their just powers from the consent of the governed." Ten of the twenty-seven grievances charged against the king directly address the issue of self-rule.
Limited government. The idea of limited government had more space than any other in both the Declaration and the Constitution. Most of the Declaration recites the ways King George III overstepped his "just powers." Eleven years later, the Constitution would carefully limit the powers given to the federal government.
Individualism. The Declaration states that "governments are instituted among men . . . to secure [the] rights" with which the creator has endowed each individual. These include "life, liberty, and the pursuit of happiness." Here is the cornerstone of American individualism. At the same time, the Declaration also talks about "one people" and "the people"—collective ideas that have to be balanced with individualism. Recall the great American debate: How do we balance individualism and communalism? The Declaration emphasizes both.
The American dream. The Declaration of Independence promises the pursuit of happiness. What does this mean? The phrase is borrowed from John Locke, who wrote that governments are instituted to protect "life, liberty, and *property.*" Jefferson, in his first draft of the Declaration, changed "property" to "happiness." But right from the start, "the pursuit of happiness"—what we now call the American dream—was entangled with the pursuit of wealth.
Equality. This idea seems clear enough: Because "all men are created equal," they all have the same rights to life, liberty, and the pursuit of happiness. But do we as a society need to feed the hungry and clothe the poor to ensure that everyone has an equal shot at the pursuit of happiness? This remains a controversial matter.
Faith in God. The words "the Creator" appear right at the start of the Declaration. But religion soon became controversial. Thomas Jefferson, who drafted the Declaration, was not a religious man. (As a deist, he thought that God did not interfere in human affairs.) Jefferson later ignited a controversy during his presidency when he refused to call national days of prayer as George Washington had done. Instead, Jefferson argued that there must be "a wall of separation between church and state." But Jefferson's wall raises as many questions as it resolves, as debates and court cases have attested for generations.

These ideas were not new. Political philosophers, especially the English thinker John Locke, had used very similar language. In his *Two Treatises on Government*, published more than a century earlier, Locke argued that in nature, there are no rules. Life is ruled by force and violence. To secure safety and freedom, people contract with one another, enter into civil society, and form governments that can protect one another's life, liberty, and property. Locke was enormously influential in revolutionary America. One curious indicator: The elegant furniture of this era, which often featured carved busts of writers, includes more carvings of John Locke than anyone else.[6]

As a statement of governing ideals, the Declaration of Independence was—and still is—breathtaking. In 1776, it was also a far cry from reality. Thomas Jefferson, who drafted much of the document, was a slave owner. The Declaration essentially invites future cruelty when it refers to "merciless Indian savages." Its authors did not live up to their noble sentiments. We do not fully live up to them today. Even so, the document stands as the great statement of American idealism—something every generation can fight for.

Grievances

The second part of the Declaration lists twenty-seven grievances against King George III. These tell us what the American colonists cared about as they began the Revolution. Three complaints dominate the list:

- *Violations of the right of representation.* This complaint comes up in ten of the twenty-seven charges against England. It is by far the most intensely felt grievance described in the Declaration.
- *Maintenance of a standing army not under civilian control.* In particular, British soldiers acted in peacetime without the consent of American legislatures. Five complaints are about the British military.
- *Loss of an independent court.* This violation of traditional justice comes up six times.

Today the Revolution is often boiled down to the colonists' slogan "No taxation without representation." The Declaration emphasized *representation* much more than taxation; taxes did not show up until way down the list, as grievance number seventeen ("Imposing taxes on us without our consent"). Economics did matter, of course. Many of the British steps that preceded rebellion, from new taxes to tighter trade rules, were essentially economic challenges. However, those which reverberate most forcefully in the Declaration of Independence are the *right of representation* and the *consent of the governed.*

 **The Bottom Line**

» The Declaration of Independence asserted philosophical ideals as the basis of the new American government.

» The first part of the Declaration features five ideals that sum up the nation's political principles.

» The second part of the Declaration lists twenty-seven grievances that led to the break. They emphasized the right of representation and consent of the governed.

The First American Government: The Articles of Confederation

When the United States declared its independence, it linked the thirteen former colonies—now states—into a **confederation**, or *alliance of independent states.* Although this first American government lasted only a little more than a decade, it taught the new nation valuable lessons about effective government.

Confederation: A group of independent states or nations that yield some of their powers to a national government, although each state retains a degree of sovereign authority.

Independent States

The states organized their governments to reflect popular desires. They introduced annual elections, extended the right to vote, and opened their legislative deliberations to public view. Some states built benches in the assembly halls so that the public could watch their representatives in action. States also enlarged their legislatures so that members would be more responsive to citizens.

Of course, the new rules still left many people out. Women had participated in the Revolutionary War. Some dressed as men and fought; others cooked, worked as nurses, and cleared the battlefields after combat. The English estimated that "women and waggoners make up half of their [American] army."[7] Nevertheless, women could not vote in most states. And, despite the Declaration of Independence's ringing statement of "unalienable rights," slavery persisted in every state.

Still, the revolutionary spirit unleashed a powerful egalitarian urge. States from Massachusetts to Virginia pondered the abolition of slavery. In some states, such as New Jersey, women with property were allowed to vote. And across the nation, state legislatures were, as historian Gordon Wood stated, "probably as equally and fairly representative of the people as any legislatures in history."[8]

The National Government

The Continental Congress approved its first constitution, called the Articles of Confederation, in November 1777. The document, which reflected Americans' recent experience with England, kept the national government weak and dependent on the states. The Articles named the new nation the United States of America and described the central government as "a league of friendship" among states: "Each . . . retains its sovereignty, freedom and independence, and every power, jurisdiction and right." In a sign of what was to come, Congress had to wait more than three years to get approval from all thirteen states for the Articles of Confederation.

Supermajority: An amount higher than a simple majority (50% plus one)—typically, three-fifths or two-thirds of the voters.

There was no chief executive (the states would implement the laws), no central authority to tax (all revenues would come from state governments), and no central power to muster an army (the states supplied the troops). Each state had a single vote in Congress. Important matters required the vote of nine states. Any changes to the Articles of Confederation required the agreement of all thirteen states. Today, we call such extra-large majorities **supermajorities**. The Articles created a very weak central government.[9]

Some Success . . .

Americans had good reason to be proud of their new government. Power remained close to the people. The new government overcame incredible odds and, by April 1783, had defeated the most powerful military force in the world. The population grew rapidly in the 1780s—the fastest rise of any decade in American history. After a brief postwar recession, the economy also expanded. Americans considered themselves both democratic and prosperous.[10]

The Continental Congress also won a major policy success when it stopped the squabbling among states over claims to western land. Instead, the Northwest Ordinance of 1787 outlawed slavery in the territory and established a

● A series of legends have grown up around Molly Pitcher, whose real name was Mary Ludwig Hays McCauley. The most famous has her stepping in to take the place of her fallen husband at the cannon during the Battle of Monmouth. The stories are most likely a composite of descriptions of many women who fought with the American army.

process by which individuals could buy western lands. When an area attracted a minimum number of settlers, it could apply to be a state with all the same powers and privileges as the existing states. With this act, the United States established its mechanism for western expansion.

. . . And Some Problems

But four major problems plagued the new American government.

First, Congress could not raise taxes and had no money of its own. The states were reluctant to provide funds. The Continental Congress had trouble supplying (much less paying) the army throughout the Revolutionary War. George Washington drew a lesson that would always guide his politics: *The new republic needed a vigorous national government if it was to survive.*[11]

Second, the requirement of unanimity made it impossible to amend the Articles. When Congress tried to fix its financial problems by levying a 5 percent tax on imported goods, Rhode Island's legislature blocked the proposal, calling it "the yoke of tyranny fixed on all the states."[12] When loans from France and Holland came due, there was no way to pay them. Again, many leaders drew a lesson: *A vigorous national government needed a stable source of revenue.*

Third, state governments were dominated by their legislatures, which operated without any checks or balances. The result was often bias and even chaos. Legislatures wrote (and repealed) laws to benefit individuals. They forgave debts. They seized private property. Leaders eventually reached yet another important conclusion: *Different sources of government power should balance one another, governors should balance legislatures, and the central government should balance the states.*

Fourth, the weak national government had a difficult time standing up to foreign powers. Spain closed the Mississippi to American vessels. Britain's trade policy played the states against one another. Pirates brazenly seized American ships in North Africa. National-minded Americans drew an obvious conclusion: *a weak central government left the nation vulnerable.*

One event, Shays's Rebellion, dramatized the problems of government under the Articles. Captain Daniel Shays, a veteran of the Revolutionary War, led a rebellion that broke out in western Massachusetts in August 1786 and spread across the state. Thousands of farmers, facing rising interest rates, took up their muskets and shut down courthouses to stop foreclosures on their farms. When Governor James Bowdoin summoned the local militia to defend the Worcester courthouse, members refused; some joined the rebellion. The same thing happened in Concord, just forty miles from Boston. By December, the rebels had seized six courthouses and an armory. Governor Bowdoin appealed to the national government for help, but Congress had no army and no money. Finally, Bowdoin hired an army and broke the rebellion. Shays's sympathizers shifted strategy: They won seats in the legislature the following year and legislated the debt relief the farmers had been fighting for—to the chagrin of the financiers who had loaned them the money.[13]

● *Captain Daniel Shays led a rebellion in protest of farm foreclosures in 1786.*

● *Alarmed by spreading chaos, the Continental Congress called for a national meeting in Annapolis. Only twelve delegates from five states arrived at Mann's Tavern in Annapolis (picture above)—not enough to do official business. With Shays's Rebellion raging, the delegates requested each state to appoint representatives to meet in Philadelphia the following May, in 1787, and so quietly authorized a convention that would write an entirely new constitution—and permanently transform the United States.*

For many national leaders, Shays's Rebellion was the last straw. Under the Articles of Confederation, neither the national government nor an individual state was strong enough to protect public property (e.g., courthouses) or private property (the repayment of loans). Shays's Rebellion pushed the most influential men in the colonies to write a new constitution. Not everyone agreed. Many Americans thought that problems such as Shays's Rebellion were the growing pains of a more democratic government that reflected the people and their desires.

Secrecy

Spring 1787 arrived cold and blustery, delaying many of the delegates on their way to Philadelphia. James Madison from Virginia got there first, with a plan for a new constitution. Madison was short, shy, and balding; today, we recognize him as one of America's greatest political thinkers. The next delegate from Virginia arrived with more fanfare. As George Washington approached, church bells pealed, cannons thundered, army officers donned their old uniforms to ride escort, and local citizens lined the streets and cheered. The presence of the great American hero made the convention's success more likely.

On the first day, the delegates unanimously elected George Washington to chair the convention. Then they agreed on a controversial rule: The deliberations would be completely secret. Guards were placed at the doors. Windows were shut and remained closed, even after the Philadelphia summer turned stifling. George Washington made only three comments during the convention—and

---

What Do YOU Think?   Your Advice Is Needed

If you could go back and offer advice to American leaders in 1787, what would you tell them? Should they stick with the Articles of Confederation or write a new constitution?

Yes, stick with the Articles of Confederation. A strong, central government can become tyrannical—forcing the people to pay taxes or house soldiers without their consent and depriving them of their rights to express their beliefs, practice their religion, or own guns. More power should reside with local government, which is closer to the people. Citizen militias can defend communities without a national army to tempt leaders to intervene in foreign conflicts.

No, build a new central government. The national government under the Articles is weak and chaotic. The national government needs to be powerful enough to repel foreign threats, to oversee national development, and to facilitate trade and good relations between the states.

I am divided about this. The Constitution will enable the United States to eventually become a wealthy and powerful nation—but it will be less democratic than the local and state governments that dominated under the Articles.

one was to rebuke a delegate who had carelessly dropped a copy of proposed resolutions. Most of what we know about the convention comes from James Madison himself, who took a seat at the front of the room and kept meticulous notes—though they were not made public until 1837, a year after Madison's death.

Was it a good idea to impose secrecy? The young republic had only recently opened up its political process to the people. Thomas Jefferson called the decision to close the convention "an abominable precedent." In a republic, he argued, the people should always know what their leaders are doing.[14]

● *James Madison was the most diligent delegate. Small, shy, and unimpressive looking, he stood just five feet tall. No one would notice Madison standing next to the tall and muscular Washington or the charismatic Franklin. However, Madison was a brilliant thinker and one of the chief architects of the Constitution and Bill of Rights. He had more influence over the shape of the final text than any other single individual.*

However, the delegates wanted to speak their minds freely without worrying about how their words would appear in the newspapers. Many also believed that powerful politicians in their home states would withdraw their delegation as soon as they heard that the convention was debating an entirely new constitution. Without secrecy, they might have to abandon their bold plan and simply amend the Articles of Confederation—which was, after all, what they had been asked to do.

The Bottom Line

» Under the Articles of Confederation, thirteen independent states bound themselves into a confederation with a weak central government that had to rely on the states to implement its decisions.

» Though feeble, this first U.S. government was, by the standards of the time, a very democratic one.

» Delegates to the Constitutional Convention convened to fix the problems with the Articles of Confederation but chose to go much further and propose a new American government.

🔘 The Constitutional Convention

As they thought about reorganizing their new government, American leaders balanced the two political dangers they had recently encountered.

- British officials' behavior warned them that a powerful central government could strip the people of their rights.
- Experience with the Articles of Confederation warned them that a weak national government could fail to protect their rights.

The delegates debated from May into September 1787. They touched on almost every aspect of government, ranging from how to elect the legislature to what to do about slavery. Throughout the discussions, six major themes dominated their attention.

Learn about the founders.

1. How Much Power to the People?

Most Constitutional Convention delegates believed the states had gone too far in empowering the voters. Too much democracy, they thought, had led to chaotic government. Several put their views bluntly right at the start of the convention. "The evils we are experiencing flow from an excess of democracy," argued Elbridge Gerry of Massachusetts. "The people . . . are the dupes of pretended patriots." Roger Sherman, a shrewd Yankee from Connecticut, summed up this perspective: "The people . . . should have . . . little to do . . . [with] government. They want [or *lack*] information and are constantly liable to be misled."[15]

The delegates faced a dilemma. They wanted their government to answer to the public; that was why they had fought the Revolution. Recent experience, however, also made them fear a system that responded too readily to the people. The delegates wished to represent the public through better educated, wealthier, and more experienced leaders—men like themselves.

Over the course of the convention, the delegates developed a view of representation that Madison called *filtration*, or *indirect elections*: The public would vote for men (and later women) who would in turn vote for public officials. Examples of filtration appear throughout the Constitution. The speeches during the convention's first days are a bit shocking to us today. The delegates wanted to make the public *less* involved in government than they had been in the eleven years since the United States declared its independence. The new Constitution would permit the public to vote for only one federal office—members of the House of Representatives.

The debate about public involvement did not end with the Constitution. Over time, Americans would play a more active role in their governance. Citizens would win more control over presidential elections beginning in the 1820s, when voting reforms were passed on the state level; they started voting directly for senators after passage of the Seventeenth Amendment in 1913. The "public" also would expand over time. Women became voters with passage of the Nineteenth Amendment in 1920; four years later, Congress ensured Native American voting rights. African Americans, who won the right to vote in 1870 (with the Fifteenth Amendment), were later violently denied suffrage, and finally won the right all over again with the Voting Rights Act of 1965. Younger Americans (eighteen- to twenty-year-olds) became eligible to vote in 1971.

The debate that began at the Constitutional Convention continues to this day. It animates one of the key ideas we discussed in Chapter 2: self-rule, balanced between direct democracy and indirect representation. At a still more fundamental level, the debate speaks to one of the great questions of American politics: *Who governs?*

● *Over time, common men began voting in American elections. This painting, by George Caleb Bingham, shows the raucous results. Note the heavy drinking—and how this, like all early American elections, was a completely male event.*

Public involvement in government has grown dramatically over the centuries, but Madison's principle of filtration still keeps the people at arm's length from their government in many areas.

2. National Government Versus State Government

The Articles of Confederation left most power with the states. Madison's plan for the new government took that power and vested it in a strong national government. The very first motion that the delegates debated called for "a national government . . . consisting of a *supreme* legislature, executive, and judiciary." In fact, Madison's original plan would have shifted most governing authority to the national level.[16]

Many delegates disagreed with this dramatic change. They believed that state and local governments were closer to the people and could more accurately reflect public sentiments—precisely what Madison was trying to avoid. Some pro–states' rights delegates charged Madison and his allies with trying to "abolish the State Governments altogether." Ultimately, delegates from New York walked out of the convention; Rhode Island refused to send any delegates in the first place. The convention was soon down to eleven of the thirteen states.[17]

In the end, the delegates compromised on a system that included both national and state power. The federal government took over many functions—but far fewer than Madison had originally proposed. The states kept many duties—but far fewer than the states' rights advocates wanted. This mixed system, with a stronger national government that leaves considerable power with the state governments, is called **federalism** (and we'll discuss it in Chapter 4). The debate about how to balance national government power and state power continues to the present day.

Federalism: Power divided between national and state government. Each has its own sovereignty (independent authority) and its own duties.

3. Big States Versus Small States

Another intense dispute at the Constitutional Convention revolved around a division we rarely notice today: the large, more populous states (led by Virginia and Pennsylvania) versus the smaller states (led by New Jersey and Delaware). Large states argued that representation should be based on population; small states wanted each state to have an equal voice. That debate led to two different plans, one put forward by Virginia (a big state) and the other by New Jersey (on behalf of the small states).

The Virginia Plan.   Governor Edmund Randolph of Virginia presented Madison's original plan for the Constitution. A powerful speaker, Randolph addressed the delegates for four hours. The plan, which became known as the **Virginia Plan**, had five key points.

Virginia Plan: Madison's plan, embraced by the Constitutional Convention delegates from larger states; this plan strengthened the national government relative to state governments.

1. Congress would have two chambers, a form known as a **bicameral** legislature, with representation in both chambers based on state population.

2. Citizens would vote for members of the House of Representatives; the number of representatives would reflect the size of the state. The House of Representatives would, in turn, vote for senators from a list of candidates provided by the state legislatures. This limited the states' role and is an example of filtration, or indirect elections.

3. Congress would elect the president. Here the Virginia Plan suddenly turned vague and did not specify whether the president would be one man or a committee; nor did it say how long the executive would serve. Madison told George Washington that he had not made up his mind.

Bicameral: Having two legislative houses or chambers—such as the House and the Senate.

4. A national judiciary with one or more supreme courts would be established, and the judges would have life tenure.

5. Congress would have broad powers to legislate in all cases where the states were "incompetent." A "council of revision" made up of the president and the Supreme Court would have the authority to review and nullify any state law.

Delegates who had not already been briefed by Madison were stunned. Randolph was urging them to build a robust national government. The Virginia Plan empowered Congress to "call forth the force of the union" against any state "failing to fulfill its duties" under the new constitution. The federal government could strike down state laws. Early votes indicated that the Virginia Plan enjoyed a small majority at the convention.

Delegates from small states were especially critical of Madison's blueprint and feared they would soon "be swallowed up." Each state had "its peculiar habits, usages, and manners," small-state advocates insisted, and these must be protected. Under Madison's plan, three states (Virginia, Pennsylvania, and Massachusetts) would have enough members in Congress to form a majority all by themselves. Representatives from the smaller states repeatedly threatened to walk out of the convention.[18]

New Jersey Plan:
Put forward at the Constitutional Convention by the small states, this plan left most government authority with the state governments.

Unicameral: Having a single legislative house or chamber.

The New Jersey Plan. The small states pushed back with their own plan, introduced by William Paterson of New Jersey and known as the **New Jersey Plan**. Rather than construct a new national government, this plan focused on strengthening the Articles of Confederation. It had four key points:

1. Congress would have only one chamber, a form known as a **unicameral** legislature. Each state would have one vote in Congress, regardless of its size—exactly the same as in the Articles. However, congressional acts would be the supreme law of the land, making the new constitution stronger than the Articles of Confederation.

2. Congress would elect a committee to serve as the federal executive for one term only.

3. The executive committee would select a supreme court, which would be responsible for foreign policy, economic policy, and the impeachment of federal officials.

4. The national government could tax the states and would have the exclusive right to tax imports.

The New Jersey Plan left the states at the center of American government but took a step toward union by building a stronger national government, one that could raise its own taxes and exercise more authority over interstate commerce. When the vote was called, only three states supported the New Jersey Plan.

The Connecticut Compromise. Convention delegates decisively approved the Virginia Plan's bicameral Congress with a House and a Senate. They voted for a House of Representatives based on population. Then debate turned to the Senate. If the delegates voted with the Virginia Plan—in which the House of Representatives would vote for senators—the big states would essentially win the debate. Tempers grew short. "I do not, Gentlemen, trust you," declared Gunning Bedford of Delaware. He hinted darkly that the small states would look for foreign allies if they lost this vote. William Paterson announced that he would rather "submit to a monarch, a despot," than accept the Virginia Plan. Luther Martin, a garrulous delegate from Maryland, wrote home that the convention was on the verge of breaking up over this issue.[19] Big states pushed back: "Will it require 150 voters from my state [Pennsylvania]," asked James Wilson, "to balance 50 from yours [New Jersey]?"[20]

Big states seemed to have the votes to carry seven states and win the Virginia Plan's version of Senate elections. But when the roll was called on July 2, one big-state supporter from Maryland and two from Georgia slipped out of the convention hall. With their exits, both states shifted, and the vote came out a tie: five states for the Virginia Plan, five against, and one evenly split.

To break the deadlock, the delegates formed a committee, which was tilted toward the small states. The committee came up with a compromise, brokered by Roger Sherman of Connecticut and therefore known as the Connecticut Compromise. The House would be based on population; the Senate would have two representatives for each state, chosen by the state legislature. (Americans did not vote directly for their senators in all states until 1913.) Because legislation had to pass through both houses, the public and the states would each have a say. Because the delegates wanted power over taxes and spending to be in the people's hands, they required that all finance-related bills had to be introduced first in the House.

● Louis Glanzman's recent painting of the Constitutional Convention. Washington towers over everyone at the center in a black frock coat. To his right stands James Madison. Alexander Hamilton is the red-haired man standing sixth from the right. Aged Benjamin Franklin, eighty-one-years-old, sits at the center of the room chatting with Hugh Williamson, a delegate from North Carolina.

The compromise squeaked through—five states voted "yes," four "no," and one split. The big states won the House of Representatives; the small states got their way in the Senate. The compromise continues to give rural states a great deal of clout in the Senate, engendering a debate as to whether small, mostly rural states like Vermont or Utah have too much power in Congress.

4. The President

Even the master planner James Madison arrived at the convention without a clear design for the presidency—also known as the *executive authority* because it *executes* (or puts into effect) the laws. The delegates even wavered about whether executive authority should be placed in one individual or a committee.

Committee or Individual?   Many delegates worried that a single executive would grow powerful and become, as Governor Randolph put it, "the fetus of monarchy." Madison and his allies, however, feared that the Connecticut Compromise opened the Senate door to the same petty state politics that had wrecked the Articles of Confederation. They therefore decided that the president should be one individual, independent of Congress, who could represent the public. After much back-and-forth, they settled on a four-year term and permitted reelections. (In 1951, the Twenty-Second Amendment limited the president to two terms.)

The Electoral College.   How would the United States choose the president? The Constitution's framers saw a problem with every option. They did not think the

Electoral College: The system established by the Constitution to elect the president; each state has a group of electors (equal in size to that of its congressional delegation in the House and the Senate); the public in each state votes for electors, who then vote for the president.

people had enough information or wisdom. They did not trust state legislators to put aside their own narrow concerns and think about the national interest. Delegates from the big states no longer wanted to give Congress the job now that state legislators were picking the senators. What could they do? In response, they came up with the most complicated rigmarole in the Constitution: the **Electoral College**. Each state would select individuals known as *electors*—the delegates hoped that they would be well-known individuals with sound judgment—and the electors would then choose the president.

How many electors would each state have? Another compromise: Each state would have the same number of electors as it had members of Congress. That meant a state's population would matter (given proportional representation in the House) but also that every state was assured of two more votes (reflecting their representation in the Senate). If no individual received a majority of electoral votes—which last happened in 1824—the House of Representatives would choose from among the five candidates with the most votes. They would vote by state, and each state would get just one vote—again, a concession to small states.

Who would elect the electors? The convention simply left this question to the states. At first, the state legislatures got the job of voting for the electors. But in the late 1820s, the states ceded this right to the people (again, white men, although by then they did not need to own any property). The people voted state by state for their electors—as we still do (see Figure 3.3).

Today, all the electors in a state generally cast their votes for the candidate who won the state (although only twenty-six states require them to do so). As we saw in Chapter 1, the system has elected five men who lost the popular vote—but won in the Electoral College. After the 2016 election, seven members of the Electoral College refused to vote for the candidate who won their state – the most "faithless electors" in history (excepting 1872 when the Democrat, Horace Greeley, died before the Electoral College met).

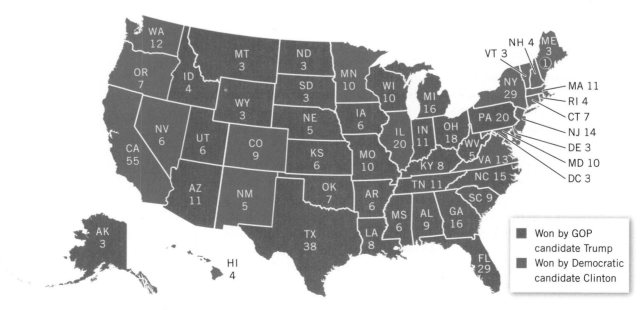

● **Figure 3.3** *Electoral College map for the 2016 presidential election. For the second time in the last five elections, the candidate who lost the popular vote became president by winning the Electoral College.*

The President: Too Strong or Too Weak?   All these details can obscure a crucial fact about the Constitution and the presidency. The delegates arrived at the Constitutional Convention less certain about this office than any other. Some feared putting too much power in one person's hands. Others recognized the need for a leader who could energetically pursue the nation's interests. Despite all that was at stake, arguments about the presidency never got very heated. Why? Because every delegate in the room knew exactly who the first president was going to be. There sat George Washington, calmly presiding over the convention. Knowing that Washington would almost certainly be thrust into the role of president cooled the tempers in the room. In the end, the delegates built a general framework and left many details to be defined by the presidents themselves.

Sometimes, the presidency has been a very powerful office. At other times, it has seemed perilously weak. We explore this paradox when we examine the presidency in Chapter 14.

5. Separation of Powers

One idea that evolved during the convention was the separation of powers. Each branch of government—the president, Congress, and the judiciary—has its job to do: The delegates vested "all legislative powers" in Congress, the executive power in the president, and the judicial power (to try cases) in the courts. The Articles of Confederation had created only a national legislature; in Britain, power was also concentrated in Parliament, their national legislature. Now, the United States would have three independent branches.

The framers added a crucial twist: checks and balances. Each power the Constitution grants to Congress or the presidency or the judiciary is balanced by a "countervailing" power assigned to another branch. Each branch is involved in the others' business. In this way, as Madison later put it, one branch's ambition for power would always check the other branches' ambitions (see Figure 3.4).

For example, Congress passes legislation but needs the president to sign a bill into law. The president can veto (reject) the bill (checking Congress); Congress can override the veto by a two-thirds vote of both chambers (balancing the president).

The president is commander-in-chief, but the Constitution gives Congress the power to declare war and set the military's budget. The president negotiates treaties, but the Senate must ratify them by a two-thirds vote. The president appoints Cabinet officials and Supreme Court justices, but the Senate must approve (or confirm) them. Congress holds the ultimate power over all federal officers. The House can impeach (or formally accuse) the president or any other officer in the executive or judicial branch of "Treason, Bribery or other high Crimes and Misdemeanors"; the Senate looks into the accusation and decides whether to actually remove the person from office. What are "high crimes and misdemeanors"? Well, they have never been fully defined and Congress must use its judgment. We review some of the considerations below.

These checks and balances are among the most distinctive features of the American Constitution. The French political philosopher Montesquieu wrote an influential treatise, *The Spirit of the Laws* (published in 1748), which argued that to avoid tyranny, the executive, legislative, and judicial functions of government must be separated from one another—and never placed in a single individual or body. However, very few governments have ever developed this principle as fully as the U.S. Constitution.

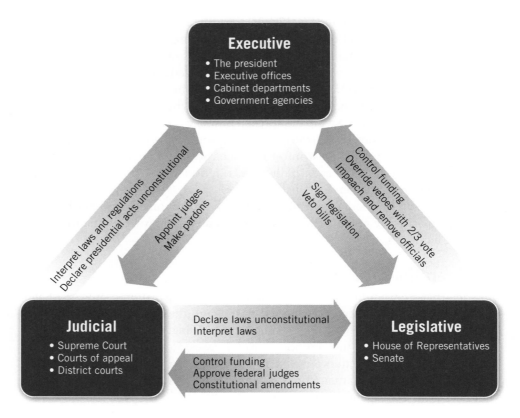

Executive
- The president
- Executive offices
- Cabinet departments
- Government agencies

Interpret laws and regulations
Declare presidential acts unconstitutional

Appoint judges
Make pardons

Sign legislation
Veto bills

Control funding
Override vetoes with 2/3 vote
Impeach and remove officials

Judicial
- Supreme Court
- Courts of appeal
- District courts

Declare laws unconstitutional
Interpret laws

Control funding
Approve federal judges
Constitutional amendments

Legislative
- House of Representatives
- Senate

● **Figure 3.4** *Separation of powers—the checks on the federal level. Multiply these checks across state and local levels and a vital question of American politics arises: Is this chaotic and fragmented state ready to take on the world? Americans have been posing this question since 1787.*

Checks and balances continue to spark disagreement in the present. Many scholars argue that American-style separated systems are too prone to gridlock—a paralysis of governing institutions—than other democracies. The danger of gridlock is that major issues such as climate change or the national debt become harder to address. An even greater potential danger: Are people growing so tired of stalemate they vote for leaders who are willing to ignore the constitutional limits?[21] We get into this question in Chapter 14. Has the U.S. government developed too many checks and balances to meet the challenges of the twenty-first century? Or do the Constitution's checks and balances remain in good working order, controlling power and preserving self-rule—just as James Madison planned?

6. "A Principle of Which We Were Ashamed"

The convention rethought almost every aspect of government—except slavery. Why? For some delegates, the answer came down to self-interest. Of the fifty-five delegates, twenty-five were slave owners. George Washington brought three slaves with him to Philadelphia. In three states—Georgia, South Carolina, and Virginia—slaves made up more than one-third of the population. And the men and women in bondage were a source of wealth and power. Each time the subject of slavery came up, delegates from South Carolina and Georgia offered the convention a stark choice—protect slavery or form a union without us.

In the end, the delegates wanted a strong union more than they hated slavery. The Constitution includes three major references to slavery—without ever mentioning the word itself. Each time, the slave-holding states got what they wanted.

The Three-Fifths Compromise.   Slavery was first thrust on the convention's agenda with the question of how to count slaves when allocating seats in the House of Representatives. As Table 3.2 shows, nearly four in ten of Virginia's residents were slaves. If slaves were counted as part of the population, southern states would have as many members in the House of Representatives as the northern states.

As soon as the issue came up, James Wilson of Pennsylvania sprang to his feet and offered a compromise. For the purpose of apportioning representation, Wilson proposed, let the total number of slaves count as three-fifths of the free people of a state. The strange fraction came from the Continental Congress. When it was trying to raise revenue from the states, Congress calculated each state's wealth on the basis of population. It then arbitrarily estimated that slaves would generate three-fifths as much wealth as free people.

This crude calculation now came back to haunt the Constitution. The delegates accepted the Three-Fifths Compromise. Its actual wording is as peculiar as the rule itself.

> *Representatives . . . shall be apportioned among the several states according to their respective numbers, which shall be determined by adding the whole number of free persons, including those bound to service for a term of years [indentured servants] and excluding Indians not taxed, three fifths of all other persons.*

The Constitution never says "slave," but simply "three fifths of all other persons." In fact, a reader who did not know that the passage refers to slavery would have a hard time understanding it. Why did the Constitution's framers—who were usually so precise—write such a convoluted sentence? They did not want the word *slavery* to appear in the Constitution. John Dickinson, a thoughtful delegate from Delaware, put it best: The awkward wording was, he said, "an endeavor to conceal a principle of which we were ashamed."[22]

TABLE 3.2 **Enslaved Proportion of the U.S. Population in 1790**

STATE	TOTAL POPULATION	SLAVES	PERCENTAGE OF POPULATION ENSLAVED
Connecticut	237,655	2,648	1.1
Delaware	59,096	8,887	15.0
Georgia	82,548	29,264	34.5
Maryland	319,728	103,036	32.2
Massachusetts	378,556	0	0.0
New Hampshire	141,899	157	0.1
New Jersey	184,139	11,423	6.2
New York	340,241	21,193	6.2
North Carolina	395,005	100,783	25.5
Pennsylvania	433,611	3,707	0.9
Rhode Island	69,112	958	1.4
South Carolina	249,073	107,094	43.0
Virginia	747,550	292,627	39.1
Source: U.S. Census			

The Slave Trade.   A second question involved the slave trade. Could the federal government regulate or abolish it? Many delegates were repulsed by the idea of stealing human beings from Africa, chaining them into the hulls of ships bound for America, and selling the survivors to the highest bidder. George Mason from Virginia rose and gave the most prophetic speech of the convention: "Every master of slaves is born a petty tyrant. They bring the judgment of heaven on a country. As nations cannot be rewarded or punished in the next world they must be in this. Providence punishes national sins, by national calamities." It was a powerful speech. However, Mason himself owned more than three hundred slaves. Their worth would rise if the slave trade were abolished.

No one else at the convention was willing to follow Mason's attack. In the end, backers of a strong Constitution struck a bargain and permitted the slave trade for another twenty years, in exchange for more national power over interstate commerce and the authority to tax imports. Historian William Beeman calculated that by permitting the slave trade for another twenty years they condemned 200,000 Africans to slavery—almost equaling the total (250,000) from the preceding 170 years.[23]

Fugitive Slaves.   Finally, in August, as the convention was winding down, delegates from the slave states proposed a fugitive slave clause—requiring the rest of the nation to assist in returning runaway slaves. This time there were no deals and barely any debate. The northern delegates simply accepted the proposal. Northern merchants, after all, benefited from the slave trade right alongside Southern planters. Every region was complicit in the tragic decision.

"The National Calamity."   Many Americans revere the document that has guided the nation for more than 225 years. However, George Mason was right when he predicted a "national calamity." Seventy-two years later, Abraham Lincoln would echo Mason as he reflected on the carnage of the Civil War in his second inaugural address: "God . . . gives to both North and South this terrible war as the woe due to those by whom the offense [of slavery] came."

The Constitution's slavery passages— as with the Civil War that led to their repeal—remind us that the Convention was the beginning of an American journey. Each generation has to face the same challenges that confronted the founders. *Who are we?* Can we try to make the United States more just, more democratic, and more inclusive? The Declaration of Independence gives America its ideals: All people are created equal. The Constitution, in turn, provides the rules. Americans have struggled over the meaning of the ideals and the implementation of the rules ever since these documents were written.

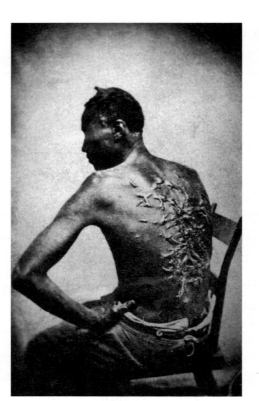

● *A vivid example of slavery's brutality. Fifty years after the Constitutional Convention, abolitionists rose up and denounced the Constitution as a "covenant with death and an agreement with hell" because of its slavery compromises. Advertisements for runaway slaves reported identifying marks—such as horrific scars from whipping and even branding.*

The Bottom Line

» The constitutional framers balanced two dangers: government that was too strong (the king of England) versus government that was too weak (the Articles of Confederation).

» The debates focused on five central issues:

1. Should the people be directly involved in government? Most delegates believed in filtration, or indirect elections.

2. National versus state power, which came down to a standoff between larger and smaller states. Big states backed Madison's Virginia Plan. Small states countered with the New Jersey Plan. The Connecticut Compromise offered a solution: House members were elected on the basis of population, but every state had two Senate seats.

3. The nature of the presidency.

4. How best to separate governing powers, answered through a system of checks and balances. For the most part, these limits on concentrated authority would continue to develop long after ratification.

5. Slavery: Pragmatic compromise in the name of union overcame moral concerns. Delegates took care not to use the word *slavery* in the Constitution, but several clauses enabling the institution to expand would lead to the greatest conflict in the nation's future.

An Overview of the Constitution

By September 17, after four months of deliberation, the Constitutional Convention had done its work. Thirty-nine of the original fifty-five delegates lined up to sign the document. Benjamin Franklin, pointing to a sunburst painted on the back of the president's chair, reflected on how he had gazed at that sun throughout the convention "without being able to tell if it was rising or setting. But now . . . I have the happiness to know that it is a rising and not a setting sun."[24] A more pessimistic observer might have pointed out that sixteen delegates—almost a third—had either left the convention or refused to sign: a portent of the battles ahead.

There are only seven articles in the Constitution, each broken down into multiple sections. (Their full text appears in Appendix II.) These passages remain the institutional foundation of the American political system.

What does the Constitution do? Get a brief tour.

Preamble

The Constitution begins with a preamble, the most elegant sentence in the document:

> *We the people of the United States, in order to form a more perfect union, establish justice, insure domestic tranquility, provide for the common defense, promote the general welfare, and secure the blessings of liberty to ourselves and our posterity, do ordain and establish this Constitution for the United States of America.*

The Constitution's authority rests not on the states, but on "we the people." As we have seen, the Constitutional Convention produced a weak version of the people—one that permitted slavery, excluded women, and permitted "we the people" to vote for exactly one branch of Congress. The next phrase—"in order to form a more perfect union"—addresses these limitations. Americans still struggle toward that more perfect union.

The preamble also offers six goals for a successful government. Ask yourself how you would rate the U.S. government on each of them today (see What Do You Think?).

Article 1: Congress

Article 1, the longest in the Constitution, describes the new Congress. Section 2 of the article establishes a House of Representatives elected every two years. In 1789, the average size of a House district was around 33,000 people—today the size of an average district has grown to just over 750,000 people. Representatives must be twenty-five years old and have been a citizen for seven years. Section 3 establishes a Senate with two members from every state, elected every six years; they must be at least thirty years old and have been a citizen for nine years.

Section 8 is the most important passage in Article 1—and perhaps the entire Constitution. Its seventeen short paragraphs tell Congress what it may do, including the "power to lay and collect taxes," declare war, regulate interstate commerce, coin money, and raise an army.

Think about the reach of congressional authority. The largest and most expensive program that Congress oversees is Social Security, which pays monthly pensions to older people. If you read all of Section 8, you may be puzzled—nothing in it remotely justifies paying for retirement pensions. How, then, could Congress create the Social Security program? Because the very last paragraph of Section 8 empowers Congress "to make all laws which shall be necessary and proper for carrying into execution the foregoing powers, and all other powers vested by this Constitution in the government of the United States." That phrase, known as the *necessary and proper clause*, gives Congress—and the government—a great deal of creative leeway. What are the limits of the power granted to Congress by this clause? This is another point on which the delegates in Philadelphia disagreed. Not surprisingly, scholars still argue about how far the necessary and proper clause stretches congressional authority. The states of the Confederacy broke away from the Union in 1861 and wrote their own constitution; although it

What Do YOU Think?   **Have We Achieved These National Goals Today?**

Think about the goals listed in the preamble to the Constitution. Then give a grade to each: An "A" if you think the United States has lived up to its goals, and a . . . well, we're sure you know all about grades!

Goal:	Grade Today:
Form a strong union	_____
Establish equal justice for all	_____
Insure domestic tranquility (that is, peace at home)	_____
Provide for the common defense (today, we might say homeland security)	_____
Promote the general welfare	_____
Secure liberty for ourselves and posterity	_____

largely mirrored the original, it ruled out using a necessary and proper clause to expand government authority.

Section 9 of Article 1 lists the things Congress may *not* do. Its second prohibition is especially important today: "The privilege of the writ of habeas corpus shall not be suspended unless when in cases of rebellion or invasion the public safety may require it." *Habeas corpus* means that government cannot hold prisoners without formally charging them with a crime. The U.S. government may not simply throw someone in jail without a charge.

Article 2: The President

The Constitution's second article shifts focus from the legislature to the executive branch. The president, Article 2 specifies, must be a natural-born American at least thirty-five years old and is chosen by electors for a four-year term. Today every state has turned the power to choose electors over to the public. Very few nations use the American process for selecting the head of state (see Comparing Nations 3.2).

Whereas Article 1 lists congressional do's and don'ts in detail, Article 2 spells out presidential powers and duties in much less detail. The president is commander-in-chief of the army and the navy.[25] Presidents can make treaties if two-thirds of the Senate approve; they appoint ambassadors, Supreme Court justices, and other officials—again with the advice and consent of the Senate.

Although these seem like a limited set of powers, the Constitution includes another clause that has permitted an enormous expansion of presidential powers: "The executive power shall be vested in a President of the United States." What

COMPARING NATIONS 3.2	The U.S. Government Is Different from Most Democracies			
Of these twelve advanced democracies, only two—Argentina and Brazil—mirror the American Constitution on all three dimensions. Most democracies are parliamentary systems, in which the lower house selects a chief executive (a prime minister). Ironically, that was the idea in both the Virginia and New Jersey Plans, the original drafts of the Constitution. None of the other democracies has as many checks and balances as the United States.	**NATION**	**HEAD OF GOVERNMENT ELECTED BY**	**FEDERALISM**	**CHECKS/ BALANCES**
	United States	Public/electors	Yes	Yes
	Argentina	Public	Yes	Yes
	Australia	Parliament (lower house)	Yes	Some
	Brazil	Public	Yes	Yes
	Canada	Parliament (lower house)	Yes	No
	France	Public	No	Sometimes
	Germany	Parliament (lower house)	Yes	Some
	Great Britain	Parliament (lower house)	No	No
	India	Parliament (lower house)	Yes	No
	Israel	Parliament	No	No
	Japan	Parliament (lower house)	No	No

that "executive power" is, and how far it can stretch, has been debated throughout American history. President Obama, for example, facing a Congress unwilling to act on immigration reform, in 2012 unilaterally declared a "Dreamers" policy that allowed young children brought illegally into the United States to apply for work permits and avoid deportation. How could he do so? The administration claimed he was using his authority to execute the laws that govern immigration. President Trump eagerly reversed the order—although he has taken an expansive view of presidential power on other issues. Where does that leave the Dreamers? The Congress and the Supreme Court will have to weigh in.

Section 4 allows for removing a president "on impeachment for, and conviction of, treason, bribery, or other high crimes and misdemeanors." Three presidents have faced formal impeachment proceedings, although only one, Richard Nixon, resigned his office. The grounds for impeachment remain highly contested; back in 1970, future president and U.S. House minority leader Gerald Ford remarked "An impeachable offense is whatever a majority of the House of Representatives considers it to be at a given moment in history."[26]

Article 3: The Courts

Article 3 creates the Supreme Court and authorizes Congress to organize additional courts. Alexander Hamilton called the Supreme Court "the least dangerous" branch of government, and the Constitution describes it only briefly. The justices are selected by the president, approved by the Senate, and have tenure for life—still another buffer against democratic politics. Article 3 grants the Supreme Court power over all cases "arising under this Constitution, the laws of the United States and treaties made."

The Constitution is silent on the Court's most formidable power: May it overrule an act of Congress? Or an executive declaration by the White House? Sixteen years after the Constitutional Convention, Chief Justice John Marshall, in deciding a case called *Marbury v. Madison*, ruled that the Court could strike down an act of Congress. (We review this case in detail in Chapter 16.) In other words, because the Court has authority over all cases "arising under this Constitution," Marshall claimed it also had a responsibility to review the constitutionality of legislation. The delegates debated this power but, in the end, sidestepped the controversy and left the language vague. Ever since Marshall's decision, however, the courts have ruled whether Congress and the president are abiding by the Constitution's rules.

Notice how the powers of each branch have evolved over time. Americans are constantly challenged to read and interpret precisely what the Constitution requires.

Article 4: Relations Between the States

Article 4 defines the relationship between the states that had so plagued the Articles of Confederation. A state may not discriminate against citizens of other states, and each must give "full faith and credit" to the official acts of other states and guarantee every state a republican form of government.

The "full faith and credit" clause can be explosive. When some states passed same-sex marriage legislation, others refused to recognize these unions; Congress passed the Defense of Marriage Act that permitted states to refuse "full faith and credit" for same-sex marriages conducted in other states. After more than a decade, the Supreme Court took the issue off the table by striking down the federal law and all state laws that limited marriage to a man and a woman. Now you know where they got the authority to do so: the Supreme Court's authority to judge which laws and regulations violate the rules laid down by the Constitution.[27]

Article 5: Amendments

Article 5 authorizes amendments to the Constitution. However, the process is extremely difficult. Two-thirds of both the House and the Senate must approve the amendment. Then three-fourths of the states must ratify it—either through their state legislatures or through state conventions. The only amendment to be ratified the second way is the Twenty-First Amendment, which in 1933 repealed the prohibition on alcohol.

Over one hundred thousand amendments have been suggested since 1791 (when the first ten amendments, or Bill of Rights, were ratified); some 11,000 have been proposed in Congress; only seventeen have passed into law. When Americans disagree with a Supreme Court ruling, they sometimes try to push through a constitutional amendment. As you can see, they very rarely succeed.

The Constitution forbids amendments on two matters: No amendment could stop the slave trade before 1808, and no state could be denied equal suffrage in the Senate (two seats) without its approval. In this way, the two fiercest debates at the convention were placed beyond the reach of future generations.

Article 6: The Law of the Land

Article 6 makes the Constitution the supreme law of the land. It also specifies that there must be no religious test for holding any federal office. Some states, however, had religious tests (requiring adherence to a specific religion, usually Protestant Christianity) for holding state and local office and even for voting, up until the 1830s.

Article 7: Ratification

Article 7 announced that the Constitution would go into effect after nine states had ratified it—a controversial move, because the United States was still operating under the Articles of Confederation, which could be amended only by all thirteen states.

The Missing Articles

Many Americans thought that the original Constitution was missing something important. Only a handful of individual rights were mentioned in the document. It said nothing about free speech, a free press, freedom of religion, jury trials, or the right to bear arms. The debate over ratifying the Constitution would quickly expose this weakness. As we will see, ratification helped introduce an important addition: the ten amendments known as the Bill of Rights.

 **The Bottom Line**

» The Constitution is a brief, elegant document with a preamble and seven articles (or major sections).

» The articles of the Constitution address (1) Congress, (2) the presidency, (3) the judiciary, (4) relations between the states, (5) instruction for amending the Constitution, (6) an assertion that the Constitution is the supreme law of the land, and (7) a process for ratifying the Constitution.

🔵 Ratification

The new Constitution now went to the states, where ratifying conventions would vote it up or down. Although most states were closely divided, the Constitution had two big advantages. First, it offered a clear plan in a time of trouble; opponents could only say "no" and force the nation to start all over again. Second, the convention had attracted many of the most prestigious men in America, beginning with Washington and Franklin. Supporters of the Constitution were known as *Federalists*—making their opponents the *Anti-Federalists*.

The Anti-Federalists

Classical republicanism:
A democratic ideal, based in ancient Greece and Rome, that calls on citizens to participate in public affairs, seek the public interest, shun private gain, and defer to natural leaders.

The Anti-Federalists based their argument against ratification in **classical republicanism**. Popular government, in this view, should model itself on ancient republics such as Athens and Rome. Republics should be small and local, permitting maximum popular participation in public affairs. When we discussed the idea of self-rule in Chapter 2, we introduced the idea of direct democracy (celebrated by Thomas Jefferson); classical republicanism is the original version of that idea.

The Anti-Federalists were not interested in a centralized nation–state such as the European empires. They had four major criticisms of the new Constitution:

- First, it stripped political control from citizens and placed it in a powerful national government over which the people would not have much influence.
- Second, the president looked too much like a king.
- Third, standing armies and navies were a threat to peace and liberty. Republics relied on citizen militias—which could be mustered during wartime—to protect the people.
- Fourth, and most important, the Anti-Federalists hammered away at the Constitution's missing piece, a bill of rights.[28]

Politics also played a role in the Anti-Federalist argument. Many of the men who opposed the Constitution were powerful political figures in their own states. A national government would diminish their influence.

Many of the Anti-Federalist (and civic-republican) arguments remain alive today. Americans often criticize the federal government and cheer the idea of restoring power to state and local officials, who are closer to the people. The Anti-Federalists may have lost the debate in 1788, but their fear of federal power and their yearning to return authority to the people endures—and shapes one answer to our great question, *Who are we?*

The Federalists

The arguments in favor of the new Constitution were summarized by an editorial dream team. James Madison and Alexander Hamilton (with a little help from John Jay, who would become the first chief justice of the United States) wrote eighty-five short essays that appeared in newspapers to explain and defend the Constitution. Known as the *Federalist Papers*, these essays achieved three very different purposes. First, they are pro-Constitution editorials, even propaganda; the authors were fighting to get New York to approve the new Constitution, and they did not pretend to be neutral. Second, they are the single best guide to the thinking that guided the Constitution. However, we have to read them carefully, always weighing the *Papers* as persuasive rhetoric on the one hand and as explanations of constitutional logic on the other. Finally, the *Federalist Papers* are outstanding theoretical essays about politics and government.

The two most famous *Federalist Papers*, no. 10 and no. 51, are reprinted in Appendix III to this book. Their eighteenth-century language sounds strange to our ears, but the argument is brilliant. *Federalist* no. 10 argues, surprisingly, that a large national government can protect liberty more effectively than small local governments. Madison begins the essay by introducing the "mortal disease" that always destroys popular government. You might think that he was referring to tyrants like George III. Instead, he points to *factions*—groups that pursue their self-interest at the expense of others. And in the United States, said Madison, factions usually reflect economic interests. This issue still haunts American foreign policy today: Removing tyrants will not achieve stable popular government until the factions that divide the country are controlled.

How can we diminish the effects of factions? Not through local governments, argued Madison. In each local area, one economic interest is likely to predominate— farmers, merchants, big manufacturers, or even poor people eager to tax the rich. Because the same local group will always be in the majority, it is difficult to stop that group from taking advantage of the minority.

Madison's realistic assessment was a breakthrough in political theory. The classical view assumed that for popular government to survive, the people—that is, the voters—had to be virtuous and respect one another. Madison introduced a modern take: expect people to pursue their own self-interest. As he wrote in *Federalist* no. 51, "if men were angels, no government would be necessary." If popular government is to survive, it must be organized to protect minorities from majorities who are going to pursue their own self-interest.

How can we do this? Move the debate to the national level, said Madison. A larger political sphere— a bigger government—will always have a great many diverse interests, arising from all the states. With so many different factions, no one interest will be able to dominate. Each faction will form a small minority of the whole and will therefore need to form alliances. As the issues change, so will the groups that are in the majority and the minority. As a result, no one faction will have an incentive to impose its will on the minority for very long – they might need that minority for the next issue. Madison's idea would run into trouble, however, if the same two sides face off against one another on every national issue. When that occurs, there is no need to form shifting alliances. That's what happened in the slavery debate in the 1850s. Some political scientists worry that the intense party divisions today might again be creating a fixed division on issue after issue. (We discuss that concern in Chapter 11.)[29]

Two Strong Arguments

To this day, both sides—Anti-Federalist and Federalist— sound persuasive. The Anti-Federalists tapped into a deep American yearning for local governments that respond directly to popular concerns. The Federalists argued that only a national government could really protect the people's rights and turn the new nation into a great power.

● *The ratification of the Constitution was a close call. Patrick Henry, a powerful orator, led the opponents (known as Anti-Federalists) in Virginia. Virginia was one of seven states where the vote was close.*

A Very Close Vote

The small states got their way at the Constitutional Convention, and, not surprisingly, they ratified quickly and unanimously—Delaware, New Jersey, and Georgia all signed by January 2, 1788. In Pennsylvania, some members of the assembly hid to slow down the process. Enthusiastic mobs found the reluctant members and marched them to the deliberations. The public crammed into the hall and gathered outside the building. After a month, Pennsylvania ratified the Constitution forty-six to twenty-three, and Benjamin Franklin led a cheering throng through the streets to Epple's Tavern for celebratory toasts (see Table 3.3 for a summary of the voting).

In Massachusetts, Governor John Hancock, who had been the first delegate to sign the Declaration of Independence, dramatically switched to the Federalist side—on one crucial condition. He asked that amendments protecting individual rights be introduced to the new Constitution. Even with his switch, the Constitution won ratification in Massachusetts only narrowly, 187 to 168. Once the votes were counted, the Anti-Federalists announced that they would "support the Constitution as cheerfully and as heartily as though [they] had voted on the other side." Other states followed the two Massachusetts precedents: request a bill of rights and unite after the debate.

After Maryland and South Carolina voted for the Constitution, the action moved to Virginia—the largest state and the most intense contest to date. Anti-Federalist opposition was led by Patrick Henry, known as "the son of thunder" for his rhetorical power; at one point he spoke without notes for seven straight hours. Governor William Randolph, who had presented the Virginia Plan at the convention, and George Mason, who had scorched the slave trade, both refused to sign the Constitution and joined Henry on the Anti-Federalist side. Despite the strong opposition, Virginia voted for the Constitution eighty-nine to seventy-nine.

TABLE 3.3   Final Vote for the Constitution

STATE	DATE OF RATIFICATION	VOTE IN STATE CONVENTION
1. Delaware	December 7, 1787	Unanimous (30–0)
2. Pennsylvania	December 12, 1787	46–23
3. New Jersey	December 18, 1787	Unanimous (38–0)
4. Georgia	January 2, 1788	Unanimous (26–0)
5. Connecticut	January 9, 1788	128–40
6. Massachusetts	February 7, 1788	187–168
7. Maryland	April 28, 1788	63–11
8. South Carolina	May 23, 1788	149–73
9. New Hampshire	June 21, 1788	57–47; required two meetings
10. Virginia	June 25, 1788	89–79
11. New York	July 25, 1788	30–27
12. North Carolina	July 21, 1789 (after the election of Washington)	194–77
13. Rhode Island	May 29, 1790 (first Congress in session)	34–32

Key: *Easy ratification*   *Tough fight*   *Originally refused*

New York was even more contentious than Virginia. New York City supported the Constitution, but the rest of the state opposed it. In the end, the new Constitution squeaked through by thirty to twenty-seven.

Not every state voted in favor. Rhode Island town meetings voted against holding a convention to debate the Constitution. Rhode Island would reluctantly join the union after George Washington had been president for two months. North Carolina initially rejected the Constitution by a lopsided vote of 184 to 83. In New Hampshire a convention met, refused to ratify, and adjourned; four months later the delegates reconvened and voted yes, and on June 21, 1788, New Hampshire became the ninth state to ratify. The Constitution would now be the law of the land.

Ratification was a very close contest. If a total of just 3 percent of the delegates across Virginia, Massachusetts, and New York had changed their vote, the Constitution would have gone down to defeat. Americans came within a whisker of rejecting the Constitution that now defines the nation and its government.

● *New York celebrated ratification by cheering Alexander Hamilton—still remembered as a major intellectual force. Here, Broadway hit* Hamilton *recalls the most forceful Federalist. Original cast members, from left, Daveed Diggs, Okieriete Onaodowan, Anthony Ramos, and Lin-Manuel Miranda in the musical* Hamilton.

A Popular Surge Propels People into Politics

The Federalists ultimately won the constitutional debate and created a strong central government far removed from the people. At first it seemed as if Roger Sherman's comment at the convention had won the day: "The people . . . should have . . . little to do . . . [with] government." But something unexpected happened. The Revolution set off a democratic surge that liberated popular energies. Not everyone was included— not women, not black people, not Native Americans. But the idea that ordinary citizens should be kept at arm's length from government was soon swamped by a great tide of participation that many of the founders neither imagined nor desired.[30] People raced to participate in both economic and political life. However, American history is not a simple story of ever-expanding participation. Rather, the battle for a more perfect union has been long and unpredictable. Over more than two centuries, rights, liberties, and democracy have been gained and lost and gained again.

The Bottom Line

» The debate over ratifying the Constitution featured two visions of American government.

» The *Federalists* argued that only an energetic national government could protect the nation and secure liberty. The *Anti-Federalists* called instead for a modest government that left power in state and local hands.

» The state-by-state voting on ratification was very close, and it was well over a year before the Constitution was approved.

» More than 230 years later, Americans are still debating the same question—How strong should the federal government be?

Passing the 13th Amendment

Bill of Rights: The first ten amendments to the Constitution, listing the rights guaranteed to every citizen.

Changing the Constitution

Although most Anti-Federalist leaders eventually rallied to the new Constitution, they insisted on a crucial addition to the Constitution: a bill of rights. The state ratification conventions proposed over two hundred amendments. When the first Congress met, in 1789, most members did not want to bother with amendments. The Constitution was ratified, Congress elected, and President George Washington's administration organized. However, one representative insisted on adding liberties to the Constitution. James Madison had been through a tough election campaign and had pledged to support a bill of rights. With his word of honor at stake, Madison took the two hundred proposed amendments, boiled them down, and pushed his reluctant colleagues, who passed seventeen. The Senate reduced the list to twelve; the states ratified ten.

The Bill of Rights

Today, the first ten amendments to the Constitution, known as the **Bill of Rights**, form a crucial feature of the Constitution and of American government. *These set out the rights and liberties—the protections from government—that every citizen is guaranteed.* Freedom of speech, freedom of the press, freedom of religion, the right to bear arms, and the long list of additional rights are an essential part of America's identity. Table 3.4 summarizes the amendments that make up the Bill of Rights.

Originally, the Bill of Rights applied only to the federal government. The First Amendment reads, "Congress shall make no law . . . abridging the freedom of speech." At the time, states that wanted to limit speech or set up an official religion were free to do so.

TABLE 3.4 Summarizing the Bill of Rights

1. Congress may not establish a religion or prohibit the free exercise of religion; it may not abridge freedom of speech or of the press or of the people's right to assemble and to petition government.
2. Citizens have the right to bear arms.
3. No soldier may be quartered in any house without the consent of the owner.
4. There must be no unreasonable searches or seizures. Government authorities may not break into your house without a search warrant.
5. No one may be forced to testify against him- or herself (declining to do so is now known as "taking the Fifth"), and no one may be deprived of life, liberty, or property without due process of law. The government may not take private property (if, for example, it wants to build a highway) without just compensation.
6. Certain rights are guaranteed in criminal trials.
7. Accused persons are guaranteed the right to trial by jury.
8. The government may not force citizens to pay excessive bails and may not impose cruel and unusual punishments.
9. The enumeration of certain rights does not diminish the other rights retained by the people.
10. Any powers not given to the federal government are reserved for the states and the people.

The Fourteenth Amendment, ratified after the Civil War in 1868 to protect the former slaves, commands that no *state* may deny "any person . . . the equal protection of the laws." In theory, this amendment extended the Bill of Rights to the states—meaning state governments must honor each right just as the national government must do. However, the Fourteenth Amendment only kicked off a long process, known as **incorporation**: The Supreme Court applied (or "incorporated") each right to state government, one right at a time. That process continues down to the present day: The Supreme Court "incorporated" the right to bear arms in 2010. As a result, no state or city may violate the second amendment right to bear arms. Where exactly does this leave gun control laws? That debate continues—stay tuned!

Ratifying the Constitution and the Bill of Rights was just the start of a long debate. We return to the story of the Constitution and individual rights in Chapter 5 and explore how they guide government today.

Incorporation: The process by which the Supreme Court declares that a right in the Bill of Rights also applies to state governments.

The Seventeen Amendments

After the Bill of Rights was passed, constitutional amendments became rare events—only seventeen have passed since 1791. Successful amendments all do at least one of four things: They *extend rights*—for example, guaranteeing the right to vote to eighteen-year-olds (seven amendments extend rights). They *adjust election rules*—for example, limiting the president to two terms (eleven amendments focus on elections). They *change government operations*—for example, switching Inauguration Day from March to January (four amendments focus on government rules). Or they *affect governmental powers over individuals*—for example, prohibiting alcohol and then (fourteen years later) permitting alcohol again. Table 3.5 summarizes the seventeen amendments that have been ratified since 1791.

Apart from formal amendments, American government—and how we interpret the Constitution—is always changing. We constantly debate how to apply the Constitution and its amendments to current issues. May Congress limit the money corporations give political candidates? May a woman have an abortion? Does the First Amendment protect those advocating violent overthrow of the government? May universities consider an applicant's race as part of admissions decisions? May a Christian student group pray before class in a public school? The wording of the

● *A group of children pray together in their elementary school class. Does the Constitution permit prayer in public schools? Or would that mean the government was endorsing (or "establishing") a religion—violating the First Amendment? The issue takes many forms. For example, the Texas Attorney General went to court to permit Bible quotes on one schoolhouse door but recently raised concerns about Muslim students reading the Koran.*

TABLE 3.5 **Amendments to the U.S. Constitution**

AMENDMENT	DESCRIPTION	YEAR RATIFIED	RESULT
11	Required state consent for individuals suing a state in federal court	1795	Modified government operations
12	Separated votes within the Electoral College for president and vice president	1804	Shifted election rules
13	Prohibited slavery	1865	Expanded individual rights
14	Provided citizenship to former slaves and declared that states could not deny civil rights, civil liberties, or the equal protection of the laws	1868	Expanded individual rights
15	Granted voting rights to members of all races	1870	Expanded individual rights
16	Permitted national income tax	1913	Expanded government powers over individuals
17	Provided direct election of senators	1913	Shifted election rules
18	Prohibited alcohol	1919	Expanded government powers over individuals
19	Extended the vote to women	1920	Expanded individual rights
20	Changed Inauguration Day from March to January	1933	Modified government operations
21	Repealed Prohibition	1933	Adjusted government powers over individuals
22	Limited president to two terms	1951	Shifted election rules
23	Extended the vote for president to citizens in Washington, DC	1961	Expanded individual rights
24	Prohibited a poll tax (one way to keep black people from voting)	1964	Expanded individual rights
25	Established a succession plan in case of president's death or disability	1967	Modified government operations
26	Extended the vote to eighteen- to twenty-year-olds	1971	Expanded individual rights
27	Established that congressional pay raises could not go into effect until the next election	1992	Modified government operations

Constitution permits different interpretations. These questions—and many more—require Americans to read the Constitution and reflect on what it tells us, more than 225 years after it was ratified.

The Constitution Today

The political life of the American colonies prepared the way for something no nation had done before: The United States organized a new government around a Constitution, written in the people's name and voted on by the people's representatives in every state. The document still guides American politics today. Who are we? Reading the U.S. Constitution is one important way to find out.

View *The 10-Minute Guide to the Constitution* from Cornell University.

What Do YOU Think?   How Strictly Should We Interpret the Constitution?

After considering the two approaches to interpreting the Constitution known as originalism and pragmatism, choose a position.

I'm an originalist. Contemporary justices should not try to substitute their judgment for that of the Constitution's framers. We cannot avoid the arbitrary use of power if we permit everyone to read the Constitution as they like. Before long, the Constitution will not mean anything at all. When the Second Amendment protects the right to bear arms, we must interpret that literally and allow individuals to purchase guns.

I'm a pragmatist. Times change and conditions evolve. The modern world imposes challenges (and features new technologies) that the Framers could not have imagined. Failing to permit the text to evolve would turn the document into an eighteenth-century straitjacket. The Founders' idea of the right to bear arms protected state militias, not individual gun owners. We should consider the historical context when we interpret the Constitution.

I'm in the middle. I believe the difference between these positions is far less stark than it appears at first glance. Even if we try very hard to get back to the document's original meaning, we always read the Constitution in light of the present. Every effort to interpret the Constitution will be guided by our own ideas and our own times. (We will come back to the debate over the Second Amendment in Chapter 5.)

But there is a catch. Americans disagree about how to read the Constitution. One view, called **originalism**, or strict construction, insists that Americans are bound to the literal meaning of the Constitution and its amendments, as their original authors and debaters understood them. From this perspective, the Constitution's meaning does not change with the times.

Another view was first articulated by Thomas Jefferson, who warned Americans not to view the Constitution with "sanctimonious reverence," as if it were "too sacred to be touched." The nation's founders should not be worshiped, he said, noting wryly that as one of the founders he was all too aware of their limitations. "I know also," concluded Jefferson, "that laws and institutions must go hand in hand with the progress of the human mind."[31] Many scholars and politicians have followed Jefferson's advice. They see a living, breathing, changing Constitution—one that speaks to each generation a little differently. This view of an evolving Constitution is known as **pragmatism**. *We cannot help bringing our own background, ideas, and judgments to bear as we think about the meaning of the document.*

As we will see throughout this book, it is often hard to tell exactly how the Constitution applies to our times. Different people reading the document come to very different conclusions—even if they are searching for the original meaning. In the end, the difference between originalism and pragmatism may not be as large as their proponents think.

Originalism: A principle of legal interpretation that relies on the original meaning of those who wrote the Constitution.

Pragmatism: A principle of legal interpretation based on the idea that the Constitution evolves and that interpretations of the Constitution must be framed in the context of contemporary realities.

Amend the Constitution Today?

ON WHAT ISSUE?

In the nearly 230 years since the Bill of Rights was ratified, just seventeen more amendments to the U.S. Constitution have been adopted—the most recent in 1992. Yet proposals keep coming, with more than 750 introduced in the U.S. House or Senate since 1999. Here are the most frequently proposed amendments over this period.

THINK ABOUT IT

What issues do most proposed amendments address? Which of these would you support? Why or why not?

If you could propose a constitutional amendment not on this list, what would the subject be? Protecting data privacy? Abolishing the Electoral College? Send your best idea to your senators or representative, and just maybe they will introduce it in the next session of Congress!

Source: Pew Research Center

Balanced budget is the most frequently proposed constitutional amendment since 1999

Most common subjects of proposed amendments, 1999–2017

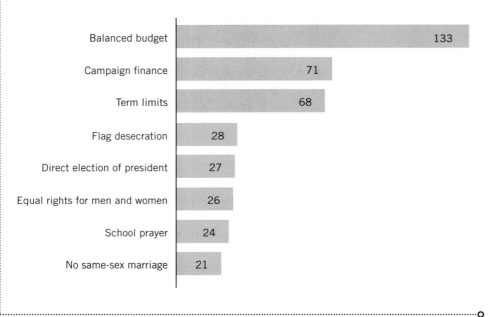

Subject	Count
Balanced budget	133
Campaign finance	71
Term limits	68
Flag desecration	28
Direct election of president	27
Equal rights for men and women	26
School prayer	24
No same-sex marriage	21

The Bottom Line

» The Bill of Rights comprises the first ten amendments to the Constitution, which define the rights of American citizens.

» Seventeen more amendments (out of more than one hundred thousand proposals) followed over the next 215 years.

» American politics is always changing, but the Constitution still stands as the American political rulebook. However, the Constitution must be interpreted, for it is often unclear what the document means and how it applies to contemporary cases.

Conclusion: Does the Constitution Still Work?

Every chapter that follows will focus on a different feature of the Constitution as it operates today—federalism, civil liberties, civil rights, Congress, the presidency, and so on. As you explore these institutions, keep asking yourself: Does the world's oldest constitution still work? Most Americans believe that it does. That is why it has lasted so long. But some disagree. Robert Dahl, a much revered political scientist, argued that the Constitution is just not democratic enough.[32] It does not include modern rights. Checks and balances are sometimes too cumbersome, making it difficult to pass needed laws. Congress no longer checks the president when it comes to war. The general effect, explained Dahl, is to water down American democracy.

The debate takes us back to the very first question we asked in Chapter 1. Who governs? Do "we the people" still rule? Or has real power slipped away to the rich and powerful? These are questions that every chapter will address.

Regardless of whether you are an *originalist*, a *pragmatist*, or someone in between, you should check to see what the Constitution says every time you study another feature of American politics. Start with the Constitution and you will know the basic rules of American politics.

CHAPTER SUMMARY

⬤ The Constitution provides the ground rules for American politics. However, it is often unclear exactly how the Constitution applies to contemporary issues. We have to interpret its meaning.

⬤ The colonial experience prepared America for thinking about a constitution. The English practice of *salutary neglect* permitted the colonies to develop their own political institutions, centered on their legislatures. Americans became used to *delegated*, or *actual*, *representation* (reflecting voter sentiment), which contrasted with the British view of *trustee*, or *virtual*, *representation* (representing the whole nation regardless of public opinion).

Check your understanding of Chapter 3.

Need to review key ideas in greater depth? Click here.

● The Declaration of Independence has two parts. First, it states the American ideal: all people "are created equal" and "endowed by their creator with certain unalienable rights" including "life, liberty, and the pursuit of happiness." Second, it lists colonial grievances, emphasizing the rights of free people to elect their legislatures.

● The first American government, under the Articles of Confederation, was an alliance of independent states that maximized popular participation. This government had some great successes, but many leaders felt that it was too weak and left the United States vulnerable to foreign powers.

● The Constitutional Convention, convened to fix the problems with the first American government, focused on six broad issues: popular involvement, national versus state power, big versus small states, checks and balances, the presidency, and slavery.

● Ratification of the Constitution involved an extremely close battle between Anti-Federalists, who opposed the Constitution, and Federalists, who supported it. The first ten amendments, known as the Bill of Rights, came out of the ratification debates and were approved by the First Congress. Seventeen more amendments followed in the next 215 years. American politics has changed enormously, but the Constitution continues to stand as the basic blueprint for American political life.

Flashcard review.

KEY TERMS

Bicameral, p. 73
Bill of Rights, p. 90
Classical republicanism, p. 86
Compact, p. 60
Confederation, p. 67
Constitution p. 57
Covenant, p. 60
Delegate representation, p. 61
Electoral College, p. 76

Federalism, p. 73
First Continental Congress, p. 64
Incorporation, p. 91
Indentured servant, p. 60
Mercantilism, p. 63
New Jersey Plan, p. 74
Originalism, p. 93
Pragmatism, p. 93

Second Continental Congress, p. 65
Supermajority, p. 68
Trustee representation, p. 62
Unicameral, p. 74
Virginia Plan, p. 73

STUDY QUESTIONS

1. Describe five ways that the colonial experience prepared the United States for a constitution.

2. Winning the French and Indian War drove two wedges between England and the colonies. What were they?

3. What is the difference between delegate or actual representation and trustee or virtual representation? How did the difference lead to the American Revolution?

Optional assignment: A colonist from Virginia and a member of the English Parliament get into a furious debate about the true nature of representation. You are lucky enough to overhear them. Describe what each says during the debate. Try to make both sides sound reasonable.

4. What are the five overarching ideas introduced by the Declaration of Independence? In your opinion, how close are we to achieving those aspirations today?

5. Describe the first government that Americans organized after they broke away from England. Where was most of the power located? What problems arose under this government? What was successful about it?

6. When it came to writing the Constitution, the delegates had to balance two fears. One emerged from the battle with England, the other from American experience under the Articles of Confederation. Describe these two fears.

7. What did Madison mean by "filtration of representatives"? List two examples of filtration in the original Constitution.

What do you think? *Would you support filtration or the direct election of representatives?*

8. Describe the differences between the Virginia Plan and the New Jersey Plan. If you had to choose between them, which would you choose, and why?

9. Describe what the Constitution says about the following:

How the House of Representatives is elected.

How the president is elected.

How the Supreme Court is chosen.

How amendments can be added to the Constitution.

10. Describe the differences between the Federalists and the Anti-Federalists. Which side would you be on? Why?

Optional assignment: Choose one of the thirteen original states. Now, write a speech to be presented before its ratifying convention arguing for or against the new constitution.

Go to www.oup.com/us/Morone to find quizzes, flash cards, simulations, tutorials, videos, and other study tools.

4 Federalism and Nationalism

"NOW HE'S ASSAULTING MY DAUGHTER."

Victoria Mesa-Estrada, a Florida attorney, was alarmed. She was advising a client with an abusive partner who had begun to molest her daughter. Mesa-Estrada told the woman to go straight to local law enforcement for protection. But the client is an undocumented immigrant and feared that she would be arrested by the police and deported back to Mexico—without her daughter who had been born in the United States and was therefore an American citizen. Victoria's client, like many of the roughly twelve million undocumented people in the United States, lives in the shadows—afraid to report a crime, visit a school, drive a seriously ill child to a hospital, seek police protection from an abusive partner, or take action against employers who refuse to pay them.[1]

In response, almost 500 cities have become "sanctuary" or "welcoming" cities—the police do not ask about legal status during routine encounters. That way, undocumented individuals can rely on the basic services and protections—police, hospitals, schools, and so on. Many Americans argue that offering sanctuary protects basic human rights that everyone deserves.

Others oppose the idea of sanctuary cities. During his 2016 campaign, President Donald Trump turned up the heat on this issue by publicizing the case of Jose Ines Garcia Arate who was on trial, but later acquitted, for the murder of a thirty-two-year-old woman in San Francisco—a sanctuary city.[2] Opponents of sanctuary cities worry that undocumented immigrants take jobs away from American citizens (Figure 4.1); that by condoning unauthorized immigration, sanctuary cities compromise the rule of law; or that the existence of undocumented immigrants divides the society and makes it more difficult to win higher wages and expand social welfare policies—a fear expressed in Europe as well as in the United States.[3]

Some states have cracked down on sanctuary cities with laws requiring local police to check the status of anyone they suspect may be undocumented. In 2018, Florida's house of representatives voted to end sanctuary practices, but the bill died in the state senate. Likewise, in Texas, state

● Dreamer Gloria Mendoza demonstrates on behalf of the Deferred Action for Childhood Arrivals (DACA), a program that grants legal status to young undocumented individuals. Immigration is classic federalism: national, state, and local governments are all involved.

In this chapter, you will:

● Learn what federalism is.

● Explore the strengths of federal and state governments.

● Examine how federalism works—and how it has evolved.

● Explore American nationalism, the force that binds and shapes our federalist polity.

● Review the contemporary conflicts that surround both federalism and nationalism.

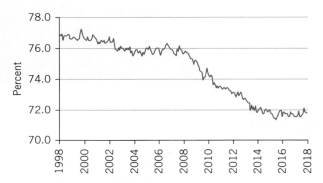

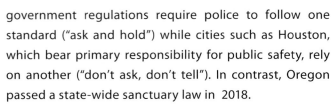

Percent

● **Figure 4.1** *Labor force participation rate among men aged twenty-five to fifty-four. Experts from across the political spectrum believe there is no relationship between immigration and the "flight from work" among white men. Are they right? Or has Donald Trump and his economic nationalism struck a chord with some of the men who have exited the work force? (Bureau of Labor Statistics)*

Watch a U.S. House
debate on a refugee
bill.

Assess current
debates on
immigration.

government regulations require police to follow one standard ("ask and hold") while cities such as Houston, which bear primary responsibility for public safety, rely on another ("don't ask, don't tell"). In contrast, Oregon passed a state-wide sanctuary law in 2018.

The standoff is complicated by the complexities of federalism. The Constitution gives the federal government—not the cities or states—authority over immigration. The Supreme Court recently affirmed that immigration is a federal issue. However, the states and the cities have independent responsibility over most law enforcement; proponents of the sanctuary city movement say local officials *do* have the authority to set policy for local law enforcement—unless the state overrides them. As you can see, in the immigration debate, the lines of authority—flowing between federal, state, and local governments—have gotten all tangled up.

Who governs? All levels of American government—local, county, state, and federal. Welcome to the politics of federalism. In the United States, most problems and many programs fall under multiple jurisdictions—national, state, and local. The lines of responsibility between levels of government are often blurred and constantly renegotiated.

In the last chapter, we traced the constitutional checks and balances between Congress, the executive, and the courts. Now we explore an even more intricate balancing act: federalism. Federalism is the relationship between different levels of government, sharing power while they squabble over who gets how much over what. This complex interplay between national and state governments stretches all the way back to the founding-era clash between Federalists (who wanted a strong national government) and Anti-Federalists (who sought more power for the states).

Who are we? A nation of divided loyalties and governments. We are from the United States *and* Texas *and* Houston, from the United States *and* Ohio *and* Columbus. The results are innovation, liberty, and confusion. Fires in California, an oil spill off Alaska's coast, food poisoning at Chipotle, or a mass shooting in Las Vegas bring out local authorities, state officials, and national agencies, all scrambling to get on the same wavelength. The same goes for addressing the opioid epidemic, setting the minimum wage, protecting clean water, managing public schools, and legalizing pot. Federalism is ingrained in our Constitution, our institutions, and our national culture.

This chapter explains how federalism works. The story in a nutshell: Federalism is a source of creativity and innovation, but it makes effective and efficient governance far more difficult.

BY THE NUMBERS

Federalism and Nationalism

Estimated number of governments in the United States	**89,004**[4]
Number of national governments	**1**
Number of state governments	**50**
Number of county or parish governments	**3,031**
Number of counties in Texas, each with its own government	**254**
Number of town or city governments or districts	**87,025**
Town and city governments as percentage of all American government	**96.6**
Number of nonmilitary personnel who work for the federal government	**2.7 million**[5]
Number who work for state governments	**5.3 million**
Number who work for local governments	**13.7 million**
Percentage of Americans who say they trust their national, state and local governments to do what is right most of the time:	**19, 62, 71**[6]

What level of government—local, state, or national—touches your life?
Which governments do you interact with the most?

Forging Federalism

Early American government began on the state level—although at the time the states were called colonies. Americans' first loyalty was to Virginia or Pennsylvania or New York. When Americans declared independence, leaders had to unite thirteen very different states under a national government. History gave them two choices about how to organize their union: a unitary government or a confederation. After trying each, the Americans invented a third approach.

Unitary government: A national polity governed as a single unit, with the central government exercising all or most political authority.

Confederation: A group of independent states or nations that yield some of their powers to a national government, although each state retains a degree of sovereign authority.

Most nations in the 1780s had **unitary governments**. The national government—the king and Parliament in England, for example—made policy for the nation and local governments carried out their decrees. To this day, most nations are organized this way. Local government is an administrative extension of national government. Because Americans rebelled against Britain's unitary government, most did not want to reintroduce the same system all over again.

A second traditional form, **confederation**, leaves most power in the states or provinces while a weak central authority provides common defense or economic benefits. Today, the European Union is struggling to make a confederation work, especially after the United Kingdom's "Brexit" vote to depart the European Union. Americans tried this system under the Articles of Confederation. As we saw in the previous chapter, it proved too weak.

At the Constitutional Convention, the delegates devised a hybrid: a *federal system* in which power is divided and shared between national and state governments. The Constitution gives some decisions to the national government (e.g., declaring war, coining money); others reside with the states (establishing schools); and some are made at both levels (raising taxes, running courts, regulating business). Over time, the shared tasks mushroomed. Because each level is independent and their powers overlap, conflict is built into the system.

To complicate matters, the United States also has independent local governments at the town, city, and county levels. These add still more layers of elected officials, government employees, services to provide, taxes to be paid, and seats at the table when decisions are made. However, local governments are *not* sovereign units. Local jurisdictions derive their authority from the states—this is known as Dillon's rule, named after an 1868 legal treatise. Some states grant their local governments broad powers, known as *home rule*; others jealously hold onto authority and approve or reject every local government action. Even states that allow home rule sometimes overrule local government decisions. When Denton, Texas, forbade fracking (an oil-extraction process that raises concerns about environmental damage), the state government stepped in and rejected the local regulations. When New York City proposed congestion pricing (charging vehicles a toll during peak hours), it was the state that decided whether they could go ahead. All the overlap and conflict between federal and state governments gets replicated—sometimes with even more intensity—between state and local governments.

On the surface, the state and local governments might seem to have a built-in advantage in any conflict with the national government. As Figure 4.2 shows, the more local the government, the more the people trust it. Yet Americans also express an unusually strong *nationalist* outlook—Americans tend to be very patriotic. As we will see, that unusual distrust of national government combined with strong patriotism is distinctively American—and directly affects our politics and government.

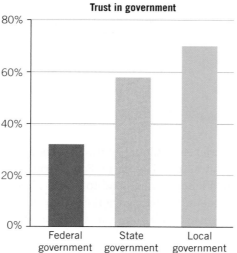

● **Figure 4.2** *Trust in government gets stronger as government gets closer to the public. (Gallup)*

The Bottom Line

» The United States rebelled against a *unitary* system and rejected a *federation* after trying one for a decade.

» The Constitutional Convention created a new hybrid form of government: a federal system of shared and overlapping power. Power is divided and shared between national and state governments.

» American federalism is further complicated by local governments, which are reliant on state government for their authority.

Who Holds Government Authority?

A federal system constantly poses the same question: Who should have the authority over a wide array of policies? Political scientists see some advantages to leaving things up to the states. And others for making decisions on the national level.[7]

Advantages of State-Level Policy

First, proponents of state-level policy argue that states are *more responsive* to citizen needs and desires. The United States is a vast nation spanning states with very different problems and attitudes. Maine and Minnesota do not need to regulate water in the same way as desert states such as Arizona and Nevada. Large cities try to curb gang violence with curfews and gun buy-back programs that would not make much sense in rural areas. Citizens of Delaware expect more government services (and pay higher taxes) than people in Florida. In short, state and local government can match policies to local conditions and values without a "one-size-fits-all" national policy.

Second, states sometimes offer more *protection for individual rights*. Same-sex couples found success on the state level long before federal officials were willing to support their right to marry. In the nineteenth century, national officials ridiculed the idea of women voting while feminists were busy winning voting rights in the Western states. On the other hand, states vehemently denied African Americans the right to vote, forcing supporters of racial equality to take the fight to the national level (we explore all these topics in Chapters 5 and 6).

Third, federalism fosters *political innovation*. Different states can experiment with new programs, trying them out on the local and state levels

● *Environmental regulations differ dramatically from state to state. Some states, like Louisiana and Texas, have few regulations; others, like California, have stringent environmental protections. The Obama administration prodded low regulation states to add restrictions on polluters; the Trump administration has sought to roll back regulations in all states. The debate between local culture versus national standards goes on.*

before they get debated on the national level. Supreme Court Justice Louis Brandeis put it famously: "A single courageous State may . . . serve as a laboratory; and try novel social and economic experiments without risk to the rest of the country."[8] Ever since, states in a federal system have been called "laboratories of democracy"—allowing us to test policy options. Throughout American history, innovations have bubbled up from the states, often diffusing from state to state, before going national. The list includes Social Security pensions for retirees, environmental protection laws, worker safety rules, direct election of senators, welfare reform, child nutrition programs, alcohol prohibition, and marijuana legalization. This process of testing and spreading ideas is known as **diffusion**.

> **Diffusion:** The spreading of policy ideas from one city or state to others, a process typical of U.S. federalism.

Finally, a more controversial point: Some argue that federalism gives people more *choices*. Each state offers a different bundle of costs and services (see Figure 4.3). People who want or need many government services can move to Connecticut or Alaska. Those who want a more limited government can choose the South or the "red states" of the Rocky Mountain West. Likewise, people who care about tough environmental standards can choose places with stringent rules such as California or Oregon.

This last point is disputed. Opponents point out that many Americans are not free to simply move. If a policy is a good one, they argue, all Americans deserve to enjoy it—which brings us to the advantages of national policies.

The Advantages of National Policy

First, national policy is often fairer than state or local policies. A single mother working full time for nine dollars an hour can be treated for breast cancer under

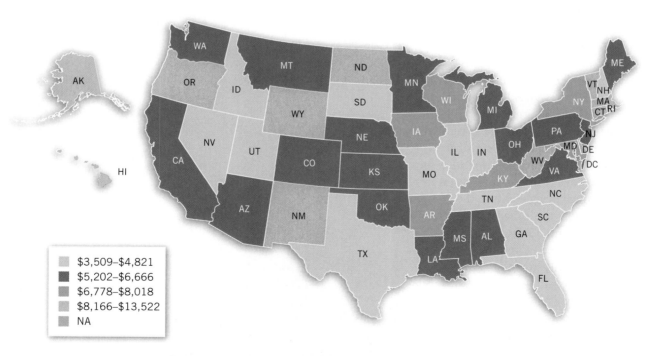

Legend:
- $3,509–$4,821
- $5,202–$6,666
- $6,778–$8,018
- $8,166–$13,522
- NA

● **Figure 4.3** *Per capita state spending on healthcare. Some states spend more than others per person. You can think of this as a choice between values: Some states emphasize individualism (less government spending) whereas others aim to implement positive freedoms (more spending). Here's the tough question: Can Americans really pick up and move to a state that reflects their own values? (The Kaiser Family Foundation)*

New York's Medicaid program but is not eligible for any treatment at all in Texas. Health advocates charge that this discrepancy is unjust and call for uniform national policies. Likewise, environmentalists argue that every citizen should have clean air and clean water regardless of their state's history of supporting regulation (they also note that air and water pollution don't stop at state boundaries). Gun rights advocates point to the inconsistencies between Ohio, which permits residents to openly carry firearms; New York, which restricts "open carry" to pistols; and Massachusetts, which restricts all guns. Finally, America's racial experience suggests that, at least sometimes, national decisions are required to overcome local prejudices.

This desire for fairness leads critics to worry that competition between states and localities leads to a *race to the bottom*. Leave social welfare policy to the states, argue defenders of national standards, and the result is a bidding war in which each state tries to cut programs (and taxes) more than neighboring states to attract middle-class people and new business. Although the race to the bottom hypothesis is hard to measure, political scientists have found some evidence that states do follow one another as programs are cut and benefits are reduced.[9]

Second, national policies can *equalize resources across the nation*. Every time there is a crisis—Hurricane Harvey in the Gulf of Mexico, a terrorist attack, raging wildfires—all eyes turn to the U.S. government, which can bring more resources and expertise to bear on the problem than individual states can. Those resources also can make day-to-day policies work across all fifty states. That way, even poorer states can have the resources they need.

Third, national policies can *standardize best practices* across the nation. After new policies are tested in the state "laboratories of democracy," a national policy can ensure that the lessons are spread to everyone. Minimum standards ensure that no state chooses inadequate health or education policies for its children.

Finally, leaving authority in state hands introduces *problems of coordination* among federal, state, and local agencies. All respond to crises. All address chronic problems such as poverty, pollution, and crime. Simply getting all the first responders onto the same communication frequency has taken many years and millions of dollars. With many different agencies responding to multiple layers of authorities, using different procedures, and trying to achieve slightly different goals, the result can be chaos. A patchwork of rules and regulations across the states can leave citizens and national companies bewildered about which rules apply where.

In sum, the ambiguity in federalism sets up a constant dispute about where to place authority. Do we leave decisions with the states because they are closer to the people? Or do we place them on the national level to try to promote equality and high standards across the country, even if local people resent them? For many Americans, the answer shifts with the issue.

Should federal laws criminalizing marijuana possession override state efforts to decriminalize it? Liberals generally say no and support local choice. Should stricter national clean air standards override state pollution regulations and expanded national healthcare standards override state insurance regulations? Now most liberals switch sides and say yes, while conservatives disagree. These debates began at the Constitutional Convention and rage around every major problem and policy. They are built into our federal institutions and are an integral part of our federalist system. Recognize one key institutional point: *Federalism gives advocates on both sides many different political venues in which to address problems, challenge policies, and assert rights.*

Regulatory Policies
DIFFER BY STATE

How does your state combat the opioid epidemic? As with so many policy matters in the federalist United States, rules may differ dramatically from one state to the next. For example, states may restrict the number of days that the prescriptions can cover (without being renewed), require substance abuse disorder assessment prior to issuing a prescription, mandate that the pharmacists check ID before dispensing the opioids, and educate clinicians who prescribe these drugs.

THINK ABOUT IT

Connecticut, New York, and Massachusetts have low rates of opioid use. Which of the regulations have each of these states adopted? Based on this evidence, are the regulations successful? What can other states learn from these three states?

What regulations does your own state have to fight the opioid epidemic? Do you believe they are excessive, sufficient, or not extensive enough? Do you think it would be better if the federal government mandated these policies?

Source: Athena Health

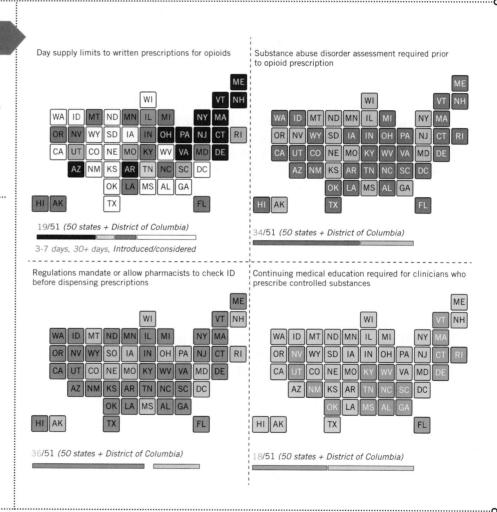

Day supply limits to written prescriptions for opioids

19/51 *(50 states + District of Columbia)*

3-7 days, 30+ days, Introduced/considered

Substance abuse disorder assessment required prior to opioid prescription

34/51 *(50 states + District of Columbia)*

Regulations mandate or allow pharmacists to check ID before dispensing prescriptions

36/51 *(50 states + District of Columbia)*

Continuing medical education required for clinicians who prescribe controlled substances

18/51 *(50 states + District of Columbia)*

What Do YOU Think?   Preserving Local Values or Promoting Consistent National Policy?

In 2014, Colorado permitted adults to buy up to an ounce of marijuana in licensed stores. Four years later, ten states and the District of Columbia had followed Colorado's lead, and legalized recreational marijuana. There was just one problem: Federal laws outlaw the possession, manufacture, and sale of marijuana. Growing ninety-nine plants, which is now legal in Colorado, can bring lifetime imprisonment in other states. After Colorado legalized marijuana, the Obama administration announced it would not prosecute legal users in the state—essentially setting aside the federal laws. Meanwhile, cities such as Colorado Springs moved to forbid local marijuana stores, called dispensaries. Neighboring states that want to uphold the federal prohibition have sued states that legalized the drug. In 2018, the Trump Administration rescinded the Obama rule. Should we leave marijuana use to the states, or insist on a national standard?

I'm a federalist; leave to each state to decide.
Because cultures differ by state, marijuana regulation should be handled state-by-state. Socially progressive states should have the right to legalize marijuana. Other states can learn from their experiment, assess the advantages and the disadvantages, and decide what policies to adopt.

I'm a nationalist; we should have one consistent standard.
The patchwork of changing laws—including within a single state—is both confusing and counterproductive. Furthermore, the legalization of pot might negatively impact neighboring states as stoned drivers and tainted merchandise cross borders. The national government should establish a policy that is best for all Americans.

Not sure.
On this, like many other policies raised in this chapter, it can be hard to come down definitively on one side. Would you have stronger feelings about other illegal drugs—should they be controlled by national, state, or local laws?

 **The Bottom Line**

» The most important question in federalism is where to place responsibility—on the state or national level.

» State-level policy has at least four advantages: it responds to local needs, enables innovation in the laboratories of democracy, protects individual rights, and enhances individual choice.

» National-level policy also has four main advantages: it enhances fairness (avoiding a race to the bottom), equalizes resources, promotes national standards and best practices, and facilitates coordination.

» Understanding the pros and cons of federalism is important as we decide whether to create national standards and programs or whether to leave judgment to local populations. This question is generally decided issue by issue and program by program.

How Federalism Works

So far this chapter's message is clear: Federalism offers endless opportunities for confusion and discord, as different layers of government tussle over who has responsibility for what. However, there are well-defined patterns to this contest. Americans have hammered out rules that enable our federalist system to function pretty well—most of the time. These rules evolve with time and are not always clear or straightforward. Even the terminology can be elusive: Americans routinely call the national government the "federal government," a practice we follow in this chapter, even though that term formally refers to the whole system of shared powers stretching across national, state, and local units.

The Constitution Sets the Ground Rules

The Constitution can be read two ways. In some respects, it restricts the national government in favor of the states; in other ways, it empowers the feds.

The Constitution Empowers National Authority. Article 1, Section 8, lists nineteen powers vested in the national government: Congress has the authority to pay debts, raise an army, punish pirates, establish a post office, handle U.S. foreign policy, and so forth. Because they are set out in black and white, scholars call these **delegated powers**—also known as *expressed* or *enumerated powers* (you can read them in the Constitution in Appendix II). This section of the Constitution is crisp and clear about the limited list of national government powers.

An especially important enumerated power grants the national government authority over international and interstate commerce. How far does that authority extend? A loose reading gives Congress power over everything touched by goods shipped between states. For example, Congress used the **commerce clause** to forbid racial discrimination in restaurants—after all, their salt and sugar come from out of state. This broad reading is increasingly controversial. What do you think? Is it appropriate to use the interstate commerce power to outlaw racial discrimination?

The final clause adds another ambiguity by authorizing Congress to make all laws *necessary and proper* for carrying out the delegated powers—*or any other power the Constitution vests in the national government.* The **necessary and proper clause**, also known as the *elastic clause*, stretches national government authority to include anything implied in the Constitution's text. Over two centuries, the elastic clause—especially when it is combined with the interstate commerce clause—has expanded national authority to include everything from creating banks to regulating airlines to overseeing zoos. These new areas of jurisdiction are known as **implied powers**—powers that are implied by, but not specifically named in, the Constitution's text.

The **supremacy clause**, found near the end of the Constitution in Article 6, buttresses these granted (or explicit) and implied powers. The clause declares that the national government's laws and treaties are the "supreme law of the land" and are superior to state laws whenever the two clash—provided the power is granted to the federal government. As you might imagine, fierce debates (and court cases) regularly turn on whether national officials indeed hold the authority to overturn state decisions.

Federal officials also wield a set of **inherent powers**—not explicitly named or strongly implied in the Constitution, but growing out of the very existence of a national government and its offices. For example, the federal government manages the list of communicable diseases requiring quarantines; or presidents raise the minimum wage for federal workers. These rely on inherent powers rather than a clear constitutional claim. As you might expect, the extent of these powers is a subject of intense debate.

Delegated powers: National government authority listed explicitly in the Constitution.

Commerce clause: The Constitutional declaration (in Article 1, Section 8) empowering Congress to regulate commerce with foreign nations, between states, and with Indian tribes.

Necessary and proper clause: The constitutional declaration (in Article 1, Section 8) that defines Congress's constitutional authority to exercise the "necessary and proper" powers to carry out its designated functions.

Implied powers: National government powers inferred, but not specifically named, in the Constitution.

Supremacy clause: The constitutional declaration (in Article 6, Section 2) that the national government's authority prevails over any conflicting state or local government's claims, provided the power is granted to the federal government.

Inherent powers: Powers that, although neither specified or implied by the Constitution are necessary for the president or Congress to fulfil their duties.

The Constitution Protects State Authority. At the same time, the states have their own authority guaranteed by the Tenth Amendment—the final amendment in the Bill of Rights. This "reserves" to the states all powers not specifically granted to the national branches in Washington. Small-government advocates brandish the Tenth Amendment to bolster their argument. Republican conservatives in the 115th Congress (2017–2018) proposed a Tenth Amendment Restoration Act that required a full review of every national executive agency (the Environmental Protection Agency, the Internal Revenue Service, and right on down the bureaucratic roster) to determine whether its existence violated the Tenth Amendment—if so, they argued, the agency would be eliminated. The bill failed but it illustrates the political importance of the Tenth Amendment.

The states' **reserved powers** include public education, public health, public morality, commerce within the state, and organizing elections. Police, prisons, and local courts are also in each state's hands. State and local officials carry out most investigations, arrests, trials, and incarcerations—unless a federal law has been violated. The vast majority of American court cases are adjudicated in state courts, and state prisons and local jails hold nearly 90 percent of the inmates in the United States.

The Constitution Authorizes Shared Power. It is a mistake to think of federalism simply as conflict between government levels. State and national authorities share many responsibilities, termed **concurrent powers**. Both national and state governments have the power to raise taxes, build roads, construct bridges, build railways, update telecommunications networks, borrow money, and regulate business. The next time you are stuck in traffic inching past a sign announcing new transportation construction, look it over carefully: You will usually see a combination of national, state, and local funds listed in support.

Federalism also involves relations among the states. The Constitution directs each state to give **full faith and credit** to the actions of other states. For example, your driver's license, issued in your home state, is honored everywhere else in the United States.

The Constitution also sets up some definite barriers to the states. A state may not launch its own navy, sign treaties with another country, or coin its own money. The Bill of Rights—though it originally applied only to the federal government—imposes a long list of limits on government in the name of individual rights and freedoms. In short, the Constitution empowers and limits both the national and the state governments. Figure 4.4 illustrates powers shared by and reserved to the different levels of government.

Emphasizing some parts of the Constitution—inherent powers, the interstate commerce clause, the necessary and proper clause, the supremacy clause—justifies a robust national government. This reading of the Constitution enables a national government that regulates toxic spills, forbids racial discrimination, enforces airport security, and prosecutes the war on drugs. Emphasizing other clauses—like the Tenth Amendment—yields a more modest national government that defers to the people of each state. That is the reading that leaves states alone to decide environmental rules or regulate state universities.

Again we return to a vital point: American government is a perpetual argument, a work in progress. The Constitution's ground rules for federalism are open to interpretation and

Compare federal and state authority.

Reserved powers: The constitutional guarantee (in the Tenth Amendment) that the states retain government authority not explicitly granted to the national government.

Concurrent powers: Governmental authority shared by national and state governments, such as the power to tax residents.

Full faith and credit clause: The constitutional requirement (in Article 4, Section 1) that each state recognizes and upholds laws passed by any other state.

Federalism as a source of interstate conflict: should New York City, with strong gun laws, be required to honor other states' much more lenient gun-carrying rules?

Federal system

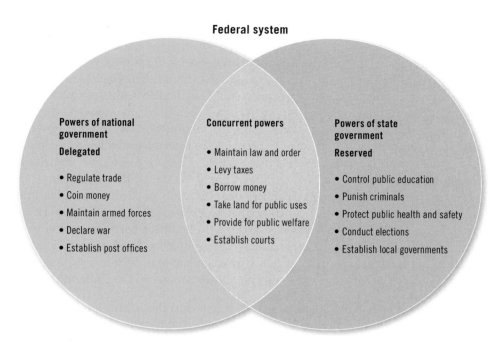

Powers of national government

Delegated

- Regulate trade
- Coin money
- Maintain armed forces
- Declare war
- Establish post offices

Concurrent powers

- Maintain law and order
- Levy taxes
- Borrow money
- Take land for public uses
- Provide for public welfare
- Establish courts

Powers of state government

Reserved

- Control public education
- Punish criminals
- Protect public health and safety
- Conduct elections
- Establish local governments

● **Figure 4.4** *The Constitution delegates some powers to the federal government, reserves some to the states, and allocates some to both. Those joint (or concurrent powers) have stretched dramatically over the years.*

reinterpretation. They have guided a long, often creative debate about which level of government should be doing what.

In different eras, Americans have organized the federal system in different ways. The next sections introduce the most important shifts that have occurred over the years.

Dual Federalism (1789–1933)

Dual federalism: Also called layer cake federalism, the clear division of governing authority between national and state governments.

For its first 150 years or so, the United States practiced a form of **dual federalism**, in which state and national governments had relatively clear responsibilities. The state governments wielded at least as much authority as the federal government. American historians with an eye for metaphor describe this arrangement as "layer cake" federalism: The different levels of government—national, state, and local— fell more or less into separate layers. Each level of government was supreme within its own band of influence (Figure 4.5).

This division of labor left the national government in charge of three major areas. One was international relations—trade, war, diplomacy, and immigration. This was a significant role, as the United States deployed troops overseas 165 times in its first 150 years—and that count does not include the long and bloody series of conflicts with Native American tribes.

Second, the national government was responsible for "internal improvements" such as transportation, a single currency, and overseeing westward expansion. In early America, it was cheaper to ship iron from London to Philadelphia than it was to move it fifty miles inland from Philadelphia. Developing transportation networks— roads, canals, and railroads—solved the problem of moving freight (and people). And perhaps most important of all, the federal post office united an increasingly far-flung people and placed at least one federal official—the postmaster—in every village across the nation.

American federalism

Layer cake or marble cake?

Layer cake federalism has a clear division of governing authority between national and state governments.

Marble cake federalism mingles governing authority with functions overlapping across national and state governments.

● **Figure 4.5** *Different federalist styles throughout U.S. history.*

● *Constructing canals, bridges, roads—and later, railroads—was a major national government responsibility in the nineteenth century, as was delivering the mail, a task that briefly included the Pony Express (right).*

Finally, the federal government regulated relations and commerce between the states. This became an explosive issue when slave states demanded assistance in capturing men and women running for their freedom.

During this era, states retained control over almost everything having to do with individual citizens. The states oversaw education, marriage, divorce, professional regulation, business contracts, driving, drinking, and burials. To this day, state governments wield the primary responsibility over individual behavior, although the federal government now touches most of these matters directly or indirectly.

The layer cake was never quite as clear-cut as the metaphor suggests. The national government distributed land in unsettled territories. Before the Civil War, it wrestled endlessly with the slavery issue. In the 1870s, it used control of interstate commerce to crack down on pornography, restrict contraception, and fight abortion. In 1920, the Eighteenth Amendment forbade the transportation and sale of intoxicating liquors. State and national authorities had overlapping jurisdiction in enforcing this act[10]—and when states like New York decided to ignore the ban on liquor, federal officials stepped in to enforce it (a 1920s version of the marijuana debate). Still, despite many exceptions, government activity remained, very roughly, separated into layers.

Cooperative Federalism (1933–1981)

During the New Deal of the 1930s, the dual arrangement collapsed. President Franklin Roosevelt (FDR) and large Democratic majorities in Congress vigorously responded to the Great Depression by passing policies that decisively strengthened the national government's role. Roosevelt presided over a shift toward **cooperative federalism**, characterized by a far more active federal government and blurred lines of authority (Table 4.1). A new bakery metaphor emerged: a *marble cake*, in which the various ingredients—the different government functions—were all swirled together. In one program after another, the responsibilities of federal, state, and local governments were mingled: funding, rules, administration, implementation, and execution all cut across the different layers of federalism.

Officials in Washington provided federal funds through **grants-in-aid**—national funds accompanied by specific instructions to state and local officials about how the money could be spent. Governors and other state leaders, desperate for resources during the Depression, accepted these national grants for roads, bridges, hospitals, healthcare clinics, Social Security support for seniors, welfare payments for poor people, and the list goes on. Most of the funds came with Washington rules and oversight.

Cooperative federalism: Also called marble cake federalism, a system of mingled governing authority, with functions overlapping across national and state governments.

Grants-in-aid: National government funding provided to state and local governments, along with specific instructions about how the funds may be used.

TABLE 4.1	Comparing Dual and Cooperative Federalism	
DUAL FEDERALISM	**COOPERATIVE FEDERALISM**
NATIONAL POWERS	
Enumerated: The national government may only wield powers specifically listed in the Constitution.	**Elastic:** The national government may wield powers "necessary and proper" to support its function.
LOCATION OF SUPREME AUTHORITY	
Separate sovereignty: National and state governments each have authority within their own spheres.	**National supremacy:** States retain important powers but are subordinate to the national government except where the Constitution strictly forbids it.
KEY PRINCIPLE	
States' rights: Each state is largely free to govern its own affairs.	**Power sharing:** National and state officials work together whenever possible; this principle was later extended to include local officials, who became more prominent after the 1930s.

After World War II, many state and local officials began expressing resentment at the national meddling in their affairs. Federal funds continued to flow, however, and during this era, supported items ranging from school lunches to modern highways and up-to-date hospitals. Few politicians were going to deny their constituents this national bounty.

Cooperative federalism, and Washington's domination of many policy areas, lasted from the New Deal (starting in 1933) through the 1970s. Senator Everett Dirksen (R-IL) quipped in 1964 that if the trend toward increasing national power continued, only mapmakers would care about the state boundaries.[11]

New Federalism

New federalism: A version of cooperative federalism, but with stronger emphasis on state and local government activity versus national government.

Block grants: National government funding provided to state and local governments with relatively few restrictions or requirements on spending. Block grant programs introduced a trade-off for state officials: more authority, fewer funds.

Ronald Reagan's presidency (1981–1989) ushered in another significant change in American federalism, enthusiastically termed **new federalism** by its advocates. Reagan and fellow conservatives tipped the pendulum of power away from national officials, promoting more authority by state and local officials. In place of grants-in-aid, with national officials carefully specifying the rules and regulations that accompanied the funds, the Reagan administration relied more heavily on **block grants:** Federal dollars flow to specific policy areas, such as education or transportation or health, but leave the program's details to state and local officials. Block grants had been developed and expanded throughout the 1970s under presidents Richard Nixon (1969–1974), Gerald Ford (1974–1977), and Jimmy Carter (1977–1981); Reagan used them to rethink federalism.

One feature of block grants has made them controversial. The grants-in-aid that marked cooperative federalism often provided unlimited funding for a specific purpose—for example, everyone who qualifies for Medicaid receives hospital coverage, and every eligible person gets food stamps. In contrast, block grants provided a fixed amount of funds for healthcare or nutrition. State and local officials get to do what they think best with the funds; however, the federal government limits its contribution, forcing state officials to make hard choices about who qualifies for the program and who does not. Notice that new federalism does not restore the neat layers of dual federalism—if anything, the lines of authority are even more swirled together than ever. Now, federal, state, and local authorities all compete for influence over programs. Perhaps you can think of this scenario as a many-flavored marble cake.

Progressive Federalism

The Obama administration, building on the George W. Bush administration, introduced **progressive federalism** in 2009: The national government sets program goals and relies on state innovations to achieve them. Note the mix of traditional Democratic approach (national goals) and Republican values (state innovation).[12] The Obama administration deployed this approach across a host of policy areas—education, healthcare, the environment, and more.

Education. The Obama administration announced a program called Race to the Top. It encouraged states to compete for national dollars, rewarding creative education policies. By promoting *competition* among states, the administration sought to nudge states toward desired policy goals without relying on overbearing national regulations.

Healthcare. Perhaps the most controversial program during the Obama Administration, the Affordable Care Act (or ACA), aimed to deliver healthcare to the fifty million uninsured Americans. Congress mandated that all uninsured people buy coverage. The federal government issued rules and regulations (defining the insurance products); the states were incentivized to build insurance exchanges where individuals could shop among competing health insurance plans. If the states were not up to the task—or simply opposed to the policy—the federal government came in and built the website that sold the insurance plans. In 2017, Republicans in Congress repealed the mandate but left the rest of the ACA intact.

In progressive federalism, the federal and state governments are partners who constantly negotiate the outlines of their joint program. Sometimes the debate is friendly, sometimes adversarial; it sometimes takes place through the courts or in Congress or across the media. The key point is that programs are defined in an intricate back and forth between federal and state negotiators.

"In Two Words, Yes And No"

● Struggles over the extent of cooperative federalism, captured in 1949—and still an issue, seventy years later.

Progressive Federalism: Approach that gives state officials considerable leeway in achieving national programs and goals.

Federalism Today

In many fields, the Trump administration is trying to go back to Reagan-era new federalism: Fewer federal dollars, fewer federal regulations. The administration planned to eliminate the $3 billion block-grant program for infrastructure projects and slash or end funding for nearly all of the twelve other largest social services, health, and housing block grants. However, the Republican Congress refused to go along and most survived in the 2018 budget. The Trump administration aimed to weaken federal regulations by giving states authority over certain programs, such as those protecting endangered species. Democrats resisted both block grant cuts and weakened environmental regulations. How will these clashes be settled? Perhaps by the outcome of the 2020 election.

Navigate federal and state healthcare policy.

Today, federalism has become a playing field for the heightened partisan battles. During the Obama administration, many states actively resisted federal policies. They asserted themselves on a wide range of policies—from enacting more muscular immigration restrictions to filing suits against Obamacare.[13] The conflict escalated further during the Trump administration. When the president opted to pull out of the international climate-change treaty known as the Paris Accord, more than twenty states and some 230 counties and large cities signed an "America's Pledge" to meet the greenhouse gas reductions at the heart of the Paris agreement. State attorneys general (the chief legal officer in each state) have filed lawsuits against White House policies on everything from immigration policy to healthcare subsidies. During Trump's inaugural year in office (2017), twenty-seven such lawsuits were filed. In contrast, a total of eight such suits were filed across the first years of the Reagan (1981), Clinton (1993), and Obama (2009) administrations put together. Time will tell whether the Trump era has ushered in a new era of hyper-polarized federalism.

The Bottom Line

» The Constitution grants the national government both delegated (or enumerated) powers and implied powers. You can read it to emphasize broad national powers, using the elastic clause, or state dominance, emphasizing the Tenth Amendment.

» Successive eras of federalism since the early twentieth century include: dual federalism, with clearly demarcated authority (the layer cake); cooperative federalism, arising with FDR's New Deal, which introduced federal dominance and blurred the lines of authority (the marble cake); President Reagan's new federalism, which shifted more decision making about spending those monies back to the states; and Presidents Bush and Obama's progressive federalism, which set national goals but relied on state innovations to achieve them.

» President Trump's term to date has featured an effort to shift back to Reagan era new federalism and more polarized relations between national and state/local governments.

Issues in Federalism

Dual, cooperative, new, and progressive—these successive versions of federalism point to the perpetually shifting nature of government power and accountability. Today, a set of long-standing debates around federalism have become all the more important. Let us take a look at some of the current issues in this debate.

Unfunded Mandates

Unfunded mandate: An obligation imposed on state or local government officials by federal legislation without sufficient federal funding support to cover the costs.

Some voices in federalism debates accept national government authority in some areas, but argue that when responsibility is passed to state or local officials, there must be resources to match. Otherwise, they claim, Washington saddles states and localities with an **unfunded mandate**—a law or regulation that imposes a duty that must be paid for primarily by state or local officials. For example, when federal regulations impose new safety requirements on commuter trains, state and local governments are left to buy and install the new technology, regardless of what shape their budget is in.

The Problems We Face: How Government Grows

Even with sufficient funding, however, serious problems often lead to a greater national government role. Sometimes local governments face problems that are beyond their capacity to solve. For example, many states' rights advocates have pushed hard to limit federal endangered species regulation. Yet after the national government cut back Environmental Protection Agency and Forest Service supervision of wildlife management, invasive species such as zebra mussels and milfoil (a plant native to Asia that has choked the life out of many American ponds and lakes) overwhelmed local wildlife agencies and caused billions of dollars in damage. Harmful plants and creatures are oblivious to local and state boundaries; many wildlife officials—including in states with conservative leadership—immediately called for a federal government response that could coordinate eradication efforts across multiple jurisdictions.

Drowned in the Bathtub? Reducing the Federal Government

The debate over federalism often reflects a particular American passion, which is especially strong among conservatives: the desire to reduce the size and scope of government. One pillar of both new and progressive federalism—at least in theory—has been **devolution**, or the transfer of responsibility for government programs from national to state and local authorities and then to the private sector. Devolutionists have fought to reduce the influence of government at every level. "I don't want to abolish government," declared conservative activist Grover Norquist. "I simply want to reduce it down to the size where I can . . . drown it in the bathtub."[14] This attack on big government gets fervent support from the conservative grassroots. Ranchers in the West have challenged federal ownership of lands for over forty years.

> **Devolution:** The transfer of authority from the national to the state or local government level.

In theory, Republicans prefer state and local control, while Democrats are more likely to seek Washington-based solutions. The reality is far more complicated: Both parties sometimes press for increased national authority and, at other times, defer to the states. Both Presidents Obama and Trump, for example, announced plans—and hundreds of millions of dollars in federal funds—to combat the opioid epidemic sweeping the United States, a scourge that has stretched many state and local governments' ability to cope.

On Both Sides of the Issue

Why do both Democratic and Republican administrations regularly stray from their parties' images? Partially because elected officials must confront complicated problems, and struggle to make troubled programs more effective. There is also a political dimension. Republicans are often criticized for being hard-hearted budget cutters. In response, Republican administrations tend to introduce new social policies designed to show compassion and energetic management. For the last seventy-five years, every Republican president has sponsored new, often very innovative, healthcare programs (except, so far, the Trump Administration). The two largest expansions of the Medicare program, the health insurance program for people over sixty-five, came under Republicans,

● *Members of an armed antigovernment militia monitor the entrance to the Malheur National Wildlife Refuge Headquarters near Burns, Oregon, in 2016. The occupation of a wildlife refuge by armed protesters in Oregon reflects a decades-old dispute over land rights in the United States, where local communities have increasingly sought for more voice in the use of public land.*

As this cartoon humorously shows, which level of our federalist government a politician supports generally depends on the issue in question. (Nick Anderson)

Ronald Reagan (who covered high or catastrophic health costs—later repealed) and George W. Bush (who expanded the program to cover prescription drugs).[15]

The Democrats face the opposite criticism: too much federal government spending. As a result, Democratic administrations also regularly go against type and rely on state innovation and initiatives. Bill Clinton's Democratic administration rewrote welfare policy to shift authority and discretion to state and local governments. Clinton ended Aid to Families with Dependent Children (often known simply as "welfare"), a program that provided unlimited funds to support roughly one in six American children. In its place, the administration (working with Republicans in Congress) introduced a block grant program called Temporary Assistance for Needy Families (TANF). TANF makes funds available and leaves most details up to the states.

What happens when the states want more innovation than the federal government? When states such as California passed legislation for strong environmental measures, the Republican Bush administration overruled them through **preemption**. The Obama administration quickly reversed that policy and encouraged states to launch forceful environmental protections. The Trump administration reversed course again and has challenged California's tough environmental standards. Notice how the old rule of thumb is reversed: Democrats urged strong state action; Republicans try to overrule it with (weaker) federal regulations.

Preemption: The invalidation of a U.S. state law that conflicts with federal law.

In a Nutshell: Our Three-Dimensional Political Chess

These examples tell us to put aside the simple idea that conservatives want less federal government and liberals more. A more sophisticated view of federalism is to see it as a kind of three-dimensional political chess. Policy debates take place in Washington and in fifty state capitals, with thousands of municipalities also weighing in. Each decision about where to locate authority over a program advances some perspectives and limits others. At times, the raucous debates look more like wrestling than chess. Chess or wrestling, it is all part of the institutional framework that shapes American politics and policy.

Today, relations between national, state, and local levels take a dizzying array of forms—sometimes they work in partnership, sometimes they are locked in combat. The one contemporary constant is *connection*: There are almost no issues in which the different levels of government exert separate functions, as in the old dual federalist system.

The Bottom Line

» Devolution transfers responsibility back to state and local governments.

» Unfunded mandates and challenges that cross state borders require close cooperation between states.

» Conventional wisdom suggests strong conservative support for state over national government. In reality, both parties in office take a pragmatic approach that belies the simple expectation that Democrats seek national programs while Republicans try to devolve power to state and local authorities.

Federalism in the Courts

Most federalism disputes are about drawing a line where national power ends and states' authority begins—and how best to ensure that the division of power is honored in practice. One explanation for the historical shifts in federalism is simple: The party in power changed. The Roosevelt administration initiated a new (Democratic) era in Washington and soon introduced cooperative federalism. The Nixon and Reagan administrations brought Republicans to the center of power and introduced new federalism. Republicans took control of Congress in 1995 and immediately passed limits on unfunded mandates. The Democratic Obama administration introduced progressive federalism. And highly partisan federalism may become the Trump administration's legacy.

What does it mean to incorporate the Bill of Rights?

Another key to the tides of federalism lies in the courts. U.S. courts early on became a key player in allocating powers between the states and the nation. Judges have typically played a balancing role when it comes to federalism. Supreme Court decisions favored national prerogatives during the early republic, when many individual states had more power and prestige than the federal government in Washington. In a series of landmark decisions, the Supreme Court—led by Chief Justice John Marshall—protected national government powers from state incursions.

The first such case was *McCulloch v. Maryland*, decided in 1819.[16] Maryland's legislature had sought to impose a tax on the Baltimore branch of the first U.S. national bank. The bank refused to pay and was sued by the state. The Maryland Supreme Court ruled that the Constitution is silent about the federal power to establish a bank—and that the bank was therefore unconstitutional; Maryland was perfectly free to tax it. Writing for the Supreme Court, Marshall overruled the Maryland court and struck down the state tax. Invoking the necessary and proper (or elastic) clause, he ruled that Congress could draw on "implied powers" required to operate a national government and that states impairing the bank—in this case, by levying a tax on it—violated the Constitution. In these and later decisions, Marshall and many other officials in the early republic were anxious to keep dual federalism in balance. At the time, doing so meant expanding national power.

As we will see in Chapter 16, in some eras—such as the period between the 1880s and the 1930s—the Court tilted away from federal authority to states and private corporations. On the other hand, the rise of activist government during the 1930s probably would not have been possible if the Supreme Court had not, quite

TABLE 4.2 **Recent Supreme Court Decisions on Federalism**

FAVORING NATIONAL GOVERNMENT
• *Arizona v. United States* (2012). Struck down key provisions in an Arizona immigration law, upholding federal-government authority to set immigration policy and laws.
• *King v. Burwell* (2015). Ruled that premium tax credits provided under the Affordable Care Act (ACA) applied in every state, though several conservative-led states had argued otherwise. Compare to the 2012 ACA case below.
• *Obergefell v. Hodges* (2015). Requires all states to issue marriage licenses to same-sex couples and to recognize same-sex marriages validly performed in other jurisdictions.
• *Cooper v. Harris* (2017). Ruled that North Carolina violated federal voting-rights laws by moving thousands of African American voters into congressional districts that had already elected African American Democrats.

FAVORING STATE GOVERNMENTS
• *Bond v. United States* (2011). Extended to individuals the right to challenge federal statutes on the grounds that these statutes interfere with powers reserved to the states.
• *National Federation of Independent Business v. Sebelius* (2012). This decision on the Affordable Care Act (ACA) struck down the national government's power to set standards for expanded Medicaid eligibility across the states.
• *Shelby County v. Holder* (2013). Reversed a long-standing provision in the Voting Rights Act that required states with a history of voting discrimination to obtain federal permission before making changes to their election laws.
• *United States v. Windsor* (2013). Struck down a section of the federal Defense of Marriage Act (DOMA) and declared that same-sex couples who are legally married deserve equal rights to all federal benefits that other married couples enjoy.
• *United States v. Texas* (2016). Invalidated Obama Administration's executive act protecting from deportation certain unauthorized immigrants (parents of U.S. citizens, or legal permanent residents), and granting them work permits. Twenty-six states, led by Texas, challenged the White House policy.
• *Murphy versus NCAA* (2018). Invalidated a federal law prohibiting states from authorizing sports gambling. The Court ruled that states may legalize sports gambling – and that Congress does not have the power to stop them. Does this signal a major shift toward state authority based on the 10th Amendment? Perhaps. Stay tuned!

dramatically, reversed its course and accepted New Deal legislation beginning in 1937. This transition to federal power led later Courts to uphold congressional actions such as the Civil Rights Act (1964) and the Voting Rights Act (1965), which limited the ways that state and private actors could discriminate. It also led the Court to strike down state actions, as when they denied Texas' right to ban abortion (*Roe v. Wade*, 1973), or, in 2015, struck down several states' "three strikes" laws that jailed people for life, often for minor offenses.

In recent years—beginning under Chief Justice Rehnquist in the mid-1990s and gaining strength with a consistently conservative majority under Chief Justice Roberts since 2005—the Supreme Court has emphasized local and state power. In fact the Rehnquist Court (1994–2005) struck down more acts of Congress than any previous Court in U.S. history; many of these decisions defended state power. A series of prominent cases has tended to shift power away from the national government toward the states (see Table 4.2). The Roberts Court (2005–current) has continued this trend. If history is a reliable guide, the current judicial trend will fade over time, as the pendulum of state and national power swings yet again.

 **The Bottom Line**

» The Supreme Court protected the powers of the federal government from state governments in the early years of our nation.

» With some exceptions, the courts have trended toward returning power to state and local government in recent years.

🗨 Nationalism, American Style

Federalism trains our focus on the Constitution (the elastic clause vs. the Tenth Amendment), on how institutions evolve (dual federalism vs. cooperative federalism, layer cake vs. marble cake), and on the clash of national versus state (seeking equity vs. "drown it in the bathtub!"). However, something deeper holds the entire complicated apparatus in place. It is the elusive cultural sentiment known as *nationalism*: the American public's sense of identity as Americans. Nationalism helps maintain the federal balance by instilling loyalty to nation, state, and locality. But it can also turn inward and exclude others—as we will see when we turn to civil rights. In this section, we explore the development of American nationalism—in its positive and negative variants.

The Rise of American Nationalism

In the excitement of the Revolution, former colonists from New Hampshire to Georgia celebrated the defeat of the British army. Yet, after the revolution, the sense of "Americanhood" began to wane.[17]

Restored national sentiment came from an unlikely source—a piece of parchment. The Constitution became a touchstone for Americans' shared sense of belonging. Following ratification in 1789, celebrations broke out across the new nation. In Boston, a three-day festival featured a town feast for twelve thousand. North Carolina's capital, Raleigh, greeted the Constitution with so many twenty-one-gun salutes that elderly residents feared the Revolutionary War had started again. The Marquis de Lafayette, the French general who had fought next to George Washington, wrote home to Paris that he was astonished to be "in the midst of perpetual fêtes [celebratory parties]."[18] It was the start of the nationalism that lives on to this day.

Powerful nationalism is a double-edged sword. Political scientist Elizabeth Theiss-Morse noted that on the one hand, a strong sense of national identity fosters mutual support and loyalty. On the other hand, the most enthusiastic nationalists are those most likely to draw strict boundaries around who counts as an American. "Help and loyalty are offered only to 'true Americans,' not Americans who do not count and who are pushed to the periphery of the national group," she argued.[19]

America's Weak National Government

Americans have long exhibited a passionate nationalist sense—and ironically, this strong nationalism is linked to relatively weak governing institutions. How does a U.S. government that is described by many of its own citizens as "overbearing" and even "tyrannical" count as *weak*? Today, we measure the strength of central governments by looking at three main principles: size, authority, and independence.

Size. For many years, American national government was dramatically smaller than those in other nations. It grew in leaps during World War I, the Great Depression, World War II, the Cold War, and the Great Society of the 1960s. Each growth spurt brought protests and efforts to cut the government back to size. In the 1930s,

● *The Pledge of Allegiance still evokes strong nationalist sentiment among many Americans.*

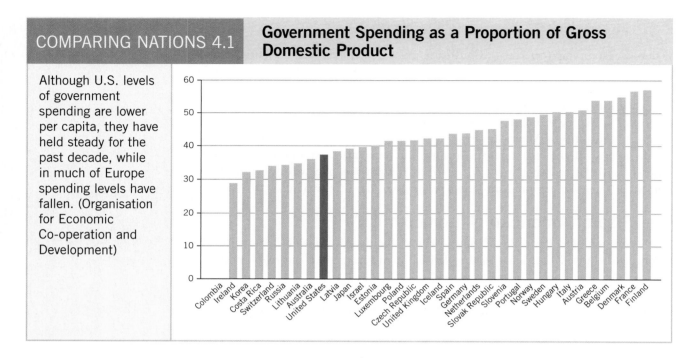

COMPARING NATIONS 4.1 **Government Spending as a Proportion of Gross Domestic Product**

Although U.S. levels of government spending are lower per capita, they have held steady for the past decade, while in much of Europe spending levels have fallen. (Organisation for Economic Co-operation and Development)

opponents, fearful of the growing New Deal bureaucracy, called President Franklin Roosevelt a communist, un-American, and worse. Critics have blasted recent presidents for adding thousands more federal employees. Despite all the fears—or perhaps because of them—the U.S. government spends less than the governments of most other wealthy nations—and leaves more to the private sector (see Comparing Nations 4.1).

In areas like education, the U.S. Department of Education spends far, far less per pupil in public schools than its counterparts in democracies like France. Does this mean the American government ignores education? Hardly: Our federalist system shifts much education spending to state and local sources. American public education funding runs over $630 billion a year and involves a huge array of decision makers: the federal government, fifty state governments, and thousands of local school boards across the nation.[20]

Authority. By the mid-nineteenth century, most developed nations—from France and Germany to China and the British colonies in India—had powerful and efficient national bureaucracies, known as the civil service. In sharp contrast, nineteenth-century American government engaged its citizens without a strong central administration or bureaucracy. European observers were stunned at the haphazard, chaotic nature of American administration.

Communal activity stretched well beyond the government. American **civic voluntarism** presented a virtually unprecedented spectacle in the nineteenth and early twentieth centuries: Robust nationalist feeling stimulating widespread individual effort in cooperation with other community members. Elsewhere, strong central governments in Paris or Tokyo or Buenos Aires took care of most civic needs. The American spirit of voluntary participation has lived on for generations, inspiring mass public involvement in everything from town-meeting government to bowling leagues to civil rights organizations.[21]

Contemporary administration reflects these roots. In France today, the minister of public instruction sets education policy for the entire nation. He or she knows what the students are doing in every meticulously regulated schoolroom across France at

Civic voluntarism: Citizen participation in public life without government incentives or coercion (speaking at a town meeting vs. paying taxes, for example).

every hour of the day. In the United States, no public official has anything near that type of power—or knowledge of what happens inside the schools. Local school boards are made up of volunteers. Most stand for election before they take their turn at overseeing education in their community. They may not be experts, but they generally understand their town or city and its values. The same spirit pervades every area of American government today.

In short, the United States has always emphasized community participation over centralized administration. The same local spirit that helps define federalism limits the authority of national officials.

Independence. In a powerful centralized system, government officials can act forcefully—as long as their superiors approve. In contrast, Americans separate and divide governing power more extensively than any other modern country. Federalism operates along a vertical dimension, with power shared among different levels of government—national, state, and local.

● *Civic voluntarism in action—a source of wonder for nineteenth-century European visitors such as Tocqueville—and a key feature of American-style federalism and nationalism.*

At every level and within every branch and institution there are further internal checks. All but one American state legislature, like Congress, has two chambers (Nebraska is the lone exception); all have multiple committees and subcommittees within each chamber. Each legislature faces an executive and an independent judiciary. In short, checks and balances at every level multiply federalism's horizontal division of power. No public official can act independently. Each needs cooperation from others.

The effort to advance public policies in a weak central government involves more conflict—many participants reflect many different interests. That, in turn, forces public officials to build support for their policies in creative ways: They call out the citizens to show support for an idea. They seek help from lobbyists. They mobilize powerful allies. They raise (and often share) enormous amounts of money to fund future campaigns. We explore all these modes of action in future chapters.

The Bottom Line

» Americans have long felt a strong sense of nationalism. This helps bind together a large and diverse nation with a fragmented government.

» Nationalist bonds can also turn corrosive and exclusionary. "Nationalists" claiming America stands only for Anglo-Saxons or Christians or English speakers sow division.

» "Strong nation, weak national government" is a great American paradox. A weak government means that American institutions (and officials) rank relatively low on three dimensions: size, authority, and independence.

» The political results of this paradox include an emphasis on citizen participation, the importance of building alliances, and a reliance on power and money.

🔵 Conclusion: Who Are We?

Federalism seems, on the surface, like a simple matter of government engineering: How do we decide who does what on the federal, state, and local levels? In reality, federalism reflects an intense philosophical debate, carved into institutional stone.

Conflicting views about power and democracy, fairness, and liberty have always marked American politics. Successive eras allocated power differently. Dual federalism (the layer cake) largely kept the state and national spheres separate. The era of cooperative federalism saw the national government expand its role and mix with state and local functions (the marble cake). More recently, conservatives and courts promote a new federalism that devolves more decisions to state and local governments. Obama-era progressive federalism tried to combine state innovation and national goals. The Trump administration returned to the Reagan era's effort to cut funds and regulations.

Issue after issue returns us to this question of where to locate government authority: federal, state, or local. Who should decide whether to restrict e-cigarette "vaping" by teens? Address climate change? Encourage immigrant "Dreamers" to remain in the United States? Promote educational standards? Allow—or halt—government collection of cellphone data? Protect the homeland? Permit or forbid sports gambling?

Federalism is the mark of a weak national government. However, a paradox of American politics is that weak government is balanced by a powerful nation with a robust, patriotic sense of national identity. That force helps bind together all the centrifugal institutions of a federal system shot through with checks and balances on every level of government.

Many critics suggest that the weak central government diminishes America's capacity to face the challenges of the twenty-first century. Others fear the opposite: An inexorably growing state marks the decline of American liberty. We will revisit these fears throughout this book. For now, simply recognize that this debate echoes those that engaged Federalists and Anti-Federalists in the 1780s. The conflict involves balancing the most important American values, never an easy task.

CHAPTER SUMMARY

Check your understanding of Chapter 4.

🔘 Americans are a people of multiple loyalties—to their nation, state, and home city or town. These divides are mirrored in our federalist politics.

🔘 Most other nations have more centralized unitary governments.

🔘 The American founders adopted a federalist system, in part to protect against concentrating too much power in one person or branch, but also to expand protections for individual rights,

increase government's flexibility, and enable more political innovations to flourish.

🔘 Different versions of federalism are evident in U.S. history, from dual federalism (in which the states and the national government perform largely separate functions) to cooperative and new versions that involve closer partnership across government levels. Issues such as devolution and unfunded mandates mark ongoing negotiations over the terms of the elaborate arrangement of local, state, and national governing power.

Given this divided authority, we might wonder what has held the United States together, especially given regional differences that culminated in civil war. An uncommonly strong sense of national identity is a large part of the answer. Americans' devotion to national unity was instrumental in building a robust nation—although nationalism has its ugly, xenophobic sides as well.

Alongside America's strong nation is its relatively weak national government, an anomaly among most countries with a similarly robust national spirit. This less powerful set of government institutions is found across American history in both the limited size of our federal bureaucracy and Washington's constrained capacity to act.

An abiding commitment to separated powers helps explain the persistence of this weak-government phenomenon alongside our strong nation. Debates about how to reform the United States' federalist, separated powers polity also have persisted over the years. We invite you to join the debate in the months and years to come.

Need to review key ideas in greater depth? Click here.

KEY TERMS

Block grants, p. 112
Civic voluntarism, p. 120
Commerce clause, p. 108
Concurrent powers, p. 109
Confederation, p. 102
Cooperative federalism, p. 111
Devolution, p. 115
Delegated powers, p. 108
Diffusion, p. 104

Dual federalism, p. 110
Full faith and credit clause, p. 109
Grants-in-aid, p. 111
Implied powers, p. 108
Inherent powers, p. 108
Necessary and proper clause, p. 108
New federalism, p. 112

Preemption, p. 116
Progressive Federalism, p. 113
Reserved powers, p. 109
Supremacy clause, p. 108
Unfunded mandate, p. 114
Unitary government, p. 102

Flashcard review.

STUDY QUESTIONS

1. Can you imagine the United States without federalism? Suppose that a central national authority ran the country and governors and mayors—and other subnational officials—were entirely subordinate to the national government. Describe some of the changes that would likely result. Would this shift toward a unitary state be an improvement, in your view? Why or why not?

2. Define the following: Dual Federalism, Competitive Federalism, New Federalism, Progressive Federalism. Does "partisan federalism"—marked by intense conflict between levels on issues from immigration to the environment—deserve a place alongside these federalist schools of thought, or does that strike you as peculiar to the present day?

3. You're asked to advise senior members of Congress. How would you advise them to approach the issue of federalism? Should they give more or less discretion to the states?

4. Think about your own political loyalties. Are they most strongly felt for your hometown or home city, the state where you grew up (or where you live now), or the nation as a whole? What do you think accounts for your outlook? If you are not from the United States, reflect on your own sense of political identity: Is it primarily to a nation, a region, or a local place?

5. If you feel a strong sense of national pride, do you think it comes with any undesirable aspects? If you are not an especially avid American nationalist, why not? What would happen if most citizens exhibited a skeptical outlook toward the country?

6. A wide range of reforms have been suggested for improving the American system of separated powers. Are there any other changes you would make to the federalist division of power across branches and between national, state, and local governments?

Go to www.oup.com/us/Morone to find quizzes, flash cards, simulations, tutorials, videos, and other study tools.

5 Civil Liberties

SIMON TAM AND HIS DANCE ROCK BAND

named themselves "The Slants" as a way to push back against a politically correct culture that tip-toed around racism. The band members, who are Asian Americans, told interviewers that they wanted to reclaim the slur. But when they applied for a trademark, the U.S Patent and Trademark Office rejected their application because the name was "disparaging to people of Asian descent." Tam sued.

Some people agree with the copyright office, arguing that hate speech has no place in our society. Groups that have faced discrimination—for their race, ethnicity, religion, sexual orientation, gender identity, or anything else—should be protected from further insult. This issue has roiled many college campuses. If a speaker has expressed hostility or hatred toward others, say some students and faculty members, they should be stopped from speaking on campus. Across the country students have shut down events and administrators have canceled speakers.

Wait a minute, say others. The First Amendment guarantees Americans the right to free speech—to say what they wish, especially if it is unpopular and even if it is hateful. You may argue against those who speak hatefully, this side argues, but you may not take away their free speech. Allison Stanger, a political science professor who was injured when students at Middlebury College violently disrupted a right-wing speaker, put it this way: "our constitutional democracy will depend on whether Americans can relearn how to engage civilly with one another, something that is admittedly hard to do with a bullying president as a role model." The Supreme Court has upheld freedom of speech in several recent cases, in arenas from polling places to pregnancy clinics. [1]

Two important values are clashing in this case. On the one hand, a community should treat its members with respect. On the other, free speech is the basis of a free society. Which side is right?

The First Amendment to the Constitution *does* guarantee people's right to free speech. This is the bedrock of American liberty: protecting individuals when they wish to speak out, practice their religion, or assemble to protest—even if what they say, or believe, or rally for is deeply unpopular.

When Simon Tam and the Slants ended up before the Supreme Court, the Court unanimously ruled in their favor. Even if they had been using the slur against Asians in a hateful way, the Court argued, the government was

● *Simon Tam and the Slants. The Supreme Court ruled unanimously that the First Amendment protected the band's name—even if it is hateful.*

Listen to Simon Tam and the Slants' song about their legal victory.

wrong to limit free speech by denying a trademark. "The proudest boast of our free speech jurisprudence," wrote the Court majority, is that we protect the freedom to express "the thought that we hate."[2] In balancing freedom of speech versus protecting communities from hate speech, the Court came down strongly in favor of free speech.

However, every right has limits. Individual protections are always balanced by community needs or by other people's rights. And the context matters. As Supreme Court Justice Oliver Wendell Holmes put it back in 1919, every action "depends upon the circumstances in which it is done. . . . The most stringent protection of free speech would not protect a man from falsely shouting fire in a crowded theater and causing a panic."[3]

Who are we? We are a nation always wrestling with a great trade-off—majority rule versus individual liberties. On the one hand, the United States is a democratic republic, which means the majority should get its way. On the other hand, it is a nation of rugged individualism, which tilts toward protecting individual freedom and rights. What we will see in this chapter is that in our democracy, a majority—even a very large majority— cannot violate the civil liberties of even a small minority.

The tension is exacerbated because we are (and always have been) a nation of minority groups—Irish, Italian, gay, Muslim, Seventh Day Adventist, gun owner, Hmong, transgender, African American, and the list goes on. When the majority feels threatened or offended, it sometimes moves to limit the minority's rights, making civil liberties all the *more* important.

Civil liberties: The limits on government that allow people to freely exercise their rights.

What are **civil liberties**? They are the limits we put on governments (and the majorities that elect them) so that individuals can exercise their personal freedoms. Americans have long embraced the figure of the brave individual, standing up for their rights. In practice, complexity abounds.

The Rise of Civil Liberties

May an anti-abortion protester shout warnings at women entering family planning clinics? May states ban violent video games? May a skinhead stand on a street corner and urge people to attack Latinos, Sikhs, or Jews? The answer to all three questions is "sometimes." We always weigh the rights of individuals against the concerns and safety of the community. Who decides? Usually, the courts do. And there is often more than one reasonable answer when the courts take up a question.[4]

Civil Rights and Civil Liberties

Civil rights and civil liberties demand opposite things from government. Civil rights require government action to help secure individual rights; civil liberties restrict government action to protect individual rights. Until people have won their rights, the idea of protecting them is meaningless. When governments enforce civil rights for some people, they often limit the liberty of others. For example, as we

BY THE NUMBERS
Civil Liberties

Number of rights listed in the Bill of Rights	**31**
Number of rights protecting freedom of religion	**2**
Number of rights protecting people accused of crimes	**19**
Number of years after the Bill of Rights was ratified before the Supreme Court ruled that state governments could not interfere with freedom of speech	**134**
Number of years before it ruled that states could not interfere with the right to bear arms	**219**
Number of new rights secured by constitutional amendment in the past fifty years (the Twenty-Sixth Amendment extended the right to vote to eighteen- to twenty-year-olds)	**1**
Percentage of Americans who supported the death penalty in 1994 and today, respectively	**80, 55[5]**
Number of states that have not executed anyone since 1976	**16[6]**
Number of states that have not executed anyone since 2010	**37**
Total number executed in Texas, Virginia, Oklahoma, and Florida since 1976	**871**
Total number executed by the federal government in that period	**3**

How has our interpretation of civil liberties and the government's responsibility to protect them changed over time?

will see in Chapter 6, the Civil Rights Act of 1964 outlawed segregated restaurants. That legal action freed blacks and Latinos to eat wherever they wished but limited the liberty of racist restaurant owners to serve whomever they wanted to serve.

In practice, the two concepts are not opposites. The battle for civil rights led to more robust civil liberties for everyone. The fight against slavery eventually led to the Fourteenth Amendment, which—as we will soon see—is the cornerstone of

● *Legal? Sometimes! When? Read on . . .*

modern civil liberties. Without the long American struggle for civil rights, we would have many fewer civil liberties.

Both civil liberties and civil rights became increasingly important to American politics over the course of the twentieth century. In this section, we look first at why civil liberties matter. We then explain how they grew and spread.

The Purpose of Civil Liberties

Lillian Gobitas was the seventh-grade class president in a Minersville, Pennsylvania, school in 1935. She refused to pledge allegiance to the flag because, as a Jehovah's Witness, she was taught that the pledge placed the nation ahead of God. Lillian was taunted, attacked, and expelled from school. Her father, Walter, sued the school district, and in 1940 the Supreme Court upheld the expulsion (8–1), declaring that "national unity is the basis of national security." (To add insult to injury, a clerk misspelled her name and the case is known as *Minersville School District v. Gobitis.*)

The American entry into World War II in December 1941 inflamed the prejudice against the sect. Mobs beat up five Jehovah's Witnesses in Wyoming, burned a Kingdom Hall in Maine, and allegedly castrated a Jehovah's Witness in Nebraska. The Court's ruling seemed to have made matters worse. "They're traitors," declared a sheriff in Maine, "the Supreme Court says so. Ain't you heard?"[7] This is the nightmare for civil liberties advocates: The powerful machinery of government invoked against a minority group.

Three years later, in 1943, the Court reversed itself and ruled that it was unconstitutional to require children to pledge allegiance if it violated their faith. In announcing its new position, the Court made a classic statement of civil liberties: "The very purpose of a Bill of Rights was to withdraw certain subjects from the vicissitudes of political controversy, to place them beyond the reach of majorities and officials."[8]

It has taken a long time for the United States to institute those principles. Civil liberties were barely visible in the nineteenth century. "What I find most dangerous in America," wrote Tocqueville in 1835, "is not the extreme freedom reigning there but the shortage of guarantees against the tyranny of the majority."[9]

The Slow Rise of Civil Liberties

The Bill of Rights barely touched American life because it only applied to the national government. The First Amendment begins, "*Congress shall make no law*" prohibiting the exercise of religion or restricting speech. Well, what about the states? Were they also bound by the individual protections in the Bill of Rights?

● *Walter Gobitas with his children, William and Lillian. The Jehovah's Witnesses were expelled from school for refusing to salute the flag.*

In 1833, John Barron found out. Barron owned a thriving wharf in Baltimore Harbor until the city diverted the water and left his dock high and dry. Barron sued, arguing that the city had violated the Fifth Amendment by taking his property for public use "without just compensation." The Supreme Court ruled (in *Barron v. Baltimore*) that the Fifth Amendment applied only to the federal government. The Anti-Federalists, reasoned the justices, had demanded the Bill of Rights to protect them from the federal government. Washington could not strip Barron of his property rights—but Maryland or Baltimore could.[10]

The Bill of Rights eventually reached the states thanks to the quest for civil liberties. After the Civil War, Congress passed the Fourteenth Amendment (ratified in 1868) to protect the newly freed slaves. Almost every discussion of civil liberties turns the spotlight on one passage in the Fourteenth Amendment:

> ***No state*** shall . . . *deprive any person of life, liberty, or property, without due process of law; nor deny any person within its jurisdiction the equal protection of the laws.* [emphasis added]

Look again at the first two words. The amendment directly addresses the states. None may deprive any person of life, liberty, or property, which are exactly what the Bill of Rights protects. The Fourteenth Amendment *seems* to apply the Bill of Rights to the states. In 1873, the Supreme Court disagreed, ruling that the Fourteenth Amendment applied only to freed slaves and to no one else.[11]

Over time, the Court changed its mind. In 1897, the Court returned to the issue raised in *Barron v. Baltimore* and ruled that state governments could not seize property without compensation. One phrase of the Fifth Amendment now applied to state and local government as well as to the federal government. The Supreme Court had "incorporated" the right into the Fourteenth Amendment. The Supreme Court decides, case by case, which liberties apply to state governments—a process called **selective incorporation**.

The Court was very slow to force constitutional liberties on the states. In 1937, it formally declared its principle for deciding which rights to incorporate: Is the right in question essential to our idea of liberty? If so, the Fourteenth Amendment's due process clause—quoted above—required states to respect that right, and the Court then incorporated, or applied, it to the states.[12] Over time, the Court incorporated almost every phrase of the Bill of Rights beginning with freedom of speech in 1925, continuing with the practice of religion in 1940, and moving to the right to own guns in 2010 (see Table 5.1).[13] In the rest of the chapter, we examine the most important civil liberties and the issues they raise.

Selective incorporation: The extension of protections from the Bill of Rights to the state governments, one liberty at a time.

 **The Bottom Line**

» The Supreme Court neatly defined civil liberties in 1943: The Bill of Rights withdraws certain subjects from political controversy and places them beyond the reach of majorities and officials.

» The Bill of Rights did not apply to the states until the Fourteenth Amendment declared that no state could deprive any citizen of life, liberty, or property.

» The Court has applied the Bill of Rights to the states one right at a time between 1897 (no taking of property without compensation) and 2010 (the right to bear arms).

TABLE 5.1 Incorporation of the Bill of Rights into the Fourteenth Amendment

THE BILL OF RIGHTS	YEAR	KEY CASE
I.* Free exercise of religion	1940	*Cantwell v. Connecticut*
No establishment of religion	1947	*Everson v. Board of Education*
Free press	1931	***Near v. Minnesota****
Free speech	1925	***Gitlow v. New York***
Right to peaceful assembly	1937	*De Jonge v. Oregon*
Right to petition government	1963	*NAACP v. Button*
II. Right to keep and bear arms	2010	***McDonald v. Chicago***
III. No quartering of soldiers		Not incorporated
IV. No unreasonable search and seizure	1949	*Wolf v. Colorado*
No search and seizure without a warrant	1961	***Mapp v. Ohio***
V. Right to grand jury indictment		Not incorporated
No double jeopardy	1969	*Benton v. Maryland*
No forced confession	1964	*Escobedo v. Illinois*
Right to remain silent	1966	***Miranda v. Arizona***
No seizure of property without compensation	1897	*Chicago, Burlington, and Quincy Railroad Co. v. City of Chicago*
VI. Right to public trial	1948	*In re Oliver*
Right to speedy trial	1967	*Klopfer v. North Carolina*
Right to trial by impartial jury	1966	*Parker v. Gladden*
Right to confront witnesses	1965	*Pointer v. Texas*
Right to compel supportive witnesses to appear	1967	*Washington v. Texas*
Right to counsel in capital punishment cases	1932	***Powell v. Alabama***
Right to counsel in any criminal trial	1963	***Gideon v. Wainwright***
VII. Right to jury trial in civil cases		Not incorporated
VIII. No excessive bail		Not incorporated
No cruel and unusual punishment	1962	*Robinson v. California*
IX. Rights not limited to rights listed in the first eight amendments		Not relevant to incorporation
X. Powers not delegated to the national government reserved to the states and the people		Not relevant to incorporation

* Notice that the First Amendment rights were incorporated early in the process. Most protections for those accused of crimes were applied between 1962 and 1968.
** Boldfaced cases are discussed in this chapter.

🔵 Privacy

We begin with an especially controversial civil liberty that, unlike all the others we will examine, is never directly mentioned in the Constitution. Instead, the Supreme Court has ruled that it is implied by the First, Third, Fourth, Fifth, and Ninth Amendments.

"Penumbras" and "Emanations"

In the mid-nineteenth century, contraceptives were widely available. Then, encouraged by the federal government in the 1870s, every state banned them—partly because of fears that immigrants would have more children than native-born Americans. Almost a century later, the director of Planned Parenthood of Connecticut defied that state's ban and dispensed condoms at a birth control clinic in New Haven. The Supreme Court heard the case, *Griswold v. Connecticut*, in 1965, struck down the law, and declared a dramatic new personal liberty: the right to privacy.

How could the Court protect privacy if the Constitution does not even mention it? Justice William O. Douglas explained: Rights that are specifically mentioned in the Bill of Rights "have penumbras . . . that give them life and substance." The *penumbras*—literally, the shadows—of the First Amendment create "zones of privacy" in which people have a right to make their own choices free from government interference. So do the "emanations"—literally, things that flow out, from other amendments such as the Third Amendment's ban on quartering soldiers in private homes—which, Douglas pointed out, was designed to protect privacy. In addition, the Ninth Amendment declares that other rights exist besides the ones mentioned in the Constitution and that these rights are also "retained by the people." Privacy is one of those rights.

In 1787, when the Constitution was written, no one was thinking about condoms. But if you apply the logic of the Constitution to modern times, the right to privacy, and to contraceptives, emerges. These civil liberties reflect the spirit of the Constitution. After all, concluded Douglas, "would we allow the police to search the sacred precincts of marital bedrooms for telltale signs of the use of contraceptives? The very idea is repulsive." Is it acceptable to interpret the Constitution in this way—reading in rights that are implied but not stated? That question presents one of the great controversies in contemporary legal analysis.

The *Griswold* case itself did not stir much controversy. After all, most people thought married couples had every right to use condoms. In 1973, however, the right to privacy led to one of the most controversial Court decisions ever.

Roe v. Wade In *Roe v. Wade* (1973), the Supreme Court drew on the right to privacy and struck down a Texas law banning abortion. The Court ruled that the right to privacy is "broad enough to encompass a woman's decision whether

● *Off-duty police offer Robert Sanderson's body lay covered by a yellow sheet (on right) in this 1997 bombing of an Alabama family planning clinic. Decades after the* Roe *decision, abortion remains the subject of fierce debate, civil disobedience—and occasional criminal acts.*

	Yes.	**No.**	**What it means.**
Are you ready to try your first civil liberties case? How would you rule in *Griswold v. Connecticut*? Do you agree that there is "a right to privacy" in the Constitution that permitted the Court to strike down the Connecticut ban on contraceptives?	Although the Constitution does not specifically mention privacy, a modern reading of the document would conclude that privacy is a basic liberty that the courts ought to protect. In addition, the consequence—a woman's right to control her own pregnancy—is an essential part of gender equality as we understand it today.	We have to stick to the simple language of the Constitution itself. We disrespect and even damage the document by reading things into it. Those who opposed Connecticut's ban on contraceptives should have gone to the legislature and lobbied them to change it.	No matter how you voted, you're part of a long intellectual tradition. If you said yes, you agree with a school of thought (which we call *pragmatist*) that says the courts must be guided by the *general ideas* that underpin the Constitution to try and determine the best outcome in a particular case. If you voted no, you're voting with *originalism*, the school of thought that limits judges to considering the document's original intent as explicitly stated in the Constitution's text.

or not to terminate her pregnancy"—within the first three months of pregnancy (before the fetus can live outside the womb). During that first trimester, the state governments cannot *regulate* or *infringe on* a woman's right to abortion.

Roe v. Wade changed American politics. It was not immediately controversial. Within a decade, however, two very strong perspectives had emerged. People who supported the decision—known as "pro-choice"—viewed the decision as essential to gender equality, for it enabled women to control when (and whether) they have children. From this perspective, *Roe* opens the door to vocations and careers for women. It protects women's health by doing away with the dangerous "back alley" abortions that desperate women sought out before *Roe* made abortions safe and legal. Democrats, for the most part, are pro-choice.

Those who oppose the decision—known as "pro-life"—believe that life begins at conception and that abortion is murder. Many religious activists took *Roe v. Wade* as a call to enter politics. The grassroots campaign to overturn the decision became a powerful force in modern conservatism. Within a decade, the Republican Party had committed itself to overturning *Roe*.

The debate added new intensity to American politics. Activists on each side felt they were fighting for the soul of the nation: on the one side, equality for women; on the other, the rights of the unborn. The intensity has helped politicize Supreme Court appointments. Each new nomination raises the same questions. What is his or her attitude toward abortion? Will it swing the Court?

Planned Parenthood v. Casey   Challenges to *Roe v. Wade* led to a string of Supreme Court decisions. In 1980, the Court accepted a congressional ban on federal funding for abortions. In 1989, it upheld a Missouri prohibition on abortions in public hospitals. In 1992, the Court took up a Pennsylvania law that seemed to directly challenge *Roe* and many observers on both sides of the issue predicted that the Court would overturn *Roe v. Wade* and permit states to outlaw abortions.

Instead, in *Planned Parenthood v. Casey* (1992), the Court voted (5–4) to take a middle ground. The Court upheld a woman's right to terminate her pregnancy as a "component of liberty." However, it rejected *Roe v. Wade*'s trimester framework, which forbade any state limitations in the first trimester. Now the Court majority allowed states to legislate "measures aimed at ensuring that a woman's choice contemplates the consequences for the fetus." In short, the right to choose an abortion could be balanced—but not overruled—by the state's desire to protect potential life so long as state regulations did not impose "an undue burden" on the woman's choice.

The original *Roe* decision had propounded a **judicial rule**. Rules set clear boundaries between what is lawful and what is not: In this case, the states may not interfere in the first trimester. Now, *Casey* replaced the rule with a **judicial standard**. A standard establishes a more general guiding principle in place of a hard-and-fast rule. What is an "undue burden" on a woman's choice? That's a judgment call.

Abortions continue to be fiercely debated—on and off the Court. In the last three years, fifteen states passed sixty-three new restrictions on abortion. On the other side, twenty-one states passed measures to protect reproduction rights (including access to abortion and contraception). In 2016, the Supreme Court set down new rules: States may restrict access to abortion only when the medical benefits outweigh the burden imposed on a woman seeking to exercise her constitutional right to an abortion.[14]

Judicial rules: Hard-and-fast boundaries between what is lawful and what is not.

Judicial standards: Guiding principles that help governments make judgment calls.

Sex Between Consenting Adults

Does the right to privacy extend to same-sex couples? In 1986, the Supreme Court ruled it did not, upholding Georgia's antisodomy law. However, judicial mores were changing along with American culture. In 2003, the Supreme Court reversed itself in *Lawrence v. Texas* and extended the right of privacy to same-sex couples. In striking down a Texas antisodomy law, the majority echoed the original *Griswold* decision: "Liberty protects the person from unwarranted government intrusion into . . . private places." Three members of the Court disagreed and signed on to Justice Scalia's blistering dissent.

Clashing Principles

The privacy cases reflect public opinion. By 1965, most Americans believed that couples should be permitted to use birth control. *Roe v. Wade* appeared to reflect the popular pro-choice view in the early 1970s, but precipitated an enormous surge defending a right to life. Later decisions balanced the right to an abortion with state restrictions—roughly in line with popular preferences. It may seem a good idea for the courts to reflect majority opinion. But civil liberties are a bulwark *against* the will of the majority: The Constitution and the Court are designed to protect individual liberties in the face of popular opposition.

Discover how the Patriot Act raised privacy concerns.

● *John Geddes Lawrence (left) and Tyron Garner (right). The police, investigating a gun disturbance complaint, broke into Lawrence's apartment—which had gay posters prominently displayed on the walls. When Lawrence began to argue, the police arrested both Garner and him for "deviant sexual intercourse." In* Lawrence v. Texas *the Supreme Court struck down the Texas antisodomy law for violating the Constitution's privacy protections.*

They are supposed to protect the rights of unpopular minorities, such as Jehovah's Witnesses in the 1940s and gay Americans in the 1980s.

As we will see throughout this chapter, applying the Constitution is never simple. The United States is founded on two ideas that often clash. We believe in government by the people. Yet at the same time, we believe that all individuals are endowed with inalienable rights. The story of civil liberties is the story of managing the collisions between the two core principles—the needs and desires of the community versus the rights of the individual.

The Bottom Line

» The Court discovered a right to privacy implicit in the shadows of the First, Third, Fourth, Fifth, and Ninth Amendments.

» The Court applied the right to privacy to strike down laws banning abortion. In *Roe v. Wade*, the Court issued a rule prohibiting states from interfering during the first trimester.

» Later cases permitted states to balance abortion rights with protections for the unborn.

» The Court extended privacy rights to same-sex couples by striking down antisodomy laws.

🛈 Freedom of Religion

As the Bill of Rights opens, the First Amendment lays down two succinct commands regulating religion:

> *Congress shall make no law respecting an establishment of religion, or prohibiting the free exercise thereof.*

Establishment clause: The First Amendment principle that government may not establish an official religion.

The federal government may not establish an official religion—that's known as the **establishment clause**. And it may not interfere in religious practice—the **free exercise clause**.

The Establishment Clause

Free exercise clause: The First Amendment principle that government may not interfere in religious practice.

By the time the Constitution was written, Americans were practicing many faiths: Puritans (or Congregationalists) in Massachusetts, Quakers in Philadelphia, Baptists in Rhode Island, Anglicans in Virginia, Catholics in Maryland, and Jews in

Newport, Rhode Island. The Constitution posed a threat. What if the federal government imposed a national religion? The First Amendment's establishment clause is designed to prohibit that. But what exactly did it forbid the government from doing? The debate began immediately.

President George Washington (1789–1797) called for a national day of prayer each year. Was that encouraging religion? President Thomas Jefferson (1801–1809) thought so and rejected the practice. The First Amendment, wrote Jefferson, builds "a wall of separation between church and state."[15] When the Supreme Court extended the establishment clause to the state governments in 1947, Justice Hugo Black quoted Jefferson's "wall of separation."[16] Until recently, Jefferson's metaphor guided the Court's efforts.

The difficulty with Jefferson's principle is that there has never been a true wall of separation. The cash in American pockets is inscribed "In God We Trust"; children pledge allegiance to "one nation, under God"; Moses, holding the Ten Commandments, is carved into the Supreme Court building. Congress opens each session with a prayer, and presidents end their speeches with "God bless America"—a sentiment no leader would invoke in England, France, or Japan. Despite these and other interconnections, the courts have tried to separate church and state. The question is how?

The establishment clause is clearly designed to keep government officials from favoring one religion—or religion over nonreligion. In a blockbuster case, *Engel v. Vitale* (1962), the Supreme Court ruled that New York's practice of starting the school day with a nondenominational prayer violated the establishment clause.[17]

A long string of controversial decisions followed. Each decision returns to the vexing question of exactly where to construct Jefferson's wall. May public schools introduce a minute of silent prayer or meditation? (No.) May graduation include a prayer? (No.) May students lead prayers at football games? (No.) Can a city or state government display the Ten Commandments? (Yes, if it does not make a religious statement.) May a city put up a Christmas display? (Yes, if it includes secular as well as religious symbols—known sarcastically as the "two-reindeer" rule.) Can a baker refuse to provide a cake for a same-sex wedding on religious grounds? (Yes, ruled the Supreme Court in 2018.)

● *Debating the establishment clause. The Supreme Court found Kentucky's display of the Ten Commandments unconstitutional by a 5–4 vote (left), but a similar display in Austin, Texas, acceptable—also 5–4 (right). What was the difference between the two? Justice Breyer, who switched his vote from "no" (Kentucky) to "yes" (Texas) explained: The Texas Commandments had stood for forty years as one of many monuments celebrating the development of the law, while the Kentucky tablets had been recently erected as an expression of religious faith. [Texas case: Van Orden v. Perry, 545 U.S. 677 (2005); Kentucky: McCreary County v. ACLU of Kentucky, 545 U.S. 844 (2005).]*

In 1971, the Court established a test to guide decisions about separating church and state. In *Lemon v. Kurtzman*, the Court struck down a Pennsylvania law that paid teachers who taught nonreligious subjects in church-affiliated (mainly Catholic) schools. The Court promulgated what became known as the *Lemon test* for judging what government actions are permissible. First, the law must have a *secular* purpose. Second, its principal effect must *neither advance nor inhibit religion*. Finally, it must not *excessively entangle* government in religion. Paying the teachers in religious schools was, the Court ruled, an "excessive entanglement," and Pennsylvania could not do it.

As the Court grew more conservative, the Lemon test came under fire. Justice Scalia complained: "Like some ghoul in a late night horror movie that repeatedly sits up in its grave and shuffles abroad . . . *Lemon* stalks our Establishment Clause jurisprudence."[18] Today, two different perspectives have emerged. **Strict separation** still tries to separate church and state using the Lemon test and remains the guiding test. An alternative view is known as **accommodation**: Government does not violate the establishment clause so long as it does not confer an advantage on some religions or discriminate against others. Accommodation is gathering momentum, making establishment clause cases unpredictable. In 2017, the Court ruled (7–2) that when a state offers a funding program (say, for improvements to public school playgrounds), it cannot rule out church schools or other religious organizations (*Lutheran v. Comer*). Strict-separation adherents lamented, "Goodbye, Establishment Clause."[19]

> **Strict separation:** The strict principles articulated in the Lemon test for judging whether a law establishes a religion. (See "accommodation.")

> **Accommodation:** The principle that government does not violate the establishment clause as long as it does not confer an advantage to some religions over others. (See "strict separation.")

Free Exercise of Religion

The First Amendment also prohibits government from interfering with the "free exercise" of religion. Once again, the Court's view has evolved over the years.

The first landmark free exercise case was decided in 1963. Adell Sherbert, a Seventh-Day Adventist, refused to work on Saturday because it violated her faith. She was fired. South Carolina rejected her claim for unemployment benefits because she refused other jobs that also required work on Saturday. Claiming that the state was infringing on her "free exercise" of religion, Sherbert sued the state for her unemployment benefits. In deciding the case, Justice Brennan introduced a two-part test, known as the *Sherbert* or *balancing test*. First, was the government imposing a "significant burden" on an individual's ability to exercise his or her faith? Second, did the government have a "compelling interest" for imposing the burden? In this case, the Court ruled that there was a real burden on Adell Sherbert and no compelling state interest for denying her unemployment benefits.

The Sherbert test lasted until 1990, when the Court took a completely different approach. Two Oregon men participated in a Native American ritual that included taking peyote, a hallucinogen. The men were fired

● Using the neutrality test, the courts struck down a Florida law that forbade the use of animal sacrifices because it specifically targeted the Cuban Santeria religion.

What Do YOU Think?   **May the Christian Youth Club Meet in School?**

The Good News is a Christian youth club that wanted to meet in school after class hours. The school district said that this was religious worship and would amount to a public school's endorsement of Christianity. The case went to the Supreme Court. Justices Stevens (who argued against Good News) and Scalia (who supported Good News) each wrote opinions. Which opinion would you sign on to?

Justice Stevens: "Evangelical meetings designed to convert children to a particular faith . . . may introduce divisiveness and tend to separate young children into cliques that undermine the school's educational mission." The school district is right to stop the practice.

Justice Scalia: Religious expression cannot violate the establishment clause when such exercise is (1) purely private and (2) open to all on equal terms. Milford [the school district] was discriminating against a religious group because it allowed other groups to meet.

Testing These Views. As you consider whose side to take, consider how one would decide this case using the Lemon test (with Stevens) or the accommodation view (with Scalia). How did the court actually rule? The answer is in the endnote.[20]

from their jobs at a private drug rehabilitation center and then were denied unemployment benefits for violating Oregon drug laws. The men sued, arguing that they should be exempted from the peyote ban because it was essential to their religious practice. Under the Sherbert test, they might have won. However, in *Employment Division v. Smith*, the Supreme Court ruled 6–3 against the two men and, in the process, made it much more difficult to sue the government for interfering with religious expression. In this case, the Court asked simply if the Oregon drug law was a neutral law applied in a neutral way. Yes, the law was neutral. It was not aimed at Native American religious practice—because it forbids *everyone* from smoking peyote.

The *Employment Division* case replaced the *Sherbert* balancing test with a *neutrality test*. The new test asks only whether the same law applies to everyone. So long as the law does not target a religious group, the Court will permit it. Obviously, this makes it much more difficult to sue on the basis of "free exercise" of religion.[21]

Religious groups—from the Catholic Church to the *Witches' Voice*—mobilized against the Court's decision. Congress passed the Religious Freedom Restoration Act of 1993 (RFRA), which required federal and state governments to use the old Sherbert balancing test. In 1997, the Court stepped in again. It ruled that Congress lacked the constitutional authority to order the states to use the balancing test. Congress came back three years later, reaffirming its authority with the Religious Land Use and Institutionalized Persons Act (RLUIPA); in addition, twenty-one states have passed their own RFRA laws (and ten others have proposals before the legislature)—all restoring the Sherbert balancing test. In 2015, however, the Supreme Court reverted to the Sherbert balancing test. A Muslim inmate sued Arkansas, arguing that prison regulations denying inmates the right to grow beards violated his rights to free exercise. The Court ruled unanimously that the state could not burden

How do we interpret the free exercise and establishment clauses?

someone's exercise of religion without showing a compelling state reason. The decision hardly ended debates in this controversial area—but the general trend has been to restore the traditional balancing test that asks whether the government has a compelling reason to impose a burden (work on Saturday, shave your beard) on religious practices.

The Bottom Line

» The First Amendment has two clauses protecting religious rights: The government may not establish a religion (the establishment clause), and it may not interfere with the free exercise of religion (free exercise clause).

» The courts have ruled on establishment cases by trying to approximate Jefferson's wall separating church and state. Government action is permissible if it meets the three criteria known as the Lemon test: It must have a secular purpose, neither advance nor inhibit religion, and not excessively entangle government in religion. A more recent view known as accommodation simply requires that government not promote one religious view over another.

» In protecting the free exercise of religion, the courts traditionally asked if the government had a compelling interest for imposing a burden.

Freedom of Speech

Now, we turn to the civil liberty that the courts rank most important, freedom of speech. After its religious clauses, the First Amendment states:

> *Congress shall make no law . . . abridging the freedom of speech or of the press.*

Protecting freedom of speech.

A Preferred Position

The Supreme Court gives the First Amendment a "preferred position" among all the amendments to the Constitution. And among the rights listed in the First Amendment (freedom of speech, religion, press, assembly, and the right to petition government), free speech holds a "preferred position." When freedom of speech conflicts with any other right, the Court generally will "prefer," or protect, speech.[22]

Why do contemporary courts put so much emphasis on the right to express opinions? Because democracy requires vigorous debate. John Stuart Mill, a nineteenth-century English political theorist, put it this way: "However true a doctrine may be, if it is not fully, frequently and fearlessly discussed, it will be held as a dead dogma, not a living truth." Over time, the courts have followed Mill, placing their faith in the free marketplace of ideas.[23]

When the right to speak out clashes with other rights free speech usually wins. How about **hate speech**—which demeans people on the basis of race, ethnicity, gender or other characteristics? In 2017, the Court unanimously protected hateful speech, in the case involving The Slants described at the start of this chapter.

Hate speech: Hostile statements based on someone's personal characteristics, such as race, ethnicity, religion, or sexual orientation.

Political Speech

The forceful defense of free speech took a long time to develop. In every generation, political leaders are tempted to stop subversive talk—or harsh criticism. Under the John Adams administration, just ten years after the Constitution was ratified, Congress drafted the Alien and Sedition Acts. Tensions with France were running high, and the acts made it illegal to "print, utter, or publish . . . any false, scandalous, and malicious writing" against the government. The meaning of the acts was brutally simple: criticize the government and face prosecution. Some of the nation's leading editors were prosecuted and jailed.

The first modern free speech cases arose during World War I. Charles Schenck, general secretary of the Socialist Party of Philadelphia, was found guilty of violating the recently passed Espionage Act because his pamphlets urged men not to enlist for a war designed to pour profits into greedy Wall Street. Was his freedom of speech curtailed? Under normal circumstances it might be, wrote Justice Oliver Wendell Holmes for a unanimous Court in *Schenck v. United States* (1919), but this was wartime. Distributing these documents, Holmes wrote, was like falsely shouting "Fire!" in a crowded theater. Holmes then formulated the most famous test for free speech: Speech is not protected if it poses "a **clear and present danger** that it will lead to 'substantive evils.'"

Clear and present danger: Court doctrine that permits restrictions of free speech if officials believe that the speech will lead to prohibited action such as violence or terrorism.

COMPARING NATIONS 5.1   Civil Liberties Around the World

Every democracy protects civil liberties differently. Each makes choices based on its culture, its history, and who wields power. Consider some international differences.

The right to free speech is stronger in the United States. In Germany and France, it is against the law to deny that the Nazis murdered five million Jews between 1941 and 1945. In Turkey, the government will punish you for discussing the Ottoman Turks' genocide of Armenians in 1915. In Thailand, it is a serious crime to criticize the king. In Canada, there are strict limits on pornography because it demeans women. Most Americans despise Nazis, Holocaust deniers, and pornographers. However, the Constitution protects them all—at least in some cases. When it comes to speech, Germany, France, Thailand, Turkey, and Canada all tilt more toward community needs, whereas the United States distinctly emphasizes individual rights.

The United States is unique in protecting gun rights. No other nation explicitly mentions the right to bear arms in its constitution. And no other nation has so many guns.

The United States puts special emphasis on property rights. For example, the Fifth Amendment forbids the government from taking private property "without just compensation." By contrast, the Canadian constitution does not even mention private property.

Most nations forbid the death penalty. Ninety-eight countries have abolished the death penalty. Almost all industrial democracies have done so (Japan, Taiwan, and Korea are the only exceptions). Abolishing the death penalty is a precondition for joining the European Union (the federation of European nations). In 2018, authorities in the United States executed twenty-four people in eight states (and over 2,800 more have been sentenced to execution and are on death row). Only a handful of nations—China, Iran, Saudi Arabia, Iraq, and North Korea—executed more people, although tyrannical governments often murder people outside the criminal justice system and these deaths would not show up in these tallies. Americans debate whether a clause in the Bill of Rights, the prohibition on "cruel and unusual punishment," should push the United States away from the death penalty.[24]

American liberties are mostly negative: They tell the government what it may not do. Other constitutions include positive rights—things that the government must do—such as educate all citizens, provide universal healthcare, or ensure that women are well represented in the national legislature.

In the early 1920s, many Americans were anxious about foreigners, immigrants, socialists, communists, and anarchists. The Supreme Court hardened the "clear and present danger" test by ruling that judges did not have to "weigh each and every utterance." They could simply determine whether the "natural tendency and probable effect" of the speech was to "bring about something bad or evil"—even if that danger lay in the distant future.[25]

The clear and present danger test stood for decades. Then in *Brandenburg v. Ohio* (1969), the Court complained that "puny" threats, which no one took seriously except "nervous judges," were being declared a "clear and present danger." The issue arose when a Ku Klux Klan leader, Clarence Brandenburg, organized a rally at which Klan members burned crosses, waved guns, and called for "revengeance" against Jews and African Americans. The Supreme Court struck down Brandenburg's conviction and rewrote the clear and present danger test. The state may not interfere with speech, it said, unless the speech "incites imminent lawless action" *and* is likely to actually "produce such action."[26]

The result makes it very difficult to curtail political speech—even when it is highly offensive. Members of the Westboro Baptist Church picket military funerals to protest homosexuality with signs that read "Fag sin = 9/11" and "You're going to hell." Albert Snyder, the father of a Marine killed in Iraq, sued the church. Forty-eight states and numerous veterans groups supported the suit. The Supreme Court acknowledged that the protests were hurtful but protected them as an exercise of free speech. The government may limit the speech only if the bad effects—a lynching, the overthrow of the government, or a terrorist attack—are likely to happen immediately.[27]

The rise of the Islamic State, and its sponsoring terrorist acts around the globe, has caused some to call for a revision of the "clear and present danger" test. Law professor Eric Posner has called for making it illegal to share links or even read websites that "glorify" the Islamic State.[28] The Court has not backed off its emphasis on free speech. However the line between supporting ISIS (protected) and assisting it in pursuing terrorism (which is a crime) is blurry.

Test Yourself: The Simpsons Versus the First Amendment— Which Do You Know Better?

Five rights are listed in the First Amendment, and there are five members of the TV Simpson family. Thirty-four percent of Americans can name four of the five Simpsons. Only one percent of Americans can name four of the five rights.

How about you? How many First Amendment rights can you name? How many Simpsons? (Answers below.)

Source: McCormick Tribune Freedom Museum, Chicago.

Answers: The Simpsons, from left to right: Homer, Bart, Lisa, Marge, and Maggie. First Amendment rights: Freedom of religion, speech, press, assembly, and the right to petition government.

Symbolic Speech

When Clarence Brandenburg burned his cross, he engaged in a form of speech known as **symbolic expression**. He was demonstrating a point of view with an act rather than through speech. The First Amendment protects symbolic speech—within limits.

In 2003, the Supreme Court identified those limits when it took two cross-burning cases on the same day. One involved a Ku Klux Klan ceremony. The original cross burnings, after the Civil War, signaled the murder of a former slave—an emblem designed to frighten people during what amounted to a campaign of domestic terrorism. The Court drew a fine distinction. Individuals may burn crosses to express their views, but not to intimidate others. Sometimes, wrote Justice Sandra Day

The expansive reach of free-speech protections: Members of the Westboro Church cheer for "more dead soldiers" in their fight against tolerance. Here they draw counter-protests at Brown University.

O'Connor, "the cross burning is a statement of ideology, a symbol of group solidarity. It is a ritual used at Klan gatherings, and it is used to represent the Klan itself." The Constitution protects these symbolic speeches.[29] The KKK burned the cross as part of a ritual without directly threatening or intimidating anyone.[30] On the same day, however, the Court upheld the conviction of another cross burner. In this second case, two men had come home after a night of drinking and burned a cross on a black neighbor's lawn. Their act directly intimidated the neighbors. Even if there is no immediate (or clear and present) danger, intimidating people is not protected by the First Amendment.

Burning the American flag is another unpopular symbolic expression. Forty-eight states and the federal government banned flag burning. The Supreme Court narrowly struck down the laws. "If there is a bedrock principle underlying the First Amendment," argued Justice Brennan for a 5–4 majority, "it is that government may not prohibit the expression of an idea simply because society finds the idea offensive or disagreeable."[31] Congress responded by passing legislation defending the flag. The Court overturned that too.

In 2015, however, the Supreme Court narrowly upheld (5–4) Texas's refusal to issue a license plate with a Confederate flag. License plates are a form of government speech, and Texas can choose what to regulate. Notice the distinction: The government may not restrict Simon Tam's (fronting the Slants) hate speech, but it can choose what it "says." Today, that issue has boiled over across the South as the region confronts its Confederate legacy. Some argue that Confederate flags and monuments commemorate those who fought for the enslavement of African Americans; others contend that they celebrate Southern heritage. The key question: When the state speaks, what should it say?[32]

Limits to Free Speech: Fighting Words

Is there any way to rein in cross burning, gay bashing, slurs against Catholics, and other forms of hateful speech? As you can see from Comparing Nations 5.1, other democracies are much tougher on hurtful speech; so are many colleges and universities. The logic is simple: How can you build a good community if some members feel singled out, threatened, or diminished?

Symbolic expression: An act, rather than actual speech, used to demonstrate a point of view.

● *Is this symbolic speech protected? A closely divided Court ruled yes (left) and no (right).*

Fighting words: Expressions inherently likely to provoke violent reactions and not necessarily protected by the First Amendment.

One legal doctrine offers a limit to hate speech by restricting **fighting words**. The Supreme Court defined these as "personally abusive epithets which, when addressed to the ordinary citizen, are, as a matter of common knowledge, inherently likely to provoke violent reaction."[33] The Court states the principle but has been reluctant to apply it. Reformers trying to create codes of decent language generally rely on the logic of "fighting words"—but it is not easy to restrict speech unless it threatens to lead to criminal action and does not express a specific political position.

What Do YOU Think?   Free Speech on Campus

Around the country, many universities forbid hate speech on campus. They forbid harassment (oral, written, graphic, or physical) against any group that might face discrimination— African Americans, Latinos, LGBTQ people, military veterans, religious denominations, age groups, and others. These codes, in turn, provoke fierce opposition. Critics argue that restrictions on speech create taboo subjects and people with unpopular opinions could end up being expelled. What should campus leaders do?

Yes. Forbid certain hurtful types of expression.
We must protect LGBTQ students, students of color, military veterans, and any other group that faces hatred and violence. Hate speech fractures communities and hurts people. It is frightening and painful to the targeted groups. It poses a threat to teaching and destroys the community spirit necessary for learning.

No. Forbid restrictions on speech regardless of how hurtful.
Everyone has the right to an opinion—even if it is a horrible opinion. We can punish criminal behavior, but we should never punish people for simply expressing their views— especially on a college campus, where exploration of ideas is a core value.

Limited Protections: Student Speech

How about students speaking out? In the 1969 landmark *Tinker* decision, the Court announced that students "do not shed their constitutional right to freedom of speech or expression at the schoolhouse gate." That decision, however, has been qualified in a series of cases that balanced student rights with the schools' educational mission.

In 1965, John (15-years-old) and Mary Beth Tinker (13) violated school rules by wearing black armbands to protest the Vietnam War. They were suspended and told that they could return only when they were ready to abide by the school's rules. The Supreme Court overturned the suspension and established what became known as the Tinker rule: The students' right to free speech could

Joseph Frederick was suspended from Juneau-Douglas High School (Juneau, Alaska) for ten days because of this banner. The Supreme Court upheld the suspension for advocating drugs in violation of the school's antidrug policy. [Morse v. Frederick, 551 U.S. 393 (2007).]

be curtailed only if it "materially and substantially interferes with the requirements of appropriate discipline in the operation of the school."[34]

In subsequent cases, the Court found that teachers and school officials had an obligation to teach students proper conduct and could regulate speech that was vulgar, indecent, offensive (1986), or inconsistent with the educational mission of the school (1988).[35]

School speech debates now face the digital frontier. Social media and other digital communications allow widespread, lightning fast broadcast of information—as well as malicious gossip, cyberbullying, and cruel rumors. By 2018, 48 states had passed laws forbidding online cyberbullying, though some civil liberties advocates critique them as restrictions on protected speech. Across the country, schools have suspended students for posts deemed inappropriate or illegal.

The First Amendment offers students—in high schools or colleges—less protection than it offers adults. School officials may regulate speech as long as they do not do so arbitrarily.

 **The Bottom Line**

» Free speech is crucial to democracy, and the Court gives it a privileged position—even against angry public opposition to flag burning, cross burning, or homophobic displays at military funerals.

» Free speech can be curtailed if it poses a "clear and present danger." Today, the Court requires the danger to be both imminent and likely to occur.

» There are limits to free speech, including fighting words and student speech.

🔒 Freedom of the Press

Freedom of the press follows most of the same rules as freedom of speech. The written word has always been essential to politics. The form changes—pamphlets during the revolutionary period, newspapers in the mid-twentieth century, and new digital media today. Written words share the "preferred position" enjoyed by speech. Broadcast media are slightly different and subject to federal regulation (as we explore in Chapter 9).

Prior Restraint

Prior restraint: Legal effort to stop speech before it occurs.

The effort to stop speech before it occurs is known as **prior restraint**. Although the Supreme Court has permitted government officials to punish people for what they have said or printed, it has never allowed federal government agents to gag citizens before they have had their say.

In 1931, public officials in Minneapolis shut down a newspaper, the *Saturday Press*, which was published by an avowed racist who claimed that Jewish gangs were running the city. In *Near v. Minnesota* (1931), the Court ruled that the state could not suppress the paper, no matter how obnoxious, but it left the door open to prior restraint for national security reasons. The government would be justified for stopping someone from publishing information about "the number and location of troops in the field," it said, but not for publishing anti-Semitic harangues.

In one famous case of prior restraint, a State Department official leaked a rich archive of classified material, the Pentagon Papers, that exposed the mistakes and deceptions that led the United States into the Vietnam War. The Richard Nixon administration, claiming a threat to national security, went to court to block the *New York Times* from publishing the papers. Within days, the Supreme Court heard the arguments and, by a 6–3 vote, lifted the ban and permitted publication. The majority opinion emphasized the "heavy presumption" against prior restraint.[36]

The shift from print media to the Internet has profoundly changed the logic of prior restraint. In 2008, WikiLeaks, a web-based venue for anonymous whistle-blowers, published internal documents from a Swiss bank that appeared to show tax evasion and money laundering at the bank's Cayman Islands branch. The bank went to court and won a restraining order against publication of the leaked documents. Stopping a newspaper from publishing is straightforward: the court enjoins the publisher. However, because WikiLeaks operates anonymously and globally, it is almost impossible for a court to suppress the information it publishes. In the WikiLeaks case, the court tried to seal the site's American address—but the documents simply appeared on mirror sites. After two weeks, Judge Jerry White dissolved the injunction and acknowledged that the court's effort had only publicized the documents. There is "a definite disconnect," he commented, "between the evolution of our constitutional jurisprudence and modern technology."[37]

● *Freedom of the press on the big screen: Academy Awards 2018 "Best Picture" nominee* The Post, *starring Tom Hanks and Meryl Streep, retold the story of the* New York Times's *and, later,* Washington Post's *decision to publish the Pentagon Papers in 1971 despite legal threats from the Nixon administration.*

Then in 2013, Edward Snowden, a contractor working for the National Security Agency (NSA), leaked a huge cache of documents detailing the NSA's extensive data collection. The reports, published in the *Washington Post*, revealed the NSA was collecting metadata on millions of cell phone calls and tapping data from tech companies.

Both the WikiLeaks and Snowden stories illustrate how new media renders the government helpless against the spread of embarrassing and potentially harmful electronic information. By flowing anonymously across national borders and court jurisdictions, new media pose dilemmas for every nation as it tries to regulate the written word. The old question was "should prior restraint be permitted?" The new question is whether it is possible at all.

Obscenity

The First Amendment does not protect obscenity. However, the courts always face the same problem: What is obscene? Justice Potter Stewart put it famously when he said simply, "I know it when I see it." Of course, different people see "it" in different things. The Court's emphasis on free speech leads it to reject aggressive regulation of obscenity.

In *Miller v. California* (1973), the Supreme Court created a three-part test for judging a work to be obscene. The **Miller test** holds that speech is not protected by the First Amendment if it has all three of these characteristics:

> **Miller test:** Three-part test for judging whether a work is obscene (if it has all three, the work loses First Amendment protection).

1. "The average person, applying contemporary community standards, would find that the work, taken as a whole, appeals to the prurient interest" (meaning that it is meant to be sexually stimulating).

2. It depicts sexual conduct in a "patently offensive way."

3. The work lacks "serious literary, artistic, political or scientific value."

The Miller test only created new questions. What does it mean to be patently offensive? Offensive to whom? How do we rely on community standards of decency when the Internet and digital media flow across borders?

In recent years, the Court has been hostile to most efforts at banning material. It struck down a congressional effort to ban online material that showed "sexual, excretory activities or organs." In an especially grisly case, it even rejected legislation prohibiting the portrayal of animal cruelty. The ban had tried to forbid "crush videos" in which women wearing high heels crush dogs, cats, and hamsters while engaging in "a kind of dominatrix patter."[38] Congress subsequently rewrote the law to get around this Court ruling and outlawed crush videos.

Feminist scholars have tried to change the framework of this debate. Pornography, they argued, subordinates women in the same way that hate speech demeans minorities. Nations such as Canada have essentially accepted this perspective. Although U.S. courts have not taken this view—and continue to protect hate speech—the feminist position continues to be an important part of the debate.[39]

Social media has given rise to a new phenomenon, "revenge porn," in which explicit photos or videos are posted online without the subject's consent. Most states now outlaw revenge porn and Congress has expressed rare bipartisan support for making it a federal crime. The courts, however, have been skeptical, striking down laws in Arizona, Vermont, and Minnesota. The Supreme Court has yet to weigh in.

Listen to Tom Lehrer's song about *Miller v California*.

Explore current censorship issues.

● *Almost anything goes. It is very difficult to win a libel judgment. Singer-songwriter Ciara filed a $15 million suit against her then-partner, Future, for his derogatory tweets. She soon dropped the case. Defamation suits are very difficult to win.*

The Court flatly forbids child pornography—a sharp limit to free speech. Even here, the Court struck down an earlier effort, the Child Pornography Act of 1996, because it criminalized too broadly—people might be prosecuted for possession of sexual images that were digitally altered or that involved people who were not minors. Led by evangelical conservatives, Congress rewrote the law to forbid presenting material that led someone to believe it included "minors engaging in sexually explicit conduct." In 2008, the Supreme Court upheld the revised law. The case involved a man who boasted online, "Dad of toddler has 'good' pics of her and me for swap of your toddler pics, or live cam." He followed up with hard-core images of minors engaged in sexual behavior. Even in this case, two members of the Court disagreed. They argued that even under the revised law, individuals could be prosecuted for selling images that were not actually illegal but that simply fooled the buyer into thinking that they were. The Court is so sensitive to free speech that even in a case like this one, two justices insisted on being cautious.[40]

Libel

There are also limits to the false things one can write or say about someone. Written falsehoods are known as *libel*, spoken falsehoods are known as *slander*. The courts have made it very difficult for public officials or celebrities to win a libel (or slander) judgment. To do so, they must prove not just that a statement was false and that it caused them harm but that it was made with malice or "a reckless disregard for the truth."

Today, the Court allows even outrageous claims, cartoons, spoofs, and criticism directed at public officials and celebrities. By contrast, English law is just the opposite: It puts the burden of proof on the writers to prove the truth of what they have written. President Trump has repeatedly attacked the American libel laws, calling them "a sham and a disgrace." Supporters see this as part of Donald Trump's effort to shake up American politics and law, but given the Court's position on free speech, it will be difficult to make changes.[41]

 **The Bottom Line**

» The rules for freedom of the press reflect those of free speech and strongly protect free expression.

» The courts are especially skeptical of any effort to impose prior restraint. New media make it almost impossible to even try.

» Obscenity is not protected by the First Amendment. The Court has spent a long time wrestling with what counts as obscenity and now uses the three-part Miller test.

The Right to Bear Arms

The Second Amendment asserts a uniquely American right. No other national constitution includes the right to bear arms. The text in the Constitution is ambiguous:

> *A well-regulated militia, being necessary to the security of a free state, the right of the people to keep and bear arms shall not be infringed.*

On one reading, this amendment simply protects colonial-era militias. On another, it guarantees the right to own weapons. Recently, the Supreme Court has rendered a decisive ruling—by a 5–4 vote—guaranteeing the right to bear arms. Consider each side of the argument.

A Relic of the Revolution?

Skeptics question whether Americans have any right to bear arms at all. The Second Amendment, they say, protected state militias. Early Americans believed that only kings and tyrants kept permanent armies. In a republic, the citizens volunteered for service in local militias that defended their communities and their nation. The Second Amendment, in this reading, is a "relic of the American Revolution"[42] and simply forbids the national government from disarming the local militias. It does not involve a constitutional right to tote weapons.

Those who favor this view generally emphasize public safety and gun control. They argue that America's high homicide rate—over 9,300 killed or wounded in mass shootings since the Sandy Hook Elementary massacre in 2012—reflects the easy availability of rapid-fire, high capacity weapons in the United States.[43]

The Palladium of All Liberties?

Proponents of gun rights read the same constitutional sentence very differently. As Justice Scalia explained, the Second Amendment has two parts—a preface about militias and a clause that really matters, declaring that "the right . . . to keep and bear arms shall not be infringed." Many see the right to bear arms as the most important right of all—"the palladium of the liberties of the republic," as Justice Joseph Story put it back in 1833. "When all else fails," declared Charlton Heston, actor and longtime honorary president of the National Rifle Association, "it is the one right that prevails. . . . It is the one right that allows rights to exist at all."[44]

The Supreme Court has been moving decisively to defend gun rights. In 2008, the Court struck down a District of Columbia rule that restricted guns in people's homes.[45] In 2010, in *McDonald v. Chicago*, the Court finally *incorporated* the Second Amendment. For the first time, the constitutional right to bear arms applied to state and local governments. The *McDonald* decision seemed to make it more difficult for cities and states to regulate weapons—but in the years since, most state and local restrictions have been upheld. Florida's governor, in the wake of a Parkland High School mass shooting in 2018, signed into law the most significant gun restrictions in that state in decades.[46]

A seller prepares weapons for a gun show. Americans disagree about whether guns should be heavily regulated, as in most advanced democracies, or whether existing regulation should be removed.

Guns on Campus

SHOULD COLLEGES ALLOW CONCEALED CARRY?

The Second Amendment's ambiguous "right to bear arms" guarantee has been a source of much debate virtually since the Bill of Rights was first introduced. College campuses historically have enjoyed low homicide rates.[47] However, after a shooting at Virginia Tech in 2007 left thirty-two people dead, political science major Chris Brown founded Students for Concealed Carry to lift bans on campuses. The map shows which states allow concealed carry, which ban it, and which leave it up to the campuses to decide.

THINK ABOUT IT

What policies have most states adopted on this issue? Do you see trends among the more liberal states of the northeast or the more conservative states of the South?

Do students carrying concealed weapons make your campus safer? Or less safe? Why?

Source: National Conference of State Legislatures

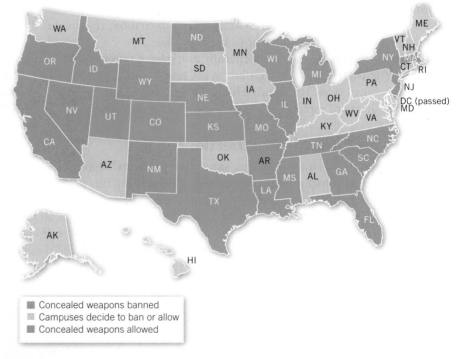

Concealed weapons laws

- Concealed weapons banned
- Campuses decide to ban or allow
- Concealed weapons allowed

Assess current debates on the Second Amendment.

Few rights issues have split Americans like the Second Amendment. Conservative and rural Americans generally defend gun rights, which they view as deeply rooted in American culture and essential to personal protection. Liberals fear carnage: domestic disputes turn deadly, children kill their friends, and urban neighborhoods become combat zones. Mass shootings keep this issue on the political agenda.

 **The Bottom Line**

» Some critics see the Second Amendment as an outmoded defense of citizen militias.

» Others see it as an important individual right—perhaps even the most important right in the entire Constitution.

» In 2010, the Supreme Court incorporated the right to bear arms as an essential individual right, though state and local restrictions have largely been upheld in lower courts.

The Rights of the Accused

The Bill of Rights places special emphasis on protecting people accused of crimes. Four amendments (Four, Five, Six, and Eight) together list thirty-one different rights for those who face criminal charges. No other issue gets as much attention. Protecting the accused involves another careful balancing act. On one hand, the courts must restrain law enforcement and defend the constitutional freedoms that define America. Yet too many curbs on law enforcement might lead to more crime. After vastly expanding the rights of the accused in the 1960s, the courts—in step with Congress, presidents of both parties, and most states—now tilt firmly toward law enforcement. However, American incarceration rates are the world's highest and especially affect minority communities—leading to calls for a renewed emphasis on rights.

In this section, we examine the most important (and controversial) protections one at a time. As you read, think about the trade-offs between safe streets and civil liberties. There are solid arguments on both sides of the issue.

The Fourth Amendment: Search and Seizure

The Fourth Amendment protects people from government officials bursting into their houses.

> *The right of the people to be secure in their persons, houses, papers, and effects, against unreasonable searches and seizures, shall not be violated, and no Warrants shall issue, but upon probable cause, supported by Oath or affirmation, and particularly describing the place to be searched, and the persons or things to be seized. . . .*

British officials in the 1770s ransacked colonial homes, searching for weapons or smuggled goods. The Fourth Amendment prevents that from happening. Justice Louis Brandeis described it as "the right to be left alone—the . . . right most valued by civilized men."[48] The police may not enter a home unless they go before a judge and explain why they suspect that evidence of a crime can be found in a specific place. The judge determines whether there is "probable cause" to issue the warrant. It sounds simple, but there are large gray areas (see Figure 5.1).

The landmark search and seizure case began in 1957 with a tip that Dollree (Dolly) Mapp was hiding a bombing suspect in her apartment. In addition, the police suspected she had illegal gambling paraphernalia there. The police knocked at her door, but she refused to let them in. They eventually broke the door down, and when she demanded to see a warrant they waved a piece of paper—not a warrant—in the air. The police searched the apartment and the basement. They never found the bombing suspect or the gambling material, but they did discover a suitcase of pornographic material—which was then illegal. Mapp was convicted on obscenity charges. The Supreme Court threw out the conviction and, in *Mapp v. Ohio* (1961, decided 6–3), devised the **exclusionary rule**: Evidence obtained in an illegal search may not be introduced in a trial. Even evidence that clearly proves someone is guilty of a crime may not be used if it was improperly obtained.

Exclusionary rule: The ruling that evidence obtained in an illegal search may not be introduced in a trial.

Twenty years later, President Ronald Reagan (1981–1989) urged both Congress and the courts to abolish the rule. Supreme Court Chief Justice John Roberts, then a young Justice Department attorney, wrote the memos supporting Reagan's criticism. During the Reagan years, the courts began making exceptions to the exclusionary rule. For example, in 1984, police arrested Alberto Leon when they discovered a large quantity of illegal drugs in his possession. Their warrant had expired, but the Supreme Court made a "good faith" exception and permitted the drugs to be introduced as evidence.[49] In 2009, Justice Roberts wrote (in a 5–4 opinion) that there was no need to exclude evidence if the police had violated a suspect's Fourth Amendment rights because of "isolated negligence."[50]

Do police need a warrant to . . .

Install a wiretap/listening device on phones?	Strip search a student?	Search a cell phone, or track someone's location via their smartphone?	Search garbage left on the curb?
Sometimes	Yes	Yes	No
Search a college/university dorm room?	Search a car?	Search a student's belongings?	Pat down "suspicious looking" people on the street?
Sometimes	No	No	No
Use a drug sniffing dog?	Use thermal imaging?	Use GPS to track a car?	Aerial search?
Sometimes	Yes	Yes	No

● **Figure 5.1** *When are search warrants required?*

In 2011 the Supreme Court crossed an important threshold. It permitted officers to break into a house without a warrant. The officers in the case knocked, identified themselves, and heard movements that sounded like the destruction of evidence of drug use. Only one justice dissented. This ruling would, wrote Justice Ruth Bader Ginsburg, seriously curtail the use of warrants by police. Writing for the majority, Justice Samuel Alito took a hard line. Residents who "attempt to destroy evidence have only themselves to blame." In 2016, the Court ruled 6–3 that evidence would have to be excluded "if there were flagrant police misconduct." In short, the courts have increasingly loosened—but not eliminated—the exclusionary rule.[51]

The Fifth Amendment: Rights at Trials

The Fifth Amendment lists a long series of rights focused largely on criminal trials. Consider them one clause at a time.

> *No person shall be held to answer for a capital, or otherwise infamous crime, unless on a . . . indictment of a Grand Jury.*

Before the government can prosecute, it must persuade a jury. A **grand jury** does not decide on guilt or innocence but only on whether there is enough evidence for the case to go to trial. The grand jury meets secretly and hears only from the prosecutor, so, as one New York judge once quipped, a decent prosecutor should be able to get a grand jury to "indict a ham sandwich."[52] As the Supreme Court has never incorporated the grand jury, this provision does not apply to the states. After the grand jury indicts, a petit (or small) jury of six to twelve individuals hears the case, weighs the evidence, and delivers a verdict.

Grand jury: A jury that does not decide on guilt or innocence but only on whether there is enough evidence for the case to go to trial.

> *. . . nor shall any person be subject for the same offense to be twice put in jeopardy of life or limb.*

An individual cannot face **double jeopardy**, or be tried twice for the same offense. ("Jeopardy of life and limb" refers to the old colonial practice of punishing people by lopping off an ear or damaging other limbs.) Without this provision, the government could simply keep trying people over and over.

Despite this prohibition, individuals sometimes face multiple trials. They can be tried on different charges, tried in federal court after being acquitted in state court, and—if they are acquitted on criminal charges—sued for damages. In a famous case, former football star O. J. Simpson was acquitted of murdering his wife and her companion, only to lose a civil judgment for damages to the victims' families.

Double jeopardy: The principle that an individual cannot be tried twice for the same offense.

> *. . . nor shall be compelled in any criminal case to be a witness against himself.*

The Constitution aimed to protect citizens from torture and coerced confessions. The liberal Warren Court affirmed this right by requiring police officers to inform suspects that they have the right to remain silent, now known as the **Miranda warnings**, after *Miranda v. Arizona* (1966). In this case, the Court ruled that any evidence acquired before the warning would not be admissible in court. The ruling created an enormous outcry. Richard Nixon used *Miranda* in the 1968 presidential campaign as evidence that the United States had grown "soft on crime." Congress tried to pass a law to get around the ruling, which the Court eventually struck down.[53]

Miranda warnings: A set of rights that police officers are required to inform suspects of, including the right to remain silent.

Over the past forty years, the courts have limited the *Miranda* rights—permitting confessions made to a police officer posing as another inmate (1990), carving out an exception for public safety (1984), and limiting the rules when defendants take the stand in their own defense (1970).[54]

The controversy subsided long ago, however, and the Miranda warnings have become "part of national culture," as Chief Justice William Rehnquist put it. Every TV cop show ends with the police nabbing the criminal while intoning, "You have the right to remain silent." Some defense lawyers claim, half seriously, the phrase is now so familiar that what defendants actually hear is, "We've caught you, and you're in big trouble now."

The Sixth Amendment: The Right to Counsel

The Sixth Amendment guarantees a speedy and public trial decided by an impartial jury. It includes another important provision, the right to counsel:

> *In all criminal prosecutions, the accused shall . . . have the assistance of counsel for his defense.*

The Supreme Court weighed in on this issue in an explosive case known as the trial of the Scottsboro Boys. In 1931, nine young African American men riding a freight train in Alabama were accused of raping two white women. Although the charges were false (one woman immediately recanted), angry mobs gathered, and eight of the young men were rushed through trials and condemned to death. In *Powell v. Alabama* (1932), the Court ruled that, at least in a capital case (a case that could end in the death penalty), the defendants are entitled to lawyers, who must be given enough time to meet with their clients and prepare their case. The Scottsboro case was a civil rights breakthrough for another reason: None of the African Americans unfairly accused of raping a white woman were executed—though seven of the nine spent years in jail.

In 1963, the Court expanded the right to counsel to all felony cases (a felony is a crime punishable by at least one year in prison). Clarence Gideon, a Florida drifter, was allegedly caught breaking into a poolroom from which he had stolen beer, soft drinks, and change out of the jukebox. When he came to trial, he demanded a lawyer, but the Florida court denied the request. Gideon was convicted and sentenced to five years, but from his jail cell, working with legal texts, he scrawled an appeal. "Something astonishing . . . happened," wrote Anthony Lewis in a book on the case. "This loser's plea made it all the way to the Supreme Court." In *Gideon v. Wainwright*

The Scottsboro Boys, with their attorney Samuel Leibowitz.

(1963), the Supreme Court ruled that the Sixth Amendment supported his claim and that the state must provide a lawyer to defend those who cannot afford one. With a competent lawyer, Gideon was acquitted. Attorney General Robert Kennedy commented, "An obscure Florida convict changed . . . the whole course of American legal history."[55] A network of public defenders soon spread across the country.

In 2012, the Court dramatically increased the scope of the right to competent counsel by holding that defendants have a constitutional right to effective attorneys during plea bargain negotiations (in a 5–4 ruling). Today, almost all federal (97%) and most state (94%) felony charges involve a plea bargain, in which the defendant pleads guilty in exchange for a lighter sentence without actually going through a formal trial. With American courts clogged by arrest backlogs, this is one way to get the cases through the system.[56]

In practice, the right to counsel has grown increasingly difficult to maintain. The public is reluctant to spend tax revenues on lawyers who defend poor men and women accused of crimes. Public defenders face huge caseloads and small salaries—a Department of Justice study reported legal aid attorneys handle as many as 900 felony cases per year.[57] At the state level, the caseload is also overwhelming. The forty-nine public defenders in Rhode Island handled 15,000 cases in 2017.[58] For all the problems, however, publicly funded criminal defense remains an essential—if endangered—part of civil liberty and American justice.

The Eighth Amendment: The Death Penalty

The Eighth Amendment introduces the question of capital punishment.

> *Cruel and unusual punishment . . . shall not be . . . inflicted.*

Is execution cruel and unusual punishment? Around the world, 101 nations have abolished the death penalty—including all the nations of Western Europe, where it is considered a violation of human rights. In contrast, the United States executed twenty-three people in 2017 and 366 in the last decade. Although the number of executions has been falling steadily, more than 2,800 men and women have been sentenced to capital punishment and are waiting on death row (see Figure 5.2). Public support for the death penalty has fallen below 50 percent and is now at a forty-four-year low.

Proponents argue that some crimes are so terrible that justice demands capital punishment. It brings closure to grieving families. It may deter future murders (although there is no definitive evidence one way or the other). Moreover, they argue, some criminals are so dangerous that they should be executed to protect other prisoners, prison officials, and the general public.

Opponents respond that killing people is immoral and that no government should be given the power to "play God." Because social systems are imperfect some—perhaps many—innocent people will be executed. The system is tilted against African Americans; blacks make up 12 percent of the population but, from year to year, between a quarter and half of those executed. In 2018, 41 percent of the inmates on death row were African American and another 13 percent were Latinos. Repeated studies have shown that in capital cases, the race of the victim is a crucial matter—members of minority groups accused of murdering white people are the most likely to receive the death penalty.[59]

What Do YOU Think?   End the Death Penalty?

Many citizens call for ending the death penalty. Is capital punishment a form of "cruel and unusual punishment" and therefore banned by the Eighth Amendment?

No.

Some crimes are so terrible that they require this punishment. Justice demands it. It brings closure to the victims' families. American public opinion supports it. If there is a deterrent effect, executing criminals might save innocent lives. Some criminals are so hardened that they pose a safety threat to other prisoners, to prison officials, and to the public. Finally, multiple safeguards are in place to guarantee that innocent people are not executed.

Yes.

It is time for the United States to join the other industrial democracies. Executions are unfair and are meted out almost entirely to poor and black and Latino defendants accused of killing white victims. No government should have this power. Killing is morally wrong, and two wrongs do not make a right. Furthermore, it is impossible to ensure that no innocent people will be killed. The deterrent effect has not been proven. Tellingly, the American Medical Association refuses to let physicians participate in administering the death penalty.

Executions by State

■ States that executed in 2017-18
■ States that executed in the last five years
■ No executions in the last five years

● **Figure 5.2** *Map of executions in the United States (Death Penalty Information Center).*

In 1972, the Supreme Court halted all executions, arguing that state laws were so vague that similar cases produced different outcomes. "The death standards are cruel and unusual," wrote Justice Potter Stewart in *Furman v. Georgia*, "the same way that being struck by lightning is cruel and unusual"—meaning that death sentences seemed to be meted out randomly. Thirty-five states drafted new capital punishment laws using *Furman* as a guide. In 1976, the Court permitted executions to go forward when state statutes included clear criteria to guide judge and jury in weighing death sentences. However, nearly three-fourths of all executions since 1976 have taken place in seven states (all in the south).[60]

Beginning in 1992, a network of law students and their professors began to use DNA evidence to review capital cases. Working together as the "Innocence Project," they have documented false convictions of over 354 inmates, 161 of whom were convicted of capital crimes. All those exonerated have now been released.[61]

The Court has imposed additional death-penalty limits. It has ruled that it is "cruel and unusual" to execute people convicted of crimes other than murder, striking down five state laws that allowed execution for child rape (2008). It has forbidden the execution of mentally ill individuals (2002) and of juvenile offenders (2005). In a much-discussed case, however, the Court ruled that lethal injections did not constitute cruel and unusual punishment despite the claim that they caused "an intolerable risk of pain" (2007).[62]

 **The Bottom Line**

» The Bill of Rights places special emphasis on the rights of those accused of crimes. Even so, American incarceration rates are the highest in the world.

» The police may not search or seize without a warrant (with minor exceptions); they must inform suspects of their right to remain silent; the accused have a right to legal counsel. The courts have widened the right to counsel, but it is often limited by a lack of funding for public defenders.

» Under current interpretation, capital punishment is not considered "cruel and unusual punishment." However, the number of executions has been falling and public support has waned.

» Between 1962 and 1968, the Supreme Court vastly expanded the rights of the accused. Recent Court decisions have tilted the balance back toward law enforcement.

Terrorism, Non-Citizens, and Civil Liberties

After the terrorist attacks on September 11, 2001, Congress passed the **USA Patriot Act**. In the fear and emotion of the terrible moment, only a few criticized the legislation. The act enhanced security by removing restrictions on law enforcement. Removing restrictions, however, means limiting rights. The Patriot Act, the broader campaign against terrorism, and continued terrorism around the world have revived a long-standing national debate: How do we balance civil liberties and public safety?

USA Patriot Act: Legislation that sought to enhance national security, passed in the aftermath of the September 11, 2001, terrorist attacks.

Contacts with Forbidden Groups

The federal government enhanced rules that bar Americans from offering aid to terrorist organizations. For example, some 150 Americans were arrested for assisting ISIS, a terrorist organization that posted grisly beheading videos as recruitment tools.[63] Although the law forbids aiding terrorist organizations, expressing general support for such an organization is protected speech.

Drawing the line between public safety and free speech remains hotly contested. For now, U.S. courts permit the government to prosecute web postings if they provide funding or other specialized assistance to terrorist groups. What do you think? Is there an obvious balance between protecting free speech and fighting terrorism?

 *Terrorist attacks and mass shootings raise the question of how to balance national security with privacy rights.*

Surveillance

Domestic surveillance requires a warrant. To prevent terror attacks, however, the Bush, Obama, and Trump administrations all permitted the NSA to conduct international surveillance without a search warrant. Major controversy erupted in 2013 around the Snowden leaks described earlier in this chapter. Snowden revealed that the NSA has been collecting bulk data—over a trillion pieces of information—on phone calls, computer searches, texts, and more. The phone data include the caller, receiver, date and time of the call, and length of the call—but not a transcript of the conversation itself. While the revelations created an uproar and calls for reform, Congress eventually reauthorized the surveillance program for six years without major new protections.[64]

The Rights of Non-Citizens

The war on terror prompted many questions around a more general question: What are the constitutional rights of non-citizens? A long body of case law, going back to the nineteenth century, extends most basic Constitutional rights to non-citizens—if someone is stopped by the police, for example, they have the same Miranda rights whether they are citizens, legal immigrants, or people without documentation. State governments may not pass laws that single out immigrants and discriminate against them.

There is one major difference, however: Immigration laws apply to non-citizens and, in that context, the procedural standards are different and ruled by the immigration laws themselves. There are still some rights—the right to remain silent and the right to legal counsel—but they are far more restricted.

The Trump administration's vigorous push against undocumented individuals or immigrants from certain countries puts this issue in a spotlight and raises a still more complicated issue: How does the Constitution apply to immigrants not yet in the United States (standing before a customs agent at the airport, for example)? The courts will be grappling with that question for a long time to come.

The Bottom Line

» The response to 9/11 and subsequent terrorist attacks created a debate about the balance between civil liberties and public safety.

» With the Snowden revelations, controversy arose about the NSA data collection of phone records and Internet surveillance.

» Although Congress passed legislation with some limits after the revelations, in 2018, Congress reauthorized the surveillance without major new protections.

» Most Constitutional rights apply to non-citizens. However, they are also ruled by immigration laws that offer more limited rights.

🔵 Conclusion: The Dilemma of Civil Liberties

How should the government balance its duty to keep the public safe, or to uphold public moral standards, with its responsibility to protect civil liberties? This is one of the most important issues facing American democracy today. If we tilt too far toward combating terrorism or outlawing practices considered socially unacceptable, Americans will lose the liberties that have defined the nation since 1776. If we tilt too far the other way, the nation may be vulnerable to attacks or lose its moral core. Getting the balance right is a major challenge facing Americans. The courts take the lead in protecting rights, but elected public officials define the policies that the courts are weighing. Ultimately, the balance between communal needs and individual rights is in the hands of the voters.

Isn't that exactly where it belongs? No. Recall the Supreme Court's judgment in 1943 when it reversed its earlier decision and protected the Jehovah's Witnesses: "The very purpose of a Bill of Rights was to withdraw certain subjects from the vicissitudes of political controversy, to place them beyond the reach of majorities and officials and to establish them as legal principles to be applied by the courts." A core point of civil liberties is to protect the rights of individuals—even if it means overruling the majority of the country.

CHAPTER SUMMARY

🔘 Civil liberties are the limits we put on governing bodies (and the majorities that elect them) so that individuals can exercise their rights and freedom. Disputes are usually resolved by the courts and guided by the Bill of Rights.

🔘 The Bill of Rights did not apply to the states until the Fourteenth Amendment required that *no state* could deprive any citizen of life, liberty, or property.

🔘 The Supreme Court applied the Bill of Rights to the states, one right at a time. It began in 1897 (no taking property without compensation) and continued until 2010 (the right to bear arms limits state and local governments). This process is known as *incorporation*.

🔘 The Court discovered a right to privacy implicit (in the shadows) in the First, Third, Fourth, Fifth, and Ninth Amendments. The Court applied the right to privacy to strike down laws banning abortion. In *Roe v. Wade*, the Court issued a rule prohibiting states from interfering during the first trimester. In *Planned Parenthood v. Casey*, the Court replaced the rule with standard forbidding laws that put "an undue burden" on the right to privacy. The Court extended privacy rights to same-sex couples by striking down antisodomy laws in 2003.

🔘 The Constitution includes two religious restrictions on government. The Establishment Clause bans the government from establishing (or favoring) a religion. In one view, this means separating church and state. For many years, the three-part Lemon test guided judicial decisions in cases involving religion. A more recent view requires simply that government not promote one religious view over another.

🔘 The Constitution also forbids government from interfering with religious practice (the free exercise clause.) The courts traditionally

Check your understanding of Chapter 5.

asked if the government had a compelling interest for imposing a burden—the Sherbert test. In 1990, the Court shifted and required only that the government action be neutral and that it would apply to everyone. Congress, state governments, and religious groups pushed back and the courts have, once again, returned to the traditional Sherbert test.

🔵 Free speech is crucial to democracy, and the Court gives it a privileged position—even against angry public opposition to flag burning, cross burning, or homophobic displays at military funerals. Free speech can be curtailed if it poses a "clear and present danger." Today, the Court requires the danger to be both imminent and likely to occur. There are limits to free speech involving fighting words, student speech, commercial speech, and obscenity.

🔵 Some critics see the Second Amendment as an outmoded defense of citizen militias. Others see the right to bear arms as an important individual right—perhaps the most important liberty in the Constitution. In 2010, the Supreme Court ruled it an essential constitutional right.

🔵 The Bill of Rights places special emphasis on the civil liberties of those accused of crimes. Even so, American incarceration rates are the highest in the world. The police may not search or seize without a warrant, they must inform suspects of their right to remain silent, and the accused have a right to legal counsel. Under current interpretation, capital punishment is not considered "cruel and unusual punishment—but public opinion appears to be slowly changing."

Need to review key ideas in greater depth? Click here.

Flashcard review.

KEY TERMS

Accommodation, p. 136
Civil liberties, p. 126
Clear and present danger, p. 139
Double jeopardy, p. 151
Establishment clause, p. 134
Exclusionary rule, p. 150
Fighting words, p. 142

Free exercise clause, p. 134
Grand jury, p. 151
Hate speech, p. 138
Judicial rules, p. 133
Judicial standards, p. 133
Miranda warnings, p. 151
Miller test, p. 145

Prior restraint, p. 144
Selective incorporation, p. 129
Strict separation, p. 136
Symbolic expression, p. 141
USA Patriot Act, p. 155

STUDY QUESTIONS

1. What are civil liberties? How are they different from civil rights?

2. In *Barron v. Baltimore*, the Supreme Court ruled that the Fifth Amendment did not protect a landowner if the state took his property. Why?

3. Describe how the Bill of Rights was applied to the state governments. First, describe the constitutional amendment that directly addressed the states. Then describe the process of incorporation by which the Supreme Court applied the Bill of Rights to the states.

4. Describe how the Supreme Court declared the right to privacy. Discuss the case from a pragmatist's and an originalist's perspective. Would you vote to maintain the right to privacy? Or would you overrule the precedent? Explain your reasoning.

5. Describe the three-part Lemon test for determining whether a state action violates the establishment clause. The late Justice Scalia was highly critical of the Lemon test. What was his view? Do you agree or not? Explain why.

6. Sometimes the Court permits a racist to burn a cross—and sometimes forbids it. Explain the reasoning in each case. Do you agree with the Court's distinction, or would you rule differently?

7. There are two interpretations of the Second Amendment right to bear arms. Describe each. Which do you support? Why?

8. The Supreme Court gives free speech a "privileged position" among the rights in the Bill of Rights. What does that mean? How does the Court justify that position?

9. Feminist scholars argue that privileging free speech in pornography cases actually undermines free speech. What is their argument? Do you agree or disagree? Explain why.

10. How does NSA surveillance raise questions about the balance between public safety and civil liberties? How do you think civil liberties should be balanced with protection against terrorism? If you had to emphasize one goal more than the other, which would you emphasize? Why?

Go to www.oup.com/us/Morone to find quizzes, flash cards, simulations, tutorials, videos, and other study tools.

6 The Struggle for Civil Rights

IN AUGUST 2017, hundreds of white supremacists arrived in Charlottesville, Virginia, to protest the city's decision to remove a statue of Confederate General Robert E. Lee. On Friday night, holding torches, they marched across the historic University of Virginia campus and chanted "you will not replace us," "Jews will not replace us," "white lives matter," and "blood and soil," a Nazi slogan. Counter-protesters greeted them with cries of "No Nazis! No KKK! No fascist USA!" and "black lives matter." Fights erupted. Police arrived, declared the assembly unlawful, and shut it down.

The next day, a larger group of white supremacist neo-Nazis, some carrying shields, pikes, and rifles, marched toward the statue of Robert E. Lee in Emancipation Park. Members of the college community, gathering in counter-protest, were shocked to face the mass bigotry. Thirty ministers locked arms in prayer at the entrance to the park in an attempt to keep the protesters out. As fights flared up amid more taunting, the police separated demonstrators and counter-demonstrators.

Then a sad day turned tragic. One of the white supremacists roared his car into the crowd that had come to stand up against racism. Nineteen were injured and thirty-two-year-old Heather Heyer lay dead.[1] Americans were stunned. President Trump sparked an uproar by saying "there were good people on both sides." Neo-Nazi websites hailed the reaction.[2] Suddenly, the ugliest features of America's racial past seemed to have leapt into the present.

Who are we? A profoundly diverse nation, founded on the idea that all people are "created equal" and "endowed" with "unalienable rights" including "life, liberty and the pursuit of happiness." We are also a nation that often fails to live up to its noble founding vision.

Civil rights are the freedom to participate in the life of the community—to vote in elections, to enjoy public facilities such as parks, and to take full advantage of economic opportunities like good jobs. People face discrimination when they are denied rights and opportunities because of their race, gender, ethnicity, religion, disabilities, age, or other personal characteristics. Once citizens have won their rights, public attention shifts to protecting them. We covered those protections—known as civil liberties—in Chapter 5. The long battle to win civil rights is perhaps the most powerful story in American history. It reveals the deepest truths about the United States and its values. It tells us who we are—and who we strive to be.

In this chapter, you will:

- Explore the seven steps to winning civil rights in the United States.

- Review the African American experience that set the pattern for civil rights.

- Assess women's quest for economic and political rights.

- Examine the political experience of Hispanics, Asians, and Native Americans.

- Consider the civil rights of other groups, including disabled people, same-sex partners, and transgender individuals.

Civil rights: The freedom to participate in the full life of the community—to vote, use public facilities, and exercise equal economic opportunity.

● White supremacists and neo-Nazis marched on Charlottesville, Virginia, clashing with Antifa, a violent left-wing group, and local counterprotesters. These events shocked the nation.

We can view the history of civil rights in two different ways. Some observers see a steady march toward a deeper and richer American equality. Sixty years ago, white supremacists would not have faced so many counter-protesters. African Americans were still restricted from voting in many southern states, and prestigious professions were closed to them. Today African Americans are CEOs of *Fortune* 500 companies and head elite academic institutions—and one recently served two terms as U.S. president. Forty years ago, only one woman in American history had won a U.S. Senate seat in her own right. Today, the Senate includes twenty-four women and the U.S. House more than one hundred, both the most in history. From this perspective, the American promise faces many obstacles but marches relentlessly on.[3]

Other observers, however, believe that there is nothing inevitable about civil rights. Sometimes rights expand, sometimes they contract. Yes, Asians won full rights, but Native Americans did not. African Americans scaled the old barriers, but many still face the daily stress of racism. Black Americans are more likely than whites to live in poverty or face jail time. There is nothing inevitable about American equality, say proponents of this perspective, and citizens should never take it for granted.[4]

As you read this chapter, ask which view seems most accurate to you: Has the United States advanced consistently toward greater civil rights for all? Or has the progress been unsteady? Whatever your answer, continue to ask: What can and should we do to ensure fair treatment for everyone?

Winning Rights: The Political Process

How does a group win political rights? Each civil rights campaign has its own unique history. However, the efforts usually involve the following stages—not necessarily in order.

Seven Steps to Political Equality

1. *A group defines itself.* Discrimination usually stretches back through time and seeps into the way the powerful view others: whites ruled blacks, men took responsibility for "the weaker sex," Indians were "savages," society pitied the disabled, and psychiatrists defined homosexuality as an illness. In the first step toward civil rights, a group embraces its shared identity and redefines itself as a victim of discrimination. Groups usually reject their old, often-demeaning label and adopt a new name: Negroes, Miss, queers, and cripples became African Americans, Ms., LGBTQ individuals, and persons with disabilities.

2. *The group challenges society.* The next step involves entering the political arena and demanding rights. Civil rights campaigns often go beyond normal politics and include marches, demonstrations, creative protests (such as kneel-ins before segregated churches), and even riots.

BY THE NUMBERS
Civil Rights

Number of black mayors in 1965	**0**
Number of black mayors in 2019	**Over 600[5]**
Percentage of southern students who attended integrated schools eight years after *Brown v. Board of Education* (ruling in 1954)	**1**
Percentage of southern students who attended integrated schools eight years after the passage of the Civil Rights Act of 1964	**91**
Percentage of white and black Americans, respectively, who were poor in 1959	**18, 55**
Percentage of white, black, and Hispanic Americans, respectively, who are poor today	**8.7, 21, 18[6]**
Number of Hispanic members of Congress in 1990, 2000, and 2019 respectively	**10, 18, 42**
Year the Supreme Court struck down laws forbidding marriage between blacks and whites	**1968**
Percentages of whites, blacks, Hispanics, and Asians, respectively, married to a member of a different race today	**11, 18, 27, 28[7]**
Percentage of whites, Latinos, and blacks, respectively, who report "a great deal" or "a fair amount" of confidence in the police	**61, 45, 30[8]**

How far have we come in achieving civil rights for all people? How far do we have to go?

3. *The stories change.* Civil rights always involve a contest over the stories that a society tells about a group. Why does the United States discriminate against people in the first place? Because the majority portrays a group as dangerous, inferior, or helpless. Winning rights requires changing the story. As you read about efforts to secure rights—past and present—be alert to the many different stories we tell about the groups in our society.

4. *Federalism comes into play.* Civil rights politics splashes across local, state, and federal governments. Because many minority groups are concentrated

How does the 14th Amendment apply to different groups?

in certain states and regions, discrimination often begins on the local level. Furthermore, state and local officials control many of the policies that affect civil rights: education, law enforcement, and voting rules. In other cases, states and localities first introduce reforms: Before the Nineteenth Amendment established women's suffrage nationally, women won voting rights in western states.

5. *The executive branch often breaks the ice.* Presidents can issue executive orders (rules that have the force of law but do not require congressional approval) that can create opportunities and momentum for a civil rights campaign. President Truman desegregated the U.S. military in 1948, and President Obama extended protections for gender identity in 2014.

6. *Congress passes blockbuster legislation.* Typically, it is Congress that passes the great changes that finally secure civil rights and echo through history. The Fourteenth Amendment to the Constitution, ratified in 1868, still dominates every effort to win rights. The Civil Rights Act of 1964 profoundly changed the quest for civil rights in the United States.

7. *It all ends up in court.* The courts are the ultimate arbiters of civil rights. Individuals and groups challenge laws they consider unjust. The courts consider what the Constitution requires and weigh the laws, rules, regulations, and private actions for what is permissible and what is not.

Notice how many moving parts there are in the reform process. We have already seen why this is so: American government is unusually fragmented, marked by overlapping actors and institutions all balancing one another. That usually makes it difficult to change deep social norms such as racial or gender discrimination. Reformers have to win over many different power centers—state legislatures, Congress, governors, the judiciary, the media, and the public.

Strict scrutiny: The standard by which courts judge any legislation that singles out race or ethnicity.

● Lucretia Mott, who helped organized the Seneca Falls (New York) convention for women's rights, is attacked by a mob of angry men. Women who challenged their own subordination faced violence in the nineteenth century.

How the Courts Review Cases

Because civil rights generally end up in court, the judicial framework is important. The courts use three categories for determining whether acts violate "the equal protection of the laws" guaranteed by the Fourteenth Amendment.

Suspect Categories. Any legislation involving *race, ethnicity, religion,* or *alienage (immigration status)* faces **strict scrutiny**. The Supreme Court is primed to strike down any law that singles out a race or ethnicity or religion unless there is a very strong reason for doing so. The Court will ask: Does the government have a *compelling government interest* in singling out a race, immigration status, or ethnicity?

Quasi-Suspect Categories. In 1976, women's advocates won a special category for gender cases: **quasi-suspect categories**. Any legislation—federal, state, or local—that introduces sex-based categories has to rest on an *important state purpose*. This is not as strong a test as a *compelling* interest, but it is still a powerful requirement, one that can touch many aspects of politics, economics, and society. For example, in 1996 the Court ruled that excluding women from the Virginia Military Institute (VMI), a state-funded school, did not serve an important state purpose. VMI had to open its doors to women cadets or forgo state funding.

Nonsuspect Categories. Other categories do not face special scrutiny—at least not yet. Legislation based on age, sexual orientation, gender identity, or physical handicaps simply has to have some rational connection between the legislation and a legitimate government purpose. This is the weakest test, but it can still bar discrimination. Using this test, for example, the Court ruled that there was no rational basis for a Colorado constitutional amendment that forbade any protection for gays and lesbians.[9]

This threefold division is the framework for civil rights law. As with almost everything else in American government, politics produced these categories. Groups argued, lobbied, demonstrated, and sued to win stricter scrutiny.

● *A civil rights effort helped lift the ban on women in combat in 2013. Since 2016, women can perform all combat jobs—including joining the Navy SEALs.*

Quasi-suspect category: A legal standard that requires governments to have an important state purpose for any legislation that singles out sex or gender. This is not as strong as the *suspect category*, which requires strict scrutiny.

The Bottom Line

» The battle for civil rights generally involves seven characteristics. The group seeking rights must define itself, challenge society, and change the way it is viewed. The contest for rights spills across all branches of government and involves states, the executive, Congress, and the courts.

» Courts interpret charges of discrimination using three standards: suspect, quasi-suspect, and nonsuspect.

Race and Civil Rights: Revolt Against Slavery

ON A HOT SUMMER DAY in Ferguson, Missouri, a police officer confronted a black man accused of stealing some cigarillos from a convenience store. Reports differ about what happened next but there is no doubt how it ended: Officer Darren Wilson fired twelve bullets at Michael Brown. The Ferguson police then left his body bleeding on the street for four hours. The next day's vigils soon turned to protests and ultimately into a movement: "Black Lives Matter."

In the following months, a stunning series of images flashed before the public: A video of Eric Garner wrestled to the ground on Staten Island, New York, and choked to death as he gasped, "I can't breathe." In Baltimore, Maryland, police arrested Freddie Gray and chained his legs in the back of a police wagon; a week later he was dead of a severed spinal column. In Baton Rouge, Louisiana, Alton Sterling was shot to death by police after being pinned to the ground for illegally selling CDs outside a convenience store. As the death toll of unarmed black people swelled, the Black Lives Matter movement grew. Beneath the protests lay a profound message: A century and a half after slavery was abolished, many Americans still do not feel fully equal and empowered.

African Americans came to America chained in the holds of slave ships, sold at auction, separated from their families, and killed for challenging their oppressors. After emancipation, leaders of the black community were systematically murdered by the thousands. Over time, people of color faced lynching, especially if they were successful; voting restrictions that almost completely disenfranchised them in the south; discrimination in the north; restricted access to housing, schools, hospitals, hotels, and restaurants; and the list goes on.

Yet African Americans constantly fought against bias and furnished the United States with many of its stars in science, art, literature, politics, medicine, sports, and entertainment. In fighting injustice, African Americans developed the tactics that other groups would use in their own battles for civil rights. Black movements forged the laws, amendments, and judicial doctrines that opened the door to civil rights across society. The black quest for freedom included two powerful crusades, one in the nineteenth century and one in the twentieth.

The Clash over Slavery

Slaves were permitted to have churches, and in the early nineteenth century, religion offered leadership, organization, and a powerful message. Black leaders drew on the Christian Bible to compare Africans to the Israelites, bound in slavery but waiting for deliverance to freedom. By the middle of the nineteenth century, the dream of freedom had become a kind of religious faith in the slave quarters.[10] Three additional forces precipitated a national crisis over slavery: a moral crusade for abolition, economic interests, and political calculations.

Abolition: A nineteenth-century movement demanding an immediate and unconditional end to slavery.

Abolition.   An **abolition** movement rose up, branded slavery sinful, and demanded its immediate end. The abolitionists were unusually diverse for the time; the movement's leadership included women and people of color (most famously, Frederick Douglass). It was small and considered radical, but its newspapers and pamphlets created a furious reaction. Many Americans—in both the South and North—feared the abolitionists would incite the slaves to rebellion. Most people preferred to ignore the issue.

Economics.   It was impossible to avoid the slavery question for a fundamental economic reason. As the United States spread west, every new settlement prompted the same question—would it be slave or free? Northerners opposed slavery on the frontier for moral reasons as well as economic ones—the spread of slavery robbed them of the opportunity to settle into new lands. Southerners insisted that slavery needed to spread into new states to survive—or the south would fall into economic ruin.

Politics.   Because the federal government controlled territories until they became states, the question—slave or free?—constantly haunted Congress. Given that every state has two senators, an equal number of free and slave states permitted the South to defend its "peculiar institution." The slaves (who each counted as three-fifths of a person for the purposes of representation—as we saw in Chapter 3) gave Southern states an additional thirty-six seats in the House of Representatives.

The Senate managed to negotiate the tensions with a series of shaky compromises. The **Missouri Compromise** of 1820 drew a line through the Louisiana Territory (see Figure 6.1). All new states and territories north of the line except Missouri would be free; everything south of the line would be open to slavery. In 1845, as Americans moved west, Congress extended the line to include Texas. In 1850, California wanted to enter the Union as a free state. The solution was the **Compromise of 1850**, which permitted California to enter as a free state and turned the decision in Kansas and Nebraska over to the residents—a policy known as popular sovereignty.

Dred Scott v. Sandford In 1857, the Supreme Court stepped in with a shattering decision that upset all the careful compromises. A slave named Dred Scott sued for his freedom. He argued that he had been taken to live in a free territory before returning to Missouri and that, as a result, he should be free. Chief Justice Roger Taney ruled that Scott was not free, because neither the territories nor the federal government had the power to limit slavery or give a black man rights. What about the Missouri Compromise? Unconstitutional, ruled Taney. Popular sovereignty? Also unconstitutional. The ***Dred Scott v. Sandford*** decision ruled that no territory could restrict slavery, much less elevate blacks to citizenship.

The *Dred Scott* decision created a political crisis. The Republican Party rose to national prominence by explicitly rejecting it. In 1860, Abraham Lincoln won the presidency on a platform that flatly opposed the extension of slavery into any

Missouri Compromise: An agreement to open southern territories west of the Mississippi to slavery while closing northern territories to slavery.

Compromise of 1850: A complicated compromise over slavery that permitted territories to vote on whether they would be slave or free and permitted California to enter the Union as a free state. It also included a strict—and hugely controversial—fugitive slave law forcing Northerners to return black men and women into bondage.

Dred Scott v. Sandford: A landmark Supreme Court decision holding that black men could not be citizens under the Constitution of the United States. It created a national uproar.

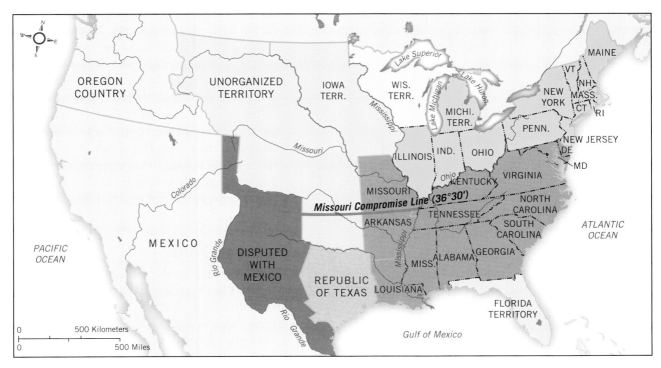

● **Figure 6.1** *The Missouri Compromise—all new American territory below the line would permit slavery; all above (except Missouri) would be free.*

territories. When Lincoln won, southern states began withdrawing from the United States, and the Civil War erupted. In the four years from 1861 to 1865, more people lost their lives than in all the other American wars combined. However, from the blood and ashes arose a second American founding.

The Second American Founding: A New Birth of Freedom?

In his Gettysburg Address, President Lincoln announced "a new birth of freedom" and declared that the United States had been "conceived in liberty and dedicated to the proposition that all men are created equal." Lincoln expressed a view of self-government that the Declaration had not fully embraced and the Constitution had rejected: "Government of the people, by the people, for the people."[11] With this simple declaration, Lincoln rewrote the American idea of freedom.

Emancipation Proclamation: An executive order issued by President Abraham Lincoln that declared the slaves in all rebel states to be free.

Lincoln's bold innovation was institutionalized in four documents. In 1863, Lincoln's **Emancipation Proclamation** freed the slaves—but only in areas that were still rebelling. Ironically, Lincoln freed the slaves in the states where he had no power to enforce his decree. The slaves themselves, however, bolted by the thousands toward the Union Army and transformed it, as one historian wrote, into "a reluctant dragon of emancipation."[12] When the Civil War was finally over, Congress wrote three "Civil War amendments" that gave full legal force to Lincoln's new birth of freedom.

The *Thirteenth Amendment*, ratified in 1865, abolished slavery.

The *Fourteenth Amendment*, ratified in 1868, made anyone born in the United States, crucially including former slaves, a U.S. citizen. The central passage of the Fourteenth Amendment comes in its declaration that *no state shall "deprive any person of life, liberty or property without due process of law; nor deny to any person . . . the equal protection of the laws."* Through this language, as we saw in Chapter 5, the Fourteenth Amendment applied the federal Constitution and the Bill of Rights to the states. The key phrase—**equal protection of the laws**—would become a core legal weapon in the battle for civil rights. It might be the single most important addition to the Constitution in the last two hundred years. It forbids any law designed to harm a group.

Equal protection of the laws: The landmark phrase in the Fourteenth Amendment that requires equal treatment for all citizens.

The *Fifteenth Amendment*, ratified in 1870, guarantees that voting rights "shall not be denied . . . on account of race, color, or previous condition of servitude." Do you notice what is not mentioned? Gender. Women had reasoned that because they were citizens, their right to vote should not be "denied or abridged," but the Supreme Court rejected this interpretation in 1875.

Freedom Fails

What happened to the former slaves? The era after the Civil War began with soaring hopes—and ended bitterly. Black families torn apart during slavery joyously reunited. African Americans formed communities, organized churches, voted, entered politics, and demanded respect from their former owners. Two

● *During the Civil War, some 200,000 African Americans, most of them former slaves, fought for the Union—a crucial factor in the war of attrition with terribly high casualties on both sides.*

African Americans were elected to the U.S. Senate and twenty-one to the House of Representatives. However, black empowerment met fierce resistance. Some whites were outraged when the freedmen no longer stepped aside on the sidewalks; many whites faced economic hardship, even ruin, after their land was destroyed and their labor force had disappeared.

Southern state and local governments reacted by passing *black codes*. These regulations tied blacks to the land, restricted their movements, and stripped them of rights such as voting, owning guns, and buying property. Legal restrictions were backed up by the violent Ku Klux Klan (KKK), which sought to prevent them from exercising their new rights by intimidating former slaves, often lynching the rising cadre of black leaders.

For a time, Congress supported the former slaves. In an effort known as **Reconstruction**, it tried to rebuild the South around a vision of racial justice. Congress organized a Freedmen's Bureau to assist the former slaves. The Civil Rights Act of 1866 guaranteed African Americans the same property rights as white Americans; the Civil Rights Act of 1875 limited private racial discrimination in hotels, restaurants, and theaters.

However, dreams of racial equality began to slip away. The North, weary of the conflict, withdrew armed forces from the South in 1877. Congress repealed the laws that implemented the Civil War amendments; no national mechanism was left to enforce "the equal protection of the laws." In the Civil Rights Cases of 1883, the Supreme Court struck down the Civil Rights Act of 1875, ruling that Congress did not have the authority to stop private discrimination. It took eighty-nine years before the Civil Rights Act of 1964 would find a way around this barrier.[13]

By the 1890s, southern state governments (with the tacit agreement of northern political leaders) had gutted the Fifteenth Amendment right to vote. *Grandfather clauses* forbade people from voting if their grandfathers had not voted; obviously, if a person's grandfather was a slave, he did not vote. *Poll taxes* required voters to pay a fee that most black people could not afford. **Literacy tests** required voters to read and interpret any passage in the state constitution. These new rules did what violence and intimidation had failed to accomplish—they drove blacks out of politics. African Americans have been the only group in any democracy, notes political scientist Richard Valelly, to enter the electorate and then be cast out all over again.[14]

The white majority in the south built a system of segregation known as **Jim Crow**, named after minstrel shows in which white singers and dancers blackened their faces and pretended to be Africans. Jim Crow laws segregated the races. African Americans could not go to white schools, play in the park, visit the zoo (Thursday eventually became "black day" at many zoos), eat at a white restaurant, stay in a white hotel, drink from a white fountain, go to a white hospital, pray in a white church, or vote. The small African American population in the

Reconstruction: The failed effort, pursued by Northerners and Southerners, to rebuild the South and establish racial equality after the Civil War.

Literacy test: A requirement that voters exhibit an ability to read; in reality, a way to restrict black suffrage.

Jim Crow: The system of racial segregation in the U.S. South that lasted from 1890 to 1965, and that was often violently enforced.

● *Thomas Shipp and Abraham Smith were taken from prison cells beaten and hanged in front of thousands of white men, women and children in Marion, Indiana. Among the brutal techniques used to deny African Americans their civil rights, lynching was the most horrific. Organized white mobs tortured and killed blacks—then left their bodies hanging from a tree or lamppost for days, as a warning to others who might advocate civil rights or racial equality.*

Plessy v. Ferguson: An 1896 Supreme Court case that permitted racial segregation.

north also faced racial discrimination, but it was more subtle and not built into the legal system in the same way as the Jim Crow laws.

In 1896, the Supreme Court ruled in ***Plessy v. Ferguson*** that there was nothing inherently discriminatory in requiring separate but equal facilities for the black and white races. "If one race be inferior to the other socially," wrote the majority, "the Constitution of the United States cannot put them upon the same plane." In practice, the facilities were separate but not at all equal. A year later, in *Williams v Mississippi*, the Supreme Court unanimously upheld the poll tax and literacy test, announcing that it was not convinced "that their administration was evil, only that evil was possible under them." The court looked the other way as African Americans were driven right out of politics.[15]

The entire system of southern segregation was held in place by the raw brutality of lynching—the ritualized murders of black men (and occasionally women) who had violated the codes. These murders were not crimes of mob passion but organized killings, with police directing traffic around the scene and white families posing for pictures around the victim's mutilated body. They served as a horrific way to enforce racial separation. The *Negro Year Book* recorded 1,799 blacks lynched between 1882 and 1920.[16] The white majority directed extraordinary fury at men and women who fell in love across the racial divide—interracial couples threatened the entire structure of segregation.[17]

How could the majority accept such repression? Once again, white separatists repeated a false story about black men's supposed sexual lust for white women. Novels, plays, and films portrayed dangerous black men threatening white women and white culture. The story in its most blatant form provided the plot for one of the seminal works in cinematic history. *The Birth of a Nation* (1915) features lust-filled black men, backed by federal troops, menacing white women until the KKK saves the day. In one of the film's last triumphant scenes, the Klan disarms the skulking black men and stops them from voting. Woodrow Wilson screened the film in the White House, and it became one of the top-grossing films of all time.[18]

By 1915, the dreams of equality had collapsed, and African Americans were, once again, denied almost all of their civil rights. Another generation—black and white together—would have to take up the fight again.

See clips from and analysis of *The Birth of a Nation*.

 The Bottom Line

» The clash over slavery eventually led Lincoln to redefine the American idea of self-rule: "Government of the people, by the people, for the people."

» *Institutional changes* marked the rise and fall of civil rights. The president issued the Emancipation Proclamation, Congress passed the Civil Rights Acts, and the states ratified the Thirteenth, Fourteenth, and Fifteenth Amendments.

» The Fourteenth Amendment contains the crucial legal rule for civil rights: "No state shall . . . deprive any person of . . . the equal protection of the laws."

» Later, courts struck down some civil rights laws, Congress repealed laws implementing the Civil War amendments, and the states introduced segregation, which the Supreme Court accepted.

» However, it was *culture*—the terrible stories that white Americans told about their fellow citizens—that fixed the new legal chains in place by inducing the majority to ignore the violations of black rights.

The Fight for Racial Equality

A great population shift marked the next civil rights movement. Beginning in the 1910s, many African Americans left the South and moved to factory jobs in the northern cities—a journey known as the **Great Migration**. By the 1950s, 40 percent of the black population lived in the North, where they faced a different kind of racial discrimination.

Two Types of Discrimination

There are two types of discrimination. Legal discrimination—known as **de jure discrimination**—involves laws that explicitly deny civil rights. By the time the civil rights movement ended, around 1970, Americans had conquered de jure discrimination—an enormous achievement.

A second type of discrimination—known as "in fact" or **de facto discrimination**—exists without the support of explicit laws and is more subtly embedded in society. Segregated residential neighborhoods are an example; this type of discrimination can be much harder to address. Today, Americans argue about whether de facto restrictions still exist—and, if so, to what extent.

The Modern Civil Rights Campaign Begins

In 1909, black leaders formed the **National Association for the Advancement of Colored People**, or **NAACP**, and began fighting segregation. In 1941, they won the first executive order on race since Reconstruction. President Franklin Roosevelt signed an order barring racial discrimination by defense contractors and created the Fair Employment Practices Committee to ensure compliance. What pushed Roosevelt to act? Black leaders, led by A. Philip Randolph, threatened to organize a massive protest march on Washington just as the United States was gearing up to fight the racist Nazi regime in World War II.

Over one hundred thousand black troops fought in the war only to be greeted by racism when they returned home. They added their voices to the call for equality—and helped change the American cultural image of black people. In 1948, Harry Truman desegregated the armed forces, making the military the first racially integrated federal institution in the United States.

The Courts

The NAACP also went to court and chipped away at Jim Crow laws enforcing segregation. Democratic President Franklin Roosevelt (1933–1944) appointed eight Supreme Court Justices during his twelve years in office. The result: a Court sympathetic to blacks' civil rights claims. In 1944, the Supreme Court struck down the all-white Democratic primary in *Smith v. Allright*, rejecting the idea that a political party was a private organization and could discriminate if it wished to.[19] The Court struck down segregation in many venues—including interstate buses, law schools, and graduate schools—and then took a monumental step.[20]

Great Migration: The vast movement of African Americans from the rural South to the urban North between 1910 and the 1960s.

De jure discrimination: Discrimination established by laws.

De facto discrimination: More subtle forms of discrimination that exist without a legal basis.

National Association for the Advancement of Colored People (NAACP): A civil rights organization formed in 1909 and dedicated to racial equality.

"Separate but equal" for George McLaurin meant a desk in the hallway. McLaurin, who was pursuing his Ph.D. at the University of Oklahoma, sued the university, and the Supreme Court ruled against segregated classes in graduate school.

● Elizabeth Eckford, one of nine black teens who integrated Little Rock High School in 1957, had to brave a gauntlet of jeering whites.

Brown v. Board of Education:
The landmark Supreme Court case that struck down segregated schools as unconstitutional.

In May 1954, in **Brown v. Board of Education**, the Court ruled that segregated schools violated the equal protection clause of the Fourteenth Amendment. In public education, ruled the court, "the doctrine of separate but equal has no place." Separate facilities were inherently unequal.[21]

Brown was a momentous decision. The follow-up to the ruling, however, was far less dramatic: almost nothing changed. The Court did not impose a strong timetable or implementation plan. National officials did little to support *Brown*, and state and local leaders did much to oppose it. A decade after *Brown*, less than one percent of the schools in the South had been desegregated.

Where desegregation did occur, the results could be explosive. The day before schools opened in 1957, Governor Orval Faubus came out against the desegregation of Central High School in Little Rock, Arkansas. The Arkansas National Guard turned away the nine high school students who tried to enter the school the next day.

The governor backed off in the face of a court order. When the African American students came back two weeks later, the National Guard had been replaced by what the *New York Times* called "a mob of belligerent, shrieking hysterical demonstrators" shouting racial epithets. President Dwight Eisenhower, a Republican, reluctantly dispatched the 101st Airborne to enforce the court order and desegregate Central High.

Elected officials throughout the South could not help but notice that Governor Faubus had become a local hero among whites and was returned to office for an unprecedented third term. Many white politicians reacted by staunchly fighting civil rights and desegregation. Years later, some white protesters would try and reconcile with the black students they had jeered, and some local politicians would publicly regret what they had said and done. But it was clear at the time that, without political support, even a major court decision like *Brown v. Board of Education* could neither crack segregation nor integrate the schools.

The Civil Rights Movement

What defeated segregation was not the Supreme Court or the paratroopers from the 101st Airborne, but ordinary American people who rose up and seized the moment. There had been scattered demonstrations throughout the country for years, but the organized movement began in Montgomery, Alabama, on a December afternoon in 1955.

Rosa Parks was riding the bus home. The white section filled up, and when a white man got on board, the driver called out that the whites needed another row. Everyone in the

● The civil rights movement took courage. Here, protesters sitting at a whites-only lunch counter have been taunted and doused with ketchup.

first black row was expected to get up. Parks refused to relinquish her seat and was arrested. The local NAACP called a boycott of the Montgomery bus lines and put twenty-six-year-old Martin Luther King, Jr. in charge. That night, King addressed thousands of people from the pulpit of the Holt Street Baptist Church and launched a campaign of Christian nonviolence.[22]

It took more than a year and direct intervention by the Supreme Court to desegregate the buses in Montgomery. But the pattern was set: The Court had opened the legal door. Protesters braved arrest, scorn, and violence to win change on the ground.

In February 1960, four black college students from North Carolina A&T University sat at a white lunch counter and inspired a tactic that spread throughout the South. Within a year, seventy thousand people—black and white—had sat at segregated counters while onlookers jeered, poured ketchup on the sitters, and held cigarette lighters to the women's hair. From lunch counters, the sit-ins spread to movie theaters, parks, pools, art galleries, libraries, and churches.

In 1961, activists came up with a new tactic. Groups of young people rented Greyhound buses and drove as **Freedom Riders** to protest segregated interstate bus lines and terminals. The first bus was pursued by a "citizens' posse" and set ablaze. Angry men tried to hold the doors of the burning bus shut, and the students narrowly escaped—only to get a vicious beating with bats and pipes.[23]

Despite the protests, segregation *still* did not yield. The stalemate was finally broken in Birmingham, Alabama. Young marchers tumbled out of churches and walked, singing and clapping, straight into appalling police violence. Fire hoses sent them sprawling as police dogs snarled and snapped. Television blazed the images around the world. The police overreaction horrified the nation.

The Democratic Party at the time was divided between northern liberals and southern segregationists. The Kennedy administration was reluctant to embrace civil rights for it did not want to lose support from Southern Democrats. The images from Birmingham forced the issue, and the administration finally submitted strong civil rights legislation to Congress.

A major obstacle for all civil rights activists is the **free rider problem**. Civil rights protesters faced dog bites, criminal prosecution, and even death; those who stood on the sideline reaped the same political benefits without any risks. Yet, in the early 1960s, hundreds of thousands of Americans (including many whites) ignored cost-benefit calculations and joined protests and marches. Why did they put themselves in harm's way? Was it the idea of freedom? Their moral convictions? Or perhaps it was the communal exuberance of fighting for something larger than themselves.

Freedom Riders: Black and white activists who rode buses together to protest segregation on interstate bus lines.

Free rider problem: A barrier to group or collective action arising because people who do not participate still reap the benefits.

1963 March on Washington: A massive rally for civil rights that included Martin Luther King's "I Have a Dream" speech.

Congress and the Civil Rights Act

Despite the protests, Congress blocked civil rights legislation—as it had done many times in the past. This time, however, activists prevailed. In May and June 1963, a great wave of protests followed Birmingham. Media stories about demonstrations, violence, and arrests fostered a sense of crisis. The **1963 March on Washington** marked the high point of the peaceful

● *Freedom Riders narrowly escaped the burning bus—only to be beaten bloody.*

Civil Rights Act of 1964:
Landmark legislation that forbade discrimination on the basis of race, sex, religion, or national origin.

protest movement; the entire nation watched Martin Luther King put aside his prepared text and declare, "I have a dream."

In November 1963, President Kennedy was assassinated, and action on civil rights became, as President Lyndon Johnson would put it, a martyr's cause. The **Civil Rights Act of 1964** was powerful legislation. It forbade state and local governments from denying access to public facilities on the basis of race, color, or national origin. The law prohibited employers from discriminating on similar grounds, and barred discrimination in private motels, hotels, theaters, and other public accommodations. There would be no more "black Thursdays" at city zoos or whites-only water fountains. Congress relied on its Constitutional authority over interstate commerce to forbid private businesses from discriminating—no more restaurants or hotels that served only whites.

Opponents sued, claiming that private businesses such as motels should be free to choose their own patrons. The Supreme Court ruled that because motels served people from other states, Congress could use its power over interstate commerce to stop owners from discriminating. Ollie's Barbecue in Birmingham, Alabama, did not have patrons from other states. However, in *Katzenbach v. McClung*, the Court ruled that because it received supplies through interstate commerce, it too fell under congressional jurisdiction. The era when traveling African Americans had to sleep in their cars was finally over.[24]

The Civil Rights Act also empowered the federal government to withhold funds from segregated schools. In less than a decade the number of southern schoolchildren in integrated schools jumped from almost none to over 90 percent (see Figure 6.2). Today, court decisions on civil rights continue to cite this blockbuster legislation.

The following year, Congress passed the Voting Rights Act of 1965. This law protected the right to vote, struck down voter suppression tactics such as the literacy test, and empowered the attorney general and the U.S. District Court of Washington, DC, to weigh any voting change in suspect areas for its potentially discriminatory effect. The legislation effectively secured the Fifteenth Amendment guaranteeing the right to vote. African Americans surged to the ballot boxes, and in their wake came black elected officials (see Table 6.1). Over time, the number of elected black officials skyrocketed—increasing 129-fold in forty years. However, African Americans, who comprise over 12 percent of the American population, still make up only about 2 percent of all elected officials.

Watch Martin Luther King's "I Have a Dream" speech.

Black power: A slogan that emphasized pride in black heritage and the construction of black institutions to nurture black interests. It often implied racial separation in reaction to white racism.

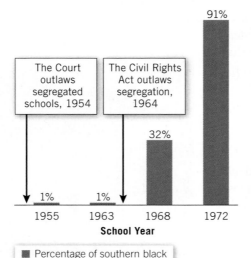

● **Figure 6.2** *The Civil Rights Act of 1964—rather than the* Brown v. Board of Education *Supreme Court decision in 1954—led to rapid integration of southern schools.*

The Court outlaws segregated schools, 1954

The Civil Rights Act outlaws segregation, 1964

91%

32%

1%   1%

1955   1963   1968   1972
School Year

■ Percentage of southern black children in integrated schools

Divisions in the Movement

In the summer of 1964 alone, eighty civil rights workers were beaten in Mississippi, four were killed, and more than a thousand were arrested. The unrelenting violence eventually provoked a backlash. After the relentless hostility, harassment, and violence, many activists rejected nonviolent protest and seized instead on **black power**—the idea that African Americans should forget about integration and empower

TABLE 6.1 **Total Number of Black Elected Officials**

	1964	1970	1980	1990	2019
Mayors	0	81	205	314	600 (est.)
Members of Congress	5	9	19	19	56
Total black elected officials in the United States	70	1,469	4,914	7,370	More than 10,500 (est.)

Sources: Congressional Research Service; African American Mayors' Association; Joint Center for Political Studies

the black community to act on its own. The civil rights movement split over strategy: Some continued to follow King and his campaign of nonviolent protest. Groups such as the Black Panthers armed themselves and vowed to answer violence with violence. Still others, such as the Nation of Islam, sought separation from whites.

Eventually, years of frustration burst into urban riots—also known as insurrections—between 1964 and 1969. The deadliest erupted in Watts, Los Angeles in August 1965 (34 deaths) and Detroit in July 1967 (43 deaths). Most outbursts had a local cause—often incidents involving all-white police forces. White liberals who had energetically supported civil rights began to turn away from the movement. The era of civil rights gave way to a desire for "law and order"—a slogan that presidential candidate Richard Nixon used to great effect on the campaign trail in 1968.

Learn about the KKK's failed attempt to conceal their identity.

 **The Bottom Line**

» The NAACP won a series of cases against segregation, culminating in *Brown v. Board of Education*; however, implementation proved difficult.

» In the early 1960s, ordinary men, women, and children—black and white—organized in mass movements to turn the legal promise of the *Brown* decision into a practical reality. As the images from marches became more dramatic, surging public opinion pushed Congress to pass the Civil Rights Act of 1964 and the Voting Rights Act of 1965.

» Taken together, these institutional changes ended de jure segregation in the United States.

» The black movement set the model for future civil rights campaigns by many other groups.

The Post Civil Rights Era

After the successful challenge to *de jure* segregation, civil rights reformers faced the perplexing problems of subtle, de facto discrimination. Protesters can kneel in front of a segregated church, but how do they challenge dead-end jobs and shabby neighborhoods?

● *In cities like Boston, busing led to protests, riots, and even killings. In 1976, these protesters attacked Ted Landsmark, an African American attorney.*

Affirmative action: Direct steps to recruit members of previously underrepresented groups into schools and jobs.

Disproportionate impact: The discriminatory effect of some policies, even if discrimination is not consciously intended.

Apply affirmative action laws.

School busing: An effort to integrate public schools by mixing students from different neighborhoods.

Affirmative Action in the Workplace

In the 1960s and 1970s, a new approach emerged to assist groups that had faced discrimination. **Affirmative action** involves direct, positive steps to increase the representation (especially in schools and workplaces) of groups that have faced discrimination in the past. The strategy started with race and then grew to redress other forms of discrimination, such as those based on gender and ethnicity.

In 1971, the Supreme Court propounded a doctrine called **disproportionate impact**. Companies could not hire or promote employees in way that created "built-in headwinds' for minority groups [that] are unrelated to measuring job capability." Companies who never hired women or had zero minority managers would be suspected of those "built-in headwinds."[25]

Affirmative action raises difficult issues. The goal is *equality of opportunity*—giving each person the same chance to achieve success. But some critics charge that it actually produces *equality of outcome* by reserving jobs or opportunities for individuals based on their race or gender. Is this the only way to make up for past discrimination? If so, how long should the programs stay in place? And is it unfair to white men that minorities and women are getting jobs and promotions? Americans faced a dilemma: How could they address the results of years and years of discrimination without creating cases of reverse discrimination against white males? The issue is so complicated because it mixes race and economics. Perhaps all populations that have historically been poor—rural whites as well as blacks, for example—should have some claim on affirmative action?

Affirmative action soon sparked a backlash and the Supreme Court began to narrow its use. In 1986, the Court warned that such programs could be used only in cases of "severe discrimination" and should not "trammel the interests of white employees."[26] By 1995, a more conservative Court rejected the entire idea of explicitly setting aside places for members of racial groups.[27]

In 2009, the New Haven, Connecticut, fire department began requiring a written exam for promotions. The top scorers on the test were all white. If the city accepted the test results, black and Hispanic firefighters could sue under disproportionate impact, arguing that the test created "headwinds" unrelated to fighting fires. But when New Haven threw out the test results, white firefighters who had scored well sued. The Supreme Court agreed, 5–4, that New Haven should not have dismissed the results. The case is difficult because both sides have a good argument: The New Haven fire department needs diverse leadership, but ignoring the test results seems unfair to the individuals who did well.

Affirmative Action in Education

Civil rights advocates believed that if children from different races and ethnicities went to school together, they would shed the prejudices that marked their parents and grandparents. The problem, however, was that because many children lived in single-race neighborhoods, local schools were inevitably segregated. One solution, known as **school busing**, aimed to achieve racial integration by driving students to other neighborhoods. Busing declined after the 1980s and observers still disagree over whether it was an idealistic often-successful effort to create a new generation that could move beyond racial divisions or liberal social engineering that only whipped up racial animosity by using children to right old social wrongs.

A major controversy over affirmative action surrounded programs that reserved places in universities for members of minority groups. Many schools sought to make up for past discrimination and at the same time enhance the diversity of their student body. These quotas, too, created a backlash. One landmark case focused on the medical school at the University of California at Davis, which held sixteen places in its entering class of one hundred for members of minority or economically disadvantaged groups. Allan Bakke, a white man who had been rejected by the medical school, sued, arguing that his academic scores were higher than the scores of minority applicants who had been accepted. In a 5–4 decision in *University of California v. Bakke* (1978), the Supreme Court ruled in favor of Bakke; setting a quota, as the university had done, violated the equal protection guarantee of the

● Should the University of Texas aim to expand diversity? These protesters disagree with the university's effort to do so. In Fisher v. The University of Texas the Court permitted (4–3) university officials to use multiple factors, including race, in creating a diverse student body.

What Do YOU Think?   Higher Education and Affirmative Action

One of the most difficult problems in politics is how to make up for past injustice. What do we, as a society, owe to groups who have faced violence and discrimination for many generations? Consider higher education—the path to success in contemporary society. Which of the following positions would you support?

I favor affirmative action in college admissions.

Preferential admissions for members of long-marginalized groups makes up for many generations of discrimination. And it's good for everyone by promoting diversity—drawing on people from different backgrounds makes for a stronger community and a richer educational experience. It also builds a more equal society if races, classes, and genders socially interact and learn to work together in their formative years. Over time, affirmative action in education will help a whole generation look past ascriptive categories such as race, gender, and ethnicity.

I oppose affirmative action in college admissions.

Past discrimination does not justify special treatment now. In *Grutter v. Bollinger* (2003), the Supreme Court implied that the correct period should last roughly three generations, or sixty years (1965–2025). Although male students comprised 58 percent of the student body in the 1970s when affirmative action went into effect, they now make up only 44 percent.[28] Furthermore, affirmative action is tantamount to reverse discrimination against hard-working individuals from overrepresented groups, such as whites and Asian Americans. Education should have only one yardstick: merit!

Fourteenth Amendment. Although the Court barred racial quotas, it accepted the use of race as a "plus" factor in the admissions process. In 2016 the Court narrowly upheld the use of affirmative action in admissions decisions—ruling that the University of Texas' admission policy, which factors in diversity without setting quotas, met the standards of "strict scrutiny." This ruling was weakened in 2018, when the Trump Administration announced a reversal of executive-branch guidance on race in college admissions that was reaffirmed by the Obama Administration.[29]

The Court has painfully picked its way through the minefield of equal opportunity. Crucial questions abound: How does a nation make up for past discrimination? How long should preferential programs last? And what about people who feel they are losing out today because of efforts to address past injustice? Should historically poor white populations have their own claim on affirmative action? Should we put aside the terrible racial past, and simply worry about all poor people? The cases are difficult because there are important values on all sides.

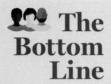 **The Bottom Line**

» To make up for past discrimination, legislatures and courts turned to affirmative action in the 1960s and 1970s. Employers and schools that had previously excluded Hispanics, Native Americans, African Americans, or women now set aside places for them.

» The courts initially sponsored affirmative action programs but are increasingly skeptical of any race-based categories, including those designed to ameliorate past injustice.

Women's Rights

In the early nineteenth century, an American woman had no political rights. She could not vote, serve on a jury, or enter into a contract after marriage. Her husband controlled her property, her wages, and even her body. Husband and wife are one, mused Justice Hugo Black, and "that one is the husband."

Suffrage

The struggle for women's rights in the United States has been interconnected with the fight for racial equality. When women joined the abolition movement, they quickly grew frustrated by the barriers that confronted them. They could lecture to other women but not men (for that would be "promiscuous"); they could join abolitionist societies but not be elected officers.[30] The first American gathering for women's suffrage, the 1848 **Seneca Falls Convention**, grew directly out of frustration over the gender barriers in the abolition movement.

In the 1870s, the women's movement gained momentum. The Women's Christian Temperance Union attacked alcohol as a cause of male violence against women. It championed voluntary motherhood (no more marital rape), suffrage for women, and decent wages. Two other groups focused on winning the vote. Led by Carrie Chapman Catt, the American Woman Suffrage Association emphasized winning voting rights state by state. The National American Woman Suffrage Association (NAWSA), galvanized by Alice Paul, fought for a constitutional amendment that would give every American woman the right to vote.

Seneca Falls Convention: The first convention dedicated to women's rights, held in July 1848 in Seneca Falls, NY.

Success came first in the West, beginning with the Wyoming and Utah Territories, which granted women the vote in 1869 and 1870—partially because gender roles were less settled in those territories, partially because strong populist reform movements swept through the West. By 1916, women voted in every state of the West and Midwest except Texas and New Mexico. The issue remained contentious, however. Four northern states voted to reject suffrage during the 1916 presidential election, and the South remained strongly opposed for fear that women might reject segregation (see Figure 6.3).

During World War I, women took on new roles throughout the economy. Led by Alice Paul and NAWSA, they increased the pressure for suffrage. Paul was jailed for her activism. Eventually, President Woodrow Wilson grudgingly supported suffrage as a "wartime measure." The Nineteenth Amendment—giving women the right to vote—cleared Congress over stiff opposition in the Senate and was ratified by the states in 1920.

Although they had secured suffrage, women were slow to win political office. Montana elected the first woman to Congress, Jeanette Rankin, in 1916 (even before the amendment passed—again, the western states in front of the curve). Still, in the first fifty years after the amendment, only three women were elected to the U.S. Senate for full terms and, after the 1970 election, there were eleven women in the House of Representatives (just 2% of that chamber) Then, during the 1970s–80s, beginning at the local level and reaching Congress in the 1990s, the number of women officeholders soared (see Figure 6.4).

Despite these gains, the United States in 2018 ranked 100th worldwide in the percentage of women in its legislature (see Comparing Nations 6.1). In the United States, women are less likely than men to leap into the contest. The good news is that women who do run win just as often as men do. The 2018 midterm elections marked a banner year for women candidates, as a record 277 women ran for Congress and governorships, with new all-time highs in the Senate (24) and House (more than 100).[31]

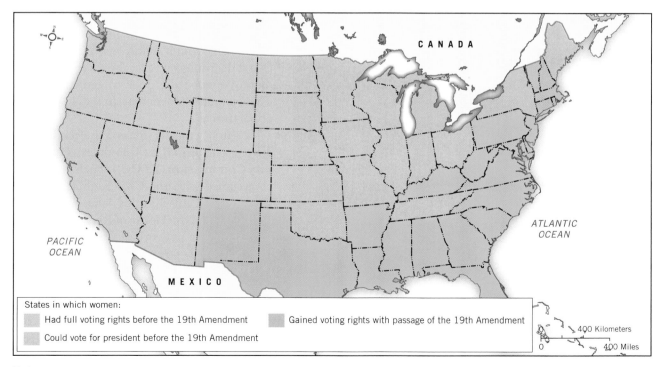

States in which women:
Had full voting rights before the 19th Amendment   Gained voting rights with passage of the 19th Amendment
Could vote for president before the 19th Amendment

PACIFIC OCEAN

ATLANTIC OCEAN

CANADA

MEXICO

400 Kilometers
400 Miles

● **Figure 6.3** *Before the Nineteenth Amendment, women had full voting rights in the West, limited rights in the Midwest, and almost none in the South and East. For women, winning the vote took a difficult political campaign that lasted more than eighty years.*

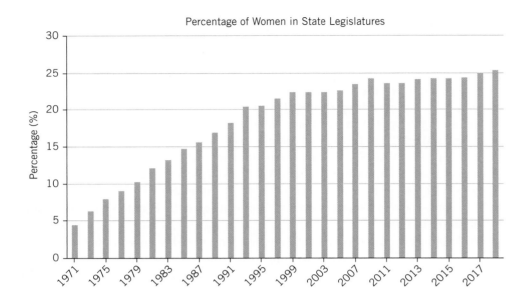

Percentage of Women in State Legislatures

● **Figure 6.4** *Number of women in state legislatures. Note the steep rise in the 1970s–1980s and the leveling out after 1992.*[32] *(Center for American Women and Politics)*

Equal Employment Opportunity Commission (EEOC): Federal law enforcement agency charged with monitoring compliance with the Civil Rights Act.

National Organization for Women (NOW): An organization formed in 1966 to take action for women's equality.

● *The cheering fans don't realize how the Civil Rights Act changed their world.*

The Civil Rights Act of 1964

The breakthrough in the struggle for gender rights slipped into the Civil Rights Act of 1964. This landmark law, as we have seen, was designed to bar racial discrimination. Congressman Howard Smith, a segregationist from Virginia, proposed adding a single word—"sex"—to the legislation with the hopes of making a mockery of the entire bill and killing it. The tactic did not work, and the Civil Rights Act passed, barring discrimination based on "race, color, religion, *sex* and national origin."

At the time, no one predicted that the gender provision in the Civil Rights Act would have the same far-reaching consequences for gender rights as *Brown v. Board of Education* had for African Americans—but it did. As with the Supreme Court decisions on race, the Civil Rights Act merely opened the door to gender change. The women's movement had to seize the opportunity.

At first, officials ignored the gender provision. The **Equal Employment Opportunity Commission (EEOC)**, which monitored compliance with the Civil Rights Act, considered it a "mischievous joke perpetrated on the floor of the House of Representatives." In response, a network of women organized the **National Organization for Women (NOW)**, drawing directly on the tactics of the civil rights campaign—demonstrations, rallies, lobbying, and litigation.

Congress and the EEOC began to pay attention. For example, in 1972, Congress passed federal education amendments that denied federal funds for programs that discriminated against women (Title VI) and that required equal athletic opportunities for men and women (Title IX). Underfunded women's sports programs began getting the same treatment as the men's varsity programs.

Notice how a single piece of legislation can have far-reaching consequences. The next time you watch a women's basketball game on national television, thank Congressman Smith for dropping the word "*sex*" into the Civil Rights Act of 1964.

COMPARING NATIONS 6.1	Percentage of Women in National Legislatures: Selected Countries	
WORLD NATION % WOMEN IN RANK		**LOWER (POPULAR) HOUSE**
1	Rwanda	61.3
2	Bolivia	53.1
3	Cuba	48.9
10	Norway	41.4
14	France	39.0
39	United Kingdom	32.0
54	Afghanistan	27.7
59	Canada	27.0
67	Iraq	25.3
71	China	24.2
77	United States	23.2
80	Venezuela	22.2
92	Pakistan	20.6
99	Saudi Arabia	19.9
116	South Korea	17.0
122	North Korea	16.3
128	Russia	15.8
146	India	11.8
158	Japan	10.1
178	Iran	5.9
189	Yemen, Papua New Guinea	0.0

Many countries outdistance the United States in the percentage of women in national legislatures: note Saudi Arabia, where women were forbidden to drive till 2018, two places ahead of the United States. Achieving balance is simpler in a Parliamentary system, where candidates are selected by the parties.

Source: Inter-Parliamentary Union; authors' compilation.

Equal Rights Amendment

Equal Rights Amendment:
An amendment, originally drafted by Alice Paul in 1923, passed by Congress in 1972, and ratified by thirty-five states, that declared: "Equality of rights . . . shall not be denied or abridged . . . on account of sex."

Reframe an issue: To redefine the popular perception of an issue.

The politics of Civil Rights spilled into other areas of gender politics. Feminists introduced an **Equal Rights Amendment (ERA)** in Congress every year between 1924 and 1972. The amendment was simple: "Equality of rights under the law shall not be denied . . . on account of sex." By 1972, it had become uncontroversial, and Congress passed it by lopsided margins. Five years later, the ERA was just three states short of ratification. Then Phyllis Schlafly, a Republican activist, organized the STOP ERA movement. Schlafly argued that the ERA threatened traditional family life. "What the libbers don't understand," said Schlafly, is "that most women want to be a wife, mother, and homemaker."[33] By **reframing the issue**, Schlafly halted the Equal Rights Amendment in its tracks. Nearly half the states have adopted sex-equality language in their state constitutions, but Congress has not voted again on the issue for more than thirty-five years.

The Courts

The women's movement also echoed the black civil rights movement in targeting the courts. Led by Ruth Bader Ginsburg (now a Supreme Court justice), advocates challenged discriminatory state laws, case by case. Because gender was a *nonsuspect category*, the courts upheld any state law as long as it had some "rational connection to a legitimate state purpose." In a series of cases, culminating in *Craig v. Boren* in 1976, the Court lifted gender into a new category of *heightened scrutiny*—not as rigorous a test as the scrutiny the courts give racial classifications, but a more rigorous test than that applied to other social groups. Ironically, the case—a major victory for women's rights—involved men challenging an Oklahoma statute that set the drinking age for beer as eighteen for women and twenty-one for men.

The courts also applied the prohibition on gender discrimination in the Civil Rights Act to sexual harassment. In 1998, the Supreme Court expanded the protection by ruling that an employee did not have to prove a specific instance of sexual harassment if there was a hostile workplace environment, which might include sexual advances, lewd comments, or general attitudes. The Court ruled that even if employers were not aware of specific instances of harassment, they remained liable for the general culture of the workplace.

Women's advocates raised the issue of differential pay more than a century ago. Today, women working full time earn, on average, four-fifths as much as men—although the exact amount of the disparity is hotly disputed and varies from 80 percent to 95 percent, depending on the methodology.[34] In a famous case, Lilly Ledbetter sued after a nineteen-year career as a supervisor with Goodyear Tire Company because she had been paid less than men in the same position. A jury found Goodyear guilty of pay discrimination, but the Supreme Court reversed the judgment by a 5–4 vote. The majority ruled that Ledbetter should have sued within 180 days after Goodyear set her pay—long before she knew about the salary differential. In 2009, President Obama signed equal-pay legislation—known as the Lilly Ledbetter Act—that permits an employee to sue 180 days from her last paycheck (resetting the clock each time she gets a lower paycheck).[35]

Class action: A lawsuit filed on behalf of an entire category of individuals, such as all public housing residents in a state or all female managers in a large company.

Recent Supreme Court decisions have made it more difficult to sue businesses for discrimination. In a major case decided in 2011, the court turned down a **class action** suit brought against Wal-Mart. The suit alleged that the company systematically discriminated against women by offering them less pay and fewer promotions. The Supreme Court ruled—once again by a 5–4 margin—that simply showing that women received less pay was not enough to prove discrimination. Rather, the plaintiffs (the women suing) needed to demonstrate a specific company-wide policy that set lower wages for all the women involved in the class action.[36]

TABLE 6.2 **Women CEOs of** *Fortune 500* **Companies**

YEAR	2000	2010	2015	2017	2018
WOMEN CEOs	3	15	23	32	24

Source: Zameena Mejia, "Just 24 female CEOs lead the companies on the 2018 Fortune 500—fewer than last year." May 21, 2018. CNBC.

Progress for Women—But How Much?

There had never been a woman Supreme Court justice until Ronald Reagan named Sandra Day O'Connor to the bench in 1981; in 2018, three of the nine justices are women. In 1964, 7 percent of American women received bachelor's degrees (compared to 12% of men); in 2016, 33.7 percent of women do (now surpassing the 33.2% of men). There had never been a woman CEO of a Fortune 500 company until 1972. In 2018, the number was up to thirty-two and then in 2018, fell back to 24—just under five percent of the total (see Table 6.2).[37]

Gender politics raise provocative questions about social roles and power. When women demanded the right to vote in the mid-nineteenth century, they met with anger and violence. Today, issues such as abortion, equality, and women's rights in the workplace continue to generate conflict. The #MeToo movement burst on the scene in 2017–2018. After years of tolerating sexual assault and harassment, women began to speak out—and a long list of male celebrities in every field were exposed for indecent behavior. The movement is both a bracing sign of progress and a harsh reminder that we still have a long way to go to reach gender equality.

 **The Bottom Line**

» In nineteenth-century law, women's political rights operated through their husbands. When women organized to win rights, they met with ridicule and violence.

» Women first won voting rights in the states—especially in the West and Midwest—before finally securing the Nineteenth Amendment, which guaranteed the right to vote regardless of gender.

» The Civil Rights Act of 1964 bars gender discrimination. As with the civil rights movement of the 1950s and 1960s, the women's movement organized to take advantage of legal changes. The law transformed American gender roles in political and professional life.

» Following *Roe v. Wade* in 1973 and the unsuccessful fight for the Equal Rights Amendment in the mid-1970s, gender politics became especially controversial, spilling into many other issues.

Hispanics

Hispanics, or Latinos (we use the words interchangeably), play a powerful and growing role in American politics and culture. Hispanics are the largest minority group, making up over 17 percent of the American population in 2018—up from just 6.4 percent in 1980.

Latinos have long faced discrimination in the United States. They were already living in the Southwest—in Arizona, California, New Mexico, and parts of Colorado, Nevada, Utah, and Texas—before the United States took those lands from Mexico in 1848. As white settlers poured into the new territories, they often displaced Latino residents from their homes and farms. As the nation urbanized, Latinos were pushed into segregated schools, excluded from jobs, and barred from housing in white neighborhoods. They also faced hostility and violence.

Today, despite enormous success in achieving the American dream, Hispanics still face challenges. They are incarcerated at a much higher rate than white non-Hispanic Americans. They are more likely to be poor, less likely to have health insurance, and underrepresented in almost every political venue. Despite all this, Latinos have a higher life expectancy than most other American groups.

Challenging Discrimination

Latinos established the League of United Latin American Citizens (LULAC) in 1929. Like the NAACP, the organization fought segregation through lawsuits. In *Mendez v. Westminster*, decided in 1947, the court struck down Latino school segregation in Orange County, California; the case was an important precursor to *Brown v. Board of Education* and involved some of the same lawyers.

During the 1960s, young Latinos turned to activism. In 1968, high school and college students called a massive student strike that reverberated throughout the Southwest. The students pushed mainstream Latino organizations to fight more aggressively against discrimination; they challenged immigration policies that restricted movement across the Mexican border. Young people took a slur against Mexicans, *Chicano*, and turned it into a movement they labeled **Chicanismo**—a defiant pride in their heritage and culture.

At the same time, the **United Farm Workers** (**UFW**) organized the most vulnerable population—migrant workers who picked crops up and down the West Coast. The UFW became a symbol of Latino mobilization. Throughout the 1960s and 1970s, traditional organizations such as LULAC, activist students, and farm workers all challenged discrimination. Their efforts prepared the way for the entry of Latino elected officials into every level of government.

Today, the central questions for Latino politics turn on immigration, language, and—perhaps most important—just how the very diverse Hispanic population might mobilize together for political action.

The Politics of Immigration

Despite Hispanics' long heritage in the land, Hispanic politics is wrapped up with immigration. Although the United States is an immigrant nation, the door to foreigners has historically swung from wide open to shut tight. Restrictions in the 1920s strictly limited

Chicanismo: A defiant movement expressing pride in Latino origins and culture in the face of discrimination.

United Farm Workers (UFW): An influential union representing migrant farm workers in the west.

● During the early twentieth century, Latinos began to organize for civil rights. This replica of a 1929 Texas restaurant sign helps illustrate why.

immigration—President John Kennedy sadly noted forty years later that America no longer offered a beacon for immigrants. After his assassination, Congress lifted the restrictions, in 1965, and a new era of immigration began. Today, one in eight American residents was born abroad.

Ancient Fears. Immigrants trigger fears that are repeated for every new group: They will undermine American values and culture; they will take away jobs; they will cling to their own languages, and remain loyal to their countries of origin and their supposedly un-American ideas. All this was said about the Irish back in the 1840s—and they were also persecuted for being Catholics; in 1900, one U.S. Senator justified a mob that killed eleven Italians after a jury exonerated them of a murder, by arguing that Italians were natural criminals.[38] The sentiments grow stronger in periods of high immigration—from early in the nation to the present day. As president, Donald Trump has made limits on legal and illegal immigration one of his signature issues. At one private meeting, the president ignited controversy by deploring immigration from "shithole countries"—though he was referring to Haiti rather than Mexico. Senator Marco Rubio (R-FL) immediately tweeted that immigrants should be judged "on who they are, not where they come from."[39]

This remains a powerful issue. In 2016, almost 1.5 million foreign-born people moved to the United States. Americans hotly debate whether to build a border fence with Mexico (57% say no) and whether to allow undocumented immigrants who were brought to the United States as children to become citizens (75% say yes).[40] The rights of immigrants depend on their legal status.

Three Categories. Immigrant groups fall into three different categories with very different legal claims on civil rights.

1. Those who were born in the United States or have become American citizens (66% of the Latino population) claim the same rights as any citizen. They are in the same protected legal category as African Americans. Any law that singles them out is "suspect" and subject to strict scrutiny by the courts.

2. Foreigners who have not become citizens fall into a second category, which the U.S. government terms *resident alien*. They number approximately 13.1 million. They may work in the United States and they pay taxes, but they cannot enjoy the benefits of citizenship: They may not vote in most elections and many government safety-net programs, such as Medicaid, explicitly exclude them.

3. An estimated eleven million people are not legally authorized to be residents. Most arrived on a temporary visa, got a job or fell in love, settled down, and simply remained after their legal time in the country expired. Others slipped across the borders (310,000 were arrested doing so in 2017). Unauthorized border crossings have plunged since the start of the Trump administration, falling some 25 percent in 2017 to the lowest number in 46 years.[41] Undocumented individuals have limited constitutional rights and, when caught, are subject to immediate deportation—despite resistance by many state and local governments, as described in Chapter 4.

Undocumented Individuals.   The debate over people who are not legally authorized to be in the United States is especially intense. Some argue that they are part of the American economy and society. They live in fear of jail and deportation. As a result, many are wary of going to a hospital, visiting their children's school, or reporting crimes against them. Many Americans want to bring these individuals out of the shadows. They should be able to obtain driver's licenses (12 states currently do so) and attend universities (Figure 6.5). Ultimately, the United States should give its undocumented a path to legal status.

Opponents respond that the undocumented have broken the law and should not be rewarded. They argue that it would be unfair to those who have waited patiently for years to receive authorization. They also fear that immigrants will take jobs and depress wages—particularly in occupations that do not require advanced education or training. Finally, they say, illegal immigration undermines the social cohesion, the sense of solidarity, within a society.

In 2012, President Obama signed an executive order—bypassing a deadlocked Congress—aimed at protecting over one million undocumented individuals who were brought to the United States as children. The Supreme Court blocked an extension of the program and President Trump ended it, arguing that the president did not have the legal authority to protect these "Dreamers." Instead, Trump pointed out, this was something Congress could (and should) do. The conflict goes on, in courts, in Congress, and within the administration.

Even Hispanic citizens whose families have lived on American soil for many generations may be subject to discrimination due to immigration politics. It may lead police to single out Latinos, a practice known as **racial profiling**. Currently research indicates that although police are as or less likely to stop Hispanic drivers on the road, those who are stopped are 30 percent more likely to receive a ticket.[42] Hispanic immigration is a major contributor to the fundamental American question: *Who are we?*

Racial profiling: A law enforcement practice of singling out people on the basis of physical features such as race or ethnicity.

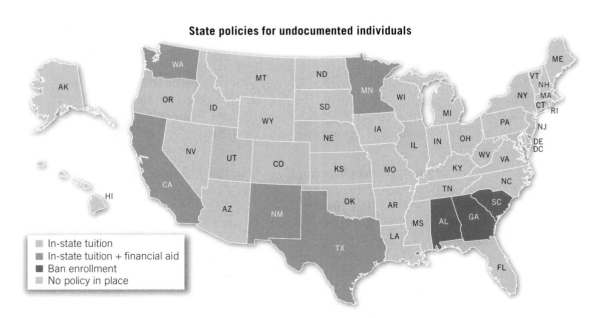

State policies for undocumented individuals

- In-state tuition
- In-state tuition + financial aid
- Ban enrollment
- No policy in place

● **Figure 6.5** *States' varied higher education rules for undocumented students, ranging from eligibility for financial aid to forbidding enrollment. (Education Commission of the States)*

Language Controversy: Speak English!

As long ago as 1752, Benjamin Franklin worried that there were so many Germans in Philadelphia that "instead of them learning our language, we must learn theirs or live as in a foreign country." In recent decades, Spanish language use has become a major issue. In 1974, the Supreme Court ruled in *Lau v. Nichols* that equal protection required schools to assist students whose primary language was not English. Many school districts established bilingual education programs. Opponents argue that bilingual education divides the community, undermines traditional American culture, and disadvantages students who fail to learn English.

Political Mobilization

Hispanic Americans face other challenges. More than one in five lives below the poverty line—two and a half times the rate for non-Hispanic whites. They have less health insurance coverage and face tensions with law enforcement.[43]

When they turn to politics to address these issues, Latinos face both barriers and advantages. The biggest barrier lies in the nature of the Hispanic community itself. In fact, *Hispanic* is a misnomer. Hispanic people come from many different places, each with its own interests and concerns (see Figure 6.6).

For Mexican Americans, who are concentrated in the Southwest, the politics of immigration looms very large. In contrast, Puerto Ricans, the second-largest Hispanic population in the United States, are American citizens by birth; immigration is less relevant to them. Salvadorans, now the third-largest Latino group, face the problems of more recent immigrants—poverty, social integration, and community building. Cuban Americans offer still another contrast. They have high average incomes, generally do not share the same political concerns as most other Hispanic groups, and have traditionally voted strongly Republican—though Cuban youth now break evenly between the parties.[44]

Is there a common political denominator across this diverse population? Today, a pan-Latino movement seeks to find common ground and mobilize voters around issues that transcend any one country or group. Shared political influence, if Latinos seek to exercise it, figures to be formidable: The Hispanic population has grown three times faster than the general population in the last two decades. Latino leaders note that Mexican American voters moved California decisively into the Democratic column in the last twenty years.

In 2006, when the Republican-led Congress proposed tough new restrictions on undocumented individuals, massive demonstrations sprang up around the

Learn about Hispanic and other civil rights groups.

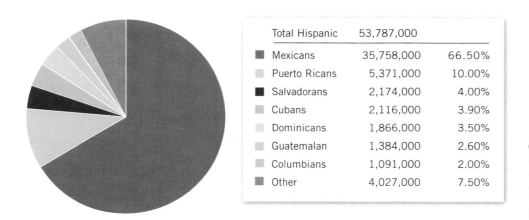

Total Hispanic	53,787,000	
Mexicans	35,758,000	66.50%
Puerto Ricans	5,371,000	10.00%
Salvadorans	2,174,000	4.00%
Cubans	2,116,000	3.90%
Dominicans	1,866,000	3.50%
Guatemalan	1,384,000	2.60%
Columbians	1,091,000	2.00%
Other	4,027,000	7.50%

● **Figure 6.6** *Countries of origin— Hispanics in America. Some two-thirds of Latinos who live in the United States were born here. This figure shows their national heritage. (U.S. Census)*

● *More than 250 years earlier after Benjamin Franklin expressed his concern, the owner of Geno's Steaks in Philadelphia announces that people should speak English. This is a hot issue—and always has been.*

United States. In the past, Latino protesters had waved Mexican flags and symbols. This time, they marched under a sea of American flags. Researchers who were undertaking a major survey of Hispanic Americans at the time discovered that the protests made Hispanics feel significantly more American.[45] Further rounds of protests came in 2018 after Trump Administration rejection of the "Dreamers" program.

The surge in demonstrations reflects the convergence of three important trends: the rapid growth of the Latino population, a sense of shared identity within that population, and an increasing identification with the American homeland. This combination may prove to be one of the most important political developments in future elections, determining not only who gets elected but which political issues receive attention.

The Bottom Line

» Latinos, the largest immigrant group, were for decades the fastest growing population in the United States; the rate of increase has slowed in recent years.

» Latinos are a diverse people with different national identities, histories, cultures, and concerns. Hispanic Americans have won civil rights advances in recent decades—and suffered setbacks.

» A key political question is whether Latinos will mobilize around shared interests and concerns. If they do, they will become an even more formidable political force.

🔘 Asian Americans

Asian Americans are the third-largest minority in the United States after blacks and Hispanics and, according to the U.S. Census Bureau, have in recent years been the fastest growing (see Figure 6.7).[46] Unlike Latinos, they do not share a common language; unlike African Americans, they do not share a common historical experience. As you can see from Figure 6.7, Asian Americans range from Indians to Vietnamese, from Koreans to Filipinos.

As a group, Asian Americans have the highest education level and the highest median personal income of all American population groups. However, the statistics mask as much as they reveal, for Asian Americans range from Indian Americans with high income and education levels to Hmong from the mountains of Laos with income levels about one-third the U.S. average.

Asians have a long history of negotiating the complicated American lines between "us" and "them." In 1882 Congress passed the Chinese Exclusion Act in 1882

■ Chinese	4,948,000	24
▨ Indian	3,982,000	20
■ Filipino	3,899,000	19
▨ Vietnamese	1,980,000	10
■ Korean	1,822,000	9
▨ Japanese	1,411,000	7
▨ Pakistani	519,000	3
■ Cambodian	330,000	2
■ Hmong	299,000	1
▨ Other	1,015,000	5

● **Figure 6.7** *Countries of origin. The national identities of about 20 million U.S. residents whose heritage is Asian. (U.S. Census)*

barring immigration and declaring Chinese people ineligible for citizenship. By 1917, Congress had extended the ban to "all natives of Asia including the whole of India." The California Alien Land Law of 1913 forbade "aliens ineligible for citizenship"—that is, Asian immigrants—from owning land. Each restriction came amid painful stereotypes. The Chinese were excluded because, as one California congressman put it, "His ancestors have bequeathed to him the most hideous immoralities."[47]

After the Japanese attack on Pearl Harbor in 1941, President Roosevelt ordered the army to round up Japanese Americans and place them in cold, miserable internment camps. They lost their liberty, jobs, property, and bank accounts. The Supreme Court upheld the internments.

The wartime camps marked only the most extreme case. Schools and neighborhoods were strictly segregated—giving rise to "Chinatowns." San Francisco established separate schools for Chinese Americans in the 1880s and maintained them until the *Brown* decision. Across the United States, Asian Americans found themselves straddling the racial binary of black and white, particularly in the Jim Crow South.[48]

Perhaps the oddest cultural twist of all is the stereotype that emerged in the 1960s. Many Asian groups were perceived as the "model minority": a hardworking group that makes its own way without any demands for rights or privileges. It may seem that this is a "good" stereotype, but by reducing each person to nothing more than a member of a group, stereotypes demean individuals and stoke social tensions.

Unlike Latinos or African Americans, Asian Americans do not form a majority in any federal electoral district except Hawaii—although some districts in California come close. Thus, Asian Americans must reach out to other groups and build broad coalitions to win elections.

● *West coast white supremacy nineteenth-century style.*

Is there anything to tie together the vast populations and interests? Perhaps. About one out of three Asian Americans reports facing discrimination and slurs. A 2018-19 lawsuit against Harvard suggests that some elite U.S. universities may be excluding Asian American candidates. An internal Harvard study found that Asian Americans have a lower chance of gaining admission than similarly-qualified white, Latino, or black candidates. Is this a new form of exclusion? The courts—and U.S. population—will debate that question in coming years.[49]

The Bottom Line

» Asian Americans, the third-largest minority group in the United States, are the fastest growing.

» Asian Americans have faced discrimination—including today, the image of "a model minority" that, as with any stereotype, is simplistic and hurtful.

» Asian Americans are a tremendously diverse group made up of people who, on the surface, appear to have little in common with one another. The key to their political effectiveness as a group lies in finding (and acting on) common interests as well as forging ties to other groups.

Native Americans

The original natives of the United States own the saddest story about rights denied. Before the Europeans arrived, an estimated ten million American Indians lived on the land that would become the United States. As the colonists spread, they introduced deadly diseases, denied indigenous peoples' sovereignty, fought bitter wars, and slowly pushed the tribes from their ancestral lands.

The Lost Way of Life

The dark side of American expansion was "Indian removal." As European settlers moved west, Indian tribes were forced from their homelands. By the time the United States stretched from coast to coast, fewer than a million of the estimated ten million natives remained.

Recent historians have warned us against simply seeing Native Americans as the passive victims of American westward expansion. The Indians built their own empires and, at times, forced the white settlers to retreat. During King Philip's War (1675–1678), natives destroyed or damaged one in five Massachusetts villages. (The war was named after the Native American leader Metacomet, known to the English as "King Philip.") Between 1750 and 1850, the Comanches dominated economic and military life in the Southwest and pulled white settlers, Spanish colonies, and other tribes into what amounted to an imperial system. Tecumseh (a Shawnee warrior) forged an alliance of Native American peoples across the Midwest to resist American expansion. With much blood and conflict, the federal government had forced most of the Native Americans into reservations by the late 1800s.

On the reservations, the tribes were pushed to adapt European lifestyles. The Dawes Act of 1887 divided reservation lands into individual parcels to destroy traditional ownership customs and encourage farming. Boarding schools educated and assimilated native children. By halting the transmission of cultural legacies, it was hoped that whites could "kill the Indian" and "save the man." Even Sitting Bull, famed Lakota seer and fierce opponent of white settlement, sent his son to be educated to ensure him a place in an uncertain future.[50]

Indians and the Federal Government

Native Americans have an ambiguous legal status. In 1831, the Supreme Court ruled that Indian tribes were "**domestic dependent nations**"—essentially, a separate people but without the rights of an independent nation. Native Americans were not considered citizens and were not protected by the Constitution until Congress passed the Indian Citizenship Act in 1924. Even today, their legal status remains ambiguous. Of a total Native American population of some two million in the Continental United States, about half live on tribal reservations, which are independent jurisdictions subject to federal but not state governments. These Indians are both American citizens and members of self-governing independent lands. Another three million Alaskan natives became U.S. citizens when Alaska joined the union in 1959.

● *Assimilation of Native Americans, often forced, was official U.S. government policy well into the twentieth century. Pupils at Carlisle (PA) Indian Industrial School, c. 1900.*

Domestic dependent nation: Special status that grants local sovereignty to tribal nations but does not grant them full sovereignty equivalent to that enjoyed by independent nations.

The primary connection of Native Americans on reservations to American government is bureaucratic rather than electoral. The Bureau of Indian Affairs (BIA) is responsible for Native American issues. The early placement of the bureau offers a telling symbol: It was part of the Department of War. Later, Congress moved it to the Department of the Interior, whose chief purpose is to promote and protect natural resources and public lands. Native Americans joke that BIA stands for Bossing Indians Around.

Social Problems and Politics

Native Americans face poverty rates almost double the national rates: 26.2 percent, compared to 14 percent for the nation as a whole. Life on the reservations is especially difficult. Most are located in rural areas with few jobs or resources. Native Americans tend to suffer from low education levels, high infant mortality rates, and lower life expectancies.

Native Americans civil rights politics divides roughly into two camps. The *ethnic minority* perspective argues that Indians should engage American democracy and mobilize for rights and equality. The alternative is the separatist *tribal movement*, which advocates withdrawing from American politics and society and revitalizing Native American culture and traditions.

The 1960s civil rights protest movements spread to Native American activists. Led by the American Indian Movement (or AIM), tribes occupied the Bureau of Indian Affairs in Washington, DC, for six days in November 1972. They "captured" Alcatraz Island in San Francisco Bay and occupied the site of the infamous prison for nineteen months between 1969 and 1971. They seized control of the village of Wounded Knee on the Pine Ridge Indian Reservation, the site of a massacre of Indians in 1890, for seventy-one days, declared the reservation a sovereign nation and exchanged occasional gunfire with federal marshals. During this Wounded Knee Incident, AIM brought its grievances before the United Nations General Assembly.

● *The cultural clash spills into sports. In 2015, a federal court ruled that the Washington NFL team's "Redskins" name was no longer protected under U.S. trademark law. Across the country teams debated names and mascots that, in the eyes of many, disparage Native Americans.*

Native Americans and the Courts

As with their contemporaries in other civil rights struggles, Native Americans fought for legislation and sought judicial redress. In *United States v. Sioux Nation of Indians*, the Court ruled in 1980 that the federal government wrongly allowed lands reserved to the Sioux to be settled without purchasing them for fair market value. The settlement awarded, including a century's worth of interest, was approximately $105 million. Now totaling over $1 billion, the settlement remains unclaimed, as doing so would relinquish the Sioux Nation's claim to the disputed lands. In another closely watched case, the Supreme Court in 2018 let stand a lower court ruling that required Washington State to protect longstanding Native American fishing grounds, in a boost for tribal sovereignty.[51]

In recent years, some tribes have used their exemption from state laws to create highly profitable gambling businesses and resorts. The Supreme Court ruled in 1987 that because tribes are considered sovereign entities, they are free from state prohibitions on gaming.[52] According to the gaming industry, 233 of the nation's 565 tribes run casinos. Whether this is a positive development—for the tribes, for the communities around them, and for the United States—is a matter of much dispute.

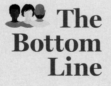 **The Bottom Line**

» Native Americans lost their way of life in the face of colonial settlers' disease, armies, and forced removal.

» The Supreme Court gave American Indians a special status: a separate people without rights. Although they retain the special status, Native Americans became U.S. citizens in 1924.

» Native Americans support two different civil rights strategies: The ethnic minority approach argues for winning political rights and benefits. The tribal movement approach prefers to withdraw and to emphasize a separate Indian society and culture.

📍 Groups Without Special Protection

The idea of demanding rights has spread to other groups that were not mentioned in the Civil Rights Act and have never received special scrutiny from the courts.

People with Disabilities

Before 1970, children in wheelchairs did not go to school, and most blind children never learned how to read. People with disabilities lived outside mainstream society. A political breakthrough came in an unnoticed provision that liberal congressional staff slipped into an obscure bill. **Section 504** of the 1973 Rehabilitation Act borrowed language directly from the Civil Rights Act of 1964 and applied it to the disabled: "No . . . handicapped individual . . . shall, solely by reason of his handicap, be excluded from participation in, or be denied the benefits of . . . any program or activity conducted by an executive agency." Suddenly, any university receiving federal funds—and all government agencies—had to accommodate disabled people.

Section 504 gave activists a political focus. When the government was slow to issue regulations, for example, sit-ins at regional offices pushed the matter forward. Notice the dynamic: Congressional staffers dreamed up a change, giving advocates a focus for action. People with handicaps and their advocates mobilized. Local health boards, planning agencies, and school officials all began hearing from the advocates. The political pattern resembles that followed by African Americans after *Brown v. Board of Education* and feminists after the Civil Rights Act: Government action provided new legal rights; the group then organized and demanded further change.

Advocates went from requesting welfare benefits to demanding civil rights. The process culminated in 1990, when Congress passed the Americans with Disabilities Act (ADA). The ADA forbade companies of twenty-five or more employees from discriminating against disabled people. It also required companies to make "reasonable accommodations" for a wide range of disabilities.

Unlike racial discrimination, however, a business can avoid making accommodations if it would be expensive or inconvenient to do so. Courts constantly weigh the costs and benefits. What is reasonable to require of a firm or a store or a university to accommodate special needs? Even with this delicate balancing of costs and access, the ADA created what amounts to a massive affirmative action program for people with disabilities. Public transportation, schools, shops, and businesses all must help facilitate a normal, mainstream life for people with special needs.

Section 504: An obscure provision in an obscure Congressional act that required all institutions that received federal funds to accommodate people with disabilities.

Sexual Orientation and Gender Identity

The movement for same-sex rights began with a riot. In June 1969, police raided a New York City gay bar named the Stonewall Inn. Traditionally, gay people had submitted to such raids. This time, the gay community broke the unwritten rules. The civil rights movement had, in the past decade, inspired many different groups – including the gay people who defied this routine police raid. The Stonewall riot marks the moment that the LGBT community stopped apologizing and affirmed its identity. Coming out and disclosing sexual orientation became a major vehicle for raising political consciousness in the 1970s. In 1973, the American Psychiatric Association removed homosexuality from its list of mental disorders.

In the early 1980s, gay communities were devastated by a mysterious plague—AIDS. No one knew what the illness was or how it was transmitted—only that diagnosis meant death. The disease pushed gay groups into local politics. In every city, gays organized and established links to the medical community, local governments, and social service networks.

Few recent changes in American politics and culture are as dramatic as the transformation of same-sex civil rights. In 1993, newly elected Bill Clinton ran into a firestorm when he promised to open the military to gay men and women.

Eighteen years later, the Obama administration ended the policy; the quiet reaction in Congress reflects the changing cultural norms.

The same arc—from fierce resistance to broad acceptance—marked same-sex marriage. Back in 2000, Vermont recognized civil unions, legal arrangements that conferred some of the same rights and duties as marriage. The state erupted in protest. What happened next was a revolution in public opinion (which is covered in Chapter 7). Approval of same-sex marriage leapt from 35 percent in 2001 to 62 percent in 2017.

Political institutions followed the revolution in public opinion. Massachusetts became the first state to permit same-sex marriage. Other states followed. The Supreme Court, in *Obergefell v. Hodges* (2015), narrowly (5–4) enshrined same-sex marriage as a national civil right. The majority held that both the Fourteenth Amendment's *due process clause* ("no state shall deprive any person of life, liberty or property without due process of law") and its equal protection clauses ("nor deny to any person . . . the equal protection of the laws") forbade the states from discriminating among couples on the basis of sexual orientation. Notice how the Amendment, put in place to benefit former slaves after the Civil War, continues to offer broad protection against discrimination. But it took activism and public opinion—led by the attitudes of younger Americans—to achieve political change. Few civil rights areas—in politics, law, or public opinion—have evolved as quickly as this one.[53]

Even so, one in four LGBTQ Americans still report serious employment discrimination. Twenty states have put employment protection in place that forbid employers from discriminating on the basis of sexual orientation or gender identity. The EEOC could extend the Civil Rights Act of 1964 to cover the LGBTQ community.[54] However, the Justice Department under the Trump Administration weighed in during a private lawsuit, in July 2017, and argued that the 1964 Civil Rights Act does not protect workers on the basis of sexual orientation. Such protections, it argued, would have to be passed by Congress. "Without a federal law," summarized one employment attorney, "many people could be exposed to discrimination just because they are gay." An appeals court ruled in 2018 that employers may not discriminate on the basis of sexual orientation. The issue is likely to head to the Supreme Court.[55]

LGBTQ individuals, in most places, still face formidable barriers to full civil rights—in employment, housing, education, and public accommodations.[56] One example illustrates the state of the debate. In February 2016 the city of Charlotte passed an ordinance prohibiting businesses, such as restaurants and stores, from discriminating against LGBTQ customers. In addition, the ordinance ensured that transgender individuals could use the restroom for the gender with which they identify.[57] Concerned that this would open the door for sexual predators to target children in the bathroom, conservatives in the North Carolina legislature rushed through House Bill 2, which required individuals to use public bathrooms that match the biological sex on their birth certificate.[58] The law set off a major backlash that cost the state $3.7 billion in revenues. The NCAA relocated championship games, companies such as PayPal and Adidas backed out of constructing facilities in the state, and a federal court blocked the statute.[59] Stung by the outcry, the state repealed the bathroom clause but continued to forbid cities from legislating protections to LGBTQ individuals. Will it stand? Public opinion data suggests that this is one area that could change rapidly, given that the younger generations across political perspectives overwhelmingly support LGBTQ rights. Stay tuned!

Protections for Sexual Orientation and Gender Identity

HOW DO EMPLOYMENT LAWS VARY BY STATE?

In February 2018, Jocelyn Morffi, a first grade teacher at Saints Peter and Paul Catholic School, received notice that she had been fired. She had just returned from her Florida Keys wedding to her same-sex partner. Morffi had no legal course of action at the local or state level: Miami-Dade County has an ordinance that protects against employment discrimination, but exempts religious institutions.[60] As the map shows, some states have instituted laws to protect individuals from discrimination in the workplace; Florida and others have not.

THINK ABOUT IT

How do protections vary geographically? Where are the states that grant the most protections located? Where are those that grant the least?

What protections against employment discrimination does your state provide? What protections do you think it should provide?

Source: Human Rights Campaign

EMPLOYMENT

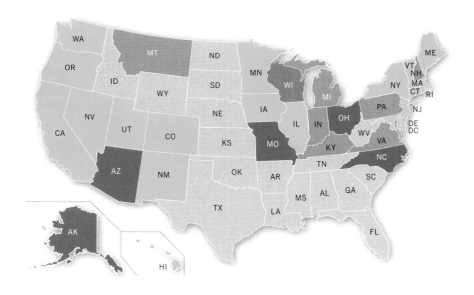

The Federal Equal Employment Opportunity Commission is currently accepting complaints of sexual orientation and gender identity discrimination in employment based on Title VII's prohibition against sex discrimination.

*Transgender individuals receive protection against discrimination in Florida and New York.

*North Carolina's executive order enumerates sexual orientation and gender identity. However, this order has a bathroom carve-out for transgender employees making the executive order not fully inclusive.

Prohibit discrimination based on sexual orientation and gender identity (20 states & D.C.): California, Colorado, Connecticut, Delaware, District of Columbia, Hawaii, Illinois, Iowa, Maine, Maryland, Massachusetts, Minnesota, Nevada, New Jersey, New Mexico, New York, Oregon, Rhode Island, Utah, Vermont, Washington

Prohibit discrimination based on sexual orientation only (2 states): New Hampshire, Wisconsin

Prohibit discrimination against public employees based on sexual orientation and gender identity (6 states): Indiana, Kentucky, Michigan, Montana, Pennsylvania, Virginia

Prohibit discrimination against public employees based on sexual orientation only (5 states): Alaska, Arizona, Missouri, North Carolina, Ohio

No protections

The Bottom Line

» People with disabilities used an obscure bureaucratic rule to mobilize, and eventually won sweeping civil rights with the Americans with Disabilities Act. The goal is to mainstream disabled people as much as possible.

» Gay, lesbian, bisexual, and transgender communities have moved toward the mainstream, driven in part by strong public opinion support from younger Americans. The Supreme Court ruled that states may not discriminate against same-sex partners when issuing marriage licenses. Still, LGBTQ Americans still face challenges in employment, education, housing, and other venues.

The Fight for Civil Rights Goes On

How close has the United States come to achieving racial equality and civil rights? A few key indicators measure how the past half-century of movements has changed America—and how far we still have to go. Fifty years ago, there were no black mayors in the United States. Today, there are over 600. The original civil rights movement also inspired a host of other groups—and provided them with new legal structures such as the Civil Rights Act of 1964 and the Voting Rights Act of 1965. Yet, the data—on poverty, employment, health, education, incarceration rates, and more—suggest that despite great progress, the struggle for many groups continues. Let's focus on the state of equality in three important areas: voting rights, socioeconomic well-being, and incarceration.

Voting Rights Today

During the 2018 election season, twenty-two states debated bills to make voting more difficult. That's on top of sixteen states that introduced new restrictions for the 2016 election, such as government-issued voter ID, no more same-day voter registration, limited early voting, reduced number of polling stations, and limits on out of state students casting ballots where they go to school. Proponents argue that these measures will reduce voting fraud. Critics respond by pointing to very few documented instances of voter fraud and charged that the measures were put into place to depress black, Latino, and young turnout—all groups that tend to vote Democratic. In general, Democrats have tried to make voting easier, Republicans to make it more difficult. Each party stands to gain from the changes it proposes.

The Supreme Court made restricting the vote easier in 2013 when it struck down the central requirement in the Voting Rights Act of 1965: Southern states that had once denied African Americans the vote were no longer required to clear voting rights changes with the federal Justice Department. Chief Justice Roberts declared that the country had changed in the half-century since the rules went into place. If Congress discovered voting problems, it could target discrimination where it is still taking place. In 2018, the Court (in a 5-4 decision) further backed away from the Voting Rights Act by accepting ten of eleven Texas voting districts that a lower court had viewed as problematic.[61]

Economic and Social Rights Today

Equality has many dimensions. Are Americans more equal when it comes to health, wealth, and social justice? Again, we find a mixed story: much progress and a long way left to go.

Health. In 1950, before the civil rights movement, whites lived over nine years (or 14%) longer than African Americans. By 2017, that racial difference had fallen to just 3.2 years (or 4%). Moreover, Asian and Hispanic Americans have longer average life expectancy than whites (Table 6.3).

Income. In 1959, just before the sit-ins began, 55 percent of African Americans lived in poverty. By 1979, the poverty rate among blacks was 31 percent, and in 2017, it stood at 22 percent. Few groups have experienced such a rapid rise out of poverty as African Americans did between 1959 and today. Still, for the entire half-century, the black poverty rate has remained at nearly three times the white poverty rate. The percentage of Hispanic and Native Americans who live in poverty is significantly higher than the white rate (Table 6.4).

For a different perspective, turn to the CEOs in America's 500 largest corporations. As we saw earlier, there are 24 women in that corner office. There are also eleven Hispanics, nine Asian Americans, three blacks (compared to six as recently as 2012), and no Native Americans. The number in 1995 for every one of these groups: zero. Although there remains a long way to go, Americans of every description keep pushing the boundaries of civil rights.

Incarceration. One final twist to the American civil rights story introduces a new source of alarm. As Figure 6.8 shows, African American men are seven times as likely to be in jail as whites. Latinos are three times as likely. Is this "**The New Jim Crow**," as civil rights advocates have argued?

Some suggest that people of all races benefit from tough law enforcement. But most observers believe that the United States has gone too far in sending people to jail, especially for minor offenses. Studies have repeatedly suggested a racial bias throughout the criminal justice system, starting in the way Americans perceive criminals. For example, when subjects were asked to "imagine a drug user," 95 percent pictured a black person. In reality, 72 percent of users are white.[62] There are subtle forms of racial and ethnic discrimination.

A formidable new front has opened in the long battle for civil rights.

The New Jim Crow: The idea that mass incarceration of African Americans has the sweeping effects of Jim Crow discrimination laws. The term is the title of a book by Michelle Alexander.

TABLE 6.3 Average Life Expectancy by Ethnic and Racial Group	
Asian American	87.3
Hispanic	83.5
White	78.8
Native American	76.9
African American	75.6
Source: Kaiser Family Foundation	

TABLE 6.4 Percentage of People in Poverty, by Race	
White	8.8
Hispanic	19.4
African American	22
Native American	28.3
Asian American	10.1
Source: U.S. Census	

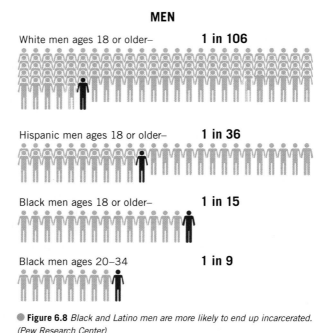

Figure 6.8 *Black and Latino men are more likely to end up incarcerated. (Pew Research Center)*

The Bottom Line

» Voting rights remain a source of fierce political debate today.

» When we turn to health, poverty, and criminal justice, we find a familiar story: The United States has made great progress—and has a long way to go to achieve full civil rights.

Conclusion: Civil Rights . . . By the People

Race. Gender. Latinos. Asians. Immigrants. Native Americans. People with disabilities. Sexual orientation. Transgender individuals. The struggle for civil rights—in many ways, the struggle to secure American ideals—spans the nation's history and engages every generation. We have seen how each group described here reached for civil rights. We also have seen how true civil rights still remain something to fight for.

No American idea is more powerful than the idea of inalienable rights, and none generates more arguments. Government actions are crucial in advancing decisions about rights. One important lesson to draw from this chapter is that laws and court cases have far-reaching consequences. The 1964 Civil Rights Act, for example, ended de jure segregation, focused the women's movement, changed gender relations in schools and workplaces, and inspired the disabilities rights movement; its influence continues even today.

The Supreme Court has been at the center of the storm across the last half century of debates about civil rights. Liberals argue that the Court must ensure that past discrimination does not hobble future generations. Conservatives, in contrast, call on the judiciary to end programs that benefit some individuals simply because of race, gender or any other factor.

America's civil rights movements marked an extraordinary attempt to overcome centuries of injustice, targeting minority and marginalized groups of all types. But did the nation do enough to give every member of society a genuine opportunity to succeed?

Ultimately, the power to make a change lies not with the Court or the Congress or the government, but with the people. The *Brown* decision became an enormous force for change only after the civil rights movement sprang into action. Throughout this chapter, we have seen people transform the politics of rights—marching into violence in Birmingham, prodding a reluctant government to implement the gender provisions in the Civil Rights Act of 1964, waving American flags over immigrant rights in Chicago, holding sit-ins to hurry implementation of disability rules in Washington, and fighting for same-sex marriage when it seemed like an impossible dream. It was people who helped shape the meaning of the legislation and the court decisions. Through their passion and their activism, the people are constantly pushing the United States to live up to its founding ideals.

Each generation faces the same challenge: How to expand civil rights to deserving groups in ways that advance inclusivity for all. That challenge is what drew the two of us to political science. It is our own hope that the mostly young adults reading our book will, like so many Americans in the past, lead the United States toward greater civil rights.

CHAPTER SUMMARY

● The battle for civil rights generally includes seven stages. A group seeking rights must define itself, challenge society, and change the cultural story. The contest for rights spills across the different levels of federalism and the different branches of government: The executive branch can break the ice, Congress is the key to deep social change, and the courts are the final arbiters of civil rights.

● The Fourteenth Amendment contains the crucial legal rule for civil rights: "No state shall . . . deprive any person of . . . the equal protection of the laws."

● A great mass movement featured ordinary men, women, and children turning the legal promise of the *Brown v. Board of Education* decision into practical reality. Protests eventually led to the Civil Rights Act of 1964 and the Voting Rights Act of 1965. The black civil rights movement set the model for future civil rights campaigns by many other groups.

● To make up for past discrimination, legislatures and courts turned to affirmative action in the 1960s and 1970s. The courts, and the public, have become increasingly skeptical of these programs.

● Women first won voting rights in the states—beginning in the West—before finally securing the Nineteenth Amendment, which guarantees the right to vote regardless of gender.

Check your understanding of Chapter 6.

The Civil Rights Act of 1964 bars gender discrimination. The women's movement organized to take advantage of these legal changes. The results transformed American gender roles in political and professional life.

Latinos, the United States' largest immigrant group, are a diverse people with many different national identities, histories, cultures, and concerns. A key political question is whether they will mobilize around shared interests and concerns. If they do, they will become a formidable force, poised to advance civil rights claims for "Dreamers" and other Hispanic Americans.

Asian Americans are the third-largest minority group in the United States and now comprise 5 percent of the population. They are also a tremendously diverse group, misleadingly stereotyped as a "model minority."

Native Americans lost their way of life in the face of disease, armies, and settlers. The Supreme Court gave them a special status: a separate people without rights. Though they retain the special status, they became U.S. citizens in 1924.

People with disabilities leveraged an obscure bureaucratic rule, used it to mobilize, and eventually won the sweeping rights of the Americans with Disabilities Act.

Gay, lesbian, bisexual, and transgender communities have moved into mainstream politics. Nevertheless, they still face discrimination at work, in school, and over housing.

Need to review key ideas in greater depth? Click here.

Flashcard review.

KEY TERMS

1963 March on Washington, p. 173

Abolition, p. 166

Affirmative action, p. 176

Black power, p. 174

Brown v. Board of Education, p. 172

Chicanismo, p. 184

Civil rights, p. 161

Civil Rights Act of 1964, p. 174

Class action, p. 182

Compromise of 1850, p. 167

De facto discrimination, p. 171

De jure discrimination, p. 171

Disproportionate impact, p. 176

Domestic dependent nation, p. 191

Dred Scott v. Sandford, p. 167

Emancipation Proclamation, p. 168

Equal Employment Opportunity Commission (EEOC), p. 180

Equal protection of the laws, p. 168

Equal Rights Amendment (ERA), p. 182

Free rider problem, p. 173

Freedom Riders, p. 173

Great Migration, p. 171

Jim Crow, p. 169

Literacy test, p. 169

Missouri Compromise, p. 167

National Association for the Advancement of Colored People (NAACP), p. 171

National Organization for Women (NOW), p. 180

The New Jim Crow, p. 197

Plessy v. Ferguson, p. 170

Quasi-suspect category, p. 165

Racial profiling, p. 186

Reconstruction, p. 169

Reframe the issue, p. 182

School busing, p. 176

Section 504, p. 193

Seneca Falls Convention, p. 178

Strict scrutiny, p. 164

United Farm Workers (UFW), p. 184

STUDY QUESTIONS

1. Name the seven steps involved in civil rights campaigns. Draw on the historical material in this chapter or your own reading/studies to describe: How did the steps work for Latino equality? For African Americans? For LGBT people? Which step seemed most important in each case.

2. Describe the Civil War amendments. Why was the Fourteenth Amendment so important?

3. What was Jim Crow legislation? What happened to Jim Crow practices?

4. Describe the sit-ins and Freedom Rides of the civil rights movement. What was their point?

5. Describe three effects of the Civil Rights Act of 1964.

6. What is affirmative action?

For further reflection: Write your own Supreme Court decision. Would you accept affirmative action in your college or university? Why or why not?

7. What is the Lilly Ledbetter Law?

For further reflection: Why do you think President Obama chose this to be the first law to sign as president?

8. Although same-sex marriage has won national acceptance in courts and public-opinion polls alike, LGBT people continue to face discrimination. Discuss recent examples of limits on gay or transgender citizens' civil rights, and how these might be redressed.

 Go to www.oup.com/us/Morone to find quizzes, flash cards, simulations, tutorials, videos, and other study tools.

7 Public Opinion

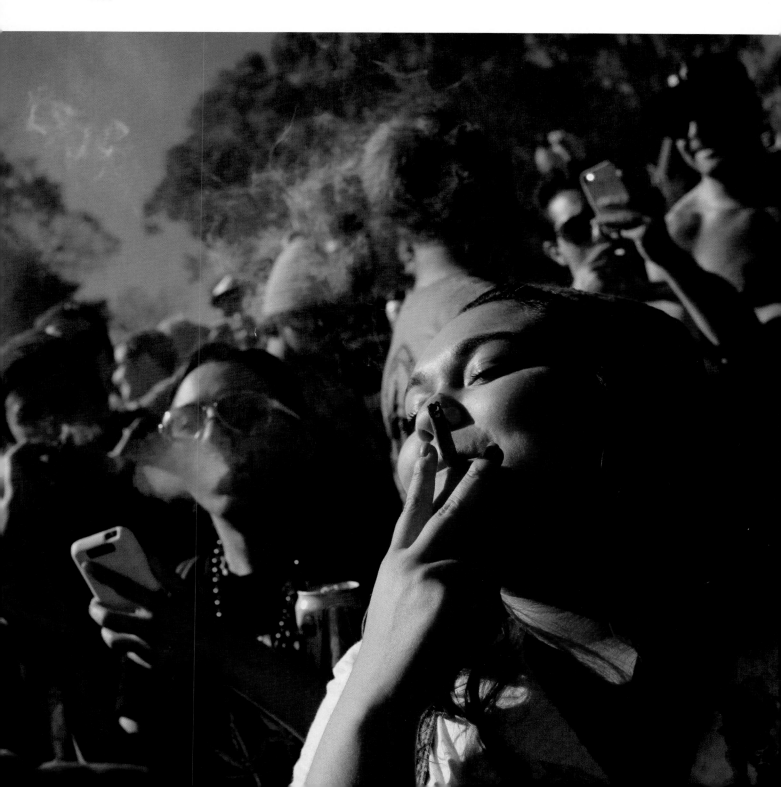

MAUREEN DOWD, a columnist for the *New York Times*, sat in her Denver hotel room and nibbled a caramel chocolate-flavored marijuana bar. Nothing. She ate some more. Suddenly, it hit her. "I lay curled up in a hallucinatory state for the next eight hours," she told her readers, "panting" and "shaking with paranoia." The next day, she found out that the bar should have been cut into sixteen pieces. To many older people, like Dowd, what Colorado had done when it legalized recreational marijuana seemed—for better or for worse—like a social revolution. After all, twenty years ago, only one in four Americans supported legalizing marijuana. Then the number began to rise. Why? Because pollsters started asking a new generation with a very different outlook (Figure 7.1).[1]

Millennials (born early 1980s–2000) strongly support recreational pot (71% in 2017). Even Republican millennials agree (63%). That is a far cry from the oldest cohort, where a large majority still disapproves. A new generation led the change in public opinion—and that led to new government policies. In 2018, thirty states had legalized marijuana in some form—up from zero twenty years ago. Is that the end of the story? Perhaps not. Many people still oppose the change. The Trump administration Justice Department reminds citizens that marijuana remains a federal offense and greenlights federal prosecutors who want to bring federal cases regardless of state laws. Still, with Colorado marijuana sales topping $1 billion a year, most observers think the change is here to stay.[2]

Same-sex marriage reflects a similar story. Public approval leapt up from 31 percent in 2001 to 62 percent in 2017. Again, a new generation came along with different opinions and changed the results (Figures 7.2 and 7.3). As we saw in Chapter 6, state legislatures started approving same-sex marriage laws and in one courtroom after another, judges ruled that banning it violated the Fourteenth Amendment's guarantee of "equal protection under the law."[3]

However, strong public views do not mean strong government action: take global warming. Seventy-four percent of Americans believe in global warming (Figure 7.4). And yet the Obama administration and a large Democratic majority in Congress failed to act back in 2009; Republicans signed a "No Climate Tax Pledge," which promised opposition to any climate change bills that required government spending. President Trump brushes aside the majority view and the scientific consensus, and calls it "a hoax." A minority—but one with very strong feelings—agrees with him. Much of this climate change denial is supported by fossil-fuel industry leaders. In the past decade,

● *Marijuana users in one of the 30 states that had legalized the drug in some form by 2018—reflecting a major shift in public opinion.*

% who say marijuana should be made legal

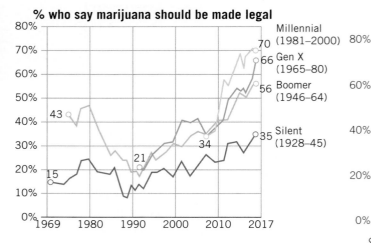

Millennial (1981–2000) 70
Gen X (1965–80) 66
Boomer (1946–64) 56
Silent (1928–45) 35

43
34
21
15

● **Figure 7.1** *Millennials set the pace. Growing support for legal marijuana reflects a change in public opinion between generations. (Pew Research Center)*

% of U.S adults who favor/oppose same-sex marriage (2001–2017)

— Favor —Oppose

● **Figure 7.2** *Support for same-sex marriage has risen dramatically. (Pew Research Center; Gallup)*

% of U.S adults who favor same-sex marriage, by generation (2001–2017)

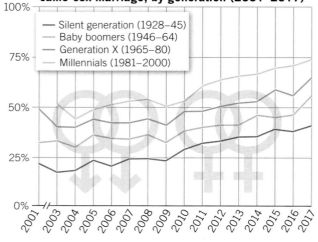

— Silent generation (1928–45)
— Baby boomers (1946–64)
— Generation X (1965–80)
— Millennials (1981–2000)

● **Figure 7.3** *. . . with Millennials setting the pace. (Pew Research Center)*

% who say ...

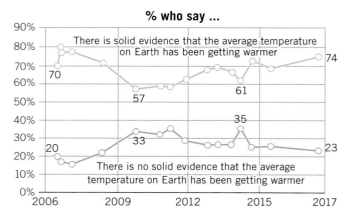

There is solid evidence that the average temperature on Earth has been getting warmer
70
57
61
74

There is no solid evidence that the average temperature on Earth has been getting warmer
20
33
35
23

● **Figure 7.4** *Americans' views on global warming. (Pew Research Center)*

Democrats and Republicans have developed sharply different views of whether government should address climate change—making action far more difficult.[4]

Who are we? The world's oldest democracy. Public opinion takes us to the very heart of self-rule: The people's views are paramount in government. Isn't this exactly the way it should be?

Not necessarily. Remember that the Constitution limits direct popular rule through the Electoral College, lifetime appointment for federal judges, the system of checks and balances, and many other institutions. American government is designed to balance public opinion and the judgment of public officials. And the minority have many opportunities to act on their views—especially if they are organized and well-funded.

No democracy can ignore its people for long. But public opinion raises a lot of tough questions: Can we trust the people to have informed opinions? Or are members of the

BY THE NUMBERS
Public Opinion

Year that "public opinion" was first mentioned by a public official (in France)	**1788**
Year the French Revolution began	**1789**
The first American president to use opinion polls to guide public policy	**Franklin Roosevelt**[5]
Percentage of the American public who can name their U.S. House member and percentage who say he or she is overpaid, respectively	**37, 65**[6]
Percentage of millennials and the "Silent Generation" (aged sixty-five and over), respectively, who approve of marijuana legalization	**71, 35**
Percentage of these generations, respectively, who believe abortions should be legal in all or most cases	**62, 48**
Percentage of these generations, respectively, who would rather have a smaller government providing fewer services	**38, 64**
Percentage of baby boomers, Gen X, and millennials, respectively, who expect that Social Security will provide no benefits by the time they retire	**28, 50, 51**[7]
The authors' predicted probability that there will be no Social Security by the time the millennial generation retires	**0.001**[8]

What role does public opinion play in democratic governments? What role should it play?

public simply parroting their friends, or professional talking heads, or some vague idea that may change tomorrow? What happens when the public is divided? How do we tell when public opinion is correctly measured? And even if we know precisely what the public thinks, perhaps politicians should do what they believe is the right thing, regardless of the polls.

These are the issues we discuss in this chapter. They all revolve around the most basic question in any democracy: How responsive should the government be to the people's views?

🔵 Sources of Public Opinion

Public opinion is simply the sum of individual beliefs and opinions. Your views about how the United States should handle relations with North Korea, whether to cut taxes or raise the minimum wage, whether sports betting should be legal, and whether *Game of Thrones* is too violent for television—along with the views of everyone else in the country—make up public opinion. The central theme for this chapter: What role should your preferences play when public officials make policy? But before pondering that, we turn to a more basic question: Where do opinions come from?

Political Socialization

Political socialization:
The process by which individuals acquire their political values and outlooks.

Why do white Americans trust the police more than black or Latino Americans do? How come some of your friends—but not others—support a strong military? Why is one classmate a staunch Republican and another completely uninterested in politics? We call the many forces that shape our political attitudes and values **political socialization.**

President Lyndon Johnson (LBJ) once remarked, "Tell me where a man comes from, how long he went to school, and where he worships on Sundays, and I'll tell you his political opinions."[9] LBJ, a big-talking Texan, may have exaggerated a bit. But basic life details are strong agents of socialization. And, yes, as Johnson claimed, they help predict where people stand. Let us look at some of the major sources of political socialization.

Parents and Friends. Many people absorb the political attitudes of their parents and caregivers. Mark Losey, running for a U.S. House seat, told his audiences a typical story about how he chose his party: As a child he used to go walking on his grandfather's farm. On one of those walks, recalls Losey, I asked, "'Grandpa, are we Democrats or Republicans?' My grandpa, who grew up on a farm during the height of the Great Depression, paused. 'Before Roosevelt became president, our family almost starved to death,' he replied. 'Grandpa Wren is still a Democrat. So am I.'"[10] Of course, some people—a minority—react against the attitudes they grew up hearing as children. Senator Orrin Hatch, a Utah Republican who retired after forty-two years in Congress, was raised a Democrat. In college, recalls Hatch, "I learned that personal responsibility . . . was supremely better for businesses and individuals than an intrusive federal government that led to personal dependency."[11] That belief turned him into a Republican. Social networks—friends and colleagues—exert a major influence in shaping public opinion. We tend to adopt views expressed by the people around us.

Education. Education is a major agent of socialization. Many of us were influenced by our teachers, going right back to kindergarten when students begin to say the Pledge of Allegiance. Those who seek graduate degrees are more likely to lean to the left—those with advanced degrees identify as 54 percent liberal

🔵 Friends, pastimes, and public rituals all influence political socialization.

and 24 percent conservative. College professors in the United States are far more likely to identify as liberals than conservatives.[12]

Gender. Gender also has a major effect on political views. Men are more likely to support nuclear power plants, fracking to extract natural gas, and testing products on animals. As you might guess from these examples, women lean Democratic by an average of five percentage points. That may not sound like much, but if only women were allowed to vote in American presidential elections, the only Republican candidate who would have won in the last fifty years is Ronald Reagan in 1984.

Race. As we have already seen, race plays an enormous role in American politics and history. African Americans are more likely to be regular churchgoers, more supportive of government spending on social services, and more Democratic. Hispanics tend to be socially conservative on issues such as abortion (see Figure 7.5) but liberal on government services (see Figure 7.6). They also have trended strongly toward the Democratic Party. White Americans lean Republican: Donald Trump won 62 percent of votes cast by white men, and 52 percent by white women in the 2016 election. On the other side, Democratic candidates for president have averaged just 39 percent of the white vote since 1980.

Religion. Religion shapes public opinion on major value questions—from support for food stamps to views about abortion. White evangelicals vote strongly Republican (between 70 and 80%). Catholic voters tend to be split. Black Protestants, Latino Catholics, Jews, and Muslims all trend decidedly Democratic.

Life Events. As we grow up, major events shape our outlooks. The plunge into a Great Depression (in the early 1930s), the attack on Pearl Harbor (in 1941), the assassination of Martin Luther King (1963), the 9/11 terrorist attack (2001), the Great Recession of 2008—all can influence people, particularly young people who are just forming their political opinions. Each generation grows up with its own shared events, technologies, and expectations.

Views on abortion, by religion and nativity
% of Hispanics in each group who say abortion should be illegal in all or most cases OR legal in all or most cases

	All–mostly Illegal	All–mostly Legal
All Hispanics	53%	40%
Catholic	54%	38%
Evang. Prot.	70%	24%
Mainline Prot.	46%	45%
Unaffiliated	35%	58%
Attend worship services		
Weekly+	69%	25%
Monthly/yearly	46%	44%
Seldom/never	35%	58%
Foreign born	58%	33%
U.S. born	43%	49%
General public	40%	54%

Figure 7.5 *Hispanics tend to be socially conservative on issues such as abortion and religious observance . . .*

Role of government
% of Hispanics in each group who prefer smaller government with fewer services or a bigger government with more services

	Smaller, fewer services	Bigger, more services
All Hispanics	53%	40%
Mexican	54%	38%
Puerto Rican	70%	24%
Cuban	46%	45%
Salvadoran	35%	58%
Dominican	35%	58%
Catholic	54%	38%
Evang. Prot.	70%	24%
Mainline Prot.	46%	45%
Unaffiliated	35%	58%
Men	54%	38%
Women	70%	24%
Foreign born	54%	38%
U.S. born	70%	24%
General public	40%	54%

Figure 7.6 *. . . but liberal on the role of government. (Pew Research Center)*

Explore polls to discover how different factors influence opinion.

In sum, there is much truth in Lyndon Johnson's crack about understanding how a person votes. He just did not have enough variables to give a full account of political socialization. Family, friends, education, gender, race, generational context—tell us all those things and we can make a pretty good guess about where you stand politically.

Party

Party preference has become an even stronger predictor of individual opinions than factors such as race and religion. Most politically active Americans are aligned with either Democrats or Republicans and generally stay committed to their party (even if they call themselves independents, most stick to one party or the other). In recent years, the differences between the parties have grown on almost every issue.[13] "From immigration reform to food stamps to student loans," commented one respected pollster, "Republicans and Democrats inhabit different worlds."[14] Your party choice reveals more about your opinions than even strong demographic factors such as race and religion.

For a time, political scientists believed that elected officials were far more partisan than the public at large. Political scientist Morris Fiorina and his colleagues argued that, at least on cultural issues such as abortion, most Americans are moderates. More recent polling suggests a major surge in partisan polarization within the public.[15]

Self-Interest: Voting Our Pocketbooks

Some experts believe that economic self-interest matters most. According to this perspective, people with more money will vote for lower taxes, while people with less will vote to expand social programs.

In practice, economic interests are important, but they are only one factor among many. In a book entitled *What's the Matter with Kansas?*, liberal economist Thomas Frank pointed out that Kansas has some of the lowest average incomes in the country but votes for a congressional delegation made up of Republicans who support cutting taxes and social programs. If these voters focused on their economic interest, argued Frank, they would be more likely to vote for Democrats. Recent studies in states such as Wisconsin, Mississippi, and Kentucky have reached the same conclusion.[16] In general, however, poorer Americans are more likely to affiliate with Democrats, while wealthier Americans are equally divided between the parties (see Table 7.1). Wallets are not everything—but they explain a lot.[17]

TABLE 7.1 **Party Affiliations by Income Level (in percentages)**

FAMILY INCOME	REPUBLICAN (%)	DEMOCRAT (%)	INDEPENDENT (%)
$150,000+	29	29	38
$100,000 to $149,999	30	30	37
$75,000 to $99,999	30	29	38
$50,000 to $74,999	27	30	38
$40,000 to $49,999	24	33	40
$30,000 to $39,999	19	33	43
Less than $30,000	17	35	42
Source: Pew Research Center			

Elite Influence

Stop for a moment and think about whom you listen to when you make up your mind about an issue. Many people turn to friends and family. A series of studies, most notably by the political scientist John Zaller, suggests that people also look to **political elites**. Americans routinely receive signals from political leaders and embrace those that are consistent with their prior beliefs.[18]

Some people look up to "experts" —academics or media personalities such as Megyn Kelly or Anderson Cooper. Others follow very visible public figures such as Oprah Winfrey. And politicians shape opinions: President Trump's tweets are followed by millions and help shape supporters' views.

● *After a stirring speech at the Golden Globes film awards, Oprah became a dream candidate for starstruck Democrats.*

When elites compete to win over the public's views on a topic, they are trying to *frame* the issue—to give the issue a particular slant. For example, when obesity became a source of widespread popular concern, many leaders joined the food industry in framing the issue as one of personal responsibility: Obesity is, they said, a problem of self-control. The simple solution: eat less, exercise more.

Others framed the problem as a "toxic food environment"—too much high-fat, low-nutrition food is available cheaply, from fast-food drive-throughs to school cafeterias. As the public health consequences of obesity became clearer, the toxic food environment perspective gained traction. The framing battle reached a fever pitch when New York Mayor Michael Bloomberg proposed banning sugary drinks larger than sixteen ounces—prompting cheers from public health advocates and scorn from conservative critics sounding off against the "nanny state" meddling in Americans' private lives.

Political elites: Individuals who control significant wealth, status, power, or visibility and consequently have significant influence over public debates.

Wars and Other Focusing Events

Americans pull together during crises. Tragedy, terrorist attacks, and the start of wars generally produce consensus—and a spike in the government's approval ratings. Ninety percent of Americans backed the decision to invade Afghanistan a few weeks after the September 11, 2001, terrorist attacks on the World Trade Center and the Pentagon.

Wars inspire a strong sense of "we're all in this together," but that sentiment generally fades, often quite quickly. After President Bush launched the Iraq war in March 2003, almost 80 percent of the public approved; four years later, approval for American involvement in Iraq had fallen to barely 30 percent.[19] Ninety percent initially supported the war in Afghanistan, but today, only one in five Americans thinks the United States is winning, and large majorities say the war was a "mistake." The same backlash confronted President Harry Truman (over Korea) and Lyndon Johnson (Vietnam).[20]

Most dramatic events have a similar, if smaller, effect on public opinion. When a bridge collapsed in Minnesota or a drilling platform exploded causing a massive oil spill in the Gulf of Mexico, there was a spike in support for infrastructure spending and environmental regulation—only to see both surges fade away. However,

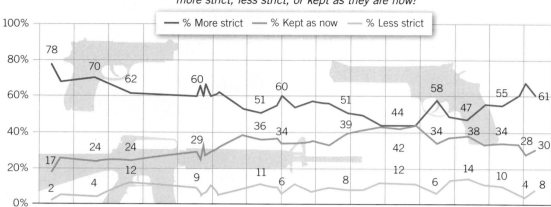

In general, do you think the laws covering the sale of firearms should be made more strict, less strict, or kept as they are now?

— % More strict — % Kept as now — % Less strict

● **Figure 7.7** *Percentage of those who approve of enhanced gun controls spikes after shootings as happened after the December 2012 Sandy Hook Elementary School shooting and the Stoneman Douglas High School February 2018 shooting. (Gallup)*

there are exceptions. When a shooting rampage in 2018 killed seventeen high school students in Parkland, Florida, their classmates mobilized, spoke out for gun control, and pushed the Florida legislature into taking action. Savvy political scientists discount the spikes in public opinion, knowing that the poll numbers generally come back down again (Figure 7.7). The key to keeping an issue alive: Organizing a group—as we explore in Chapter 12.

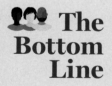 **The Bottom Line**

» Political socialization refers to the factors that shape our political opinions. These include family, friends, education, gender, race, religion, and major life events.

» Party identification has become the most reliable predictor of public opinion in recent years.

» Self-interest and political elites also influence political attitudes.

» How issues are framed can shift individual and collective views.

» Dramatic events, especially wars, also have a powerful role in shaping our opinions.

Measuring Public Opinion

Opinion poll: Systematic study of a defined population, analyzing a representative sample's views to draw inferences about the larger public's views. Also termed *survey research.*

How do we know what the people are thinking? Professional polling firms such as Gallup and Rasmussen, major media organizations, partisan outfits, and academic research centers all jostle to provide the most up-to-date **opinion polls**. Candidates for office commission private polls to tell them how they are performing; presidents and governors retain pollsters to gauge public opinion on various policy items. Let's take a look at why good polling techniques are essential, how reliable polls are designed, where not-so-good polls cut corners, and—most important— how to recognize each kind.

Polling Bloopers

Well-designed scientific polling techniques could have averted polling's first major embarrassment. Back in 1920, a magazine named the *Literary Digest* helped introduce the idea that polls could predict presidential elections. The magazine relied on postcards sent in by subscribers and boasted that it had never failed to predict the winner. Then, in 1936, the *Digest* forecast a lopsided defeat for incumbent President Franklin D. Roosevelt—who instead won the biggest landslide in a century. Why was the *Literary Digest* so far off base? Because its readers tended to be wealthy people who did not like President Roosevelt or his policies.

The biggest polling blooper of recent years? The 2016 presidential election. Scores of polls gave Hillary Clinton a solid lead. Reading the polls, experts pegged the probability of a Clinton victory at between 71 and 99 percent. Pollsters scrambled after the election to explain: How could their scientific predictions be so wrong? As the pollsters point out, they did predict the popular vote: Clinton won by 2 percent of the national vote—close to the consensus prediction of 3 percent. But the polls were off in a few key states – upsetting the predictions for the Electoral College results. The lesson: Polling is an inexact science. But some polls are better than others.[21]

▷

Listen to excerpts from Roosevelt's fiery 1936 campaign speech, helping him overcome opposition among wealthier voters.

Polling 101

Imagine that you are hired to conduct a public survey about the next mayoral election. Where do you start? You could ask a few friends in your American government class who they plan to vote for, but that would not offer you a reliable way to predict the winner. Here is how to improve your poll.

The Random Sample.   One foolproof way to predict the election would be to interview every voter. That would take years and cost too much. Instead, pollsters pick a random selection of individuals who reflect the entire population. All relevant people should have an equal chance of being interviewed. Otherwise, your results will be as misleading as the *Literary Digest* poll—skewed to the wealthy, or the young, or people who just happened to surf to your website.

Sampling Frame.   If your poll is to accurately forecast public views, your survey respondents must reflect the population. That means they must mirror the population's *age, education, income, gender, race* or *ethnic group,* and many other factors that reflect who will vote in the mayoral election. Asking only your classmates would bias the poll toward college-educated and younger people. A good representative survey includes **demographic groups** in rough proportion to their presence in the population.

Refining the Sample.   Do you want your poll to represent *all* city residents, or only those who will probably turn out and vote? Choosing **likely voters** will more accurately predict the outcome of most elections—but determining exactly who will turn out makes the pollster's job more difficult. One explanation for why pollsters got the 2016 election wrong: Their samples in key states were skewed toward people with higher education levels (who traditionally are more likely to vote).[22]

Timing.   Before you start knocking on doors or dialing numbers consider the *timing* of your survey. When do you conduct the poll? If you do it during the day, people with jobs will be busy or away from home; if you conduct a telephone poll

Random sample: A sample in which everyone in the population has an equal probability of being selected.

Sampling frame: A designated group of people from whom a set of poll respondents is randomly selected.

Demographic group: People sharing specific characteristics such as age, ethnicity/race, religion, or country of origin.

Likely voters: Persons identified as probable voters in an upcoming election. Often preferred by polling organizations, but difficult to specify with great accuracy.

Pollsters Face Growing Challenge

HOW CAN THEY PERSUADE AMERICANS TO PARTICIPATE IN POLLS?

Political campaigns and major issues now attract dozens of polls from a host of sources. News stories routinely cite polling results. Yet even as professional pollsters expand in number and influence, Americans' willingness to participate in polls has plummeted.

THINK ABOUT IT

How have the three rates (contact, cooperation, and response) displayed in the infographic changed over the last fifteen to twenty years? Can we trust poll results based on shrinking percentages of the population?

How could pollsters reverse this decline in cooperation? What would encourage *you* to spend twenty to thirty minutes on the phone with a polling organization?

Source: Pew Research Center

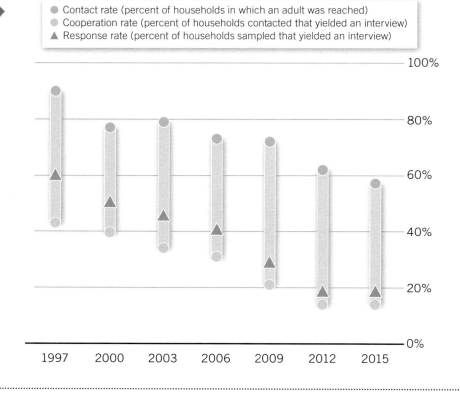

● Contact rate (percent of households in which an adult was reached)
● Cooperation rate (percent of households contacted that yielded an interview)
▲ Response rate (percent of households sampled that yielded an interview)

on a Friday evening, younger residents are less likely to be home—skewing your results to older people's opinions.

Wording.   Once you have chosen your sampling frame and decided when to ask questions, you face an even more important concern: What exactly will you ask? If this were a chat with your classmates, you might ask simply, "Who do you support in the 2019 mayoral election?" But surveys must take into account **framing effects**: The *way* pollsters ask a question often influences the response.

For example, researchers from the Pew Research Center asked people to choose between a tax cut and "funding new government programs." The public overwhelmingly picked the tax cut, 60 percent to 25 percent. Then the pollsters adjusted the question and asked respondents to choose between a tax cut and funding for "programs on education, the environment, health care, crime fighting and military defense." Now, 69 percent opted for the government programs and only 22 percent for the tax cut. The wording made all the difference. Slight rephrasing can dramatically change the results. Does government provide too much assistance to the poor? Only 6 percent say yes. Does government provide too much *welfare* (which is the same question with a new word)? Now, 40 percent say yes.[23]

In other cases, these wording biases can be subtle. In obscure political races (other than president, governor, or large-city mayor), many survey respondents prefer the candidate who is named *first*, no matter what party or other identifying details are included in the question. A really good poll will pretest the questions to sniff out the subtle biases that creep in with different wordings. International polling also has grown more sophisticated (see Comparing Nations 7.1).

Lies, Damn Lies, and Polls.   Campaigns or advocacy groups often *want* to skew their survey results and use framing effects to their advantage. Some polls actually try to influence respondents' views. These surveys—which do not even pretend to be legitimate efforts to measure opinions—are termed **push polls**. Such "polls" have more impact on unsuspecting respondents because they are campaign advertisements masquerading as scientific surveys.

For example, people who answered the phone during the 2018 California primary were first asked questions about the infamous contamination of the water in Flint, Michigan, and then asked whether they supported a water fee increase in California. The pro-fee pollsters, having duly primed their respondents, then announced that 69% favored the increase. This, of course, was more an advertisement than a serious poll.[24]

Technology and Error.   Younger Americans are especially hard to reach and survey. Can you guess why? Many young people—and 47 percent of all phone users—rely on

● *Mocking bias in the polls.*

Framing effects: The way the wording of a polling question influences a respondent

How do we know what "the people" think?

Push poll: A poll question designed to get a certain result – often a negative campaign ad that masquerades as a regular opinion survey or a poll.

COMPARING NATIONS 7.1 | Top Global Threats: Polling Around the World

When people in different nations are asked about the greatest global threat, Americans, Russians, and Western Europeans point to Islamic terrorism; South Americans and Africans worry about global climate change; Japanese cite cybersecurity; South Koreans and Vietnamese worry about China's rising global influence; and Turkey, a longtime ally, now names "U.S. power and influence" as the greatest threat to the globe. (Pew Research Center)

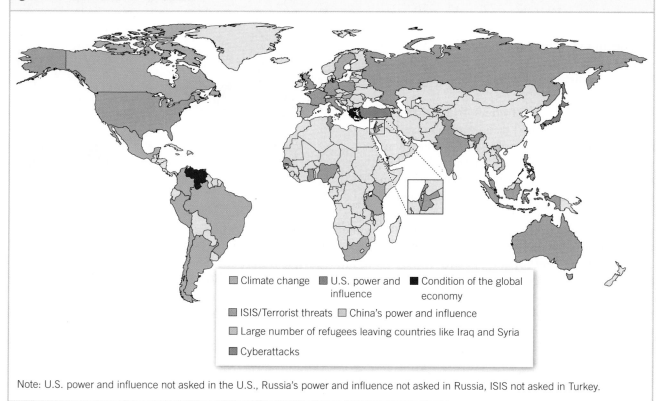

- ▢ Climate change ■ U.S. power and influence ■ Condition of the global economy
- ▢ ISIS/Terrorist threats ▢ China's power and influence
- ▢ Large number of refugees leaving countries like Iraq and Syria
- ■ Cyberattacks

Note: U.S. power and influence not asked in the U.S., Russia's power and influence not asked in Russia, ISIS not asked in Turkey.

mobile phones rather than landlines.[25] To save time and money, most professional pollsters use *automated* dialing for landline calls. Machines dial dozens of numbers at once; when a caller answers, the "robo-dialer" transfers the call to a human surveyor. Pollsters cannot autodial cell phones because most states do not allow it.

Sampling Error and Response Bias.   Finally, you have collected the raw data from all of your surveying. Time to tell the world about the details of your poll? Not so fast. You still need to determine your poll's "confidence interval," or **margin of sampling error**, a statistical measure of how accurate your results are. By carefully designing their poll, national surveys are able to achieve small errors with as few as one thousand respondents (see Figure 7.8).

Pollsters also must consider **response bias** in publicizing their findings. Studies show that some respondents purposely mislead pollsters. Response bias can reflect animosity toward pollsters or the all-too-human tendency to align with "acceptable" views. Survey questions that might elicit unpopular attitudes, such as racism or sexism, can lead respondents (consciously or unconsciously) to shift their answers in a more socially acceptable direction.

A classic example of response bias arose when Tom Bradley, the first African American mayor of Los Angeles, ran against a white candidate, George

Margin of sampling error: The degree of inaccuracy in any poll, arising from the fact that surveys involve a *sample* of respondents from a population, rather than every member.

Response bias: The tendency of poll respondents to misstate their views—often to avoid "shameful" opinions such as sexism or racism.

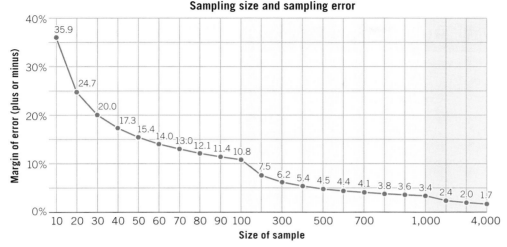

Sampling size and sampling error

Figure values (plotted points, margin of error vs. size of sample):
35.9, 24.7, 20.0, 17.3, 15.4, 14.0, 13.0, 12.1, 11.4, 10.8, 7.5, 6.2, 5.4, 4.5, 4.4, 4.1, 3.8, 3.6, 3.4, 2.4, 2.0, 1.7

Y-axis: Margin of error (plus or minus), 0% to 40%
X-axis: Size of sample — 10, 20, 30, 40, 50, 60, 70, 80, 90, 100, 300, 500, 700, 1,000, 4,000

Figure 7.8 *Sampling errors decline with larger sample sizes (MEER Research).*

Craft and interpret surveys to advise Congress.

Deukmejian, for governor of California in 1982. Bradley had a comfortable double-digit lead in opinion surveys as Election Day approached—but lost the race. Today pollsters must be alert to what is now known as the Bradley effect: The possible inclination of some survey respondents to avoid appearing racist or racially motivated. Pollsters speculate there may have been "shy" Trump voters in 2016—people reluctant to reveal that they supported Trump. Still another potential source of bias: Democrats may be more willing to respond to polls than Republicans.

Sample size, framing effects, and margin of error: Account for all these, and you are well on your way to conducting a truly scientific public opinion survey. One important reason to understand the design of polls is so that you can distinguish the good from the bad. Table 7.2 summarizes some of the tips.

How Did They Do? After pollsters' poor performance in 2016, many reworked their methodology to take account of a changing electorate. In the days before the 2018 election, polls showed control of the U.S. House flipping to Democrats.

TABLE 7.2 **Tips on Reading Polls**

1. *Check out the margin of error.* A 3 percent margin of error means plus or minus 3 percent—turning a 50 percent approval rating into one that could be as low as 47 or as high as 53 percent. If the margin of error is too large (say over 5%), then approach the poll with caution.
2. *What is the timing?* The farther away from Election Day, the less meaningful the results.
3. *The random sample is the gold standard.* If the respondents chose themselves (by deciding to take the survey), then it may be fun to read . . . but it is probably not an accurate picture of the public.
4. *What is the sample size?* Be wary of polls that interview a small number of people. For a national poll, 1,000 to 1,500 respondents is typical. Too few respondents means a hefty margin of error.
5. *Compare across polls.* Because every poll has biases, read a range of polls, toss out the extreme findings, and average the rest.

What Do YOU Think? Is Polling Bad for Democracy?

More than 350 surveys of Americans were conducted on the 2016 presidential election. Is that bad for democracy? *What do you think?*

Too Much Polling. Candidates who lead in the polls might use the bandwagon effect to convince undecideds to join them and thus unfairly influence the results of the election. Moreover, the media obsession with who's up and who's down drives out serious discussions of ideas and policies. In 2016, there was more than four times as much news coverage of the horse race than of policy stands.[26] We should focus less on the race and more on the issues.

Let a Thousand Polls Bloom. Polls communicate the people's views and values to candidates and elected officials. As candidates assess how well they are doing in a given geographic region or with a demographic group, they hone and target their message, which becomes the campaign promises that they work to deliver once elected to office. Furthermore, the more polls, the less likely a candidate will be able to falsely claim they have a lead—and convince undecideds to join them.

Although the average predicted outcomes of polls in some state races were off by as many as three percentage points, the House indeed flipped to Democrats—and, also as predicted by most pollsters, the Senate remained in Republican control.[27]

Do Opinion Surveys Influence Us?

Could the profusion of polls also affect the decisions we citizens make—including how to vote? They sometimes seem to. Candidates who are leading in the polls sometimes pick up support from voters who were undecided or who weakly supported the opponent. The **bandwagon effect** in polling varies considerably from place to place and election to election. It can be exaggerated by media coverage: In 2016, many observers attributed Donald Trump's unexpected nomination as the Republican Party candidate to the bandwagon effect.[28]

A close cousin of polling's bandwagon effect is the **boomerang effect**. Here, a candidate who has been consistently ahead in opinion surveys underperforms on Election Day. Supporters see a big lead for their candidate, figure that he or she will win without any difficulty, and so do not bother to vote.

Scrambling the issue further, some voters also appear to follow the *opposite* of the bandwagon effect. America loves rooting for the underdog—the one we do not expect to win—and this tendency also appears in public opinion polling. The **underdog effect** is invoked when a candidate losing in the polls performs better than expected. There is less empirical evidence for this phenomenon, though one study showed that candidates who told supporters they were "barely losing"—triggering the underdog effect—received 55 percent more donations than those reporting they were ahead in the polls.[29]

Bandwagon effect: When people join a cause because it seems popular or support a candidate who is leading in the polls.

Boomerang effect: The discrepancy between candidates' high poll ratings and election performance, caused by supporters' assumption that an easy win means they need not turn out.

Underdog effect: Sympathy for a candidate behind in the polls, contributing to a higher-than-predicted vote total—and sometimes a surprise election victory.

The Bottom Line

» Scientific surveys have come a long way since their origins in 1936. Professionals now design well-specified polls that capture popular views with a high degree of accuracy.

» Indeed, poll results can affect public opinion, in ways ranging from the bandwagon effect to the underdog effect.

» Sampling errors, response bias, and other potential flaws inevitably confer a measure of uncertainty on any survey.

Public Opinion in a Democracy

If the public is to have a meaningful role in governing, political leaders must listen to their views. But here is the uncomfortable question: Do the people know enough to shape government decisions? We have seen that the founders were wary of the public when they framed the Constitution. The question continues to provoke disagreement. Is the public rational and capable of self-government? Or are we, as political scientist David Sears argued in a recent essay, "an ignorant and easily duped electorate?"[30] Let us look at two different views.

Ignorant Masses

"The masses are asses!" insisted Walter Lippmann in his pathbreaking book *Public Opinion* (published in 1922). Lippmann, a well-known political journalist and cultural critic, dismissed the young "science" of public opinion as undeserving of the name. In his view, the typical American was distracted by celebrity shenanigans and minor scandals, rarely followed policy issues closely enough to understand the details, and yet readily offered up personal views on any topic. Paying attention to the uninformed masses was no way to run a country. Lippmann, along with many others, believed that governing involved technical decisions that were best left to well-trained experts.[31]

Some modern thinkers embrace a similar view. Most Americans cannot answer basic questions about our political system. In a 2017 survey, only a quarter of respondents could name the three branches of government, and over one-third (37%) could not name a single right protected under the First Amendment.[32] Critics describe America as an "ignorant democracy." Popular whims and cleverly packaged slogans, they say, win out over serious political deliberation.[33] Public opinion, in this view, is a tool for manipulation by savvy message consultants and political marketers.

In 1960, four University of Michigan professors published a book that hit America like a thunderclap. Not only were most citizens uninformed, but even more damning, *The American Voter* described the scientific poll—the instrument widely used to capture public opinion by the 1950s—as all but useless. One of the authors, Philip Converse, later coined the term **nonattitudes** to describe the response of many Americans to polls. When people were asked the same questions at different times, they tended to change their answers—sometimes radically. Moreover, changes in their responses were random: People did not switch their positions in response to new information or in changing contexts, but rather offered up different and even diametrically opposed views for no apparent reason.[34]

TYPES OF POLLS

Benchmark polls. Conducted by a campaign as the race begins, these surveys provide a basis for comparison, or a "benchmark," for later polls.

Straw polls. Informal polls carried out by local party organizations or news outlets; they often involve actual (nonbinding) votes cast by party members. Media organizations (and the straw poll winners) tout the results, but they can be misleading.

Brushfire polls. Internal surveys conducted by a campaign once election season begins. They provide details about how a candidate is performing; if things are going poorly, the campaign can work to put out the bad news or "brushfire" (which burns hot and spreads fast).

Exit polls. Performed on Election Day, these surveys intercept voters as they exit the voting location. Media reporters often rely on exit polls to call results for one or the other candidate, even if ballots haven't been counted yet.

Nonattitudes: The lack of a stable perspective in response to opinion surveys; answers to questions may be self-contradictory or may display no consistency.

The American Voter shook the confidence in the value of both public opinion and the scientific methods used to measure it. If Americans spewed random thoughts in response to survey questions, what use were opinion polls? This perspective extends right down to the present. Titles of recent books repeat the old story: *Do Facts Matter?* Or, more pointedly, *Uninformed* and *Just How Stupid Are We?*[35]

Recent research echoes this pessimistic view suggesting that most people do not function as "rational actors" who seek and analyze information, weigh evidence, and choose candidates (or support policies) that advance their preferred views. People rationalize preconceived biases and may not even be aware of why they are making the choices they make.[36] In short, there are reasons to be skeptical about the people's wisdom in governing the nation.

The Rational Public

Other commentators defend the American public, arguing that ordinary Americans, not elite technocrats, are the best judges of what government should do. This alternative view gained force in the 1980s, helped by a book-length response to *The American Voter* called *The Rational Public*.[37] The authors, Benjamin Page and Robert Shapiro, agreed that most voters are generally inattentive to policy issues and uninformed about political details. However, measured across large groups of people, public opinion moves in coherent, stable ways that signal shared views about policy issues. Although a single person may hold inconsistent or even self-contradictory notions, these are submerged in the collective outlook of tens of millions. Taken as a whole, the public can differentiate among alternative policies, in ways that accurately reflect its shared values and beliefs.

Information shortcuts: Cues about candidates and policies drawn from everyday life.

Page and Shapiro argued that most of us use **information shortcuts** to arrive at reasonable judgments about politics and government. These shortcuts often derive from our direct personal experience. Homeowners grasp the importance of interest-rate changes, and shoppers feel inflation's effect on rising prices. Both homeowners and shoppers develop an intuitive sense of the performance of the economy. Likewise, citizens notice the impact of other policy outcomes on their daily live: Do trains or buses run on time? Does the mail arrive late? Does filling up the SUV cost more than it did last month? Through a steady and often unwitting process of making everyday evaluations, voters and poll respondents can arrive at reasonably well-established positions on candidates or policy issues.

Is there any way to reconcile the two views: ignorant individuals on the one hand, a rational public on the other? The writer James Surowiecki offered one solution, summarized by the title of his book: *The Wisdom of Crowds*. Even if any one individual does not have clear views, argued Surowiecki, a large crowd can add up to a rational public. In fact, a random collection of people is, in many cases, wiser than a group of experts.

Surowiecki built on the work by the French thinker Nicolas de Condorcet, who in the eighteenth century demonstrated that, although each member of a jury may not do much better than a coin flip in accurately judging guilt or innocence, taken as a whole the jurors are likely to reach a correct decision. Likewise, a group of people may include those that are ignorant about details or eccentric. However, if the group is big enough—at least a few dozen—and members feel free to speak their minds, they will zero in on a good collective decision. Often these are innovative, outside-the-box

What Do YOU Think? How Closely Should Elected Officials Follow Public Opinion?

Should the government approve a giant pipeline delivering gas from Canadian tar sands to Texas refineries? When the debate began, the public supported the project but, in 2015, the Obama administration refused to issue a permit to build the pipeline, aligning itself with a Democratic Party concerned about global climate change and the environment. The Trump administration reversed the decision in response to Republican desires for energy independence—and despite the fact that public support has dropped and polls show that the public disapproved of the pipeline, 51 percent to 42 percent.[38] Is it okay for presidents to override public opinion? (You may recognize this as a concrete example of the debate about self-rule back in Chapter 2).

Elected officials must lead.
We elect leaders and expect them to fulfill their campaign promises. As opposition to the pipeline rose among Democrats, President Obama responded to the people who voted him into office. President Trump did the same – he responded to his base. Furthermore, presidents can be privy to more information about an issue than the general public. In these cases, they must override the opinion of the majority.

Public opinion should dominate.
Even though individuals may not know all the details of a policy issue, a large group of people tends to provide reliable information and make good choices that are reflected in polls. Furthermore, polls measure and communicate the values and views of the people. Elected officials should look to these polls to inform their decisions.

---

solutions. Experts, on the other hand, are typically trained in similar ways and are subject to **groupthink**: They tend to reinforce one another's existing prejudices.

Surowiecki illustrated his point by describing a nineteenth-century country fair in England. A prize was offered to whoever could guess the correct weight of a giant ox. Cattle experts weighed in with their informed guesses, but all were off the mark. More than eight hundred locals offered up guesses as well. Although no one hit the correct weight (1,198 pounds), an average of the crowd's collective estimate came out at 1,197—just one pound below the correct total, and closer than that offered by the agricultural experts.[39]

Of course, crowds can be dangerous too—they can turn into angry mobs, losing any semblance of rationality altogether. That is exactly why the Constitution has so many checks and balances. Recall the great question when we discussed the Constitution (in Chapter 3): Does American government have too many checks and balances? Or not enough?

Groupthink: The tendency among a small group of decision makers to converge on a shared set of views; can limit creative thinking or solutions to policy problems.

James Surowiecki discusses the power—and danger—of crowds, including online "mobs."

● How much does this ox weigh? Ordinary fairgoers' collective guess outperformed that of agricultural experts in a famous nineteenth-century contest—a testament to the wisdom of crowds.

The Bottom Line

» Since the founding era, some Americans have viewed public opinion as an unreliable, even dangerous, guide to government policymaking based in part on voter ignorance.

» Others argue that, in practice, a "rational public" is the best source of democratic decision making.

» One way to resolve these clashing views is to focus not on what individuals know about politics but on how many different popular views add up to the "wisdom of crowds."

Public Opinion and Governing

The optimistic view about the crowd's wisdom restores traditional hopes about self-rule. However, if public opinion is to guide government, three conditions must be met.

1. The people must know what they want.
2. The public must clearly communicate its desires to political leaders.
3. Political leaders must pay attention to public views—and respond.

Each step is full of difficulties. Consider each in turn.

Do the People Know What They Want?

Even when polls suggest that the public have distinct preferences, they are often too vague to guide policy. For example, after the economic collapse in 2008, polls showed that a majority of Americans were angry at Wall Street banks. By large margins, the public favored tough legislation: slash financial industry CEOs' pay, throttle back on trading in exotic financial instruments that few people understand, and make banks pay for the economic mess they helped create.

But when Congress and the Obama administration tried to translate this public discontent into concrete legislative solutions, popular consensus evaporated. Should we regulate derivatives as we do stocks and bonds so that their trading is transparent? Half the public said yes, half said no. Limit CEOs' pay or the multimillion dollar bonuses the financial wizards receive each year? Maybe, or maybe not, Americans told pollsters. Deep in the details, the crowd did not

Public opinion alerted politicians to the anger at big banks—but did not provide an answer for what to do about it.

have the knowledge to formulate a solution. In the end, Congress passed the "Dodd–Frank" bill regulating the financial industry in 2010, but this did not satisfy many people. Republicans rolled back the regulations in 2018. After the next crash, the public will again demand regulation and the cycle will begin anew.[40]

The public knows what it wants—generally. But usually that's not enough to guide informed policymaking.

How Do the People Communicate Their Desires?

It is difficult for the people—even a clear majority—to convey their views to policymakers. None of our instruments for adding up and transmitting millions of people's views are particularly effective.

As we have seen, survey research can offer snapshots of public opinion on policy issues. However, polls have margins of error; they can be spun to advance partisan interests. They offer general impressions, not a guide to crafting policies and making decisions—as we just saw in the case of widespread public anger at Wall Street. And with so many competing polls, often with different results, it can be difficult to pin down what the public really wants. Still, sometimes forceful shifts in public opinion leap out from the polling cacophony and lawmakers get a clear message.

Of course, democracies also rely on elections. Candidates who win often claim they have a **mandate**: The people have spoken. But it is difficult to translate an election into support for any single policy. In 2016, Republicans won the presidency and both chambers of Congress. But even with that mandate, they failed to eliminate Obamacare, build a border wall, or rewrite the immigration laws. As previous administrations learned, even a clean sweep of the elective branches does not automatically translate into policy success.

Interest groups and political parties also work to collect and transmit popular views. However, their messages about what the people want generally come with a partisan spin.

Mandate: Political authority claimed by an election winner as reflecting the approval of the people.

Do Leaders Respond to Public Opinion?

On the surface, the answer seems to be unambiguous: yes! Opinion surveys are everywhere, and politicians seem hooked on them. President Trump routinely tweets out any uptick in his **approval rating**, while Democratic critics are quick to report that Trump had the lowest ratings of any modern president in his first year. American politicians spend more on pollsters, by far, than leaders of other nations; in national elections, presidential and congressional candidates spend more than a billion dollars on opinion surveys. President Bill Clinton was said to poll on everything—including where to go on vacation.[41]

However, attention to public views does not necessarily mean that politicians slavishly follow the poll results. Rather, polls guide political leaders in their efforts to persuade the public to embrace their own views—and criticize the opposition and their ideas.[42]

Polls clearly matter in setting the **policy agenda**. Public opinion helps shape which topics governing officials pay attention to in the first place. If the public thinks something is important, political leaders will usually respond.

Approval rating: A measure of public support for a political figure or institution.

Policy agenda: The issues that the media covers, the public considers important, and politicians address. Setting the agenda is the first step in political action.

You can enjoy this trail today thanks to a shift in public opinion back in 1910.

Big changes in public opinion have an especially significant effect on elected leaders. Members of Congress and state legislatures are often reluctant to legislate in the face of strong popular opposition. Americans may ignore many topics, but when large numbers of us pay attention and begin supporting or opposing an issue, politicians generally respond—as we saw in the chapter opening with legalizing marijuana and recognizing same-sex marriage.

Public opinion also enables presidential actions that might otherwise be blocked. Theodore Roosevelt (1901–1909) was a popular president, but he had to abandon his ambitious plans for a national system of protected forest in the eastern United States because of public indifference. His less popular successor, William Howard Taft (1909–1913), signed the Forest Reserve Act into law. How did Taft succeed? After a massive forest fire known as the "Big Burn" raged across three western states and killed more than one hundred young firefighters, public opinion swung decisively in support of environmental protection. If you have hiked on the Appalachian Trail, vacationed in the Smoky Mountains, or gone leaf-peeping in New England, you have benefited from a program made possible by shifting public opinion.

Although collective public opinion holds some sway, the opinions of some groups matter more than others. As we have seen, pollsters target the opinions of likely voters—individuals they expect to participate in elections. Social movements, interest groups, and political parties work to collect and transmit their views and can have a more direct influence on public policies. By participating in the political system, your voice is more likely to be heard.

The Bottom Line

» If public opinion is to guide politics, three conditions must be met: The public must know what it wants, its views must be effectively communicated, and leaders must pay attention.

» Even strong public opinion may not be specific enough to offer policy guidance.

» U.S. government officials devote more resources to polling operations than do top officials in other nations.

» Popular views can help set governing agendas. Polls most often guide officials in determining how best to win over the public to their policies. And occasionally, when a clear majority expresses its opinion, politicians follow suit.

👤 Conclusion: Government by the People

Americans founded their nation on an inspiring idea: the consent of the governed. Lincoln put it beautifully, in his Gettysburg address, when he prayed that "government . . . by the people shall not perish from the earth." But just how do we maintain those democratic dreams? They demand that public opinion guides—or at least influences—the government and that the people get involved in government affairs.

Public opinion surveys are the most widely used effort to understand the popular mind. Scientific techniques have refined polling to a point of remarkable accuracy—especially when elections draw near.

Yet, a great debate swirls around public opinion itself. Many have called it whimsical or uninformed—even the framers of the Constitution were skeptical. Others are more optimistic: Collective decisions—the wisdom of crowds—are often wiser than those made by well-trained experts.

Today, our smartphones and laptops stream even more information, enabling each of us to instantly research any issue. But more information is not always better. Research by Barry Schwartz, a political psychologist, shows that an overabundance of choices and details tends to paralyze individual citizens, rather than empower them.[43]

The current torrent of polls, some of them carefully slanted by advocates or politicians trying to influence us, similarly spews out overwhelming reams of data. Politically attentive citizens (like you) and passionate advocates for a candidate or cause alike need to hone their skills at reading polls—drowning out the noise, picking the more accurate reflections of public sentiment.

Our sprawling intersection of politics and polls most often results in ambiguous public views. But, at times, massive shifts in public opinion—as with marijuana reform—change officials' views and lead to policy change. A rising generation's attitudes can decisively influence our public policies.

Ultimately, no public opinion poll can replace the central act of governance: elected leaders, with an eye to public sentiment (and all the surveys measuring their approval ratings) deciding what issues to promote and then voting "yes" or "no." On the issues where Americans are not sufficiently informed and uncertain, public officials have a major effect in setting the agenda, framing issues, and signaling popular views. They can take the lead in encouraging us to be better stewards of democracy.

CHAPTER SUMMARY

🔘 Scientific surveys have come a long way since the *Literary Digest* in 1936. Professionals now design well-specified polls that capture popular views with a high degree of accuracy. However, be cautious when reading polls, such as those without a well-defined sample (e.g., online surveys). Always pay attention to the margin of error when interpreting results.

🔘 Political socialization is the study of the forces that shape public opinion. The most important are family and friends, race, gender, religion,

Check your understanding of Chapter 7.

economic interests, demographics, party affiliation, the view of political elites, and defining events such as war.

● In a democracy, public opinion should guide the government. But are the people capable of self-rule? From the Constitutional Convention to contemporary social scientists, many experts consider public opinion to be uninformed and unreliable—and therefore a dangerous guide to decision making.

● Others respond that the public, taken as a whole, is a rational, reliable source of government decisions. Even if individuals do not know much, there is wisdom in crowds.

● The United States devotes more resources to polling operations than other nations. Polls have become the everyday mechanism for gauging public opinion. But while scientific techniques have made polls more accurate, rising costs, plummeting response rates, the difficulty of predicting turnout, and hostility to pollsters can make all polls miss.

● Public officials generally balance public opinion with their own beliefs about the best decisions. If they are seen as overly faithful to poll results, the paradoxical result may be that their approval rating falls. Polls often guide administrations, not in selecting a policy, but in determining how best to win over the public to their policies.

● Popular views can be especially important in setting the agenda: If something seems important to the public (and the media), politicians respond. Congress, in particular, pays attention to spikes in public opinion. Presidents find it easier to get their policies passed when public opinion is strongly in favor of those policies.

Need to review key ideas in greater depth? Click here.

Flashcard review.

KEY TERMS

Approval rating, p. 221
Bandwagon effect, p. 216
Boomerang effect, p. 216
Demographic group, p. 211
Framing effects, p. 213
Groupthink, p. 219
Information shortcuts, p. 218

Likely voters, p. 211
Mandate, p. 221
Margin of sampling error, p. 214
Nonattitudes, p. 217
Opinion poll, p. 210
Policy agenda, p. 221

Political elites, p. 209
Political socialization, p. 206
Push poll, p. 213
Random sample, p. 211
Response bias, p. 211
Sampling frame, p. 214
Underdog effect, p. 216

STUDY QUESTIONS

1. "The masses are asses," wrote one observer of American politics. He was summarizing a perspective that public opinion is not a reliable guide to government. Why, exactly, do some say that public opinion is unreliable? Be sure to include the effect of *The American Voter*.

2. Other scholars insist that public opinion is a legitimate guide to government decision making. Summarize this alternative view, noting the argument made in *The Rational Public*.

3. For further contemplation: Which of these perspectives on public opinion seems more powerful to you? Do you believe the public is basically ignorant? Or collectively wise? (Yes, you may opt for a bit of both.) Defend your answer.

4. "Public officials must always balance public opinion with their own beliefs."
   a) Explain why.
   b) What problems face political leaders who *always* follow the polls in deciding what to do?
   c) What problems face political leaders who *never* follow the polls in deciding what to do?
   d) How can polls help leaders who already know what they want to do?

5. Define the following terms: *push poll*; *sampling frame*; *margin of error*; *Bradley effect*.

6. What does it mean to "frame an issue"? Illustrate using the issue of obesity, or a hot-button issue in the headlines that interests you.

7. Given limitations on polling, can you imagine other ways that the public's opinion could best be conveyed to political leaders? (You'll encounter some alternatives in the next chapter as well.)

Go to **www.oup.com/us/Morone** to find quizzes, flash cards, simulations, tutorials, videos, and other study tools.

8 Political Participation

A FLORIDA CAR SALESMAN named Gene Huber, who salutes a cardboard cutout of President Trump every morning, was invited onstage by the president during an appearance in Melbourne, Florida. Not previously active in politics, Huber eventually quit his job to attend Trump rallies and otherwise support the president full-time. Both during and after Trump's 2016 campaign, millions of Americans from every walk of life have attended these rallies, drawn by Trump's call to "make America great again."

Even as Huber was helping to inspire the Trump faithful, appearing at presidential events from Phoenix, Arizona, to Raleigh, North Carolina, opposing voices also were drawn into civic action. From women marching by the millions across the United States the day after Trump's inauguration in 2017 to pro-"Dreamers" Deferred Action for Childhood Arrivals (DACA) support rallies, political engagement surged among many other traditional nonparticipants. Voter registration, subscriptions to mainstream media outlets, public demonstrations: All have continued to rise since Inauguration Day.[1]

Those drawn into political participation by the Trump presidency took to newer forms of engagement as well—sometimes crossing the line into aggression. Trump supporters regularly "troll" (flood online accounts with nasty messages) public figures who the president singles out for criticism, often on Twitter. At a congressional baseball game, a former campaign volunteer for Democratic presidential hopeful Bernie Sanders opened fire on Republicans, wounding five.[2] Meanwhile, the number of Twitter followers of the violent antifascist movement Antifa skyrocketed—even as that group hurled Molotov cocktails and stoned police in Berkeley, California.[3]

Most, however, remained civil. During President Trump's State of the Union address, actress Alyssa Milano issued a call for "digital counterprogramming," expressly rejecting violent protest. Across the United States, a "Civil Conversations Project" is one of many efforts to bring together those of different viewpoints to *enhance* political participation during a polarized time.

Who are we? Heirs of the revolutionary Americans who took to the streets and town centers to throw off the British yoke? A nation where every generation finds new ways to participate, sometimes violently? A country where thousands show up to political rallies to cheer long-shot candidates? A democratic

● *Florida car salesman Gene Huber was attracted to politics by the Donald Trump campaign; he later quit his job to support the president at rallies.*

● Explore the long-standing paradox of America exhibiting strong *and* weak political participation.

● Learn the three types of participation: traditional politics, direct action, and civic engagement.

● Examine why people participate.

● Identify the benefits and drawbacks of an emerging "clickocracy," as political engagement moves online.

● Consider whether there can be too much popular participation in a democracy.

Actress Alyssa Milano calls on fellow critics of White House immigration policies to join a #StateOfTheDream campaign during President Trump's 2018 State of the Union Address.

Alyssa Milano
@Alyssa_Milano

(Follow)

Please join us! Resist and persist with digital counter-programming to Trump's #SOTU! Check out and share this google doc for instructions and more info.

#StateOfTheDream

nation in which 100 million people do not even bother to vote? We are all of these.

Participation in public life is always changing. The millennial generation, like many before them, have found new ways to participate that revolve around social media—called **clicktivism**[4] or #politics, and it takes many forms. Perhaps your friends dumped ice water on their heads and challenged people in their network to do likewise or pay up for a good cause? That, too, is a form of public participation.

Clicktivism: Democratic engagement in an online age: point your mouse or scan a QR code, click, and you have donated funds, "liked" a candidate, or (in some states) even cast your vote.

Traditional participation: Engaging in political activities through the formal channels of government and society.

How We Participate

Political participation in the United States arises from a paradox. In some ways, Americans are highly engaged in politics, while in other ways Americans are downright apathetic. In this chapter, we explore the many pathways to participation in the political system; some stretch back over two hundred years. Others are just now emerging on the political scene. Pathways to participation break into three broad categories: traditional participation, civic volunteerism, and direct action.

Traditional Participation

The 2020 election campaign has already begun to fire up millions of people. Will Donald Trump run for—and win—a second term? Will a Republican challenge him in the primary election? Can former Vice President Joe Biden or Senator Elizabeth Warren capture the Democratic nomination, or will a member of the rising generation take the helm? Many of these candidates' supporters engage in traditional politics. **Traditional participation** means getting involved in politics through formal government channels—organized by federal and state constitutions and developed over time. Voting, working for a candidate, signing petitions, or writing letters to the newspaper are all ways of becoming active (see Table 8.1).

TABLE 8.1 **Rates of Traditional Political Participation**

22% of Americans have attended a political meeting on local, town, or school affairs.
13% have been an active member of a group that tries to influence the public or government.
10% have attended a political rally or speech.
7% have worked or volunteered for a political party or candidate.
7% have called into a live radio or TV show to express an opinion about a political or social issue.
1.7% have donated to political campaigns.
0.03% have donated $200 to political campaigns.
Source: Pew Research Center

BY THE NUMBERS
Political Participation

Percentage turnout of voting-age population, U.S. presidential election, 1940	**63**
Percentage turnout of voting-age population, U.S. presidential election, 1980	**58**
Percentage turnout of voting-age population, U.S. presidential election, 2016	**56**
Estimated number of political-themed blogs, 2001	**500**[5]
Estimated number of political-themed blogs, 2018	**more than 100,000**[6]
Percentage of American millennials (aged 17–35) expressing trust in U.S. government, 2018	**20**[7]
Percentage of Americans under age thirty expressing trust in U.S. government, 1961	**81**
Proportion of U.S. college students who report volunteering for public service, including informal volunteering such as helping neighbors, 2015	**82**[8]
Proportion of baby boomers (aged fifty to sixty-eight, roughly) who report volunteering when they were of college age	**44**
Percentage of Americans under thirty who consider themselves to be politically engaged or politically active, 2018	**29**[9]
Percentage donated to U.S. election campaigns by the top 0.5 percent (one half of one percent, by income), 2015–2016	**70.3**[10]

How is the way Americans participate politically—through social media, for example—changing?

Voting. Voting is the foundational political participatory act in any democracy. Yet over 120 million eligible Americans did not turn out at the polls in the 2018 midterm elections. Recall from Chapter 2 that the Constitution leaves most election details up to the states. There are many subtle ways that a state can encourage (or discourage) voters by making it easier (or harder) to vote. If you have voted, you know the basic drill. First, register to vote. Seventeen states and the District of Columbia make the process much easier by permitting registration and voting on the same day. Oregon was the first state to automatically register voters.

Second, cast your vote. Only a few years ago, this meant arriving on Election Day at your assigned polling place. But today, thirty-seven states now permit early voting—and more than a third of the ballots are cast before Election Day. Washington and Oregon conduct elections by mail.

If you do vote on Election Day, bear in mind that some states limit voting facilities—creating long lines, which discourage some voters. In November 2018, voters waited over three hours in Reno, Nevada, so that all voters in line had a chance to cast their ballots. Record turnout—the highest for a midterm election since 1966—meant late poll closings in Texas and Georgia, and some Maryland polling stations ran out of ballots.

Once you get to the head of the line, you may encounter polling workers. They are usually unpaid volunteers—another form of political participation. They will direct you to a voting booth, often adorned with distinctive blue curtains. Inside, you find one of many different voting mechanisms. Some jurisdictions use touch screens; some states use voting machines with levers; and in others you mark paper ballots much as the first U.S. voters did in 1789 (although there were no curtains back then—everyone voted in public). In 2016, an allegedly Russian-sponsored hacking of Democratic Party servers led to congressional hearings and federal investigations about electronic voting machines being tampered with, and even calls for a return to paper balloting.

Electoral activities: Public engagement in the form of voting, running for office, volunteering in a campaign, or otherwise participating in elections.

If many different offices are listed on the ballot, perhaps along with an issue referendum or two (which we discuss in Chapter 10), it might take you several minutes to work your way down the ballot and make all your choices. In local elections featuring just a handful of races, you may finish voting in thirty seconds or so.

Electoral Activities. Beyond voting, Americans engage in other **electoral activities**. They volunteer to get out the vote for favorite candidates. They go to meetings and rallies. They post signs on their lawns and bumper stickers on their cars. They donate money.

Political Voice. Political engagement continues after the election is over. According to Pew Research, one in five Americans contacts a government official in the course of a typical year. They get in touch about potholes, immigration

● Why is voting turnout lower in the United States than in many other countries? Perhaps it is because some governments make it difficult. Here, long voting lines in Atlanta, Georgia, 2018.

policy, nuclear weapons agreements with Iran, or the school lunch menu. Obviously, the key is finding the right official: Do not call the White House about potholes or the mayor's office about an international trade deal. To the surprise of many people, legislators—and especially members of Congress—devote considerable time to constituent inquiries.

If Americans turn out less, they are quick to express political opinions. On average, Americans exercise their **political voice** more often and more openly than citizens of many other countries. Teachers and students walk out of high school classes to advocate for higher teacher pay; small business owners contribute campaign funds to politicians challenging Obamacare. In addition, Americans, particularly millennials, express their voice through the market. Advocates on the left have boycotted companies who exploit workers or spoil the environment; conservative activists similarly have boycotted companies that end sales of semi-automatic rifles, such as Dick's Sporting Goods.

Political voice: Exercising one's public rights, often through speaking out in protest or in favor of some policy change.

Civic Voluntarism

Not all participation runs through politics. Many Americans—young, middle-aged, and seniors alike—volunteer for causes or donate money for local charities. These are forms of **civic voluntarism**, working together to address problems through society.

Civic voluntarism has a long pedigree. When the French visitor Alexis de Tocqueville, who we met earlier in this book, traveled through the United States in 1831–1832, he was struck by Americans' propensity to get involved. In *Democracy in America*, Tocqueville repeatedly remarked on the way Americans join together to build roads, schools, and hospitals; in France, he noted, such projects would require elaborate layers of government approval—and in England, would need the patronage of a lord.[11]

The US is still at or near the top of the international charts on volunteering.[12] And the millennial generation—again, adults between late teens and early thirties— is the most active in modern U.S. history when it comes to volunteering their time for worthy causes. Over the past decade, the proportion of teenagers who volunteer has more than doubled. Résumé padding for career advancement? Recent studies say no, or at least not exclusively. Figure 8.1 shows the major reasons millennials get involved.

Voluntary engagement comes in many forms. People serve in a food bank, teach English as a second language, join a volunteer fire department, or help raise money for high school basketball uniforms. Many Americans respond to crowd funding requests on sites such as Kickstarter, GoFundMe, and others.

Volunteers may not see their work as political, and indeed, getting involved is often related to a hobby or

Civic voluntarism: Citizen participation in public life without government incentives or coercion – for example, getting together to build a public playground rather than just paying taxes and leaving it to public officials.

● Getting involved in civic action comes in many forms. Vendors such as Ruth Wagner were part of the Earth Day celebration at the University of Texas at Brownsville.

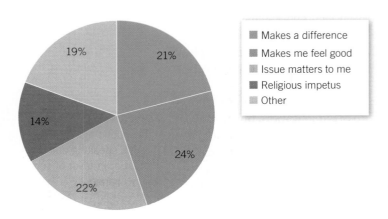

- Makes a difference
- Makes me feel good
- Issue matters to me
- Religious impetus
- Other

● **Figure 8.1** *Americans aged 15 to 25: Reasons for volunteering. (Brookings Institution)*

Direct action: Participating outside of normal political and social channels through civil disobedience, demonstrations, and even riots.

Civil disobedience: Protesting laws one considers unjust by refusing to obey them—and accepting the punishment.

enthusiasm rather than public spirit. Whatever the motivation, voluntary activity tends to draw people into the common sphere. And once there, the payoff is clear. If you volunteer, you are more likely to vote, pay attention to political affairs, and otherwise engage in public life. As we saw in Chapter 1, successful democracies require a vibrant civic spirit.

Direct Action

When people feel that the traditional forms of participation are not working, they sometimes seek change outside of normal channels and take **direct action**. This is the world of demonstrations, marches, armed standoffs, and riots.

Protest politics can invoke the highest American aspirations. Or they can reflect nativism, prejudice, and unbridled anger. The goal is generally to call attention to a cause and to foster a movement around it. Of course, direct action can blur into electoral politics. Protests can foster political movements that then penetrate national institutions. The #MeToo movement against sexism and gender inequity arose in part from the women's marches noted at the start of this chapter. A record number of women candidates and victors in the 2018 midterm elections represents an institutional change growing out of protest.[13]

Occasionally, direct action goes further and violates the law—sometimes through proud acts of **civil disobedience**. Protesting slavery in 1849, Henry David Thoreau urged his countrymen: "if [the law] requires you to be the agent of injustice to another, then, I say break the law. Let your life be a counter friction to stop the machine." Martin Luther King picked up this theme in his eloquent letter from a Birmingham jail, where he explained to white liberals why black Americans would break unjust laws rather than waiting quietly for reform.

The line between traditional participation and direct action can blur. Recall that the First Amendment guarantees the right to assemble—although local authorities normally require a permit before people can march in the street. We label all marches and demonstrations direct action—whether the protesters have a permit (making their assembly legal) or not (making it civil disobedience).

Direct action is not always part of the proud democratic legacy. Violent protests in Seattle cost an estimated $20 million—and put antiglobalization on the political agenda. White supremacists in Charlottesville claimed they were defending Southern heritage when they clashed with counter-protesters in 2017 and again in 2018. Were they taking political action on behalf of a despised group? Recklessly destroying property and endangering lives? Or both?

As the Charlottesville demonstration shows, direct action includes the dark legacy of violence and injustice. Recall how the entire system of Jim Crow was kept in place by a tradition of lynching—a form of American terrorism.

More common, great American rallies mark high points in our political history. Environmental activism offers a classic example. After millions of Americans gathered to promote cleaner air and water at the first Earth Day in April 1970, Congress passed major clean air legislation within a month, and a Clean Water Act soon after that. A series of "Rally for Life" marches in the 1980s–1990s, including

Go back to the Civil Rights protests pictured on pages 172 and 173—young people at a sit-in are humiliated, those on a Freedom Bus beaten and almost burned alive. College students carried out the sit-ins and Freedom Rides. A question for you— one we often ask ourselves: **If you were in college between 1960 and 1962, would you have joined in?** It would have taken conviction, courage, and (for most students) a willingness to ignore parents horrified by the risks.

What would you have done? Explain why. Now consider the protests taking place on campuses today. How are they similar? How are they different? Have you considered taking part yourself? Explain why.

a National Mall event attracting more than 700,000, helped advance the anti-abortion cause in Congress and many state legislatures. That type of political voice is the lifeblood of American democracy.

The Participation Puzzle

This chapter confronts us with a puzzle: American voting rates are very low compared to those in other nations. Under 60 percent of the voting age population turns out in presidential elections and just 35 to 40 percent in midterms. In contrast, Belgium or Sweden see election turnout rates in the high 80 percent range; in South Korea and Israel they run to the high 70s. Yet Americans are quick to get involved in direct action. Low American voting rates are puzzling, especially when they are coupled with relatively high levels of direct action.

Perhaps the level of citizen participation reflects the rules that govern the electoral institutions (that second "I" from Chapter 1). Low **voter turnout** may simply reflect the barriers to voting that many states have erected over the years: registration requirements, voting on a working day, the disenfranchisement of former felons, and so on. After all, rules can make it easier or more difficult for citizens to participate.

Perhaps historic barriers restricting the African American vote in the south and the immigrant vote in the north contribute to low turnout today. For example, Mississippi had very high barriers to voting; in 1938, the two million citizens of the state (49% of them black) cast a total of only 35,439 votes for all five seats in Congress.[14] Limits in that era, like poll taxes and literacy tests (more on those below), no longer exist. But critics still ask: Do American government officials *want* the public involved in their work? Some democracies go so far as to *require* voting.[15] High participation rates make a democracy more robust—but they also slow things down and raise controversy. Of course, erecting barriers to traditional participation always invites the larger disruption of direct action.

Here's the fundamental question: Is the American system a miracle of mass participation? Or one designed to limit citizen access? Or, in the spirit of American federalism, is it a state-by-state patchwork of both?

Voter turnout: A measure of which proportion of eligible voters actually cast a legitimate ballot in a given election.

Compare voter participation by country and group.

The Bottom Line

» Traditional participation involves engaging politics through formal government channels. Voting is the most familiar form of traditional political participation.

» Americans participate in politics year round. One in five contacts a public official in the course of a year.

» Civic voluntarism is a form of engagement with public life that operates outside of government—but enhances democracy.

» Direct action seeks immediate and sweeping change. It has a long legacy in the United States that goes back to its founding and includes some of the nation's great reform movements.

Why People Get Involved

Political scientists pay particular attention to who gets involved, how much, and why. Americans participate with extraordinary vigor in many aspects of public life. Nearly half of American adults are likely to volunteer time to an organization, and 73 percent are likely to help a stranger. By comparison, adults in other countries volunteer at an average 20 percent rate (just 5 percent in China, for example) and only 44 percent in other countries are inclined to help strangers (25 percent of Japanese and 31 percent of Czechs are likely to do so.)[16] Yet whether we are voting, volunteering, or expressing our political voice, some Americans feel more inspired to participate than others.

What makes some Americans more likely to engage in political activity? Let's look at five major factors: background, friends, community, mobilization, and government benefits.

Background: Age, Wealth, and Education

Age. Age is a strong predictor of political engagement: Older people vote more often. Figure 8.2 displays voting rates for different American generations. Notice that *young* adults vote less, in election after election. At the same time, younger voters are more likely to try and influence politics through direct action, are far more likely to engage politically online (clicktivism), and practice greater political expression than did young Americans in recent decades (see Figure 8.2).

Learn about the role of the younger Americans in the 2012 election.

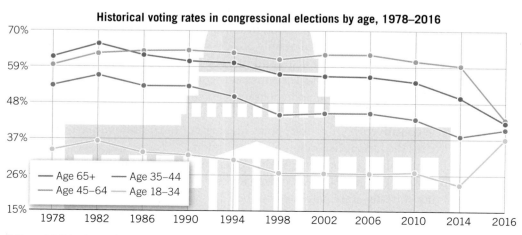

Historical voting rates in congressional elections by age, 1978–2016

Age 65+ — Age 35–44
Age 45–64 — Age 18–34

70%
59%
48%
37%
26%
15%

1978 1982 1986 1990 1994 1998 2002 2006 2010 2014 2016

Figure 8.2 *Voter turnout in congressional elections, by age (U.S. Census Bureau, Current Population Survey).*

Wealth.   Income is another strong predictor of political participation. Top earn-ers tend to be much more engaged in politics than those farther down the income ladder—and the higher the income, the more likely individuals are to get involved. Just 1.3 million people—around 0.42% of the U.S. adult population—contributed over 70 percent of total funds raised in the 2018 campaign.[17]

Americans' behavior has run in cycles: Sometimes, the political system per-mits (and even facilitates) vast differences in wealth—what Mark Twain called a gilded age. National resources flow to those at the top. At other times, a back-lash develops against growing inequality. In these egalitarian eras, national and state policies limit the accumulation of outsized wealth. However, in every era, wealthy people have more access to political leaders and more influence over politics.

Education.   Education also predicts political involvement—and education closely tracks income. As Figure 8.3 shows, the more education, the higher the voting levels. Less than 30 percent of people who did not finish high school normally vote in presidential elections, whereas citizens with a college degree are more than twice

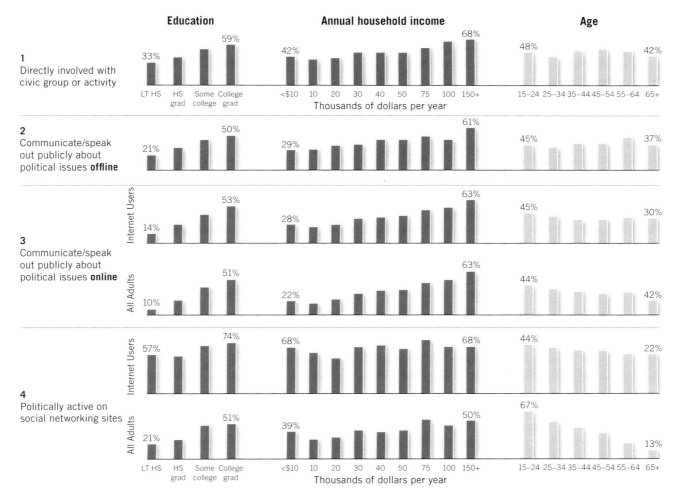

● **Figure 8.3** *Percentage involvement in civic activities by education, income, and age (Pew Research Center).*

Note: *"LT HS" indicates the population with less than a high school education.*

Public Rallies

WHAT ISSUES DRAW PEOPLE TO PROTEST?

Americans are drawn to participate in politics for many different reasons, as this section shows. As the number who participates in public rallies has climbed in recent years, what topics prove most likely to draw people into the streets to march? As of 2018, here are the top twelve issues. They include both liberal (women's and LGBTQ rights, environment/energy, minimum wage) and conservative (abortion, gun rights, removing Confederate monuments) staples, but at least in the present cultural moment, more protesters come from the left.

THINK ABOUT IT

Look back at issue polls from the year you were born, or even just five years ago (both Pew and Gallup websites list these year by year). Which topics seemed most of interest then? What has changed in the United States to explain the shift to this set of issues?

Any issue(s) that you would add to this list, as likely sources of mass protest in coming months? Anything you'd *like* to see on the list that isn't—something that arouses your passion enough to join a march or rally?

Source: Washington Post *and Kaiser Family Foundation.*

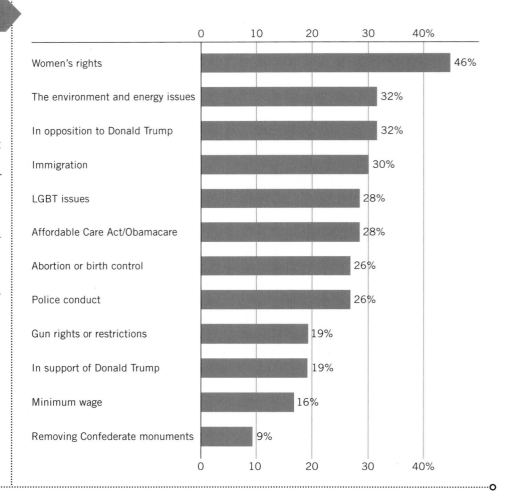

Issue	Percentage
Women's rights	46%
The environment and energy issues	32%
In opposition to Donald Trump	32%
Immigration	30%
LGBT issues	28%
Affordable Care Act/Obamacare	28%
Abortion or birth control	26%
Police conduct	26%
Gun rights or restrictions	19%
In support of Donald Trump	19%
Minimum wage	16%
Removing Confederate monuments	9%

as likely to vote. Voters with less education, however, played a critical role in 2016 due to their strong support of Donald Trump.

Race. If we were writing this book fifteen years ago, we would have had to add another major reason for lower turnout: race. Traditionally, African Americans voted in lower numbers than white Americans. Gradually, however, the gap began to close, and in 2012, for the first time in U.S. history, blacks voted at a slightly higher rate than whites. A significant contributor to that change was Barack Obama's presence on the ballot; African American turnout dropped in 2016 to pre-2012 levels.[18] Latinos and Asian Americans still vote at a lower rate than whites: Under 50 percent of eligible voters in these communities cast ballots, for reasons researchers still debate.[19] However, as their numbers grow, they are becoming an increasingly important political force.

● *Social capital on the big screen. Characters from* It's A Wonderful Life, *a 1946 film that portrays the power of social networks and civic engagement.*

Friends and Family

Another way to predict whether someone will vote or volunteer is to find out whether their parents and closest friends do. On average, someone whose family or peers vote regularly is likely to do so as well. An even more powerful inspiration is being *asked* to vote, volunteer, or otherwise exercise political voice by people close to you. Political science studies find that face-to-face encouragement is the most reliable route to political activity. Being asked to vote, even by a stranger, as long as it is in person, tends to get results.[20] This finding appears to hold for many forms of participation—and in many nations. Protesters are often part of personal networks.

Community

The type of community you live in also seems to make a difference. In areas where neighbors are more trusting and civic participation is strong people are more likely to get involved—both in local activities, such as block watches or school fundraisers, and in voting for national office. Social scientists refer to these kinds of relations as **social capital**.

Such communities, organized around a commitment to building social capital, tend to house happier, healthier residents. Through active communication and a strong foundation of trust among citizens, Americans can realize the benefits of engagement on a wide scale. One related worry about millennials: They exhibit lower levels of trust, generally speaking, than previous groups of young Americans. This makes social capital harder to generate in the rising generation.[21]

People who live in areas high in social capital are more deeply involved in activities such as book clubs, community gardens, and bowling leagues; they spend more time connecting informally with one another than in places where people live more anonymously and watch a lot of television. It may sound simple: A key to political participation is to live in a highly participatory community. But transforming a neighborhood into one with strong social capital—or sustaining civic connections

Social capital: Relations between people that build closer ties of trust and civic engagement, yielding productive benefits for the larger society.

● *Social capital in Detroit, where residents in low-income neighborhoods joined together to paint vacant homes.*

Political mobilization:
Efforts to encourage people to engage in the public sphere: to vote for a particular candidate (or donate money, work on the campaign, etc.) or to get involved in specific issues.

Issue advocacy: Organized effort to advance (or block) a proposed public policy change.

once they exist—is no easy task. How might you help to cultivate a spirit of engagement in your surrounding community?

In one neighborhood in the city of San José, Costa Rica, residents developed their own technique for boosting social capital. The neighborhood had experienced a sharp rise in crime. Residents got together and agreed to leave for work a few minutes earlier each morning, taking that extra time to greet and talk at least briefly with their neighbors. The practice became informally known as *El Ley del Saludo* (Law of the Greeting), and it helped reduce crime markedly—as well as boost voting rates and other markers of political participation. Likewise, a low-income area of Detroit banded together and used social media to call out people dumping trash in their neighborhood. Once they began taking action, they found new ways to get involved: They painted vacant homes and started community gardens in the empty lots.[22]

Connections between family and participation may run deeper than our tendency to imitate the behavior of those closest to us. Recent studies suggest that we may *inherit* a tendency toward political participation. In other words, your desire to vote or volunteer is determined by your genes—but only partly.[23] Political involvement is shaped by several influences simultaneously, so genetic inheritance, as with the level of social capital in a community, is only one factor among many.

Political Mobilization

Party organizations have traditionally done the work of **political mobilization**. Both major parties remain powerful sources of encouraging millions of people to get involved—especially at election time. (We'll talk about political parties in Chapter 11.)

In some cases, charismatic political figures are a source of mass mobilization. John F. Kennedy, inspiring young people to "ask what they could do for their country" in the early 1960s; Ronald Reagan, drawing evangelicals into politics in the 1980s; and Donald Trump, arousing many formerly uninvolved white working-class voters (like Gene Huber, whose story opened this chapter) in 2016, are all examples.

On **issue advocacy** campaigns, when professional and amateur organizations promote public involvement in a specific cause, interest groups become our mobilizers in chief. At times, issue advocacy campaigns and social movements threaten to take over a party—as happened with the Tea Party Movement and the Republican Party after 2009.[24]

● *Chance the Rapper speaks out about youth education in his native Chicago; some apply the term* raptivist *(rapper + activist) to such engaged figures.*

In the eyes of professional political mobilizers—advocacy groups, campaign strategists, and other members of the enormous Washington, DC–based "political industry," each of us is a potential resource. Activists constantly test ways to inspire people to sign a petition, write our congressional representatives, get out and vote, or otherwise engage politically.

Government Beneficiaries

A fifth factor encouraging participation in public life may strike you as odd at first glance: receiving some type of government benefits. If, for example, you are covered by your parents' health insurance past age twenty-one or you receive a federally guaranteed student loan (which keeps interest rates low), you are a beneficiary. Receiving such support can boost active participation later in life. Researchers have shown that when the government rewards service—as when returning soldiers receive free or discounted college tuition through the GI Bill—recipients are considerably more likely to get involved as volunteers and to exercise their public voice.

However, not all government programs are alike. As political scientist Joe Soss has shown, programs that treat beneficiaries with respect generate social capital. But programs aimed at poor people—called "means tested" because government officials check on your income (or means) before approving the benefits—appear to depress political participation.[25]

These spurs to participation all focus on individual factors. There is a larger backdrop to participation as well.

Historical Context

Major shifts in the economy and in politics affect both the intensity and favored types of participation. In the rural South during the 1950s, for example, an infestation of boll weevils (tiny insects that feed on cotton plants) devastated the cotton crop. Many African American subsistence farm workers, their livelihood gone, moved to southern cities where they became recruits for the civil rights movement.

Context deeply influences opportunities for political engagement.[26] During some historical periods, Americans have been more likely to engage in public life than at other times. For example, workers (in the 1930s) and students (1960s) flocked into direct action politics in massive numbers. Today—with Americans organizing across the political spectrum, including on many college campuses—we appear to be in another high participation moment.

HOW MOBILIZERS SEE US

Political strategists and mobilizers have a language of their own. Below are some of the terms you'll hear if you work in advocacy or campaign politics long enough.

• **Grassroots:** A movement for political reform that is sparked at the local level, "from the ground up"— figuratively speaking, from the grass roots.

• **Astroturf:** A movement for reform that *appears* to be grassroots but is actually mobilized by political professionals.

• **Dog whistling:** Using insider, "coded" language to rouse constituents or interest-group members who care strongly about an issue. (The rather crude analogy is from training dogs, which hear high-frequency whistles that other animals—including humans—cannot.)

 **The Bottom Line**

» Participation in politics and government is influenced by personal factors: background characteristics such as income and education; family and friends; communities and social capital; political mobilization; and receiving government benefits from programs that treat beneficiaries with respect (i.e., Social Security).

» Americans participate in political life at very different rates. A few engage passionately, a larger number are moderately engaged, and the majority of us are only sporadically involved. This contributes to the appearance of high *and* low participation in the United States.

» Political mobilization also is influenced by the larger social and historical context.

HOW MOBILIZERS SEE US
(*Continued*)

• **Actorvist:** A professional actor involved in political issue campaigns, an increasingly valuable way to win attention for one's cause. George Clooney and Oprah Winfrey, both of whom speak out in favor of gun control, Chuck Norris, who actively supports a strong military, and Demi Lovato, on mental health, are among the many "actorvists" engaged in American policy mobilization efforts today.

• **Raptivist**; a term describing rappers who get involved in political causes: Chance the Rapper, for example.

The paradox of voting:
For most individuals, the cost of voting (acquiring necessary information, traveling to polling site, and waiting in line) outweighs the apparent benefits. Economic theory would predict very low voter turnout, given this analysis.

What Discourages Political Participation?

Back to the participation paradox: Although Americans are more actively engaged in politics then citizens of other nations, voter turnout in the United States is low (see Comparing Nations 8.1). Why? Political scientists list many reasons:

- Elections are held on Tuesdays—when many people are at work. Many other nations vote on weekends.
- The United States holds more frequent elections—national, state, and local—which can cause "voter fatigue" from repeated trips to the polls.
- The United States also holds primary elections, which are staggered throughout the year in different states.
- Finally, registering to vote can be burdensome and complicated.

Economist Anthony Downs famously asked why anyone should vote. His theory, the **paradox of voting**, suggests that it makes little sense for an individual to expend the time and resources necessary to vote. One person is not going to change an election. The paradox: apparently rational people show up by the millions to vote each year. Downs could have said the same thing about joining a protest march or posting online. Here again, Americans regularly take to the streets or post petitions on Facebook. Why?

As we saw in the previous section, people get many benefits from participating: a sense of involvement, of duty performed, of belonging to a community. So some political scientists flip the question: Instead of asking why anyone bothers to vote, given the time it takes to learn about candidates and get to the polls, they ask the opposite. Why don't **more** people vote, given the value of participation? Four broad reasons explain why people of all ages, income levels, and educational backgrounds do not participate in political life: alienation, barriers to participation, complacency, and shifting mobilization patterns.[27]

Alienation

Alienation from public life may be described as a feeling of powerlessness, or an inability to control one's own political fate. Most alienated people ignore politics. When they get involved, it is usually not through traditional channels but through direct action—intense and even violent protest. Historically excluded groups, such as African Americans, are most likely to report a sense of alienation.[28] Younger people and recent immigrants also feel higher levels of alienation. Recently, alienation levels have soared among white men who failed to finish high school.

These findings raise a question: Do some groups feel alienated because they lack a history of participation? Remember, one predictor of whether a person will get involved in politics is whether his or her parents or peer group are actively engaged. Or perhaps immigrants, minorities, and young people *want* to participate in politics and feel alienated because they are shut out? In a moment we will look further at institutional barriers that discourage participation.

● *A negative ad in a 2018 Pennsylvania campaign for the U.S. House. Relentless attack-style politics can help mobilize highly partisan voters—while turning moderates away from participating.*

COMPARING NATIONS 8.1   Voter Turnout in Selected Countries

The United States has one of the lowest voter turnout rates in the developed world. Most stable democracies register voter turnout rates in the 65 to 80 percent range, far higher than America's. In one of the top five countries, Australia, voting is *compulsory*—required by law. In the United States, although a high percentage of registered voters turn out—around 65 to 70 percent in presidential election years—many voting-age Americans do not bother to register. VAP and RV turnout are derived from different data sources and consequently, VAP is lower than RV in some countries. *Source: Pew Research Center*

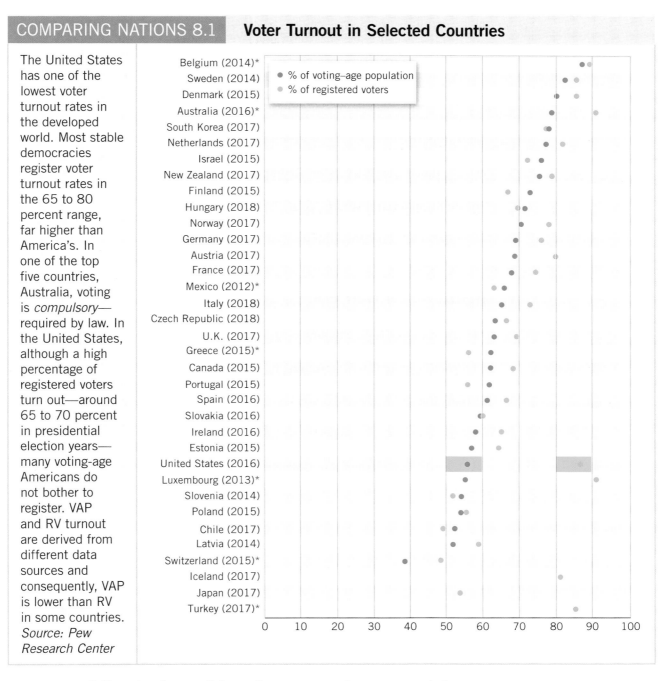

A sense of alienation from politics and government also can come in less extreme forms. The sheer number of elected offices and the high frequency of U.S. elections can result in public weariness and eventually disengagement, especially when campaigns feature seemingly endless negative advertisements.

Sharp partisan differences also play a role. Many polls chronicle a widening gulf between liberals and conservatives in U.S. political debates. The angry debates accompanying this polarization have led many Americans to "hate politics and politicians." The millennial generation appears to be particularly uncomfortable with the high levels of conflict between the parties.[29]

Finally, alienated citizens charge the political establishment with focusing on matters that avoid real problems. Government officials, they contend, seem more

Consider how this negative ad influences you.

Why do some countries have higher voter turnout than others?

interested in winning elections and appeasing the rich and powerful. They do not address the deeper issues that many people care about—growing inequality, a sense of being left behind, or the erosion of the nation's moral fabric. The 2016 presidential election featured two candidates, Donald Trump and Bernie Sanders, who embodied this alienation—and stunned political observers with their unexpected success. Trump's victory was one of the great election upsets in American history.[30]

In countries with totalitarian or oligarchic political systems, alienation can become pervasive. Large majorities of the population are turned off completely from government and politics. Compared to those in such places, Americans exhibit much lower levels of alienation (see Comparing Nations 8.2). But the phenomenon is present. Looming changes in American society raise important questions about alienation. As the United States becomes a "majority–minority" country, will white voters tend to feel more alienated? Will minority groups feel less alienated? The 2018 midterm elections, with the highest turnout in a half-century, suggest that alienation can be overcome.

Institutional Barriers

When Will Walker, a young black farmer, arrived to cast his vote in Tuscaloosa, Alabama, in 1964, he was first required by state law to pass a literacy test, one supposedly designed to prove that he was capable of exercising political judgment. None of the white voters streaming past Will to the voting booths had to take such a test. Will shrugged and turned to the paper before him, brandished by an unfriendly poll worker. He had brushed up on his basic U.S. government facts, and he knew plenty about the various candidates running for election. Yet no amount of studying could have prepared Will for questions like these:

- The electoral vote for president is counted in the presence of two governmental bodies. Name them: _____ and _____.

- The president is forbidden to exercise his or her authority of pardon in cases of _____.

- If the president does not wish to sign a bill, how many days is he or she allowed in which to return it to Congress for reconsideration? _____ days.

- At what time of day on January 2 each four years does the term of the president of the United States end? _____

Will filled out as many of the twenty questions as he could; he did better than most political science majors might today. But he was turned away from the polls. Alabama allowed only black voters with a perfect score to vote. Owing to this and other deliberate efforts to block participation, many counties across the Jim Crow South featured voter registration rates among African Americans that approached zero.

Most of these overtly racist obstacles to participation were eliminated during the 1960s. Nevertheless, some critics continue to point out structural barriers to participation in American public life, such as the disenfranchisement of individuals convicted of a crime, even after they have served their sentence.

The incentives and barriers to voting can be subtle: How difficult is it to register? Are there plenty of opportunities for early voting before Election Day, including on weekends? How long are the lines at polling places?

COMPARING NATIONS 8.2   **Trust in Government**

American trust in government is low by historical standards—but around the middle of the pack compared to other nations today. (Source: Edelman)

Few worldwide have a lot of trust in their government

How much do you trust the national government to do what is right for our country?

	A lot	Somewhat	Total
Canada	20%	47%	**67%**
U.S.	15	36	**51**
Netherlands	24	47	**71**
Germany	26	43	**69**
Sweden	15	52	**67**
Hungary	9	48	**57**
UK	14	35	**49**
Poland	14	28	**42**
Italy	1	25	**26**
France	3	17	**20**
Spain	5	12	**17**
Greece	1	12	**13**
Russia	20	47	**67**
India	39	46	**85**
Indonesia	30	53	**83**
Vietnam	31	51	**82**
Philippines	36	44	**80**
Japan	6	51	**57**
Australia	7	41	**48**
South Korea	2	21	**23**
Israel	14	37	**51**
Jordan	13	35	**48**
Tunisia	11	18	**29**
Lebanon	2	13	**15**
Tanzania	48	41	**89**
Ghana	51	19	**70**
Kenya	28	40	**68**
Senegal	37	23	**60**
Nigeria	34	20	**54**
South Africa	22	22	**44**
Venezuela	14	15	**29**
Brazil	2	22	**24**
Argentina	10	12	**22**
Mexico	2	15	**17**
Chile	5	10	**15**
Colombia	7	5	**12**
Peru	4	8	**12**

Note: Question not asked in Turkey.

Democrats have generally tried to simplify voting rules. They have sponsored reforms such as the National Voter Registration Act of 1993, usually referred to as the **motor voter law**, which permits citizens to register to vote when they receive their driver's license. On the other side, Republicans in many states have tightened restrictions on voting. They argue that more careful monitoring reduces fraud and that voting should be treated as a privilege that takes time and energy. Accordingly, many states have introduced new voting regulations: tougher identification requirements, limits on same-day registration, reductions in the voting periods, purging

Motor voter law: Passed in 1993, this act enables prospective voters to register when they receive their driver's license.

people who have not voted in six years from the list of registered voters, and so on. Opponents call this voter suppression and charge that it is an effort to limit young people, minorities, and others from voting. In 2018, the Supreme Court took a largely hands-off approach to state government voting actions. The debate about institutional barriers to voting goes on.

Complacency

Some people do not participate because they are satisfied with their lives. Without urgent problems they want solved, why bother to get involved? Large membership-based interest groups tend to attract more new members and receive a boost in financial contributions when the group's core issues are threatened. The election of President Trump boosted membership in the American Civil Liberties Union (ACLU) and other liberal groups. Mass shoot-

● *Donald Trump, after winning election in 2016 thanks in part to mobilizing new voters, continued to hold campaign-style rallies as president—here, in Michigan in 2018.*

ings generally increase membership applications to the National Rifle Association, as gun supporters fear government restrictions. When the news cycle turns to new concerns, the groups find it harder to mobilize support as concerned people move to a newly endangered cause.

A different view of political apathy comes from the economist John Kenneth Galbraith, who coined the phrase "culture of contentment" to describe America. His view was that the upper-middle class and those at the top of the wealth distribution will fight hard to sustain their "contented" way of life. Those who are less well-off will be increasingly discouraged from participating in political life.[31]

Is there still a culture of contentment in pockets of American life? What do you think: Do you see evidence of contentment complacency around you?

Shifting Mobilization Patterns

Before the 1960s, when political parties were Americans' main source of political mobilization, wealthy and poor people were organized to participate in roughly similar proportions. The main focus was on getting people out to vote, so intensive door-to-door canvassing at election time was the norm. A surge in advocacy-group organizing since the 1960s has boosted the public's collective voice in politics. Movements on behalf of consumer rights, the environment, and many other causes represent major gains in public leverage.

These gains, however, have primarily benefited the relatively well-off, who can devote resources of time and money to public involvement. Political sociologist Theda Skocpol noted that "Americans who are not wealthy or higher-educated now have fewer associations representing their values and interests, and enjoy dwindling opportunities for active participation."[32]

Cycle of nonparticipation:
Resistance by political parties to mobilizing disengaged Americans to vote—because their lack of involvement makes their allegiance to one or the other party suspect.

This shift from parties to advocacy groups as the main agents of political mobilization adds up to a **cycle of nonparticipation**. If people are so disengaged that they do not affiliate with either political party, party organizers are unlikely to reach out to them at election time—because they might vote for the wrong side.

The Bottom Line

» Participation in civic life tends to vary by age, income level, and education.

» Several other factors have fueled a decline in Americans' political participation in recent years. These include alienation, barriers to participation, complacency, and shifting mobilization patterns.

» The tendency to disengage is most pronounced among millennials, which includes most college students today.

New Avenues for Participation: The Internet, Social Media, and the Millennial Generation

The millennial generation is the most wired group in history. New technologies have engendered new forms of participation—liking a candidate's Instagram feed, commenting on an online opinion piece, or retweeting political leaders' views. Today, political participation has expanded to include online activities and social media. Like many new styles of politics, clicktivism (or #politics) has triggered a hot debate.

Is clicktivism a powerful new form of participation that can change the way we do politics for the better? Or is it a threat to popular government? Or, less dramatically, does "participating" on a laptop or smartphone screen negatively affect the experience of civic involvement? Once again, there are multiple sides to the story. Some observers predict a vibrant new era of citizen participation. Others take a much less sunny view and warn about fragmented communities, central government control of emerging outlets, and viral malice.[33]

Scenario 1: Rebooting Democracy

First, optimists begin by pointing out how *active* Internet users are. People seek out news, follow links, and access a world of information (see Figure 8.4).

Second, people can easily respond. The Internet offers multiple opportunities for talking back: swipe on a "Like" icon, comment angrily or wittily on a political blog, or communicate with a network of like-minded people. Democracies, when they are working well, *hear* their people. New technologies give individuals many opportunities to exercise their political voice.

Third and related, the Internet vastly expands the range of commentary. Traditionally political pundits were limited to a small circle of well-known personalities and authors. Today, if you have something to say, you can launch a blog, send a tweet to dozens or hundreds (or millions) of followers, or post news stories or opinions for your Facebook friends. Some have had terrific success. The *Daily Kos*, launched by Markos (Kos) Moulitsas Zúniga, boasts one and a

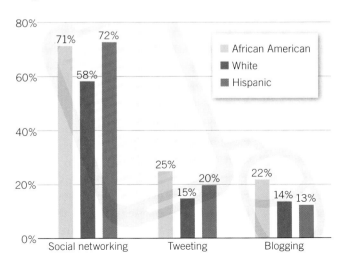

● **Figure 8.4** *Who is socially active online? A view by race and ethnicity (Pew Research Center).*

Use social media to urge people to action.

quarter million Facebook followers; on the opposing (conservative) side, Michelle Malkin has more than 2.1 million Twitter followers. Other familiar sites include the *Drudge Report* (conservative), *Talking Points Memo* (liberal), and NewsBusters (conservative). Of course you do not need a blog—YouTube videos and Instagram stories go viral all the time. People post petitions on change.org. Crowdfunding platforms like Kickstarter raise significant funds for civic and political causes.

Fourth, as we will see in Chapter 9, the new media democratizes news production. Rather than wait for a news van and reporters, bystanders capture important events and upload them. Suddenly, everyone sees a shooting or an angry candidate blurt out a racial slur.

Fifth, the Internet offers new ways for politicians and parties to reach out. Barack Obama refined this technique and turned his 2008 and 2012 campaigns into a type of movement, galvanizing millions of carefully targeted followers. Others learned the lesson and adapted the technologies. Donald Trump continues to treat his Twitter followers—now more than fifty million—to a daily stream of pungent observations and stinging insults.

In sum, optimists argue that social media and other Internet-based sources promote active users; link people to one another; permit citizens to bypass the talking heads and make their own comments; and offer politicians a powerful tool to mobilize, connect, and collect. None of these factors ensures that clicktivism will help refresh American democracy. But they suggest a great deal of promise.

Scenario 2: More Hype and Danger Than Democratic Renaissance

All this potential, however, might be squandered. Technological change may not enhance democracy and, according to some skeptics, is already harming it. Critics level three main charges against the Internet and social media as keys to political participation.[34]

First is the sustained power of *central control*, by governments or corporations, over the Internet and its users. "Facebook has more power in determining who can speak and who can be heard around the globe than any Supreme Court justice, any king or any president," noted law professor Jeffrey Rosen. Social media companies determine what speech violates their community standards, when to cooperate with security agencies, and how to monetize information about your shopping habits.[35] Competing with public officials and tech companies for control are cyber-criminals, as hackers constantly seek to steal sensitive political information (the Pentagon, for example, is attacked by hackers millions of times *each day*).[36]

Din: Shorthand for the sheer volume of information and noise generated by online sources; can be a disincentive to participate politically.

Second, with more than 1.8 billion websites on the Internet, the sheer volume and variety of available information are mind-boggling. The resulting chaos and noise—known as **din**—can overwhelm participation as well as enhance it. Researching a specific topic often involves wading through a forest of hearsay, contradiction, malice, and deliberate misinformation.

Try to do an Internet search for this chapter's topic, "political participation" and related terms, for example. As of 2018, we found more than thirty million relevant Internet sources. Which ones provide valuable or even usable details about participation in the public sphere? Merely to scan each site for one minute would take sixteen years.

Third, the Internet incubates lies, malice, and falsehood. Rumors start and spread. Racism, anti-Semitism, misogyny, and character assassination all flourish in the hyper-connected, often-anonymous new media. No, Hillary Clinton was not running a child-sex ring out of a Washington, DC, pizza parlor—though a man who saw that "news" online travelled from North Carolina and fired three rifle shots to "save the children." Like so many others, this dangerous falsehood metastasized on the Internet. The democratic promise of the Internet comes with a dark side.[37]

In sum, critics worry that the Internet and social media will have a corrosive effect on American democratic participation. They point out that the government monitors Internet behavior; meanwhile, corporations gather information from every click and swipe. Yes, people can post and blog, but not many develop an audience. Finally, the Internet generates malice, misinformation, and trolling as easily as communication and community.

Does Social Media Increase Political Participation?

Whatever their downside, the new social media have become a fact of political life. They open more and more opportunities for broad participation and policy innovation. For example, Mobile, Alabama, engages Instagram to fight urban blight. Fairfax County, Virginia, uses social media to boost pet adoption rates. Government "hackathons" invite people to pitch their civic-improvement ideas. And everywhere citizens use smart phones to publicize what their public officials are doing. Social media users are also more likely to participate in politics than the general public (see Table 8.2).

What explains this correlation between social media and participation? Perhaps individuals who are inclined to become involved in politics are more likely to be social media users. Or do people get engaged by what they see and hear online—and then act on it? Or is there a bandwagon effect—watching others comment on posts or joining groups stimulates individuals to jump in and do likewise?

The bandwagon effect has been successfully employed in the past to encourage voter turnout and other kinds of political participation. In Barack Obama's 2008 presidential campaign, an advisory group recommended that the campaign's messages encouraging supporters to vote on Election Day be revised to read "A Record

TABLE 8.2 Social Network Site (SNS) Users' Participation Rates

	% OF SNS USERS WHO HAVE DONE THIS	% OF ALL ADULTS WHO HAVE DONE THIS
"Like" or promote material related to political/social issues that others have posted	38	23
Encourage other people to vote	35	21
Post your own thoughts/comments on political or social issues	34	20
Encourage others to take action on political/social issues that are important to you	31	19
Belong to a group that is involved in political/social issues or working to advance a cause	21	12
Follow elected officials, candidates for office, or other elected officials	20	12
Source: Pew Research Center		

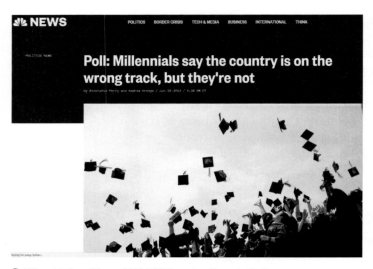

● *Millennials in politics: a 2018 NBC News headline says it all.*

Turnout Is Expected." This proved more effective than other types of appeals.[38]

Skeptics point out that although the bandwagon effect within social media may galvanize participants in the short term; it is unclear whether it will sustain traditional political engagement. Although the critics offer valuable caveats, participation via new social media is here to stay. It will continue to morph and change—and with it the ways we participate in politics.

How the Millennial Generation Participates

Millennials vote less than other age groups both in the United States and in many other nations. They are less likely to get involved in political campaigns. They do not identify strongly with either political party—as of 2018, 45 percent of millennials called themselves independents. That is far more than any other generation—no other age cohort reaches 40 percent independent (see Figure 8.5). Millennials are also more likely to identify as liberals than does any other generation.[39]

Millennials participate in their own distinctive way: From working in hospitals to helping out in programs for at-risk kids, young adults today volunteer at unusually high rates. And they are willing to endorse the government more than any other generation. Should we have a bigger government doing more things such as guaranteeing healthcare for all? Only the millennials say yes, at a 57 percent rate. In contrast, only 30 percent of the silent generation, enjoying the two largest government programs—Social Security and Medicare—agree (see Table 8.3). Why?

Younger generations display a higher level of trust in public officials, but relatively low levels of trust in their fellow citizens (see Figure 8.6). When asked whether "Most people look out for themselves," 70 percent of millennials agreed—in contrast, only 40 percent of "matures" (Americans over sixty-five) agreed. A similar gap was present for the statement "Most people would take advantage of you" (56% of millennials, compared to 29% of matures). Millennials also called themselves

| TABLE 8.3 | **Support for Bigger Government Highest Among Millennial Generation** |

PERCENTAGE WHO WOULD PREFER A BIGGER GOVERNMENT PROVIDING MORE SERVICES							
	1980	**1989**	**1996**	**1999**	**2007**	**2011**	**2014**	**2017**
Total	32	48	30	43	43	41	42	48
Millennial	–	–	–	–	68	56	54	57
Gen X	–	–	53	54	51	45	46	50
Boomer	45	52	24	41	33	35	35	43
Silent	25	35	19	34	30	25	27	30

Source: Pew Research Center

less patriotic—49 percent said yes compared to 75 percent of boomers (patriotic) and 81 percent of the oldest generation.[40]

How does a generation that is skeptical of their fellow citizens but not of government institutions participate? You probably know the answer to that: through social media and the Internet. This generation of "digital natives" comments on politics, captures (and uploads) the world around them, and networks online. For millennials and the generations that follow, the future of political participation lies in the question we posed above: How will clicktivism affect our democracy?

As we saw in Chapter 7, this is the generation that has already rewritten national attitudes on issues ranging from same-sex marriage (74% approval) to legalizing marijuana (70% approval). A strong majority (85%, in a 2018 GenForward poll[41]) believe undocumented immigrants should have a chance to become citizens. Millennial political voice has already changed public policy—and it will continue to do so.

Political scientists have one concern about this generation. Alternative forms of political participation—both direct action and online—are powerful forces for

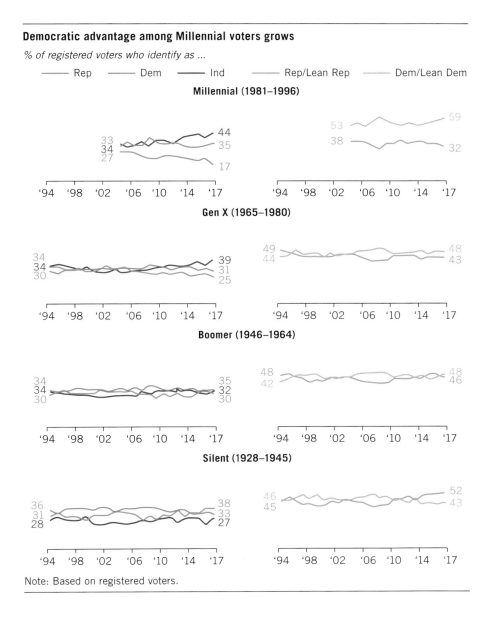

Figure 8.5 *Recent trends in party identification, by generation (Pew Research Center).*

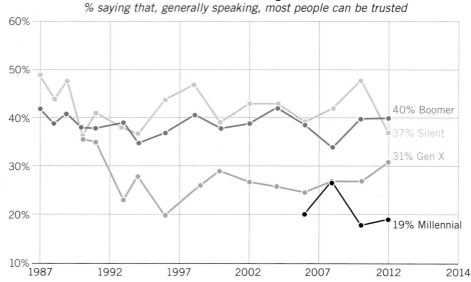

Millennials less trusting of others
% saying that, generally speaking, most people can be trusted

40% Boomer
37% Silent
31% Gen X
19% Millennial

● **Figure 8.6** *Millennials less trusting of others (Pew Research Center).*

disruption and change. However, they cannot produce stable, long-term democratic governance. The millennial generation participates in voting and other forms of political engagement at low levels, and participation trends tend to persist over time. Young America is diverse, eager to build social capital by volunteering, and feels strongly about many political issues. But it has not been moved to translate that energy into traditional modes of political action.

The vital question is why. Perhaps the new generation finds subtle political barriers to participation built into the political process—complicated election rules, long lines, reduced voting periods, and so on. Or perhaps the fault lies with the parties that they are so disinclined to join: Negative advertising diminishes turnout, and the issues atop older Americans' agendas may not address a new generation's major concerns, including debt, education, employment, and inequality. Research suggests another possibility: Those high-volunteering millennials also are much more apt than previous generations of young Americans to switch their interests swiftly among different policy areas: fighting homelessness today and advocating for cleaner water tomorrow. Such shifts make it difficult to develop a sustained interest in any particular topic, and ultimately, any sustained interest in civic action more generally.[42] Finally, it may simply be that the digital-natives generation is less interested in collective solutions and traditional politics. *What do you think?*

 **The Bottom Line**

» The Internet, and especially social media, has launched a revolution that is changing the way Americans participate politically.

» An emerging age of activism and connection may refresh American democracy—or troubling developments may diminish it.

» New methods of participation are emerging online.

» Millennials participate in these new methods, but are less likely to vote, belong to a party, or get involved in traditional politics.

🕐 Conclusion

Participation is always in flux. Today, young Americans are less likely to participate in traditional politics—voting at lower rates than other generations did, for example. At the same time, millennials volunteer, build social capital, and engage politically through social media.

A rising generation that spurns traditional politics bodes trouble for popular government. It reminds us of Ben Franklin describing the newly formed government: "A republic, if you can keep it" (Chapter 1). Keeping the republic means revitalizing the traditional channels of political participation.

When our behaviors threaten ourselves or those around us, should public officials step in to help encourage the "right" kind of participation? Governments have intervened in other areas such as using resources such as electricity and water more responsibly, for example, or boosting our inclination to save money for retirement. Traditionally, governments have adopted coercive, top-down answers, relying on official regulations: Everyone *must* conserve water by taking shorter showers, or everyone *must* wear a seat belt or use a motorcycle helmet. Some governments, in fact, require their citizens to vote. Should we? (See What Do You Think?)

Americans resist such restrictions on individual behavior. When we participate in politics, it tends to be on our own terms, not because laws or political leaders require us to.

Another possibility is to provide gentler *nudges* toward participation. Faced with a wide array of choices, most of us tend to go with the simplest option. Take the example of organ donations. Spain had a relatively low proportion of organ donations in the early 1990s, but within a decade, its rate of donations had soared. The shift saved many lives. How did Spain manage it? By changing the default option. Previously, Spanish citizens—like Americans today—had to "opt in" to organ donor

---

What Do YOU Think?   Should Voting Be Required by Law?

Americans vote at relatively low rates. One proposal is to require voting (you'd risk a fine by not voting). Countries where voting is required have much higher participation rates.

Yes! A vibrant republic requires active participation by the people.
If everyone voted, elected officials would genuinely represent all the people. It would make our politics more inclusive. And it would avoid a grave danger: Apathetic people soon lose their rights and liberties.

No! Voting is a privilege as well as a right.
People should inform themselves and take the extra effort to cast a vote. We shouldn't make voting too easy—it's probably a good thing if uninformed people stay home. It makes politics and governing more efficient.

Not sure?
Today, political observers make arguments on both sides. Democrats are usually eager to expand voting—and are usually in the yes column. Republicans have increasingly been voting no on this issue. We hope you'll have a stronger, better-informed opinion by the time you've finished this book.

programs, a process involving several steps. Spain's government shifted to an "opt out" default, so that Spaniards were presumed organ donors unless they went through the process of indicating otherwise. Should state governments find a way so that citizens who turn eighteen have to opt out of voting? What about other forms of participation?

Whatever you think of these nudges, Americans today face the task of revitalizing the formal channels of participation. There is enormous political energy across the political spectrum—from fervent Trump supporters on the right to calls for social justice on the left. The key to the future lies in finding a way to channel that energy into everyday politics. Finding a way to make traditional politics vital and relevant is the key to "keeping the republic."

CHAPTER SUMMARY

Check your understanding of Chapter 8.

● Participation in civic and political life is a long-standing American tradition—helping, in the view of nineteenth-century visitors like Tocqueville, to distinguish the United States as a rising nation. Today, although Americans still exhibit higher levels of voluntarism than citizens of other countries, our rates of participation in politics and government have fallen to disturbing levels.

● People participate in public life in three broad ways:

- First, by participating through traditional political mechanisms: Voting, going to rallies, contributing to campaigns, contacting public officials.

- A second mode of participation involves contributing to civil society through volunteering and getting involved in the community.

Need to review key ideas in greater depth? Click here.

- Third, Americans have been quick to get involved in direct action when traditional mechanisms seem unresponsive. This is the politics of demonstrations, protest movements, and even armed confrontations.

● Whether someone engages in civic life depends on both personal factors—those with politically active family members and close friends, or with higher education levels, are more inclined to participate—and political context. During periodic outbursts of direct participation, many people who might ordinarily stay on the sidelines are drawn to participate.

● Another key to this push–pull of participation: Americans simultaneously get involved in civic affairs, especially in their local communities, and express high dissatisfaction with U.S. government institutions. That dissatisfaction helps to drive down participation in direct political activity like voting.

● Millennials exemplify this tension: They engage in voluntary public service activities at record rates but tend to mistrust politics and government. They also increasingly connect with others through social media, a force that is transforming political participation in fast-evolving (and, for the most part, poorly understood) ways.

● Mass engagement in politics and other civic activities is the lifeblood of American democracy, helping to explain why analysts are so anxious to expand participation.

KEY TERMS

Civic voluntarism, p. 231

Civil disobedience, p.232

Clicktivism, p. 228

Cycle of nonparticipation,
   p. 244

Din, p. 246

Direct action, p. 232

Electoral activities, p. 230

Issue advocacy, p. 238

Motor voter law, p. 243

Paradox of voting, p. 240

Political mobilization, p. 238

Political voice, p. 231

Social capital, p. 237

Traditional participation, p. 228

Voter turnout, p. 233

Flashcard review.

STUDY QUESTIONS

1. This chapter describes three forms of political participation: traditional political participation, civic volunteerism, and direct action. Describe each. Which do you think is most important? Why?

2. What are some of the benefits of participating in civic and political life? Why do so many Americans—especially younger people in their teens and twenties—choose not to participate through formal mechanisms?

3. Why do many Americans have a difficult time articulating a sense of the "public," compared to private life or affinity groups?

4. Describe the factors that encourage and discourage political participation.

5. Forms of direct participation appear to be rising even while voting rates remain low. What explains this paradox?

6. Which features distinguish the millennial generation when it comes to participation in civic and political activities?

7. Do you consider social networking sites a source of *enhancing* or *discouraging* participation in public life? Which evidence might you consider in support of your claim?

8. What explains the strong turn in recent years to "nudges" in U.S. policymaking? Does this trend strike you as a benefit or a drawback for American democracy?

Go to www.oup.com/us/Morone to find quizzes, flash cards, simulations, tutorials, videos, and other study tools.

9 Media, Technology, and Government

IN 1961, THE AMERICAN MEDICAL ASSOCIATION enlisted actor Ronald Reagan to help fight President John F. Kennedy's healthcare plan. Reagan cut a record (on vinyl) that the medical association sent (by snail mail) to every physician's home. "If this program passes," warned the future president, "one day we will awake to find that we have socialism. . . . We will spend our sunset years telling our children and our children's children what it was like in America when men were free." The record asked doctors' wives to invite their friends, serve coffee, play Reagan's message, and then write letters to Congress opposing government health insurance. Congress voted down the program, although another version passed four years later and is now known as Medicare.

In 1993, the Health Insurance Association of America aired television ads opposing President Bill Clinton's health plan. The ads featured "Harry and Louise," a pleasant middle-aged couple who were concerned that national health insurance would create a bureaucratic monster and wreck their health-care. "They [the Washington bureaucrats] choose," intones a voice at the end of the ad. "You lose." Congress soon buried the Clinton health proposal. It took nearly two decades until a later president, Barack Obama, succeeded in getting a comprehensive healthcare plan passed.

In 2016, Republican presidential nominee Donald Trump took to the social media platform Twitter to publicize his vow to end that health law, known as the Affordable Care Act (ACA) or "Obamacare." In 140-character bursts, Trump channeled outrage at this Big Government intrusion—and kept right on going once he took office. As President Trump's Twitter following swelled to over fifty million, his attacks on the ACA were retweeted and "liked" by tens of thousands of followers—encouraging Republican officeholders to repeal it.

Each snapshot captures the media technology of a different era—and the politics they have channeled. In 1961, a recording reached an elite audience, which responded by mailing letters to Congress. In 1993, a TV ad ran in select markets and then spread farther on television via pundits—and helped bring down a signature presidential initiative. A quarter-century later, a posting instantly reached millions of social-media followers, generating reaction in new

● *Media photographers swarm Facebook CEO Mark Zuckerberg during his appearance before a joint hearing of the Senate Judiciary and Commerce committees.*

● **Learn how media coverage of politics is changing.**

● **Consider the democratic promises and pitfalls of mainstream and social media.**

● **Explore how the media is (and is not) biased.**

● **Understand the rules that channel the media into its current forms.**

● **Discover how U.S. media is distinctive.**

● **Assess how media coverage influences politics, campaigns, and elections.**

media formats (Instagram, blogs, Facebook) and traditional ones (newspapers, radio, TV). Three major changes mark the evolution of issue campaigns across more than fifty years:

- First, *information is cascading faster and faster.* As media outlets multiply, consumers rush to keep up with the never-ending flood of news.

- Second, *today's media includes many more voices and formats.* Proliferating media options contribute to a more polarized public, as people follow sources that align with their interests or ideological outlook.

- Third, *the new media permits the public to be much more active.* You can comment on an Instagram or Facebook posting more easily (and in more ways) than you could respond to a record in 1961 or a TV commercial in 1993. The public also can act as media watchdogs and information providers, by recording and posting events on cell phones—supplying coverage formerly controlled by large media organizations.

What is the media?[1] It is all the ways people obtain information about politics and the wider world: Instagram, television, Facebook, radio, newspapers, Snapchat posts, Reddit threads, blogs, Twitter feeds, and more. Media outlets are the major information bridge between citizens and government.

The successive rise of radio, television, and the Internet each had a profound impact on American political culture. Fifty years ago, everyone heard the same newscast and took part in the same debate. Today, each position on the political spectrum tunes in to its own news source and links to its own network. *What do you think* about the **new media**: Does the vast expansion in outlets enhance democracy? Diminish it? Or perhaps some of both?

Hear Reagan's "Operation Coffee Cup" recording.

See the Harry and Louise ad.

New media: On-demand access to information through digital devices that increasingly feature interactive participation with content.

Donald J. Trump
October 31, 2017 ·

It's time to repeal and replace Obamacare once and for all. I will FIX it, but the Washington Democrats must END the obstruction. Americans WILL get the top quality healthcare they deserve!

TELL DEMOCRATS END THE OBSTRUCTION

50K   7.5K Comments 6.2K Shares 921K Views

● *From LP record albums to tweets and Facebook posts: Evolving media technologies have changed American politics—and journalism.*

Who are we? From the start of this book, we have seen that the United States is an immense, ongoing argument over political ideas. The media brings the people into political debates; it is the great link between leaders and citizens. The national media reflects America itself: raucous, fast-changing, multicultural, forceful, loud, and lucrative. It sparks intense policy debates at home. It broadcasts America to the world.

BY THE NUMBERS
The Media

Number of daily newspapers in print in the United States in 1850	254^2
Number in 1900	$2,226^3$
Expected number in 2020	700^4
Percentage of Americans who get news from social-media sites, 2018	68
Percentage of Internet-using Americans who trust information from social media sites	33
Percentage of Americans who trust information from traditional news sources	72^5
Percentage of Republicans and Democrats, respectively, approving of how news media performs its "watchdog" role, 2011	58, 58
Percentages in 2018	$38, 82^6$
Number of journalists for broad-interest websites (such as Slate.com) accredited to cover the U.S. Senate, 2009	2
Number accredited in 2019	more than 90
Percentage of news-media advertising revenue earned by digital sites, 2011	20.4
Percentage in 2017	43.6^7

Is anything important lost about news reporting and publishing in the great transition from analog (newspapers) to digital? Do you trust traditional/mainstream news sources or web-based ones more? Why?

Media and American Democracy

Media outlets perform three essential functions in a democratic system: providing information, acting as a public watchdog, and helping shape the political agenda. Let us take a closer look at all three.

Providing Information

First, media coverage *informs the public*. Without media bridging the gap, the public would be ignorant of most political events: Most of us cannot attend sessions of Congress, the Supreme Court, or our local city or town council—much less keep track of the literally thousands of policy issues and public problems that government addresses each year. When the media does its job well, we are more informed voters, more avid politics watchers, and more engaged citizens.

Are there limits to this information-providing role? Imagine that you are a Republican with lots of Democratic friends. You come across a detailed news article that crushes one of their cherished beliefs. You send it to them with a snide comment—and what happens? Rather than changing their minds, the story strengthens what they already believe. New information rarely influences people who have strongly held opinions. Instead, new information reinforces existing opinions, regardless of the story's content.[8]

However, new items can have an impact on people who have not yet made up their minds. About a third of the public does not have strong political views and is less likely to follow the news. This group *is* open to influence by the media. Here is a paradox: The news media is most likely to influence the people who pay the least attention to it. Because this group does not follow politics and government very closely, only news stories with a **loud signal** are likely to reach them and influence their views.

Loud signal: Media stories with very broad coverage and an unambiguous message.

Public watchdog: Media coverage that alerts the public when a problem arises in politics or society.

Fact-check the media.

Watching Political Leaders

Second, the media serves a **public watchdog** function, scrutinizing government for corrupt or illegal acts, misleading statements by leaders, failed consumer protections, and other flawed decisions or government processes. *Washington Post* reporters brought down the Nixon presidency by reporting doggedly on the Watergate scandal. In the run-up to the 2020 election, candidates' public statements (on social media, during debates, or in campaign appearances) are scoured by media outlets for accuracy and consistency. Is a candidate misleading the American public? Reporters keep careful score.

Politicians often complain about media coverage, but Donald Trump fights back directly, denouncing journalists who criticize his views or those who ask questions he considers unfair. More than half a million people "liked" President Trump's July 2017 post of himself appearing to beat up a man with the CNN logo as his head.[9] Serving as a watchdog for democracy has never been easy.

Shaping the Political Agenda

Editors and reporters have enormous influence on what Americans think *about*. Media executives listen to the political din and pluck out one or two stories to headline and a dozen others for the second tier. Those become the topics that politicians address, Congress investigates, talk shows debate, and you discuss and post and retweet. When an issue commands widespread attention, we say it is on the political agenda, also known as the **policy agenda**. The first step toward political action is to get your issue—homelessness, immorality, animal cruelty, whatever— onto the policy agenda, which often requires an attentive journalist.

Setting the agenda is one of the most important influences the news media has on American politics. Politicians, think tanks, interest groups, citizens, and experts all try to influence the agenda, but issues can arise seemingly out of nowhere. During the 2016 National Football League preseason, San Francisco 49ers quarterback Colin Kaepernick—incensed by what he felt was the inequitable treatment of African Americans—remained seated and later knelt while the national anthem was played. No one appeared to notice, until after the 49ers' third preseason game. As media coverage mounted, other athletes—professional, college, and high school—joined Kaepernick, further feeding news coverage. Many Americans, including President Trump, felt that the athletes were disrespecting the U.S. flag and those who died defending it. Media attention kept these issues on the national agenda well into 2018–2019. As we will see in Chapter 17, getting onto the agenda is only one step in the long political process.

Does the public attend to an issue because the media covers it? Or does the media cover an issue because the public is interested? In a classic study, two political scientists asked subjects what issues they thought were most important. Then the researchers broke the subjects into groups, and over four days, gave each group a tailored version of the nightly news emphasizing different issues— pollution, defense, inflation, and so forth. For the most part, the issues that the subjects saw on the news became more important in their own minds.[10] When the media focuses on an issue, its importance—or salience—generally rises in public perception.

The media's focus on some stories and not others affects public perceptions of policy issues as well as candidates and officials. This influence is known as **priming**. For example, because the Republican Party generally supports smaller government, stories about government incompetence prime the public to see the world through Republican eyes. Stories about the plight of the elderly or hard-working poor people prime voters to think along Democratic Party lines.

There are many ways to cover an issue, and each offers a slightly different perspective. When a media outlet emphasizes a particular slant, it is **framing** an issue. Consider the decision in 2018 by Republicans in Congress and the Trump administration to scrap the "Volcker Rule," passed in the wake of the financial meltdown of 2008–2009 to prohibit banks from making risky investments with customer deposits. Business-friendly outlets, such as *Fortune*, framed the story as relief from overzealous regulators, in stories like one headed, "It's Time to Just Kill the Volcker Rule"; on the left, headlines read "Republicans Are Sowing the Seeds of the Next Financial Crisis."[11] Mainstream media organizations tend to seek balance, often describing for their audience two or more competing frames. The *New York*

● Reporters serving as "watchdogs"— revealing foibles and misdeeds—can become targets of sharp coverage themselves.

Policy agenda: The issues that the media covers, the public considers important, and politicians address. Setting the agenda is the first step in political action.

Priming: Affecting public perceptions of political leaders, candidates, or issues by reporting on topics in ways that either enhance or diminish support.

Framing: The way an issue is defined; every issue has many possible frames, each with a slightly different tilt in describing the problem and highlighting solutions.

● *Colin Kaepernick's protest spotlighted the mistreatment of African Americans—and, fuelled by media coverage, sparked a backlash among conservatives for not respecting the flag.*

Times view on the Volcker Rule, for example, was headlined "Bankers Hate the Volcker Rule. Now It Could be Watered Down."[12]

Often, media framing is invisible to the public because it reflects the dominant social values of the time. The issue of equality was once framed as a problem concerning white men: Could they achieve the American dream in an industrial system devoted to profits? Later, mass social movements reframed the issue as one that spoke directly to race, ethnicity, and gender.

In short, framing defines the nature of the problem, organizes potential solutions, and wipes out alternative policies. A lesson all political (and business, nonprofit, etc.) leaders learn quickly: If you are not actively shaping the terms of debate, your opponents will. An academic article's title puts it perfectly: "Frame or Get Framed."[13] Media coverage plays a crucial role—often, *the* crucial role—in issue framing.

The Bottom Line

» A vast change is under way in media formats, driven by rapid technological advancement.

» Media outlets continue to perform essential democratic functions: providing information, acting as "watchdogs" to protect the public trust, shaping what news is reported (agenda setting), setting the context for a topic (priming), and describing it in specific ways (framing).

U.S. Media Today: Traditional Formats Are Declining

Media technology changes quickly, and each change remakes the connections between citizens and their leaders. The media affects the news we get, the arguments we hear, and the deliberations we engage in.

Where People Go for News

Our lead story is simple. Fifty years ago, three national TV networks and the daily paper all delivered essentially the same news to an audience with few options for challenging (or even responding to) reporters' coverage. Most households subscribed to one newspaper. Your grandparents' choices were simple: tune in or not. Today, new technologies—and the giant Internet companies that invent and manage them—give Americans a host of options that are shaking up both media and government.

As Figure 9.1 shows, digital sources are replacing traditional media, especially television. Back in 2002, TV was the chief source of news for 82 percent of the public; by 2017 that figure had fallen to 50 percent—down seven percentage points in just one year. Americans under fifty-five have switched decisively to digital sources. Newspapers and magazines continue a long slide from their one-time dominance. In contrast, radio hangs on—almost everyone listens to it, in the car or on podcasts.

What are the implications of this shifting media world? Social media sites such as Facebook or Instagram generally do not perform their own reporting: They rely on a combination of links to traditional news sources, partisan sites, and public comments. New media formats include podcasts, crowd-funded reporting, and multimedia platforms that combine digital media in telling stories, such as the hugely popular "Serial" podcasts that include short videos, letters, maps, and other clues online. More than 200 stories are now funded each year through Kickstarter and similar sources; this removes traditional gatekeepers such as producers and editors from the work of agenda setting, or deciding which issues receive priority coverage.

What does this fast-changing landscape mean for the media, for politics, and for democracy? We can learn more by focusing on developments in each of the major media.

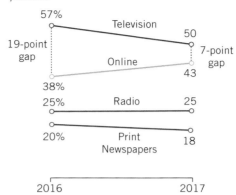

% of U.S. adults who _often_ get news on each platform

Figure 9.1 *Sources of political news. (Pew Research Center)*

Newspapers and Magazines: Rise and Decline

Newspapers have always been midwives to American democracy. The *Federalist Papers* (still vital commentaries on our Constitution) first appeared as articles in the *New York Independent Journal*. George Washington subscribed to ten newspapers. His most famous communication, the Farewell Address, was actually a letter addressed to his "fellow citizens" and printed in the papers.

In the 1830s, newspapers became the first **mass media**—just when the vote expanded to include all white men. Papers cost one penny and reflected the raucous, highly partisan, and often corrupt politics of the era. The *New York Herald* hired reporters to go out and dig up facts, and gave the readers what they wanted—murder, fire, suicide, and crime. That profit-driven journalism disgusted the old elites but made the *Herald* the most widely read newspaper in the world.

Newspaper influence grew steadily. The Spanish-American War, in 1898, is known as the first media-driven war because banner headlines blamed Spain for sinking an American battleship in Havana Harbor (there was no evidence for the charge) and helped bully the McKinley administration into the conflict. By the turn of the twentieth century, there were more than 2,200 newspapers in the United States.[14] Even after the rise of radio and television, newspapers remained the major source for political information. A typical metropolitan newspaper ran seventy stories in a day, including national, local, and business news—add sports and society features and the total ran to more than a hundred. By contrast, the

Mass media: Information and entertainment for broad popular audiences including newspapers, magazines, radio, and television.

half-hour television news had time for only ten or twelve stories. Now, after more than two centuries at the center of the news media, the newspaper is waning, with magazine circulation falling as well. The advertisers who once guaranteed profits have migrated to the Internet, and so have readers.

The result is a dramatic decline in big-city newspapers. Between 2000 and 2015, American newspapers slashed 40 percent of their staff, especially foreign correspondents and those covering local beats.[15] Declines continue: Some major papers stopped printing and have moved entirely to the Internet. Occasionally an "angel investor" comes along—Jeff Bezos, the Amazon founder and chief executive officer, spent $250 million in 2013 to buy the *Washington Post* and its affiliated papers—but such investments are rare.

Radio Holds Steady

The first commercial radio stations began airing in the 1920s. President Franklin Roosevelt seized the new technology during the Great Depression of the 1930s and delivered weekly radio addresses known as "fireside chats." The talks were informal, as if the president were talking to his listeners right by their own firesides. Hearing Roosevelt's voice personalized the relationship between Americans and their president. Indeed, political scientists link this development to the rise of the **personal presidency**.

The radio also gave new immediacy to wartime reports during World War II—and to baseball games. It accelerated the velocity of news and information. The medium made the nation, and the world, a smaller place.

Radio's golden era lasted just thirty years. By the mid-1950s, television had become king. However, radio still has a role in national politics. Conservative talk radio arose in the late 1980s after the Reagan administration cleared the way (we discuss the government connection later in this chapter). After Rush Limbaugh—a talented, pugnacious host—syndicated his daily talk show, a stream of fellow conservatives followed him onto the airwaves. Limbaugh pioneered the argument that became an article of conservative faith: The rest of the media is biased, so dial in here. Liberals tried to counter with their own talk shows, but their efforts foundered, perhaps because liberals are less likely to complain that the media is biased.

Compared to television, public radio has a large presence in the United States: National Public Radio's (NPR) audience is over thirty-eight million listeners a week, and has grown in recent years. Roughly 15 percent of NPR's funds come from the federal government, prompting ferocious criticism from conservatives, who argue that taxpayers should not be supporting "liberal" radio shows. Supporters respond that rural areas often have no other source of radio news. (The independent organization AllSides, which estimates media organizations' political leanings, rates NPR news programs as centrist, though found their editorial commentary to be inching left in late 2017–2018.)[16]

Personal presidency: The idea that the president has a personal link to the public. Made initially possible by twentieth-century media.

Franklin Roosevelt used the new medium—radio—to speak directly to citizens in their homes. One result: the rise of the personal presidency. The change in the media helped introduce a change in politics.

Podcasts also have enabled radio to thrive as a news provider. As the fastest-growing media format at present, podcasts attract millennial listeners alongside typically older radio news consumers, and launch investigative stories of their own. Online media companies such as Slate, as well as traditional organizations like the *Washington Post*, host multiple podcasts on their sites.

Television: From News to Infotainment

Television burst onto the American scene in the 1950s and revolutionized both entertainment and politics. President John F. Kennedy sensed TV's power and gave the first live press conference in February 1961. An incredible sixty-five million people—one in three Americans—tuned in. The young, charismatic president was a natural TV performer, and, once again, a new media technology intensified the link between the people and their president.

The Rise of Cable.   Two networks, CBS and NBC, monopolized the television news business during the 1960s and 1970s. Interested Americans all watched the same version of the day's events, solemnly read during the evening news shows by celebrated anchors.

Technology broke the monopoly. Cable stations began airing in the 1970s and attracted small slices of the network audience. They lingered on the fringe of the media until 1991, when an upstart named Cable News Network (CNN), showed a live video of American rockets exploding into Baghdad, the capital of Iraq, at the start of the Gulf War. CNN introduced a new model: It reported news all day long. No more waiting until 6 p.m. for the national network news. A new format was born: the twenty-four-hour news cycle. Thirty years ago, White House staff, and the reporters who covered them, all relaxed when the news cycle ended around 5 p.m. Today, the cycle never ends.

In 1996, Rupert Murdoch launched Fox News, a network with a conservative slant. As Republican viewers headed for Fox, other cable networks—most notably MSNBC—moved to the left and developed shows with a liberal spin.

Eventually, cable channels filled every niche along the political spectrum—Fox offerings such as *Hannity* on the right, shows like *Hardball with Chris Matthews* in the center, and *Last Week With John Oliver* and the *Rachel Maddow Show* on the left (see Figure 9.2). Political science analyses affirm that, as households switched to cable, presidential communications tended to reach only members of their own party.[17]

Infotainment.   As cable channels proliferated, the line between news and entertainment began to evaporate. Late night talk shows got into the political act. Hosts gleefully lacerated the political losers of the day. Politicians responded by lining up as on-air guests. A major threshold of the new era was crossed when Senator John McCain, the Republican nominee for president in 2008, announced his candidacy on the *Late*

▷

President Trump chats with Fox & Friends hosts in 2018.

● *Kennedy pioneered the televised news conference—and his approval rating soared to 70 percent. Presidents now had to be telegenic in live performance. Once again, the media had shifted the expectations and role of the presidency.*

News sources believed to be objective

	All Americans %	Republican %	Independent %	Democrat %
FOX	24	60	16	3
CNN	13	4	11	21
NPR	10	1	12	15
Local News	5	4	5	5
BBC	5	3	7	9
MSNBC	4	0	4	7

Figure 9.2 *Political polarization fuels Americans' belief that the media (especially that favored by the other side) is biased. Here, trust levels vary by political outlook. (Gallup/Knight Foundation)*

Show with David Letterman—with bandleader Paul Shaffer in pink shades blasting out "Hail to the Chief." Donald Trump has elevated blurred lines to an art form, regularly appearing on (and retweeting clips from) Fox News' "Fox and Friends" morning show, and reportedly speaking directly with the network's most popular anchor, Sean Hannity, as often as several times a day.[18]

Amid this colorful scene, network and cable news gained viewers during the 2016 campaign and its aftermath, after several years of decline. This partly reflects the irresistible spectacle of Donald Trump, who bluntly stated to the *New York Times* while president "newspapers, television, all forms of media will tank if I'm not there because without me, their ratings are going down the tubes."[19]

Overall, the TV picture reflects the state of the entire American media. A broadly shared view of the world, as interpreted by the nightly network news, has shattered. TV now runs the gamut from left to right and from formal news to frothy entertainment. The line between news and entertainment continues to blur—leading to the hybrid now known as **infotainment**. One worry raised by scholars and media executives alike: as infotainment spreads, Americans already inattentive to politics tend to become even less interested—and are less likely to vote or otherwise participate politically.[20]

Infotainment: The blurred line between news and entertainment.

The Rise of the New Media

There is much to celebrate about engaging with news and other political information online. Active readers can click a Facebook link, read content from, say, the *Wall Street Journal*, post a comment on Instagram, debate classmates in an online chat room, and surf over to YouTube for a related clip from CNN—or one posted by an eyewitness. The reader, not an editor or producer, chooses the material. Digital media permits readers to respond immediately, to share, to network, and to learn more—often through multiformat platforms.

Media analysts raise three concerns about the new media. First, traditional organizations still do the vast majority of basic reporting. Web-based outlets aggregate news and sometimes provide background, links, and multiple perspectives, but most stories are still developed by traditional reporters. If newspapers and TV networks cannot generate revenue, they will not survive. Where will we get the basic facts and stories? Will the reporting function migrate to another media institution? This is already happening in some cases, with online reporters for sites such as *Vox* or *Slate*. Digital media outlets doubled their reporting staffs from 2008 to 2017, but they are still dwarfed by traditional news organizations.

Second, important stories may get lost. Local media—newspapers, local TV news—always covered the "hot" topics (war, murder, and high school sports) along with less exciting civic issues (such as school board meetings and wetland controversies). Because everything was bundled together into one package, the popular stories paid for the civics lessons. As mainstream media, especially local newspapers, downsize staff and try to sell stories by the piece on the Internet, there may be no way to subsidize coverage on limited-interest (but very important) issues such as local education. A related concern: Traditional media must generate ever more dramatic headlines to keep up with the alluring "clickbait" fare online, dulling audiences' attention to vital but complicated policy stories. Political scientists who study media report that this effect is particularly strong among the millennial generation: "When the goal is to attract young viewers, sensational and novel [stories] often drown out news of more significance that lacks excitement."[21]

Third, traditional media tend to include a variety of viewpoints. Conservative and liberal columnists tend to appear side-by-side on the op-ed page; pundits from left and right serve on the same Sunday morning news show panel. Facebook and Instagram deploy algorithms (or individuals configure their Twitter feeds) to filter stories based on viewer preferences, emphasizing newsfeed items that fit a user's worldview.[22] The result: Each of us inhabits a shrinking "echo chamber," encountering mainly or perhaps only media reports that fuel our existing views and prejudices.

As diverse viewpoints disappear in the new-media age, **fake news**—stories that are made up, or that are twisted to promote a particular viewpoint—appears to be on the rise.[23] A natural tendency, fueled by a president who criticizes virtually all mainstream media as fake-news purveyors, is to characterize as "fake" news with which one does not agree. But empirical evidence suggests that deliberately misleading views, or ideology masquerading as fact, is more common among proliferating digital-media sites—particularly on scientific subjects such as climate change or environmental harms.[24] Americans are increasingly concerned about misinformation both online and offline (Figure 9.3).

On the other hand, some observers predict the new media will usher in a golden era of citizen participation. The Internet and social media sites turn us all into potential news providers. Traditional news always awaited the arrival of a camera team and/or print reporters. Now anyone can record an event on his or her smartphone, post it to YouTube, Instagram, or Twitter, and watch it go viral.

Learn about the first Pulitzer Prize awarded to an online-only news site.

Fake News: The deliberate spread of falsehood or misinformation— often a charge leveled by politicians against unfavorable stories.

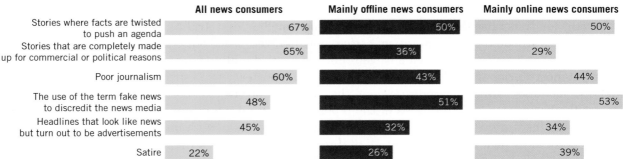

Percent Concerned about Type of Misinformation

	All news consumers	Mainly offline news consumers	Mainly online news consumers
Stories where facts are twisted to push an agenda	67%	50%	50%
Stories that are completely made up for commercial or political reasons	65%	36%	29%
Poor journalism	60%	43%	44%
The use of the term fake news to discredit the news media	48%	51%	53%
Headlines that look like news but turn out to be advertisements	45%	32%	34%
Satire	22%	26%	39%

● **Figure 9.3** *Proportion who are very or extremely concerned about each type of misinformation by main source of news. (Reuters Institute/Oxford University Press)*

Private citizens recording instances of young black men killed by police in recent years helped inspire the Black Lives Matter movement, for example.

Likewise, new technologies enable us to trace events that were much harder to track when people communicated via (untapped) telephones. Today, public officials' texts or email trails can connect them to scandalous revelations. In 2018, the *New York Times* obtained a cache of emails and other documents from the political analysis firm Cambridge Analytica, showing that the firm used data illegally obtained from Facebook to target individual voters. The evidence caused Cambridge Analytica to cease operations, and landed Facebook in its biggest political crisis.

Search engines and Internet portals link mainly to stories posted by traditional news sources—three-fifths of those populating Table 9.1. Both mainstream media and citizens worry that the portals and search engines grab the revenue. News aggregators such as *Huffington Post* or *Daily Beast* rely on traditional news sources but avoid paying them, while also generating their

TABLE 9.1	Top-Visited News Sites, June 2018

1. Reddit
2. CNN
3. Google News
4. *New York Times*
5. *The Guardian*
6. *India Times*
7. Yahoo News
8. Fox News
9. Weather.com
10. *Forbes Magazine*
Source: Alexa News Aggregation

own content. The people who gather the news—for old and new media alike—find it difficult to eke out a livable salary. As these sources cut their own costs, news coverage gets thinner and less reliable. Ultimately, the old media's downward spiral affects most of the stories that people read on their laptops and cell phones.

The Bottom Line

» Thirty years ago, a few outlets—three networks, a weekly news magazine, and the local newspaper—delivered roughly the same news. Today, media outlets cater to every perspective—left, right, and center. Americans no longer share a single source of news.

» Previous waves of rising "new" media—newspapers, radio, and television—changed the nature of news reporting and altered political institutions such as the presidency.

» Today all of these now-traditional institutions are in serious decline. Newspapers, newsmagazines, and network and local television are all losing ground as the place Americans go for news. Internet sources, especially social media platforms, are taking their place—especially among young people.

» The new media raises several major concerns, including: Do the benefits—everyone's ability to contribute to "news" and increased transparency—outweigh losing traditional reporting sources and the rising incidence of "fake news"? Will these more democratic formats find large audiences, or are we too fragmented into individual niches? And can new media invent revenue sources that enable them to cover vital but sometimes obscured stories, especially about local issues?

Is the Media Biased?

Although both Republican and Democratic officeholders have long complained that media organizations are biased against them, charges of bias are finding wider public agreement. In 1984, a substantial majority of Americans (58 to 42) supported the view that media are careful to separate fact from opinion. Today, those proportions are reversed: just 32 percent agree with this statement of media objectivity, while 66 percent view media as *not* separating fact and opinion. Nearly half of Americans, in a recent poll, could not name a single "objective" news source.[25]

On the right, traditional news organizations are decried as hostile to conservatives, their reporters overwhelmingly liberal: "97 percent of donations from mainstream media [reporters] go to the Democrat[ic] party," complained a Republican Congressman in 2017.[26] On the left, media is viewed as biased toward corporate power, given that nearly all outlets are privately owned—many by huge media conglomerates. Bernie Sanders and his supporters charged during his 2016 presidential campaign that "the corporate-owned media is inherently biased against the slate of issues his 'revolution' is built upon due to their business interests."[27]

Learn about organizations that monitor the media.

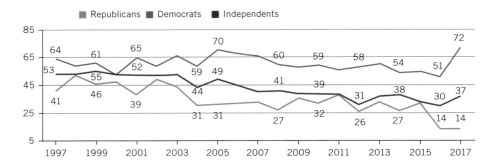

● **Figure 9.4** *Trust in U.S. Media. (Gallup)*

Such widespread charges of bias are worth taking seriously. When the public no longer trusts media organizations, U.S. government as a whole suffers—given the importance of a free press to American democracy. As Figure 9.4 shows, Republicans and independents continue to view the media with high degrees of suspicion, even as Democratic support rose in the wake of President Trump's victory.

Are Reporters Politically Biased?

Conservatives are correct about the press corps' personal attitudes. Mainstream media reporters are much less likely to identify as Republican (7%, in a 2014 study) than the national population (around 25%). Most call themselves independent, especially those in local media, where the number runs well above 60 percent.[28] This may partly reflect geography: As Figure 9.5 displays, a much larger proportion of mainstream and online journalists live among other coastal elites—in cities and counties that vote overwhelmingly Democratic—than compared to just a few years ago.[29] Just as you are more likely to share the political opinions of those living around you, so (the argument goes) do reporters.

Scholars have searched for bias in campaign coverage and in the types of stories that are aired. Though a few studies have found favoritism, dozens of studies fail to show a systematic bias among mainstream media reporters. Perhaps reporters' views creep into their framing of which issues matter? Researchers find no reliable evidence to suggest that policy frames in mainstream media systematically favor liberal views.[30]

What about the left-wing claim that corporate ownership encourages journalists to favor the status quo, and avoid hard-hitting stories on poverty, marginalized people, or radical social movements? One well-known political science study found that news organizations that stood to benefit financially from legislation (the 1996 Telecommunications Act) covered the Act more favorably than outlets realizing no financial gain. Other research demonstrates that newspapers tend to run content

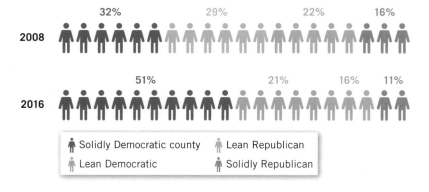

● **Figure 9.5** *Jobs in media are increasingly clustered in counties that lean Democratic. (Politico)*

biased in favor of advertisers.[31] But a pervasive inclination to ignore less well-off Americans in favor of the wealthy and powerful: A raft of scholarship has turned up no such practice among mainstream media organizations.

There *is* hard evidence of a much deeper bias that runs through the news media—the need to attract a larger audience. Media organizations' principal bias arises in their core purpose: attracting coverage and making money. Media outlets print or say or film with an eye to drawing an audience.

Profits Drive the News Industry

What does the media actually sell? The answer is not news about government actors or election campaigns. Media sells its audience to advertisers. As a result, the prime directive is to expand the audience. When ratings rise, the business prospers; when they fall, networks replace anchors and newspapers cut staff. As Sam Zell, former CEO of the media giant Tribune Company, bluntly said to his reporters: "You need to help me by being a journalist who focuses on what readers want and therefore generates more revenue."[32]

These financial realities give the news media a strong incentive to pitch its own politics near the views of its audience. For the large networks, that means the political center, where most Americans are comfortable. Hence people on both the left and right complain about bias; the center—where most stories are in fact pitched— *is* to the left of conservatives and to the right of liberals.

At the same time, each publication and network seeks its own audience. More conservative communities usually tune in to more conservative sources, and vice versa. In short, the market forces each news source toward the politics of its audience. That pressure is just the start of audiences' influence on the media. Other market biases include the search for drama, conflict, and scandal.

Drama Delivers Audiences

Journalists find it relatively difficult to generate audience excitement about a school board meeting or a healthcare proposal. Miners trapped below the earth: now that pulls people to their televisions and Twitter feeds. A good drama must have a narrative arc with a beginning, middle, and end. It should have a protagonist (the miners), pathos (anxious spouses), a villain (the coal company or government regulators), drama (will they be rescued before they run out of air?), an ending (tired but jubilant miners hugging their families), and a take-home message (we need to worry about mine safety).

Do not be fooled by the political moral at the end of the episode. Real mine safety raises complicated—and potentially boring—policy issues that will not attract much of an audience. You can be sure that when the state legislature debates mine safety, the cameras and reporters will be off chasing the next drama.

Local news gets much of its drama from crime. A classic rule of thumb guides the local TV news: "If it bleeds, it leads." Many good

Explore the role of the media in agenda setting.

● *Media outlets chase audiences with sensational stories— especially about violent crimes such as carjacking. This image led the news in West Palm Beach, Florida, although car thefts had fallen by 66 percent over the previous two decades.*

● Conflict sells. In the wake of Hurricane Harvey's devastation of Houston, multiple news outlets ran stories about looting and crime. Houston Mayor Sylvester Turner reacted by declaring that "looting will not be tolerated" and ordered a city-wide curfew. The initial stories proved to be greatly exaggerated; Houston saw far fewer property crimes (and no shootings) in Harvey's aftermath than during normal times.

things may have happened that day, but the lead story will feature the most grisly event. The images are familiar to the point of cliché—a breathless reporter live on the scene, yellow tape blocking the area, grim-faced cops or fire-fighters in the background, weeping relatives in a daze, and perhaps a blank-faced perpetrator blinking into the camera.

The need for drama transforms election coverage as well. Election reporting rarely focuses on the issues—an audience turnoff. Instead, the dramatic spotlight is on the protagonists, their families, their strategies, their dirty tricks, and their blunders. Elections have a built-in narrative arc as well: a *beginning* (the candidates throw their hats into the ring), a *middle* (who is ahead? who had the best week?), a *conclusion* (someone wins), and a *take-home message* (the loser had a fatal flaw that other candidates should avoid). In 2016, media outlets debated whether Americans' thirst for drama-filled coverage led reporters and editors to provide Donald Trump with more free publicity than any other candidate.[33]

Political debates—whether about the environment, gun rights, education, or taxes—generally reflect the same pressure to build a narrative. Regardless of the issue, media coverage focuses on drama and conflict, heroes and villains, winners and losers. This tendency exacerbates media bias. For example, despite a dramatic drop in U.S. crime rates over the past twenty years, most Americans believe that crime is actually rising.[34] The constant coverage, especially of local news, misleads viewers to imagine that criminals are running rampant everywhere.

Click on your favorite news website. Can you see the dramatic narrative that frames the lead story? Pundits criticize media stories for lacking substance. However, as a student of political science, you have learned to examine the *institution* and its incentives. The media, seeking a large audience to serve up to advertisers, covers whatever attracts the most attention. Simply calling for serious coverage will not change the incentives built into the media market.

Investigative "Bias"

Other media biases have to do less with the market and more with the profession of journalism. Two are especially powerful: skepticism and fairness. Back in the early 1960s, Washington reporters were a small, white, male club with a code that winked at extramarital affairs in the White House or falling-down drunks in Congress. Then a series of events transformed the media's stance toward powerful men and women: The moral intensity of the civil rights movement, administration efforts to manipulate the press during the Vietnam War, and the **Watergate scandal** all made the old accommodations seem irresponsible. How could reporters go easy on segregationists or liars?

Watergate was especially significant in fostering skepticism. Reporters investigated a burglary of Democratic Party headquarters that led directly to the White House. President Nixon had secretly taped conversations in the Oval Office, and while pursuing the case of the botched burglary, the Supreme Court forced the

Watergate scandal: A failed effort in 1972 by Republican operatives to break into Democratic Party headquarters in the Watergate office complex in Washington, DC. President Nixon tried to cover up the event—eventually causing him to resign from the presidency.

What Do YOU Think?   Is the Media Objective? Should It Be?

After Congress repealed the Fairness Doctrine that forced media outlets to provide opposing viewpoints, some media sources began to cater to partisan audiences. Today, 46 percent of Americans cannot name an objective news source, and many feel that the media is not doing a good job serving our democracy.[35]
Do you agree?

—Not enough objectivity. Media organizations should serve as a platform for the expression of opposing views—vital to the democratic process. They also should do a better job of distinguishing facts from opinions to restore public trust in media—and other governing institutions.

—Enough objectivity. Even though some media sources are partisan, the public has access to a range of sources—from Fox to CNN to MSNBC, providing the public access to a wide range of viewpoints. I can gather a fuller picture of critical issues and arrive at a better interpretation of events by following multiple sources.

—Too much objectivity. Media reports too often bend over backward to give all sides a fair hearing. Journalists are very knowledgeable about politics; I want to hear their views, not just their "unbiased" recitation of facts and politicians' opinions.

release of the tapes. Their content stunned Americans. Now the public could hear their president order aides to "stonewall" the Watergate investigations. Even more shocking, the presidential tapes bristled with ethnic slurs, anti-Semitism, and foul language. (The newspaper transcripts were full of the notation "expletive deleted.")

In response, reporters redefined their roles. Rather than acting as chummy insiders, they became skeptics, aiming to pierce through official propaganda and find the hidden truth. Media emphasizing their "watchdog" function led relations between the press and politicians to turn more adversarial. Each time the members of the press felt misled by an administration, their skepticism grew. For example, George W. Bush insisted that Iraq owned dangerous weapons that threatened the United States. (It did not.) Barack Obama promised Americans, "If you like your health plan, you can keep it." (Not all could.) Media outlets have kept a running tally of President Trump's false or misleading statements—beginning with the size of his inaugural crowd. In the new environment, the reporter's mission became uncovering lies and bad behavior.

The Fairness Bias

The effort to be fair introduces an unexpected bias. Reporters energetically try to present both sides of each issue. However, when issues do not have two equal sides, the effort creates the impression of a debate that does not exist. Companies that market tobacco, unhealthy foods, or toxic products, for example, have learned that they do not need to win the debate. They simply sponsor research and announce that there are two sides to the issue. The fairness bias then leads the media to report the two sides as equivalent—even if one of the sides was manufactured by an interested party.

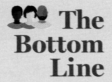

The Bottom Line

» Both conservatives and liberals complain of media bias. However, the media generally reflects the politics of its audience—which is to the left of conservatives and to the right of liberals.

» The media's deepest bias comes from its need to win ratings and appeal to advertisers. That puts an emphasis on drama, scandal, and conflict—exacerbating partisan political divisions.

» Media efforts to be objective and balanced can introduce their own biases, such as "fairness."

How Governments Shape the Media

We have seen how technology constantly changes the media. The media, in turn, changes politics. In this section, we examine how political rules shape the development of the media.

Democratic nations organize their media in three different ways: First, the *government can fund* media outlets. This **public ownership** model is familiar in many nations—but, for the most part, not the United States. Second, the government can *regulate* the media to ensure that it operates in the public interest. Third, the government can stand aside and let the *market* guide the media; the assumption of the market model is that private companies will give the people (and the advertisers) what they want.

Public ownership: A situation in which media outlets are run by the government and paid for by tax dollars.

The First Amendment Protects Print Media from Regulation

You have already encountered the primary political rule governing print media—the First Amendment: "Congress shall make no law . . . abridging the freedom of speech or of the press." As we saw in Chapter 5, the Supreme Court has been strict about forbidding government interference with the press. Compared to most peer nations, it is very difficult to censor news (a practice known as prior restraint), to convict someone of slander or libel (spoken or written lies), to restrict pornography, or to forbid hate speech. Reporters are also fierce in protecting their sources. A *New York Times* reporter, Judith Miller, went to jail for three months rather than reveal her source for a story about a CIA agent named Valerie Plame.

Market forces and audience feedback impose the limits that do exist. American newspapers, paid for by local advertisers, generally reflect local mores. They are tame compared with, for example, the English tabloids. Web-based news outlets likewise reflect the outlook of their parent companies and of their audience. New-media consumers can respond swiftly to coverage they see as biased or inappropriate, through "comments" sections and organized Twitter and Facebook campaigns. When the gossipy site Gawker printed an article outing a gay Condé Nast executive, readers tweeted a torrent of objections, calling the story an unwarranted example of "gay shaming." Gawker soon removed the article and issued a promise to uphold higher standards in the future.

Regulating Broadcasters

Radio and television fall into a separate category. They have been subject to government regulations from the start. As radio stations spread in the 1930s, their signals began to interfere with one another. In 1934, the Franklin Roosevelt administration created the Federal Communications Commission (FCC) to referee the industry. The agency was founded on a basic political philosophy: the airwaves belong to the public. The FCC would license stations on a given frequency—preventing signals from overlapping—but in exchange, stations were required to be "socially responsible." When a station secured or renewed its license, it had to show that it operated in the public's interest. When television emerged, the FCC expanded its jurisdiction to include it.

In 1949, the FCC issued an important regulation, the **fairness doctrine**. The fairness doctrine required radio and TV stations to give equal time to each side of a public issue. The rule reflected the era's expectations: sober, nonpartisan coverage of news and politics. Even though it was not strictly enforced, the fairness doctrine led stations to shy away from political controversies altogether; that way, they avoided the bother of achieving a balance.

In the 1980s, the Reagan administration challenged the entire idea of public responsibility enforced by regulatory agencies. It promoted a different political philosophy, viewing media as a private commodity rather than as a public good: end government regulations and let the consumers use the market to enforce what they value. The FCC repealed the fairness doctrine in 1983. The consequences were huge. Under the fairness doctrine, each talk show with a point of view had to be balanced by another talk show from the opposite perspective. A station that broadcast conservatives such as Rush Limbaugh would be required to air an equal amount of liberal programming. Repealing the rule opened the door to the media landscape we have today: a rich and raucous menu of news and politics that reaches across the political spectrum.

As with Internet news outlets, government regulation of new media operating in cyberspace is evolving as technology changes. In 2015, following a vigorous debate pitting new-media companies such as Netflix and large Internet service providers such as Comcast against consumer rights advocates, the FCC established "net neutrality" rules. These prohibited Internet providers from charging more for certain content or from giving preferential treatment to certain websites ("pay to play"). Three years later, net neutrality was killed by a party-line vote of FCC commissioners. Some states, including California and Washington, wrote their own net neutrality laws—and were sued for interfering with interstate commerce. Will high-paying customers have access to faster Internet service? Can customers be charged a premium for using certain popular social-media sites, such as Instagram? Without guaranteed net neutrality, no one can say for certain.

Fairness doctrine:
Regulation that required media outlets to devote equal time to opposite perspectives.

● *Fierce political support for net neutrality did not change FCC commissioners' minds in 2018.*

Consolidation: The process whereby a media company grows, acquires other companies, and threatens to dominate the market.

Telecommunications Act of 1996: A major overhaul of communications law that opened the door to far more competition by permitting companies to own outlets in multiple media markets such as radio, television, and magazines, and removing or reducing limits on how many outlets one company can own.

Protecting Competition

The market model is based on competition. If one corporation captures too much of the market, might it diminish consumer choice? This question arose when corporations moved to control companies across different media markets—print, radio, and television. Some observers warned that a few companies may come to dominate and stifle the marketplace of ideas. The top two radio companies, Clear Channel and CBS, control so many stations that they broadcast to a larger audience (263 million strong) than all twenty-four of the remaining radio networks combined. **Consolidation**, from this perspective, threatens free speech and fair debate.

Those who favor deregulation respond that today's media takes so many different forms, from radio stations to online news, blogs, and tweets, that stiff competition for consumer attention is inevitable. The **Telecommunications Act of 1996** reflected this second view and permitted many forms of cross-ownership. One result evident more than twenty years later: Media companies have consolidated to the point that a few companies control vast swaths of American media.

 **The Bottom Line**

» Democratic nations organize their media in three ways: government ownership, regulation, and markets. The United States has historically relied on the latter two models, regulation and markets.

» The First Amendment protects print media from most government regulation.

» Broadcast media in the United States was originally regulated by agencies such as the FCC, which imposed the fairness doctrine—a reflection of a less partisan era. The FCC is still active, but reduced its own power further by ending "net neutrality."

» Deregulation, new technologies, and the rise of multiple media have created the spectrum of perspectives and views that mark American media today. At the same time, a handful of giant media companies now control much of the content we see and hear. This contributes to our partisan and conflicted politics.

🔘 Media Around the World

The American media is different from that of other nations. (Have you noticed how many times we have said that about American politics?) The "watchdog" tradition, combined with near-absolute freedom of the press to write or say what they wish, is stronger in the United States than most other countries. Most nations also began with government-operated broadcast media—the one option the United States has little pursued, apart from public television (PBS) and radio (NPR). However, the differences may be eroding. The American media has gone global, and in some countries, leaders even complain about the "Americanization" of their media—moving from public to private ownership.

Media Consolidation

WHO PRODUCES, DISTRIBUTES, AND OWNS THE MEDIA?

Our fast-changing media landscape reflects a remarkable degree of consolidation. Three decades ago, media content—
what Americans read, watch, and hear—was spread across more than 50 companies.

CIRCLES SIZED BY MARKET CAPITALIZATION

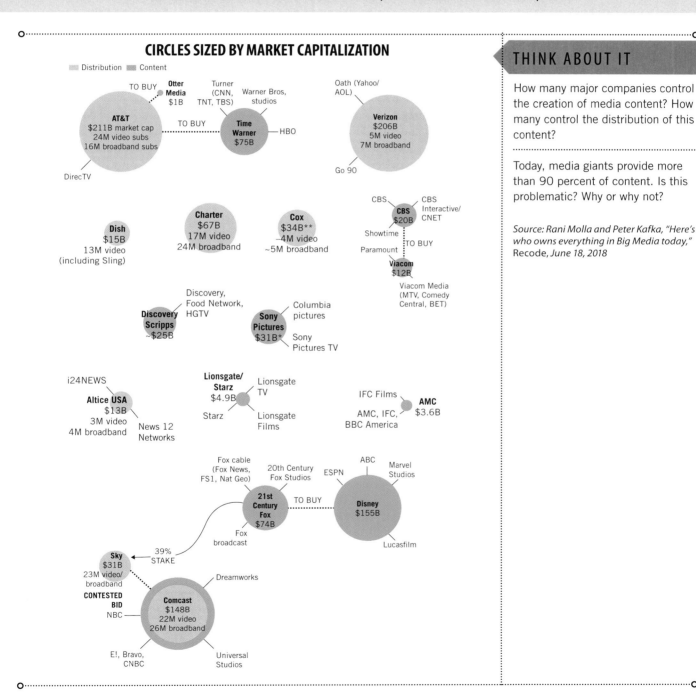

Distribution   Content

TO BUY **Otter Media** $1B

Turner (CNN, TNT, TBS)

Warner Bros, studios

AT&T $211B market cap 24M video subs 16M broadband subs

TO BUY

Time Warner $75B — HBO

DirecTV

Oath (Yahoo/ AOL)

Verizon $206B 5M video 7M broadband

Go 90

Dish $15B 13M video (including Sling)

Charter $67B 17M video 24M broadband

Cox $34B** ~4M video ~5M broadband

CBS   CBS Interactive/ CNET

CBS $20B

Showtime

TO BUY

Paramount

Viacom $12B

Viacom Media (MTV, Comedy Central, BET)

Discovery, Food Network, HGTV

Discovery Scripps ~$25B

Columbia pictures

Sony Pictures $31B*

Sony Pictures TV

i24NEWS

Altice USA $13B 3M video 4M broadband

News 12 Networks

Lionsgate/ Starz $4.9B

Lionsgate TV

Starz

Lionsgate Films

IFC Films

AMC, IFC, BBC America

AMC $3.6B

Fox cable (Fox News, FS1, Nat Geo)

20th Century Fox Studios

ABC

ESPN

Marvel Studios

21st Century Fox $74B

TO BUY

Disney $155B

Fox broadcast

Lucasfilm

Sky $31B 23M video/ broadband

39% STAKE

Dreamworks

CONTESTED BID

NBC

Comcast $148B 22M video 26M broadband

E!, Bravo, CNBC

Universal Studios

THINK ABOUT IT

How many major companies control the creation of media content? How many control the distribution of this content?

Today, media giants provide more than 90 percent of content. Is this problematic? Why or why not?

Source: Rani Molla and Peter Kafka, "Here's who owns everything in Big Media today," Recode, *June 18, 2018*

275

Government-Owned Stations

When radio developed in the 1920s, leaders in many democratic nations worried about the new medium's potential power. What if demagogues seized the airwaves? Rather than leave radio and, later, television programming to private entrepreneurs, most democratic countries introduced public stations that were owned by the government and funded through taxes. To this day, the publicly owned BBC is the largest network in Britain, attracting 32 percent of the TV market; in contrast, the largest commercial network (ITV) draws under 22 percent.[36] Most other democracies also have popular public stations. A cautionary tale told across Europe is that of Italy, where for forty years the Berlusconi family has controlled the top three national TV channels. Silvio Berlusconi parlayed that control into four terms as prime minister; despite his conviction for tax fraud, in 2018 Berlusconi's new *Forza Italia* party was in the governing coalition.[37]

Now consider the United States, where public television draws barely 2 percent of the TV audience. Are there reasons to be concerned about private control of the airwaves in the United States? Or is this a fine example of the market at work? In many democratic countries, rising American-style commercial media has cultural leaders concerned that the U.S. mix of infotainment and polarized news outlets will soon follow.[38]

Censorship

A different media model dominates authoritarian nations: The government directly controls the media and censors every story. This was historically common practice around the world. Government censorship, limiting open information and political debate, has always been the tool of tyrants. Democracies can only operate with the free flow of ideas and information.[39]

New media challenges the ability of authoritarian regimes to control information (see Comparing Nations 9.1). When the Internet is blocked, innovative

---

COMPARING NATIONS 9.1   **Censorship Under Pressure?**

Zhang Guanghong, a human-rights activist in China, used the WhatsApp social-media site to send a letter critical of Chinese president Xi Jingpin. Even though WhatsApp is not often used in China, he was soon detained by police, and faced serious charges of insulting China's government and the Communist Party.[40] Although new media has shaken up information control in many countries, censorship in China and other restrictive states is expanding almost as fast as the Internet itself.

A few years back, a high speed Chinese train was rammed from behind, killing thirty-nine people and injuring 192. Messages from inside the wrecked train described bloodshed, chaos, and slow response; they were reposted up to 100,000 times. The official state-run media tried the usual narrative—bad weather, a heroic response, many saved. But twenty-six *million* posts from ordinary Chinese citizens overwhelmed that story. Both government and news agencies apologized, changed their approach, and launched an investigation into the crash. As one state-run newspaper put it, the government responded to its "netizens."[41]

The apology in China suggests that new media can shake up authoritarian governments and censorship. At the same time, Zhang Guangdong's story affirms the Chinese government's ability to crack down on "outside media" sources. Facebook, Google, YouTube, and Twitter are blocked in China, and current rules require all images and words from even partly foreign-owned companies to be approved by government agencies before being broadcast in China.

networks can spring up to spread the news; new technologies permit people to receive content outside official channels. A key future question is whether (and how) citizens in authoritarian countries will successfully seize the democratic potential of new media forms. Whatever the answer, the crucial link between media and popular government extends far beyond the United States to every nation.

American Media in the World

American media industries have enormous reach. In one typical week in June 2018, *Jurassic World: Fallen Kingdom* was the highest grossing film in fourteen of twenty-five countries tracking box-office receipts, from Italy to South Africa to Turkey; *Ocean's Eight* was on top in three others, including Australia and Colombia; *Avengers: Infinity War* led in China; *Solo: A Star Wars Story* in Singapore; and *Deadpool 2* was box-office king in Japan, Argentina, and the Czech Republic. American television has a similarly wide influence, both in entertainment and news; CNN is a staple on cable in virtually every corner of the world. The U.S. media model, with its emphasis on markets and consumer choice, has a major impact in both democracies and authoritarian nations.

Every nation has its own media style. Governments remain a major content provider (and regulator) in most industrial nations. Looking abroad illustrates how distinctive the U.S. model remains. Few other nations have organized a system of private entrepreneurs operating within a framework of very light (and heavily criticized) regulatory oversight.

 **The Bottom Line**

» Rapidly changing media outlets link citizens to their politics around the world. An open media is a vital key to making democracy work.

» The American model of media as private enterprise is spreading. However, most other democracies retain more government regulation than the United States.

» Authoritarian nations censor their news reporters. Increasingly, new media forms are challenging government control of the news, but the censors are keeping pace.

Understanding the Media in Context: War, Terrorism, and U.S. Elections

Every aspect of the media's influence on politics is on display during two dominant American events: military conflicts, including responses to terrorism; and election campaigns. Framing issues, emphasizing drama, and "infotainment"; the fragmenting of story lines in our new-media age: all come to the fore.

Covering Wars and Terrorism

When America engages in military conflicts, reporters are embedded with the troops. Mathew Brady's portraits of Civil War carnage helped establish photography's mass appeal. Wars and terrorist attacks feature no shortage of drama, playing

Vietnam War coverage. Images such as these—a South Vietnamese general shooting a handcuffed Vietcong prisoner in the head, and Vietnamese children fleeing a U.S. napalm attack on their village— triggered protests and opposition to the war. Were they too violent for objective news?

naturally to media's inclination to cover striking conflicts. Questions arise in every war about whether media is "sensationalizing" the conflict by providing particularly gruesome images.

Others warn that wartime media coverage must not give "aid and comfort to America's enemies," as a U.S. general lamented darkly during the Vietnam conflict. Debates were sparked during the Iraq War by media reports of alleged American military misdeeds, such as "waterboarding" torture and other mistreatment of prisoners at the notorious Abu Ghraib detention facility. Did the coverage portray U.S. soldiers unfairly, diminishing support for the war back home? What responsibility do journalists have for balanced reporting, including of atrocities by our wartime enemies? And how able are traditional media outlets, most of which have slashed budgets for foreign correspondents, to provide big-picture coverage of conflicts as complex as those in Afghanistan and Iraq?

Media coverage of terrorist attacks also raises questions about journalistic ethics. Should the media faithfully report on any government claim about foiled terrorist plots, for example? Some experts worry that extensive media coverage of terrorism may actually heighten the chance of a subsequent attack, as misguided actors seek journalistic fame through terrible crimes. Should the Islamic State, for example, be given the media's "oxygen of publicity" for beheadings and other horrific acts?

Political science research suggests that reporting inadvertently *does* lead to further terrorist acts. One recent study concluded that a *New York Times* article about a terrorist attack in any specific country increased the number of ensuing attacks in that country by as much as 15 percent. Scholars calculated that each additional *Times* article—or other mainstream global coverage—resulted in between one and two casualties from another terrorist attack within the next week.[42]

The Campaign as Drama

U.S. election campaigns involve political rather than armed conflicts, of course, though media's influence is amply on display. As noted earlier, reporters cover electoral campaigns like horse races—obsessed with who will cross the finish line first. With the advent of digital media, the pace of information is even swifter; one result is that now the coverage of presidential campaigns devotes much less time to the candidate's actual views. In 1968, the average clip of a candidate speaking on the news, called a **sound bite**, ran uninterrupted for over forty seconds. Today, the average clip has fallen to under eight seconds. After those few seconds, you might see the candidates gesture and move their lips: merely the backdrop for the anchor or pundit's analysis, which is often centered on (you guessed it!) why the candidate is winning or losing.

Throughout the campaign, reporters' antennae are always up for gaffes and hints of scandal. When one appears, the entire media throngs to it. Every speech and debate is carefully combed over for blunders; sites such as "FactCheck.org" review all candidates' claims during stump speeches and debates. Does this media whirlwind really matter to election outcomes? The short answer: rarely. Effective campaigns develop rapid-response teams that deal with whatever crisis gusts through the media on that day.

Media coverage of terrorist attacks: the aftermath of a New York City trail of mayhem in a rented truck. Could 24/7 reporting raise the chances of further attacks?

Sound bite: A short audio clip; often refers to a brief excerpt from a politician's speech.

Without the charge of a presidential race, midterm campaigns like 2018's can seem more distant and even dull. Media influence is evident here as well, however. Scandals, endlessly reported by journalists desperate for material beyond the candidates' daily stump speeches, can knock a candidate out of a race: or, as ex-Governor Eric Greitens of Missouri discovered in summer 2018, out of office—after steamy revelations of an affair with his hairdresser. And any attention at all, in (say) a U.S. House open seat or state lieutenant-governor roundup of candidates, is welcome; so-called "free media" can amplify a message—and validate it (*The Wall Street Journal* wrote about my candidacy!") in ways that resonate with voters.

Candidate Profiles

Campaign coverage often features a powerful narrative. The media sketches a profile of each candidate—simplistic, exaggerated, and very hard to escape. That image then shapes future coverage. Once the portrait develops, it reverberates through the world of infotainment. Behavior that "fits" immediately gets airtime, reinforcing the narrative.

Once the media paid attention to Bernie Sanders's 2016 presidential race, they pictured Sanders as an insurgent, whose critiques of U.S. financial institutions attracted progressive Americans, especially college students and other young voters. Hillary Clinton became an Establishment figure, with reporters noting her long history in Washington institutions such as the State Department, the U.S. Senate, and the White House as First Lady. As the primary season shaped up as an anti-Establishment year in both parties, Sanders's surprising staying power was in part thanks to the framing of his candidacy by reporters.

Campaigns respond to shrinking sound bites by creating visual images that will speak louder than the inevitable punditry. Waving flags, cheering crowds, or bales of hay down on the farm all convey images—regardless of media voiceovers.

Campaigns spend extraordinary sums on advertising. Some ads have become classics, usually because of their wicked stings. In 1964, President Lyndon Johnson's campaign ran perhaps the most famous ad—just once—raising fears that electing Republican presidential candidate Barry Goldwater might result in a nuclear war. A little girl plucked petals off a daisy, counting down "10...9...8..." Then an ominous male narrator took over, counting down to 1, when the screen filled with a nuclear mushroom cloud. In 1988, Republicans skewered presidential Democratic nominee Michael Dukakis with an ad featuring Willie Horton, a convicted murderer who was released from a prison on a weekend-furlough program approved by then-Governor Dukakis. While on release, Horton committed a rape; the story was used to paint Dukakis as a hapless, "soft-on-crime" liberal. Political advertisements become especially effective if they seep into the news coverage and become part of the campaign narrative. That can amplify the signal enough to reach the voters in the middle who are not paying much attention.

New media raises the prospect of great changes in campaigning. Social media outlets such as Facebook and Twitter give candidates a targeted way to circumvent the mass media and speak directly to supporters. (As we shall see in the Presidency chapter, Donald Trump's use of online media propelled him right into the White House.) Digital messaging creates a sense of movement, of belonging. It offers a way to mobilize supporters behind a cause without relying on traditional media coverage. Ironically, the mainstream media eagerly reports on successful new media campaigns—amplifying that success by publicizing it.

See the controversial "Daisy" ad from the 1964 Johnson campaign.

 **The Bottom Line**

» Reporting on war and terrorism has long attracted more viewers than almost any other political story. Ethical questions about the nature of media coverage continue to reshape editors' approach to these dramatic stories.

» Media coverage of campaigns reflects the general patterns of the contemporary media. It emphasizes drama, conflict, and the horse race narrative.

» Campaigns attempt either to influence the media or to bypass it and speak directly to supporters. These efforts in turn become part of the media coverage.

Conclusion: At the Crossroads of the Media World

The media reflects the United States—and broadcasts it to the world. American media has many critics. Conservatives blast the mainstream media's "liberal bias"; progressives lament the stifling influence of corporate media ownership. Another line of concern: Millennials, engaging media through smartphones, find it hard to filter the endless stream of news and information arriving from every social-media corner. We should remember what makes the American broadcast media unusual: It has always been a commercial enterprise. Whatever draws an audience survives and flourishes.

America's media reflects the nation and its people. The fifth-largest network in the United States is the Spanish-language Univision. In fact, the dozen Spanish-speaking networks on American television today boast a total of more than 400 affiliates. Together, they reach more local stations than any one of the major networks. And the foreign-language media does not stop at Spanish. In San Francisco, Comcast offers thirty-five foreign-language channels, and the Dish satellite menu includes a hundred foreign-language stations. Sixty million Americans (including one of your authors) have at least one parent born abroad, and the media reflects that reality.

What else does the media tell us about who we are? Here is another important indicator: The ten largest religious networks have more than 350 affiliates. The largest, INSP (formerly the Inspiration Network), reaches an estimated eighty-five million households. By way of comparison, ESPN reaches ninety million.

As we have seen, television in every demographic is being squeezed by the Internet and the new media. Netflix, for example, now has more than 125 million subscribers, and by some estimates will be the largest U.S. "TV network" within the next few years. In this booming new category, it is America's young people who are driving the change—pioneering new technologies and picking winners and losers among sites and applications. What once appeared to be a great digital divide is now shrinking, as African American and Latino youth catch up to white youth. In forums such as Twitter, they have nudged their way to the top among the young. The United States consumes programs in hundreds of languages. *Who are we?* A multinational and multicultural society, bustling with changes and beaming its images to the world—through television, cinema, blogs, Instagram posts, streaming Netflix shows, and tweets.

Pessimists lament the collapse of our national community. Every political side now has its own news shows. Americans do not just disagree about values—they do not even hear or see the same reality. Mainstream newspapers and networks are losing money, and as a result, their capacity to collect the news is declining. As the details about national and international events get sketchier, the void is filled by loud, ill-informed opinions. The entire news apparatus dashes after drama, conflict, and scandal. Important issues such as education, the environment, and healthcare are downplayed in this chase for an audience. To pessimists, today's media—fragmented, declining, sensationalist—exacerbates the conflicts in American politics.

In contrast, optimists see a thriving democracy in which people are active and engaged. Debates in Washington may be long and loud, but that only reflects an energetic nation undergoing enormous change. As media outlets expand and go digital, people's choices grow richer. Today, the United States has a broad lineup of news, information, and analysis. Members of the traditional media try to present objective reports as best they can. Cable channels and radio stations get partisans excited about their ideas and their parties. And new media—Internet-based outlets such as Instagram and Facebook—permit people, especially young people, to engage in political dialogue as never before. The media stirs up the best features of American politics: broad participation and strong opinions that leaders cannot help but hear.

CHAPTER SUMMARY

Check your understanding of Chapter 9.

The media—and the stories editors and users choose to emphasize—helps set the political *agenda*, *prime* the electorate, and *frame* issues.

Media stories affect public opinion—primarily among people who do not have strong opinions. Because these people tend to pay less attention to the news, stories with clear signals (heavy coverage, a strong perspective) will change their views.

Media platforms have expanded from the traditional television, radio, and newspapers to include online news sites, podcasts, Facebook, Twitter, and more.

Media technology changes very rapidly, and each change reshapes the connection between citizens and their leaders—a crucial criterion for democracy. A big question runs through this chapter: Does today's media strengthen American democracy or weaken it?

News sources are changing. Newspapers, magazines, television, and radio are all facing very different business models, and rushing to fill the void with new formats such as on-demand streaming and podcasts. Online news is rising fast. Today, it is the number one source of news for people under thirty. The enormous number of news sources spans the political spectrum and blurs the line between entertainment and news.

Yes, the media is biased. Reporters in the mainstream press are less conservative than the general population, but they do not seem to tilt election coverage or other news. The deepest bias—across the entire news media spectrum—comes from the media's purpose: It is a business that needs an audience to generate revenue. Therefore the news emphasizes drama, conflict, and scandal.

In most other democracies, the government ran the first radio and TV stations and still plays a large role in the media world, although commercial media is rising. In authoritarian countries, the new social media poses a threat to the old model of information control and press censorship.

The new social media is changing the nature of news and information. On the upside, users are more active. They can choose, respond, report, comment, critique, create, and share. Candidates and parties have new ways to connect. On the downside, the ready availability of news on the Internet has challenged the pay models of traditional print outlets, leading to a new media environment that facilitates the spread of rumors and even lies. All of this means that we as a society do not share the same news.

This influence gives media leaders considerable power over American politics. Whether that power is used for the public benefit is a much-debated question—perhaps most sharply when it comes to covering urgent topics such as war, terrorism, and election campaigns.

In many ways, the media reflects America. What we watch and hear tells us who we are.

Need to review key ideas in greater depth? Click here.

KEY TERMS

Flashcard review.

Consolidation, p. 274

Fake News, p 265

Fairness doctrine, p. 273

Framing, p. 259

Infotainment, p. 264

Loud signal, p. 258

Mass media, p. 261

New media, p. 256

Personal presidency, p. 262

Policy agenda, p. 259

Priming, p. 259

Public ownership, p. 272

Public watchdog, p. 258

Sound bite, p. 279

Telecommunications Act of 1996, p. 274

Watergate scandal, p. 270

STUDY QUESTIONS

1. Where do most Americans get their news—local television, network television, newspapers, or the Internet?

2. Which sources do millennial Americans rely on most for their news?

3. Name two problems most analysts see in the decline of the newspaper. Do you agree that these are problems? Why or why not?

4. How is the American media biased? Describe three of its biases.

5. Name three ways in which the American media is different from that of other nations. Be sure to consider the questions of ownership, objectivity, and investigation.

6. Choose a news source and look at today's headlines. Can you find a "media narrative" in these stories? Do you see a narrative arc, drama, conflict, good guys, and bad guys? Can you come up with a more objective way to present the story?

7. Research a potential presidential candidate for the 2020 election. What does she or he stand for? Now design a campaign commercial for that candidate. Put him or her in the best possible light using visuals and voiceovers. Post your creation on YouTube.

8. Pick a story. Read its coverage in the *New York Times*. Now compare this coverage with that of two other sources: the BBC and Al Jazeera. Identify at least one difference in the way the other two outlets covered the story.

THE RULES FOR WINNING THE PRESIDENCY

were clear. Raise a lot of money, build a sophisticated team, and win over the party leaders.[1] The 2016 presidential campaign seemed perfectly predictable. Team Jeb Bush raised a whopping $116 million. On the Democratic side, Hillary Clinton was not far behind. Then Donald Trump broke all the rules: He seemed indifferent to fundraising, he did not build a serious campaign organization, he did not run any commercials, and he was crude and insulting—to Latinos, African Americans, U.S. prisoners of war, women, immigrants, newscasters, donors, and even Republican elder statesmen.[2] Trump mocked many of the sixteen other Republican candidates who could not get airtime—as the media obsessed over the latest Trump outrage. By the end of the campaign, estimates suggested that Trump had swung $2 billion worth of free media coverage—much of it negative. Yet he won primary after primary. Despite the cold shoulder from almost every past Republican presidential candidate and most officeholders ("trickle-down racism," charged former presidential candidate Mitt Romney), Trump won the nomination. On the Democratic side, Senator Bernie Sanders—a rumpled, little known, 74-year-old democratic socialist with a Brooklyn accent representing Vermont—also broke the rules: He lashed the rich, lambasted party leaders for ignoring everyday people, and won 23 contests and 43 percent of the votes in the Democratic primary.

When political scientists published their models before the general election, the median (or middle one) predicted correctly that the Democratic presidential candidate Hillary Clinton would get 51 percent of the popular vote. A surge of white (mostly male) voters from economically distressed communities, however, gave Trump the Electoral College and powered one of the biggest upsets in American campaign history. It was a very close call. If 78,000 votes in Wisconsin, Michigan, and Pennsylvania (out of a total of 12 million) had gone the other way, Hillary Clinton would have won.

But here's the thing about American politics: There's always another election coming up. Two years later, the 2018 midterm shook up American politics. Republicans gained ground in the Senate, but Democrats won control of the House of Representatives and made inroads with suburban voters. What's next? Another election, of course. All eyes turn on the next great prize: the election of 2020.

● *Republicans and Democrats confront one another during a raucous campaign event. The question for political scientists and citizens: How much do campaigns matter?*

In this chapter, you will:

● Learn what is unique (and what is not) about American elections.

● Examine how democratic American elections are today.

● Discuss the influence of money in elections.

● Explore presidential and congressional campaigns.

● Identify the keys to a successful campaign for Congress.

● Consider election reforms.

● *Alexandria Ocasio-Cortez, a former Bernie Sanders organizer, jolted the political establishment by upsetting powerful Democrat Joseph Crowley in a New York City primary. She became an instant star and in January became the youngest member ever elected to Congress.*

Sometimes, political scientists suggest, campaigns barely matter. More fundamental factors—such as the economy and the sitting president's approval rating—determine who wins the election. Not the hyped-up, media-saturated, roller-coaster campaign.

In fact, campaigns are essential to electoral outcomes. This chapter will show you how and why.[3] We won't just focus on the White House. Thousands of candidates run for positions from U.S. senators to judges to municipal drain inspectors. *Who are we?* A nation of elections. Americans vote more often and for more officers—on every level of government—than the people of almost any other nation. Through elections, Americans choose leaders, guiding philosophies, programs and policies, and the nation's attitude toward the rest of the world.

Both Donald Trump and Bernie Sanders pose an overarching question for campaigns and elections in the United States: Is the electoral system, the rules that govern our voting, designed to reflect the people? Should it better reflect public views? Or perhaps, as some of the founders thought, American electoral machinery should be *less* sensitive to the whims of public opinion.[4]

How Democratic Are American Elections?

Time, place, and manner clause: The constitutional clause that delegates control of elections to the state governments.

The Constitution sidestepped a crucial matter: Who votes and how. It left the election details—the **"time, place, and manner"**—up to the states. Every state builds its own electoral process—and our federalist conflicts have always filtered right into the voting rules. For example, felons can vote from jail in Maine, only after they have passed through parole and probation in Texas, and almost never in Florida. We can evaluate how well elections enhance popular rule by focusing on four dimensions: frequency, breadth, voting barriers, and the role of money.

Frequent and Fixed Elections

One way to hold public officials accountable is to require them to face the public frequently. The United States schedules elections for national office more often than most other democratic countries. House members are chosen every two years, presidents every four, and Senators every six. Add state and local elections and there is never a year in the United States without major elections.

In parliamentary democracies, the prime minister generally decides when to hold an election as long as there is at least one within a set period, usually five years. In contrast, American national elections are on a fixed date (chosen back

BY THE NUMBERS
Campaigns and Elections

Years in which American women first voted (in New Jersey)	**1797–1807**
Year in which women in all states could vote	**1920**
Number of people filing to run for president in 2016	**1,812**
Number filing who were "serious" Republican candidates	**17**
Number of candidates named Prince of Darkness, Satan Lord of the Underworld H. Majesty	**1**
Sequential rank of Iowa and New Hampshire in presidential primary season	**1, 2**
Percentage of U.S. population that is non-Hispanic white, 2017	**61.3**
Percentage of Iowa's and New Hampshire's population, respectively, that is white	**86, 91**
Number of Americans who voted in the 2016 presidential race	**128.7 million**
Number of Americans who did NOT vote in the 2016 presidential race	**100 million**
Percentage of Americans who support limits on money spent in political campaigns (2018)	**77[5]**
Percentage of voting-age population who turned out for midterm elections in 2010 and 2014 respectively	**41, 36.7**
Percentage of voting-age population who turned out for midterm election in 2018	**47**
Number (and percentage) of House or Senate incumbents who lost in 2016	**4 House (0.9%), 2 Senate (2%)**

Who participates in campaigns and elections and how does that influence our democratic process?

COMPARING NATIONS 10.1	**Election Timetables for National Government**	
How does the United States compare to other selected advanced democratic countries in election frequency?	**FREQUENCY**	**GOVERNMENT BODY**
	2 years	**U.S. House of Representatives**
	3 years	House of Representatives in Australia, New Zealand, El Salvador
	4 years	Parliaments in Argentina, Costa Rica, Germany, Japan, South Korea, Switzerland; **U.S. president**; president and lower chamber of legislature in Brazil
	5 years	Parliament in Ireland; president in South Korea; congress in Peru; *maximum term* for prime minister (and parliaments) in Canada, Denmark, France, Italy, United Kingdom, many others
	6 years	Argentinian, Australian, and **U.S. senators**
	8 years	Senators in Brazil and Chile

in 1845)—politicians do not have the luxury of deciding when to stand before the people. On the first Tuesday after the first Monday in November of every even-numbered year, we elect all House members and a third of the Senate; every fourth year, we elect a president. However, special elections are held if an office holder dies or resigns, and each state sets the date of the primary elections that determine which candidates represent a political party for each office. The timing and frequency tilts U.S. elections in a more democratic direction.

Do you see any drawbacks to frequent elections? All that campaigning consumes a great deal of time, money, and energy. House members are always running for reelection. As a Canadian prime minister once remarked, "In your system, you guys campaign for 24 hours a day, every day for two years. You know, politics is one thing, but we have to run a government."[6]

Over 520,000 Elected Officials

Not only are American elections unusually frequent, but an enormous *number* of positions are elected—from presidents to municipal drain inspectors. The United States was the first nation to choose its chief executive—and later judges—by popular election. Today, thirty-nine states elect judges (87% of all state judges). No other country elects judges, as they are supposed to be above politics. Critics charge that fundraising and campaign promises compromise the impartiality of state judges. But elections remain the American way.

To get a feel for the numbers, see Table 10.1, which lists elected officials in Iowa City, Iowa. Count them up: there are 58 elected officials for the 74,398 residents. From Anchorage, Alaska, to Zapata, Texas, more than 520,000 officials stand for election at the local, state, and national level. That's one measure of democracy in action. Is this a good way to give the people influence over government? Or does it make informed judgment impossible by overwhelming them with too many choices? What do you think?

TABLE 10.1 **Who Do You Vote for in Iowa City?**

NATIONAL OFFICIALS	
1 U.S. president	
2 U.S. senators from Iowa	
1 U.S. representative from Iowa's Second District	

IOWA STATE OFFICIALS	
1 governor	
1 lieutenant governor	1 secretary of state
1 attorney general	1 state treasurer
1 agriculture secretary	1 state auditor
1 state senator	1 state representative
7 Iowa Supreme Court justices (appointed for one year by governor, then must win a public "retention election" every eight years)	

COUNTY OFFICIALS	
1 supervisor	1 sheriff
1 treasurer	1 attorney
1 auditor	1 recorder

TOWNSHIP/CITY OFFICIALS (IOWA CITY IS BOTH A CITY AND A "TOWNSHIP")
1 clerk
3 trustees
7 school board members
4 education agency directors
7 city council members (who in turn elect one member as Iowa City mayor)
9 agriculture extension members
1 soil and water conservation commissioner

What Do YOU Think?   **Elected Appointed Positions?**

There are too many elective positions.
The public is asked to vote too often. Few voters can learn about so many races. The United States should appoint more experts to handle the technical aspects of government.

No, we need to encourage people to vote more often.
Reducing the number of elected officials would be unhealthy for our democracy. Voting permits the people to hold their public officials directly accountable. It's the best check on government officials.

Barriers to Voting

As we saw in Chapter 8, there are plenty of barriers to voting. Registration requirements were introduced in the nineteenth century to limit voting; today eight states strictly require a photo ID and many others make registration burdensome; 33 states restrict voting by felons after they have done their time. Other states purge voting lists (which makes it harder to register), offer fewer voting stations in some neighborhoods (check out the long lines featured on all the news feeds on Election Day), and the list goes on. On the other hand, some states make it easy: seventeen states permit same day registration (including the six with highest turnout in 2016) and sixteen states saw more than half the population vote by mail or vote early. The point: It's all up to the states. Some encourage voting, others raise barriers. Why? Usually, the majority party protects itself by adjusting the voting rules—a tendency that goes all the way back to the first elections.[7]

Financing Campaigns: The New Inequality?

Enormous sums flow through U.S. elections, triggering another set of fears. Does money tilt the process?

Too Much Money?   The price tag for the 2016 presidential and congressional races combined: 6.5 billion (Figure 10.1). Those billions raise a perennial question: Is there too much money in American political campaigns?

Many critics say yes. Public officials on every level devote enormous amounts of time and energy to raising money. As a result, some people fear that wealthy people may be able to buy influence and bury candidates and (more important) political issues that they do not like. Polls consistently show overwhelming majorities want to reduce the role of money in U.S. elections. In 2002, Congress responded with the Bipartisan Campaign Reform Act (known as McCain–Feingold), which limited the amounts individuals, corporations, and organizations could give.

Bipartisan critics pushed back. Both Mitch McConnell (R-KY), the Republican Senate leader, and the American Civil Liberties Union, argued that supporting campaigns is a form of free speech. The Supreme Court has largely accepted this perspective. In *Citizens United v. The Federal Elections Commission*, the Court ruled (5–4) that the free speech clause of the first amendment protects corporations, unions, and other groups who wish to support candidates or causes. In *McCutcheon v. Federal Elections Commission*, the Court struck down limits on the total donations an individual can make (again 5–4). The law still limits how much you can give an individual candidate running for office, but not how much you spend overall by donating to parties, to multiple candidates, and on issue ads.[8]

There was no great outcry over these Court decisions. Americans oppose the rising tide of campaign cash, but for most, the issue is not a high priority. After all, think about those campaign numbers in context: The $6.5 billion spent on all

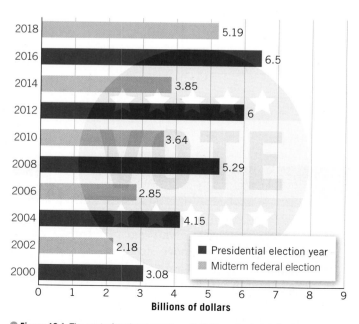

● **Figure 10.1** *The cost of national elections (inflation-adjusted dollars)*
(Open Secrets)

national races in 2016 was less than two-thirds of what Americans spent at Taco Bell and less than a third of the estimated amount spent on pornography during the same year. What do you think: Is contributing to campaigns a citizen's right? Or is it turning our democracy over to the wealthy?

Democracy for the Rich?   Do the wealthy dominate elections—perhaps even squeezing out the people's influence? There are three major concerns.

First, does one party get an advantage? Some groups do contribute mainly to one party. Labor unions back Democrats (by a ten-to-one margin, in recent elections), and some industries—such as oil and gas companies—largely support Republican candidates. But most business sectors traditionally split their donations about evenly between the two major parties. In 2016, for example, Comcast gave $1.9 million to Democrats, $2.1 million to Republicans; Northrup-Grumman, the fourth largest defense contractor, contributed $1.8 million to Democrats and $2.5 million to Republicans. Most corporate sectors wanted a seat at the table in both parties. Are the Republicans now pulling ahead, as many Democrats fear? If so, it has not begun to show in total spending. In the 2018 midterms, Democrats outraised Republicans by more than by more than $300 million in the House and $140 million in the Senate. The entire price tag for the midterm: 5.2 billion.[9]

Second, incumbents generally overwhelm their challengers. In 2018, sitting senators amassed $14.6 million on average. Their opponents scraped together just $1.9 million. Perhaps that's one reason the reelection rates in 2018 were 93% (House) and 89% (Senate). This kind of lopsided funding has a big impact, not in the headline presidential contest and big contested Senate races, but down the ballot in the low profile congressional and state level races —which receive less media attention.[10]

Third, critics worry that the need to raise funds—always more and more money—makes office holders especially sensitive to their funders. Big donors confidently chuckle that they are "buying a seat at the table"—they can always get in the door to talk to elected officials. Mick Mulvaney, now director of the Office of Budget and Management, put it bluntly. Back when he was in Congress, he said, "If you're a lobbyist who never gave us money, I didn't talk to you."[11] Still, research has not yet found a systematic link between contributions and political influence.[12]

In sum, campaign money does not seem to matter in high profile races—such as the presidency—when both sides will get their message across. It's farther down the ballot, in less visible races, where money counts. Incumbent members of Congress only rarely face well-financed opposition.

Major Donors: Easier to Give.   OK, you have made your fortune and you want to contribute to your favorite candidate. What are your options? First, many corporations and advocacy groups organize **political action committees** (**PACs**) to donate to candidates. PACs, which must include fifty or more contributors, may legally contribute $10,000 to any one candidate—$5,000 for the primary campaign, $5,000 more for the general election.

Want to contribute more? The **super PAC** was born in 2010 after the Supreme Court struck down laws limiting "independent" political spending by corporations and unions (in *Citizens United v. FEC*). Super PACs, formally known as "independent expenditure-only committees," may raise unlimited sums from virtually any source—business firms, unions, or individuals—and spend as much as they like to openly support or oppose political candidates. Unlike traditional PACs, they are not supposed to directly contribute to or coordinate with the candidate's political

Political action committee (PAC): An organization of at least fifty people, affiliated with an interest group, that is permitted to make contributions to candidates for federal office.

Super PACs: Organizations that raise and spend unlimited amounts of money to promote a candidate or publicize a cause. However, they may not directly contribute to a candidate or coordinate with a campaign.

Money in Elections

THE NEW RULES

Since 2010, the Supreme Court rulings in *Citizens United v. FEC*, *McCutcheon v. FEC*, and others have weakened the limits on campaign contributions and enabled super PACs to emerge. Although per-candidate and per-PAC limits still exist, the caps on the number of candidates or PACs a donor can contribute to have been lifted.

THINK ABOUT IT

How has the amount of money a single donor can contribute to candidates, party committees, PACs, and super PACs changed?

How does the lifting of caps affect wealthy donors who hedge their bets by contributing to multiple candidates? How will this affect elections and democratic representation overall?

Sources: Washington Post Information Graphics; Open Secrets

		2010	2018
Candidates	Limit for each candidate	House and Senate candidates $5,200 each	House and Senate candidates $5,400 each
	Limit for all candidates in an election cycle?	YES Total possible contribution: $48,600	NO LIMIT By giving each candidate the maximum amount. one donor could contribute $2,527,200
Party committees	Limits	$74,600	$1,197,400
PACs	Limit for each PAC	$5,000 each	$5,000 each
	Limit for all PACs	YES Total possible contribution: $74,600	NO LIMIT By giving each PAC the maximum amount. one donor could contribute $Millions
Number of super PACs		0	Over 2,300

campaigns. But that rule is difficult to enforce as close associates generally run the super PACs lined up behind a candidate.[13]

Despite all this, Shaun McCutcheon, a conservative Alabama businessman, was frustrated by the campaign finance laws that capped his overall donations. In *McCutcheon v. FEC*, the Supreme Court agreed (5–4). The law still limits how much you can give an individual candidate, but not how much you spend overall by donating to parties and outside groups. The top seven contributors in 2018 gave just under $300 billion, evenly split between the parties.

What is left after the Court's ruling is a patchwork of regulations. No one may contribute more than $2,700 to any individual candidate or $5,000 to an old fashioned PAC (not to be confused with super PACs, which have no limits). One way around that limit is through **bundling**: convincing colleagues and friends to donate at or near the maximum amount, then delivering all the checks together.

Still another source of campaign-related funds: **527 groups**. These are named for the section of the U.S. tax code that regulates them; 527 groups are forbidden from advocating directly on behalf of any candidate's election. However, they can accept and spend unlimited amounts for "issue advocacy." They may not explicitly support or oppose a candidate, but the ads they run can be indirectly supportive— or scathing. "Senator Jones is a tree killer who hates the environment" is an acceptable message for a 527 group; "Vote against Senator Jones" is not.

PACs, super PACS, bundlers, 527s: In the 2016 presidential contest, these outside groups spent an estimated $1.04 billion—beyond the roughly $1.5 billion raised by the presidential campaigns. Each innovation raises a fresh round of questions about democracy and campaign spending. As the limits on campaign spending are eliminated, one very wealthy individual can essentially fund a presidential candidate through the primaries.

All this money has swamped another reform: public financing. During presidential primaries, party nominees who raise $5,000 in small donations ($250 or less) in each of 20 states qualify for federal matching funds—a lump sum ($96 million in 2016). There's one catch. If they accept the money, they must limit their total spending. In 2008, candidate Barack Obama declined public funds and badly outspent Republican John McCain, who accepted them and was barred from raising further funds. Since then, no presidential candidate has accepted public financing for a general election.

Does contributing funds to a legislator "buy" anything valuable for donors? Should the system be changed to reduce the influence of monetary contributions? Or is spending money on campaigns a vital form of free speech? These are the essential questions of American campaigns.

Bundling: A form of fundraising in which an individual persuades others to donate large amounts that are then delivered together to a candidate or campaign.

527 groups: Organizations that raise and spend unlimited amounts for "issue advocacy" but are forbidden to coordinate their efforts with any candidate or campaign.

 **The Bottom Line**

» Are American elections truly democratic? Americans vote more often and for more offices than the citizens of most other democracies. But they also face barriers to voting in many states.

» The most familiar question today focuses on the role of money in election campaigns. PACs, super PACs, and 527s have become fixtures in national elections. Recent court decisions have significantly expanded the ability of wealthy donors and outside groups to contribute large sums.

Presidential Campaigns and Elections

The presidency is the greatest electoral prize but winning it is brutal. Running is expensive, exhausting, and often humiliating. Yet, in every presidential race, dozens take up the challenge.

Who Runs for President?

Onetime candidate Morris "Mo" Udall, who ran in 1976, said afterward, "You have to be a little crazy to run for president." The U.S. Constitution, however, only requires that candidates be American citizens, aged 35 years or older who have resided in the country for 14 years or more.

Serious presidential candidates generally have experience as elected officials—and in the last half-century, both parties have nominated candidates with one of three offices on their résumé—vice president, governor, or senator. The last president to have come directly out of the House of Representatives? James Garfield in 1880. Businesspeople with no experience in public office? None ever won the presidency—until Donald Trump in 2016 (Table 10.2). In all American history, Donald Trump is the first newcomer to navigate the political process. How did he do it? Read on.

The Three Phases of Presidential Elections

Presidential campaigns involve distinct stages—the nomination process, the party convention, and the general election. Each stage requires very different political strategies, played out amid the white-hot lights of global media coverage.

TABLE 10.2 **The President's Résumé**

YEAR	WINNER	PREVIOUS POSITION	LOSER	PREVIOUS POSITION
1960	John Kennedy	Senator	Richard Nixon	Vice president (1953–1961)
1964	Lyndon Johnson	Vice president (1961–1963)	Barry Goldwater	Senator
1968	Richard Nixon	Vice president (1953–1961)	Hubert Humphrey	Vice president (1965–1969)
1972	Richard Nixon	Incumbent	George McGovern	Senator
1976	Jimmy Carter	Governor	Gerald Ford	Vice president/incumbent
1980	Ronald Reagan	Governor	Jimmy Carter	Incumbent
1984	Ronald Reagan	Incumbent	Walter Mondale	Vice president (1977–1981)
1988	George H. W. Bush	Vice president (1981–1989)	Michael Dukakis	Governor
1992	Bill Clinton	Governor	George H. W. Bush	Incumbent
1996	Bill Clinton	Incumbent	Bob Dole	Senator
2000	George W. Bush	Governor	Al Gore	Vice president (1993–2001)
2004	George W. Bush	Incumbent	John Kerry	Senator
2008	Barack Obama	Senator	John McCain	Senator
2012	Barack Obama	Incumbent	Mitt Romney	Governor
2016	Donald Trump	Real estate developer, Reality TV star	Hillary Clinton	Secretary of State, Senator, First Lady

Winning the Nomination

The grueling process begins with the invisible primary (also known as the money primary). Candidates toss their hat in the ring and then build an organization, compete in televised debates, and scramble for media attention. Before the first vote was cast in the 2016 race, five candidates had already dropped out—doomed by low polls, anemic fundraising, and weak debate performances.

Next, the candidates run the gauntlet of state contests. Iowa begins with a **caucus** where activists in each precinct meet to select delegates who will vote for a candidate. Here's an opportunity to break out of the pack—or suffer an unexpected setback. In the 2016, Texas Senator Ted Cruz won 27.6 percent of the vote, followed by Donald Trump (24%) and Florida Senator Marco Rubio (21%). After only 186,000 voters had spoken, Republicans had their frontrunners. On the Democratic side, the presumed nominee, Hillary Clinton, barely held off Vermont Senator Bernie Sanders, 48.8 percent to 49.6 percent—Sanders showed he was a serious contender.

Next, on to New Hampshire's *primary.* In a **closed primary**, only party members go to the polls and vote for a nominee. In an **open primary**, voters can participate in either party's elections. New Hampshire's primary is semiclosed because independents may vote in either party's primary. New Hampshire produced a political earthquake: Donald Trump won easily, making him the Republican frontrunner with Ohio Governor John Kasich a distant second. And Bernie Sanders smashed to victory with over 60 percent of the vote.

After that, candidates face contests in many states, each with its own rules, norms (some states tolerate more negativity than others), and methods (endorsements matter more in some, farm issues in others). Candidates hopscotch the country trying to amass delegates (while raising money)—until **Super Tuesday** when both parties schedule multiple elections on a single date. Party leaders generally hope to have a winner by Super Tuesday so that the nomination process does not drag on too long and damage the eventual nominee. But in 2016, Hillary Clinton won 511 delegates, Bernie Sanders hung on with 348 of his own, and the contest continued. On the Republican side, Cruz, with 232 delegates, continued to challenge Trump who by then had 332.

Caucus: A local meeting of voters to select candidates to represent a political party in a general election or to choose delegates who select candidates at a convention.

Closed primary: A vote cast by party members to select candidates to represent the party in the general election.

Open primary: A vote cast by any eligible voter to select candidates to represent the party in the general election.

Super Tuesday: The date on the presidential primary calendar when multiple states hold primaries and caucuses.

● *Presidential candidate Vermin Supreme (left) placed fourth in the 2016 New Hampshire Democratic primary on a platform of time travel research, zombie alert preparation, and ponies for all.*

What Do YOU Think?   Why Iowa and New Hampshire?

Two years before each presidential election, politicians, campaign advisors and the media descend on two small states. By tradition, Iowa's caucuses and New Hampshire's primary are the first two presidential contests—giving them an outsized influence in the process. Should they continue to have such an important say in choosing the president?

Yes.
Small states like these test the candidates' abilities through one-on-one meetings with small groups—a very different challenge than the media campaigns reliant on heavy fundraising that follow in the large states. These small states reveal the men and women behind the slick media presentations.

No.
Iowa ranks thirtieth in population and is 86 percent white; New Hampshire forty-second in population and 91 percent white. Two highly unrepresentative states eliminate many candidates before any large state has even had a chance to vote.

Winner-take-all: The candidate winning a simple majority (or, among multiple candidates, a plurality) receives all electoral votes or primary delegates; sometimes called "first-past-the-post."

Proportional representation: The allocation of votes or delegates on the basis of the percentage of the vote received; contrasts with the winner-take-all system.

Both parties require that a winning candidate attract a majority of the convention delegates. In 2020, the magic number is 1,237 for Republicans and 2,382 for Democrats. The parties assign each state a number of delegates based on state population and party loyalty in the last election. In the 2016 Republican race, for example, Texas had 155 delegates and Vermont 16.

In the past, Republicans used a **winner-take-all** system, under which the winning candidate receives all the delegates for that state. Democrats, in contrast, have generally employed a system of **proportional representation**, allocating delegates based on the proportion of the vote a candidate wins. In 2016, the GOP primaries required proportional representation until mid-March, when states could choose to allocate all their delegates to the outright winner (seven states did so). Why all this rigmarole? Republican Party activists wanted a process that did not get decided too soon—before their candidate had been fully tested (as happened with John McCain in 2008)—but they did not want the contest to drag out so long as to damage the winner (Mitt Romney in 2012).

The traditional rules are clear: Primary season candidates must make strong first impressions; compete well in state after state; avoid errors or outrageous statements in a dozen or more debates; and manage a campaign team that, as the contests continue, can swell to thousands of people. They also may have to carefully calibrate their issue positions.

In 2016, Donald Trump once again broke the rules. He made outrageous statements and did not bother with a professional campaign team.

So, why did he win the primary? First, day after day, he did what he needed to do to dominate the news feeds. Trump had already attracted the public attention as a businessman and celebrity, from his best-selling book, *The Art of the Deal*, to his own reality television show, *The Apprentice*. Trump had been a symbol of economic success to many. Trump's misstatements during the primary only continued to place him in the limelight. *The Art of the Deal* explained why: "Good publicity is preferable to bad, but . . . bad publicity is sometimes better than no publicity at all. Controversy, in short, sells."[14]

Second, Trump emphasized American economic decline even as the Obama administration touted a solid growth rate. Trump understood that many individuals felt left out of the economic recovery—and he targeted his pitch directly to them.

These individuals formed a vital component of his early base of supporters.

Third, questions of identity have grown increasingly intense and prominent in American politics. What appeared to be mistakes—bashing immigrants, racially insensitive language, and so on—spoke to a segment of voters that resented cosmopolitan, urban, coastal, multicultural elites. Recent work in political science suggests that the Trump campaign managed to mobilize the issue of white identity, especially among white voters with low education—some of whom had voted for President Obama.[15]

Finally, both Trump's success and Bernie Sanders's strong showing can be attributed—in part—to the nature of voter turnout in primary elections. Far fewer Americans turn out for primary elections than for general elections, and those who do vote tend to be more ideologically driven than the more centrist fall electorate. Conventional political wisdom holds that candidates must therefore run more to the extreme—farther left for Democrats, farther right for Republicans—to capture the nomination and then move back to the middle for the general election. Both candidates deeply energized their base supporters—ardent conservatives and progressives, respectively. Each, in a very different way, conveyed an authenticity to an electorate deeply cynical about politics and politicians. And, as the contest moved on to the next stage, Trump broke yet another convention: He doubled down on his own base instead of tacking to the center.

● *Chicago—1968 Democratic National Convention: Angry protests both in and outside the hall created an image of disarray and crisis. This convention symbolized the collapse of the old Democratic coalition. Republicans would take the White House in five of the next six elections.*

Organizing the Convention

Political party conventions showcase the party's presidential nominee on a national stage; they also gather party insiders from across the United States for several days of meetings and celebration. Advocacy groups and corporate interests flock to the conventions as well. Everyone jockeys to be noticed by a potential future president and his or her closest advisers.

When it works well, the convention can provide the nominee an **electoral bounce**, a temporary boost in the polls. A star-studded Democratic convention gave Hillary Clinton a bounce, despite furious opposition from Sanders supporters. That boost vaulted her into a lead she never relinquished in the polls—until Donald Trump won the election.

Electoral bounce: The spike in the polls that follows an event such as a party's national convention.

The General Election

After the convention, the campaigns shift into overdrive. With just three months between the convention and Election Day, every hour matters. Campaigns scramble to stage media events, blast the opposing candidate, tweet, post, and meet with donors.

See the 1960 Nixon–Kennedy debate.

General elections usually feature three debates between the nominees, as well as one vice presidential debate. Pundits scrutinize the performances, search for gaffes, and report the overnight polls. The truth, however, is that most viewers have already made up their minds and debates normally have only a slight impact on the race.

Winning Presidential Elections

The CIA, the FBI, and the National Security Agency jointly reported that Russian President Vladimir Putin had run a sophisticated operation to tilt the election to Donald Trump. The Russians spread disinformation through Internet trolls, hacked the computer systems of both major parties, and leaked the emails of Democratic leaders online ahead of the Democratic National Convention.[16] Most analysts, however, are skeptical that Russian social media or cyberactivities influenced the results of the elections.[17] What factors did—and do—influence who wins presidential races? Along with the candidates themselves—their speeches, gaffes, debate performances, and responses to the unexpected— a variety of factors help determine the winner.

The Economy.   Bill Clinton's headquarters in 1992 featured a famous whiteboard reminding campaign staffers: "It's the Economy, Stupid." If the economy is performing poorly, the party holding the presidency suffers.

Even with a fairly strong economy in 2016, the growing difference between the haves and the have-nots proved to be a major issue. In the Democratic primaries, Bernie Sanders spoke to frustrations over America's growing inequality. Donald Trump painted a dark picture of the state of the nation that baffled prosperous elites but resonated in the towns and small cities of middle America.

Demographics.   Once upon a time, each party worked to build a winning coalition by relying on its base of likely supporters and reaching out to undecided groups in the middle. After the 2012 election, the Republican Party did an "autopsy" to explain why it had lost the presidency and slipped (minus two seats) in the Senate. Major conclusion: The party failed to appeal to growing ranks of millennials and minorities, especially Hispanics. In 2016, Republican primary voters spurned that advice and turned to a candidate who shouted out the perils of immigration and disparaged immigrants. The criticism propelled Trump to victory in the primaries and then, rather than pivot for the general election, Trump doubled down on anti-immigrant rhetoric. A party that already appealed to older, whiter, and more male voters spoke directly to those demographics. White voters had not given a Democratic nominee more than 43 percent of the vote in 35 years. Democrat Hillary Clinton overwhelmingly won the black vote (an estimated 88%), Latino (65%), Asian (65%), and people under 30 (55%). But she only managed 37 percent of all whites voting.[18]

● *Over 70 million Americans tuned into the Kennedy and Nixon debate in 1960—launching the age of televised campaigning. The more charismatic Kennedy won the White House by the slimmest of margins—.001 percent.*

War and Foreign Policy.   Most Americans pay far more attention to domestic issues, especially those that touch their pocketbooks, than foreign ones. Occasionally, however, foreign-policy issues become pivotal, especially when the nation is at war. In 2004, for example, the 9/11 attacks—which had occurred three years earlier—helped George Bush win reelection. In 2016, Republicans sharply criticized Hillary Clinton for a terrorist attack in Benghazi, Libya, that killed four American embassy officials during the time she served as secretary of state, although she took far more hawkish (or aggressive) views than Donald Trump.[19] However, 2016 was a normal year: Few voters named foreign policy as a major influence on their choice of candidate.

Still, Trump questioned support for traditional U.S. allies and alliances (e.g., NATO, the alliance that won the Cold War) and expressed admiration for Russian leader Vladimir Putin.[20] Most Washington insiders were aghast at Trump's foreign-policy statements.

Domestic Issues. Every presidential candidate has a list of favorite programs and strategies. Bill Clinton discussed education, energy, Medicare, and Medicaid so often that his staff started calling his campaign E2M2. Donald Trump promised job creation, infrastructure, a hard line on immigration, and a strong nationalist trade policy—the United States would not be pushed around anymore. The candidates' issue preferences are important, not because they will decide the election (highly unlikely), but because they set the agenda for the presidency.[21]

Explore domestic issues and party platforms.

The Campaign Organization. One truism that every would-be president knows is that it is essential to assemble a team of talented, loyal advisors capable of charting a plan for victory. Building a large, multistate organization—often from scratch—is an enormous job that tests every candidate's executive skill. [22] Again, Donald Trump was unusual. He relied on his own instincts and the advice of a small circle—despite Republican pleas that he defer to seasoned political managers. Instead he kept shaking up his team, bringing on Steve Bannon, who the BBC described as a "bare knuckled populist," to direct the final months of the campaign.[23]

Trump supporters chant "Build the Wall" (on the Mexican border).

Parties Matter. Many analysts expected moderates to abandon Donald Trump and go over to Clinton in droves. He was too toxic, too divisive, too racist, too sexist, and too unpredictable. What analysts overlooked was the force of party attachment in a partisan era (see Chapter 11). Even a candidate that blasted many of the party's traditional policy positions still commanded the loyalty of the vast majority of Republicans. In the end, 92 percent of Republican men and 91 percent of the women came home to vote for the party's nominee.[24]

The Electoral College and Swing States. Because almost all states are winner take all, presidential elections usually hinge on a small number of states. Democrats know they will win in New York and California. Republicans know they will sweep the Deep South. Both parties compete to win swing states—states that might go either way in a race—to amass 270 Electoral College votes. Swing states keep changing. In 2016, the battle was in some 10 to 12 states including Colorado, Florida, Iowa, Nevada, New Hampshire, North Carolina, Ohio, Pennsylvania, Virginia, and Wisconsin.[25]

Hillary Clinton won the popular vote by 2.9 million votes—48.2 percent, compared to Trump's 46.1 percent. So how did Trump win the Electoral College? Razor thin margins in three states the Democrats had held for 24 years—Michigan (10,700 votes out of 4.7 million cast), Wisconsin (22,000 votes out of 4 million), and Pennsylvania (44,000 out of 6 million)—gave the Trump campaign all 46 Electoral College votes in those three states and the election. In addition, Democrats tend to concentrate in urban areas. As a result, Clinton won the popular vote by large margins in several states with the largest concentration of urban populations. In California and New Jersey, where approximately 95 percent of the population lives in urban centers, Clinton won 61.7 percent and 57.3 percent of the popular vote, respectively.[26] Republicans are more efficiently (at least for maximizing Electoral College votes) spread out over rural and suburban America (Figure 10.2).

But here is a crucial historical point: The states are always evolving. Forty years ago, California was reliably Republican, Texas Democratic. American politics is fluid, dynamic, and always changing.

Finally, the biggest number in the 2016 national elections was 100 million. That's the number of people who did NOT vote in 2016—and it is almost as large as the number who voted for the two major candidates *combined* (128.7 million). All those nonvoters could just be a blockbuster source of change—if a party or a candidate hit on a way to get them to the vote (Figure 10.3).[27]

That Elusive Winning Recipe.   There is no sure recipe for winning a presidential election. They occur so rarely—the 2016 contest was only the eighteenth since World War II—and involve such an immense array of influences that journalists, historians, and political scientists spend years trying to draw lessons from each campaign.

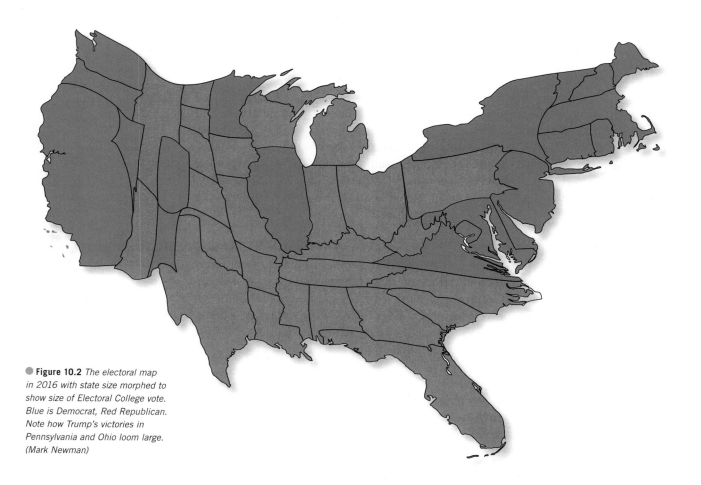

● **Figure 10.2** *The electoral map in 2016 with state size morphed to show size of Electoral College vote. Blue is Democrat, Red Republican. Note how Trump's victories in Pennsylvania and Ohio loom large. (Mark Newman)*

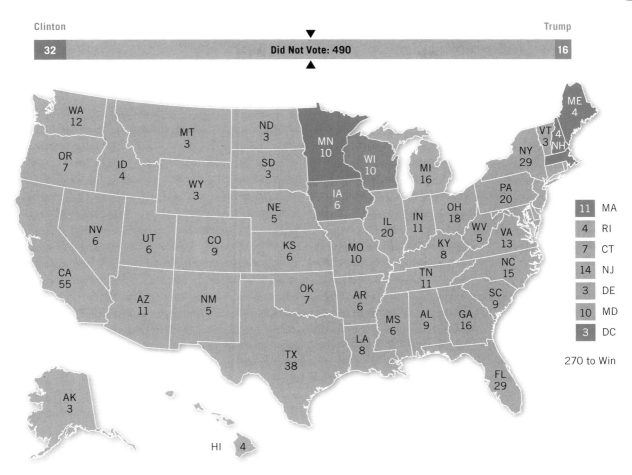

● **Figure 10.3** *If "not voting" had been a candidate for the 2016 presidential race, "not voting" would have won the Electoral College in almost every state. (270 to Win)*

In 2016, demographics mattered (Figure 10.4). White working-class people (especially men) had long tilted Republican (Figure 10.4). Now all Americans with

two-year college degrees or less—especially whites—strongly favored Trump. Suburban and rural America went Republican, as well. Trump spoke to the economic anxieties of those left behind in an era of jarring inequality. He channeled the grievance some people felt toward cosmopolitan urban elites. Rural, middle America believed that urban and coastal areas did not share their values and received an unfair portion of government benefits—a point one political scientist emphasized in charting the changes to Wisconsin politics—even before the 2016 election.[28] That resentment may be exacerbated by uneasiness with immigration, racial changes, and the prospect of a majority–minority nation.[29]

Still, a great question hangs over the Republican future: Will they find a way to reach out to minority and millennial voters as those populations grow? In 2016, the white vote, which typically breaks Republican, fell from 72 to 70 percent of eligible voters—still a majority but a steadily diminishing one. Meanwhile, voters who lean Democratic grew: Hispanics rose from 10 to

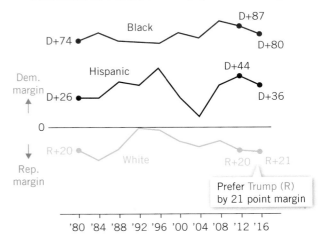

In 2016, Trump won whites by virtually the same margin as Romney in 2012

Presidential candidate preference, by race or ethnicity

● **Figure 10.4** *Whites supported the Republican candidate in 2016 by roughly the same margin as in 2012, but the education gap widened. (Pew Research Center)*

11 percent of all voters, Asians from 5 to 6 percent, and black voters held stable at 13 percent. Those changes helped boost the Democratic Party's presidential chances. The first indicators from the 2018 midterm suggested the trend continues. As in the recent past, African Americans voted in high numbers, comprising approximately 12 percent of all voters. Hispanic turnout, however, jumped: Hispanics made up 8 percent of all midterm voters in 2014, but 12 percent in the 2018—a 50 percent increase. These voters pose a major challenge for both political parties: Historically, two-thirds of Hispanic voters have supported Democratic Party candidates. Will Democrats continue to win them over on issues such as undocumented immigration? Or can Republicans make inroads by stressing moral values and the American dream? However the votes trend, the future of electoral politics may lie in these rising demographic groups.[29a]

Predicting Presidential Elections

Do you want an easy way to start a conversation with strangers? Ask which candidate will win the next presidential election. Predicting presidential outcomes is a national pastime, attracting pollsters, political scientists, pundits, and all the rest of us. Social scientists have developed sophisticated models to predict on the basis of fundamentals long before the election. Some even believe that all the campaign excitement is irrelevant: Mathematical models will pick the winning party.

What goes into a model? Each has a slightly different recipe but most political science models emphasize the economy; whether the country is at peace; presidential approval; and fatigue with the party in power—with just one exception, no party has controlled the White House more than two consecutive terms in the last 72 years.

How did the political science models do? Table 10.3 shows the results: The models were amazing—and still wrong. Eight of the 11 models, all run months

TABLE 10.3 **Political Science Models Predict the Elections**

FORECASTER	PERCENTAGE OF TWO-PARTY VOTE CLINTON WILL WIN	PERCENTAGE POINTS BY WHICH THE MODEL MISSED (0 = PERFECT)
Michael Lewis-Beck and Charles Tien, *Political Economy*	51.0	0.0
James Campbell, *Convention Bump and Economy*	51.2	−0.2
James Campbell, *Trial Heat and Economy*	50.7	0.3
Brad Lockerbie, Economic *Expectations and Political Punishment*	50.4	0.6
Bruno Jerôme and Veronique Jerôme-Speziari, *State-by-State Political Economy*	50.1	0.9
Christopher Wlezien and Robert Erikson, *LEI and Polls; Post Conventions*	52.0	−1.0
Thomas Holbrook, *National Conditions and Trial Heat*	52.5	−1.5
Andreas Graefe, J. Scott Armstrong, Randall Jones, and Alfred Cuzan, *Pollyvote*	52.7	−1.7
Alan Abramowitz, *Time for a Change*	48.6	2.4
Helmut Norpoth, *The Primary Model*	47.5	3.5

Source: Oxford University Press (OUPblog)

before the voting, came within 1 percent of the results: Clinton wins 51 percent of the two-party vote. Yet the models face limits. They could not deal with the jagged permutations of the Electoral College.

 **The Bottom Line**

» Presidential elections, despite their grueling intensity and duration, attract many aspirants every four years.

» Nearly all serious candidates for the presidency are experienced politicians. No candidate without any experience in the public sector had ever won the presidency—until Donald Trump.

» The three phases of the campaign—the nominating process, party conventions, and the general election—require different political strategies.

» Election outcomes are influenced by many factors: the economy, wars, organization, party loyalty, demographics, and the Electoral College. Add the role of accident and luck, and election outcomes are often difficult to predict.

Congressional Elections

In contrast to the focus on two presidential candidates, congressional elections feature a colorful kaleidoscope of races across the country. Every two years, all 435 House districts hold an election, with an additional 33 or 34 Senate seats in play as well. It's a political junkie's dream.

Candidates: Who Runs for Congress?

Almost anyone can seek a seat in Congress. Convicted felons, rodeo clowns, college professors, and reformers in their mid-twenties have won unexpected victories. As Table 10.4 shows, there are few limits on candidacy.

But winning is not easy. The average House race costs over $1.7 million; to make it to the Senate, you will need on average $10.5 million (depending on where you're running, of course).[30] Most candidates spend hours on the phone raising money. The personality traits that inspire candidates to run for Congress—self-confidence, leadership ability, and interest in politics—increase as people move up the political ladder.

TABLE 10.4 **Requirements for Running for Congress**

Age	Successful House candidates must be at least 25 years old to take office; senators must be at least 30.
Citizenship	House candidates must have been a U.S. citizen for at least seven years; Senate candidates for at least nine.
Residence	Candidates must live in the state, though not necessarily the House district, where they are seeking election.

The median net worth of House and Senate members in 2018 was $511,000 (meaning half are above, half below). More than a third are millionaires.[31] However, congressional races attract relatively few top American business leaders, wealth holders, or celebrities—there are not many Mark Zuckerbergs, Warren Buffetts, or Oprahs in Congress. And when the famous or wealthy mount a run, they do not always win. Maryland businessman David Trone spent $13 million of his own money seeking the Democratic nomination for an open House seat in 2016 and lost. World Wrestling Entertainment CEO Linda McMahon spent $100 million on her two failed Senate races in 2010 and 2012—although the publicity helped make her President Trump's head of the Small Business Administration.[32]

Each time one party targets a Senate candidate, the other party matches it. The price tag for Texas's Senate race in 2018 approached $120 million, close to the record set in Pennsylvania's 2016 contest. Even little New Hampshire's 2016 Senate race cost more than $100 million. The results reflected what political scientists have long found: Money alone rarely swings high profile congressional elections. But with 468 races, the big money makes it hard to challenge most incumbents.[33]

If neither money nor celebrity guarantees a seat, here is a more promising shortcut to Congress: Be related to a member. One in eight members of Congress has a relative who already served (including 20 members who hold their parent's seat). Since 1947, there usually has been a Kennedy in office—today, Congressman Joe Kennedy (D-MA). Other families—Bush, Adams, Roosevelt, Clinton—have built dynasties over the years.[34]

Still, political amateurs dominate each crop of new candidates challenging sitting members of the House for their seat. Typically, about one in six of these challengers is an elected official, usually from the state legislature; another 10 percent or so serve in nonelected government positions—often as former congressional staff. The remaining three-quarters of the total are new to government service and often inspired by an issue or a cause. Senate candidates, because they run statewide, tend to be more experienced and most are political veterans.

● Left: Frederick Frelinghuysen, New Jersey delegate to the Continental Congress (1779) and later U.S. Senator (1793–1796). Right: Frederick's great-great-great nephew Rodney Frelinghuysen served in the U.S. House from 1995 to 2018. He was the sixth Frelinghuysen to represent New Jersey in Congress.

Women on average are just as likely as men to win elections to Congress, but the parties have been slower to recruit them as candidates, women were less eager to run, and when they ran they were more likely to draw primary challenges than men.[35] In 2018, however, an astonishing 3,379 women were running for political office. When the votes were counted, there were over 100 in the House of Representatives and over 125 in both chambers breaking the previous record—101 in the previous Congress. By party, women representatives break over five to one toward the Democrats.

Members of large minority groups (African Americans, Latinos, and Asian Americans) tend to run much less often than Caucasians. As we saw in Chapter 5, their ranks are slowly growing, especially in the House Democratic Caucus.

● A new generation: 2018 saw the largest number of women ever run for and win election to Congress. Here, California Republican Young Kim stops on the campaign trail, poised to become the first Korean-American women in Congress.

Talent and experience are vital in congressional races. Party leaders know that recruiting skilled candidates gives them an advantage. A candidate's background also has an impact on the quality of representation in Washington. How well Congress carries out its work depends on the ability of its members.

The Power of Incumbency

If you talk to sitting members of Congress about reelection, you will see the worry wash over their faces. House and Senate officeholders face a more volatile American electorate than they did a quarter-century ago: Voters are less predictable and harder to reach through traditional advertising. Now that virtually every utterance is digitally preserved, candidates have to be more careful about what they say. The popular Senator George Allen of Virginia, cruising with a 20 point lead in 2006 against little-known Democratic challenger James Webb, was caught on videotape at a campaign rally calling an Indian American Webb staffer "macaca," a racial slang insult. The clip went viral, Allen tried to deny it, to laugh it off, and eventually apologized, but he could not shake the media storm and wound up narrowly losing—dooming his presidential aspirations as well. Allen never recovered. Since then, many candidates have been caught saying embarrassing things that come back to haunt them.

Despite this more treacherous electoral environment, most incumbent House and Senate members fare very well in their quest for reelection. Even in 2010 when Republicans won back the House in the largest Republican landslide since 1890, more than nine of every ten incumbents won another term. In 2018, 93% of House members and almost 88% of Senators won reelection. The power of incumbency held again. But there is one caveat: Twenty six mainly moderate Republicans retired in this election cycle—perhaps fearing a backlash against the party in power.

At first glance, this **incumbency advantage** is a mystery. As we explore in Chapter 13, Americans overwhelmingly give Congress a thumbs down. In 2018, approval ratings for Congress hovered between 13 percent and 20 percent—not the lowest on record, but close. What did the voters do? They voted the rascals right back in. Incumbents won more than 90 percent of the races (see Figure 10.5).

Hear Senator George Allen's "macaca moment."

Incumbency advantage: The tendency for members of Congress to win reelection in overwhelming numbers.

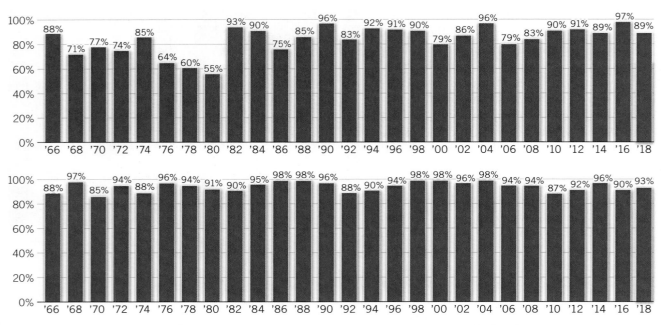

● **Figure 10.5** *Senate (top) and House (bottom) reelection rates, 1964–2018 (Open Secrets).*

What explains these consistently high incumbent success rates? For one thing, members have become very skilled at running *against* Congress. They position themselves as reasonable individuals fighting against a dysfunctional institution—a position known as Fenno's paradox (named after a much loved political scientist): And the way Congress operates—stalemate on the big issues, lots of little favors to constituents—makes the stance an easier sell. "I'm for expanding aid to needy children," say liberal members, "but I can't get it past the Republicans on Capitol Hill. Oh, and how about that new aquarium I funded?" GOP members tell a similar story.[36]

And back to money. Most congressional races feature very well-funded incumbents running against underfunded challengers. In short, members are attentive to constituents, raise a great deal of money, and already have staff and name recognition. Most win reelection. Here is the paradox: People despise Congress but defend their own representatives.[37]

Patterns in Congressional Elections

Here's another familiar pattern: In most **midterm elections**, the president's party loses congressional seats—termed **midterm loss**. In the last 40 midterm elections (going back to 1938), the president's party picked up seats in either chamber of Congress only five times—and only a few seats each time. In contrast, the president's party lost double-digit House seats eight of 12 times In 2018, the pattern held in the House: The Democrats picked up over 30 seats and won control of the chamber. But Republicans gained at least 3 Senate seats—the best showing by an incumbent party in more than 50 years (see table 10.5).

Another intriguing pattern involves elections when America is at war. Although we might expect voters to "rally around the flag" and support the president's party during wartime, in fact, the opposition usually wins seats in the congressional elections following a war's outbreak. Presidents Woodrow Wilson (World War I),

Midterm elections: National elections held between presidential elections, involving all seats in the House of Representatives, one-third of those in the Senate, 36 governorships, and other positions.

Midterm loss: The president's party loses congressional seats during the midterm elections. This has occurred in most midterm elections.

TABLE 10.5	Midterm Congressional Election Results, 1970–2018		
ELECTION YEAR	PRESIDENT	SEAT GAIN	
		HOUSE	SENATE
2018	Trump (R)	**D+32***	**R+3***
2014	Obama (D)	R+13	R+9
2010	Obama (D)	R+63	R+6
2006	G. W. Bush (R)	D+30	D+6
2002	G. W. Bush (R)	**R+8**	**R+2**
1998	Clinton (D)	**D+5**	(No change)
1994	Clinton (D)	R+54	R+8
1990	G. H. W. Bush (R)	D+8	D+1
1986	Reagan (R)	D+5	D+8
1982	Reagan (R)	D+26	(No change)
1978	Carter (D)	R+15	R+3
1974	Ford (R)	D+48	D+3
1970	Nixon (R)	D+12	**R+1**

*The president's party has won seats in a midterm election only four times (indicated in **bold**) in the past 42 years.*

*Results as of November 16, with some races still too close to call.

Franklin Roosevelt (World War II), Harry Truman (Korea), Lyndon Johnson (Vietnam escalation), and George H. W. Bush (Gulf War) saw their parties suffer big losses in the first election after war was declared. George W. Bush (Iraq War) beat the cycle for two years but then his party lost the House and Senate, as well as the presidency.

Redrawing the Lines: The Art of the Gerrymander

How does gerrymandering work?

Fifty-one Democrats in the Texas House fled the state and holed up in Oklahoma. Legislative leaders called the Texas Rangers, the Federal Aviation Administration, and the Department of Homeland Security to "round 'em up and bring 'em home." What was going on?

Republicans had won control of the Texas legislature, and they immediately whipped out their red pens to redraw the congressional districts. Democrats claimed that Republicans were unfairly stacking the districts to assure Republican winners—just what the Democrats traditionally did. Because they were going to lose a vote that they considered unfair, the Democrats fled the state to deny the majority a quorum (the number of members a legislature needs to have present to do official business). Sure enough, they eventually limped home and lost the vote over redistricting and five House seats in the next election.

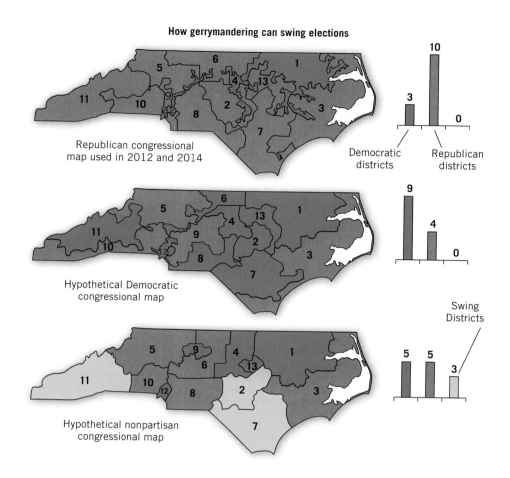

How gerrymandering can swing elections

Republican congressional map used in 2012 and 2014

Democratic districts   Republican districts

Hypothetical Democratic congressional map

Hypothetical nonpartisan congressional map

Swing Districts

● **Figure 10.6** *Both parties eagerly redraw the lines. Here, three versions in North Carolina yield completely different congressional delegations. (Daily Kos)*

Reapportionment:
Reorganization of the boundaries of House districts, a process that follows the results of the U.S. census, taken every ten years. District lines are redrawn to ensure rough equality in the number of constituents represented by each House member.

Gerrymander: Redrawing an election district in a way that gives the advantage to one party.

Redrawing congressional districts can have a significant impact on who gets elected (Figure 10.6). How does this work?

The House of Representatives has been fixed at 435 members for over a century. Every ten years, the census measures American population shifts, determines which states have gained or lost population, and **reapportions** House seats. In 2010, Texas gained four new seats, Florida gained two, and New York and Ohio each lost two. Following reapportionment, states redraw the boundaries of the election districts in a process called redistricting. Sometimes two U.S. House representatives will find themselves running against one another when their districts are combined.

In a **gerrymander**, the party in control of the state legislature draws the lines to help itself. See Figure 10.7 for a hypothetical example. Imagine a state called PoliSciLand that has two districts that are 100 percent Republican (A and B) and one district that is 100 percent Democratic (C): PoliSciLand sends two Republicans and one Democrat to Congress. Then an enterprising Republican on the redistricting committee says, "Hey, we're the majority in this PoliSciLand legislature. Let's redraw the congressional districts our way."

Check out the result: By drawing the district lines horizontally instead of vertically, Republicans take the Democratic district and split its voters into three different congressional districts. Instead of one district with 100 percent Democratic voters and two that are 100 percent Republican, PoliSciLand now has three districts, each 33 percent Democratic and 66 percent Republican. Without changing a single vote, our imaginary PoliSciLand state now has three House Republicans . . . and no Democrats.

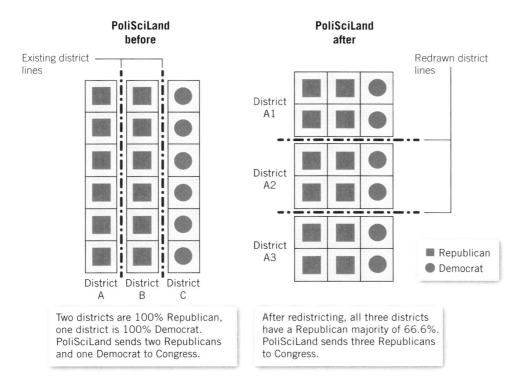

PoliSciLand before

Existing district lines

District A · District B · District C

Two districts are 100% Republican, one district is 100% Democrat. PoliSciLand sends two Republicans and one Democrat to Congress.

PoliSciLand after

Redrawn district lines

District A1

District A2

District A3

■ Republican
● Democrat

After redistricting, all three districts have a Republican majority of 66.6%. PoliSciLand sends three Republicans to Congress.

● **Figure 10.7** *How gerrymandering works—a hypothetical case of highly political redistricting.*

The term *gerrymandering* goes back to 1812, when Massachusetts governor Elbridge Gerry signed a bill that redrew the districts to help his party. One of Gerry's new districts looked like a salamander, which at that time was seen as a sort of mythical dragon. "Gerry" + "salamander" = "gerrymander," and a great American contribution to the art of politics was born.

Today, with sophisticated information technology, state legislatures can carefully craft political boundaries. Two main techniques are "packing," or placing all the like-minded voters into one district, and "cracking," or spreading them out so that they form a minority in many districts. Because Democratic voters are crowded into cities, they are easy to pack. Our imaginary PoliSciLand cracked the Democratic district.

Savvy political observers carefully watch who wins the state legislatures in the round years ('10, '20, '30, . . .), because those results determine the majority that gets the job of redrawing the lines after the census numbers are announced. This is especially difficult if your state is losing population.

Redistricting processes in most states are messy and politically charged. Many results look at least as bizarre as the original gerrymander. Together, the political parties have perfected the practice—although Republicans dominated the 2010 state level elections and became masters of

THE GERRY-MANDER.

● *The original gerrymander: Massachusetts, 1812.*

the art. In 2016, Republicans won the total popular vote for Congress by less than 1 percent but reaped a big advantage in number of seats held: 241 to 194. Partially this is because of gerrymandering, and also—as noted above—because Republicans tend to be spread out in less populated cities, and Democrats crowd into fewer, more urban districts.

As you can see, the election contest for House seats and state legislative seats usually begins in earnest—long before anyone starts running—when the state legislature sits down to draw the district. That has led some observers to quip that Congress selects their voters rather than voters selecting Congress.

Nonpartisan Districting and Minority Representation

Does all this seem unfair to you? Some reformers would like to put the whole process of drawing electoral districts into the hands of a nonpartisan commission that would divide states into natural communities and not tilt to any political side. California passed a law to do just that after the 2010 census—as have other states since (Figure 10.8). State legislative districts were redrawn by a "Citizens' Redistricting Commission" rather than by elected politicians, who naturally seek to protect their personal and partisan interests. The result was compact, contiguous districts faithful to existing geographic communities—and a lot of angry legislators at the state and U.S. House levels, who had to scramble to figure out their new district lines.

One guideline the California commission and others have to follow is to preserve communities of interests—such as ethnic groups—intact. In the past, some states used gerrymanders to create majority-minority districts—packed with African American voters. For black Democrats, it was an anguishing call because it split two sides of their political identity: It delivered more black representatives, but fewer Democrats. In 1995, the Supreme Court ruled that race could not be the predominant factor in creating congressional districts, and this packing was halted.[38] Despite dire predictions, the black congressional caucus continued to grow, jumping from 29 House members in 1995 to 56 after the 2018 election.

Assess current debates on redistricting.

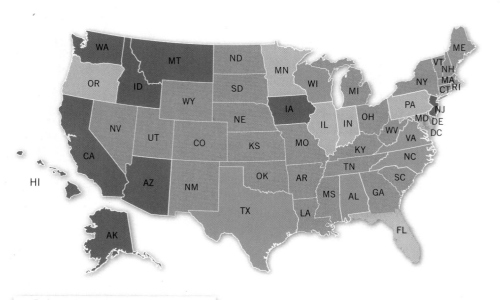

● **Figure 10.8** *As gerrymandering becomes more bare-knuckle, more states have moved toward nonpartisan commissions. (Reclaim the American Dream)*

■ Reforms instituted
■ Ongoing and recent reform efforts
■ Ongoing and recent legal challenges
■ Both legal challenges & reforms

In 2018, the Court unanimously permitted highly partisan districts in North Carolina, Wisconsin, and Maryland, then bitterly divided (5–4) in a ruling on a Texas case. The majority held that courts should "presume" that states are acting in "good faith" and not aiming to suppress minority votes. Four liberal justices dissented and two saw "undeniable proof of intentional discrimination." The Supreme Court sent some of the cases back to the lower courts where redistricting battles continued, even as the clock ticked down to Election Day.[39]

Gerrymandering
Texachusetts

The Bottom Line

» Every two years, all 435 House seats and a third of the Senate seats are up for election.

» Very few restrictions govern who may run.

» House and Senate incumbents have powerful built-in advantages when running for reelection.

» The president's party generally loses House and Senate seats during midterm elections.

» Decennial redistricting of House seats can result in some strangely shaped—and politically motivated—districts, known as gerrymanders.

» Both parties gerrymander. In 2010, Republican control over state legislatures led to election districts that gave the Republicans an advantage in the House of Representatives.

Congressional Campaigns

Congressional candidates continue to navigate a changing political landscape, with the rise of new media, the influx of ever-greater sums of money into elections, and other developments. In this section, we examine how these trends are shaping the way candidates run for Congress.

Candidate-Centered Elections

In most democracies, political parties run campaigns—mobilizing voters and choosing slates of candidates to run under the party banner. Ask a classmate from another country who runs the government back home, they will usually respond with a party name: Tories, or Socialists, or Liberal Democrats. Not in the United States. Over the past four decades, Americans have shifted to **candidate-centered elections**. Candidates themselves decide to run, raise money, grab airtime, and organize their own campaigns.

Why is the United States so different from other major democracies? It hasn't always been. Once upon a time the party bosses in many states quietly picked the candidates (puffing on cigars in smoke-filled rooms).[40] But primaries spread in the 1970s. They required candidates for most offices to win a primary election. Anyone can leap in and run—undermining the party's ability to pick candidates. As social media expanded, candidates broke free from party databases, outreach, and fundraising.[41] Individual candidates now control their own destiny—deciding to run, raising their own money, choosing their issues, and organizing their team.

Candidate-centered elections: A system in which individual candidates decide to run, raise their own money, and design their own strategy—as opposed to party systems, in which political parties play these roles.

However, another trend limits a candidate's independence from the parties. As partisanship has risen, the party faithful who eagerly vote in low-turnout primaries have grown increasingly intolerant of moderates in the middle. Republicans who vote for a tax increase or Democrats willing to compromise on environmental standards have become endangered political species. Gerrymandered districts reinforce the trend by creating **safe districts**—where voters are likely to vote for one party over another by a large ("safe") majority. Legislators are safe from the other party, but not from activists in low-turnout primaries who charge that the legislators have betrayed the party's values.

Safe district: a district consisting of voters who have historically voted for one party over the other by a large majority.

How to Run for Congress

Now that you know about campaigns and elections, are you ready to run your own race for Congress? It won't be easy, but following our advice will increase your chances. Here are our four keys to winning a congressional election—*money, organization, strategy,* and *message.* Even if you are not planning to run, remember these as you watch congressional races.

Running a campaign for a House race

Key 1: Money.   First, you will need funds to mount a legitimate challenge—up to two million dollars in many House districts and five or six times that if you are running for the Senate. Where does all the money go? Media and direct mailing take a big chunk, followed by database and demographic data, consultants, offices, phone banks, computers, and lawn signs. Unless you are wealthy, you are going to have to "dial for dollars." Your staff will prepare **call lists** and you will spend your days desperately filling your war chest.

To boost your chances of winning and reduce the cost of campaigning, you may want to wait and run for an **open seat**—one with no incumbent running because of a member's retirement. Taking on an incumbent costs more each election cycle. Along with raising money, savvy newcomers find ways to get lots of media attention.

Call list: A long list of potential donors who candidates must phone.

Open seat: A seat in Congress without an incumbent running for reelection.

Key 2: Organization.   You also will need a well-constructed team to run for Congress. Somebody has to recruit and train your speechwriters, fundraisers, social media coordinators, and supportive community leaders. Back before the era of candidate-centered politics, parties took care of that work. Today, challengers like you usually have to create an organization from scratch.

There is a side benefit to assembling a talented campaign organization. Political insiders see hiring established pollsters, media experts, and so forth as the sign of a competitive campaign. Funders, recognizing a possible winner, will start directing more money your way. Although most new congressional candidates publicly decry the "professionalization" of campaign politics, almost all of them hire established members of the Beltway insiders' club.

● *A biannual ritual: The picture of the freshman congressional class.*

Key 3: Strategy.   A fat bankroll and seasoned organization cannot compensate for a common rookie mistake—the lack of a well-conceived campaign strategy. Uncertainty is a central fact in every election, given fast-shifting political winds, opponents' moves, and the power of unexpected events. Incumbents tend to stick to the strategy that worked the last time. Challengers must invent a strategy that plays well to their political and personal strengths.

Two elements of successful congressional campaign strategies are vital: building a coalition of supporters and connecting with voters. Every state or district includes local business leaders, political activists, religious leaders, and spokespeople for identity groups. Strategically attracting some of them is essential. A coalition-building strategy also targets broader groups likely to vote for a party's candidate.

During the 1980s and 1990s, House Republican candidates in district after district forged coalitions of conservative, middle-aged, white, Protestant, relatively affluent voters. By 2006, this reliable lineup had fragmented in many places, and Democrats won forty-seven of forty-eight contested House seats to retake control of the chamber. By 2010, a new Republican coalition, now fueled by Tea Party activists and featuring a larger proportion of lower-income, disaffected white voters, regained control of the House. Notice how fast the winds shift in contemporary electoral politics.

Candidates primarily reach voters through the media. Candidate strategies need to include plenty of high-profile events—speeches, press conferences, visits to hospitals or nursing homes—that attract media coverage. If you cannot build crowds because of your low **name recognition**, you may resort to more creative approaches—bring in a local celebrity. Anything for airtime!

You also will need a smart social media strategy. Instagram, tweets, Google banner ads—anything to grab eyeballs for your campaign.

But don't forget old-fashioned politicking. Knocking on someone's door and meeting face to face is still, by far, the best way to win votes. As a House challenger in 1974, Bill Clinton announced his intention to "shake every hand in the district." Clinton lost that race but employed the strategy in his next race for Arkansas governor, which he won. "I'd go to the store," reported one local, "there was young Bill Clinton. Go to the movies—there he was at the entrance, hand out. Eventually I told him I'd vote for him if I just didn't have to shake his hand anymore!"[42]

Sadly, there's another effective strategy: **negative campaigning**. This usually involves strewing seeds of doubt in voters' minds about your opponent's policy positions, ethics, and character. Much as you may find this strategy repugnant, many argue that "going negative" works. However, good news: Recent work in political science suggests that negative ads may not change many minds or actually win elections.[43] The jury is still out, so in the meantime, expect that the other side's opposition researchers will portray you in the least flattering light possible. The point is not to change people's minds but to discourage the weaker supporters on the other side—going negative is thought to keep them home on Election Day.

Key 4: Message. Finally, you have to give people a good reason to vote for you. Candidates with a clear, powerful message sometimes topple better-financed and more elaborately organized opponents. In 2014, an unknown economics professor with a shoestring budget ($200,000) named David Brat upset House Majority Leader Eric Cantor. In 2018, a 28-year-old progressive activist Alexandria Ocasio-Cortez upset

CAMPAIGN LINGO

If you're running for Congress, you will want to know what your advisers are talking about. Here are a few insider terms from the campaign trail.

• **Robocall:** Automated phone call used to contact thousands of voters; often features a recorded message by the candidate or a popular party personality—or an attack on the opponent.

• **Advance team:** Campaign staffers who arrive at the site of major events ahead of time to organize the site and build crowds.

• **Field/GOTV:** The staff and volunteers who engage one on one with the public on behalf of the candidate.

• **Retail campaigning:** Attracting supporters or votes one by one, through door-to-door visits or small meetings.

• **Wholesale campaigning:** Reach hundreds or thousands at once through a speech, targeted advertisement, or robocalls.

• **Oppo:** Conducting research on the opposition to identify weakness.

• **Text-to-donate:** Use of text messages to donate funds to a campaign. Tightly regulated by the Federal Election Commission: for example, donations to any one candidate are limited to $50 per phone billing period.

Joe Crowley, the fourth most powerful Democrat in the House, with just one-tenth his budget. Both long shot candidates had the same message: Their opponents had lost touch with the district. In 2018, Brat himself lost to a candidate, Abigail Spanberger, with a clear message: women and health care.

In the relatively rare case that a first-time challenge like yours is victorious, what can you expect as a freshman member of Congress? (Yes, *freshman*: the term is the same as in high school or college, and the learning curve is just as steep!) What comes next?

A *new campaign*, starting immediately. For House members, the next election looms just two years away. Senators have a more relaxing six years—but must run statewide, which in high-population or sprawling states is very time consuming. The legendary House speaker Sam Rayburn told each incoming House freshman class that "a member of Congress can be elected by accident, but seldom reelected by accident." Voters back home will watch a first-term member especially closely, as will his or her colleagues on Capitol Hill.

As a sitting representative or senator, you may join your colleagues in denouncing Washington as corrupt and in need of reform. That message gives incumbents a quick-shot electoral boost but it has corroded Americans' support for their national legislature in recent decades. And this decline in support raises an important concluding question: Is the American electoral system in need of reform? And if so, how?

 **The Bottom Line**

» To run successfully for Congress, follow a few vital steps: raise sufficient funds (and then raise more), organize a talented team, develop a strategy that plays to your strengths, and hone your message.

» If you win, you become a freshman. Well done! Now, start running—your reelection campaign has begun.

Conclusion: Reforming American Elections

Does the U.S. electoral system work? In this chapter we highlighted a variety of concerns—from gerrymanders to incumbency rates to the influence of money in politics. Is it a problem that we keep sending the same representatives back to Congress, up to 98 percent of the time? Is it a problem that big spenders often win elections? Many reforms have been proposed. Here we focus on three.

Start with *gerrymanders*. We could try to end partisan battles over legislative districts by asking neutral panels to draw the lines—eight states do so for congressional districts, fourteen for state legislators. The goal: rational, compact, community-based districts that don't tilt to either party. The proposals always face the same challenges: Can we really trust the experts to find truly neutral districts? Indeed, is there any such thing? Iowa has tried to address the objections by giving the job to a nonpartisan panel and then forwarding the plans they draw up to the state legislature for an up or down vote. This reform debate heats up every time one party draws another outrageously biased district.

Next comes *money*. Do we really want our legislators spending hours each day, every day, raising funds? Do we want them piling up so much cash that no one can afford to run against them? Although the current system is highly unpopular, there is little agreement about how to change it. One simple reform, proposed by Democrats in 2016: forbid anonymous donations (known as "dark money"). Let the public know exactly who is funding that oppo (negative research) shop. More ambitious reformers call for publicly financed elections, in which (as in most other advanced democracies) the government provides equal funding to each candidate and allows relatively small donations from the public. This would create a much more even playing field between incumbents and challengers. Several states—including Arizona, Connecticut, and Maine—have passed laws publicly funding statewide elections. However, the courts have repeatedly struck down laws limiting contributions.

We also reviewed concerns that money buys influence. Surely cochairing a fundraiser or bundling tens of thousands of dollars will win you a politician's gratitude. The connection seems obvious to many critics, but political scientists, examining the data from every angle, have had a very hard time proving anything like direct "pay-to-play" schemes—contributing to a campaign in expectation of a policy payoff after the election. Big donors enjoy personal access to their representatives, but tracing actual votes or favors back to contributions has so far come up empty. However, subtle forms of influence, especially over small issues (e.g., items in the tax code) are difficult to measure.

Finally, large donors pay to protect incumbents who support their perspective. Environmentalists support green legislators; oil and coal companies write checks for politicians who fight them.[44]

Campaign finance reform polls well, but it also has strong critics—including a narrow Supreme Court majority that has repeatedly blocked efforts in the name of free speech. If a candidate excites you, why shouldn't you send money to him or her? Those who disagree point to who can spend: Should we give large organizations—such as corporations and labor unions—the same right to free speech as citizens? The Supreme Court in *Citizens United* narrowly said yes.

Another concern is that a single very wealthy individual can simply bankroll a candidate, or target a candidate, especially on the state level where relatively small amounts of money and negative research can sink a legislator or a judge. Congress has been reluctant to move boldly toward finance reform, with many Republicans especially skeptical. And the Supreme Court (again by a 5–4 majority) has overruled bipartisan legislation that both Congress and the states have crafted. The debate remains intense, but the institutional barriers to finance reform, in both Congress and the courts, have gotten steeper.

● Complaints about corporate influence go far back in American history. In 1889, cartoonist Joseph Keppler suggested that large corporate trusts were the real "bosses of the Senate." The Senate of that era was eventually reformed. Does ours need reform as well?

How about *term limits*? The president is limited to two terms, as are many governors. Why not limit members of Congress to, say, 12 years of service? Here, many political scientists are skeptical. The problem with this reform is that good legislating takes skill. Term limits clear out legislators just when they have learned how to become effective.[45] Although 21 states instituted term limits on state legislators, starting in the 1990s, six have rolled them back—with others considering the move. The reform did introduce fresh faces but the turnover had an unexpected downside. Seasoned lobbyists—no term limits for them—stepped in to "guide" the steady flow of rookie legislators. Still, proponents of the reform reply that incumbents become most savvy at staying in office—term limits would open up Congress to fresh ideas and talent.

These are three of the most popular reform ideas. Individual states have tried versions of each, but nationally we still have partisan gerrymandering in most states, few (and declining) limits on campaign spending, and no term limits for Congress. In the end, the vast majority repeatedly win reelection to a partisan Congress that often bogs down in stalemate—and receives worse grades than almost any other institution in American life.

Is the system broken? Do the Electoral College, the barriers to voting, the role of money, and partisan gerrymanders derail majority rule too extensively? Or is American politics doing what it has always done: giving a raucous people their voice while muddling through just fine? We will look at this issue from different angles when we study Congress in Chapter 13 and the presidency in Chapter 14.

Whether the system needs reform or not, campaigns and elections provide avenues to participation for the many groups in American society. Despite all the barriers and problems, repeated waves sweep new people, new voices, and new ideas into office. Each generation of Americans decides whether to shake up the system of campaigns and elections or to leave things in place. Every election brings new excitement, new voters, and new ideas into American politics. In 2016, the totally unexpected won out; 2018 saw a surge of victories for women, people of color, and a rare increase for the incumbent party, the Republicans, in the Senate.

We are especially proud of our many students who have run (and won!) seats in state legislatures and in Congress. We hope that you get engaged too. If you have read this chapter carefully, you now better understand all the challenges we face. But engaging in elections remains the one and only way to ensure government by the people.

CHAPTER SUMMARY

Check your understanding of Chapter 10.

🔵 Elections define democracies. They give the people a say over who governs them.

🔵 A key question in this chapter is: Are American elections democratic enough?

🔵 American electoral systems are unique because:

- We vote on a huge number of offices—over 520,000.

- We vote often compared to other nations.

- Federal elections for the House of Representatives take place every even-numbered year.

- In some places, there are elections every single year.

🔵 The Constitution puts the states in charge of running elections, instructing them to manage "the time, place, and manner." But it is silent on crucial matters—such as who has the right to vote.

🔵 In the last 60 years, all presidents have had one of just three jobs on their résumés: vice president, governor, or senator. Donald Trump became the first president in American history with no public sector experience.

🔘 The road to the White House passes through three stages: primaries, the party convention, and the general election.

🔘 The most familiar question about American democracy today involves the role of money in election campaigns. PACs, super PACs, and 527s have become fixtures in national elections.

🔘 The only constitutional limits to running for Congress are age, citizenship, and residency in the state.

🔘 Winning a race for Congress takes money, organization, strategy, constituent service, name recognition, and a good knowledge of the district.

🔘 Every ten years, the state legislatures redraw their congressional districts to keep up with changes in the population. The *gerrymander* is a district that is redrawn to help one party. Across time, some striking patterns have emerged in congressional elections: The president's party loses seats in the midterm elections, results have grown more volatile (with the party in power shifting often), and war spells trouble for the president's majority.

Need to review key ideas in greater depth? Click here.

KEY TERMS

Flashcard review.

527 groups, p. 293
Bundling, p. 293
Call list, p. 312
Candidate-centered
   elections, p. 311
Caucus, p. 295
Closed primary, p. 295
Electoral bounce, p. 297
Gerrymander, p. 308

Incumbency advantage, p. 305
Midterm elections, p. 306
Midterm loss, p. 306
Name recognition, p. 314
Negative campaigning, p. 314
Open primary, p. 295
Open seat, p. 312
Political action committee
   (PAC), p. 291

Proportional representation,
   p. 296
Reapportionment, p. 308
Safe district, p. 312
Super PACs, p. 291
Super Tuesday, p. 295
Time, place, and manner
   clause, p. 286
Winner-take-all, p. 296

STUDY QUESTIONS

1. Describe the limits that the Constitution places on popular participation in elections. Which one federal office could people originally vote for directly? Which people were generally not permitted to vote?

2. For further study: Is the American system of elections democratic enough for the twenty-first century? Defend your position by pointing to features that make it more (or less) democratic.

3. Describe the American system of campaign finance. What are PACs? How about super PACs? What influence did the 2014 *McCutcheon v. FEC* Supreme Court decision have on the system?

4. For further study: What is campaign finance reform? Make an argument for or against

campaign finance reform. If possible, explain how recent research supports your argument.

5. Describe the three stages of a U.S. presidential campaign. What were some highlights of each stage during the rollicking 2016 contest?

6. You have decided to run for Congress. What four things will your campaign need to be successful?

7. What is negative campaigning? Why do candidates rely on it so heavily?

8. Consider this: If you were running for Congress, would you use negative campaign ads against your opponent? Why or why not?

9. Describe three reforms that have been suggested for campaigns and elections in the United States. Now, pick one and argue for or against it. Be sure to defend your position.

Go to www.oup.com/us/Morone to find quizzes, flash cards, simulations, tutorials, videos, and other study tools.

11 Political Parties

CONGRESSMAN RON MACHTLEY, a moderate Republican from Rhode Island, enjoyed playing basketball. Washington was a lonely place, with his friends and family back home, and the ball games were a great way to relax. One day, in the early 1990s, a couple of serious-looking men came up to him with a blunt message from the new Republican House leader, Newt Gingrich (R-GA): "You're playing with the enemy—Democrats. No more basketball." Gingrich believed that Republicans had grown too comfortable in the minority, where they had languished for most of the last 60 years. The path back to power, he believed, required fire and resolve.[1]

Ron was stunned. Until recently, Democrats and Republicans would battle it out during the day and then adjourn to bourbon and tall tales at night. Members of the two parties worked together to craft important laws. The Senate passed the Civil Rights Act (1965) thanks, in part, to Northern Republicans; five years later, Congress passed the Clean Air Act, a blockbuster environmental bill, almost unanimously (there was only one negative vote), and it was signed into law by Republican President Richard Nixon. In 1997, the Republican congressional majority worked with Democratic President Bill Clinton to extend health insurance to seven million children.

Cross-party majorities were not unusual because there was as much difference *within* each party as there was between the parties. The Democratic Party appealed to very conservative southerners and very liberal northerners; Republicans also stretched across the political spectrum. In the early 1990s, almost as many Republicans (86%) as Democrats (93%) agreed that the "nation needed stricter environmental laws and regulations."[2]

Those days are over. Liberals sorted themselves overwhelmingly into the Democratic Party, conservatives went to the Republicans, and now **partisanship** touches every aspect of politics. The difference between parties is greater than any of the other divisions in American politics—greater than differences in race, income, education, religion, or gender. Today, Democrats continue to support strong environmental regulations but the number of Republicans who do so has dropped 47 points. A wide divide has opened on almost every issue, leading most engaged Democrats (70%) to say Republicans make them "afraid," "angry," and "frustrated"—and most active Republicans believe Democrats will ruin the country. Today, most Americans live near, hang out with, date, and marry people

● *Sen. Jeff Flake (R) of Arizona walks with emergency responders near the crime scene of an early morning shooting in Alexandria, Virginia, in 2017. Senior Republican Congressman Steve Scalise was among five victims shot and wounded at a baseball practice ahead of an annual game between lawmakers.*

In this chapter you will:

● Learn about the role parties play in governing America.

● Explore the two-party system and compare it to parties in other nations.

● Trace the history of parties in the United States.

● Investigate why people identify with one party (or why they don't).

● Analyze the great paradox: Why Americans like parties and don't like partisanship.

● Reflect on whether or not the United States has grown too partisan.

Partisanship: Taking the side of a party or espousing a viewpoint that reflects a political party's principles or position on an issue.

As partisan divides over political values widen, other gaps remain more modest

Average gap in the share taking a conservative position across 10 political values, by key demographics

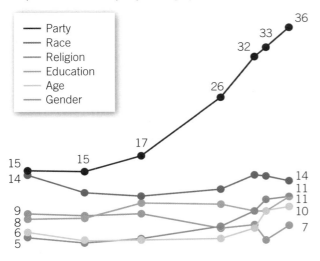

- Party
- Race
- Religion
- Education
- Age
- Gender

● **Figure 11.1** *Political party predicts people's values more than other factors—including race, education, and gender (Pew Research Center).*

Political party: A group that shares political principles and is organized to win elections and hold power.

● *Representative Roger Williams (R-TX) is placed in an ambulance after a gunman opened fire on congressional Republicans practicing for an annual charity game.*

with similar political views. In 2017, partisan antipathy reached a new height when a former volunteer for Democrat Bernie Sanders's presidential campaign opened fire on the Republican team practicing for a congressional baseball game, critically injuring one legislator and wounding several others. The gunman lived in his van and belonged to a Facebook group called "terminate the Republican Party."[3] A year later, police intercepted pipe bombs that a man living in a van plastered with Trump stickers had mailed to liberal leaders.

American party divisions are stronger today than they have been for at least a century (see Figure 11.1). Here's the big question: Is this a bad thing? Does intense disagreement make it harder to engage in civil discourse needed to govern well? Might it be splitting the country apart? Or does it enhance the public's choice between clashing political principles?[4]

Unlike almost every other institution we discuss in this book, **political parties** are not mentioned in the Constitution. Why? Because the founders despised them. President George Washington warned against their "destructive," "frightful," and "fatal" consequences. Thomas Jefferson, who actually helped organize the first party (against national government), always insisted, "If I could not get to heaven but with a party, I would not go there at all."[5]

The deep corruption of the early political parties seemed to justify the early fears (cynical politicians used to half-jokingly urge supporters, "Vote early, vote often"). By the mid-1800s, the two political parties—the rival engines of democracy—were the largest and most influential political organizations in the nation. Corrupt or not, nineteenth-century Americans discovered they could not run a democratic republic without parties. Today, parties shape national elections, congressional votes, policy decisions, judicial rulings, state government, and our own political opinions.

Who are we? A deeply partisan people who helped invent the modern political party. Parties provide a vital link between Americans and public officials. Many Americans form lifelong party attachments, fear the other party, and yet are quick to denounce partisanship.

🔘 Political Parties and U.S. Government

The Democratic Congressman was blunt. "When President Obama was elected, the Republicans did everything to defeat everything—every single

BY THE NUMBERS
Political Parties

Percentage of Americans who identified as Democrats, Republicans, and independents, respectively, September 2018 Gallup poll	*27, 26, 44*
Percentage of Americans who identified as Democrats, Republicans, and independents, respectively, November 2005 Gallup poll	*34, 33, 30*
Percentage favorable/unfavorable rating of Republican Party, August 2016	*36/58*
Percentage favorable/unfavorable rating of Republican Party, July 2005	*46/45*
Percentage favorable/unfavorable rating of Democratic Party, August 2016	*44/46*
Percentage favorable/unfavorable rating of Democratic Party, July 2005	*52/38*
Smallest proportion of Senate seats held by a major party (Federalists, 1821–1823)	*4 (out of 48)*
Largest number of House seats held by any party (Democrats, 1937–1939)	*334*
Total number of national parties fielding a presidential nominee, 2016	*9*
Total number of parties (other than Republican or Democratic) getting at least one electoral vote in the last 45 years	*0*

What is the role of political parties today? How do they aid or hinder our democratic process?

thing—he proposed." Well, it worked. The Republicans won control of Washington. Now the Democrats are in the opposition and refusing to cooperate. "Sure," continued the Congressman, "we could try and cooperate and, maybe, get some good things done. But a lot of members want to just say 'no,' make the administration look bad, and try to win back Congress in the next election." The electoral incentives for both parties are clear: Block the opposing party.[6]

That blunt assessment might tempt you to agree with President George Washington: Do we really need parties? The answer is yes. Let us see why.

What the Parties Do

Love them or hate them, political parties are an essential part of American government. They are responsible for five major jobs: championing ideas, selecting candidates, mobilizing voters, organizing postelection government, and integrating new voters into the political process.

Parties Champion Ideas.   U.S. politics reverberates with ideas, as we saw in Chapter 2, and every candidate takes a position on scores of issues. How do voters keep all these positions straight? In effect, parties create a brand that gives people an easy way to find candidates who roughly share their views. If you strongly support environmental activism, a path to citizenship for undocumented immigrants, robust social programs, a woman's right to choose, public radio, and high-speed rail, you are probably a Democrat. If, on the other hand, you care more about lowering taxes, reducing the size of government, getting tough on undocumented immigrants, supporting traditional families, and outlawing abortion, you are probably a Republican. You prefer to mix and match from the lists? You are probably an independent who belongs to neither party—though political scientists know that most independents are not really independent, as they regularly vote for one party.[7]

However parties—and what they believe—are always evolving. Every election introduces new ideas and goals. Candidate Donald Trump challenged many traditional Republican views—he opposed free trade agreements and staunchly defended Russia's government—but, once in office, he won support from a sky-high 90 percent of Republican Party members. He appeared to be successfully rewriting the Republican Party playbook.

Parties Select Candidates.   Parties choose the candidates who will run for election. Republicans began with 17 contenders running for president in 2016 and voted, state by state, until they had selected Donald Trump as their candidate. The two major parties select candidates to run for office at every level of government—except local government, which sometimes relies on **nonpartisan elections**.

Parties Mobilize the Voters.   Party leaders work to get the people to vote for their candidates. The parties raise money, hire consultants, craft advertisements, take polls, and organize phone banks. They also have become adept at suppressing the other side's votes through negative advertising.

Parties Organize Governing Activity After the Election.   Once the election is over, each party works to enact its signature programs. Leaders set agendas, line up votes, and organize their teams in Congress (as we will see in Chapter 13), in presidential administrations (as we will see in Chapter 14), and in the state governments (as we saw in Chapter 4).

Parties Help Integrate New Groups into the Political Process.   Parties are important agents of **political socialization**, transmitting basic lessons about politics and government (the details may differ depending on the party). Party messages have attracted immigrants, young voters, evangelical Christians, high-tech entrepreneurs, and many more into the American polity. Parties provide crucial communication links between 325 million Americans, spread across a continent, and their elected leaders. Savvy party leaders are always looking for overlooked groups they can rally to their cause. Barack Obama galvanized black Americans who, in 2008 and 2012, turned out at higher rates than whites for the first time in American history (though sources disagree on 2008).[8] Four years later, Republican nominee Donald Trump galvanized white males without a college degree—who felt abandoned by both Democrats and Republicans.

Nonpartisan election:
An election in which candidates run as individuals, without any party affiliation. Many towns and cities feature nonpartisan elections.

Political socialization:
Education about how the government works and which policies one should support; provided by parents, peers, schools, parties, and other national institutions.

● *Parties socialize new groups into politics. When evangelical Christians started getting involved in politics in the 1970s and 1980s, Republican leaders were there to show them the ropes. Here, President Ronald Reagan speaks to evangelical leaders.*

● *Barack Obama supporters celebrate his presidential reelection. For the first time in history, African Americans voted at a higher rate than white voters when Obama ran for president.*

Political parties provide an efficient, effective solution to these five issues.[9] Is there anything especially distinctive about the American **party system**? Yes: the United States is unusual because it relies on just two major parties.

Two-Party America

In January 2019, all 435 members of the House of Representatives, 98 out of 100 senators, and every governor were either Democrats or Republicans. Why is the United States so resolutely devoted to the number "two" when it comes to party politics?

One reason for this two-party tradition rests on American ideas (see Chapter 2). Democrats and Republicans often take different sides in the great American debate over ideas. For example, Republicans see liberty as freedom from government coercion while most Democrats emphasize "freedom from want" and support government programs that will ensure everyone has the basics.

As you know by now, institutions invariably reinforce ideas. In this case, the winner-take-all electoral rules, described in Chapter 10, keep third parties out. The Libertarian or the Green Party may amass a great many votes; but even a party that wins 20 percent of the national vote but does not win an outright majority in any state or congressional district is shut out of both Congress and the Electoral College. In contrast, most other democracies operate multiparty systems. Proportional representation systems would give a party that won 20 percent of the vote, roughly 20 percent of the seats in the legislature. A French sociologist named Maurice Duverger drew the conclusion: American style elections (often described with a horse racing metaphor, "first past the post") generally yields a two-party system while proportional representation produces many parties.

The result is simple and dramatic: The rules push every group to join one of the two major parties. When candidates decide to break out of the two-party system, they are accused of being "spoilers"—throwing the election to the party that does not share their philosophy at all. That's what happened in the 2000 presidential election. In Florida, Republican George W. Bush won 48.847 percent of the vote, Democrat Al Gore won 48.846 percent of the vote, and Green Party candidate Ralph Nader won 1.635 percent of the vote. Bush's 0.001 percent margin gave him all 25 electoral votes in Florida and made him president. Disappointed Democrats blasted Ralph Nader for drawing just

Party system: The broad organization of U.S. politics comprising the two main parties, the coalition of supporters backing each, the positions they take on major issues, and each party's electoral achievements.

COMPARING NATIONS 11.1	Organizing Electoral/Governing Systems

The international community features many different party arrangements. There are subtle differences among all nations, but a few main organizational styles tend to predominate, and each produces a different style of party politics.	**Multiparty systems:** The vast majority of the world's countries are governed along multiparty lines, from India to Italy and Japan to Tokelau, a tiny group of Pacific islands with about 1,400 inhabitants and three political parties. A coalition of two or more parties, with frequently shifting alliances and complex power-sharing arrangements, usually forms a government in multiparty systems.
	Two-party systems: The United States is the largest two-party state; other examples are Jamaica and Malta. Elsewhere, as in the United Kingdom and Spain, two parties have dominated, but third parties occasionally join in governing coalitions.
	Single-party systems: Only seven formal single-party states, in which only one party is allowed to contest national elections, exist today, ranging from China to Eritrea. Another 40-plus countries feature "single-party dominance" systems, in which minor parties are allowed but one powerful party wins national elections.
	Nonpartisan systems: Today, some Persian Gulf states—the United Arab Emirates, Oman, and Kuwait—outlaw political parties and officially run on a "nonpartisan" basis, though a traditional tribal family rules in each of the three nations. A few Pacific island nations also are nonpartisan, partly because their populations are so small. Many urban governments in the United States are nonpartisan—a legacy of anticorruption crusades from the early twentieth century.

enough liberals to throw the election to the Republicans. The Florida experience only reinforced a key institutional lesson: work within the two parties.

Other institutional forces reinforce the two-party system. State laws determine who gets on the ballot, and they often make it very difficult for minor party candidates. In Florida, for example, after reforms in 2011 that *eased* restrictions, a third party still needs to collect more than 112,000 notarized signatures simply to list its candidate on a presidential primary ballot—a high bar for a small party.

The advantage of America's two-party system: It is predictable and stable. In nations with many parties, each election is followed by negotiations among the parties trying to form a majority. Today in Germany, the majority coalition has two parties; in Israel, it has six; and in India, the "National Democratic Alliance" governing coalition elected in May 2014 included 16 parties with seats in the lower house. Sometimes a single group pulls out of the governing coalition and forces a new election.

There also are disadvantages to two-party dominance in the United States.[10] For starters, it is less representative. In 2016, over 15 percent of the voters in Massachusetts voted for Republican congressional candidates. Is it fair to end up with nine Massachusetts Democrats—and no

● *Die Partei is a satirical party in Germany. Their campaign poster mocks the political discussion ("Bla, Bla, . . .") and then makes outlandish promises: "If you vote for us, we will execute the 100 richest Germans." The party won one seat in the 2014 European Parliament—the first satirical party to win representation.*

Republicans—in Congress? Voters in Germany or Japan or other proportional representation systems generally have more choices for national or local office; people passionate about a cause—immigration, the environment, religion, free markets—can often find a party devoted to their cause (see Comparing Nations 11.1). Perhaps you are wondering if Americans have ever made room for additional parties. The short answer: No.

Third Parties in American Politics

Theodore "Teddy" Roosevelt is one of the most colorful figures in U.S. political history: a military hero who suffered from asthma and a big-game hunter who adopted an orphaned bear cub (giving rise to the familiar "teddy bear"). When Roosevelt came out of retirement to run as a Progressive Party candidate, he became the only third-party presidential candidate to come in second—but he still got clobbered by Woodrow Wilson, who won 435 electoral votes to Roosevelt's 88.

Reforming The Two-Party System in Iowa

Table 11.1 lists all third-party presidential contestants who gained more than 5 percent of the popular vote or more than 10 electoral votes since 1840. It is a short list, without a single candidate who came close to winning. Even in 2016, after much publicity, the Libertarian Party candidate managed just 3 percent. And most third parties lasted just one term (or four years) at the national level. Roosevelt's Progressive Party, for example, elected some 15 members to Congress and spearheaded important reforms but dissolved within four years. The Tea Party, which has attracted considerable attention, is not in fact an organized national party, but a label that candidates adopt to signal their conservative views.

On the state level, third parties have done slightly better. In 2018, there were 169 members of the Libertarians and 143 associated with the Green Party elected (remember, that's out of 520,000 elected officials—see Chapter 10).[11] Minnesota was the only state to elect a third-party candidate governor. Jesse Ventura, a former professional wrestler (known as "The Body"), rode his blend of outsized personality and blunt

TABLE 11.1 **The Road to Nowhere: The Most Successful Third-Party Presidential Contenders, 1840–2019**

ELECTION	THIRD-PARTY CANDIDATE(S), PARTY	PERCENTAGE OF POPULAR VOTE (NO. OF ELECTORAL VOTES)
1856	Millard Fillmore, American (Know-Nothing) Party	22.0 (8)
1860	John Bell, Constitutional Union Party	12.6 (39)
1892	James Weaver, People's Party	8.5 (22)
1912	Theodore Roosevelt, Progressive Party Eugene Debs, Socialist Party	27.4 (88) 6.0 (0)
1924	Robert La Follette, Progressive Party	16.6 (13)
1948	Strom Thurmond, States' Rights (Dixiecrat) Party	2.4 (39)
1968	George Wallace, American Independent Party	13.5 (45)
1980	John Anderson, National Unity Party	6.6 (0)
1992	Ross Perot, United We Stand Party	18.9 (0)
1996	Ross Perot, Reform Party	8.4 (0)

● *Wrestler-turned-governor Jesse Ventura, a member of the Reform Party.*

common sense to the governor's mansion as a Reform Party candidate in 1998. In the last quarter-century, four other states have elected governors outside the major parties: Alaska (1990, 2014), Connecticut (1990), Rhode Island (2010), and Maine (1994, 1998). All four winners were independents rather than representatives of third parties.

Despite their history of electoral failure, minor parties make valuable contributions. They open the process to alternative views, give dissidents voice, and expand civic engagement. Third-party movements have often injected strong and controversial views into the major parties. They fought for the abolition of slavery, the direct election of senators, gender equality, laws eliminating child labor, the prohibition of drinking, the income tax, limits on immigration, and smaller government.[12] When a third-party cause becomes popular, one of the major parties tends to adopt it—as they did with every issue in the previous sentence.

The Bottom Line

» America's two-party style has endured for over 200 years, with Democrats and Republicans as the main standard-bearers since 1856.

» The election rules explain the dominance of the two parties.

» Third parties arise periodically to challenge two-party dominance, but none has ever managed to break through.

America's Party Systems: Origins and Change

Political parties are always evolving. Every few decades the entire U.S. party system changes: new issues, new winners, new (or renewed) parties, and new ways of winning elections. We can identify at least six distinctive "party systems" stretching across American history.

Beginnings: First Party System (1789–1828)

Early Americans tried to avoid political parties. But they disagreed on a crucial issue: How strong should the central government be? Politicians who supported strong government became identified as Federalists and those for states' rights and limited national power became Democratic–Republicans. Political parties were born.

The Federalists, led by the immensely popular Washington, won two unanimous votes (there was no campaign) and then announced he would not accept a third term. John Adams, Washington's vice president, won the third election.

In 1800, Democratic–Republican candidate Thomas Jefferson won a bitter victory over President John Adams. This was the first contested election, and the first time the White House changed party hands. For the rest of the first party period, the Democratic–Republicans dominated national politics, winning the next six presidential elections and controlling Congress for twenty-four years (see Table 11.2). The Federalists bitterly noted that Jefferson had won by carrying the slave states, whose Electoral College count was inflated by adding three-fifths of a vote for each slave (discussed in Chapter 3). In fact, slaveholders held the presidency for most of the next forty years.

The first party system began with a distrust of party politics. George Washington struggled, through the first two administrations, to project a nonpartisan image. The idea did not last long. Party newspapers were soon showering opponents with insults that would make modern politicians blush. Politics occasionally turned deadly. Aaron Burr, a Democratic–Republican who served as Jefferson's first vice president, despised Hamilton and his Federalist followers. On a hot July morning in 1804 the two fought a duel and Burr fatally wounded Hamilton, further hobbling a Federalist Party already in decline. The party limped along until 1816, but after 1800 it never won a presidential election.

TABLE 11.2 Overview of the Six Party Systems

Notice that the sixth party system—our own—is very unusual in one way: no party dominates. This is especially true in recent times. Democrats have an edge in the presidency while Republicans have an edge in the House and Senate. Like every system, this one will likely end—perhaps with one party taking over. But which party?

	YEARS IN CONTROL					
	PRESIDENT		HOUSE		SENATE	
	FEDERALIST	DEMOCRATIC–REPUBLICAN	F	DR	F	DR
1. 1789–1828	12	28	8	26	12	22
	DEMOCRAT	NATIONAL REPUBLICAN/WHIG	DEM	NR/WHIG	DEM	NR/WHIG
2. 1829–1860	24	8	24	8	28	4
	DEMOCRAT	REPUBLICAN	DEM	REPUB	DEM	REPUB
3. 1861–1896	8	28	6	30	14	22
4. 1897–1932	8	28	10	26	6	30
5. 1932–1968	28	8	32	4	32	4
6. 1969–present						
a) 1969–1992	4	20	24	0	18	6
b) 1993–present	16	12	8	20	11	17

The first party system set a durable pattern: two main parties contesting elections and building coalitions. One party (in this case, the Democratic–Republicans) dominated until evolving rules swept in a new constellation of parties, ideas, and supporters—in short, a new party system.

Rise: Second Party System (1828–1860)

When Andrew Jackson won the presidency in 1828, some twenty thousand Democrats (many of them angling for government jobs) swarmed into Washington for his inauguration. Supreme Court Justice Joseph Story spoke for the old-style gentry: "The reign of King Mob seemed triumphant."[13] What he was really seeing was the birth of modern party politics.

In just three decades, political parties had evolved into a form that we would recognize today. Party competition grew fierce, voting rights expanded to most white males, and enthusiastic party members threw themselves into politics.

The birth of modern politics and "the rise of the common man" came with serious downsides: fewer rights for the small population of free blacks (90% of African Americans were still slaves). And elected officials dispensed jobs to their followers as the "spoils of office"—a corrupt patronage system of government (discussed in Chapter 15).[14]

Party names changed along with the institutional shifts. The Federalists had vanished. Jefferson's old Democratic–Republicans split into two factions in the 1820s. Supporters of Andrew Jackson became Democrats; a rival faction called themselves the "Whigs"—named after a British party that opposed royal tyranny.

The Democrats favored small farmers, the rising urban workers, and local control. They embraced immigrants (and stuffed ballots in their hands almost as soon as they landed). The Democrats pursued a genocidal Indian removal, plunged into war with Mexico, and increasingly became identified as the southern and pro-slavery party. Whigs favored a stronger government that would knit the country together through canals, railroads, the distribution of federal lands to settlers, and other infrastructure projects. They supported business and manufacturing, opposed Indian removal, fought to limit the influence of immigrants, and included a northern faction intent on resisting slavery's expansion.

There was no federal safety net during this pre–Civil War period. Democratic Party officials, especially in urban areas, often provided basic services in exchange for votes—the basis for the urban party machines that would grow extremely powerful by the late 1800s.

Both parties foundered on the question of slavery. Neither, however, could duck the issue. As the United States spread west, every new territory and state raised the same terrible question: Should slavery be permitted to spread? Democrats had a direct answer: Leave it to the states and the territories. Whigs were divided; those from the south fought for the expansion of slavery, those from the north opposed it—and the issue exploded the party. Out of the Whigs' demise a new party system arose—and clarified the future of slavery in the United States.[15]

● The new Irish and German immigrants, identified by the type of liquor they prefer, steal American democracy in this nativist critique of urban (Democratic) voters during the second party period.

War and Reconstruction: Third Party System (1860–1896)

Abraham Lincoln helped form a new party—the antislavery Republican Party. The Republicans strongly supported free labor (which today we call capitalism) and insisted that new western settlements should be free of slavery (free soil), because slavery's expansion would undermine the people's right to work for themselves (free labor). After Lincoln won the presidential election of 1860, the southern states feared the end of slavery, and the nation soon entered the Civil War.

During the war, Lincoln skillfully deployed the Republican Party on behalf of the Union forces. He drew on party members to recruit soldiers, name officers (party connections helped), negotiate for war supplies, and sell war bonds to finance the war effort. With no similar party apparatus in the South, Confederates faced a much more difficult task.[16]

After the war, Republicans again drew on the party to try and rebuild the nation. "Radical Republicans" promoted black rights, helping to boost many former slaves into Congress and statehouses under the Republican banner. Democrats, fighting back in the South, denounced Reconstruction's "excesses" and often resorted to violence and racist tactics that tried to limit the freedom of the former slaves to travel, to vote, or to seek employment.

After winning the war, Republicans dominated elections between 1864 and the midterm election of 1874, when the Democrats broke through and took back the House. By then, each party had a strong regional identity. Democrats controlled the former Confederate states, which became known as "the Solid South" because they reliably voted Democratic—after they violently drove African Americans out of politics and restored white dominance. Republicans grew strongest in the Northeast and the Midwest. The elections were decided by a whisker. After 1872, the presidency changed hands with each election and two (of five) winners lost the popular vote but won in the electoral college—something historians considered remarkable until it happened again in the current era (in 2000 and 2016).

During the 1870s and 1880s, large numbers of European and Asian immigrants streamed into the cities, where municipal governments featured well-developed **party machines**— powerful political organizations. Managed by **party bosses**, the machines provided immigrants with such basic services as food, shelter, jobs, contacts, and a sense of belonging. In exchange, the party (Democrats controlled the machines in most cities, Republicans in others) could count on a block of all-important votes once immigrants became naturalized citizens. The machines grew notorious for bribery and corruption. In some places they paid men to vote, stuffed ballot boxes, permitted repeat voters, and engaged in terrible brawls on Election Day.

The western lands joined the Union as solid Republican states, and party leaders no longer needed to scrape for black Republican votes in

Party machine: A hierarchical arrangement of party workers, often organized in an urban area to help integrate immigrants and minority groups into the political system. Most active in the late nineteenth and early twentieth centuries.

Party boss: The senior figure in a party machine.

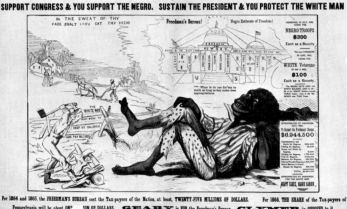

● *Reconstruction set off a fierce contest over the former slaves. Black men and women eagerly tried to build civic communities. White supremacists joined the Democratic Party and fought back. This caricature was part of the racist campaign designed to show that the former slaves were not prepared for freedom—a false charge backed by violence that eventually helped defeat racial reconstruction.*

the South. They stood aside as the Democratic politicians across the South pushed black voters out of office (see Chapter 5).

Business and Reform: Fourth Party System (1896–1932)

In 1892, a radical populist party swept out of the west and took five states and over a million votes. Then the worst economic depression until that time hit the country. In the 1894 midterm, the Democrats lost 116 seats—the biggest drop ever. In the 1896 presidential election, the populists joined the Democrats to challenge the status quo but were defeated by a Republican Party, sometimes tagged the "millionaires' party." However, after President William McKinley was assassinated in 1901, his vice president, Theodore Roosevelt, stepped into the White House, challenged the "millionaires' club" and began to sponsor reforms.

The great debates of the fourth party system featured support for the status quo and business on the one side and pressures for political and economic equality (championed by reformers, known as Progressives) on the other. Should women be given the vote? Should the government regulate emerging corporate giants such as Standard Oil or the Central Pacific Railroad? Should judges be elected? How about Senators? On the state level, should the government regulate child labor? Should it limit the workday for men and women? To the Progressive reformers, led by Theodore Roosevelt, the answer was yes, yes, yes.

This period also focused on the question of whether liquor should be prohibited. More than one in six Americans had been born abroad; drinking became associated with immigrants, big cities, political corruption, and spousal abuse. During World War I, a constitutional amendment whipped through Congress and the nation, and America banned the sale of alcohol beginning in 1920. A wave of crimes associated with illegal liquor rocked the cities while rural districts went dry with little complaint (or violence). Business leaders bitterly complained that Prohibition—a massive national effort to change American habits—was creating an era of big government.[17]

THE BOSS STILL HAS THE REINS

● Cartoonist Thomas Nast mocks one corrupt politician, Boss Tweed, at the reins of New York's democracy.

● One policy both parties agreed on for most of the fourth party system: prohibiting the sale of alcohol. The 1920s became a boom time, marked by rising new industries such as advertising, automobiles, and electricity. Then the economy collapsed in 1929–1930, taking down Prohibition and the entire "fourth party system" as well.

Depression and the New Deal: Fifth Party System (1933–1968)

Another President Roosevelt, Teddy's distant cousin Franklin, helped define the fifth party system. The Great Depression (1929–1941) unhinged party politics, crippling a Republican Party now associated with business elites and economic incompetence.

After three years of economic misery, Roosevelt frankly blamed the "unscrupulous money changers" and "self-seekers"—the old "millionaires' club"—for the nation's "dark days." Roosevelt's **New Deal** focused on jobs, infrastructure, government aid to the elderly (Social Security), temporary assistance for the needy (unemployment insurance and welfare), and new federal government agencies to manage it all. Roosevelt's Democratic Party reaped the electoral rewards, reshaping party coalitions.

The Democratic Party coalition included an unusual mix of interests: the Solid South; the big-city machines with their ethnic supporters; labor unions (the Democrats sponsored legislation that permitted the movement to grow); farmers, who saw agricultural prices rise during these years; and, starting in 1936, African Americans.

African Americans had been loyal to the Republican "**Grand Old Party**" (**GOP**) since Lincoln signed the Emancipation Proclamation. From the party's free-soil origins in 1856 up through the 1920s, the GOP was the party of civil rights. Republican governments in the western states gave women the vote long before the Nineteenth Amendment extended it to women in Democratic strongholds. Now, Roosevelt's employment programs, along with early efforts to reduce racial segregation, won many northern black voters to the Democratic Party. However, there was now a tension within the Democratic Party: Liberals, labor unions, and African Americans pressured the party to expand social programs and civil rights, while southern Democrats struggled to rein in social programs and preserve segregation. Democrats kept the coalition together—and hung on to their southern majority—for another thirty years, but as they became known as the party of civil rights, white southern voters shifted to the GOP. As the Democratic coalition began to crumble, a new generation of Republicans rose up with fresh ideas for America.

New Deal: Broad series of economic programs and reforms introduced between 1933 and 1936 and associated with the Franklin Roosevelt administration.

Grand Old Party (GOP): Long-standing nickname for the Republican Party; ironically, bestowed early in the party's history, in the 1870s.

The Sixth Party System: Parties at Parity (1969–Present)

President Richard Nixon (1969–1973) and, later, Ronald Reagan (1981–1989) developed a "southern strategy" to win middle-class white votes. They emphasized

---

What Do YOU Think? Do the 2016 and 2018 Elections Suggest a New Party System?

What do the results of the most recent national elections tell us about the immediate future of the party system? Is one party poised to establish dominance for a long period of time?

Yes.
Donald Trump's election means that the Republicans have won the White House in three of the last five elections in three of the last five elections. Although the GOP lost the House in 2018, they made gains in the Senate and hold 62 state legislative chambers. The electorate is Republican now.

Probably not.
Remember that the Democrats won the popular vote in the 2016 presidential election—and in four of the last five elections. In 2018, they took control of the House of Representatives. Control of the political system has swung back and forth.

No.
Republicans may have won in 2016—but it was a very close call. Elections are still won and lost by a hair. And a solid majority of millennials may have been on the losing side—but their influence will only grow. Demographic changes herald a very different future.

small business, limited government, and a more market-oriented vision. The Republican Party always had a conservative wing, but now this wing rose to dominance.

By 1981, Republican President Ronald Reagan launched a direct assault on the fifth party system through a powerful new conservative mantra: Government is not the solution to our problems. Instead, said the rising Republican coalition, government is the source of the problem. During the 1980s, the parties lined up in their contemporary ways: on economic and social issues alike, Democrats leaned left, Republicans right.

Republicans controlled the fourth party period and Democrats the fifth. The current party era introduces something new: Neither party is in control. Instead, very close elections swing party control back and forth. The new era, the sixth party system, is the era of very close elections. And with very close elections comes growing partisanship.

The most influential president of this period was Ronald Reagan and his new pro-market, antigovernment philosophy. Eventually, even Democrats began to abandon their old philosophy and began to echo Reagan. Democratic president Bill Clinton announced that "the era of big government is over."[18]

Perhaps the United States will experience close elections for a long time to come. However, this sixth party period is already one of the longest-lived. Political historians are watching carefully to see if one party or the other is poised to break away, establish dominance, and start a new party era. Perhaps Donald Trump's victory and the strong run by Bernie Sanders in 2016—both party outsiders—suggest that the coalitions of the sixth party system are unraveling. What do you think?

Why the Party Period Matters

Why should we care what party system we are in? Because a new party system means new politics—and new national rules. Coalitions of voters, ideas, and political leaders determine how America is governed. Will we adopt universal health insurance? Will tax cuts allow business to apply the savings to hiring new workers? Will we round up and deport undocumented people or give them a path to citizenship? These and many other decisions depend on the party—and the ideas—in power.

 **The Bottom Line**

» Two main parties have always dominated U.S. party politics—and since 1856, they have been the same two, Republicans and Democrats.

» The two parties—and the contest between them—regularly reboot the party system. Each change in party system means a change in the voters who make up each party and the ideas that inspire them.

» We count at least six party systems since the founding of the United States. The latest, which began in 1969, is the period of very close elections.

» Political historians are watching closely for the rise of the next party system.

Party Identification . . . and Ideas

Party identification: Strong attachment to one political party, often established at an early age.

Many Americans feel strongly attached to their party. That attachment is called **party identification**, and it deeply affects how individuals see politics. Where do party identities and differences come from? And exactly who is attached to each party?

Building Party Identification

As we saw in Chapter 7, political socialization and party loyalty often start with family and include demography—race, gender, age, and so on. The Democratic Party is younger. Men break Republican, women Democratic (see Figure 11.2).[19] The Republican Party is mostly white; the Democratic Party is increasingly diverse. Indeed, political scientists John Sides, Michael Tesler, and Lynn Vavreck have argued that underlying contemporary partisanship is a fierce identity politics—with white identity on the right and multicultural identity on the left. From these identities emerge views on immigration, social welfare policies, and the federal government itself.[20]

Strong groups for Democratic and Republican parties

% of each group that identifies as . . .

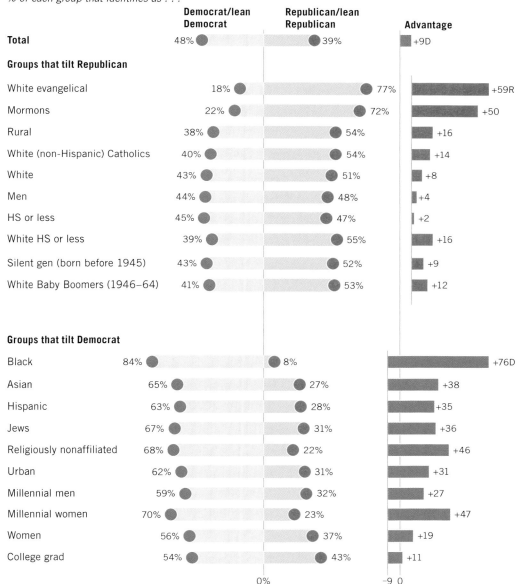

	Democrat/lean Democrat	Republican/lean Republican	Advantage
Total	48%	39%	+9D
Groups that tilt Republican			
White evangelical	18%	77%	+59R
Mormons	22%	72%	+50
Rural	38%	54%	+16
White (non-Hispanic) Catholics	40%	54%	+14
White	43%	51%	+8
Men	44%	48%	+4
HS or less	45%	47%	+2
White HS or less	39%	55%	+16
Silent gen (born before 1945)	43%	52%	+9
White Baby Boomers (1946–64)	41%	53%	+12
Groups that tilt Democrat			
Black	84%	8%	+76D
Asian	65%	27%	+38
Hispanic	63%	28%	+35
Jews	67%	31%	+36
Religiously nonaffiliated	68%	22%	+46
Urban	62%	31%	+31
Millennial men	59%	32%	+27
Millennial women	70%	23%	+47
Women	56%	37%	+19
College grad	54%	43%	+11

● **Figure 11.2** *Party demographics. White, male, older evangelical voters are more likely to vote Republican, while Black, Asian, female, young, and urban voters are more likely to vote Democrat (Pew Research Center).*

What Do YOU Think?   Personality and Party

Consider your own personality and party preference. Does recent political science research help predict your views—and the views of the people around you?	**Yes.** I believe that Democrats are generally more likely to seek new experiences and Republicans are more likely to emphasize duty and discipline.	**No.** I think there are different traits that explain party identification. (Please specify which traits you think matter most.)	**Interests, not personality.** I don't believe personality predicts politics. We are rational creatures pursuing our own self-interest regardless of personality.

Other traits also matter. Urban dwellers are Democrats, suburbanites lean Republican, and rural voters are strongly Republican. White evangelicals and Mormons are strong Republicans, secular people Democrats. Even personality seems to matter. Some studies find that people who exhibit more "openness" (eagerness to explore new experiences) are more likely to be Democrats. Those who measure high in "conscientiousness" (strong sense of duty, discipline, impulse control) tend to be Republicans.[21] Think about your own personality: Does it fit with this recent political science theory?

Another influence on party affinity comes down to the political moment when voters form attachments. Certain times seem to carry magic for a political party—John Kennedy's 1960 election drew millions into strong identification as Democrats, as Ronald Reagan's election in 1980 did among Republicans.

Although political historians are always alert to a sea change, no mass shift in party identification has shown up for the last 25 years. Current poll numbers show that approximately 27 percent of the electorate identifies as Democratic and 25 percent as Republican. Recently, we see a surge in independents who are weary of both parties—at 44 percent, their numbers larger than either party.[22] Why? The intense conviction among the party faithful may make others less willing to identify themselves. Still, most independents vote faithfully for one party or the other and feel just as strongly about the shortcomings of the other party. Only about 12 percent of the population are true independents.[23]

Still one factor may be slowly shifting the balance toward the Democratic Party: When Ronald Reagan whipped Jimmy Carter in the 1980 presidential election, the electorate was almost 90 percent white; by 2020 the percentage of the electorate that considers itself white is estimated to be down to around 68 percent—and falling. Of course, groups can and do shift parties. Still, the demographic trend seems to contain an urgent message for the Republican future: diversify the base.[24]

The Power of Party Attachment

Party identification shapes three key aspects of public involvement: voting/political participation, "filtering," and ideology.

Explore party values and factions.

Straight-ticket voter: Votes for the same party for all offices on a ballot.

Voting/Participation.   Party identity is a very strong predictor of your voting habits. In 2016, for example, 89 percent of Democrats voted for Clinton while 90 percent of Republicans voted for Trump. Analysts measuring the strength of party attachment find that strong partisans tend to be very loyal **straight-ticket voters**, sticking with their party's candidates right down the ballot. Their opposite? **Split-ticket voters**, who make their choices candidate by candidate.

Voting rates are higher among those with strong party identification. Only 60 million (27% of eligible voters) cast a ballot in the 2016 presidential primaries. The key to every election is turning out the party's **base voters**—those who deeply identify with the party—while winning over some independents. Conventional wisdom used to hold that independents were in the middle. Not anymore. Today, most lean strongly toward either the Democratic or the Republican Party.[25]

Filtering.   Party identification also plays a *filtering* role. Filters choose what signals in the media environment people are liable to accept or reject. As one political scientist wrote, "people tend to project favorable characteristics and acceptable issue positions onto the candidates of the party they favor."[26] In a set of experiments, social scientists asked respondents to rate a generic series of political candidates based on photos and detailed biographies. Each was sometimes described as a Democrat, sometimes as a Republican, and sometimes as an independent. The study found that self-identified Democrats preferred the candidates described as "Democrats," the Republicans preferred Republicans. The candidate's policy positions, appearance, or family background, were all less important than party label.

Ideology.   The parties take divergent views on issue after issue. This creates the polarization we described at the start of the chapter. Should we provide government support to people who cannot take care of themselves? Democrats say yes (71%); Republicans say no (only 24% agree). Should we make every effort to improve the position of minorities, even if it means preferential treatment? A majority of Democrats say yes (52%), while just 12 percent of Republicans agree. Do you believe in God as described in the Bible? Republicans are more likely to say "yes " (70%) than Democrats (45%). On all these indicators, differences between the parties have more than doubled in the past 15 years.[27]

Of course, even with the growing intensity of party ideology, no party is a monolith. Each includes multiple factions with different—sometimes very different— ideas. Moreover, both parties are now in flux, with some factions rising while others fade away. Let us take a look at the factions within the parties today.

Republican Factions

Republicans are often lumped together as conservatives, but significant differences exist. Consider six different Republican factions.

Populists or Trumpists.   These men and women feel left behind by economic and cultural changes. They are skeptical of elites in both parties, believing that they have turned their back on conservative values—and more generally, on America. They are strong nationalists, vehemently oppose immigration, and fear international trade deals. President Trump now leads this wing of the party. Populists cheer when he is "politically incorrect."

● *Every party has fringe groups. Strong language about immigration brought white nationalists back into the national spotlight when some endorsed Donald Trump.*

Split-ticket voter: Votes for at least one candidate from each party, dividing his or her ballot between the two (or more) parties.

Base voters: Party members who tend to vote loyally for their party's candidates in most elections.

Growing Partisanship—On Core Issues

HOW DO REPUBLICANS AND DEMOCRATS DIVIDE?

Notice how the members of different parties take very different views on two questions at the start of this book:
What does (and should) government do—and who are we?

THINK ABOUT IT

Summarize how each party sees the issues of government aid, racial discrimination, and immigration. Where do you stand on these issues? Why? Can you describe how those with the opposite view would respond to your own arguments?

Do you think it's important to try and overcome these divisions? What might be done to minimize the divide on this issue? Suggest some possible steps.

Source: Pew Research Center

% who say ...

Government should do more to help the needy

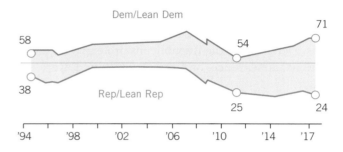

Racial discrimination is the main reason why many black people can't get ahead these days

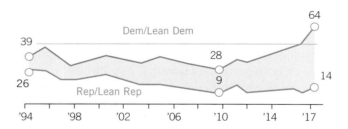

Immigrants strengthen the country with their hard work and talents

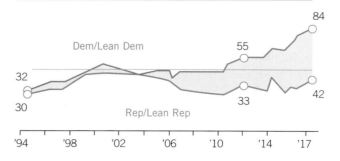

Referring to this faction of the party, Senator Bob Corker (R-TN) recently commented, "People no longer care about issues. They [only] want to know if you're with Trump."[28]

Religious Traditionalists. Some conservatives support a return to what they consider America's Christian origins. Traditionalists oppose abortion, affirmative action, and same-sex marriage; they support school prayer, gun rights, and restrictions on immigration. Some view the Bible as a guide to social and political life that is every bit as important as the Constitution.

Fiscal Conservatives. This faction supports tax cuts, opposes government spending, and identifies the large U.S. budget deficit as its major concern. Many aim to reduce the size of the federal government. They voted for the sweeping Trump Administration tax cut, but wish to see its costs balanced with cuts in the large entitlement programs—Social Security and Medicare (see Chapter 17).

Libertarians. Libertarians are strong defenders of individual liberty who promote minimal government intrusion into personal rights. Most libertarians follow a laissez-faire economic theory and are passionate advocates of free markets. Libertarians reject federal involvement in education, environmental regulations, transportation, healthcare, old age pensions—you get the idea. That may sound conservative, but because libertarians oppose all government they are liberal on social issues. They also think government has no business deciding whether you can have an abortion, smoke marijuana, or marry whomever you like. This faction has been shaken by the rise of Donald Trump but it has a long legacy in the party and is likely to be back.[29]

Watch Donald Trump's populist supporters during the campaign.

Neoconservatives. Neoconservatives support strong U.S. intervention to spread democracy and free markets around the world. The "neocons" believe that the United States should exercise its military muscle to help improve the world. This view has slipped from favor since the Bush administration, but it has deep intellectual roots and remains a mainstay of Republican foreign policy.[30]

Moderates. Moderates, a once-proud Republican faction, appear to be heading toward extinction. Moderates tend to be fiscally conservative but will consider tax increases along with spending cuts and are willing to compromise with Democrats to get things done. A quarter of self-identified Republicans describe themselves as moderates and a group of House Representatives rallies as "The Tuesday Group," but they have had trouble finding traction against their more conservative colleagues. Many populist Republicans dismiss moderates as RINOs: Republicans in Name Only.

Democratic Factions

Democrats also encompass very different groups. Today, 13 percent label themselves conservative, 50 percent liberal.[31]

Progressives. Progressives occupy the left wing of the Democratic spectrum. Progressives are skeptical of military action and wary of corporate power. They are strong environmentalists, embrace universal healthcare, support immigrant rights, advocate a woman's right to reproductive freedom, often champion gun control, and are especially concerned about economic inequality. They enthusiastically

● *Every party has fringe groups. Left-wing antifa protesters smash windows and set fires amidst reports that conservative activist Milo Yiannopoulos would come to the University of California, Berkeley campus.*

backed Senator Bernie Sanders in the 2016 primaries and responded to Trump's elections by helping launch the #MeToo Movement.

The Civil Rights Caucus.   Many Democratic Party members trace their political commitment to the spirit and the memory of the civil rights movement. They advocate for groups that have historically faced discrimination, especially racial minorities, recent immigrant communities, and women. They build "rainbow" coalitions, fight against discrimination, support social programs, and join in declaring sanctuary cities. Both Barack Obama and Hillary Clinton won their primaries with muscular support from this group. While a close look at elections data suggests some divergence between black and Latino voters, this faction works hard to bridge the divides.

Organized Labor.   Unions have been a major source of campaign contributions, votes, and ground game for the Democratic Party. President Obama won 58 percent of the union vote in 2008. Unions strongly support jobs programs, infrastructure projects, and workers' rights. Labor tends to oppose globalization and free trade, and they often break with progressives on environmental issues and, often, on immigration questions. Republicans have made major inroads, especially among white working men.[32]

Centrists.   In the 1990s, some centrist Democrats embraced a *Third Way* between the farther-left progressives in the party and Republican conservatives. For example, they sought to reduce the number of abortions while legally protecting women's right to choose. They sought to balance environmental protection with "smart growth." The "third way" theme was important during the Bill Clinton years. Today, roughly one-third of self-identified Democrats call themselves centrists. They include a congressional caucus of Blue Dog Democrats—the founding members of the caucus announced they were "choked blue" by the extremes in both parties. The Blue Dogs are down to 19 members and the 2018 election did nothing to revive their prospects. Democrats picked up nine House seats in the conservative South, but all were progressive candidates. The centrists are fiscally conservative who urge the progressive caucus to tack to the center. But in a highly polarized era, this is becoming an increasingly hard sell.

We have just identified ten factions across the two parties. Why so many? Because the parties themselves are changing. Partisanship and electoral dynamics (e.g., safe districts where the only real threat to an office holder is in the primary) have moved national officials in both parties away from the moderate camps. Populists (among Republicans) and progressives (Democrats) are feeling especially emboldened. Still, both parties include multiple perspectives. Add variations across states and regions, and the perspectives multiply. The crucial point: Parties are always boisterous combinations of views. Are you unmoved by every one of these perspectives? Then you are a genuine independent!

Organizing the Parties

With so many factions, running a party is a complicated job. The work falls on three different groups: the party organization, the party in government, and the party in the electorate. As with most American institutions we have studied in this book, each of these groups has a national, a state, and a local dimension. By now you will recognize the classic feature of American political institutions: a very complicated organizational chart.

Distinguish between the groups that make up a party.

The Party Bureaucracy.   The central organization for both parties is a national committee—the Republican National Committee (RNC) and the Democratic National Committee (DNC). These committees raise funds for the party, coordinate election strategies, decide which local races to fund, organize a national convention every four years, and prepare the **party platform**—the party's statement of purpose and its position on issues. If you are a candidate for a prominent office—from senator to mayor—your success may rest in large part on your ability to persuade the **party organization** to contribute funds to your campaign.

The committees also issue and enforce the party's rules for primary elections, from the presidential level downward. Important members of the DNC and RNC include the state party chairs and vice chairs, who are the most faithful activists in each party.

Traditionally, the party's organizational leaders are anonymous insiders that oversee the primary process. Then, during the 2016 primaries, Bernie Sanders charged that the DNC was openly siding against him. A blockbuster email trove, published by WikiLeaks (the result of a Russian intelligence hack), seemed to prove him right, as high-level staffers wrote things such as "he's never going to be president." With their behind-the-scenes activity exposed, DNC Chair Debbie Wasserman Schultz and other staffers resigned in disgrace.

Party platform: The written statement of a party's core convictions and issue priorities. Generally revised every four years, in time for the national party convention.

Party organization: The portion of a political party that includes activists, state/local leaders, and affiliated professionals such as fundraisers and public relations experts.

Party in Government.   The **party in government** gets the recognition. These are the government officials in each party—elected leaders, appointed officers, individuals running for political office, and their staffs. The party in government struggles to enact the policies they support—and to stop their rivals from enacting theirs.

There is a constant struggle for influence within each party in government. Presidents usually command their own party—as Donald Trump now does the Republicans. But beware. If public approval ratings within the party fade, presidents can face challengers. For the party that does not control the White House, the contest is more wide open. Congressional leaders, governors, and presidential candidates all vie to put their own stamp on the party.

Party in government: The portion of a political party's organization that comprises elected officials and candidates for office.

Party in the Electorate.   What is left after the party organization and officeholders? We are! Each party's followers make up the **party in the electorate**.

The Big Tent.   The media generally focuses on the famous party names. Political parties thrive, however, when all their elements—the organization, the officeholders, and the public supporters—work together. That means sharing the same message, getting enthused about shared principles, and even embracing the party symbols—right down to the bumper stickers.

Party in the electorate: The largest (and least organized) component of a political party, drawn from the public at large: registered members and regular supporters.

● Sanders's supporters at the Democratic convention protested bias of the DNC. The role of the conventions is to bring the different factions together.

American federalism makes unanimity difficult. Local officials run the party in each state. Democrats in a conservative state like Alabama often have more in common with many Republicans in their own state than they do with liberal Democrats in San Francisco or New York. The same is true for the more liberal Republicans in New York or Massachusetts.

The party organizations always make tactical calculations: Do they put their resources in a few swing states that they have a good chance of winning in the next election cycle? Or should they spread their resources across many states—even long shots—with the hope of slowly building up their party in places where it does not often win?

Federalism pushes each of the two major parties to adopt a "big tent" approach: spread themselves wide, embrace followers of divergent views, and hope any resultant ideological muddle does not turn off too many party members. However, many party members reject the big tent approach and insist on sticking to their political principles—which can make for tumultuous politics within each party.

The Bottom Line

» A substantial majority of voting-age Americans identify strongly with one of the two major parties. Others declare themselves independents—their numbers have been rising.

» Our powerful sense of party identification is a result of many factors, including parental influence, political context, and even personality type.

» Party identification in turn helps shape our voting patterns, the ways we filter political information, and our bedrock ideas about politics and government.

» Each party features several ideological factions, with most politically aware Americans aligning with one or two of these.

» Each party includes three groups: the party organization, the party in government, and the party in electorate.

Party Competition . . . and Partisanship

Parties began to lose their influence over politics and government in the mid-1960s. Interest groups muscled in on party territory, mobilized voters, and shaped issue positions. Americans began to identify with movements and organizations—civil rights, environmentalism, the right to life, and libertarianism. The parties floundered. By the 1970s and 1980s, political observers were publishing books such as *The Party's Over* and *The Decline of American Political Parties.*[33] The central role of parties in organizing elections also slipped, with the rise to greater prominence of the "candidate-centered election" that we saw in Chapter 10. Political scientists warned that there was not enough partisanship in the American system—if the parties became too much alike, they could not offer the voters a meaningful choice.

Parties Rise Again

Just as political science analysts declared the death of parties, however, their revival began. During the 1980s, changing congressional rules shifted power from committee chairs back to party leadership, strengthening the parties in Congress. A huge influx of money into politics further revitalized party organizations, buoyed by the widespread adoption of PACs in the 1980s, 527 committees in the 2000s, and super PACs in the 2010s (see Chapter 10). The DNC and RNC, along with the congressional campaign organizations, became the chief recipients of campaign funds—and directed them in turn to candidates, who became more dependent on the parties as a result.

The parties also became ideologically purer. Each party was now organized around a clear set of ideas and principles. Each side could concentrate on defeating its foes rather than on negotiating the differences within its own ranks.

Competition and Partisanship Intensifies

Today the two parties are thriving, contesting very close national elections. Since 2000, the presidency has changed party hands three times, the Senate four times, and the House three times—such successive razor-close elections have not been seen since the nineteenth century. The close contests have made parties more important and partisanship more intense (see Table 11.3).[34]

In the past, partisan differences on Capitol Hill were blurred by factions within each party. Democrats were so bitterly divided over civil rights that they could barely hold a **party caucus** during the 1950s and 1960s. Today, those differences within the parties have almost disappeared. Party factions remain, as we saw earlier, but party members are far less diverse in their views. The strongest divisions are now between the two parties. By 2010, every single Republican in the U.S. Senate was to the right (in terms of voting record) of even the most conservative Senate Democrat. For the first time, ideological conflict in both the House and the Senate breaks down perfectly along party lines. This partisan divide makes the political contest—over ideas, programs, and even the meaning of America—louder and angrier than it has been in more than a century. No matter where you look, partisanship within government is rising. It is also increasing among the public.[35]

Senator Richard Burr (R-NC), seated right, and Senator Mark Warner (D-VA) promise bipartisan cooperation in the Senate Intelligence Committee.

Talking POLITICS

PARTY ICONS AND SYMBOLS (*Continued*)

Red/Blue: Widely used by the media and the public—and party insiders—to designate states that tend to vote Republican (red) or Democratic (blue), the red/blue "tradition" dates back only to 2000, when the major broadcast networks used these colors to indicate whether GOP candidate George W. Bush or Democratic nominee Al Gore won a state.

Thomas Jefferson/Andrew Jackson: These were especially iconic figures on the Democratic side. Most state Democratic parties held an annual Jefferson–Jackson Day celebration. One problem: They were slaveholders. As the progressive and civil rights groups rise in the Democratic Party, so does skepticism toward Jefferson and Jackson.

Divided government: Periods during which at least one house of Congress is controlled by a party different from the one occupying the White House.

TABLE 11.3	**Party Control of U.S. National Institutions**		
Ten changes of control in ten elections is an unusual level of turnover.			
		PARTY IN CONGRESSIONAL MAJORITY (SIZE OF MAJORITY)	
ELECTION YEAR	CONTROL OF PRESIDENCY	SENATE	HOUSE
2000	**R (Bush)**	50–50 (later +1 D)*	R (9 seats)
2002	R (Bush)	**R (2 seats)**	R (24 seats)
2004	R (Bush)	R (10 seats)	R (29 seats)
2006	R (Bush)	**D (2 seats)**	**D (37 seats)**
2008	**D (Obama)**	D (19/20 seats)	D (79 seats)
2010	D (Obama)	D (6 seats)	**R (49 seats)**
2012	D (Obama)	D (10 seats)	R (34 seats)
2014	D (Obama)	**R (8 seats)**	R (60 seats)
2016	**R (Trump)**	R (4 seats)	R (47 seats)
2018	R (Trump)	R (3 seats)**	**D (35 seats)***

*After May 2001, when Senator Jim Jeffords switched parties, Democrats controlled the Senate.

**As of November 9 with some races undecided

Bold denotes party control switched after that year's election.

It is not clear who influences whom. Are partisan officials fanning the flames of party differences among Americans? Or do activists within each party push their leaders to take stronger positions against the opposition? Or perhaps media outlets such as Fox News and MSNBC, catering respectively to conservatives and liberals, have driven us into our party corners? The answer to all three questions is probably yes.[36]

Should we worry about the rise in partisan differences? Does it make governance worse? Public opinion surveys repeatedly report popular dismay at partisan disagreement. What is it that Americans are so worried about?

First, party divisions lead to gridlock—a slowdown in government's ability to get things done. Second, bitter partisanship, as one commentary put it, "breeds bad public policy."[37] Third, a toxic partisan climate is said to drive more public officials away from government service, because less partisan members of Congress retire early in the face of incivility and relentless conflict. And fourth, constant partisan sniping leads to disenchantment among the public.

Is partisanship really generating these types of bad government outcomes? Some political scientists break with popular wisdom and argue that the fears of partisan breakdown are exaggerated: American government—with its checks, balances, and federalism—was designed to move incrementally. Delay is part of the normal process. **Divided government** (when at least one house of Congress is controlled by a party different from that occupying the White House) has always been loud, divisive—and unexpectedly productive.[38]

Moreover, partisanship has not made congressional service less attractive. Retirements, at least until 2018 (when a record-breaking number of Republicans retired), actually lagged behind the pace of the 1980s and 1990s, and the average length of House or Senate service rose slightly in the 2000s. Is partisan rancor driving the "best and brightest" out of politics? This argument is not supported by counting up years of service.

Today, more and more political scientists are reluctantly coming around to a more pessimistic view. The parties clash over almost everything and increasingly, on every level of government. Divided government increasingly yields political paralysis. The political standoff led to a government shutdown in October 2013, and an unprecedented drop in the nation's bond rating in 2011. It meant the Supreme Court had to muddle through with eight members for over a year in 2016–2017. And the dangerous result may be that gridlock in Congress drives more power to the executive branch. Each of the last three administrations infuriated opponents by expanding executive action. Even if divided government worked in the past, the partisan differences have grown too intense. Moreover, the partisan intensity drives away everyone but the shrinking party bases—as the millennial generation's experience grimly testifies.

Which side is right? For now, be aware that there are two sides to the argument about whether rising partisanship is harming American government. However, as the debates go on, social scientists—like the general public—tilt increasingly toward the pessimistic perspective.[39]

What Do YOU Think?   Should We Be Trying to Diminish Partisanship?

When Supreme Court Justice Anthony Kennedy resigned, a political war erupted. Conservatives urged President Trump to nominate a real conservative who would tip the balance of the court to the right. Liberals vowed a fierce battle to push for someone more moderate— like Justice Kennedy. What do you think of the partisanship that fueled this and many other debates?

Yes, partisanship is harmful.
It leads to paralysis and extremism. It tempts public office holders—like justices and presidents—to dangerously expand their powers. Worse, it is turning people off from politics, and that will create problems for us in the long run.

No, partisanship is healthy.
President Trump won the election promising to appoint conservative judges. The problems of partisanship originate from strong ideas and close elections. These arguments are useful and part of the democratic process. We should encourage intense views and strong arguments—that's what introduces bold new ideas. People who oppose can have an impact where it counts—at the ballot box!

Maybe.
Some partisanship is useful, but today the parties are taking disagreement too far. Every branch of government must be a mix of strong ideas and compromise.

Conclusion: A Party System Ripe for Reform?

Calls for reforming the U.S. party system are as old as the system itself. George Washington and other founders called for an end to partisan spirit before parties even arose. Yet parties swiftly became vital to American government. Now the party spirit that the founders feared may indeed have grown excessive—though political scientists still debate the matter. What should we do? Here are three of the most commonly voiced proposals:

1. Proportional Representation. As we saw earlier, America's winner-take-all system elects the highest vote recipient in each of 435 single-member House districts—and that reduces to almost zero the number of House or Senate members who are not from one of the two major parties. A proportional representation system provides minor parties with representation equivalent to their electoral support. You would soon have representatives of the environmental party, the pro-immigration party, the anti-immigration party, and the libertarians. Would this change be a good thing?

Supporters believe that moving to proportional representation would give voters more choices, possibly increasing voter turnout. It would enhance policymaking by ensuring that a wider spectrum of options is considered, better reflecting the nation's ideological and civic diversity. Many advocates predict that more women and minority-group representatives could be elected.[40]

2. Reduce the Barriers to Third-Party Competition in Elections. If not a wholesale switch to a proportional representation system, why not make it easier for minor parties to be listed on the ballot? Why not let them join major-party candidates onstage in debates? Multiple parties might reduce the level of conflict and force groups to compromise and reach out across party lines. They might bring change and fresh ideas into American politics.

On the other hand, perhaps the two parties have effectively managed the head-spinning diversity of America. Opening the floodgates to numerous minor parties might make it even more difficult to achieve consensus.

3. Reduce Partisanship in Government. Reformers promoting this approach sometimes call for a "postpartisan" American politics. Ideas include limiting negative campaigning (unfortunately, this is hard to do), reducing the role of outside advocacy groups in campaigns (attempts to do so have been struck down by the Supreme Court), and adopting public financing (implemented in a few places, but without notable reduction in partisan polarization).

So far, the attempts at unity have been swamped by disagreements. If partisan differences are to decline in intensity, the change is likely to originate in elections. Traditionally, when one party breaks through and becomes the clear majority party, it sets the political pace. So far, proponents of each party—rooted in very separate places—have been more eager to win than to compromise. Neither has shown much inclination to change their practice: condemn partisanship while fiercely embracing one party and its ideas.

Here is a slightly different way to think about parties and partisanship. Consider the rich history of party politics in America that we have traced across six party systems. Those 230 years have often seen a spirit that the Greeks called *agonistic*—a willingness to disagree with your adversaries while acknowledging their views as legitimate. This spirit means engaging wholeheartedly in a process of debate. In a democracy, successful political ideas must not just be rationally sound. We must also contest them, and we do this through party competition. Perhaps *stronger* parties, providing clear alternatives and articulating "core commitments" in a forthright way, is an antidote to our current gridlock and hyperpolarization.[41]

After all, the United States has always been a nation based on ideas—and intense disagreements about what they mean. The great debate that now occupies the parties has been going on for more than 200 years. The important goal is that as many citizens as possible all join in. The greatest dangers come not from strongly held views but from apathy among the citizens. That, in the long run, might be the greatest risk of our charged partisan times.

CHAPTER SUMMARY

● America's two-party style has endured for over 200 years, with Democrats and Republicans its main standard-bearers since 1856.

● The foundational American ideas and the organization of our elections help explain the dominance of the two parties.

● Third parties arise periodically to challenge two-party dominance, but none has ever managed to break through.

● The system of two parties—and the contest between them—is regularly rebooted through the birth of new party systems. Each change in the party system means a change in the voters making up each party and the ideas that inspire them.

● Historians count at least six party systems since the U.S. founding: the Federalist era, the Jacksonian era, Civil War and Reconstruction, the era of rising business and Progressive reform, the New Deal, and (beginning around

Check your understanding of Chapter 11.

1972) a contemporary period of roughly equal balance between the two major parties.

● A substantial majority of voting-age Americans identifies strongly with one of the two major parties. Others declare themselves independents.

● A powerful sense of party identification is a result of many factors, including parental influence, political context, and even personality type.

● Party identification in turn helps shape our voting patterns, the way we filter political information, and our bedrock ideas about politics and government.

● Each party features several ideological factions, with most politically aware Americans aligning with one or two of these.

● Republicans include religious traditionalists, Trumpists/populists, libertarians, neoconservatives, fiscal conservatives, and moderates. Democratic factions include progressives, the civil rights caucus, organized labor, and centrists like "third way" proponents and Blue Dog Democrats.

● Each major party must work to unite under one "big tent" their key figures and followers. These include the *party in government* (elected politicians, their staffs, and affiliated political professionals), the *party organization* (party chairs, the national committees, and the state party leaders), and the *party in the electorate* (the millions of people who identify with the party).

● American parties are highly decentralized: State and local party leaders largely run their own organizations, independent of national headquarters.

● Most Americans—and many social scientists—believe that partisanship is affecting the quality of American government. The intensity of the conflict, they believe, will weaken our institutions.

● Perhaps a long period of deep conflict will have this type of dangerous effect. However, strong debates are healthy in a democracy. Remember, the United States is a nation based on ideas—and intense disagreements about what they mean. The great debate that now occupies the parties has been going on for more than two hundred years. The important thing is that as many citizens as possible join the debate.

Need to review key ideas in greater depth? Click here.

KEY TERMS

Flashcard review.

Base voters, p. 335
Divided government, p. 342
Grand Old Party (GOP), p. 331
New Deal, p. 331
Nonpartisan election, p. 322
Partisanship, p. 319
Party boss, p. 329

Party caucus, p. 341
Party identification, p. 332
Party in government, p. 339
Party in the electorate, p. 339
Party machine, p. 329
Party organization, p. 339
Party platform, p. 339

Party system, p. 323
Political party, p. 320
Political socialization, p. 322
Split-ticket voter, p. 335
Straight-ticket voter, p. 334

STUDY QUESTIONS

1. What are the two main reasons American politics is usually limited to two political parties?
2. Which reason do you consider a more important explanation for the two-party system? Explain why.
3. What is proportional representation?
4. For further contemplation:
   a) Would you support introducing proportional representation in Congress?
   b) What would be the effects of this switch?
   c) Explain why these effects would help or harm American democracy.
5. Describe four functions that parties serve in the American electoral process.
6. What are the three separate parts of the party organization? Explain what each part is responsible for.

7. Choose any one-party system in American history.

    a) Describe the era.

    b) Which party, if any, dominated the era?

    c) What replaced the party system you have chosen? (If you chose the present era, do you see any signs that this system is ending?)

8. What is party identification? Name three factors that influence party identification.

9. Describe three factions in each political party today.

10. For further contemplation:

    a) What does partisanship mean?

    b) Explain why many Americans worry about partisanship.

    c) Some suggest the fears of partisanship may be exaggerated. Do you agree with this suggestion or not? Explain why.

Go to www.oup.com/us/Morone to find quizzes, flash cards, simulations, tutorials, videos, and other study tools.

12 Interest Groups

YOU HAVE BEEN HIRED as a new congressional staffer—and today is your first day at work on Capitol Hill. (Congratulations!) You arrive during a wildly busy legislative season. The office is bustling, and nobody has time to get you oriented. In fact, you barely know where you are assigned to sit . . . and now the legislative director has asked you to prepare a detailed analysis of "papa," or at least that's what you heard her say. A sympathetic colleague explains that she meant "PAHPA," which Google tells you is the Pandemic and All-Hazards Preparedness Act. Your diligent Internet search shows only that the act is due to be reauthorized next year; the bill hasn't yet been introduced. And your analysis is due by tomorrow morning.

Where to begin?

Quick, call the Congressional Research Service, the research arm of Congress. They're glad to help you out, they say—but it will take a few weeks. *Weeks?* You have hours, at best.

You feel like slinking out of the office before anyone notices and fleeing Washington altogether. Then salvation arrives on your desk, in the form of an elegantly bound, meticulously researched report on PAHPA reauthorization. All the details you need on chemical and biological threats, as well as potential flu pandemics—which House and Senate members are pushing which views, the politics involved, even the technical details—are laid out clearly. As you debate whether to cry or laugh with relief, you wonder: Who *wrote* this? You look around to thank your angel of an officemate. Not here, your colleagues smile: over on **K Street**. An interest-group lobbyist sent it directly to you. As this chapter shows, that elegant, informative, and timely report is at the heart of what interest groups do in Washington.

Interest groups have become so central to American government that it is difficult to imagine our system without them. At the same time, lobbyists and the interest groups they represent consistently receive among the lowest approval ratings of any professionals, in or out of politics: 8 percent approval, in Gallup's most recent survey.

Who are we? We are a nation of too many lobbyists and special interests. Or are interest groups also positive contributors to American democracy? Pause and consider: How many interest groups work on *your* behalf? None, you say? Or perhaps one or two advocate for causes you care about—such as

K Street: A major street in downtown Washington, DC, that is home to the headquarters for many lobbying firms and advocacy groups—and thus synonymous with interest-group lobbying.

● *Dana Loesch, spokesperson for the National Rifle Association (NRA), one of the most powerful interest groups in America.*

the environment or tax relief or the Catholic Church? In fact, like most Americans, you are represented by dozens of groups—advocates who push for clean air, safe food, affordable federal student loans, and most everything else you care about. Your college or university likely has representatives who lobby to promote the school's concerns—at the state capitol and in Congress. Your student fees or tuition may help pay for their work. Even your favorite subject, political science, has a national association based in Washington, DC, with several advocates on staff. Whether you know it or not, you are a participant in what one expert terms our "interest-group society."[1]

More than two centuries ago, James Madison warned against interest groups—he called them "factions"—in *Federalist* no. 10, the "mortal disease" that have always killed off popular government. His solution? *Increase* the number of interest groups. That way, none would become too powerful and they would have to work together to accomplish anything. Increase the number of groups? That is one piece of advice the United States has certainly taken.

Concern about **special interests** has surged periodically since Madison published his famous warning. Jacksonian Democrats, Progressives, New Dealers, 1960s radicals, Bernie Sanders supporters in 2016: Many reform groups across U.S. history expressed a fear that a few select groups (usually big business) were getting fat off the rest of us. The entire outcry obscures a basic truth: Interest groups are not just "them"—they are us.

Again: *Who are we?* The United States is a society of interest groups that are woven into the fabric of our politics. The central puzzle in this chapter is whether their influence saps American government of its vigor and fairness—as many people believe—or whether interest groups perhaps enhance American democracy.

Special interest: A pejorative term, often used to designate an interest group whose aims or issue preferences one does not share.

 # Interest-Group Roles in American Politics

What does it take to become an interest group? Dozens of lobbyists pursuing members' goals on Capitol Hill? Inside political connections galore? A million motivated supporters? It is much simpler: We define an **interest group** as *an organization whose goal is to influence government.*

Notice two important elements in that definition. The first is *organization*: A collection of wheat farmers begins to resemble an interest group only when they meet regularly to discuss and manage their concerns. The second is *influence government*: Plenty of organized groups have no contact with public officials. When those wheat growers join the American Farm Bureau Federation and press Congress for subsidies to keep crop prices stable, then they are an interest group.

At least two hundred thousand interest groups are active in American politics today. About three-quarters of those are public advocacy or citizen groups; the remainder represents private (usually corporate) interests. AARP, which represents nearly forty million Americans, is an example of a public advocacy group. It provides financial services, insurance products, discounts at hotels, and information to people aged 50 and over. It also hires lobbyists to press government officials

Interest group: An organization whose goal is to influence government.

BY THE NUMBERS
Interest Groups

Estimated number of interest groups engaged in national, state, and local U.S. politics	**More than 200,000**
Number of members claimed by National Rifle Association	**Nearly 5 million[2]**
Estimated number of professionals lobbying the U.S. government	**90,000[3]**
Number of lobbyists registered with Congress, 2017	**11,545[4]**
Estimated percentage of former members of Congress who now work as Washington lobbyists	**43**
Percentage of registered lobbyists who serve only public interest clients	**33**
Total spending reported by healthcare interest groups, 2017	**$561,231,163[5]**
Total spending on lobbying by the city of Houston, Texas, 2018	**$260,000**
Total amount spent on lobbying by the Chamber of Commerce, 1998–2018	**$1.5 billion**
Appropriation to fund all U.S. House and Senate salaries/operations, 2019	**$2.2 billion[6]**
Reported expenditures on lobbying, U.S. corporations, 2018	**$2.7 billion[7]**
Median pay, CEO for top 50 largest Washington nonprofit trade associations, 2018	**$1.3 million[8]**

As you read through these examples, is interest-group lobbying more or less pervasive in American government than you imagined? Why?

on issues of interest to seniors, such as Medicare. A much smaller membership is claimed by the Financial Services Forum, a private lobbying association that works with government on economic and banking policy: only eight giant financial-services firms, including Goldman Sachs, JP Morgan Chase, and Bank of America.

Given that interest groups seek to influence government, how do they carry out that work? Along three main paths: informing, communicating, and mobilizing.

● *Lobbyists representing Amazon, Google, Facebook, and other tech industry giants prepare for a congressional hearing on net neutrality.*

Informing Members

Interest groups such as AARP, Financial Services Forum, and Farm Bureau perform three main functions for their members. First, groups *inform members about political developments.* The American government is sprawling—House members each represent more than 750,000 people, on average. Interest groups have become a primary link between the public and its government. Groups provide access through which members can stay informed. Most of us, whether bankers or farmers or college students, do not have time to keep up with complicated government policies—even those directly affecting our career or personal interests.

Communicating Members' Views

A second function of interest groups: *communicate members' views to government officials.* Interest groups may meet directly with these officials, but often they gain access by hiring **lobbyists**. Put simply, a lobbyist is a person who engages with government officials on behalf of a particular cause or issue. Plenty of people try to influence government—like college students, who fan out across their state capital for an annual "Lobby Day," asking legislators to oppose higher student fees or appropriate more funding for science labs. Professional lobbyists, who are paid by clients to influence lawmakers, generally enjoy greater access to the halls of power than does the average American.

The AARP hires lobbyists to communicate members' views to government on a wide range of issues affecting seniors, from Social Security benefits to disability insurance.[9] In 2006, when President Bush tried to add a new prescription drug benefit to Medicare, Democrats thought they had the votes to block the legislation on Capitol Hill. Then the AARP threw its weight behind the bill—and it passed.

Lobbyist: A person who contacts government officials on behalf of a particular cause or issue.

Mobilizing the Public

Third, interest groups *mobilize the public*: They encourage groups of people to act politically. Lobbyists develop Facebook and Instagram alerts, TV ads, urgent direct-mail postcards, and tweets, all meant to provoke action.

Many Americans care deeply about abortion policy, for example. Most are not satisfied with voting every two years for candidates who share their position. Pro-life and pro-choice groups offer members frequent opportunities to *do something* on this issue of personal concern. Interest-group mobilization activity happens on many issues, from food safety to corporate espionage. Contributing funds, writing letters, organizing rallies and protests, exchanging ideas with others of similar views, and winning audiences with policymakers: Interest groups facilitate all these means of political participation.

When groups mobilize their members, they are often pushing their own specific angle, of course. Tobacco and vaping industries and interest groups like Consumer Advocates for Smoke-free Alternatives Association promote vaping as a healthier alternative to smoking. Anti-vaping activists point out that e-cigarettes, particularly those that are fruit or candy flavored, attract teens who are then more likely to start smoking real cigarettes.[10] Tobacco and vaping-company lobbyists have mounted an "education" campaign aimed at both the public and lawmakers about the benefits of vaping, compared to smoking; public health groups have pushed back.

How well represented by interest groups are your specific political concerns? If you care about something that is already on the government agenda, groups are likely promoting your view in Washington. More obscure topics—and less powerful interests—may not get a hearing. However, if you have strong opinions about a policy that seems to be overlooked, do not despair. American political history is full of "crackpots" who believed in outlandish things—ending segregation, putting airbags in every car, slashing personal income-tax rates—that eventually won out.

● *Vaping advocates appeal to both public and lawmakers.*

Indeed, through their work informing members, communicating views to political officials, and mobilizing the public, interest groups play an important (if controversial) role in democratic societies.

What Do Interest Groups Do for Democracy?

Whether our interest-group system represents all (or most) people is a heated debate, both among political scientists and across the public. Some, in a view called *pluralism*, hold that as long as the American political process is open to a wide range of different groups, then government policies should roughly correspond to public desires. No single set of interests dominates our system, pluralists insist, and all the different groups pushing and tugging allows the collective good to shine through. Some see this view as a latter-day update of James Madison's argument in *Federalist* no. 10: The answer to the problem of interest groups is—more interest groups.

Two pessimistic theories respond to the pluralists. Many Americans fear that the proliferation of interests and groups is bogging the entire system down in stalemate: Political scientists call this **hyperpluralism**. Any time a group promotes a policy change—education reform, a new highway, privatizing Social Security, or fighting climate change—there is always another group to oppose it because they do not want to pay the taxes or fear harm to the environment. Policy "gridlock" is often the result of the immense buildup of lobbyists in Washington and state capitals—and the growth of what one scholarly article recently described as "vicious, street-fighting hyperpluralism."[11]

Others worry that the playing field is tipped toward the most powerful. This **power elite theory** portrays a group of wealthy, influential Americans—mostly from the corporate sector—who mingle regularly and thus promote their shared ("class") interests in government. Most of the power elites live and work in cities other than Washington, DC, so business lobbyists do the day-to-day work of influencing government on the elite's behalf.

Power elite analysts look at the makeup of President Trump's cabinet—nearly all leaders of high-powered American companies before joining the administration—and conclude that the theory of intersecting influences is alive and well.[12] Or they note that every current U.S. Supreme Court justice attended Harvard or Yale Law School. (Ruth Bader Ginsburg graduated from Columbia Law, after first attending Harvard Law.)

Pluralism: An open, participatory style of government in which many different interests are represented.

Hyperpluralism: The collective effect of the vast number of interest groups in slowing the process of American democratic policymaking.

Power elite theory: The view that a small handful of wealthy, influential Americans exercises extensive control over government decisions.

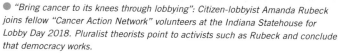

"Bring cancer to its knees through lobbying": Citizen-lobbyist Amanda Rubeck joins fellow "Cancer Action Network" volunteers at the Indiana Statehouse for Lobby Day 2018. Pluralist theorists point to activists such as Rubeck and conclude that democracy works.

Power elite theorists, in contrast, see interest groups as part of a cozy, interlocking network that perpetuates themselves in power.

One political science analysis of Washington interest-group spending came up with numbers that gave new life to the elitist perspective. Lobbying, these researchers wrote, is dominated by business: 53 percent of the lobbying organizations and 72 percent of the expenditures represent business interests. In contrast, public interest groups account for 5 percent of lobbyist spending. And groups supporting less privileged people employ just 2 percent of the lobbyists in Washington. The results, this study suggests, reflect a famous political science conclusion from 1960: This chorus "sings with a decidedly upper class accent."[13]

Which view—pluralist, hyperpluralist, or power elite—is correct? Political scientists cannot say for sure. It is difficult to tell whether big business or other powerful groups regularly win their policy aims. For every example that affirms the power of elites in the American system, another story suggests the opposite—that small business or retired people or environmental advocates prevail. Hyperpluralists note that *neither* group is getting all that much from Washington, as big bills are bottled up for years. Perhaps each theory captures part of the truth.

We return later in this chapter to the question of how well Americans are represented in general. By now you understand the central issue: the extent of interest groups' influence in American politics and policymaking.

The Bottom Line

» Interest groups, or organizations that seek to influence government, employ lobbyists to pursue benefits for their clients or membership.

» Groups serve their members by communicating political information to them, analyzing and relating members' views to policymakers, and mobilizing people to act politically.

» A long debate continues among pluralist, hyperpluralist, and power elite theorists about whether the collective public is well represented by interest groups.

🔵 Types of Interest Groups

Interest groups can do a good job promoting their members' personal interests. How well are collections of Americans—truck drivers, for example, or Latinos or CEOs or homeless people—represented in the interest-group system? What about the U.S. public as a whole? To answer such questions, we look at the various types of interest groups, and who they represent.

Political scientists divide the teeming world of interest groups into three main categories: *economic* groups, which exist primarily to serve members' financial interests; *citizen* groups, which are organized to advance the public interest (as they define it) or a particular cause; and *intergovernmental* groups, featuring one level or branch of government working to influence another.

Economic Groups

Economic groups seek financial and other resource benefits for their members; we can further classify them into three subcategories (see Table 12.1). *Business* groups promote the interests of corporations. Most large companies have their own in-house lobbyists—Google, for example, employs 13 registered lobbyists in its Washington office alone—and also hire lobbying firms with expertise in their industry to work on specific projects. Google pays more than 20 other groups to lobby on issues such as protecting high-tech patents, cybercrime, net neutrality, and immigration (Google hires engineers and other experts from all over the world).

Labor groups represent workers from nearly all large industries in the United States. The largest is the National Education Association (NEA), with 2.9 million members, most of them public school teachers. Next largest, at 1.75 million members, is the Service Employees International Union (SEIU), representing many service industries such as healthcare, hospitality (e.g., hotels and restaurants), and public employees. Both the NEA and SEIU, like other labor groups, run education and political-engagement programs. But their greatest focus is on higher pay and better benefits for their members. This effort mainly targets employers, but they also lobby government—primarily on regulations affecting working conditions, such as higher minimum wage or safety improvements.

A third class of interest groups primarily concerned with economic interests is **trade associations** and professional groups.

Trade association: An organized group representing individuals and businesses that belong to the same industry.

TABLE 12.1 Types of Interest Groups

CATEGORY	PRIMARY PURPOSE	EXAMPLE
Business groups	Economic benefits for a company or firm	Google (13 in-house lobbyists; hire 20+ additional lobby firms)
Labor groups	Economic benefits for labor union members	National Education Association (2.9 million members)
Trade or private associations	Economic benefits for businesses or professionals in a given sector	American Petroleum Institute (oil and gas company members)
Citizen groups; also called public interest groups	Organize and mobilize like-minded individuals around a shared passion, political viewpoint, or cause	Sierra Club, Christian Coalition
Intergovernmental groups	Advocate for one level or branch of government to another	National Governors Association

These organizations represent several—or even hundreds—of companies or professionals in a specific sector. The American Petroleum Institute (API) is a Washington-based trade association representing oil and gas companies: The API lobbies for tax benefits, favorable trade deals, and reducing costly regulations on their members. To join the American Architects Association, one must be—you guessed it—an architect; similarly, lawyers join the American Bar Association and doctors the American Medical Association. Although these groups are well-known, many associations are obscure: Take a guess at what PATH International represents.[14] Others may use a name that masks their purpose: A few years ago, an association called Citizens for Better Medicare spent millions of dollars lobbying for changes to Medicare, the national health insurance law. Eventually reporters noted that the "citizen" members were actually drug companies, health insurers, and large hospitals.

Citizen or Public Interest Groups

Explore PETA and other interest groups in depth.

What about interest groups not organized primarily to serve members' economic interests? Hundreds of thousands of *citizen groups*, also called *public interest groups*, exist in American politics. They cover the political spectrum, representing practically every conceivable issue and group of people, even those at society's margins. The National Alliance to End Homelessness, for example, is a well-respected Washington interest group. Single-issue organizations, such as People for the Ethical Treatment of Animals (PETA), fit into this category, as do those established to promote a political viewpoint, such as the American Conservative Union.

Material benefits: Items distributed by public interest groups as incentives to sign up or remain a member.

Expressive benefits: Values or deeply held beliefs that inspire individuals to join a public interest group.

Citizen groups do not have a built-in constituency (in contrast, most lawyers join the American Bar Association), and so must work hard to recruit and retain members. Many arise around an issue high on the policy agenda: When the Trump administration pulled out of an international "Paris Agreement" to fight climate change, for example, hundreds of citizen groups joined U.S. mayors and governors (of both parties) as well as business and university leaders to lobby under the #WeAreStillIn banner.[15] Whether long established or brand new, public interest organizations must address the problem of *free riders*. There is no evident reason that a rational person should join a citizen group, pay dues, and spend time in meetings. Others are willing to do the work and everyone gets the benefits of clean air or consumer safety – whether they pitched in or not.

Log on to the website of a public interest group—Greenpeace or the National Rifle Association (NRA) or Habitat for Humanity, which builds homes for needy people around the globe. Alongside the rhetoric about global warming or the right to bear arms, you will see major swag available. Tote bags, curated trips to Yosemite, gun-safety videos, teddy bears, travel mugs—all free or discounted for joining.

In political science terms, these **material benefits** are vital to sustaining citizen groups. Such benefits help attract new members, whose dues provide part of the funds needed to keep the lights on and lobbyists on board. Others join because of **expressive benefits:** The group expresses

● *Citizen action groups lobby across the country. Here, a New York State chapter fights proposed cuts in government services.*

values that its members share, such as social justice or individual freedom. Still other people may join an interest group for **solidarity benefits**. Think of your own experience as a Girl Scout or fraternity member: It can feel very powerful to be part of the group. Interest-based organizations tap into that feeling and engage members based on shared social fellowship.

> **Solidarity benefits:** The feeling of shared commitment and purpose experienced by individuals who join a public interest group.

Trade associations are subsidized by their sponsoring firms. Members of the American Petroleum Institute, for example, pay annual dues based on the size of their organization, starting at $1,600 and rising to tens of thousands of dollars. Citizen groups are partly supported by members, but their dues are much less, averaging around $15. Larger donations might come from foundations, government grants, or wealthy individuals, who are called "angels" in the interest-group world.

The best-known angels are big-spending donors who usually align with one or the other political party and who financially support interest groups. Charles and David Koch are prominent conservative funders. They sponsor Republican candidates for all levels of office, and run ad campaigns designed to inoculate their energy companies from political backlash. An "angel" on the other political side, George Soros, has funneled millions of dollars into liberal advocacy groups, from America Coming Together to MoveOn.org. In our highly polarized politics, angels such as Soros and the Koch brothers face bitter criticism from partisans on the other side.

Intergovernmental and Reverse Lobbying

Public officials also act like interest groups and promote their own views. Some engage in **intergovernmental lobbying**, pushing their counterparts in other branches to support their policy aims. The White House maintains a legislative affairs office to promote its views on Capitol Hill, staffed with former top House and Senate staffers. Even the president needs lobbyists!

> **Intergovernmental lobbying:** Attempts by officials in one part of the government to influence their counterparts in another branch, or at a different (state or local) level.

Presidents and Congress are also frequent targets of intergovernmental lobbying from state and local officials. The National Governors' Association (NGA) includes all fifty states' governors—conservative and liberal alike. Because states share a strong interest in federal funding for social programs (Medicare, Social Security, Medicaid), infrastructure programs (highways, bridges, and schools), and many other concerns, the NGA is in constant contact with the White House and Congress.

Government officials also lobby interest groups, termed **reverse lobbying**. Executive and legislative leaders alike regularly convene closed-door meetings of key interest groups before moving forward on a policy proposal. Hearing from all sides can generate useful information and ideas, and also may establish a compromise that wins support to push legislation through Congress.

> **Reverse lobbying:** Attempts by government officials to influence interest groups on behalf of their preferred policies.

Reverse lobbying can be controversial. President Obama used this approach to health reform when he directed advisors to meet privately with groups representing the insurance

Michael B. Hancock
@MayorHancock
Follow

Mayors are the ones implementing legal marijuana. We know what works & what doesn't. Teaming up w/ @MarkFarrellSF, @MayorJenny, @LibbySchaaf, @tedwheeler & @mayorheidi in a first-of-its-kind coalition to help cities, states & Congress prepare for legalization #MayorsMJCoalition

The Government for Responsible U.S. Cannabis Policy Coalition will push for Congress and the Administration to take action.

#MayorsMJCoalition

● *Intergovernmental lobbying in action. Urban leaders announce a cannabis coalition to defend state marijuana laws in Congress and the White House*

industry, pharmaceutical companies, hospitals, physicians, and other primary stakeholders. Republicans charged that Obama and Democratic allies had "bought off" these groups—reverse lobbying run amok.

 **The Bottom Line**

» Interest groups come in several types: Those pursuing primarily *economic* concerns include business and labor groups, along with trade and professional associations.

» *Citizen* groups include those promoting broad causes (consumer rights, civil liberties) and single-issue advocates such as PETA, as well as ideological groups.

» Governments also lobby each other, as well as engaging in "reverse lobbying"— working with interest groups to advance desired aims.

Interest Groups Past and Present

America's interest-group society has deep roots in our history. The First Amendment is among the most familiar American political creeds. Freedom of religion, speech, press, and assembly are all ingrained in the national mind. Most schoolbooks do not mention the final clause of that amendment, however: the right to "petition the government for a redress of grievances." In other words, the first amendment in the Bill of Rights guarantees the right to lobby.

After the Constitution was ratified in 1789, the first Congress gathered—and so did petitioners seeking benefits. As journalist Jeffrey Birnbaum described, "After each legislative day, hogsheads of wine and port poured freely at sumptuous meals of mutton, pork, duck, and turkey. Dinner linens are snowy white; the cutlery is burnished & English, and the check was paid by the wealthy merchants of the day."[16] These merchants were among the original economic interest groups in American politics.

As far back as the 1750s, journalists lining the halls outside Britain's House of Commons were called "lobbyists." In the early 1830s New York, the "Empire State," had the largest population and most business activity. Albany, the capital, was a constant target of privilege seekers, who became known as "lobby-agents." President Andrew Jackson, or someone on his White House staff, shortened this to "lobbyist" and hurled it pejoratively at national bankers. The name stuck, and spread to anyone seeking to influence government.

1960s Advocacy Explosion

Although economic interest groups have a long history in the United States, the number of professional lobbyists remained at a few dozen for a century, and then gradually rose to perhaps two hundred by the 1950s. Public interest groups also arose during this period, but because they were organized around a specific objective—banning liquor sales or winning benefits for Civil War veterans—the enthusiastic membership melted away once the legislative battles were done. Writing in 1963, a group of seasoned political scientists concluded "When we look at the typical lobby, we find its opportunities to maneuver are sharply limited, its staff mediocre, and its typical problem not the influencing of Congressional votes but finding the clients and contributors to enable it to survive at all."[17]

Then the old ways changed. Demonstrations for civil rights and against the Vietnam War roused massive numbers of Americans in the latter 1960s and 1970s. Spirited public engagement spread to other areas: women's rights, the environment, consumer rights, access to healthcare, protecting life, restoring the traditional family.

These movements required organizers to channel all that public passion to attain results. Enter professional public interest lobbyists. Advocacy groups such as the Sierra Club and the NAACP had existed for decades; now they expanded both their membership and political activities. As Washington churned out regulations, political and economic life became more complex—requiring a guide to explain all the intricate new rules to small businesses, farmers, local officials, and others. Enter the expert insider lobbyists. Big corporations, the target of many of these new rules (Make safer products! Increase gas mileage! Protect worker safety!), realized they needed louder voices in Washington as well. Enter the corporate lobbyists. Their demands also cascaded: Lower our taxes! Protect us from competition! Help us create jobs!

The result of all this expanded public, government, and lobbying activity: an **advocacy explosion**. After the mid-1960s, the number of professional, full-time lobbyists swelled into the thousands (see Comparing Nations 12.1). Critics who already feared interest-group power were doubly alarmed by the growth of an elaborate "politics industry" in Washington, DC.

Advocacy explosion: A vast and relatively swift increase in interest groups active in Washington, DC, beginning in the mid-1960s.

Young and Plugged In

For many Americans, the mental portrait of a lobbyist involves a potbellied, middle-aged fellow swapping yarns with his old pal the congressman. That stereotype may fit an earlier era. In recent years, lobbying has become a lot more female and a lot more youthful. Women now make up nearly half of Washington lobbyists and increasingly dominate social issue areas like healthcare and consumer rights.[18]

By the late 1990s, the *Wall Street Journal* noted that the world of lobbying was shifting to "20-somethings and 30-somethings" who had advanced degrees in policy studies and technical expertise—a far cry from the backslappers of an earlier era. After Republicans won control of Congress in 1994, the *Washington Post* profiled the new lobbying power in town, characterizing these interest-group

---

COMPARING NATIONS 12.1   **The Spread of American-Style Lobbying**

Though other countries also ramped up legislative volume and complexity during the 1960s, none has anything like America's interest-group society. Parliamentary democracies in Europe and Asia organize public and private interests into a few "peak groups," whose representatives sit with national officials to slice up the pie—deciding formally how much business and labor should get. These groups are often financed by the government and work more like collaborative partners than multiple opposing sides in a legislative scrum.

This political style leaves far fewer openings for interest groups. As a result, only the United States features lobbying *firms*, filled with hundreds of lawyer-lobbyists and their staffs. Lobbying practices overseas are beginning to resemble American styles, largely because U.S. lobbying outfits increasingly locate their offices in other national capitals. Ironically, the United States is exporting what may be the least popular feature of American government.

representatives as "young, conservative, and very plugged in." More recently, older Millennials (aged late 20s/early 30s) are lauded in headlines like "Millennials Are On the Frontlines of Political and Cultural Change in America"—and that includes lobbying.[19]

The Bottom Line

» Interest-group activity in the United States stretches back to the beginning of the republic; our modern system of thousands of active groups dates to the 1960s–1970s "advocacy explosion."

» In recent years, younger Americans and women have increasingly populated Washington's interest-group ranks.

Interest-Group Lobbyists in Action

Another Monday morning in Washington, DC: All over the capital, lobbyists are starting their workweek. Some head straight to Capitol Hill to catch up with any staffer (or, ideally, Senate or House member) they might bump into. Others gather in boardrooms for breakfast with lobbyists sharing similar interests—protecting the environment or promoting family values—to review the week's urgent legislation. Some flick through their Twitter or Instagram feeds, sifting through the latest opinions and posting a few of their own. And several dig into an ongoing research project, gulping coffee to break through the morning fog.

The Multiple Roles of Lobbyists

Lobbyists wear many different professional hats. Some interest groups are large enough to hire specialists—staff members dedicated to researching policy issues or developing media advocacy campaigns. Lobbying firms also hire outside scientists, consultants, and other experts to assist them. But most Washington representatives juggle several roles: It's all part of the job.

Researchers. The typical interest-group representative spends significant time every day studying political trends, monitoring government programs, and analyzing policy information.

As giant appropriations bills make their way through Congress and the White House each year, groups working on budget and tax policy prepare detailed briefing books for each House and Senate office.

Such research work can be very expensive. Between 2001 and 2014, the American Petroleum Institute, a trade group for the oil and natural gas industry, spent some $36 million on a single study refuting the link between benzene (a vapor produced by burning gasoline) and cancer.[20]

● Lobbyists work at all levels of government. Here, they pack a hearing in Lansing, Michigan, on the state's electricity laws.

Witnesses. Most congressional committee hearings feature testimony—on both sides—from interest groups most concerned about the issue. Executive agencies convene similar gatherings on how to implement a law, again featuring lobbyist experts. Even more lobbyists are in the audience at congressional hearings, following every utterance and move. Experienced Washington eyes can watch this crowd—a questioning look to a senator's aide here, a note passed to a witness there—and predict whether the committee will approve the legislation under discussion.

Position Takers. Washington representatives for various groups routinely issue statements outlining their organization's position on important legislation. Each January, for example, the U.S. Chamber of Commerce—which represents more than two million businesses—holds a press conference to announce the group's main goals for the coming legislative season. Even more frequently, the AFL–CIO, representing more than 60 labor unions, posts every week a "Working People Weekly List" of leading issues they are lobbying on in Washington and state capitals.

Coalition Builders. Affiliated groups often band together in **lobbying coalitions**, allowing them to share information and split the labor of contacting lawmakers. Although quantum computers—machines that rely on quantum mechanics to solve complex problems—won't exist in marketable form for years, a lobbying coalition is already seeking U.S. government support and funding. The Quantum Industry Coalition, announced in summer 2018, comprised 14 groups, including major industry players such as Microsoft, Intel, and Lockheed Martin, as well as smaller start-up companies.

Social Butterflies. There is a social side to lobbying work as well. One interest-group representative we know starts his weekdays in Longworth Cafeteria, on the House side of Capitol Hill. Strategically located at a central table, he greets the stream of members and staffers as they pick up a morning coffee or bagel, exchanging the latest political gossip.

Grassroots Campaign Builders. Join an interest group, and you will receive a steady stream of appeals to write your representative or senator: to balance the budget, to stop teen smoking, to recognize Palestine as a country, and so on. Interest groups mount these **issue campaigns** as part of their attempts to attract public support from across the country—from the "grassroots," as the term goes. Sometimes these appeals can backfire. Back in the 1980s, Texas senator Lloyd Bentsen labelled one transparent Washington-based effort to mobilize Texans as **"astroturf lobbying"**—a caustic dismissal of artificial attempts to mimic grassroots-style public concerns.

Three Types of Group Representatives

A big divide exists in Washington between lobbyists who represent economic interest groups and those who represent citizen groups or intergovernmental lobbying offices. So far, we have treated each type as similar. But their professional styles, and the demands on their time, are often different.

If you ran into Heidi Wagner on campus, you might well mistake her for a student. Wagner is quick-witted and loves indie and hip-hop music. Unlike any of your classmates, though, she is listed as one of "Big Pharma's 625 Washington Lobbyists" in a report published by the advocacy organization Public Citizen. Wagner is a highly talented healthcare lobbyist who represents a global pharmaceutical

Lobbying coalition: A collection of lobbyists working on related topics or a specific legislative proposal.

Issue campaign: A concerted effort by interest groups to arouse popular support or opposition for a policy issue.

Astroturf lobbying: An attempt by interest groups to simulate widespread public engagement on an issue.

WASHINGTON LOBBYING

Drop: Set of brochures and position papers left behind by a lobbyist after visiting a legislator's office.

Fly-in: A series of Washington meetings, usually on Capitol Hill, organized by lobbyists for their out-of-town clients.

Bird-dogging: Posing tough questions to an elected official, often at a public event. Advocacy groups often engage in this tactic to advance their cause and win attention.

Gucci Gulch: Areas outside the House Ways and Means and Senate Finance committees, which deal with tax and revenue issues; the hallways are lined with high-priced lobbyists wearing expensive shoes— sometimes by Gucci.

Rainmakers: Lobbyists adept at raising funds for politicians or causes; when they collect large sums, they are said to be "making it rain."

Talking POLITICS

WASHINGTON LOBBYING

(*Continued*)

Third House: In Washington, as well as many state capitals, lobbyists are viewed (not necessarily positively) as a co-equal "third branch" of government, given their expertise and access.

firm. Wagner exemplifies one type of private interest-group actor, the single-firm lobbyist. Though she collaborates with many other healthcare lobbyists, Wagner ultimately works for—and is paid by—one employer.

Now meet Tom Dobbins, lobbyist for the American Composites Manufacturers Association. He represents dozens of firms that make composites: everything from high-tech fiberglass boat hulls to carbon-reinforced materials that support our skyscrapers. Dobbins is a trade association lobbyist, working for a collection of firms in the same type of business. Because tobacco farmers or trial lawyers or composites manufacturers share common interests in Washington, it makes sense to have one or a few lobbyists represent their concerns.

After working for a single firm or trade association for a few years, many lobbyists go into business for themselves, representing a range of clients (usually in one issue area, though some high-profile lobbyists work across fields). These independent lobbyists are known in Washington-speak as "hired guns," though most of them hate that term. Some have dozens or even hundreds of clients: Over the last decade, a former chemical engineer turned independent lobbyist named Stu Van Scoyoc reported serving 321 different clients.

Independent lobbyists, unless their firm goes out of business or their client stream dries up, have a guaranteed income stream—sometimes a very large one. For example, Tom Donohue, the president, CEO, and lobbying face of the U.S. Chamber of Commerce, earns more than $6 million a year.[21]

Nonprofits Don't Lobby?

For many citizen groups, the very word "lobbying" has a dirty connotation. Few public interest leaders describe themselves as active lobbyists. Moreover, one study found, "most nonprofits don't know how to lobby and, worse, think that it entails cutting shady deals with sleazy characters."

Yet to successfully advocate for a group's interests, it is all but essential in today's American political system to make one's case to lawmakers in state capitals or in Washington. As the same study concluded, "to make the changes they want to see in the world, nonprofits must learn to lobby . . . and they may even learn to love it."[22] Whether cleaning up a local river, providing social services to immigrants, seeking English-only laws, or planning a march on the state capitol or White House, to succeed, citizen-group advocates must include lobbying as part of their plan.

● Lobbyists' offices on K Street. Although "K Street" remains shorthand for Washington lobbying, in reality, most interest groups in the capital locate their offices elsewhere.

The Bottom Line

» Lobbyists perform a wide range of roles, from researchers to social butterflies.

» Private sector lobbyists can represent a single firm or a trade association, or set up in business for themselves as independent lobbyists.

» Citizens' groups are often loath to engage in "lobbying," but they must to succeed.

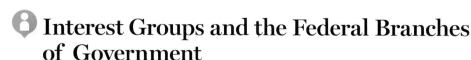 Interest Groups and the Federal Branches of Government

The traditional model of Washington power brokers depicted a closed process dominated by **iron triangles**—tight, durable links among powerful interest groups, congressional committee chairs and their staff, and administrative officials.

Consider one example: *farm subsidies*. For decades, many American farmers—growing crops from corn to tobacco—have received "price supports," or subsidies worth millions of dollars, from the U.S. government. Critics charge that this practice is a huge giveaway of taxpayer dollars. Agricultural experts explain that weather and other uncertainties endemic to farming make a system of crop insurance and production management necessary. During the 2018–2019 farm bill reauthorization, farm subsidies were targeted for cuts. Legislators in both parties pointed to the need to rein in spending, but when the smoke cleared, the price supports remained. However, the bill remained stalled over work requirements for food stamp recipients.[23]

In traditional accounts, a classic iron triangle explains the staying power of farm subsidies (Figure 12.1). Congressional members and staffers on the House and Senate agriculture committees have close relationships with lobbyists for farm groups, thanks in part to the many farmers in those members' home states. The lobbyists encourage their Congressional friends to appropriate funds for the Department of Agriculture. Farm lobbyists establish connections with Department of Agriculture officials well aware of their power to help deliver the congressional funding their programs require. If these officials balked at implementing subsidies, they might find their congressional appropriation cut the following year—so they keep the programs humming along. The combination of executive branch, legislative branch, and lobbyists—the iron triangle—is all but unstoppable.

Farm policy, given its long-established players, may be the last vestige of an old system. Iron triangles proliferated around Washington into the 1960s, given

Iron triangle: The cozy relationship in one issue area between interest-group lobbyists, congressional staffers, and executive branch agencies.

Discover how to lobby Congress on a specific issue.

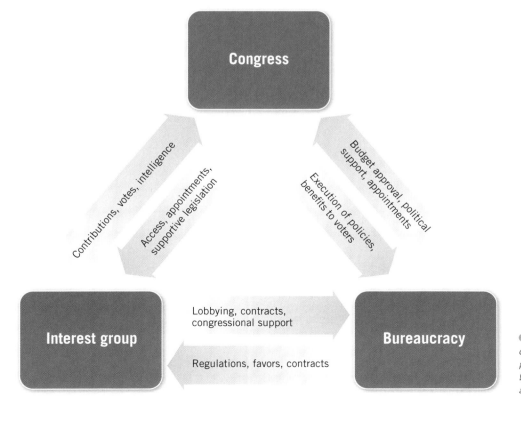

● **Figure 12.1** *Iron triangle: The classic image of interest-group power features a close relationship between Congress, interest groups, and federal government bureaucracy.*

the relatively closed environment of national policymaking. The subsequent "advocacy explosion" initially brought more lobbyists into closer contact with Capitol Hill staffers, which ensured the triangles' survival for a while.

Rise of the Issue Network

Over the past 30 years, iron triangles have largely given way to a very different image of looser, more open **issue networks**. A flood of new lobbyists representing more and more positions, in addition to the growing numbers of congressional staffers, have broken apart the cozy triangles. Political scientist Mark Peterson charts a "radical change" beginning in the 1980s, as triangles dissolved into a "far more diverse and open system" that featured "looser, less stable, less predictable, and more diverse patterns of interaction and decision."[24]

One feature that helped to strengthen iron triangles and also undergirds issue networks: Washington actors often serve sequentially as policymakers, lobbyists, and formal party officials—a phenomenon termed the **revolving door**. Research shows that more than half of current lobbyists passed through the "door"—they formerly worked in Congress or the White House.[25]

Figure 12.2 illustrates an example of an issue network focused on telecommunications policy. Notice how much more complicated than a simple triangle this network is. Welcome to the life of a Washington lobbyist today! To negotiate these networks—to faithfully represent members and attract new clients—modern interest-group representatives cannot count on a few reliable contacts with the chair of a congressional committee and a bureaucrat or two. Instead, they must cultivate connections across Capitol Hill and in multiple executive departments and agencies. They also may have to master the byzantine ways of the judicial branch.

Interest Groups and the Courts

Iron triangles and issue networks portray interest groups engaging with the two elective branches, Congress and the presidency. What about the courts, which—as you will see in Chapter 16—have a major role in federal and state policymaking? By law and

Issue network: Shifting alliances of public and private interest groups, lawmakers, and other stakeholders all focused on the same policy area.

Revolving door: The tendency of many Washington lobbyists to move from government work (e.g., as a congressional or White House advisor) to lobbying and back again.

Related Industries/Interests
AARP; Assn. of National Advertisers; American Public Power Assn.; colleges/universities; media companies such as Tribune, NPR, CC Media Holdings; manufacturers such as General Motors, John Deere; U.S. Olympic Committee (broadcast rights; telecomm for athletes); American Library Assn.; related industry groups such as Compact Particle Acceleration Corp.

Social Welfare
Privacy groups, such as Free Press, Public Knowledge; consumer-advocacy groups, such as Electronic Frontier Foundation; unions, such as Communications Workers of America; orgs. to expand Net access, such as National Disability Rights Network; Center for Long-Term Cybersecurity; Free Press Action Fund.

Telecommunications
US telecomm cos., such as Comcast, DISH, Verizon, AT&T (also organized in groups such as 21st Century Privacy Coalition); global telecomm cos., such as Deutsche Telekom; satellite cos., such as Eutelsat; trade associations, such as CTIA, Telecommunications Industry Assn., Wireless Infrastructure Assn., and A to Z Communications Coalition; small-teleco associations, such as INCOMPAS; executive branch (U.S. Trade Assn., FCC, FTC, White House); Congress (commerce committees); states/cities; Chamber of Commerce; lobbying and law firms large & small.

Free Market/Conservative
Conservative think tanks, such as Cato Institute, Heritage Foundation, AEI; free-market groups such as National Taxpayers Union, 60 Plus Association; American Conservative Union.

High-tech industry
NCTA (Internet & TV Assn.); US tech cos., such as Apple, Amazon, Facebook, Alphabet/Google; global tech cos., such as Garmin; tech trade associations, such as TechNet, Software & Information Industry Assn. (SIIA), Internet Assn., Financial Innovation Now; tech philanthropies, such as Gates Foundation, Chan-Zuckerberg Initiative.

● **Figure 12.2** *Today, scholars generally see a more extensive network of actors influencing policy than that pictured by the classic iron triangle. Here, the issue network that influences telecommunications policy. (Authors' compilation based on Berry and Wilcox)*

custom, interest groups have almost no access to Supreme Court justices and very little connection to other federal (or senior state) judges. But interest groups still manage to weigh in on judicial decision making, even without seeing judges in person to make their case. They do so in three main ways.

Lobbying on Judicial Confirmations. One way to shape court decisions is to influence the central players—to help determine who gets *appointed* as Supreme Court or federal judges. Each federal judge is approved by the Senate. That process used to be routine—current Justice Ruth Bader Ginsburg, like most of her predecessors, was confirmed by a large Senate margin, 96-3. Today, however, every Supreme Court nomination immediately prompts a multimillion-dollar confirmation fight. Interest groups spend heavily on public campaigns to influence the presidents who choose judges and the senators who confirm—or block—a president's choice.

● Supreme Court nominee Neil Gorsuch stands for a break during his Senate confirmation hearings, held in a room filled with lobbyists for interest groups—many of which spent millions of dollars seeking to influence the confirmation battle.

Filing Amicus Curiae ("Friend of Court") Briefs. Groups interested in a pending case are permitted to—and sometimes invited by a court to—write up legal memos, or "briefs," arguing their position on the case. Major cases attract dozens of such documents: In 2018, when the Supreme Court reviewed partisan "gerrymandering" (covered in Chapter 10), hundreds of groups and individuals filed more than 50 different amicus curiae briefs.

Sponsoring Litigation. It can be very expensive to take a case to court. Researching the relevant issues, paying the lawyers, and pursuing litigation through multiple appeals can cost millions of dollars. Interest groups often take up a legal cause, contributing both money and expertise. When the Supreme Court agreed to review establishment clause rules about what counts as state sponsorship of religion—for example, whether government funds can go to Catholic schools or whether a state courthouse can post the Ten Commandments—interest groups such as the American Civil Liberties Union (liberal) and the Federalist Society (conservative) provided substantial expertise and financing.

The Bottom Line

» Lobbyists working in specific areas sometimes still form "iron triangles" with congressional staff and executive branch officials.

» More fluid "issue networks" featuring lobbyists as central players increasingly characterize today's complex policymaking environment.

» Successful federal lobbyists master political information gathering and analysis, engage in political campaigns, and form close ties with one of the two major parties.

» Interest groups also lobby the judicial branch by funding confirmation battles, filing amicus curiae briefs, and financing litigation.

👤 Interest Groups and Power

Should Americans worry that interest groups are intimately involved in the details of policymaking, writing bills, and shaping legislative outcomes? Senator Henry F. Ashurst, an Arizona Democrat, once admitted bluntly: "When I have to choose between voting for the people or the special interests, I always stick to the special interests. They remember. The people forget."[26] If members of Congress are voting with or otherwise directly influenced by lobbyists, this unelected set of central actors deserves our close scrutiny—and perhaps alarm.

Political scientists lack hard evidence about interest groups' power: Did this bill pass because lobbyists said it should, or did it pass regardless of all their politicking? Instead, we fall back on typical measures of what matters in national politics: *numbers* and *money*. Washington insiders gauge the status of a White House agency or a special congressional committee based partly on how many staff it has. If interest groups are spending a lot to influence lawmakers, their financial input may be a clue to the return their clients are getting on their investment.

How many lobbyists work in Washington? Around 11,500 professionals registered as congressional lobbyists in 2018, but that number represents a fraction of the total. Lobbyists can avoid registering if they spend less than 20 percent of their time on "lobbying activities," a loosely defined term. Although legal penalties apply to those failing to disclose lobbying work, not one criminal case has been filed under this law. One interest-groups expert offers a figure closer to 100,000 based on all the grassroots advocates, political consultants, trade association representatives, and others who can claim to be under the 20 percent threshold.[27]

Tens of thousands of lobbyists, all chasing members of Congress and their staffs, as well as White House and executive branch officials—many commentators see these numbers as decisive evidence of interest-group influence. Interest groups are increasingly active in state and local government as well. Companies that used to focus on Washington are diversifying: Google had lobbyists in just two states in 2006; by 2015 they had expanded to 30 states, and through lobbying coalitions like the Internet Association now reach all 50 states.[28]

Ultimately, if you measure the influence of interest groups by simple numbers, then this sector is certainly powerful. Do the numbers suggest an ability to win policy goals? Not necessarily. Political science research suggests that, as lobbying networks become denser, interest groups are better able to block undesirable legislation, but not to advance new aims.[29] That "veto power" underscores how central interest-group lobbyists have become to national, state, and local government. But the widespread notion that lobbyists are writing most bills and arranging laws' passage: No research substantiates that claim.

Interest Group Spending

Interest groups big and small, from Wall Street financial interests to California almond growers, spend an estimated eight billion dollars each year attempting to influence Washington policymaking. This does not include spending on political campaigns, an issue discussed later in this chapter.

This $8 billion figure is inexact. Official Senate and House records indicate that *registered* lobbyists reported spending nearly $3.37 billion on lobbying activities in 2017 (see Figure 12.3). Because many of those seeking to influence Congress never bother to register, analysts estimate that total spending is about 2.5 times the reported amount.[30]

How do interest groups invest in campaigns?

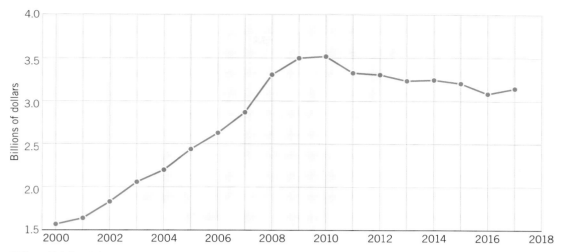

● **Figure 12.3** *Trends in spending by registered lobbyists, 2000–2017, in billions of dollars. (Center for Responsive Politics)*

Clients of private groups and members of public groups together provide those billions of dollars, which are spent on lobbyists' salaries, research costs (remember that neatly bound report!), the expense of running a Washington office, travel, and so forth. Table 12.2 lists the top-spending interest-group clients for 2017. Of the various sectors represented (healthcare, oil/gas, etc.), most of these big spenders are corporate interests. Does that confirm the "power elite" view? Or is it merely a waste of money, because business appears to lose plenty of policy battles?

When an issue of importance to a group or industry arises in Washington, affected groups tend to boost their spending. The e-commerce giant Amazon was already devoting millions to its lobbying efforts when, in 2017–2018, the Trump administration took up tax rates for online retail and U.S. Postal Service shipment costs. In response, Amazon doubled its in-house lobbying team (to 28) in one year and quadrupled lobbying spending, compared to three years earlier. Other "e-tail" firms also boosted their lobbying activities.

Some analysts look at annual growth in lobbying spending and conclude that it proves interest groups' extensive political influence. But the truth is more complicated. We might ask, for example, what Amazon and other e-commerce companies got for all their spending. An internet-sales tax that Amazon and fellow online retailers strenuously opposed was, at the last minute, pulled out of the 2018 spending bill over President Trump's objections. The battle continues—as does the lobbying swirl.[31]

Our conclusion about all that money: It probably did not influence many votes. On a high-profile issue such as Internet taxation, most members of Congress have very strong views. Seasoned politicos can predict most of the votes. What are the lobbyists spending funds on, then? They are supporting the members who agree with them, or trying to "soften up" the few members who might be persuadable on this topic. If members need facts for their speeches, lobbyists are there to provide background. That is why, in our story at the beginning of the chapter, that invaluable report landed on your desk.[32]

A clearer sign of lobbying heft may be an adjustment in a policy or specific bill. Energy companies, for example, successfully pushed to include an "offset program" in climate change legislation that allowed them to invest in projects to remove

Watch President Trump criticize Amazon in 2018— helping spur the e-commerce giant to double its lobbying force.

TABLE 12.2 Biggest-Spending Lobbying Clients, 2017

LOBBYING CLIENT	TOTAL AMOUNT SPENT
U.S. Chamber of Commerce	$82,190,000
National Assn. of Realtors	$54,530,861
Business Roundtable	$27,380,000
Pharmaceutical Research & Manufacturers of America	$25,847,500
Blue Cross/Blue Shield	$24,330,306
American Hospital Assn.	$22,094,214
American Medical Assn.	$21,535,000
Alphabet Inc.	$18,150,000
AT&T Inc.	$16,780,000
Boeing Co.	$16,740,000
Open Society Policy Center	$16,110,000
DowDuPont	$15,877,520
National Assn. of Broadcasters	$15,460,000
Comcast Corp.	$15,310,000
Lockheed Martin	$14,464,290
Amazon.com	$13,000,000
Southern Co.	$12,970,000
National Retail Federation	$12,890,000
NCTA the Internet & Television Assn.	$12,790,000
Oracle Corp.	$12,385,000
Source: Center for Responsive Politics	

carbon dioxide from the atmosphere if they were unable to meet reduced emissions targets. This technical policy change underlines an important truth: The more obscure the provision, the better the chances of winning it. The less the public is aware of a topic, the more room Congress has to deliver favors.

Regulating Interest Groups

All this talk of influence leads naturally to questions about how interest groups are regulated. What are lobbyists forbidden to do in pursuit of their policy goals? For a long time, the answer was "not much." Until 1946, there were no real limits on lobbying action, though out-and-out bribery—clearly exchanging votes for money or other favors—was prohibited. That year, Congress passed the **Federal Regulation of Lobbying Act**, which required lobbyists seeking influence in the House or Senate to:

- *Register with Congress.* An office was opened in the Capitol—today registration is online—for lobbyists to fill out forms (first annually, and eventually every three months) listing all clients on whose behalf they sought to influence Congress.

Federal Regulation of Lobbying Act: The initial U.S. statute spelling out requirements on lobbyists active in Congress, which was passed in 1946.

Amazon's Lobbying Interests

HOW DO INTERESTS EXPAND AS COMPANIES GROW?

Many companies, especially in the technology/e-commerce area, announce as they grow that they will remain out of politics—Amazon included. Yet, like most of its fellow tech companies and online retailers, Amazon lobbies on an increasing number of issues, as shown in the graph.

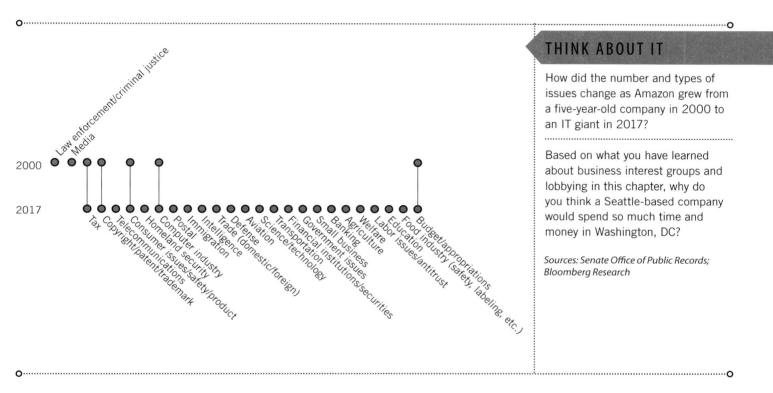

THINK ABOUT IT

How did the number and types of issues change as Amazon grew from a five-year-old company in 2000 to an IT giant in 2017?

Based on what you have learned about business interest groups and lobbying in this chapter, why do you think a Seattle-based company would spend so much time and money in Washington, DC?

Sources: Senate Office of Public Records; Bloomberg Research

369

- *Report the amount and sources of income derived from lobbying Congress.* This line-by-line list is supposed to include all of a lobbyist's clients and how much each paid, but lobbyists may exploit the rules to keep some clients out of sight.

Notice the absence of any restrictions on lobbying activity. In theory, a lobbyist could accept a large sum from one client and pass those funds on to a member of Congress as a "gift." The 1946 law merely required interest-group representatives to identify both themselves and the source/amounts of their payments for lobbying.

Tighter restrictions on gift giving were imposed in 1995, following public clamor about presents, meals, and travel "junkets" for members of Congress paid for by interest groups. The House banned virtually all gifts. On the Senate side, inexpensive items such as T-shirts and other trinkets were still allowed—up to a value of $50 per year for any senator from a given lobbyist. This **gift ban** law was designed to make it more difficult to "buy" favors from a member of Congress. Members and lobbyists insisted that gifts were simply tokens of friendship and esteem; critics thought otherwise.

Gift ban: A regulation that eliminates (or sharply reduces the permitted dollar amount of) gifts from interest groups to lawmakers.

Loopholes in the 1995 law swiftly appeared. The House prohibition on lobbyists buying meals for congressional members or their staff was clarified to cover only meals consumed while sitting down, presumably at a restaurant. "Finger food," such as hors d'oeuvres eaten standing up at parties, was a legitimate expense—enabling lobbyists to continue sponsoring fundraising events for congressional members and their staff—who always knew which events had the best food. Lobbyists also could pay for a meal with lawmakers as long as the member or staffer was a "personal friend." Imagine all the new friendships born after that ruling!

Stories like the "finger food exception" inspired a fresh round of popular outrage, sparking Congress to revisit interest-group lobbying reform. In 2007, a new Democratic majority closed many of the loopholes in the gift ban and barred senators from lobbying their former colleagues for two years after leaving the Senate. Yet today, despite continued public criticism, "junkets" and other excesses remain: Interest groups continue to sponsor plentiful trips for members of Congress or state legislators. Despite President Trump's vow to "drain the swamp"—to reduce lobbyist influence in Washington—restrictions have loosened: For example, a rule banning administration officials from lobbying their former agencies for two years was cut back to one year.[33]

 **The Bottom Line**

» Because of the difficulty of measuring interest-group influence in government, researchers turn to metrics such as the number of lobbyists and how much they spend on lobbying.

» Beginning in the mid-1960s, an advocacy explosion saw lobbyist numbers climb dramatically. Resources devoted to lobbying also rose sharply.

» Despite their extensive presence and billions of dollars in spending, lobbyists rarely change congressional minds on high-profile votes; their role is to support members who are already on the same side. Special favors are easier to win on obscure or highly technical topics.

» Regulations on interest-group activity are relatively limited in the United States. They have periodically been tightened, but extensive loopholes remain.

Are Interest Groups Bad or Good for America?

Americans remain deeply cynical about the work of interest groups in our national polity, even as we write checks to groups involved in the causes we care about or show up for "Lobby Day" at our state capitol. What is wrong with interest-group activity in American government? Throughout this chapter we have explored the question of influence—whether lobbyists have too much say in national politics. Here we summarize four primary concerns, raised at various points in this chapter.

Four Concerns About Interest Groups

1. Corruption.   The close connections between lobbyists and federal lawmakers arouse concerns about the unfair advantage enjoyed by lobbyist insiders over ordinary citizens. As we saw earlier, interest groups devote more than $8 billion annually to influence policymaking and help direct hundreds of millions more to campaigns for Congress and the presidency. Does this add up to corruption at the core of American government?

Paul Manafort would fit right into a nineteenth-century lobbyist's portrait: well connected, high living...and thoroughly corrupt. Manafort was a Washington pioneer, combining lobbying, public relations, and campaign consultancy under one roof. He represented arms dealers and foreign dictators including the Philippines' Ferdinand Marcos and Jonas Savimbi of Angola, collecting millions in unreported fees. Manafort's makeover of Ukrainian strongman Victor Yanukovych earned Manafort "walk-in" privileges after Yanukovych won Ukraine's presidency in 2010. Yanukovych was removed from power in 2014 and is currently wanted in Ukraine for "high treason." Manafort never bothered to register as a foreign lobbyist, and was indicted by the U.S. Justice Department in 2018 for that crime and for illegally hiding money overseas.[34]

In Washington, with an alert news media always ready to leap on a scandal, only one lobbyist in recent years has been charged with anything similar: Jack Abramoff, a high-living lobbyist connected to senior Congressional and White House leaders who was sentenced to jail in 2006.

2. Division and Hyperpluralism.   Critics also worry about interest groups' divisive influence. Former Harvard president Derek Bok wrote that "America no longer seems diverse; it seems divided into innumerable special interests . . . gray power, gay power, red power, black power; the sun belt and the frost belt; environmentalists and hard hats; industrial groups, professional groups, educational groups: all more conscious of their rights, all more aware of their claims on the rest of society."[35]

Bok's view taps into an old debate about whether individual preferences add up to the "public good." Does any collective interest transcend the selfish demands of specific interest groups? Alexis de Tocqueville praised Americans' tendency to form voluntary associations to

● *Lobbyist and Donald Trump presidential campaign manager Paul Manafort was sentenced to jail in 2019.*

achieve political ends. Modern public interest groups, however, seem like pale shadows of the lively civic bodies Tocqueville applauded.

A related concern, introduced earlier in this chapter, is "hyperpluralism": the fear that the crush of lobbyists hinders decisive political action. On the 2016 presidential campaign trail, former Florida governor and presidential son and brother Jeb Bush blasted the "swarms of lobbyists" holding sway in Washington—until reporters noted that he had once registered as a lobbyist himself.[36]

3. Accountability. America's leaders are accountable to the people, thanks to our frequent national elections. Interest-group lobbyists face no such public accountability, despite their significant roles in influencing debates and policymakers. No lobbyist is elected by the people, and few legal controls regulate their activities. Moreover, negative issue campaigns by interest groups appear to enhance cynicism among the public about "bureaucracy," corroding the government's accountability.[37]

4. Restricted Access. Interest groups are an increasingly important way of bringing public concerns before our national officials. Yet not all segments of the population are equally represented: Some political science research suggests that barriers to representation have become higher as interest-group mobilization has expanded in recent years.[38] Unequal access is the result. Political sociologists Theda Skocpol and Vanessa Williamson summarized the concern: "Over the past few decades, attentive and well-resourced business lobbying organizations [have] gained enormous influence over what issues came up for debate, and they were able to block or insert critical provisions in legislation making its way through Congress and in rules taking shape within administrative agencies."[39]

● Do interest groups representing large corporations have greater access—and therefore power—than other groups? This protester thinks so.

Though blatantly corrupt acts such as Manafort's may be rare, on this view the real scandal is not in lavish trips or fancy meals. Instead, the U.S. political system may face a more fundamental problem: The proliferation of interest groups and lobbyist bias tilts democracy toward the wealthy and the powerful.

These four arguments constitute a sobering set of critiques, fueling the pressure for reform that has occupied Congress for years, and that led many Americans to respond positively to Donald Trump's call to "drain the swamp" and ban lobbyist influence.

Four Defenses of Interest Groups

There is another side of the story—one not often told in a contemporary political discourse that portrays interest groups as agents of corruption and inequality—that may moderate this negative view. Early in this chapter we looked at how interest groups may be useful to group members; let us turn now to the possible benefits that interest groups provide for all of us.

1. More Democratic Representation. Pluralists hold that the proliferation of interest groups, and their links with public officials, furthers the democratization of American politics. The expanded number of groups translates into better representation of a wide range of interests. Not *all* interests, however: People seeking assistance from government typically must possess some combination of resources, organization, and a favorable political context.[40] Even so, advocates' ability to negotiate the system—and connect directly to lawmakers and party leaders—means that a great many Americans and their interests are well represented today.

2. Communication and Information. Conveying citizen views to officials and providing the population with information about government activities are essential features of any democratic polity. Such two-way communication is facilitated by constant exchanges between interest groups and the members or private clients they represent. Thanks to technological advances in communication, as well as innovative tactics developed in part by interest groups, any interested citizen has vast quantities of information available with only a few mouse clicks.

Likewise, Capitol Hill and the executive branch are inundated with lobbyists describing public (and corporate) views—permitting lawmakers to analyze more information and hear more points of view before reaching a decision. Additional information and new perspectives can inform both public and official preferences, thus enhancing the democratic deliberative process.

3. Mobilizing and Organizing the Public. America's mass political parties originally came into existence to mobilize the vast number of voters entering the system after the expansion of suffrage. Parties still play an important mobilizing role, but their work is supplemented in essential ways by interest groups. Issue advocacy, along with other group activity to mobilize public concern, appears to spur at least modest increases in voter turnout. It also may encourage more participation in other respects, as citizens are inspired to write members of Congress and otherwise get involved. In our social-media age, interest groups help connect the public with issues that arouse their passions and register their views.[41]

4. Stability. The flip side of hyperpluralism—in which the thicket of lobbyists slows down our separated-powers system of policymaking—is *stability*. One virtue of the U.S. system, in some people's eyes, is its remarkable longevity. Some 230 years after the Constitution was ratified, we see relatively few changes in our basic structures of national government.

James Madison's fundamental concern about factional influence led him to recommend the proliferation of interests, preventing any handful of powers from gaining enduring control over public policy. The legacy of that view exists today: Interest-group activity is so extensive, featuring strong positions on every side of most issues, that the policymaking system inches along very slowly. It is difficult to mount sweeping new policy programs, or even pass major legislation, given the army of lobbyists and formal party leaders seeking to rewrite, add amendments to, or kill outright most bills.

In summary, the interest-group story is a paradoxical one. One principal result of all the heaving and pushing, effort and striving, by thousands of lobbyists in Washington may be greater stability in policy formation and governance. Whether the four benefits described here outweigh the dangers we described earlier is the ultimate puzzle of interest groups and democracy.

 **The Bottom Line**

» Critics of interest groups in American governance variously claim that they are corrupt, too numerous, lack accountability, and/or enjoy access to lawmakers that ordinary citizens usually can't achieve.

» Supporters of interest groups respond that they enhance democratic representation, help communicate popular views to public officials (and in turn report on government actions to their members), mobilize people for action, or that their sheer numbers enhance the stability and predictability of American government.

Conclusion: Interest-Group Influence Revisited

To help spur your thinking on interest-group influence, we end with a final question: How might we better tap the potential benefits of lobbying activity while minimizing the dangers? If national policymakers work to keep the political process open and transparent, their efforts can enable more groups to gain access—and to help ensure something like a level playing field for all of us.

Could interest groups themselves enhance their contributions to democratic governance? Aware that *information* is at the heart of lobbying activities, two political scientists suggested a central clearinghouse that collects details on the flood of interest-group activity—allowing the public to access more of the information that interest groups provide to Congress and other policymakers.[42]

Public officials also can strive to ensure that the least well-off sectors of our society—typically those poorly represented by interest groups—receive enhanced representation. As you have seen throughout this book, some Americans are uneasy about a government that stitches together a patchwork safety net of welfare benefits, healthcare, and other essential services for people down on their luck. The powerful and the wealthy have plenty of voices looking after their concerns in Washington. A fair system can ensure that groups supporting the least powerful will get the sanction and resources needed to make our interest-group society one that embraces every member.

CHAPTER SUMMARY

● Interest-group lobbying has long been a vital feature of U.S. government and politics. Lobbyists are deeply engaged across our policymaking system, and groups have sprung up to represent virtually every professional, personal, and identity-based interest, providing their members with information about federal policies and conveying those members' concerns to Washington. Yet Americans hold lobbyists in very low regard.

● Public anxiety centers on interest groups' reputed power to affect policymaking. Groups spend billions of dollars each year to advance their views, and lobbyists swarm over Washington (and state capitals) in vast numbers. It is not clear, however, what all this activity adds up to.

● Although critics insist that lobbyist influence in shaping government outcomes is extensive, political science research has not turned up definitive evidence in support. And the proliferation of groups on all sides of most issues tends to mean that even if one sector (e.g., business) gains the upper hand in Washington, the pendulum eventually swings to the other side, and other sectors (e.g., public interest groups) win a string of policy victories.

● A long history of interest-group involvement in American national and state politics was punctuated by an "advocacy explosion" that began in the 1960s. In recent years, interest-group representatives have been getting younger—and many more women have entered the lobbying profession.

Check your
understanding
of Chapter 12.

Today, lobbyists perform a wide range of roles, from testifying on policy issues before Congress to acting as full-service "concierges" on behalf of their private or public interest clients. Advocacy or membership groups have a harder time retaining members and must appeal to a mix of benefits: material, solidarity, and expressive.

Need to review key ideas in greater depth? Click here.

● Interest groups are active in all three branches of government; in each, they both seek and provide information—the currency of politics. They also work on (and help finance) political campaigns and are closely intertwined with the leadership of both the Republican and the Democratic parties.

● The central presence of interest groups in the halls of government has led—across U.S. history—to calls for reform, including banning lobbyists altogether. At least partly balancing the dangers that interest groups pose are a set of benefits they provide, including boosting democratic representation and contributing to the long-lived stability of American politics and governance.

KEY TERMS

Flashcard review.

Advocacy explosion, p. 359
Astroturf lobbying, p. 361
Expressive benefits, p. 356
Federal Regulation of Lobbying
    Act, p. 368
Gift ban, p. 370
Hyperpluralism, p. 353
Interest group, p. 350

Intergovernmental
    lobbying, p. 357
Iron triangle, p. 363
Issue campaign, p. 361
Issue network, p. 364
K Street, p. 349
Lobbying coalition, p. 361
Lobbyist, p. 352

Material benefits, p. 356
Pluralism, p. 353
Power elite theory, p. 353
Reverse lobbying, p. 357
Revolving door, p. 364
Solidarity benefits, p. 357
Special interest, p. 350
Trade association, p. 355

STUDY QUESTIONS

1. What is an interest group, and what are their main roles in the American political system? What are the different types of interest groups? How did the groups (and the lobbyists they employ) proliferate so widely in American national politics?

2. Name the three main theories about the effects of interest groups (pluralism, for example, is one). Describe each.

3. After reading the chapter, which of the theories in Question 2 seems to you most accurate? Justify your answer.

4. Describe the traditional iron triangle. Explain the issue network that has now replaced it in large part.

5. What is the free rider problem? Name three types of benefits that interest groups provide to overcome the free rider problem.

6. Describe three ways that interest groups try to affect Supreme Court decisions.

7. One of the most important elements to lobbying success is gathering information. Explain how and why.

8. Describe four primary concerns about interest groups (summarized at the end of the chapter).

9. Describe four defenses of interest groups. Are there any you would add, based on your reading?

10. Researchers have not made much headway in specifying interest-group influence. Can you imagine any better ways to accurately measure lobbyists' influence on American policymaking?

11. Think of the interest group that represents you the best. Is it a group that works on a specific issue, such as gun control or lower taxes? Or is it one representing a specific "identity" group, as in women or Latinos or LGBTQ people? Or is it a geographically based organization, concerned

with the interests of Texans or New Englanders or mountain states residents? Or, perhaps, is the group organized around a partisan or ideological perspective? Why is that group your preferred representative?

12. What do you think the effects might be of the trend toward younger and more women lobbyists? Can you imagine any changes in how lobbyists do their work or the effect of interest groups on the policy system?

Go to www.oup.com/us/Morone to find quizzes, flash cards, simulations, tutorials, videos, and other study tools.

13 Congress

HIGH DRAMA ON THE U.S. SENATE FLOOR:

July 28, 2017. After a raucous all-night debate, John McCain—military hero, Republican Party presidential nominee in 2012, recently diagnosed with terminal brain cancer—strode into the chamber. His was the decisive vote on a bill to repeal the Affordable Care Act, a President Trump campaign promise and GOP priority. Two Republicans had already voted "no" on repeal, joining all 48 Democratic senators. McCain paused as the chamber held its breath; instead of merely speaking his vote, he extended his arm . . . and turned his thumb down, signifying a "nay" vote.

The bill had failed. The ACA would continue to provide affordable health insurance to more than 20 million Americans. And the U.S. Senate once again proved to be an institution where deliberation and compromise weigh at least as heavily as pure partisan or ideological loyalty.

The ACA story began nearly a decade earlier, in the House of Representatives. Over four months, three different House committees produced two different bills. The Speaker of the House at the time, Nancy Pelosi (D-CA)—the first female Speaker in American history—worked to combine elements of both bills into a single Act. Pelosi and her top lieutenants met with different groups in the House: conservative Blue Dogs, the liberal Progressive Caucus, the Congressional Black Caucus, the Hispanic Caucus, abortion opponents, and others. Each wanted to add to or subtract from the bill. After bargaining for seven feverish months, Pelosi brought the legislation to the House floor; after a fierce all-day debate (with sparks flying about whether abortion would be covered), the legislation squeaked through by a vote of 220 to 215 as the clock moved toward midnight.

In the Senate (with its one hundred members), two more committees produced two *more* bills—making five different versions, each one topping a thousand pages. The Senate majority leader, Harry Reid (D-NV), then hammered out a compromise Senate-style: Reid met not with separate groups but one by one with individual senators, searching for the magic sixty votes. After eight months of negotiating and compromise, an exhausted Senate voted yes at 7:15 a.m. on December 24, 2009. Now, the House and Senate had to negotiate the differences between their bills: Add

● *U.S. Senate Majority Leader Mitch McConnell (R-KY), flanked by fellow Senate leaders, speaks to reporters. Bitter party polarization in recent years, resulting in legislative inaction, has led scholars to term the modern Congress a "broken branch" of government.*

379

Assess current debates on healthcare.

three more months of horse trading. Throughout the process, only one Republican voted for the legislation. When the ACA finally passed, Republicans immediately introduced a bill to repeal the new law, and scheduled dozens more repeal votes over the next several years.[1]

Many analysts now dub Congress the "broken branch" of American government. They criticize the House and the Senate for their archaic rules and dysfunctional gridlock. "The Senate has literally forgotten how to function," sighed Senator Angus King (Independent-ME), in 2018. "We're like a high school team that hasn't won a game in five years."[2]

As the McCain drama testifies, even after the 2016 election—with Republicans controlling both chambers of Congress and the presidency—the Capitol Hill stalemate on most major issues continued. Congress did pass some 200 bills and resolutions in 2017–2018, including a sweeping tax cut. But commentators on left and right alike emphasize what *hasn't* been accomplished, from ACA repeal to major infrastructure improvements to President Trump's much-advertised wall along the United States/ Mexican border.

Who are we? A vibrant people who are suspicious of government. Congress builds that suspicion right into its governing process: It is very difficult to introduce important changes. This raises a key question about Congress today: Is it indeed "the broken branch of government"? Or does it reflect the spirit of the American nation by slowing down policymaking and ensuring that deliberation and stability reign? Keep these two different views in mind as we explore Congress, our national legislature.

🔵 Introducing Congress

The Constitution places Congress at the center of American government. The document's first and longest article provides a detailed accounting of legislative organization and authority (Table 13.1).

This is a formidable set of powers. For most of American history, Congress ruled. After the Civil War, President Andrew Johnson brooded in the White House while Congress passed bill after bill redefining the nation, including the postwar constitutional amendments ending slavery and guaranteeing voting rights to black Americans—which President Johnson ineffectually opposed. A half-century later, when Senator Warren Harding won the presidential election of 1920, one of his old Senate buddies told him to "sign whatever bills the Senate sends you . . . and don't send bills for the Senate to pass."[3]

By the middle of the twentieth century, however, Congress had become increasingly deferential to the White House, especially in foreign affairs. Today, the nation looks first to the president to manage the economy, deploy troops, address crises, and pursue policy objectives, although Congress retains its powers to introduce, debate, and pass all legislation. We call the Affordable Care Act "Obamacare," and credit President Trump for the 2017–2018 tax cut, even though Congress worked out most of the details on each.

Congress

Percentage of Americans who approved of Congress, fall 2018 polls	**19**[4]
Percentage who approved of Congress, fall 1998	**55**
Percentage of House members re-elected in 2016	**97**
Percentage re-elected in 2018	**93**
Percentage of Senators re-elected in 2016	**88**
Number of bills considered by 115th Congress, 2017–2018 (as of November 12, 2018)	**10,689**
Number considered by 95th Congress, 1977–1978	**18,045**[5]
Number of African Americans in the Senate, 1950	**0**
Number of African Americans in the Senate, 2019	**3**
Number of women in the House of Representatives, 1949	**7**
Percentage of those women who were Republicans, 1949	**57**
Number of women in the House of Representatives, 2019 (as of November 12, 2018)	**102**
Percentage of those women who are Republicans, 2019 (as of November 12, 2018)	**16**
U.S. rank out of 193 countries, for percentage of women in national legislatures (as of June 2018)	**102**[6]
Annual salary for Member of Congress	**$174,000**
House Speaker's annual salary	**$223,500**

Members of Congress collectively look more like the nation they represent, churn out thousands of bills each year, and are paid far less while in office than leaders in other fields (business, nonprofits, academia). Yet public approval ratings for Congress have never been lower. How to explain Americans' disdain for Congress?

TABLE 13.1 **Constitutional Powers of Congress**

From Article 1, Section 8 (unless otherwise noted).*
Financial. Power to raise revenue through taxes and borrowing, pay national debts, "provide for the common defense and general welfare," and regulate trade and commerce among the American states and with other countries.
Legal. Power to establish U.S. citizenship laws, regulate bankruptcy laws, issue U.S. money, punish counterfeiters, establish a patent system ("to promote the progress of science and useful arts"), fix national weights/measures standards, and enact laws subject to presidential approval. Impeach presidents and federal judges.
Institutional. Power to organize the judicial and executive branches, establish a postal system (Article 2, Sec. 2), set up and control the national capital (Washington, DC, since 1797), admit new states, and exercise control over U.S. territories (Article 3, Sec. 3). Alter or amend the time, place, and manner of states' election laws related to congressional elections (Article I, Sec. 4).
National defense. Power to declare war; regulate rules for prisoners of war; and raise and fund the U.S. Army, Navy, and other defense forces.
Additional congressional powers are provided by constitutional amendment. For example, the Thirteenth (1865), Fourteenth (1868), and Fifteenth (1870) Amendments authorize Congress to enforce African Americans' civil rights, as you read in Chapter 6.

Still, Congress remains near the center of American government. Presidents may command more public attention, but they need cooperation from the House and Senate to advance their policies. We judge presidents in part on whether their programs win approval from Congress, as you will see in Chapter 14. Moreover, Congress's importance extends far beyond the vital responsibility of lawmaking. As much as any other actor or institution in U.S. government, it is Congress that answers the question, *Who are we?*

Two Chambers, Different Styles

Congress reflects two faces of the American people in its basic makeup. Like most other national legislatures, Congress is bicameral, comprising two "houses" or chambers. The larger *House of Representatives* includes 435 members, divided among the states based on population size, along with six nonvoting delegates from Washington, DC, Puerto Rico, Guam, and other U.S. territories. All House members serve two-year terms, and each represents a district of approximately 730,000 people.

The House is organized around a relatively clear set of rules and procedures. The majority party wields centralized control through a powerful leadership team. In the **116th Congress** (2019–2020), Democrats won the majority; this positioned Nancy Pelosi, the Democratic leader to become Speaker of the House and to control which issues reach the **floor**, and frequently to get them passed.

The Senate is made up of one hundred members, two from each U.S. state, each elected for a six-year term. The Democrats lost the Senate in 2014; Republicans retained a majority after 2018. Back in the nineteenth century, an old truism (attributed to Mark Twain) declared "every senator a little king."[7] To this day, each Senator possesses a remarkable degree of autonomy, especially compared to the average House member. Any senator—even the most junior—is able to halt the entire body's consideration of a bill merely by placing a **legislative hold** on it.

For example, the Senate must vote to approve every U.S. ambassador nominated by the president. Normally, this is a routine formality. Cassandra Butts, an experienced government worker, was proposed in 2014 as new ambassador to the Bahamas. She excitedly awaited confirmation. Months, then years, passed: First Senator

116th Congress: The Congress elected in November 2018, meeting in 2019–2020. The first Congress met in 1789–1790. Each Congress is elected for two years and numbered consecutively.

Floor: The full chamber, either in the House of Representatives or the Senate. A bill "goes to the floor" for the final debate and vote, usually after approval by one or more committees.

Legislative hold: An informal way for a senator to object to a bill or other measure reaching the Senate floor. The action effectively halts Senate proceedings on that issue, sometimes for weeks or longer.

Ted Cruz (R-Texas) put a hold on all State Department nominations because he was upset about a U.S. treaty with Iran. Then Senator Tom Cotton (R-Arkansas) put holds on Butts as well as two other proposed ambassadors. What troubled Senator Cotton? A complaint about a Secret Service leak of private information, unrelated to Butts or the Bahamas. Cotton wanted the administration's attention, so he did what any senator may: bring the body to a halt with a one-man veto.[8]

Popular American culture, in films such as *Mr. Smith Goes to Washington* featuring a noble **filibuster**—"democracy's finest show"—celebrates the lone senator standing up bravely for justice. But much of the time filibusters or holds involve narrowly focused issues, such as Senator Cotton's. Actual public filibusters—taking the floor and speaking for hours or even days on end—have all but disappeared from the Senate. Instead, Senators quietly issue a legislative hold merely by informing the leadership that they object to a particular bill's moving forward, which has the same effect: bringing Senate consideration of that issue to a halt.

The two congressional chambers present a familiar contrast in the United States. Americans, as we saw in Chapter 2, embrace direct democracy—and the centralized House can move swiftly on national legislative priorities. Americans also fear government power and seek stability: Enter the independent senators, slowing legislation down with filibusters and holds. Legend has it that Thomas Jefferson, who had been in Paris during the Constitutional Convention, asked George Washington why the Constitution established two chambers in Congress. "Why," responded Washington, "do you pour your tea into the saucer?" "To cool it," replied Jefferson. "Just so," returned Washington, "we pour House legislation into the senatorial saucer to cool it." Whether the exchange actually took place, it neatly captures the traditional contrast between House and Senate.[9]

An essential question for Americans today: Is the Senate too good at the task of cooling legislation? Cooperation between the two parties, essential for getting around the filibuster or hold, has diminished—the tone in the once courtly Senate now increasingly resembles the partisan House. Across the United States, schoolteachers, police officers, state health officials, and everyone else dependent on federal funding had to wait for agonizing months in 2018 while the Senate and House bickered over a federal budget, missing deadline after deadline. Imagine trying to plan for a new school year or organize a Mars launch with no idea what your budget will be. Do we need a more nimble and responsive government in the twenty-first century? Or is the senatorial function of slowing things down more important than ever?[10]

Filibuster: Rule unique to the U.S. Senate that allows any senator to hold the floor indefinitely and thereby delay a vote on a bill to which he or she objects. Ended only when sixty senators vote for cloture.

The House and Senate Each Has Unique Roles

The Constitution also grants each branch a measure of unique authority. All budget measures must originate in the House (because until 1913 it was the only chamber elected directly by the public; now both are). The House holds the power to impeach public officials—including the president—for "high crimes and misdemeanors." After the House impeaches (or indicts) an officeholder, the Senate holds a trial and decides whether to remove him or her. The Senate also has exclusive authority over two important matters. The president negotiates

● *Swearing in a new Congress.*

See two filibuster versions: Senator Smith's noble moment, in the movie *Mr. Smith Goes to Washington*, and a real-life example from then-Senator Rand Paul.

treaties with other countries, but the Senate must approve them by two-thirds majority. Sixty-seven votes is a very high bar in today's politics, and, as we will see in Chapter 14, presidents have found some creative ways around it.

The Senate also has sole power to review presidential appointments—the Constitution calls it "advice and consent." Each nominee for the Supreme Court, for example, must win confirmation by the Senate. Here is another place where some political scientists see a broken branch: Although in the minority, Democrats delayed or blocked more than 100 of President Trump's nominees for judiciary and executive-branch positions in 2017 and 2018—responding, in part, to Senate Republicans blocking 73 Obama judicial nominees in 2016 alone. Again the question: A broken branch? Or a healthy limit on presidential power?

What Do YOU Think?   Senate Filibusters and Legislative Holds

President Donald Trump is the latest in a long line of critics to call on the Senate to end its distinctive filibuster rule.[11] Should senators be allowed to hold up legislative initiatives indefinitely, or at least until their opposition can round up sixty votes to stop their stalling action? What do you think?

Yes.	No.	Not sure.
Filibusters and holds ensure independence and protect minority rights. They are also a time-honored tradition. Slowing government down remains a good idea.	The sixty-vote rule makes a mockery of simple majority rule and causes gridlock, slowing policymaking to a crawl. It is time to rewrite Senate rules and end the filibuster and legislative hold.	You may want to ponder this question as you read the rest of the chapter; we return to this theme in a few pages.

The Bottom Line

» Congressional powers, as granted under the Constitution, are extensive and very clearly defined.

» America's Congress is bicameral: The House has 435 members (plus six nonvoting members) who are elected every two years. The one hundred senators serve six-year terms.

» House and Senate work together in many areas, most notably passing legislation; each chamber has distinctive powers, however, such as the Senate's sole authority to approve presidential appointments and treaties.

» The two chambers of Congress reflect different national priorities. Populists appreciate the responsive House; advocates of stability embrace the more deliberate Senate, where rules like the filibuster and hold make it more difficult to pass legislation.

» Less legislation and more partisanship have Congress watchers debating: Is this a broken branch of government?

Congressional Representation

Members of Congress represent their constituents in multiple ways. They must live in the same state or district—which is known as *geographic* representation. They may share views about political issues—or *substantive* representation. Some also resemble the people they represent in terms of race, ethnicity, gender, age, national origin, and so on, termed *descriptive* representation.[12]

Access an interactive map of African Americans in the House and Senate throughout U.S. history.

Does Congress Reflect America?

A half-century ago, every senator was white. Only two African American members sat in the House of Representatives. Today, Congress more closely resembles the country it represents—in some respects.

As Figure 13.1 shows, the Congressional Black Caucus (one of several **congressional caucus** groups) has grown to include over fifty members (including two nonvoting representatives from Washington, DC and the Virgin Islands). Among House Democrats, nearly one in four representatives is black. Latinos have had a slower time breaking into Congress, but their recent rise in numbers is also striking. Forty members are Hispanic. More than a dozen members are Asian and four are Native American.

Despite the growth, Congress has a long way to go before it reflects America. Overall, only 22 percent of the House and just 9 percent of the Senate are members of racial minorities—compared to 36.7 percent of the population.

Jeannette Rankin (R-MT) was the first woman elected to the House, in 1916. She fought for women's suffrage, Prohibition, and workers' rights during her first term. Many years later, in 1941, Rankin returned to the House for a second term (by then, there were six other female members). As a confirmed pacifist, she was

Congressional caucus: A group of House or Senate members who convene regularly to discuss common interests; they may share political outlook, race, gender, or geography.

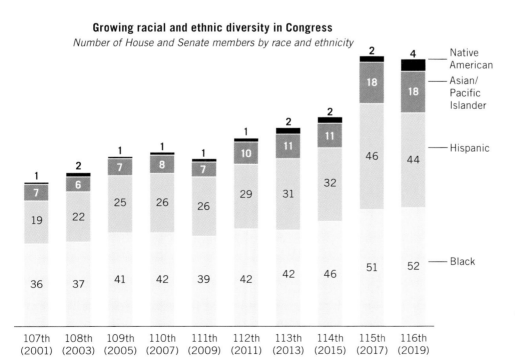

Growing racial and ethnic diversity in Congress
Number of House and Senate members by race and ethnicity

● **Figure 13.1** *Growing racial and ethnic diversity in Congress. (Pew Research Center; authors' compliation)*

What Do YOU Think?

Who Really Represents You?

Which do you consider more important—descriptive or substantive representation?	**Descriptive representation.** Race, ethnicity, gender, sexual orientation, and/or class are crucial to political representation. Someone cannot really speak for me if he or she has not experienced the world as I have.	**Substantive representation.** It doesn't matter if someone looks like me as long as he or she effectively represents my views. Someone who does not share my political outlook is not going to represent me well.	**Not sure.** There may be no right answer to this question—political theorists have long argued about which to emphasize. Think about how you might combine these two positions.

one of fifty members to vote against U.S. entry into World War I, and the only member to vote against declaring war on Japan after the attack on Pearl Harbor in 1941.

Among historically underrepresented groups, the number of women in Congress has risen most rapidly. The House had twenty female members in 1966, thirty by the late 1980s, and over one hundred in 2019. Over 23 percent of the House, compared to 52 percent of the nation, is female. In the Senate in 2019, there were a record twenty-four women—nearly a quarter of the chamber. The United States ranks below the top 90 among legislatures around the globe on the percentage of women in the larger national chamber (our House). Some nations *require* a certain percentage of women. That is easier to do in a parliamentary system, where the parties choose the candidates, than in the United States, where candidates declare themselves and run in primary elections for the nominations.

● *Representative Jeannette Rankin (R-MT), the first woman in Congress. She was first elected in 1916—before the Nineteenth Amendment legally enfranchised women in all states.*

These numbers are a far cry from parity. On the other hand, we might marvel at how things are changing. When your parents were in school, female, black, or Latino members of Congress were a rarity—and their political science textbooks did not even mention the fact. Today, the numbers are at an all-time high.

The religious makeup of Congress has changed dramatically over the last half-century. Until recently, it was overwhelmingly Protestant. Today, Catholics make up nearly a third of Congress (reflecting their proportion of the population); Jews make up 5 percent of the House and 8 percent of the Senate (more than two times the percentage in the population); there are seventeen Mormons, four Muslims, two Buddhists, one Hindu, and one atheist in Congress today.

How important is descriptive representation? If you are a conservative, evangelical woman who deeply believes in the right to life, you may not be thrilled to hear that Nancy Pelosi (a liberal who strongly supports abortion rights) is the most powerful woman in the House of Representatives. She represents you descriptively (you are both women) but not substantively (you share few of the same ideas or policy preferences). You might say that Speaker Pelosi does not represent your interests at all.

Trustees and Delegates

Each member of Congress—in fact, every representative in any organization—faces the same conundrum: Do what you think is right? Or do what your constituents want?

Do the Right Thing.   One view holds that representatives owe us their best judgment. They sit in the House or Senate, with considerably more information than their constituents. Just like your doctor or your lawyer, your House and Senate members' job is to pursue what is best for you. And if you disagree with the result, you can always vote for their opponent in the next election. This perspective, as we saw in Chapter 3, is known as the *trustee* view of representation.

On a lot of issues, members of Congress must rely on their expertise and judgment, or that of their staff. Constituents often have no strongly held views. Most people do not care whether their senators voted to approve the president's choice for deputy undersecretary of commerce, or whether the technical corrections bill updating an obscure public law passes.

Do What the People Want.   Another view holds that true representation involves House or Senate members faithfully following popular preferences. A lot of choices before Congress have to do with basic values. You do not need more information to know how you feel about the right to own guns, or whether healthcare is a universal human right. A legislator, according to this view, should take voting instructions directly from his or her constituents. This is the *delegate* view of representation.

Political scientists recognize that the rules help tilt individuals one way or another (here is the institutional perspective again).[13] When the constitutional framers required members of the House to run every two years, they favored the delegate view: Pay close attention to the people or you will be out of a job. Each senator has six years between elections; the rules practically instruct them to be trustees, to act as they think best.

What ultimately makes for good representation? The theoretical answer is simple: *Representatives effectively pursue their constituents' substantive interests.* The trick comes in figuring out what those interests are and promoting them through the complicated legislative process. Eventually, at election time, the people judge whether their members of Congress effectively pursued their interests. To political scientists, this is how a well-operating representative system works.

This theorizing barely registers with most members of the House and Senate. They come to Congress with a clear perspective that informs nearly all of their important votes. They rarely spend time pondering what stance to take on gun rights or on national health insurance. The answers are part of their basic philosophy, forged years before they arrived in Congress. Most politicians do not pander—at least not on large, visible issues. They know what they believe, and despite popular wisdom, they rarely say merely what they think their audience wants to hear.[14] However, a great outcry from the constituency over an issue will often moderate a member's strongly held views. It is often safer to do nothing and blame the other members for the outcome.

What Do YOU Think?   Two Views of Representation

The trustee and delegate views are each legitimate ways to represent people. Do what you think best—or do as your constituents direct you. On every issue, each representative must decide how to weigh these two key factors. Ask yourself how you would act as a member of the Senate or House.

Delegate.
I take my voting instructions directly from my constituents. I wouldn't be properly representing them if I didn't follow their wishes.

Trustee.
I am more inclined to do what I believe to be the right thing on behalf of my constituents. If they disagree, I will have to persuade them in the next election campaign.

Not sure.
Perhaps the answer depends on the issue. If you take this middle ground, think about the types of issues that would make you a delegate or a trustee.

The Bottom Line

» Members of the House and Senate represent Americans in multiple ways. These include:

1. *Geographic representation*: Constitutional election rules say members must live in the state or district they represent.
2. *Descriptive representation*: Does the assembly resemble the people?
3. *Substantive representation*: Do members of Congress effectively pursue constituent interests?

» Along with these different styles of representation, members can act as delegates or trustees. Representatives can faithfully follow what the people want or do as their political experience, instincts, and core principles dictate.

Getting to Congress—and Staying There

How do members of Congress spend their days? From occasional glimpses of C-SPAN, you might imagine Congress as a sustained feast of debates, but members of the House and the Senate spend relatively little time on the floor. Table 13.2 displays the typical workweek of a member of the House, taken from a survey. Not a lot of time left for quietly contemplating the major issues of the day, is there? One classic political science study suggests that the "electoral connection" occupies members of Congress more than anything else.[15]

The Permanent Campaign

Congressional members spend extensive time on the campaign trail. House members face the voters every two years—more frequently than other national legislatures. Even senators, with a more comfortable six years between races,

TABLE 13.2 Average Division of Time of a U.S. House Member

Meeting with staff (mostly in Washington)	19%
Meeting with constituents (mostly in district)	19%
Ceremonial events (in district; some in Washington)	13%
Fundraising calls/meetings	11%
Committee meetings (hearings, member meetings)	8%
Floor action (votes, debates, morning business)	7%
Office work (email, reading, legislative drafting)	6%
Informal talks (with colleagues, lobbyists, media)	6%
Caucus meetings (all-party or subgroup gatherings)	5%
Other (miscellaneous)	5%
Source: Congressional Management Foundation	

must keep their campaign operation, especially fundraising, humming along. In Table 13.2, notice that the members spend as much time raising money as they do on committee meetings or floor action. Does this constant pressure to attract donations and remind voters of their virtues discourage members of Congress, or potential candidates, from running? As we saw in Chapter 10, most representatives stay in office a long time. And when a seat in either chamber opens because of retirement or death, a lengthy list of office seekers from both parties is usually ready to run.

The Constitutional Convention grappled with a central question of democracy: Could the people be trusted to vote directly for members of Congress (as we discussed in Chapter 3)? Recall the original compromise: House members were elected directly, while senators were to be insulated from the whims of public opinion and chosen by state legislatures. In some western states, the people voted and the legislature ratified the choice; but in most states, the public did not vote for senators until 1913 when the Seventeenth Amendment was ratified. Did the state legislatures pick more elevated senators than the people did (as the constitutional framers expected)? Not necessarily. In the very first congressional elections, for example, Virginia's legislature passed over James Madison for the Senate; the people of his district had better sense and elected him to the House, where he immediately pushed through the Bill of Rights.

Home Style: Back in the District

New members of Congress—and most long-serving representatives and senators, for that matter—spend a lot of time back in their district or state. Often they are literally returning home to families who have decided to stay in Seattle or St. Louis or Scranton, rather than making the move to Washington. Today, as many as 100 House members, most of them conservative Republicans, proudly refuse to settle into a Washington residence and sleep on a cot in their office. Most members leave Capitol Hill on Thursday evenings and only return on Monday evening or even Tuesday morning, unless House or Senate votes are scheduled on a Friday or Monday.

Back home in their constituency, members are kept hopping. District staff line up events for them to attend every morning, afternoon, and evening. Members spend this time meeting with constituents, giving talks about Washington issues (and hearing plenty of advice about how to do things better), cutting ribbons on new ballparks or office buildings or schools, visiting with local party leaders and elected officials, and raising funds for their next election. And even when Senators and House members are in Washington, many hold Facebook or Skype town meetings with constituents—reflecting the high premium members place on staying in touch.

A Government of Strangers

In the past—before jets, advanced technology, and modern campaigns—members of Congress lived in Washington. Senators or representatives worked together during the day and socialized during evenings and weekends. In fact, a bar for members, called the Hole in the Wall, was located between the House and Senate chambers.

Today, most legislators are not in Washington long enough to get to know one another. They dash in, spend three days packed with congressional business, and dash home. This schedule makes it more difficult for Congress to get things done, because it is now a collection of strangers. The tortured legislative process—described at this chapter's start—is further complicated by the lack of personal relations.

Why do members insist on rushing home each week, and scheduling virtual meetings from Washington with the folks back home? Because it helps them win re-election—an ever-present concern. In fact, when political scientists build models to explain and predict congressional behavior, they often assume that re-election is a member's primary or even only goal.[16] We consider this an exaggeration. Many members are genuinely pursuing their political ideals. But there is no denying that the pressure for re-election significantly shapes congressional behavior.

 **The Bottom Line**

» Members of Congress are always running for office. Fundraising takes up a particularly large amount of time and attention.

» Members pay special attention to their home style: Most go back to their constituency every week—compressing normal congressional business into the period from Tuesday through Thursday.

» Congress has become an institution of strangers who do not know one another. Most members focus intensely much of the time on re-election.

Congress at Work

When members of the House and Senate do gather in Washington, they have a staggering to-do list: managing the nation's legislative business, investigating executive branch activities, staging public hearings about everything from auto safety to U.S. aid to Zimbabwe. And, of course, raising money for re-election. How—and where—do they accomplish all that work?

The City on the Hill

The huge Capitol building is perched on an actual hill; its majestic marble dome dominates the Washington skyline. Traditionally, no building in the District of Columbia except the Washington Monument may be taller. The Capitol building is also the heart of a small city within a city. Six grand office buildings house the members and their staff; the newer buildings feature offices the size of basketball courts. Three ornate structures house the Library of Congress, which has mushroomed from Thomas Jefferson's personal book collection into the largest library in the world.

This City on the Hill also includes a dozen restaurants, two gyms, a chapel, a bank, a post office, and a warren of "hideaways": small unmarked offices for the personal use of senior members. Add another half-dozen staff "annex" buildings, several elegant townhouses rented most nights for fundraising events, a small high school for congressional pages—young men and women who scurry around the House and Senate floor running errands for members—and even a subway, to shuttle the members back and forth between their office buildings and the congressional chambers.

Inhabitants of this "city" include the 541 members of Congress, along with more than 22,000 staff members, who range from well-paid senior policy experts to summer interns; the Capitol police force, 250 members strong; and the U.S. poet laureate, a Congress-appointed position whose occupant receives a beautiful office in the Library of Congress. And do not forget the thousands of lobbyists. It all adds up to a very busy place.

How much are members paid? As of 2019, the rate is $174,000 for House and Senate members, a figure frozen since 2009.[17] That is three times what the average American makes (see Table 13.3). Leaders earn a slightly higher salary; the House Speaker is the highest paid at $223,500. Constituents frequently complain that congressional salaries are too high. Note, however, that comparable leaders in other areas—from business managers to academic deans—are paid much more. If your primary professional aim is to make money, running for Congress is not a good bet.

Congressional staff members are a major presence in this company town. Until 1893, most members of the House had no staff support; beginning in 1891, senators were allotted one part-time staffer, paid six dollars per day. As Congress became more professional, it saw a steady increase in assistants, researchers, committee experts, legal counsel, and the like. By the 1990s, House and Senate staff leveled off at around 27,000; the number has since declined to about 22,000 today.

Each House and Senate member has a chief of staff, a legislative director, a press secretary, a scheduler, and a host of other office staffers, including legislative correspondents who handle the huge volume of constituent requests that pour into each member's office. Many college graduates take entry-level positions (like legislative correspondents), because there are many opportunities to move up quickly. We have both worked on Capitol Hill—it is an exciting job for the men and women, many of them right out of college, who dominate staff positions.

In addition, each summer, thousands of college students descend on Capitol Hill to work, usually without pay. Interning is not glamorous activity, but congressional

CAPITOL HILL BUZZWORDS

Christmas tree: A bill that is packed with "riders," or benefits for constituents: a dam in one district, a new government building in another, and a science lab or a football stadium at a state university.

Medagogue: A member who sounds loud, insistent alarms about any proposed legislative changes to the Medicare program, which provides health insurance for people over age 65. Traditionally applied to Democrats, although the Republicans have recently learned to Medagogue as well as their rivals.

Must-pass (n): A bill considered so vital that Congress *has* to enact it, such as legislation funding the annual operations of the U.S. government. Because of this necessity, must-pass items are loaded up with "rider" items (see "Christmas tree").

Senate Swamp (n): Area across from the Capitol's Senate steps where one or more Senators gather for media appearances on hot topics of the day; in recent years, issue-based rallies are held in the "Swamp" as well.

TABLE 13.3 Annual Average Salaries by Profession

CEO, top 500 company	$13.9 million
NBA player	$7.1 million
NFL player	$2.7 million
U.S. president	$400,000
Surgeon	$251,890
Senior U.S. executive branch official (capped since 2010)	$199,700
Member of Congress	**$174,000**
Lawyer	$147,950
Personal financial advisor	$124,140
Pharmacist	$121,710
Aerospace engineer	$115,300
Political scientist	$98,620
Web developer	$74,110
Elementary school teacher	$60,830
Plumber	$57,070
Child/family social worker	$48,430

Sources: Sporting Intelligence; Bureau of Labor Statistics (March 2018 report); U.S. Office of Personnel Management

offices hum with excitement and offer a ringside seat on one of the most fascinating institutions in the world.

New staffers arriving on the Hill soon hear the most common question: not *"What do you do?"* but *"Who are you with?"* Working for a congressional leader, a committee chair, or a nationally known figure can catapult even new staffers up the Washington pecking order. Many staff members feel a rush when an important bill they helped craft passes or when they prepare their boss to succeed on a major news show—or when their member meets with the president.

Capitol Hill life runs on a unique rhythm. Congress usually remains in session, apart from holidays, from the beginning of January through early August; members return after Labor Day and rush to finish for the year in early October during election (even-numbered) years, because they are anxious to focus on their campaigns. In non-election years, the session lasts longer—Obamacare passed the Senate on December 24 in 2009. When in session, the Hill buzzes with action, especially when members are in residence Tuesday through Thursday. Staffers work late into the night, while lobbyists and media swarm around the Capitol.

Congressional staff at work. With C-SPAN on TV in the foreground, staffers discuss a key upcoming vote in 2018.

Members of Congress know that they stand in the vortex of history. Every move—such as the deep bow made by clerks carrying House bills to the Senate and vice versa—reflects a legacy that may stretch as far back as the Virginia House of Burgesses, which first convened in 1619. In fact, new members of Congress make a candlelight visit to that historical site as part of their orientation.

Minnows and Whales: Congressional Leadership

When Lyndon Johnson (D-TX) served as Senate majority leader in the 1950s, he divided colleagues into two camps: "whales," who could influence landmark legislation, and "minnows," who dutifully followed others. Most "whales" are chairs of important committees or part of the formal leadership structure.

The House and Senate feature very different leadership styles. The smaller, more collegial Senate—where any member can request a hold and bring the entire body to a halt—usually requires patient, consensus-minded leadership. Majority leaders do not so much lead as manage Senate procedures, cajoling and pleading proud senators to move legislation along. Recently, the traditionally consensual Senate has begun to behave more like the partisan House, making it still harder to forge agreements. The larger House, run on majoritarian principles, permits much tighter central control from the Speaker and other top leaders; perhaps because the whole body is up for election every two years, the House has traditionally been the more partisan branch.

House Leadership

Democrats and Republicans each choose a party leader from their ranks. When a new Congress opens after an election (in January of odd-numbered years), the majority party votes its leader to the top post in Congress, the **Speaker of the House**. Speaker Paul Ryan retired in 2018, and was replaced as the 116th Congress opened by the leader of the Democratic Party. The Speaker serves as the public face of the House. He or she is simultaneously an administrative officer, a political spokesman, and a party leader.

Speaker of the House: The chief administrative officer in the House of Representatives.

As chief administrative officer of the House, the Speaker presides over the chamber on special occasions (e.g., when a president delivers the State of the Union address to Congress). The Speaker rules on procedural issues, chooses members for committees, assigns legislation to committees, and "maintains order and civility"—although civility is increasingly difficult to sustain.

The Speaker sets the House's agenda and determines which bills are considered and when. Speakers negotiate with the Senate and executive branch. And they help manage the Rules Committee, which sets the terms of the debate for every piece of legislation that reaches the House floor. Speakers sometimes work with Rules to hold the majority together or derail opposition on important votes.

As leaders of the majority party, Speakers spin issues in their party's favor and serve as the party's public face. That leads the opposition to target them—to portray them as partisan or ruthless. It takes a nimble politician to juggle the different roles the Speaker must play. Newt Gingrich brilliantly designed the 1994 Republican victory in Congress after 40 straight years in the minority. However, he proved to be more effective as a rebel than as Speaker. His combative persona and fondness for the limelight quickly made him a controversial

● *Departing House Speaker Paul Ryan (R-WI) announces his retirement in 2018.*

figure—and hurt the new Republican majority's image. In contrast, Speaker John Boehner tried to build consensus in the party, but was toppled after five years at the helm in 2015 by ultra-conservative young Republicans impatient for change.[18]

The House majority leader is the second in command. He or she acts as the majority party's floor manager, negotiator, and spokesperson. The majority leader also serves as the Speaker's eyes and ears, tracking party members' actions and preferences. Steny Hoyer (D-MD) currently holds this position.

The number-three position is the majority whip. Majority whips are responsible for party discipline—utilizing a loyal team to determine party members' position on issues, and ensuring that Republicans or Democrats vote the way the leadership wants them to. The term *whip* comes from the British Parliament, which borrowed the term from fox hunting, where the "whipper-in" was responsible for keeping the pack of hounds together—and yes, those fox hunters did the job by cracking whips. The majority whip leads a team of nine deputy whips, each responsible for members from a different region.

The minority generally has the same leadership structure, with one big difference: no Speaker. The top Republican in the 116th Congress, minority leader Kevin McCarthy (R-CA), is joined by the minority whip in trying to thwart the Democratic majority.

House whips have a challenging time persuading their colleagues to vote the way they want. They do a lot of arm-twisting and deal-cutting—and they have to be creative. Back in the 1970s, minority whip Leslie Arends (R-IL) needed one more GOP vote to win an important agriculture bill. One Ohio Republican, knowing the bill was unpopular with his constituents, simply flew home. When Arends discovered his crucial vote was missing, he called an Ohio radio station and persuaded the DJ to announce, every fifteen minutes: "If anybody spies Representative Jones, who should be representing us in Washington but isn't, tell him he's supposed to be in Washington tomorrow for an important vote." Jones flew back the next morning and sheepishly voted with his fellow Republicans.

Senate Leadership

When you think about the Senate, take all the difficulties involved in managing the House—and quadruple them. Senate rules, such as the filibuster and the hold, give each individual senator a great deal of autonomy. The Senate leadership must turn to personal skills, especially an ability to negotiate with colleagues, to advance their party's goals.

The senators elect a majority leader—currently Mitch McConnell (R-KY). However, the Senate leader does not even formally preside over the chamber. The Constitution gives that job to the vice president (VP). In practice, vice presidents rarely show up in the Senate, appearing mainly for very important votes (because the VP can break a tie) and on ceremonial occasions. Likewise, the

president pro tempore—currently Charles Grassley (R-IA)—has presiding authority at certain formal occasions. Otherwise, every senator presides in turn over the body, serving rotating half-hour stints. A staff member stands by the presiding member's side, helping him or her to negotiate the complex rules.

After Hillary Rodham Clinton, elected to the Senate from New York in 2000, served her first half-hour in the Senate's presiding chair, she told colleagues it was "the most difficult thing I'd ever done in politics."[19] Perhaps she would change her mind now, after a grueling presidential campaign preceded by service as Secretary of State. But then-Senator Clinton's line emphasizes how tortuous the Senate rules can be.

Senate whips from both the majority and minority parties serve the same functions as in the House—though they command much less power to demand party discipline, again owing to the Senate's individualistic ways. This difficulty extends right up to the majority leader. It is hard to set the Senate's agenda or command floor action in a context of unlimited debate and amendments, with the constant threat that any one senator will place a hold on legislation or mount a filibuster. The best that majority leaders and their team can muster is to influence which policies will be considered on the Senate floor, and in what order, though that is usually done in consultation with the minority leader. If the minority leader indicates that an item will be subject to a filibuster or a hold, the majority leader normally passes over it and moves to the next item on the agenda.

President pro tempore: Majority party senator with the longest Senate service.

Committees: Workhorses of Congress

The regular duties of congressional lawmaking play out mainly in committees. Committees draft legislation, sponsor hearings, oversee the executive branch, and draft the federal budget. Every year, the administration sends its priorities to Congress. Leadership duly assigns issues to committees, where many die a quiet death. Even after Obama won a big re-election victory in 2012, Republican-led congressional committees buried such presidential priorities as gun control, environmental regulation, and (in the House) immigration reform.

Learn about your representatives and the committees they serve on.

The Enduring Power of Committees

Table 13.4 lists the types of congressional committees. Legislative committees were invented in the very early days of the United States; the British Parliament still has nothing resembling the extent and power of congressional committees. The basic committee structures and operation have been remarkably resilient, despite decades of pressure for reform. How have they managed to duck calls for change?

Two reasons: First, inertia—it is hard to remake Congress, given layers of tradition and complex rules. Second, in their own way, committees work. Individual members devote extensive time to fundraising, paying attention to constituents, and shuttling in and out of Washington. The committee system permits busy members to specialize and become expert on a narrow range of topics (especially in the House, where members typically serve on one primary committee). In short, committees enable Congress to devise fairly sophisticated legislative solutions to the many issues competing for attention.

The committee system is yet another way American government separates powers. It means that Congress winds up with multiple centers of authority, making the legislative process slower and harder for the public (and the media) to follow.

TABLE 13.4 Congressional Committee Types

Standing committee	Permanent bodies, with fixed jurisdiction (Table 13.5 lists them all). House and Senate standing committees vary widely in prestige: The oldest are traditionally the most influential, though some newer ones (such as Intelligence, created after 9/11 in both chambers) deal with significant topics. Standing committees are further divided into multiple *subcommittees*, organized around areas of expertise.
Select committee	Created to investigate a particular issue; these exist for a defined period of time. Also called *special committees*. A select committee to investigate the terrorist attack on the U.S. Embassy in Benghazi, Libya, was convened from 2014–2016, for example.
Joint committee	Made up of both House and Senate members to address topics of continuing importance. These committees can remain in place for decades; the Joint Committee on Taxation has existed since 1971, for example. *Conference committees*, introduced later in this chapter, are temporary joint committees, created to consider a specific piece of legislation.

Earmark: A legislative item, usually included in spending ("appropriations") bills, that directs Congress to fund a particular item in one House member's district or a senator's state.

But the division of labor allows an institution—with distracted, busy members—to accomplish more. By dividing the labor of its members, the 115th Congress was able to dispatch more than 10,500 bills, although that number was nearly twice as high forty years ago.

The standing committees (see Table 13.5) provide a main avenue to send favored services, or "pork," home to a representative's district. Members of the Appropriations Committee—which decides how U.S. funds are spent—are informally called "cardinals," like the ruling cadre in the Vatican. Other members approach them, hat in hand, to request **earmarks** in the form of items in appropriations bills: a dam in this district, funds for highway construction in that one. Appropriations members saw their power diminished in 2012, after Congress's decision to outlaw earmarks; within a year, however, Congress found creative ways to fund the practice.

The committee system makes Congress far more efficient. But there is also a harsher reality. Committees fragment Congress into small fiefdoms, hide action from public view, and make it relatively easy to do favors for well-placed constituents (a tax break or a phone call to get a pesky regulator to back off). The fragmentation also makes it still more difficult to pass major legislation or to address large national problems. Only about 6 percent of the bills and proposals assigned to committees ever make it to the floor.

The organization of Congress raises, once again, the dilemmas of American democracy: Is the system biased toward the powerful? Does the bias against action frustrate the popular will or simply reflect the American wariness of government (or both)? What do you think?

Leadership and Assignments

After the 2018 congressional election, many House members found excuses to check in with the new Speaker: Along with fond holiday wishes, they were jockeying for preferred committee assignments. The Speaker is a key player in assigning members (and chairs) to each committee—a vital decision, given all the power committees wield. Each party votes on members' committee assignments, and seniority remains a vital factor in determining chairs, but all decisions are made with the Speaker's blessing. Over in the Senate, the decision involves more

TABLE 13.5 House and Senate Permanent Standing Committees, 116th Congress (2019–20)

U.S. HOUSE COMMITTEES	U.S. SENATE COMMITTEES
Agriculture	Aging (Special)
Appropriations	Agriculture, Nutrition, and Forestry
Armed Services	Appropriations
Budget	Armed Services
Education and the Workforce	Banking, Housing, and Urban Affairs
Energy and Commerce	Budget
Ethics	Commerce, Science, and Transportation
Financial Services	Energy and Natural Resources
Foreign Affairs	Environment and Public Works
Homeland Security	Ethics (Select)
House Administration	Finance
Intelligence (Permanent Select)	Foreign Relations
Judiciary	Health, Education, Labor, and Pensions
Natural Resources	Homeland Security and Governmental Affairs
Oversight and Government Reform	Indian Affairs
Rules	Intelligence (Permanent Select)
Science, Space, and Technology	Judiciary
Small Business	Rules and Administration
Transportation and Infrastructure	Small Business and Entrepreneurship
Veterans' Affairs	Veterans' Affairs
Ways and Means	

give-and-take but ultimately rests in the majority leader's hands. Minority party assignments are recommended by minority leaders in both chambers.

Members compete fiercely to join the most influential committees. Once they are on a committee, representatives and senators often stay for many years—gaining power and influence, and aspiring to become chair. Traditionally (but not always), the chair is the longest serving committee member. Members generally seek to join committees that reflect the concerns of their district. When political scientist David Price (D-NC) won a seat in Congress, his colleagues at Duke University wondered how his committee assignment would reflect his expertise. Price, already a savvy politician, requested a seat on the House Banking (now Financial Services) Committee because his district has a strong banking and financial service sector.[20]

Skilled committee chairs broaden the jurisdiction of their committee by claiming pieces of bills that are referred to many different committees. As we saw in the chapter opening, five different committees won jurisdiction over Obamacare. Each committee has its own process. Each has its own political slant. Committees can bury a bill, completely rewrite it, report out an unrealistic version, or boost the chances of success with a strong bill.

Jurisdictional squabbles can erupt into battles for influence between committees when their responsibilities overlap. The House and the Senate each have different committees for Homeland Security, Intelligence, and Foreign Affairs. Sometimes they all hold hearings on the same issue, and because legislation is assigned to every committee that has jurisdiction over the topic, overlapping authority means multiple committees wrestling to shape the same legislation. See Comparing Nations 13.1 to find out how this legislative process differs in other countries.

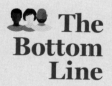

The Bottom Line

» Congress resembles a small city. Its residents include the 541 members of Congress, 22,000 staff members, and an army of lobbyists. The city includes its own amenities, traditions, and slang.

» House leadership includes a Speaker, majority and minority leaders, and ten whips. Successful leaders in the House impose discipline on their party members. The Senate allows far more individual action. Party leaders and whips have fewer institutional tools with which to impose discipline.

» Congressional committees are the workhorses of Congress. They have proved efficient and adaptable over the years. However, the committee system also fragments Congress, hides action from public view, accommodates constituents seeking individual favors, and makes it difficult to pass major legislation.

Legislative Policymaking

As the Affordable Care Act's convoluted passage testifies, congressional lawmaking can be boiled down to five words: *Complex process. Difficult to win.* The last decade saw thousands of bills submitted each year (see Figure 13.2). How many made it all the way through the process to become law? Less than 3 percent.

Why even bother pursuing legislative wins? There are other ways to make policy. As we will see in subsequent chapters, presidents can issue executive orders (Chapter 14), bureaucrats can write regulations (Chapter 15), and activists can go to the courts (Chapter 16). But nothing else has the status—symbolic as well as legal—of an act of Congress. That is why bills keep coming despite the long odds.

Americans complain about the nation's failure to face up to global warming. Or our broken public education system. Or our inability to ban abortion, ensure net neutrality, or reduce the federal budget deficit. Pundits explain these failures by invoking "American attitudes" or "American culture" or "powerful lobbyists." Here is a more accurate explanation: Congressional rules make it very hard to do any of these things—even when a majority of legislators (and the nation) are in support. What happens when a bill is proposed? Read on.

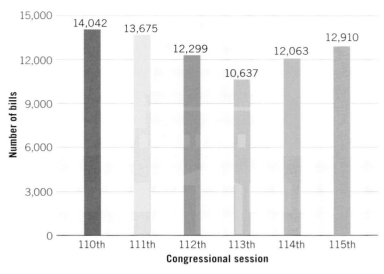

Figure 13.2 *Bills and other resolutions introduced in Congress (115th, as of November 12, 2018). (GovTrack)*

Drafting a Bill

Anyone can petition Congress to consider a bill, but only members of the House and Senate have the right to introduce one. Every piece of legislation needs at least one primary sponsor, whose name is publicly inscribed on the first page. Major bills are often referred to by the sponsors' names, with some creative exceptions (see Table 13.6).

Bills can feature any number of co-sponsors, or members who agree to have their names listed as supporters. The main sponsors usually try to sign on many members, especially powerful ones such as committee chairs, as co-sponsors. A loose rule of thumb: The more co-sponsors a bill has, the higher the likelihood of passage.

Anything can be introduced as legislation—no matter how far outside the box. Congressman Ron Paul (R-TX) once introduced a bill mandating that the Treasury buy a one-inch-wide strip of land stretching down the middle of the United States from Canada to Mexico. All goods or people crossing that line would be charged a

TABLE 13.6 **Examples of Creative Legislative Titles**	
Clarifying Lawful Overseas Use of Data (CLOUD) Act (2018)	Allows U.S. law enforcement (with a judge's subpoena) to obtain American citizens' private data from servers anywhere in the world.
EGO (Eliminating Government-Funded Oil-Painting) Act (2013)	Bans federal funding of official portraits of government officials.
Personal Responsibility in Consumption Act (2006)	Immunizes fast-food companies against lawsuits by obese consumers.
What Really Happened Act (2002)	Requires instant TV replay in all major sports.
Note: Only the first of these bills passed.	

toll, declared Representative Paul, eliminating the need for any other taxes or government fees. The bill did not make it out of committee.

Bills' sponsors rarely write the legislation themselves. Some bills include language taken from state legislation, or even other countries' parliaments. Congressional members "borrow" legislative language from each other, adapting colleagues' bills for their own use. Most serious bills go to the experts at the Congressional Research Service (CRS) for drafting help. Bill drafters also consult with outside sources, including executive branch officials, lobbyists, and academics. And members regularly copy themselves; as each new session begins, many congressional offices participate in a time-honored ritual: dust off and reintroduce bills that failed last time.

There is a great art to bill drafting. Writing legislation necessitates major political choices. How much money should we ask for in spending bills? How far can we change current laws? Do we dare test existing constitutional limits? Many bills include bargaining chips—provisions the sponsors are willing to negotiate away to win over the skeptics. Legislation to reduce average elementary school class sizes might also feature a sentence promising healthier lunches in all public schools. When the serious bargaining starts on Capitol Hill that line may be dropped to satisfy budget hawks who always focus on the costs. Fuzzy language sometimes helps avoid disagreement, but drafters are also aware that if the law passes, it may very well end up involved in litigation, which puts a premium on clarity and precision.

Once the bill is drafted and the co-sponsors have signed on, it is ready for the next step: submission.

View an example of a congressional bill, its description, supporters, and status.

Submitting the Bill

The more traditional Senate typically introduces bills as the legislative day opens, around noon on Tuesdays, Wednesdays, and Thursdays. Let's take a peek inside the chamber.

The presiding officer taps his or her gavel, bringing the stir of conversation to a halt. Members pause as the Senate chaplain recites a prayer. A swirling bustle breaks out as the chaplain concludes. Routine administrative motions (such as approving records of the previous day's proceedings) are followed by morning hour statements—short speeches that celebrate home state achievements. A constituent is turning 100 years old, or a softball team has won the state title.

Watch closely: A senator snaps her fingers. A page (usually a high school student trained for this role) dashes down the aisle, takes the senator's document, and places it in a flat wooden tray beside the bill clerk. The clerk writes a number on the first page (bills are numbered serially, starting each session with S.1), notes the senator's suggestion for committee referral, and places it in a tray. That night it is printed. A bill has been born!

The House is less ritualized, in keeping with its democratic spirit, but bill introduction continues to be an old-fashioned practice. Representatives carry proposed bills themselves down to the rostrum. They hand their legislation to the clerk or drop it in a mahogany box, called the "hopper." From there, bills are delivered to the Speaker's office, where they are assigned a number—starting each session with H.R. 1—and referred to committee.

Committee Action

As we have seen, committees are the congressional workhorses. The House leadership normally assigns each bill to committees with authority (or jurisdiction) over the area affected by the proposed legislation. Major legislation can go to as many as six different committees. Once they are assigned a bill, the committees perform four major tasks.

1. Committees Hold Hearings on Policy Topics. Witnesses submit written testimony for staff members and reporters to read; unless they are senior government officials or celebrities, they are limited to a five-minute presentation at the **committee hearing**. When they begin, a little green light goes on; at the four-minute mark, a yellow light goes on. At five minutes, a red light blinks. Nervous rookies stop mid-sentence; veterans ignore the lights and talk serenely on—until the chair bangs the gavel.

The staff assembles a list of who is testifying at each hearing. Witnesses generally include White House officials and cabinet heads—whose testimony has to be cleared with the Office of Management and Budget (OMB; introduced in Chapter 14 as "the agency that says no"). At many hearings, officials try to stick to their authorized script while critical Senate or House members pummel them, knowing full well that the government witness cannot express any views that were not cleared by the OMB.

Celebrities are popular witnesses, attracting media attention to what might otherwise be a low-profile event. Angelina Jolie has appeared before Congress five times on international aid issues; Kourtney Kardashian spoke to the Senate about safety measures in the cosmetics industry; Oprah Winfrey's Senate Judiciary testimony was cited in a National Child Protection Act; and Michael Crichton, author of *Jurassic Park*, *Westworld*, and other thrillers, explained a few years ago that global warming was pure fiction. More often, witnesses include interest-group lobbyists, think tank experts, academics, and pollsters reporting public opinion on the issues.

Hearings also can get tough. When the CEOs of three big U.S. automakers went to Congress for a bailout, their trouble began when Representative Brad Sherman (D-CA) needled them about flying to Washington on corporate jets while claiming that their companies faced bankruptcy.

● *Celebrity congressional witnesses include . . . Elmo! Elmo "testifies," with the help of music industry executive Joe Lamond, before the House Education Appropriations subcommittee in support of funding for school music programs. When he finished, Elmo tried to eat the microphone.*

Committee hearing: A way for committees to gather information and gauge members' support as legislative policymaking gets underway. Hearings usually feature witnesses who submit testimony, make an oral presentation, and answer questions from members of Congress.

Rep. SHERMAN:	I'm going to ask the three executives here to raise their hand if they flew here commercial.
Mr. MULALLY [Ford CEO], Mr. WAGONER [GM], Mr. NARDELLI [Chrysler]:	(No response.)
Rep. SHERMAN:	Second, I'm going ask you to raise your hand if you're planning to sell your [private] jet . . . and fly back commercial.
Messrs. MULALLY, WAGONER, NARDELLI:	(No response.)
Rep. SHERMAN:	Let the record show no hands went up.
Rep. ACKERMAN:	It's almost like seeing a guy show up at the soup kitchen in high-hat and tuxedo. . . . I mean, couldn't you all have downgraded to first class or jet-pooled or something to get here?

Other members asked the CEOs if they would give up their hefty compensation packages and work for one dollar a year. Nardelli, the Chrysler chairman, declined with a muttered, "I'm good." The CEOs learned their lesson: When they next testified before Congress, they rode to Washington in cars manufactured by their company.

2. Committees Prepare Legislation for Floor Consideration. Committees are the primary source of policy development in Congress. Members and committee staff, drawing on their collective knowledge, assess and revise each bill that comes before them.

Committee markup session: A gathering of a full committee to draft the final version of a bill before the committee votes on it.

Major rewrites of bills occur in **committee markup sessions**, when the committee gathers to work through the legislation's language, line by line. The result, called a "chairman's mark," is hot property among lobbyists, public advocates, and other interested parties; it contains many of the details that will become law if the legislation wins approval.

Following markup, the committee holds a vote on whether to report a bill to the full House or Senate. When the Senate Finance Committee took up a $1.5 trillion tax-reform bill in November 2017, it considered 355 amendments over four days—incorporating nearly 100 before voting to approve by a party-line vote of 14–12. All that work in just one Senate committee—and remember that at least one other committee is usually negotiating another version of the same legislation—in this case Senate Budget, which plowed through several dozen more amendments before voting 12–11 to send an amended bill to the Senate floor.

Committee votes are pivotal moments in a bill's career, as important as roll-call votes on the floor. If a bill is voted down in committee—not reported, in Congress-speak—it is usually dead. Those voted through by a narrow margin probably face tough sledding on the floor, and the Speaker may decide never to bring the closely divided measure up for a vote.

The House Armed Services Committee holds a 15-hour markup session!

3. Committees Also Kill Legislation. Of the more than four thousand bills referred to the 40 House and Senate standing committees each year, only about one in eight sees any action. Items judged less important or not particularly urgent—or not politically viable—may be quietly ignored. Some bills are proposed just to satisfy voters or score political points, and have no chance of passing; committees usually bury them swiftly. Well into modern times, bills often died in committee without any public acknowledgment of how members voted. A key reform of the 1970s required all committees to keep full records of important votes.

4. Committees Exercise Oversight. Congress's work is not done when legislation passes. House and Senate standing committees monitor the executive branch, making sure cabinet departments and agencies perform their roles properly. This supervision can be a high-stakes activity: Oversight hearings investigate scandals; review major issues such as cybersecurity and protection against terrorism; and evaluate presidential appointees. Committees also continue to monitor the programs that they have passed: Is the agency spending its budget properly? Are people benefitting from the program as promised?

Note that, as with lawmaking, the committees of Congress are the front lines in this vital interplay between the legislative and executive branches.

Floor Action

After a successful bill makes it through committee markup and is approved by all necessary committees, its next stop is the House or Senate floor. Once it gets there, its chance of becoming law increases dramatically. Of bills that make it to the floor, more than half are enacted. But legislation may take a long time to achieve floor consideration—leaders rarely call up a bill until they think they have the votes to win.

Getting to the Floor.   Floor procedures in the House and Senate are very different. After a Senate committee approves a bill, it is placed on the "business calendar," from which it will be called up for consideration on a timing schedule worked out by the majority and minority leaders. Only bills that receive **unanimous consent**— agreement by all senators—can be brought to the floor. One "nay" and the bill is put on hold.

In the House, majority party leaders exert more control over which issues make it to the floor. They may start by rewriting the legislation—sometimes because multiple committees have passed different chair's marks and cannot come to agreement among themselves. Other times, the Speaker, majority leader, and fellow leaders rewrite a bill to get the measure through.

Once it confirms a bill's language, the House Rules Committee issues a directive governing the process for the bill: for example, which type of amendments may be proposed from the floor. The membership of the Rules Committee is tilted to favor the majority party, and the committee chair works closely with the Speaker to ensure that floor action will follow the leadership's wishes. The Senate, in contrast, allows virtually unlimited consideration on the floor; amendments of all kinds just keep on coming.

In both chambers, once bills make it to the calendar, they can get stuck there—for an entire session, in some cases. A logjam of legislation may be the reason. Or it might be the result of coordination issues between House and Senate, given the requirement that legislation has to move through both chambers. Bills also may be bottled up in the Senate because of the "unanimous consent" requirement. Achieving 100 percent agreement to allow a bill to come up for a vote often involves elaborate negotiations.

On the Floor.   Eventually a bill's moment for floor consideration arrives. Supporters hope their measure will be taken up in the House and Senate around the same time, knowing that legislation often makes it only to one or the other chamber during a session—another form of death sentence. In the 115th Congress (2017–2018) bills to prohibit taxpayer funding

Unanimous consent: A Senate requirement, applied to most of that body's business, that all senators agree before an action can proceed.

● *Senator Susan Collins (R-ME), among a handful of pivotal votes on the 115th Congress's signal legislative achievement, a $1.5 trillion tax bill, surrounded by reporters. The bill was delayed reaching the floor for days while Collins and two other holdout Republican Senators decided their votes.*

Sponsor a bill on immigration reform and see if you can get it passed.

for abortion, to require all states to honor "concealed carry" gun laws, and to repeal the Affordable Care Act all sailed through the House—and died when the Senate failed to act on them.

In both chambers, floor action on legislation follows the same broad procedures. First, a bill is assigned a floor manager—usually the main sponsor, but on big issues, the chair of the committee or subcommittee that reported the bill takes up this role. The manager handles amendments as they come up and controls the time for debate. Majority and minority party members each have a specific number of hours and minutes to discuss the legislation, determined in the Senate by agreement between party leaders and in the House by the Rules Committee.

Then the political maneuvers really start. In both the House and Senate, floor action involves amendments, procedural moves, and eventually a final vote—all accompanied by a lot of talk along the way. Members rarely change any votes with their eloquence. But floor speeches are not empty oratory. Congress watchers know that who chooses to speak, and what they say, matters. "I rise to support H.R. 835" is very different from "I rise to thank my good friend for introducing this excellent bill, H.R. 835; I have just a few questions about it." Each statement offers valuable clues about the likely outcome. Whips listen especially closely and adapt their floor strategies to secure a majority in support of party-approved amendments and the final vote for passage.

The real audience for much of the speechmaking is the constituency back home eager to see their representatives fight for (or against) an issue. At times, however, the members snap at one another. Members of the minority often express frustration at the hardball tactics of the leadership. In 2016, the Senate considered six gun-control measures in the wake of a horrific mass murder at an Orlando dance club. House Republican leaders, however, refused even to hold committee hearings on the issue—leading furious Democratic members to stage a rare sit-in on the House floor.

House rules permit leaders to introduce creative strategies to get their legislation through. They can extend the time allocated for debate (while a few more arms are twisted). They sometimes permit members to vote "yes" on multiple contradictory motions knowing only one (the last vote or the one with the most votes) will really count; this procedural antic permits members to tell angry constituents, "don't blame me, I voted for that bill" (yes, they did—but they also voted against it when it really counted).

Senate leaders, far from inventing new rules, are more likely to breathe a sigh of relief after steering a bill past the potential member holds and simply getting it to the floor. There, a related danger lurks: the filibuster or legislative hold. A senator may halt all activity in the chamber by refusing to yield the floor or issuing a hold; the only way to stop him or her is through a **cloture vote**, which requires the approval of three-fifths of the Senate—sixty votes.

Filibusters used to be rare events. Between 1927 and 1960, there were only 18 efforts to break a filibuster (or

Cloture vote: The Senate's only approved method for halting a filibuster or lifting a legislative hold. If sixty senators—three-fifths of the body, changed in 1975 from the original two-thirds—vote for cloture, the measure can proceed to a vote.

● *House Democrats demanding floor action on gun control.*

cloture filings). Not a single one succeeded in *invoking cloture*, or stopping the filibuster and permitting a vote on the issue. As you can see in Figure 13.3, the effort to invoke cloture grew more common in the 1970s (which averaged 32 filibusters every two-year session); it became a common tactic in the 1990s and 2000s, when the legislative hold became a regularly used tactic. Both Democratic and Republican majorities averaged 72 cloture filings (seeking to break a filibuster or lift a hold) each session. The new Republican minority (2007–2015) broke all records and averaged 161 cloture filings a session. Pushing back, Democratic opposition required more than 190 filings in the 115th Congress (most cloture requests are caused by the minority party). Sixty votes has effectively become the new Senate threshold for passing legislation.

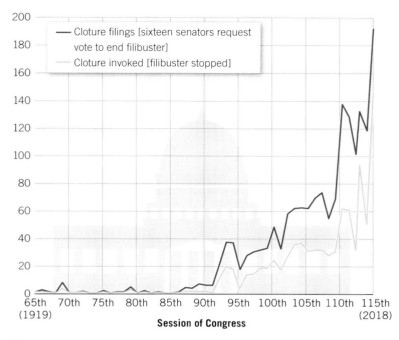

● **Figure 13.3** *Cloture votes are called to end a filibuster or hold. When they are successful, cloture is invoked and the blockage ends. Notice how they used to be rare events. The 113th Congress (2013–2014) broke the all-time record for cloture votes until the 115th Congress (2017–2018) when the numbers spiked again. (U.S. Senate)*

The Vote

Once amendments are voted down or adopted, the time for speeches has expired, and the leadership reckons it has a winning majority, it's time for a final floor vote. On uncontroversial matters, a **voice vote** of all members is sufficient. But several dozen votes each session are judged important enough to require a **roll-call vote**. In the Senate, a clerk still calls the roll, alphabetically scrolling through senators by last name, with each responding "yea" or "nay" (or "present," if they wish to abstain). Because the much larger House would take hours to vote if it proceeded in this way, roll calls are now done electronically. Representatives use a voting device about the size of a credit card that they plug into kiosks located around the House chamber.

Roll-call votes on major bills are among the most important public acts a member of Congress performs. These votes attract a great deal of attention from constituents, lobbyists, the media, and potential campaign opponents—who might use an unpopular vote to attack an incumbent.[21]

Conference Committee

Legislation must pass the Senate and House in identical form to be ready for presidential action. If different versions of a bill pass—and technically a single comma in a five-hundred-page bill counts as a "difference"—a **conference committee** must reconcile them. These special sessions, made up of lawmakers from both chambers, provide a golden opportunity for disgruntled members or attentive lobbyists to revisit a bill. Interested parties who failed to get a favorite item included during committee or floor action now have another chance. "An apple and an orange could go into conference committee," lamented President Ronald Reagan, "and come out a pear."[22] No joke: The conference can write a significantly new bill, though sections that were the same in House and Senate versions cannot be altered in conference.

House–Senate conferences, if successful, yield a single version of a bill. Each chamber then has an "up-or-down" floor vote—no further amendments

Voice vote: A congressional vote in which the presiding officer asks those for and against to say "yea" or "nay," respectively, and announces the result. No record is kept of House or Senate members voting on each side.

Roll-call vote: A congressional vote in which each member's vote is recorded, either by roll call (Senate) or electronically (House).

Conference committee: A special House–Senate committee that must reconcile differences between House and Senate versions of the same bill.

To track your House and Senate members' votes, go to Congress.gov and enter their names.

● *C-SPAN televised live the December 2017 House–Senate conference committee to resolve differences in their respective versions of a tax reform bill.*

permitted. Opponents in the Senate may launch another filibuster, hoping to win over new members who object to the compromises made with the House. If the majority beats the filibuster in the Senate and a majority of both houses votes in favor, the bill has passed Congress.

In recent years, however, the two chambers have increasingly negotiated with one another prior to passage in a process known as "ping pong." That yields bills that match and do not have to go to conference committees. The number of conferences has declined dramatically – from more than fifty a session (in the 1990s) to under ten today.[23]

Presidential Action: Separated Powers Revisited

Even after all that, legislation still faces another hurdle. No bill becomes law until the president takes action, usually by signing it (bills also become law within 10 days of congressional passage, if Congress remains in session). On important issues, a signing ceremony often takes place in the White House Rose Garden. Presidents sign multiple copies of the bill, handing out pens to the original sponsors and other high-ranking congressional members in attendance.

Veto: The constitutional procedure by which a president can prevent enactment of legislation passed by Congress.

Presidents can also **veto** legislation. Here is yet another place a bill can falter. If the president says no, Congress has one more shot at passing the legislation. It is a high bar, though. To deny or override a veto, both chambers need a two-thirds majority: at least sixty-seven senators and 291 members of the House have to say no to the president. Only in this way can a bill become law without presidential approval. Figure 13.4 summarizes the process of how a bill becomes law.

We will cover more details about veto practices in Chapter 14 on the presidency. Fortunately for most legislative advocates, presidential opposition is rare: George W. Bush and Barack Obama vetoed 12 bills each. President Trump did not exercise the veto power during his first two years in office.

The Bottom Line

» Transforming a policy idea into a federal law is extremely difficult. Why bother? Because legislation remains the central act of American domestic government. Important laws have far-reaching consequences.

» The power of an officially sanctioned law inspires the introduction of thousands of bills in Congress each year. Most proposed legislation (97%) never gets through the process to become law.

» Congressional committees are the central actors in legislative policymaking, holding hearings and marking up (or deleting) bills to prepare them for floor action.

» Floor procedures are another intricate part of the process. Once passed by both House and Senate, legislation may still face a conference committee, a presidential veto, or both.

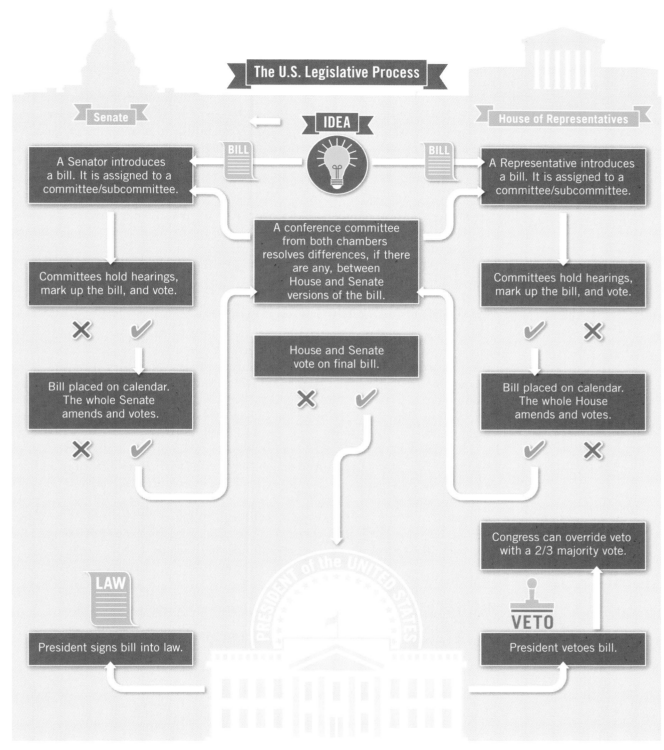

● **Figure 13.4** *How a bill becomes a law.*

Why Is Congress So Unpopular?

Congress, the "people's branch," might be expected to win the most public support among our national political institutions. Not even close—it is by far the least popular branch. For a half-century, polls have reported the popularity of Congress, the sitting president, and the Supreme Court, along with other institutions. Since the 1970s, Congress has come in last in virtually every survey, often by a great margin. Today, Congress is less popular than at any other time in modern history and less popular than, well, almost anything—including the Internal Revenue Service, witches, zombies, and hipsters (see Figure 13.5).[24] And yet, as we saw in Chapter 9, Americans re-elect over 90 percent of their representatives, year after year. Why?

Constituents tend to like their own representatives and senators, who receive far higher approval numbers than Congress as a whole. And individual members have become adept at raising money (to drive off talented challengers) and running against the Congress they serve in. But what makes the institution itself so unpopular? The public dislikes both partisan fighting and gridlock. Let us look more carefully at each complaint.

Partisan Polarization in Congress

Congress has exhibited partisan differences since its origins. Strong party disputes, fueled by regional and racial divisions, led nineteenth-century members to carry swords, pistols, or Bowie knives into chambers. Following a rousing anti-slavery speech by Senator Charles Sumner of Massachusetts in 1856, a southern House member, Preston Brooks, slipped onto the Senate floor and beat Sumner unconscious with a cane. Sumner was unable to resume his Senate duties for nearly three years.

Subsequent combat in the House or Senate was mostly, but not entirely, limited to words. During the 1950s and 1960s, large Democratic majorities in both chambers masked differences—mostly between southern conservatives and liberals from other regions of the country—within the Democratic caucus. Cross-party conflict rose during the 1980s, as Republicans gained congressional seats. When the GOP won control of the Senate in the 1980s and challenged Democrats for control of the House after 1990, the fault lines between the parties cracked open.[25]

Explore why incumbents are reelected despite Congress' unpopularity.

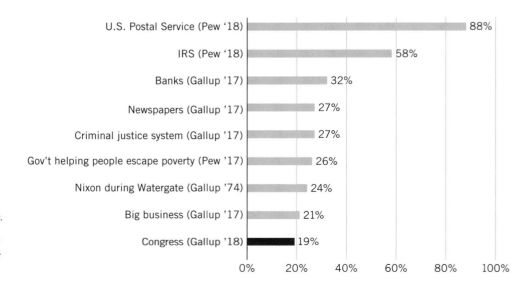

● **Figure 13.5** *Public approval of Congress, compared to other institutions, ideas, and individuals. Across 2018, Congress's approval rating remained between 15 to 19 percent; it fell as low as 7 percent in 2014 (Gallup).*

U.S. Postal Service (Pew '18) — 88%
IRS (Pew '18) — 58%
Banks (Gallup '17) — 32%
Newspapers (Gallup '17) — 27%
Criminal justice system (Gallup '17) — 27%
Gov't helping people escape poverty (Pew '17) — 26%
Nixon during Watergate (Gallup '74) — 24%
Big business (Gallup '17) — 21%
Congress (Gallup '18) — 19%

0%   20%   40%   60%   80%   100%

Partisan Polarization

HOW HAS IT CHANGED OVER TIME?

For more than one hundred years, Congressional parties displayed considerable ideological overlap, represented by the narrow gap between median Democratic and Republican voters on the upper left (1994) display.

Democrats and Republicans more ideologically divided than in the past

Distribution of Democrats and Republicans on a 10-item scale of political values

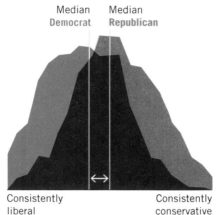

1994

Median Democrat · Median Republican

Consistently liberal — Consistently conservative

2004

Median Democrat · Median Republican

Consistently liberal — Consistently conservative

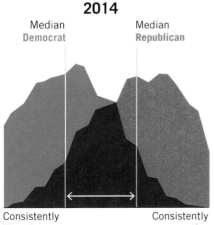

2014

Median Democrat · Median Republican

Consistently liberal — Consistently conservative

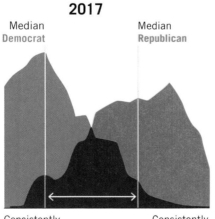

2017

Median Democrat · Median Republican

Consistently liberal — Consistently conservative

THINK ABOUT IT

How has that gap changed since 1994?

While this growing gap between the parties is usually criticized, are there any *advantages* to such a wide ideological divide?

Think about yourself and your politically engaged friends and relatives. Do you prefer highly partisan candidates? What impact might your choices have on the work of Congress?

Source: Pew Research Center

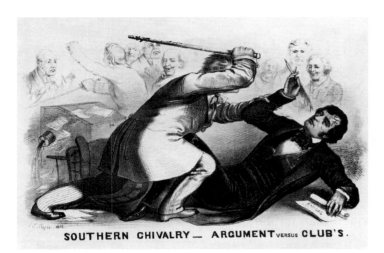

SOUTHERN CHIVALRY — ARGUMENT versus CLUB'S.

● *Congressional partisanship, Civil War era-style. A northern cartoonist vividly renders the 1856 caning of Senator Sumner.*

The proportion of House votes in which a majority of Democrats voted against a majority of Republicans increased by more than 50 percent during the 1990s and early 2000s.[26] In a similar telling measure, party cohesion—the proportion of each party's House or Senate members who vote with the party majority—remained at or above 90 percent each year after 1990, after historically varying from the mid-60s to the low 80s. In other words, the parties were no longer divided; instead, parties dug in against one another with fewer and fewer members willing to look for middle ground or vote with the other side.

Titles and subtitles of recent books about Congress underscore the point. These include: *Fight Club Politics: How Partisanship Is Poisoning the House of Representatives*; *The Broken Branch: How Congress Is Failing America and How to Get It Back on Track*; and, by an actual sitting House member, *Drain the Swamp: How Washington Corruption is Worse Than You Think.*[27]

There are two perspectives on polarization. Most political scientists believe the parties are now, for the first time in modern U.S. history, sorted by ideology.

What Do YOU Think?   Is a Partisan Congress a Good Thing?

Should Congress seek more cross-party agreement? The answer may not be so obvious—especially if you view politics in terms of principles, not merely the pursuit of self-interest. Today's "partisan" Congress features a significant ideological divide between conservative Republicans and progressive Democrats. Partisanship helps guide how members pursue the goals they believe in and try to persuade the public. What do you think?

Yes, a partisan Congress is a good thing.
It permits the public to choose between very different political philosophies. Take undocumented immigration, for example. For decades, both parties in Congress had largely indistinguishable positions. Now, Republicans introduce bills to increase deportation and build a wall, while Democrats fiercely denounce the GOP for separating children from parents at the U.S./Mexican border and call for an extension of the "Dreamers" program to permit young immigrants to attend college and work.

No, Congress has gotten too partisan.
The parties may disagree with one another, but they do not reflect the views of most Americans. Most people are moderates who do not feel well represented by the strong party views that fail to listen to the other side. More important, rising partisanship hampers cooperation necessary for Congress to pass important legislation and respond to the American public's preferences. Congress should seek compromises in the national interest.

It depends.
Context matters. For example, in times of economic suffering, people should put aside their political philosophy (whether pro- or antigovernment) and pass legislation for relief. But on other matters (such as abortion or gun control) members should stick to their principles.

Republicans have moved steadily to the right over the past quarter century, and Democrats more recently are swinging leftward; this encourages both parties to be more partisan. Others see "asymmetrical polarization": The Republicans, inspired by a fiery conservative movement, are the ones who have pressed the partisan fight in the name of their ideals.[28]

Divided Government

How to explain the rise in partisan "gridlock" over the past quarter century, which has intensified conflict during the past decade or so? Divided government, say some.[29] Divided government occurs when each party holds at least one of the three nationally elected institutions: the presidency, the House, or the Senate. Include state governments and the courts, and party division and gridlock get even worse. One or both houses of Congress led by a party opposed to the president, the argument goes, will result in a legislative standoff—as well as more aggressive congressional investigations of the White House and a slowed-down policymaking process. Although for many years prominent political scientists questioned this connection, suggesting "divided we govern,"[30] more recent studies have suggested that divided government leads to gridlock and policy stalemate.[31] One result: a "virtual disappearance of regular order in Congress"—that is, bipartisan lawmaking according to long-established norms.[32]

 **The Bottom Line**

» Congress has grown more partisan. Today, the parties themselves are more ideologically consistent. This makes for sharper conflict, but it also gives people clearer choices.

» Does divided government lead to more gridlock? Political scientists argued in the past that it does not, but today it appears that developments, such as the growing ideological purity of the parties and the regular use of legislative holds, signal that divided government now means an inability to solve America's problems.

Some Popular Reforms—and Their Limits

Should we care that Americans do not like Congress? Many observers—and thoughtful members—worry that continued public disapproval will erode the effectiveness of Congress as an institution. Our national legislature will not disappear as a result of unpopularity, but the laws Congress enacts will have less sanctity, compel less attention and obedience, if the institution passing them is increasingly viewed as corrupt or hapless. Others worry that potential political talent, especially our most promising young people, are discouraged by deep public disapproval from considering a congressional career (as either staffers or members). Still another danger: A deadlocked Congress will permit power to leak into the executive branch, which will increasingly make policy on its own. We will explore that worry in Chapter 14.

Each year, reformers propose various fixes to improve Congress. We have already discussed two such reforms: increasing third parties and imposing term limits (see Chapter 10). Here we discuss two other popular reforms: limits on lobbyists and public education about what Congress really does.

● *Public disapproval of Congress.*

Limit Lobbyists

Americans have called for years for reductions in lobbyists' influence in Congress. Chapter 12 chronicled extensive lobbying reforms, including bans on gifts and meals that lobbyists once provided to members. Both reform packages were greeted with yawns from the public: Congressional approval ratings actually dropped after each was implemented.

Remember James Madison's surprising conclusion from *Federalist* no. 10: Because groups inevitably promote their own interests, liberty is best protected when many groups pursue their interests right out in the open. That way, the different interests will check one another and people will have a choice among a great many perspectives. The solution to special interests: more special interests.

Madison could not have imagined the vast array of interests swarming over Capitol Hill today. But, as we discussed in the previous chapter, one person's special interest is another's cherished protector of a vital program. Lobbyists represent virtually everyone. And they link together our vast public and the complicated structures of national governance.

Even so, congressional organization—with its arcane ways, complicated processes, and multiple committees and subcommittees—creates many opportunities for special interests to quietly win favors and block initiatives they do not like. The problem is not their power over the big issues, on which members have strong views and votes are in the limelight, but in the minute details or obscure items to which few pay attention, even though millions of dollars (or other benefits) can be gained or lost with a few strokes of a legislator's pen.

How to limit such deals and favors? Perhaps James Madison had the best answer. When energy companies seek special benefits, environmental groups blow the whistle (and vice versa); when public hospitals push higher pay for CEOs, taxpayer groups challenge their arguments. Perhaps the solution to the problem of interests really is more interests. That would mean reforming the way Congress does business—to make sure that a wider array of interests are heard on every issue—rather than focusing on eradicating lobbying.

Educate the Public

Some reform proposals include an earnest plea for better education about Congress. Many Americans do not know their House member's name and cannot begin to explain how bills become law. Perhaps with a little more knowledge, the public would be more sympathetic.

Political scientists John Hibbing and Elizabeth Theiss-Morse argued, on the other side, that Americans' real problem with Congress is not lack of knowledge. The underlying problem is deeper: Americans dislike logrolling and bargaining; we dislike committees and bureaucracy; we dislike political partisanship (and parties); we despise interest groups. Americans disdain the slow pace of congressional lawmaking: We disapprove of multiple stages, veto points, and extended House and Senate debates—which inevitably involve hashing things out, bickering, and backscratching. Or, to put it differently, concluded Hibbing and Theiss-Morse, many Americans disapprove of some of the core features of democracy in practice. Although Americans love democracy in the abstract and demand transparency in politics, we do not enjoy watching the congressional process playing out with all its messy give-and-take.[33]

The Real World of Democracy

This chapter has tried to make clear how difficult, complex, and often muddled congressional policymaking is. Our ultimate goal is to increase your appreciation for the messiness of democracy, as carried out in the people's branch. Maybe all the bargaining, partial solutions, noisy debates, horse trading, and compromising faithfully reflect a diverse, divided, sometimes raucous American public. Congress is, on balance, the most open, transparent institution in our system of government. It is also inevitably full of flaws and limits—just like the humans it serves.

Why, in the end, are people's opinions of Congress so dismal? Perhaps the public laments how hard it is to get legislative results from Congress despite glowing campaign promises. Or perhaps it is discomfort with the essential realities of democracy: noisy debates, stops and starts, compromise and logrolling. Part of the fault also lies with the individual members who glide to re-election, year after year, by vehemently criticizing the institution they serve in.

The Bottom Line

» Some popular reforms propose limiting the influence of lobbying groups in Congress.

» Others emphasize the importance of educating the public, so that Americans can exercise greater oversight and develop a deeper understanding of the workings of Congress. We would recommend education about the "messy" nature of legislating in a diverse democratic nation.

Conclusion: Congress and the Challenge of Governing

Congress, as an institution, does some important things very well—representatives and senators are remarkably adept at looking after individuals who request help. Direct constituent service, at home in the district and state, is often superb. That is one reason why re-election rates are so high.

But as our individual needs have become better supported, Congress has grown less capable of solving the big societal problems—such as immigration, healthcare, crime, inequality, wage stagnation, global warming, or the byzantine tax code. By any measure, Americans' collective aspirations are at least as important as our personal concerns. The overarching question throughout this chapter is whether the U.S. Congress has lost its ability to achieve big collective aims, or whether it still muddles through precisely as the constitutional framers intended.

In the past, Congress has certainly proven capable of broad achievements. Medicare and Social Security, to take two of the largest congressional programs, have cut the rate of poverty among elderly Americans by more than half and provided seniors with generous health benefits.

Genuine democratic, popular government can be chaotic, muddled, and sometimes repugnant. But it is essential. Our representatives in Congress must find a way to continue to fulfill their democratic duties. The people's branch will have to find a way to govern effectively—and to win back popular approval—if American democracy is to flourish in the future.

CHAPTER SUMMARY

Check your understanding of Chapter 13.

⬤ Congress operates under extremely complicated rules that make action difficult. Americans debate whether Congress still works the way it is supposed to—blunting too much government action. Or whether it has become "the broken branch."

⬤ America's Congress is bicameral: The House of Representatives contains 441 members (435 voting; six others represent territories such as Guam and Puerto Rico) elected every two years; in the Senate, one hundred senators serve six-year terms.

⬤ The two chambers of Congress reflect different national priorities. Populists appreciate the responsive House; advocates of stability embrace the more deliberate Senate.

⬤ Members of the House and Senate represent Americans in multiple ways. These include:

- *Geographic representation*: Constitutional election rules say members must live in the state or district they represent.

- *Descriptive representation*: Does the assembly look like the people?

- *Substantive representation*: Do members of Congress effectively pursue constituent interests?

⬤ Members of Congress are always running for office. Fundraising takes up a particularly large amount of time and attention. Members pay special attention to their home styles: Most go back to their constituency every week—compressing normal congressional business into the period from Tuesday through Thursday.

Need to review key ideas in greater depth? Click here.

⬤ Congress is increasingly an institution of strangers who do not know one another well.

⬤ Congressional leadership in the House includes a Speaker, majority and minority leaders, and ten whips. Successful House leaders impose discipline on their party members. In the Senate, party leaders and whips have fewer institutional tools with which to keep members in line.

⬤ Congressional committees have proved efficient and adaptable over the years, preparing legislation and conducting oversight of the executive branch. However, the committee system also fragments Congress, hides action from public view, enables well-placed constituents to win individual favors, and makes it difficult to pass major legislation.

⬤ Floor procedures are another intricate part of the legislative process. Once passed by both House and Senate, legislation may still face a conference committee, a presidential veto, or both.

⬤ Congress has grown more partisan. Today, the parties themselves are more ideologically consistent. This makes for sharper conflict, but it also gives people clearer choices.

⬤ The difficult path to legislation raises a key question about Congress: Should we cheer the slow-moving process as a way to limit government? Or should we worry that the institution is not up to addressing America's vital problems?

KEY TERMS

Flashcard review.

116th Congress, p. 382

Cloture vote, p. 404

Committee hearing, p. 401

Committee markup
  session, p. 402

Conference committee, p. 405

Congressional caucus, p. 385

Earmark, p. 396

Filibuster, p. 383

Floor, p. 382

Legislative hold, p. 382

President pro tempore, p. 395

Roll-call vote, p. 405

Speaker of the House, p. 393

Unanimous consent, p. 403

Veto, p. 407

Voice vote, p. 405

STUDY QUESTIONS

1. Discuss the following reforms:

a) There should be public financing for all congressional elections, even if that means raising taxes.

b) The Senate filibuster and legislative hold should be abolished.

c) There should be more limits on lobbyists' access and/or influence.

2. How did Congress lose so much power to the president? Are there ways to get some of that power back? Should power be more balanced between the two branches?

3. Why is Congress today so partisan? Can you think of ways to reduce partisanship? Are there any advantages to drawing strong partisan lines between Republicans and Democrats?

4. Should it be easier to pass laws through Congress? What, if any, benefits do all the checks and balances provide?

5. Why is Congress so unpopular with the American people? In your view, does Congress deserve its low approval ratings?

Go to www.oup.com/us/Morone to find quizzes, flash cards, simulations, tutorials, videos, and other study tools.

14 The Presidency

GEORGE WASHINGTON, the first president of the United

States, faced a problem. He had to persuade thirteen independent-minded states to think of themselves as one unified nation. Washington decided to foster unity by touring the new country. He set out with assistants, slaves, horses, and dogs. As the party approached each town, the president mounted a great white steed and cantered handsomely into the cheering throngs, his favorite greyhound trotting at his side. Washington named the dog Cornwallis, after the British general who surrendered to end the Revolutionary War. Poor Cornwallis the greyhound died while touring the southern states, but his name reminded the people that they were part of a proud and independent nation. Everywhere Washington went the people greeted their president with ringing bells, cheers, songs, speeches, parades, and flags. The crowds felt, at least for a day, like Americans.[1]

Who are we? Each president offers a different answer. Washington may be our greatest president, not because of his domestic programs or foreign policies—at the time, critics were scathing about both. Instead, Washington embodied the new nation. He championed American ideals, spoke to national aspirations, introduced new ideas, and personified the nation's sense of identity—both to Americans and to the world. All presidents do the same, some more successfully than others.

The president's role is difficult partly because Americans rarely agree about who we are. The United States are often the *Un*-United States. Washington took slaves on his unity tour. Didn't slavery violate the new nation's ideals? Many Americans knew that it did.

Almost 230 years after Washington's tour, newly inaugurated President Donald Trump signed an executive order barring citizens from seven Muslim-majority nations from entering the United States—without consulting administrators or legal experts. The results: Chaos at the borders; civil rights attorneys dashed to the airports to defend visitors abruptly pulled out of lines; multiple federal courts put the ban on hold. The president pressed on. His administration rewrote the travel ban in light of court rulings, and eventually, a bitterly divided Supreme Court (5–4) upheld it. The Court majority was clear: The law gave the president authority over the nation's borders. Six months later the president signed another controversial order barring most transgender individuals from serving in the U.S. military. It reversed an executive order signed

● *President Trump signs a travel ban during his first week in office.*

In this chapter, you will:

● See how the Constitution defines the presidency.

● Focus on presidential power.

● Learn what presidents do.

● Reflect on presidential popularity—and greatness.

● Consider the personal side of the office.

● Tour the Executive Office of the president, and meet the team around a president.

by his predecessor, Barack Obama. Again, the president's order set off a scramble in his own agency, this time the military; a debate in Congress; and more litigation.

Many constitutional experts read these executive orders as emblematic of swelling presidential power.[2] President Obama had seized presidential authority to protect immigrants and transgender individuals; President Trump expanded that authority still further to keep people from some countries out of the United States and some Americans out of the military. Many Americans despaired as neither Congress nor the Court, both dominated by conservatives, was willing to question his authority.[3]

But there is another way to see it. The case illustrates how the president is enmeshed in a complex institutional web. The president clearly took his policy to the people during the election, then had to adjust it to address the courts' constitutional concerns, work with the bureaucracy to organize an orderly process, maintain support in Congress (which can override the bans), and work out the legal arguments with the Justice Department.

Today, the presidency raises precisely the same question the delegates debated at the Constitutional Convention: How much authority should the president wield? From Washington's tour to Trump's bans, the presidency reflects the same three themes:

> *The president personifies America.* More than any other individual, presidents tell us who we are—and what we are becoming. As Americans grow more partisan, this traditional role becomes more challenging. Most Republicans believed (incorrectly) that Barack Obama was born in Kenya—and was therefore not eligible to be president.[4] Fast forward to the present, when Democrats return the favor and chant "not my president" during frequent protests against Donald Trump.
>
> *The president injects new ideas and themes into American politics.* Our discussion of Congress emphasized the institutional rules of the game; the presidency puts more focus on individuals and ideas. President Trump promised a new approach to border security—and that quickly rose to the top of the nation's political agenda.
>
> *The president has enormous powers—at least on paper.* That authority, and how presidents use it, returns us to the fundamental question: Is the presidency too powerful for a democratic republic? Or is the office too weak to do what Americans demand of it? Perhaps the same president can be both too strong and too weak. Keep this question of authority in mind as you read the chapter.

Defining the Presidency

Time travelers from the nineteenth century would easily recognize today's Senate or Supreme Court. However, the modern White House would stun them. The presidency is the branch of the federal government that has changed the most over the decades.

BY THE NUMBERS
The Presidency

Number of presidents in the last 85 years	**14**
Split between Republican/Democratic presidents in the last 85 years	**7 from each party**
Length, in months, of the shortest presidency (William Henry Harrison)	**1**
Length, in months, of the longest presidency (Franklin D. Roosevelt)	**145**
Number of presidents younger than Barack Obama when they were elected	**2**
Number of presidents older than Donald Trump when elected	**0**
Election year of last president without a college education (Harry S Truman)	**1945**
Birth year of first president to be born in a hospital (Jimmy Carter)	**1924**
Year in which first woman (Victoria Woodhull) ran for president	**1872**
Number of presidents who were sons or nephews of prior presidents: (John Quincy Adams, Benjamin Harrison, Franklin D. Roosevelt, George W. Bush)	**4**
Estimated proportion of presidents who have had extramarital affairs	**1 in 3**
Number of presidents to hold a patent (Abraham Lincoln, for an invention to free boats trapped on a sandbar)	**1**

Who do Americans elect to the highest office—and how representative are they?

Up till eighty years ago, Americans could walk right in the front door of the White House and greet the president. In 1829, during President Andrew Jackson's inauguration, supporters mobbed the mansion and forced the president to climb out a window for his own safety; aides placed tubs with whiskey and orange juice on the lawn to lure the crowds outside. When William Henry Harrison won the presidency in 1840, so many men milled about the White House hoping to get a government job that the president-elect could not find an empty room to meet with his cabinet.

● *Different eras. After Andrew Jackson's inauguration, Americans crush into the executive mansion—aides used whiskey punch to draw the crowds outside. Today, elegantly dressed supporters snap photos of the president dancing on stage.*

Today, there are no more mobs in the White House. Presidents have redefined their roles and renegotiated their powers. The presidency is a different institution. Partly, all the changes arise because each president has the opportunity to reshape the office. One reason the presidency is so fluid lies in the job description. By now, you know where to look for that: the Constitution.

Defined by Controversy

The Constitutional Convention's delegates faced three tough questions when they defined the presidency (for more detail, see Chapter 3). First, *should the United States even have a president?* Traditional republics feared executive power. The founders feared the English king was too powerful; but also worried that the state governments did not have enough executive power and were too feeble to govern effectively. Their job was to find a happy medium. In the end, they selected a single president and established simple qualifications for the post: a natural-born citizen at least 35 years old who had lived in the United States for at least 14 years.

Second, *how long should the president serve?* The delegates at the Constitutional Convention considered terms of four, six, seven, eight, 11, and 15 years. Alexander Hamilton passionately argued that presidents should be elected for life—an elected king. They settled on four years, with no limit on the number of terms. Washington would set a precedent when he stepped down after his second term, dazzling his contemporaries by walking away from power. For a century and a half, American presidents followed Washington's example and served no more than two terms—until Franklin D. Roosevelt broke the pattern and won four elections between 1932 and 1944. The Twenty-Second Amendment, ratified in 1951, six years after Roosevelt's death, bars presidents from serving more than two terms.

Third, *how should the United States choose its president?* Delegates to the convention feared that the public did not know enough, that the state legislatures were too self-interested, and that Congress would become too powerful if given the task of appointing the executive. They finally settled on a roundabout method, the Electoral College, which you encountered in Chapter 10: The states each get electoral votes equal to the members in their congressional delegation. Who would elect the electors? The Convention simply left the matter to the states (see Chapter 3).

Political scientists still debate the Electoral College because it distorts the popular vote. Even very close popular votes often look lopsided in the Electoral College. Ronald Reagan got 50.7 percent (in a three-way race) in 1980, yet the Electoral College made these contests look like a rout, with Reagan taking a whopping 91 percent of the Electoral College vote. More important, the Electoral College has put the popular vote loser in the White House in two of the last three presidencies. Major population centers—New York, Los Angeles, Houston—are all but ignored during presidential elections because they are in states which safely give majorities (and all their Electoral College votes) to one party or the other.[5]

▷

Learn about executive privilege and other presidential powers.

The President's Powers

Article 2 of the Constitution, which defines the presidency, seems puzzling at first glance. Article 1 meticulously lists everything Congress is empowered to do: The instructions run for 52 paragraphs. In contrast, Article 2 says very little about who the president is or what the president does. Thirteen short paragraphs define the office. This vague constitutional mandate is one reason why the office keeps evolving.

The Constitution is especially terse when it gets to the heart of the presidency: the powers and duties of the chief executive. It grants the president a limited number of **expressed powers**, or explicit grants of authority. Most are carefully balanced by corresponding congressional powers. Table 14.1 summarizes this balance.[6]

Expressed powers: Powers the Constitution explicitly grants to the president.

The president draws real authority from a simple phrase at the end of the section: "Take care that the laws be faithfully executed." Congress votes on legislation and then sends it to the executive branch to put into effect. In other words, Congress grants **delegated powers** to the president. For example, Congress passes legislation that aims to improve hospital care. It delegates power to the executive branch, which issues detailed rules saying that hospitals will receive lower federal payments if patients develop infections after surgery. Vague laws increase the discretion of the executive branch which puts them into effect.

Delegated powers: Powers that Congress passes on to the president.

Presidents claim a third source of authority: **inherent powers**. These are not specified in the Constitution or delegated by legislation, but are implicit in the vague Article 2 phrase, "The executive power shall be vested in a president." During crises, presidents have often seized on "inherent" authority. During the Civil War, for example, President Lincoln took a series of unprecedented military actions with no clear legal basis. He imposed censorship, ordered a naval blockade, and issued orders while Congress was not in session. After the 9/11 attacks, President Bush exercised inherent powers to engage in foreign surveillance, to detain enemy combatants without hearings, and to authorize coercive interrogation (which critics

Inherent powers of the presidency: Powers assumed by presidents, often during a crisis, on the basis of the constitutional phrase "The executive power shall be vested in the president."

TABLE 14.1	**The President's Expressed Powers**

The president is commander in chief of the army, navy, and state militias. But Congress has the power to declare war, set the military budget, and make the rules governing the military.
The president can grant pardons and reprieves for offenses against the United States.
The president can make treaties (with the approval of two-thirds of the Senate), appoint ambassadors (with the advice and consent of the Senate), and select Supreme Court justices and other officers (again, with Senate approval).
The Constitution also authorizes presidents to appoint executive officers and solicit their opinions, and requires presidents to report on the state of the Union.

Executive privilege: Power claimed by the president to resist requests for authority by Congress, the courts, or the public. Not mentioned in the Constitution but based on the separation of powers.

THE BIG STICK IN THE CARIBBEAN SEA

● One way to expand presidential authority: President Theodore Roosevelt, who entered the White House in 1901, combined diplomacy and military might—"speak softly," he summarized, "and carry a big stick."

Executive agreements:
International agreements made by the president that do not require the approval of the Senate.

called torture). The president's claim of inherent powers is not the last word on the matter. Congress may pass legislation in response and the Supreme Court often weighs whether the president has overstepped the constitutional boundaries of executive authority.

Modern presidents have expanded presidential power in many ways. As we shall see later in this chapter, presidents regularly issue executive orders, negotiate **executive agreements** with other nations, and claim **executive privilege**—all ways of bypassing Congress. Throughout this chapter we encounter subtle ways that presidents have expanded their power.

The result is a very fluid definition of presidential power. Presidents regularly renegotiate the limits of the office through their actions at home and abroad. Crises generally expand the presidential role. More than any other institution, the presidency is a constant work in progress. The arc of presidential history begins with a vague constitutional grant of power that has grown through the years.

This discussion brings us back to the question we posed at the start of the chapter: Has the president become too powerful? We turn to that question in the next section.

COMPARING NATIONS 14.1	Chief Executives' Power
Although presidents have expanded their authority over time, chief executives in parliamentary systems, those used in most other democracies, typically are granted these powers. U.S. presidents might long to exercise any of these.	*Emergency decree powers*: Executives' authority is greatly expanded in national emergencies (and they typically get to decide what counts as an "emergency").
	Partial (line-item) *veto*: Prime ministers and other foreign leaders are able to strip out individual legislative provisions that they find objectionable.
	Exclusive right to introduce certain types of legislation, especially budgets.
	The ability to dismiss the legislature and call new elections.

The Bottom Line

» Presidents serve a four-year term and can run for re-election once.

» They are elected indirectly, via the Electoral College.

» The president has three types of powers: *expressed* in the Constitution, *delegated* by Congress, and *inherent* in the role of chief executive.

» In theory, Congress passes laws and the president executes them. In reality, presidents constantly negotiate the limits of their power—which often expands during crises.

🛈 Is the Presidency Too Powerful?

The constitutional framers wrestled with the same issue we debate today: *power.* How much authority do presidents need to protect the nation and get things done? When does the office's reach violate the idea of limited government?

An Imperial Presidency?

During George Washington's national tour, a few Americans fretted about his nine stallions, gold-trimmed saddles, personal attendants, and all that adulation. Washington, they whispered, was acting more like a king than the president of a homespun republic. They were articulating a constant American theme: The president has grown too mighty. Flash forward two centuries.

When President Obama visited Africa, hundreds of Secret Service agents arrived in advance, an aircraft carrier with a fully staffed trauma center sailed offshore, and military cargo planes hauled in fifty-six support vehicles including fourteen limousines. Likewise, when President Trump landed in London, the English press reported that 1,000 staff members came along with him. The presidential parties included lawyers, secretaries, speechwriters, military aides, physicians, and personal chefs. For the English visit, they required 750 hotel rooms. U.S. fighter jets flew in shifts, providing continual air cover. Today, American presidents travel like emperors.[7]

What about weaker individuals? Washington's successor, President John Adams, did not have to worry about cheering crowds. Critics mocked the chubby second president as "His Rotundity." Adams attracted so little attention that he regularly swam naked in the Potomac River (until a female reporter allegedly spied him, sat on his clothes, and demanded an interview). Even Adams, however, aroused widespread fears about executive power when he signed the Alien and Sedition Acts, which gave the executive broad powers to deport "dangerous aliens" and punish "false, scandalous, and malicious" speech. The president seemed to be trampling the First Amendment by silencing criticism.

Many presidents have stretched the limits of the office. One approach, the **unitary executive theory,** defends the expansion of power. This view contends that the Constitution puts the president in charge of executing the laws, and therefore no one—not Congress, not the judiciary, not even the people—may limit presidential power when it comes to executive matters. Many executive decisions demand swift, decisive, and sometimes secretive action. Only an empowered president, the argument goes, can make those instantaneous calls.[8]

The unitary executive theory is controversial. Arthur Schlesinger, Jr., a celebrated historian, warned of an **imperial presidency**. Very powerful presidents, he feared, become like emperors: They run roughshod over Congress, issue secret decisions, unilaterally deploy force around the world, and burst past the checks and balances limiting presidential power. Critics worry that imperial features have slowly become part of the presidency itself. Republicans bitterly argued that the Obama administration's overreach embodied the imperial presidency. Now Democrats say the same about the Trump administration. Many contemporary scholars echo this fear: As Congress grows more deadlocked, suggested political scientist

Unitary executive theory: The idea that the Constitution puts the president in charge of executing the laws and that therefore no other branch may limit presidential discretion over executive matters.

Imperial presidency: A characterization of the American presidency that suggests it is demonstrating imperial traits, and that the republic is morphing into an empire.

🔵 *President Obama arrives in Los Angeles aboard Marine One—surrounded by support aircraft.*

Francis Fukuyama, supporters cheer when presidents act decisively—even if it pushes the boundaries of presidential power. Power appears to be flowing to the president.[9]

At issue are two vital principles: We need a president who is strong enough to lead the country and face our problems. But if presidents become too strong, we lose our republican form of government. This is a deep paradox of American politics: *We need powerful leaders; we fear powerful leaders.*

A Weak Office?

At the same time, the presidency can sometimes seem very weak. Every modern president has complained about his inability to get basic goals accomplished. Congress, the courts, the opposing political party, the media, interest groups, and bad luck can all humble a president. Since 1960, only four (of 11) presidents have completed two full terms. What kind of "imperial" presidency is that?

Presidents often appear weakest when they wrestle with domestic issues. Even under the best of circumstances, as we saw in the previous chapter, it is difficult to get major legislation through Congress. The president nominally runs the executive branch, but the bureaucracy is immense and often difficult to control—and cabinets are staffed by officials the Senate must approve. Introducing changes through the American political process is extremely difficult, even for the savviest presidents.

For a case study in the weak presidency, take Jimmy Carter. Congressional relations turned frosty early in his term after Carter unexpectedly vetoed a spending bill. Carter's major legislative proposals stalled on Capitol Hill. Then the economy soured; interest rates spiraled toward 20 percent, and unemployment topped 10 percent. Gas prices soared, forcing customers in some regions to wait in long lines at gas stations.

Carter did not seem to have an answer to all the woes besetting the nation. A mischievous editor at the *Boston Globe* captured one reaction to Carter's speech when he designed a mock headline, "Mush from the Wimp." By mistake, the headline ran in the *Globe*'s first edition.[10] A few months later, militant Iranian students took 53 Americans hostage at the U.S. embassy in Tehran and held them for 444 days. A weak president seemed to be completely overwhelmed by events all around him.

Even President Trump, who made progress on many of his goals (rolling back regulations, cutting taxes, restricting immigration from Muslim countries, winning conservative Supreme Court appointments) struggled to get much of his agenda through Congress: He failed to repeal Obamacare (by a single vote in the Senate), to build a border wall, to change the immigration laws, or to slash federal spending.

Back and forth goes the debate. Is the president getting too powerful and breaking free from popular control—both the formal institutional limits and the more subtle mores? Or do presidents need more power and authority if they are to effectively govern a superpower in the twenty-first century? To answer these questions, let us take a closer look at just what presidents do.

 **The Bottom Line**

» Americans want a powerful president; simultaneously, Americans fear a powerful president.

» The executive branch has grown far stronger over time, especially when it comes to foreign policy.

» In significant ways, presidential power also is limited, especially when it comes to solving domestic problems.

What Presidents Do

Over time, presidents have taken on many jobs. Some are described in the Constitution. Others arise organically during national crises. Presidents seize still other powers as they jockey for political advantage. By now, the president has accumulated an extraordinary number of hats (and helmets).

Commander in Chief

The Constitution lays it out simply: "The president shall be the Commander-in-Chief of the Army and Navy of the United States and the militia of the several states." Congress declares war and presidents manage it.

For many years, the United States had a small standing army and called men and women to service in wartime. After each war, the army quickly demobilized. This approach reflected classical theory. In great republics like Athens and Rome, citizens took up arms when enemies loomed and then returned home when the crisis had passed—just as George Washington had done during the American Revolution. Peacetime armies were, according to the traditional perspective, a recipe for empire or monarchy.

This tradition changed after World War II, when the United States faced off against the Soviet Union in the Cold War. An army of around 250,000 (after World War I) grew into a force of over two million and spread across the globe. Back in 1835, Tocqueville mused that the Constitution gave the president "almost royal prerogatives which he has no occasion to use." Now the occasion had arrived, and the president's power grew.[11]

Today, America's active-duty force numbers over 1.3 million, with another 808,000 in reserve (Figure 14.1). Military spending fell sharply between 2011 and 2015—partially because of troop reductions in Iraq and Afghanistan—and then began to rise again in 2016, topping $681 billion in 2018. And that does not include the Department of Veterans Affairs, the Department of Homeland Security, intelligence agencies, and other related efforts. The military operates about 750 installations around the globe. In short, the commander in chief oversees the world's largest fighting force. That role, by itself, makes the president one of the most powerful individuals in the world.

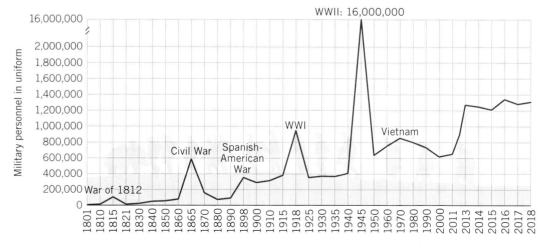

Figure 14.1 *The military and how it grew, 1800–2018: Traditionally, the United States called soldiers to war and then demobilized after the war. The United States began to play a global role after the Spanish-American War. (Historical Statistics/Statistical Abstracts and US Department of Defense)*

What Do YOU Think?

Who Should Deploy American Troops?

The Constitution gives Congress the power to declare war and makes the president commander in chief. However, Congress has not declared war since 1941—the start of World War II. Since then, the United States has fought wars in Korea, Vietnam, the Persian Gulf, Kosovo, Afghanistan, Iraq, and more—without a congressional declaration. The War Powers Act only requires the President to seek approval 60 days after committing troops. Should the president have the power to dispatch troops without prior authorization from Congress?

Yes.
Today, dangers arise in minutes, not months. Enemies have sophisticated weapons that can threaten the United States or its allies at any time. New surveillance techniques alert the executive about terrorists planning an operation, troops massing on a border, or unusual communications patterns. In the modern world, the United States cannot afford to leave decisions to deploy military power to the slow, partisan, very public congressional process.

No.
The founders were clear that decisions over war and peace should be debated in Congress. This is one of the most important roles that Congress has and a public debate is crucial for democracy. Open public debate, caution, and the ability to hear all sides are just as important—perhaps even more important, than speed when it comes to deploying troops. Besides, giving the presidents this power makes it too easy to deploy America's powerful arsenal. Anyone who feels this section of the Constitution is out of date must follow the rules and propose a constitutional amendment.

Meanwhile, checks on the commander in chief have faded. The Constitution authorizes Congress to declare wars, but since the nuclear age dawned in 1945, presidents have rarely waited for Congress to act. Facing the doomsday threat of nuclear missiles, military response time is measured in minutes—too fast for congressional deliberation.

In an effort to regain some of its authority, Congress passed the War Powers Act (1973). The act permitted the president to send American forces into combat "in case of a national emergency created by an attack on the United States . . . or its armed forces." When presidents deploy troops, however, they must notify Congress within 48 hours and gain its approval within 60 days. In practice, presidents have unilaterally deployed troops and treated the War Powers Act with contempt. Even when they sometimes do turn to Congress, it is very difficult to vote no when Americans are in combat.[12]

Presidential powers have always waxed during wartime. Franklin D. Roosevelt's attorney general once quipped, "The Constitution has not greatly bothered any wartime president."[13] Three developments have further increased the president's military authority: America's powerful military machine, always poised for deployment; new technologies, such as drones, that permit presidents to target enemies around the globe; and perceptions of perpetual threat—first from the Soviet Union, now from terrorists.

Presidents are deeply engaged by their military role. They traditionally start each day with a security briefing that reviews all the dangers stirring around the world. They have a large national security staff. And—the great symbol of our nuclear age—they are never more than a few feet away from "the football."

If you see the president in person, or a wide-angle shot on television, you can glimpse a military officer standing about 20 feet away and clutching a medium-size black briefcase, known as "the football." What is in the bag? The answer is classified, but over the years the public has learned that it is a mobile communications center locked into the American nuclear arsenal. Every minute of every day, the American president is steps away from a kit that would enable him or her to launch an attack that could obliterate any nation from the face of the Earth.

Top Diplomat

The Constitution gives presidents the lead role in foreign affairs. Presidents and their international advisors set an overall framework for the U.S. role in the world. Some administrations emphasize international alliances; they work closely with foreign powers and build multinational institutions. Others prefer to go it alone—they ignore the United Nations and are reluctant to sign treaties for fear that they will bind the United States to foreign governments.

Global statecraft is full of unexpected snares. When President Obama met then–British Prime Minister Gordon Brown for the first time, the English press howled about "humiliation." Brown had given Obama a valuable pen carved from the timbers of a nineteenth-century British warship; Obama's gift was a pile of DVDs. Did the then popular president really mean to hu-

A uniformed officer with "the football"—a briefcase that contains launch codes for the nuclear arsenal. The football is never more than a few feet away from the president.

miliate the relatively unpopular prime minister? Certainly not; the administration had simply slipped up.

Foreign policy crises differ vastly from everyday domestic politics. Passing laws is a long, complicated process full of compromise and constraint. During international crises—hostage situations, terrorist attacks, the outbreak of war, or simply international negotiations—all eyes turn toward the president and his team. Often presidents must make fast decisions with immediate consequences. John F. Kennedy captured the intensity, a few weeks after taking office, in a late-night phone call to former vice president Richard Nixon during his first international crisis. "It really is true that foreign affairs is the only important issue for a president to handle, isn't it?" queried Kennedy. "I mean who gives a shit if the minimum wage is $1.15 or $1.25 compared to something like this?"[14]

Foreign diplomacy is not just about trouble spots. The State Department manages 305 embassies, consulates, and diplomatic missions around the world. Presidents must hash out American relations with nearly two hundred nations that range from "special friends" to distant allies to avowed enemies. Intricate questions arise about how to approach each country: Should the president shake hands with

● *Body language and diplomacy: President Trump confronts the G-7 leaders including German Chancellor Angela Merkel (center) and Japanese Prime Minister Shinzo Abe (with folded arms).*

Assess current debates on climate change.

our nation's enemies? Every smile or snub sends a diplomatic message. A president sets the tone and the policy for all these relationships.

President Trump has stunned allies by disparaging their leaders and their policies—attacking the prime minister of Canada as "very dishonest and weak" and calling Great Britain's Brexit plan "very unfortunate."[15] Although President Trump's comments have violated the polite language of classical diplomacy, he has pursued a larger goal: fundamentally reorient American foreign policy. After World War II, American leaders from both parties built a web of alliances to promote Western and—sometimes—global interests: military alliances such as NATO, economic agreements to lower tariffs and facilitate free trade, and special accords on issues like climate change (the Paris Climate Accords). Promoting his America First policy, President Trump has bluntly questioned whether many of these institutions serve U.S. interests.

The president charged that NATO members were not paying their fair share for the alliance and insisted that they speed up their agreement to increase their military budgets to 2 percent of GDP by 2024; then in a meeting with the allies, he upped that goal to 4 percent of GDP (more than the United States itself was spending).[16] In an effort to push wealthy European countries to pay for their own defense, he ordered the Pentagon to study the impact of withdrawing troops from Germany (a key NATO member and ally). Congress responded with a bipartisan, nonbinding resolution supporting NATO. The exchange illustrated how the president now dominates the power over diplomacy. But it also shows how Congress could reassert its authority to influence U.S. global engagement.[17]

The First Legislator

The Constitution includes presidents in the legislative process. It authorizes them to *recommend measures* for Congress's "consideration," report to Congress *information on the state of the Union*, and *veto legislation* they oppose.

Recommending Measures. Until modern times, presidents generally avoided legislative affairs. In 1840, William Henry Harrison devoted his inaugural address—the longest and dullest in history—to denouncing the insatiable love of power creeping into the presidency. He pledged to honor congressional authority by avoiding legislative involvement. Dwight Eisenhower (1953–1961) was the last president to try to leave legislation to Congress. His cabinet officers complained, and before long Eisenhower was recommending measures—and blasting Congress when it failed to approve them.

Today, presidential candidates define the legislative agenda. President Donald Trump campaigned on repealing Obamacare, restricting immigration reform, cutting taxes, and renegotiating trade agreements—precisely what the 115th (2017–2018) Congress took up. Congressional leaders have their own lists. Top White House advisors lobby for favorite programs. And unexpected issues constantly spring up and require presidential attention.

State of the Union.   The Constitution invites the chief executive to report on the state of the Union "from time to time." Today, the "SOTU," as insiders term it, is an annual event, delivered with great fanfare before Congress, Supreme Court justices, cabinet members, and a national television audience. The speech announces the president's legislative program for the year.

Following the SOTU address, each program undergoes a second round of debates within the administration: Does it really fit our budget? Can we make it work smoothly? Did Congress cheer or yawn when the boss rolled it out? What was the public reaction? Most policies have friends and enemies in the administration—and if you get your favorite idea funded, I may not get mine. The process is a bureaucratic version of a knife fight. Proposals that survive go up to Capitol Hill, where they face the long, complicated congressional process we described in the last chapter.

Presidential "Batting Average."   Only members of Congress can formally propose a law, so presidents rely on supporters in each chamber to submit their bills. The White House has a congressional liaison team to negotiate and cut deals. Generally hidden from public view, the liaison is a key role in the modern presidency. No matter how talented a liaison might be, frustration inevitably sets in. To the executive branch, legislators seem overly parochial as they focus on their states and districts. Still, most presidents quickly learn the same lesson: Work closely with Congress. Managing relations with House and Senate members is one of the most important presidential skills.

One measure of a presidents success is their "batting average"—how many of their bills get through (Table 14.2). There are many different ways to keep score: successful passage as a proportion of all the bills the president endorses, of the most important bills, or of bills that the other party opposes. You can see that when the same party controls the White House and Congress, known as unified government, the batting average is much higher, usually around .800. When the opposition party controls Congress (divided government), the average usually falls below .500. Some political scientists have argued that divided government makes for a more effective legislative process. But notice how divided governments have been yielding less agreement in recent years. President Obama enjoyed the highest batting average in the past 75 years when both houses of Congress were Democratic, and the second lowest average when he faced a divided Congress.

Of the presidents since World War II, President John Kennedy signed the most legislation in his first year (684). Who signed the least number? President Trump, with 96 bills.[18]

Veto.   When Congress passes a law, presidents have the authority to sign or **veto** it (*veto* means "I forbid" in Latin). As we saw in the last chapter, a veto blocks the legislation unless two-thirds of both chambers vote to **override** it, a very high bar. Presidents have 10 days to return the legislation to Congress with a message explaining why they have rejected it. If the president does nothing, the bill becomes law in

Veto power: The presidential power to block an act of Congress by refusing to sign – and returning it to Congress with objections.

Override: The process by which Congress can overcome a presidential veto with a two-thirds vote in both chambers.

● Across the ideological divide: President Ronald Reagan (a Republican) and Speaker of the House Tip O'Neill (D-MA) negotiate the budget. "Maybe Tip and I told too many Irish stories," wrote Reagan in his diary after a long dinner together.[i]

TABLE 14.2 Presidential Batting Average: Measuring the Proportion of Congressional Bills on Which the President Took a Position That Passed

PRESIDENT	PARTY	YEARS IN OFFICE	CONGRESSIONAL CONTROL	PERCENTAGE OF CONGRESSIONAL VOTES SUPPORTING PRESIDENT'S POSITION
Ronald Reagan	R	1981–1986	Mixed control (R Senate, D House)	67.4
Ronald Reagan	R	1987–1989	Democrats control Congress	45.4
George H. W. Bush	R	1989–1993	Democrats control Congress	51.8
Bill Clinton	D	1993–1994	Democrats control Congress	86.3
Bill Clinton	D	1995–2000	Republicans control Congress	48.1
George W. Bush	R	2001–2006	Republicans control Congress	80.9
George W. Bush	R	2007–2008	Democrats control Congress	43.0
Barack Obama	D	2009–2010	Democrats control Congress	92.0
Barack Obama	D	2011–2013	Mixed control (D Senate, R House)	52.8
Barack Obama	D	2015–2016	Republicans control Congress	35.7
Donald Trump	R	2017–2018	Republicans control Congress	90.4 (Through 11/12/18)

▇ President's party controls Congress

▇ Opposition party controls Congress

▇ Congress split

10 days—unless the congressional session has expired and the president's inaction kills the legislation, a move known as a "pocket veto."

The veto is a formidable weapon. In the last 80 years, presidents have rejected more than 1,400 bills. Congress managed to override just 60 times, a congressional "batting average" of 4 percent. Recently the veto has become a more partisan weapon, as conflict between the parties has escalated. Franklin D. Roosevelt, Harry Truman, and Jimmy Carter all flourished the veto pen against a Congress controlled by their own party; in their first two years, the three presidents struck down 73, 74, and 19, respectively. In contrast, recent presidents—Clinton, Bush, Obama, and Trump—have been far more sparing in their use of their veto power (see Figure 14.2).

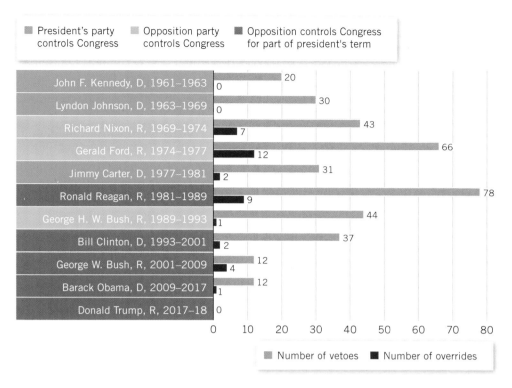

President's party controls Congress | Opposition party controls Congress | Opposition controls Congress for part of president's term

President	Number of vetoes	Number of overrides
John F. Kennedy, D, 1961–1963	20	0
Lyndon Johnson, D, 1963–1969	30	0
Richard Nixon, R, 1969–1974	43	7
Gerald Ford, R, 1974–1977	66	12
Jimmy Carter, D, 1977–1981	31	2
Ronald Reagan, R, 1981–1989	78	9
George H. W. Bush, R, 1989–1993	44	1
Bill Clinton, D, 1993–2001	37	2
George W. Bush, R, 2001–2009	12	4
Barack Obama, D, 2009–2017	12	1
Donald Trump, R, 2017–18	0	

Number of vetoes | Number of overrides

Figure 14.2 *Presidential vetoes and overrides. Note that vetoes were far more common 50 years ago, even when the same party controlled Congress and the White House. Congress rarely manages to override a presidential veto. (U.S. Senate)*

A president's veto rarely comes as a surprise. As Congress works on a law, the president's congressional liaisons are ever present. Administration officials may threaten a veto to shape the legislation in ways they prefer. When negotiations get especially intense, the president can also go public and challenge individual members or Congress as a whole. Congressional leaders in turn can threaten to bury another bill the president wants, or defy a president to veto popular bills. After all the back-and-forth, presidents have developed yet another strategy: They can voice their displeasure while signing bills into law.

Signing Statements. Bill signing has become a great Washington ritual, especially for popular legislation. Congressional sponsors flank the president, who has a big pile of pens to hand out to the program's key supporters while cameras capture the smiling moment.

In recent decades, presidents have increasingly issued **signing statements** as they sign a bill into law. These statements may offer their administration's interpretation of the law—one sometimes at odds with Congress's expressed ideas.

Chief Bureaucrat

As chief bureaucrat, the president has the powers to make appointments and issue executive orders.

Appointments. The Constitution gives the president the power to appoint the men and women of the executive branch of government, subject to confirmation by the Senate. President Washington took the top officers of the major departments and organized them into a cabinet to advise him. By 1800, the executive branch comprised five departments and two hundred officeholders.[19]

Signing statements: Written presidential declarations commenting on the bill that is being signed into law—often including criticism of one or more provisions.

Today, the executive branch includes 15 departments and 2.6 million employees—a number that has leveled off in recent years; add the military and the executive branch tops four million. Presidents appoint some four thousand **political appointees** who direct the executive agencies; the rest are **civil servants** who stay on from one administration to the next (all discussed in Chapter 15).

Political appointees: Top officials in the executive agencies, appointed by the president.

The Trump administration has shattered one record: four cabinet secretaries fired in the first year—and five in a year and half. No other president dismissed more than one. The administration's supporters cheer the full throttle, take-no-prisoners approach to governing. Others worry that large organizations like the cabinet agencies suffer when there is rapid turnover at the top. After 14 months in office, the White House had a record number of vacancies. Beyond firings and resignations, the administration had not yet nominated any individual for roughly one third of the 640 top jobs throughout the departments, leaving career civil servants or no one at all in these positions as of late 2018. (We'll explore this issue in Chapter 15.)

Civil servants: Members of the permanent executive branch bureaucracy who are employed on the basis of competitive exams and keep their positions regardless of the presidential administration.

Executive order: A presidential declaration, with the force of law, that issues instructions to the executive branch without any requirement for congressional action or approval.

Executive Orders.   As chief executive, presidents wield powers that do not need to go through Congress. They can sign **executive orders**, with the force of law, setting guidelines for federal agencies. Most executive orders specify the details needed to implement acts of Congress. Some are simply instructions for operating the executive branch: setting up a new council or office, for example. Others involve controversial decisions. They can be issued with fanfare or executed secretly. Recent executive orders include: regulatory rollbacks, bans on entry from selected countries (described at the start of this chapter), enhanced border security, restrictions on lobbying, and an effort to strip funds from sanctuary cities.

Some presidential scholars suggest that executive orders are unconstitutional—the Constitution never mentions them. However, courts generally permit the orders as part of the "inherent powers" of the presidency.[20] The Supreme Court has only struck down eight executive orders—five of Franklin Roosevelt's, two of Bill Clinton's, and one of Barack Obama's—out of more than 13,700 going back to the Washington administration.

Contemporary administrations had been issuing between 30 to 40 executive orders a year. President Trump issued 58 in his first year—more than any prior administration. The Trump administration has used executive orders to undo Obama's executive orders on immigrants brought to the United States as children (the "Dreamers") and on regulations for Obamacare. It has sued to cap refugees coming to the United States, ban transgender people from the military, restrict environmental reviews on infrastructure projects, form (and then disband) a voter fraud commission, and bar tax authorities from imposing penalties on clergy members who endorse political candidates. At least eight of the Trump Administration executive orders are still blocked by the courts.

Some observers worry that, once again, Congress is steadily losing authority. Presidents—from both parties—use a traditional form of executive power to expand the scope of their

● *President Trump signs the first bill of his administration—surrounded by administration officials and congressional leaders from both sides of the aisle.*

Executive Orders Issued, Per Day

WHICH PRESIDENTS RELIED MOST ON THIS POWER?

Presidential power is exercised in many forms. Although the Constitution separates power among the branches, presidents dating back to Abraham Lincoln have issued executive orders that have the force of law but do not require congressional approval.

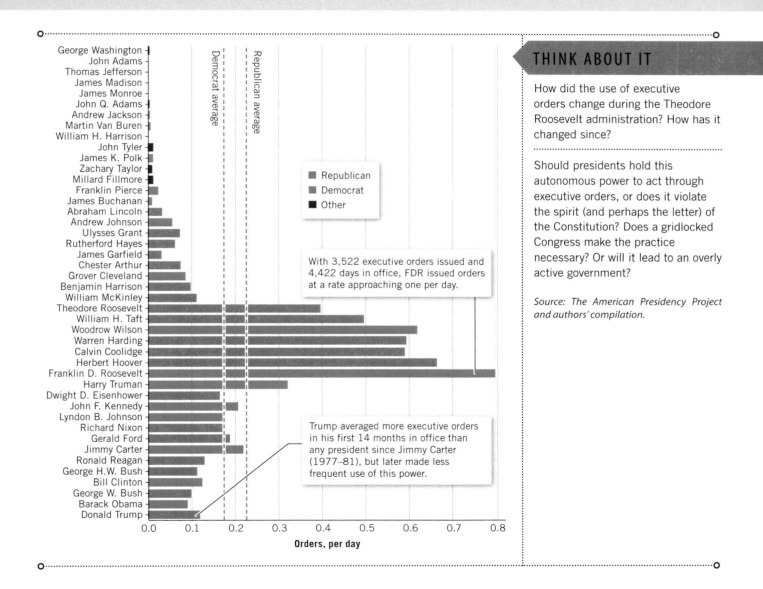

Legend:
- Republican
- Democrat
- Other

With 3,522 executive orders issued and 4,422 days in office, FDR issued orders at a rate approaching one per day.

Trump averaged more executive orders in his first 14 months in office than any president since Jimmy Carter (1977–81), but later made less frequent use of this power.

X-axis: Orders, per day (0.0 to 0.8)

Vertical reference lines: Democrat average, Republican average

THINK ABOUT IT

How did the use of executive orders change during the Theodore Roosevelt administration? How has it changed since?

Should presidents hold this autonomous power to act through executive orders, or does it violate the spirit (and perhaps the letter) of the Constitution? Does a gridlocked Congress make the practice necessary? Or will it lead to an overly active government?

Source: The American Presidency Project and authors' compilation.

office. More and more, worry the critics, they bypass Congress and make policy from the White House—and Congress, marked by partisan stalemate, has been slow to respond.[21] There is, however, an inherent weakness in governing by executive order: They are much easier for an incoming administration to repeal and replace than an act of Congress.

Economist in Chief

Economic authority is one item the Constitution definitely does *not* grant the president. It places the power of the purse—taxing, spending, borrowing, and regulating commerce—firmly in congressional hands. However, during the Great Depression of the 1930s, the Roosevelt administration seized responsibility for putting the nation back to work, launching one recovery program after another. "Take a method and try it," insisted Roosevelt. "If that fails, try another. . . . Above all try something."[22]

The idea soon took root: The president was responsible for a smooth-running economy. The year after Roosevelt died, Congress legislated the Council of Economic Advisers (CEA) to help presidents oversee the economy. Today, the president and a host of staffers monitor economic conditions. White House economists vet every plan and proposal for its impact on American prosperity; they help formulate policy on almost every issue—taxing, spending, trade deals, and the projected costs of a new federal holiday. Every new administration crowds more economists into its ranks. Presidential popularity and, as we saw in Chapter 10, the party's chances of holding onto the office in the next election, are heavily influenced by economic conditions.

During the Trump administration's first two years, the economy boomed—and, as always, credit went to the administration in power. The president himself took a very visible role: placing tariffs on aluminum and steel; launching a trade war with China, and renegotiating NAFTA (the trade deal with Mexico and Canada). Despite the deep discomfort of most economists with tariffs and trade wars, the economy continued to prosper right through most of 2018, although growth slowed across the second half of the year. What will be the long-term consequences of all these actions? Stay tuned!

● The president as head of state. President Bill Clinton and First Lady Hillary Clinton wear traditional kente cloth. They are waving to thousands of cheering Ghanaians. With them is then-president of Ghana, Jerry Rawlings.

The Head of State

Most nations have a ceremonial head of state who stands above partisan politics and represents the nation. The queen of England, the emperor of Japan, and the president of Israel all play this nonpolitical role while their prime ministers make the policies that govern their countries. Citizens of the British Isles do not need to check their political affiliation when they sing "God Save the Queen"—she represents them across the political spectrum. In contrast, the presidents of the United States play both roles. They stand for the nation even while they fight for one party.

Presidents spend a lot of time in their ceremonial role. They throw out the first pitch during the World Series, spare a turkey every Thanksgiving, light the White House Christmas tree and menorah, smash a bottle of champagne across the bow of a new aircraft carrier, congratulate national heroes, host championship sports teams, and embody America every time the Marine Corps Band plays "Hail to the Chief." When presidents travel abroad, they represent all Americans, not just their party or their supporters.

Party Leader

George Washington repeatedly warned the country against political parties and the strife they bring. However, by his second term, rival parties were not-so-quietly emerging and they thrust yet another role onto the president: party leader. This role sharpens the tension we described in the last section. There is a very fine line between leading the nation (and standing for everyone) and leading the Republicans (which means defeating Democrats).

Can anything tamp down the partisan conflict? Yes: The secret ingredient is fear. When a president grows very popular, opponents will often go along out of fear that the voters might punish them if they do not. Presidents who get more votes in a district than a House member, or more votes in the state than a senator, can be very persuasive—as long as their poll numbers remain high.

The Bully Pulpit: Introducing Ideas

President Theodore Roosevelt was bursting with ideas, opinions, exhortations, and warnings. He called the presidency itself a "bully pulpit" (today we might say "awesome brand multiplier"). Roosevelt knew that an active president has the country's ear, an opening to introduce and promote new ideas.

Most presidencies are marked by a few big ideas. In his inaugural address, John F. Kennedy called the nation to public service. "Ask not what your country can do for you," said Kennedy. "Ask what you can do for your country." As the second-youngest president in history (after Theodore Roosevelt), Kennedy projected youthful energy and vigor. The president's ideas seemed part and parcel of the man himself. Ronald Reagan championed a very different idea when he called government the source of our national problems; individuals pursuing the American dream and trying to get rich were, he declared, the real source of national vitality. Successful presidents arrive in office with powerful ideas—and persuade the public to embrace new visions of our political life.

A sign of a fading party is a cupboard bare of ideas. When Jimmy Carter won the White House in 1976, a member of his transition team wrote a strange memo. The new administration, he said, must educate its appointees about President-elect Carter's "goals and philosophy." The Democrats of that era were so vague about their ideas that the president's staff thought it necessary to instruct its troops about what their new leader stood for—even after a long election campaign.[23]

"The power of the presidency," as political scientist Richard Neustadt famously put it, "is the power to persuade."[24] Persuasion involves the ability to put something new before the public, the power to take an unfamiliar notion, and get the whole nation to talk about it. Throughout this book, we have focused on the power and importance of ideas in American politics. The presidency is the institution best geared to inject new ideas into our great national conversation.

The Impossible Job

How can anyone juggle so many different presidential roles? The honest answer is that no one can. Even great presidents cannot handle all their jobs well all of the time. Still, this is what we demand of our chief executive.

Each presidential role requires different strengths and skills. No person will have them all. The bully pulpit can help: Bold ideas bring together the many threads of this huge task. They make a presidency coherent. Without that, presidents may seem overwhelmed by the job, skittering from one task to another without a broader sense of purpose or vision.

● Theodore Roosevelt takes full advantage of his bully pulpit.

Finally, note one theme that runs through every role: Presidential authority has grown in every aspect of the office. The president's many roles are one more way to measure the swelling power and importance of the office. That brings us back again to the central paradox of the executive: The presidency grows ever more powerful, yet the role has grown so large that no one person can perform every aspect of it well.

The Bottom Line

» The president wears many hats and helmets. Some are specified in the Constitution. Others have developed over time.

» Presidential roles include commander in chief, top diplomat, first legislator, head bureaucrat, economist in chief, head of state, and party leader. Presidents also are uniquely situated to introduce new ideas—tying together these many different roles.

» The president's authority has grown in every one of these roles. At the same time, it is difficult to do so many different things effectively.

Presidential Leadership: Success and Failure in the Oval Office

Presidents try to manage perceptions of their performance. They address the public, use (and bypass) the media, schedule eye-catching events, and rely on polls to hone their message. How do we know if they have succeeded? We will examine three different measures of presidential achievement: polls, historical rankings, and the great cycles of political time.

Managing the Public

As the only nationally elected official (excepting the vice president, who is elected as a package with the president), presidents develop a relationship with the people, which they cultivate by **going public**—directly addressing citizens to win support. Each new form of media—radio, television, Twitter, Snapchat—shifts the way presidents go public.

John F. Kennedy demonstrated the full power of the media when he held the first live, televised press conference in February 1961. It was a smash hit, with 65 million viewers; Kennedy's approval ratings climbed to 75 percent and stayed high for 16 months. Kennedy had shifted how presidents connect to the public: People saw him, heard him, and related to him directly. Few people gave Donald Trump much chance in the 2016 Republican primary, much less the general election. What did they overlook? His savvy in going public.

Today, presidents continue to look for ways to connect with Americans. They give campaign speeches before large crowds—even when the next election is years away. They speak directly to the camera from the Oval Office. Their office tweets supporters. You can follow them on Instagram or Facebook. Each of these actions is an effort to win the public over—sometimes for a specific policy, sometimes for a broad presidential agenda.

Presidents deploy an entire office that directs their public outreach—and their strategies are always changing. Presidents constantly balance going public with playing "the inside game"—quietly working with Congress and the bureaucracy to get things done. Which is more effective? That depends on the time and circumstance. But every president—going public or playing the inside game—works to shape public perceptions.[25]

Images are often more important than words. Presidents hug disaster victims, play basketball with the troops, or wave to cheering throngs. The image can turn negative in an instant. President Johnson playfully lifted his beagle by the ears in front of the press (cruel!). President Ford slipped and fell in public (clumsy!). President George H. W. Bush threw up at a state dinner in Japan (you can imagine!). In a complicated world, a single picture can distil popular perception. Images have an impact—positive or negative—when they seem to reveal the president's true strengths or weakness. The key point is simple: *Presidents constantly try to manage their image in the public eye.*[26]

Our 24/7 media era, described in Chapter 9, complicates the effort to touch the public. Today the sheer volume of information flowing through the media means that only the most important events will command attention for long. The president's message now requires constant repetition, amplification, and—to grip viewers—a touch of novelty and drama. Going public is a rapidly changing art form.

The White House runs a sophisticated polling operation that guides its outreach efforts. The president's daily schedule frequently includes briefings from the administration's pollster. The president's team scrutinizes the findings, not to develop new policies but to recalibrate the ways it presents its message. President Trump has proven especially adept at bending the news cycle with his tweets—to the delight of some and the chagrin of others.[27]

Going public: Directly addressing the public to win support for oneself or one's ideas.

● *Lyndon Johnson lifting his beagle by the ears. The president was trying for a lighthearted moment but quickly felt the backlash from outraged pet lovers.*

Some political scientists caution that it is very difficult to move public opinion. The bully pulpit is most powerful, suggested political scientist George Edwards, when presidents recognize and exploit changes that are already in the political air.[28]

Approval Ratings

Every week, another wave of polls reports how Americans view the president's performance. These are used widely, inside and beyond Washington, as a rough barometer of the administration's success. Any one poll can be misleading (as we saw in Chapter 8), but if you eliminate the outliers—the occasional polls that are much higher and lower than the others—and scan the rest, you will have a snapshot of the administration's ratings that are reverberating through the media and around Washington.

A president riding high in the polls finds governing easier. Members of Congress watch the president's popularity in their own states and districts and think twice about opposing them. As the president's approval sinks, criticism rises. Congressional allies back away. Press coverage turns sour. The late night talk shows serve up an extra dose of mockery.

All administrations run through polling cycles; no president stays above 50 percent approval for an entire term. Average out differences across administrations and roughly the same pattern generally emerges: high approval scores at the start, usually above 60 percent; a slow decline that bottoms out midway through the second year; a gradual ascent and peak toward the end of the fourth year (see Figure 14.3). With luck, it rises above 50 percent in time for re-election. Then a dip after re-election and a rise at the end.[29]

Dramatic events create spikes in approval (or disapproval). The two highest ratings on record reflected boosts for George H. W. Bush after a quick, dramatic victory in the First Gulf War, and for his son George W. Bush after he responded to terrorist attacks on the World Trade Center in September 2001 by standing defiantly on the rubble with a bullhorn, surrounded by cheering firefighters and cleanup crews. Each Bush peaked at an 89 percent approval rating in Gallup polls. Such spikes in popularity are usually temporary. A year after his military triumph, George H. W. Bush's approval rating had fallen below 40 percent, and he lost his re-election campaign. The younger Bush narrowly won re-election but ended his time in office tied for the lowest ratings of all modern presidents after a full term.

Polls offer immediate public feedback, but they do not reflect an administration's historical importance or long-term success. For that we can turn to a different type of poll.

Presidential Greatness

Back in 1948, historian Arthur Schlesinger, Sr., asked a panel of historians to rank the presidents. Their choice for the top three: Abraham Lincoln, George Washington, and Franklin D. Roosevelt.

See President George W. Bush's dramatic bullhorn speech at Ground Zero.

● *George W. Bush visits the scene of the 9/11 terrorist attack. The dramatic days following the attack drove President Bush's approval ratings to one of the highest levels ever recorded by Gallup.*

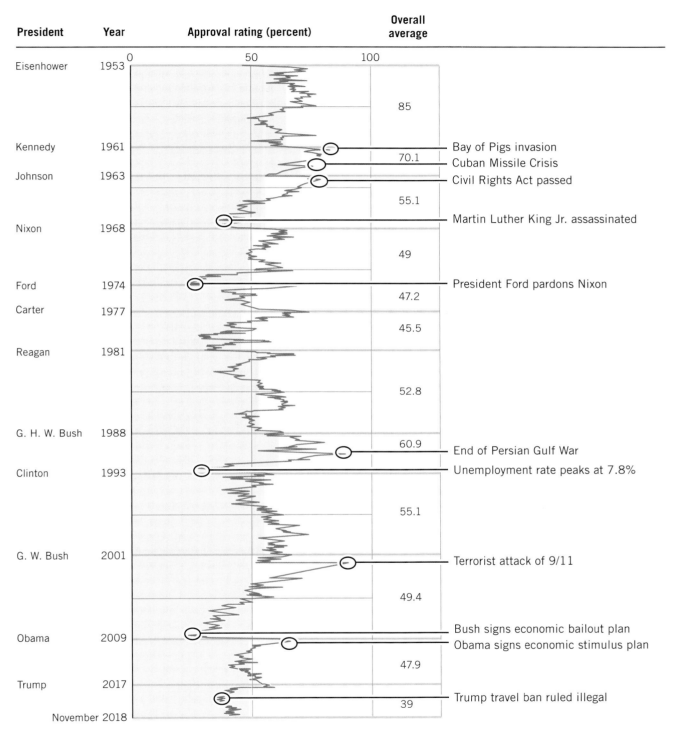

●**Figure 14.3** *Presidential job approval. Every administration goes through polling cycles. Note how important events create short-lived spikes—but a general pattern across administrations tends to repeat itself. (Gallup)*

Poll after poll followed—we list four different versions in Table 14.3. In each, a different panel of historians and political scientists ranks the presidents in order from great to failed.

TABLE 14.3 Rating the Presidents

Here are the results of four independent polls by historians and political scientists (you can find dozens of them). Historian Arthur Schlesinger polled historians in 1948; his son Arthur Schlesinger Jr. repeated the exercise with historians and political scientists in 1996; the United Kingdom Center for the United States Presidency (USPC) provided rankings from a foreign scholarly perspective; and the American Political Science Association (APSA) conducted a survey in 2018.

	POLITICAL PARTY	SCHLESINGER (1948)	SCHLESINGER, JR. (1996)	USPC 2011	APSA 2018
George Washington	None/Federalist	2	2	3	2
John Adams	Federalist	9	11	12	14
Thomas Jefferson	Dem-Repub.	5	4	4	5
James Madison	Dem-Repub.	14	17	14	12
James Monroe	Dem-Repub.	12	15	13	18
John Q. Adams	Dem-Repub.	11	18	20	23
Andrew Jackson	Democratic	6	5	9	15
Martin Van Buren	Democratic	15	21	27	27
William H. Harrison	Whig	—	—	—	42
John Tyler	Whig	22	32	37	37
James K. Polk	Democratic	10	9	16	20
Zachary Taylor	Whig	25	29	33	35
Millard Fillmore	Whig	24	31	35	38
Franklin Pierce	Democratic	27	33	39	41
James Buchanan	Democratic	26	38	40	43
Abraham Lincoln	Republican	1	1	2	1
Andrew Johnson	Democratic	19	37	36	40
Ulysses Grant	Republican	28	24	29	21
Rutherford Hayes	Republican	13	23	30	29
James Garfield	Republican	—	—	—	34
Chester Arthur	Republican	17	26	32	31
Grover Cleveland	Democratic	8	13	21	24
Benjamin Harrison	Republican	21	19	34	32
William McKinley	Republican	18	16	17	19
Theodore Roosevelt	Republican	7	6	5	4
William H. Taft	Republican	16	22	25	22
Woodrow Wilson	Democratic	4	7	6	11
Warren Harding	Republican	29	39	38	39
Calvin Coolidge	Republican	23	30	28	28
Herbert Hoover	Republican	20	35	26	36

TABLE 14.3 (*continued*)

	POLITICAL PARTY	SCHLESINGER (1948)	SCHLESINGER, JR. (1996)	USPC 2011	APSA 2018
Franklin D. Roosevelt	Democratic	3	3	1	3
Harry Truman	Democratic	—	8	7	6
Dwight D. Eisenhower	Republican	—	10	10	7
John F. Kennedy	Democratic	—	12	15	16
Lyndon B. Johnson	Democratic	—	14	11	10
Richard Nixon	Republican	—	36	23	33
Gerald Ford	Republican	—	28	24	25
Jimmy Carter	Democratic	—	27	18	26
Ronald Reagan	Republican	—	25	8	9
George H. W. Bush	Republican	—	24	22	17
Bill Clinton	Democratic	—	20	19	13
George W. Bush	Republican	—	—	31	30
Barack Obama	Democratic	—	—	—	8
Donald Trump	Republican	—	—	—	44

Liberals and conservatives rarely disagree about how the presidents rank. Ronald Reagan is an exception, though his ratings from left-leaning scholars have climbed in recent polls. Such agreement returns us to the question: What makes a great president?

There are plenty of answers. President Harry Truman said that all the great presidents were especially decisive. Political scientists Marc Landy and Sidney Milkis suggested that great presidents redefine the presidency. Our view is that great presidents redefine America; they reshape the way the nation sees itself. Or, to put it slightly differently, *great presidents tell us who we are.* Their definitions of America resonate with the public and endure over time.[30]

Greatness in Context: The Rise and Fall of Political Orders

Presidents are not masters of their destiny. The times make the presidents as much as they make the times. Individual presidents fit into national cycles of politics and power. Presidential scholar Stephen Skowronek described each presidency as part of a great historical pageant: the rise and fall of **political orders**. A political order is a set of ideas, institutions, and coalitions that dominate an era.[31] In Skowronek's telling, orders rise and fall in three steps. Every president fits somewhere in the cycle.

Step 1: A New Order Rises. Outstanding leaders take over the presidency and shake up the political system. An Abraham Lincoln, Franklin D. Roosevelt, or Ronald Reagan introduces a fresh philosophy of government. He leads a political party with new allies and new ideas into power. The public responds enthusiastically to this bold break with old political ways.

Political order: The set of institutions, interests, and ideas that shape a political era. Great presidents reconstruct the framework, launching a new order.

Step 2: The Order Refreshed. Every governing coalition eventually grows tired. The great president who boldly articulated its themes is gone. Many of the original goals are won. New problems arise that have nothing to do with the philosophy that fired up the party in the first place. The ideas begin to look out of date; the great coalition begins to unravel. If a party is lucky, a new leader will come along and infuse the party with a fresh variation of the old philosophy, renewing the aging order.

Step 3: The Old Order Crumbles. No order lasts forever. Over time, the party finds its ideas increasingly irrelevant. The old order feels outdated, a political dinosaur.

Every president comes to Washington with fresh hope and promise. Political historians look back and see that each operates within a cycle. Some (Lincoln, Roosevelt, Reagan) take office as the head of a new coalition with fresh ideas. If the rival party comes to power when the order is still strong, they will usually bend to its assumptions and general outlook. Others come to Washington at the end of an era (Herbert Hoover, Jimmy Carter). They face a far more difficult governing challenge. To some extent, the rankings we see in Table 14.3 reflect each president's place in political time.

The Bottom Line

» Presidents try to manage public perceptions of the job they are doing. They get immediate feedback from polls. A president's place in history, however, does not emerge right away.

» Great presidents change the way Americans see themselves. They change what government does. They forge a new answer to the question, *Who are we?*

» Individual presidents don't completely control their own destiny. They operate in the historical cycle of political orders.

The Personal Presidency

In at least one respect, the presidency is very simple: It is always about one individual. At the heart of the enterprise stands a person with strengths and weaknesses, quirks and foibles. The personalities of our presidents have imprinted their administrations in many ways, big and small.

Presidential Style

James Madison was just a bit over five feet tall and weighed less than one hundred pounds. He wore tall hats to add height, dressed entirely in black, and never owned more than one suit at a time. He was both diminutive and timid. Early historians blasted him for his cautious leadership during the War of 1812. But scholars have warmed to Madison. Historians now believe that the war helped define America as a united nation. Madison was guided by a fierce attachment to the Constitution that he had drafted. Who better than a small, shy, modest, man in black to avoid too much "personality" in the presidency?

Or take some darker personal qualities. . . .

Secluded in his hideaway office across the street from the White House, the fireplace crackling as the air conditioner hummed, Richard Nixon scribbled on yellow legal pads into the night. He was brilliant—and paranoid. Nixon usually dealt directly with four or five aides; their job was to keep others at bay. Sitting alone, writing away on his yellow pads, he dreamed up remarkable ideas.

At the time, the United States was locked in a cold war with two great communist powers, Russia and China. Nixon calculated that our two enemies were bitterly opposed to one another. He negotiated secretly with China. When the Russians discovered the thaw between China and the United States, they feared being left out. They too pursued closer relations with the United States. Nixon had invented a way to ratchet down the bitter cold war by playing off our enemies against one another.

Ronald Reagan: This sunny, folksy, patriotic, old-fashioned storyteller introduced a new conservative era.

Nixon also cooked up a national health insurance plan that serves as a model (for Democrats) to the present day. But, sitting alone and often drinking heavily into the night, he also stoked the personal demons that ultimately cost him the White House.

Or consider a very different political genius. . . .

Ronald Reagan loved to tell stories. He told them to make a point, to deflect people from saying things he did not want to hear, to reorient a conversation that was going the wrong way, or—well, just because he loved telling them. "He could drive you crazy [telling] . . . the same stories over and over again," reported Congressman Dan Rostenkowski (D-IL). "He really made no show whatsoever of listening to arguments. . . . He saw reality, not as a thing to bow to but a thing that could be changed and shaped."[32]

Was it really true that, during World War II, army bureaucrats granted Reagan's unit permission to destroy a warehouse full of useless files, "provided copies are made of each paper destroyed?" Who knows? The parable was irresistible: Government bureaucracies choke the life out of any enterprise.[33]

What Do YOU Think?   Go Public or Play the Inside Game

	Go Public.	**The Inside Game.**	
Pick an issue you care about: Immigration or climate change or something else. Now, what would you advise the president to emphasize?	In the era of Obama and Trump, presidencies are almost like social movements—keep your supporters mobilized.	To really make progress, you have to work quietly with individual members of Congress and the bureaucracy.	Of course, every president does both, but on every issue has to stress one or the other.

Such tall tales went to the heart of Reagan's successes and failures as president. He focused on parables rather than policies. His airy indifference to the analytic world of evidence and arguments freed him to repeat his handful of moral lessons, impressing them on American discourse. Such tales helped him reframe American politics in terms of a more rugged individualism that scorned handouts and collective action. He made it work because he wrapped that individualism in a nostalgic vision of America.

Madison's republican simplicity, Nixon's brilliance and paranoia, Reagan's pointed storytelling and gauzy vision of American free enterprise all shaped the way they governed and the mark they left. This kind of territory used to be the province of historians and anthropologists, not political scientists. But we know that it is vital to acknowledge—and study—the personal dimension of the presidency.[34]

Learn about presidential achievements.

The Burden of the Office

For another truth about the presidency, compare photographs of almost any president at the start and then at the end of their time in office: It is an exhausting job that takes a visible toll on the incumbents. Fourteen presidents and former presidents died during the twentieth century; eleven passed away prematurely. Presidents before they take office usually appear young, handsome, and smiling; by the time they step down, they often look careworn and gray.[35]

These morbid health statistics remind us that the Oval Office houses a vulnerable human being. Presidents get sick, take dubious drugs, get drunk, overeat, have affairs, contemplate suicide, fret about ailing parents, and burn with insecurities. None can escape the human condition. All wrestle with an extremely difficult job.

Presidents are usually very talented—or they would not have gotten to the White House. As with all people, however, they have strengths and weaknesses, vast skills and blind spots.[36] Confronting these personal limits returns us to a central question of this chapter: Has the presidency developed too much power for any one person to handle?

● *Young man, older man: Barack Obama as president-elect and late in his presidency.*

The Bottom Line

» Although presidential scholars generally focus on ideas and institutions, the presidency also has an important personal dimension.

» All presidents exhibit a distinctive personal style.

» Presidents are limited human beings with strengths and weaknesses. That is precisely why the Constitution located the office in an intricate system of checks and balances.

The President's Team: A Tour of the White House

When Herbert Hoover moved into the Oval Office in 1929, he presided over a presidential staff of four administrative assistants, plus 36 typists, clerks, and messengers. That was it. No speechwriter, no press secretary, no congressional liaison; no chief of staff, no drug czar, no budget director. Today, the presidency is more than a person or an idea or a party. It is a bureaucracy staffed by thousands of people.

The Political Solar System: Presidential Appointments

Every time a new president is elected, hopes spread across the country. University professors who have always dreamed of government service, college students who worked on the campaign, business executives looking for a plum position on their résumé, and supporters who believe the president-elect will make America a better place: All want to work for the new administration.

To get a job in the executive branch, do not start by being modest. You must campaign: One executive angling to be a senior Treasury Department official some years back tasked four subordinates to do nothing but promote his name to the team in charge of selecting top appointees (yes, he got the job).

Let us take a tour of the offices working directly for the president. A crucial opening point: Power is always measured by proximity to the Oval Office. The executive branch is like the solar system, with the president as the sun and everyone else rotating around him. The most impressive thing you can say in Washington, DC: "When I was talking to the president yesterday. . . ." Most people who work for the president are in an orbit somewhere past Pluto: They never get any face time. Let us look at who does.

The Vice President

Traditionally, the vice president's primary job was to stand in the wings in case the president died. That awful transition has happened eight times in American history, four times by murder. There were at least four more close calls: Assassins fired point-blank at Andrew Jackson (the gun jammed), Franklin D. Roosevelt (the shooter missed the president and killed the mayor of Chicago), Gerald Ford (a bystander grabbed the gunwoman's arm, diverting the shot), and Ronald Reagan (the bullet lodged less than an inch from his heart).

Vice President Mike Pence served six terms in the House before being elected Governor of Indiana.

Besides standing by in case of catastrophe, vice presidents preside over the Senate and cast a vote in case of a tie. There is not much power in presiding, and the vice president only appears in the Senate chamber on special occasions.

Otherwise, a vice president's responsibilities are entirely up to the president. For a long time, the role was meager. Senator Daniel Webster rejected the vice presidential nomination in 1848 with an acid comment: "I do not choose to be buried until I am really dead."[37] Bad move: Webster would have become the thirteenth president when Zachary Taylor died in the White House. Franklin D. Roosevelt's first vice president, John Nance Garner, offered an infamous assessment of the post when he said the job was "not worth a pitcher of warm piss."[38]

The weak vice presidency continued well into the twentieth century. Harry Truman had barely met with President Roosevelt when FDR's death in 1945 catapulted him into the Oval Office. "Boys," he said when he met the press the next day, "if you ever pray, pray for me now." In 1960, reporters asked President Eisenhower what ideas Vice President Nixon had contributed. "If you give me a week," quipped the president nastily, "I might think of one."[39]

The vice presidency became important during the Carter administration (1977–1981). From Carter through Trump, six of eight presidents were Washington outsiders who had never held a federal job; every newcomer chose an experienced Washington hand as his vice president, relying on him as advisor, envoy, and (in Mike Pence's case) fundraiser. Slowly, vice presidents gathered the emblems of power: a seat at cabinet meetings (1950s), an office in the White House (1970s), a vice presidential jet (Air Force 2, in the 1970s), a growing staff, and—perhaps most important in status-obsessed Washington—regular meetings with the president.[40]

The Cabinet

Members of the cabinet have two primary roles: They run executive branch departments, and they meet to discuss policy with the president in cabinet meetings. Once the cabinet served as a president's governing team. Washington's initial cabinet had four members, today there are fifteen members; add the vice president and other important presidential staff officers, and meetings are too large to serve as a real decision-making body. We discuss the cabinet, and the hundreds of thousands of federal bureaucrats who work under cabinet secretaries in the executive agencies, in Chapter 15.

In most administrations, a handful of cabinet officers rise above the rest and shape administration policy. Political scientists call them the "inner cabinet": usually, the secretaries of state, defense, the treasury, and justice—precisely the quartet in Washington's original cabinet. Most other cabinet secretaries operate far from the centers of power. Departments such as Transportation and Energy have vital roles to play. But unless the "outer cabinet" secretaries have personal connections they are rarely part of a president's inner circle.

Cabinet secretaries often come to see issues from the perspective of their own bureaucracy rather than that of the administration or the party. After all, they are surrounded by tens of thousands of employees who do a lot of work with limited resources and look to the secretary to champion their causes. Richard Nixon's close adviser John Ehrlichman groused that the administration chose solid, budget-cutting conservatives to run the cabinet departments—and then watched them run off and "marry the natives."[41]

Presidents must manage the tension between senior cabinet officials and the circle of presidential advisors in the White House. At one cabinet meeting during the Carter years, the secretary of Housing and Urban Development summed up her

President Nixon worked closely with National Security Advisor and later Secretary of State Henry Kissinger.

frustration by blurting out: "We can move government forward by putting phones in the White House staff offices and then using them." Translation: No one in the White House even returns my phone calls. The president's inner circle had shifted from the cabinet to the White House staff.[42]

The Executive Office of the President

Influence over government policy has leaked steadily into the **Executive Office of the President** (**EOP**), made up of agencies that help a president manage the president's daily activities. These administrators and advisors surround the chief executive. President Franklin D. Roosevelt organized the EOP in 1939; it now has about 1,800 employees. Many are experts who stay on from one administration to the next. Presidents who have been most adamant about expanding the EOP are conservatives frustrated that the cabinet agencies did not pursue their values. Richard Nixon created or revamped four of the EOP offices; Ronald Reagan added three more. Today, every president—left, right, or center—relies on them.

Table 14.4 illustrates the offices in the Executive Office of the President. The list reflects the hats and helmets that the president wears. Organizing a new EOP office or an office within the White House Office (discussed below) is one way for administrations to signal the things they consider most important. George W. Bush added an office for his faith-based initiatives; Barack Obama, reflecting the high-tech/information age, created an Office of Digital Strategy, and Donald Trump, the first businessman in the White House, created an Office of American Innovation.

In the Executive Office of the President, a familiar clash gets especially intense. On one hand, most EOP employees are experts on specific issues—immigration, healthcare, or the budget. On the other, they have to serve each president's political philosophy (not to mention furthering his re-election prospects). Slowly, the balance between these goals has tipped toward politics.[43] Let us visit the most important offices in the EOP.

Executive Office of the President (EOP): The agencies that help the president manage daily activities.

TABLE 14.4 Offices in the Executive Office of the President, 2019

OFFICE	EMPLOYEES	YEAR ORGANIZED	ORGANIZED BY
White House Office	450	1939	F. D. Roosevelt
Council of Economic Advisers	27	1946	Truman
National Security Staff	58	1947	Truman
Office of the U.S. Trade Representative	240	1963	Kennedy
Council on Environmental Quality	24	1969	Nixon
Office of Management and Budget	487	1921/1971	Harding/Nixon
Office of the Vice President	25	1972	Nixon
Office of Science and Technology Policy	32	1976	Ford
Office of Administration	234	1977	Carter
Domestic Policy Council	25	1985	Reagan
Office of National Drug Control Policy	84	1988	Reagan
Homeland Security Council	18	2001	G. W. Bush
Executive Residence	96 (full-time)	—	—

Central clearance: The OMB's authority to review and "clear" (or approve) anything a member of the administration says or does in public.

The Office of Management and Budget (OMB). This is the most powerful agency in the executive branch—known (not very fondly) as "the agency that says no." The OMB uses its authority over the federal budget to manage the entire executive branch. During the Reagan administration, the agency acquired its most powerful weapon—**central clearance**: the power to review and "clear" (or okay) anything a member of the administration says or does in public. All members, from the Defense Secretary to an analyst in the Small Business Bureau, must submit every speech they make, opinion piece they write, congressional testimony they deliver, and policy they propose to the OMB for its approval. Until they get the OMB's nod, they may not say or publish a word.

The OMB vets every administration proposal. When Congress passes a bill, the OMB coordinates various White House officials' recommendations about signing or vetoing the legislation. Officials at the OMB often get the last word as well. Imagine how frustrating it must be for energetic new secretaries to take over their departments, only to learn they must clear all their formal statements and policy proposals with the budget office.

Before the Nixon administration organized the OMB in 1971, fiscal control was much looser. President Lyndon Johnson famously low-balled his economic estimates. One day, instructing a young senator from Massachusetts named Ted Kennedy, Johnson warned him not to let economic projections slow up his favorite bills and illustrated the point with Medicare. "The fools [at the Bureau of the Budget] had to go projecting [Medicare] down the road five or six years, and when you project it the first year it runs $900 million," Johnson told Kennedy.[44] Those anticipated costs, complained LBJ, cost him votes in Congress; he advised the new senator to stop economists from interfering with important proposals. Today, the OMB requires cost-benefit analyses for all White House policy moves. The era of simply suppressing cost estimates is long past. The formal rules now empower an economic perspective. Still, every savvy political operator knows plenty of ways to massage the numbers.[45]

The Council of Economic Advisers (CEA). Meet another clutch of economists. The Council and its chair keep an eye on the whole economy, private as well as public. CEA staff performs economic analysis for the president: unemployment predictions, productivity measurements, economic forecasts, and all the rest.

The National Security Council (NSC). The NSC brings together the powerful officers who make national security policy: secretaries of state, defense, energy, and the treasury (economists again); the chair of the Joint Chiefs of Staff; and others who the president selects. The national security advisor directs the council and must work for consensus across all the different perspectives and formidable personalities: diplomatic, military, and economic. In some administrations, the national security advisor is as influential as the secretaries of state or defense—although the Trump administration saw an unprecedented three NSC advisors in its first 14 months (see Chapter 18).

Settle a military crisis from the White House.

The Heart of Power: The White House Office (WHO)

Our tour ends at the heart of power. The White House Office is part of the Executive Office of the President, but it also stands apart. This group of four hundred or so advisors, aides, and associates works directly for the president, most of them in the West Wing. At the center sits the **Chief of Staff**, the president's gatekeeper, traffic cop, and coordinator. Other important offices include speechwriters, White House counsel (the president's official lawyer), and the legislative affairs team.

Chief of Staff: The individual responsible for managing the president's office.

Until President Obama, the two parties organized their White House Office very differently from one another. Franklin D. Roosevelt set a mixed example for future Democrats: creative chaos. Roosevelt surrounded himself with gifted intellectuals, gave them overlapping tasks, and let them freelance from issue to issue. Many Democratic administrations tried to mimic Roosevelt. John Kennedy valued broad-minded intellectuals and encouraged them to weigh in on any subject. So did Bill Clinton; early in his administration, staffers would jump in and out of meetings and conversations regardless of their assigned tasks. The bull sessions went on deep into the night.

In contrast, Republicans like clearly defined organization and tasks. You will find no vague or dotted lines on their personnel tables. Republican executives usually model their organization on the military or traditional business: crisp lines of authority flow from the president to the Chief of Staff. Everyone has a clearly defined role.

Now, that has all changed. The Obama White House was tightly organized—almost Republican in style. President Trump seems to thrive on creative chaos—encouraging aides and confidantes to drop by the Oval Office, hiring and firing White House officials at an unprecedented clip, and assigning tasks to people he trusts regardless of their background.

No matter the style, the Chief of Staff makes the White House run. He or she directs traffic through the president's office, oversees the schedule, sums up the decisions that are made, and follows up to see that those decisions are understood and implemented. The position requires a strong, talented, smooth, competent administrator familiar with the levers of power. In the past, some presidents tried to act as Chief of Staff (Jimmy Carter) or to bring in a political neophyte (Bill Clinton chose his pal Mack McLarty, whom he'd known since kindergarten); chaos followed. Someone has to follow up each meeting and summarize what has been decided. Otherwise, everyone remembers something different. The other extreme is equally dangerous. If the chief of staff seems arrogant, aloof, or rude, the White House loses support and cooperation.

The White House staff is like a little village, full of odd folkways and habits that reflect the way the president wishes to run the country. For example, Ronald Reagan

SPEAK LIKE A WEST WING INSIDER

Want to learn to talk like a member of the White House staff? Start practicing now. Casually toss off something like: "I'm given to understand that WHO is the real force in the EOP." Those are two indecipherable acronyms (the more the better) and, of course, the passive voice: You don't want to risk revealing your sources!

put special emphasis on his speechwriting team; they spent hours watching tapes of his past speeches to learn his rhythms and his way of thinking. The president reworked their draft speeches with great care. Reagan's successor, George H. W. Bush, thought the president should speak more plainly and rejected all the attention on crafting speeches. He demonstrated the new order by stripping the speechwriting team of its White House Mess (dining hall) privileges. The village recognized a major demotion.

When a new president comes to town, attention focuses on his cabinet selections. The wise observer knows to track more subtle appointments to the White House Office. After all, no matter how brilliant the secretary of labor or how experienced the secretary of health and human services, they will have to rely on unseen advisors in the White House to convey their ideas, programs, and problems to the president. The route to influence—the path to "yes" on any program—usually runs through the White House Office staff.

Unlike the high-ranking members of the cabinet agencies, most EOP staffers are not subject to Senate confirmation. They are elected by no one, overseen only by the Chief of Staff, and often have regular access to the president's ear. Should the president's advisors, rather than the experienced cabinet secretaries confirmed by the Senate, run the executive branch? Again, we confront the fundamental issue: power and control versus democracy and enhanced accountability. Perhaps granting authority to White House staff makes the whole federal leviathan more responsive to the will of the people. Most democracies are, ultimately, ruled by experts. American government is run in part by men and women with a sharp eye on winning the next election.

One final feature of the White House staff strikes most newcomers: Its members are young—much younger than the staff running other governments, large corporations, universities, or major nonprofit organizations. Cabinet secretaries with years of experience often complain that their access to the president is governed by young people in their twenties and thirties.

What Do YOU Think?   Do Presidents Need Such a Large Staff?

The Executive Office of the President (EOP) now houses more than 1,800 staff members, from economic and foreign policy advisors to communications specialists. All answer directly to the president and his top aides; most do not even require Senate confirmation. By comparison, President Lincoln had four personal assistants, and when Franklin D. Roosevelt took office 82 years ago, he had a staff of 36. Does the modern presidency require such a large staff?

Yes, absolutely.
Given the office's immense range of responsibilities, presidents need reliable, trustworthy experts and assistants to analyze intelligence and economic data, to assess overseas threats, and to help manage public perceptions of the president. In fact, it's surprising there isn't more support (Congress, after all, has more than twenty-five thousand staffers).

No—start staff cuts immediately.
Modern technology could make the presidency far more efficient. If CEOs can run major companies with far fewer staff reporting to their office, and other sectors are able to function with far fewer personnel, so could the White House.

Not sure.
The huge array of presidential staff reportedly work incredibly hard, and the White House certainly has a plateful of duties. But perhaps the large staff reflects too much power in the executive? If Congress reasserted its traditional powers, we could cut back the EOP army.

The First Spouse

One team in the White House Office does not fit any traditional political category: the office of the president's spouse. Traditionally, the "First Lady" role was simply that of hostess. Eleanor Roosevelt broke the traditional mold and pioneered a new role: the First Lady as activist. Eleanor was a powerful liberal voice, a popular symbol of the New Deal, and a forceful advocate for Franklin D. and his policies. In effect, she became a one-woman campaign for liberal social policy. A *New Yorker* cartoon captures the First Lady's spirit of tirelessly campaigning for social and labor reform. Deep underground, two sooty coal miners stop their labors as one remarks with surprise: "For gosh sakes, here comes Mrs. Roosevelt!"

● The first spouse in the media storm: Melania Trump set off much commentary when she traveled to an immigrant children's center on the U.S. Mexico border wearing a jacket labelled, "I really don't care, do u?" Was she criticizing the media for its treatment of the president's border policy? Or the president's policy itself?

Few First Spouses were as active or committed as Eleanor Roosevelt, but she set a pattern of policy engagement that her successors have followed. Lady Bird Johnson chose "beautification" of American cities and highways as her policy focus. Nancy Reagan became a spokesperson for the war on drugs. Mrs. Reagan was the first to achieve that mark of status, an office in the West Wing. Bill Clinton assigned his wife, Hillary, the signature policy initiative of his presidency, national healthcare reform. In fall 1993, Hillary Clinton's performance in a series of Congressional Hearings drew praise from both parties; it did not save the health plan but signaled the start of her own political career—and established a new ceiling for First Ladies' contributions to presidential action.

Melania Trump has focused on children; her "Be Best" program centers on child well-being, cyberbullying, and opioid abuse. Political scientists—especially those interested in gender and power—have begun to pay particular attention to the role of the First Spouse.[46]

What did Melania Trump mean?

The Bottom Line

» Each president directs a massive organization—the executive branch of the federal government.

» Cabinet secretaries manage the great executive-branch bureaucracies, but only a few have influence in the White House.

» Over time, executive branch policymaking has migrated from the cabinet to the Executive Office of the Presidency—the network of offices that help the president manage the government.

» The president's innermost circle is the White House Office. These close advisors—often relatively young—include the Chief of Staff, speechwriters, the legislative liaison, and the office of the First Spouse.

Conclusion: The Most Powerful Office on Earth?

In 2017 a new president arrived, bursting with ideas and campaign promises—and raising, once again, the fundamental question about the presidency. President Trump seemed to make policy on the fly: threatening leaders of other countries, holding high profile summits, announcing the rollback of regulations, renegotiating treaties and trade deals, pushing Congress to cut taxes, naming conservative justices to the courts. At the same time, the president fumed over Congress's refusal to change immigration law, to allocate money for a border wall, or to cut spending.

The presidency is a far more powerful office than it was a century ago. Has it grown too powerful for a republic? Or is it too hobbled to carry out the mandate of the public? Perhaps it is most accurate to say that the same president can be both too powerful and too weak, depending on the issue, the circumstances, and the incumbent. As you watch the Trump administration, ask yourself whether the president is too powerful—or not powerful enough.

The Trump presidency also raises another concern among political scientists: Does Donald Trump violate norms—a basic civility toward political opponents, respect for judges and courts, respect for a free press, deference to the rules—that protect democratic institutions?[47] Strong democracies rely not just on formal laws, as Alexis de Tocqueville put it, but also the "reason and mores" that limit power and guide behavior. Once they are broken, they may be hard to re-establish.[48]

Who are we? The president offers us an answer—actually, several different answers. Americans seek a powerful, confident figure at their government's center. At the same time, we fear strong executives and hem them in with a labyrinth of checks and balances. We want our collective democratic voice ringing in the ears of our national leaders but also want our security protected in ways that may require secrecy and fast, decisive choices. We are a people who demand small government, yet complain when every need is not speedily met by the executive branch. We are a complicated, diverse, paradoxical people—just like the presidency that reflects and serves us.

CHAPTER SUMMARY

Check your understanding of Chapter 14.

● *The president personifies America.* More than any individual, the president tells us who we are—and what we are becoming.

● *The president injects new ideas into American politics.* Our discussion of Congress emphasized the institution and the rules of the game; the presidency puts more focus on individuals and ideas.

● The president has three types of powers: Those expressed in the Constitution, those delegated by Congress, and those inherent in the role of chief executive.

● The executive branch has grown far more powerful over time, especially when it comes to foreign policy.

● The office of the president constantly raises the same fundamental question: *Is the president too powerful for a democratic republic? Or is the office too weak to accomplish what Americans demand of it?* We may also consider whether the president is both too strong and too weak at the same time.

● The president wears many hats and helmets. Presidential roles include commander in chief, top diplomat, first legislator, head bureaucrat, economist in chief, head of state, and party leader. The president's authority has grown in every one of these many roles. At the same time, it is difficult for one person to do so many different things effectively.

● Presidents try to manage public perceptions of the job they are doing by going public and getting feedback from polls. Individual presidents do not completely control their own destiny. They operate in the historical cycle of *political orders*.

● The presidency always has a personal dimension. Presidents are limited human beings with

strengths and weaknesses. That is precisely why the Constitution located the office within an intricate system of checks and balances.

● Over time, executive branch policy has flowed from the cabinet secretaries to the Executive Office of the Presidency—the network of offices that help the president manage the government.

● The president's innermost circle is the White House Office. These close advisors—who are often relatively young—include the Chief of Staff, speechwriters, the legislative liaison, and the office of the First Spouse.

 Need to review key ideas in greater depth? Click here.

KEY TERMS

 Flashcard review.

Central clearance, p. 448
Chief of Staff, p. 449
Civil servants, p. 432
Delegated powers, p. 421
Executive agreements, p. 422
Executive Office of the
   President (EOP), p. 447

Executive order, p. 432
Executive privilege, p. 421
Expressed powers, p. 421
Going public, p. 437
Imperial presidency, p. 423
Inherent powers of the
   presidency, p. 421

Override, p. 429
Political appointees, p. 432
Political order, p. 441
Signing statements, p. 431
Unitary executive theory,
   p. 423
Veto power, p. 429

STUDY QUESTIONS

1. Some people have suggested changing the president's term to one seven-year term without the possibility of re-election. How would that proposal shift the incentives that currently face a first-term president?
2. Why is the Constitution considerably more vague about presidential than congressional powers? What problems—and benefits—does that ambiguity create?
3. What do you think: Is the president too strong or too weak? Defend your opinion.
4. Name seven different roles the president plays. Which do you consider the most important right now? How well do you think the president is carrying out this role today?
5. How well do you think President Trump "goes public"—appealing to the American public to support his policies? Do *you* respond positively to his speeches and legislative requests?

6. Should presidents care about their approval ratings from the American public? Why or why not?
7. Explain how presidents help Americans understand (and define) who we are. What does the president tell the world about the kind of nation and people we are?
8. Explain the role of the OMB. What does this agency do? What perspective was it designed to bring to policy debates?
9. Describe the role of the First Spouse. Despite getting involved in policies, spouses are often more popular than their presidential partners. Why do you think that is so?
10. Describe the three stages of every political order. Where do you think we stand today in the great cycle of presidential political time?

 Go to www.oup.com/us/Morone to find quizzes, flash cards, simulations, tutorials, videos, and other study tools.

15 Bureaucracy

In this chapter, you will:

- Learn how the bureaucracy developed, how it is meant to work, and why programs and processes sometimes fail.

- See how federal agencies do their job.

- Examine the different types of agencies that comprise the public service.

- Consider who—if anyone—controls the bureaucracy.

- Review possible reforms—and affirm what works well in our massive, sprawling federal bureaucracy.

THE MISSOURI "BOOTHEEL" is a rural region in the southeast corner of the state—and, yes, on the map it does look like a boot's heel. As the 2010s dawned, the region faced a public health crisis. There were not enough hospitals, clinics, or health providers to serve this Mississippi Delta area of farmland, small towns, and rolling hills. Obesity and diabetes rates were rising sharply, and newer scourges such as opioid addiction left resources even more stretched.[1]

The Bootheel was not unusual. Healthcare providers are often scarce in rural America. Health care advocates in the Bootheel did something that may surprise you: They called for help from bureaucrats. The Health Resources & Services Administration, a part of the Department of Health and Human Services, responded with a solution: A digital network connecting six far-flung health centers across the region that would coordinate care and advise residents in each neighborhood when a service provider or mobile clinic was coming to their area.[2]

Health outcomes in the Bootheel improved after the network went into place.[3] Note the unexpected heroes who improved health care: Bureaucrats in Washington, DC, working with bureaucrats in Missouri and local health professionals, as well as private advocacy groups (such as The Bootheel Network for Health Improvement).

Bureaucrats helping? That's not a story most people expect to hear. Most Americans hold a very low opinion of the federal bureaucracy. Sixty percent, in a 2018 poll, agreed that "unelected or appointed officials in the federal government have too much influence in determining federal policy."[4] Politicians often campaign for office against faceless bureaucrats in Washington, portraying the executive departments as "armies of regulators descending like locusts," in the words of U.S. Senator Ted Cruz (R-TX). President Obama in his first inaugural address promised to shrink government programs "that do not work."[5] The Trump Administration pushed an elaborate reorganization plan that would merge and cut entire agencies.

This chapter tells a different story about the federal bureaucracy. Yes, we'll look at the standard critiques—and the important points they make. But we also present the other side reflected in the Bootheel story: Health policy bureaucrats partnered with local leaders to improve lives in rural Missouri.

● *Rural regions such as Missouri's "Bootheel" have fewer physicians, clinics, and hospitals and are underserved by health professionals. That's where government bureaucrats are able to help.*

Bureaucrats, despite their terrible reputation, perform valuable, even life-saving services. The bureaucracy is what makes government run.

The criticism of generic bureaucrats generally melts away when pollsters ask about specific agencies. For example, two-thirds of Americans give high marks to the U.S. Postal Service, the Centers for Disease Control, and NASA.[6] Bureaucrats look a lot better when we focus on what they actually do.

Who are we? In many ways, a country of bureaucrats: U.S. national departments and agencies employ 2.6 million civilians (and nearly 4 million including active-duty military). Nineteen million Americans work for state and local governments. These numbers add up to some 23 million people on government payrolls—more than one in every ten working-age adults. What's more, the federal bureaucracy resembles the population it serves more than any other branch of government (Figure 15.1). Remember that Congress is overwhelmingly white, male, and middle-aged; all presidents have been male and, except for Barack Obama, they have all been white. But the U.S. civilian bureaucracy is far more diverse, although Trump Administration appointees to federal agencies and departments have reversed a decades-long trend toward increased diversity.

Does its diversity make the bureaucracy more representative? Not necessarily. One of the great challenges every national bureaucracy faces is how to synchronize its work with the people's will. A vital question for this chapter: How can a bureaucracy of 2.6 million unelected federal workers govern democratically? An efficient and effective federal bureaucracy is essential to good government. How does it best fit with democratic governance?

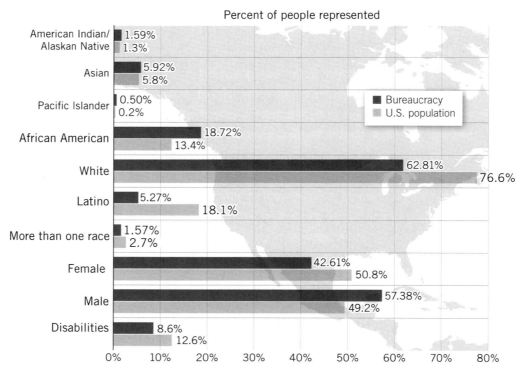

● **Figure 15.1** *U.S. civilian bureaucracy demographic characteristics (U.S. Census).*

BY THE NUMBERS
The Bureaucracy

Number of cabinet departments, U.S. executive branch, 2019	**15**
Number of official independent agencies/commissions, such as the CIA or Postal Service	**67**[7]
Number of departments during the George Washington administration (1789)	**4**
Number of departments during the Theodore Roosevelt administration (1905)	**7**
Number of ministries (e.g., cabinet departments), Japanese government, 2001	**20**
Number of Japanese ministries in 2019, following extensive restructuring in recent years	**12**
Total federal bureaucracy workforce	**3.9 million**
Percentage of that total who are active-duty military	**34**
"Hidden workforce" of federal contractors and grantees	**5.3 million**[8]
Number of women, in U.S. history, who have headed cabinet-level departments	**36**
Number of those named since 1975	**34**
Miles of hallways in the largest U.S. federal building, the Pentagon	**17.5**
Maximum annual salary earned by a civil servant (GS-15, top of scale), 2019	**$136,659**
Average layers of upper management in large U.S. cabinet departments	**64**

The federal bureaucracy was modernized in the 1890s. How has it changed over the century and a quarter since?

The Trump administration illustrates the tension. It came to Washington claiming a mandate to shake up American government and immediately ran into a bureaucratic wall: rules, rules, rules. The president soon discovered that announcing (or tweeting) a policy change had to be followed by a very careful and rigorously defined process. How does that process work? Read on!

How the Bureaucracy Grew

Predicting storms near Miami, keeping tabs on elections in Brazil, Nigeria, and India, and tracking suspected terrorists worldwide all require large, well-coordinated bureaucracies—as the National Oceanic and Atmospheric Administration (NOAA), the State Department, and the Central Intelligence Agency (CIA) are intended to be. This section examines where the U.S. bureaucracy came from, how bureaucracies are organized, and some of the problems that can hamper their success.

Birth of the Bureaucracy

In the nineteenth century, U.S. government jobs were political prizes. Men got their posts—as officers in the army, postmasters in rural towns, or tax collectors in ports—because they helped politicians win elections. When George Washington Plunkitt, a colorful New Yorker, decided to enter politics, he went to the local party boss with a marketable commodity: votes. He got his start in politics by delivering the votes of all his friends and neighbors.[9]

This system was inefficient, unfair, and corrupt. Senator William Marcy, another New Yorker, gave the system its name when he declared, "To the victor belong the spoils." Giving jobs to political friends became known as the **spoils system**.

Reformers fought for years to break this corruption. Jobs, they insisted, should be distributed on the basis of merit, not political connections. These good-government advocates championed **universalistic politics**: a government of impartial rules that apply equally to everyone. That ideal was the basis for bureaucratic government in the United States.[10]

Battles erupted between reformers and defenders of the spoils system. In 1881, a crazed office seeker assassinated President James Garfield. Suddenly, the reformers had a martyr for their cause. The spoils system, they said, had caused the president's assassination. Popular outcry pushed a reluctant Congress to pass the **Pendleton Civil Service Act** (1883), which required the federal government to hire well-qualified individuals, who took demanding exams to achieve their posts. It was the first step toward building the civil service—another name for the bureaucracy—that runs the government today.

Spoils system: A system in which government jobs are given out as political favors.

Universalistic politics: A government that is run according to transparent rules, impartially applied.

Pendleton Civil Service Act: The law that shifted American government toward a merit-based public service.

Reformers fighting for a more efficient government had a big advantage: There were jobs that needed doing. As American society and economy grew more complex, the spoils system (which too often attracted the lazy and the incompetent) failed to answer the nation's needs. Five key forces pushed the United States toward a more efficient bureaucracy.

War. Each time the United States mobilized for war, the bureaucracy grew. Matters of life and death could not depend on political hacks; military efforts spurred a search for competent administrators and well-organized offices. After each war, government maintained some of the new jobs. The number of civilian employees doubled during World War I and tripled during World War II. World War II, more than

James Garfield is assassinated in the Baltimore train station by a frustrated job seeker. Reformers blamed the spoils system and used the tragedy to introduce the civil service.

any other force in American history, created the large national bureaucracy we have today.[11]

Morality. Nineteenth-century observers often noted that the U.S. government was very active in regulating morality. Enforcing moral rules required the creation of increasingly sophisticated agencies. For example, the effort to outlaw all liquor (under Prohibition, which lasted from 1920 to 1933) created a powerful new law enforcement agency in the Department of the Treasury.[12]

Economics. Over time, the federal government assumed responsibility for economic performance. This created many new government offices—commissions designed to regulate business (starting in 1887 with efforts to manage the giant railroads); the Federal Reserve, intended to stabilize banking (created in 1913 after a series of financial panics); and a host of offices and agencies in response to the Great Depression (in the 1930s).

"Your Honor, this woman gave birth to a naked child!"

● *Late nineteenth-century moral reformer Anthony Comstock and his quest to stamp out any signs of smut. His effort helped build a sophisticated postal bureaucracy.*

Geography. The United States spread rapidly across the continent. Keeping the far-flung nation together required a more sophisticated postal service (including, briefly, the famous Pony Express), new forms of transportation, the distribution of public lands to homesteaders, and repeated military actions against Native Americans.

Race/Ethnicity. Slavery and civil rights constantly engaged the federal government—leading, most dramatically, to the Civil War and the Reconstruction-era occupation of southern lands by the federal army. Likewise, shifting immigration policies, often based on ethnicity (the Chinese Exclusion Act of the 1880s, for example), required a huge network of federal officials deciding who was permitted to settle in the United States.[13]

Each of these forces—war, morality, economics, geography, and race/ethnicity questions—pushed the United States toward more efficient national bureaus and agencies. The Pendleton Act of 1883 laid the cornerstone for the civil service that developed into a professional national bureaucracy by 1900 (after the Spanish–American War). By 1946 (after World War II) the country had developed many of the agencies that govern America to this day.

The Bureaucratic Model

What is a bureaucracy supposed to look like? The German social scientist Max Weber (1864–1920) reduced it to five characteristics that, in theory, mark all modern bureaucracies—including the American civil service. As we consider each, remember that this is how the bureaucracy is *supposed* to operate, not how it always does.[14]

Hierarchy. All bureaucracies have a clear chain of command. Each individual reports to the person above him or her all the way up to the president—or the queen,

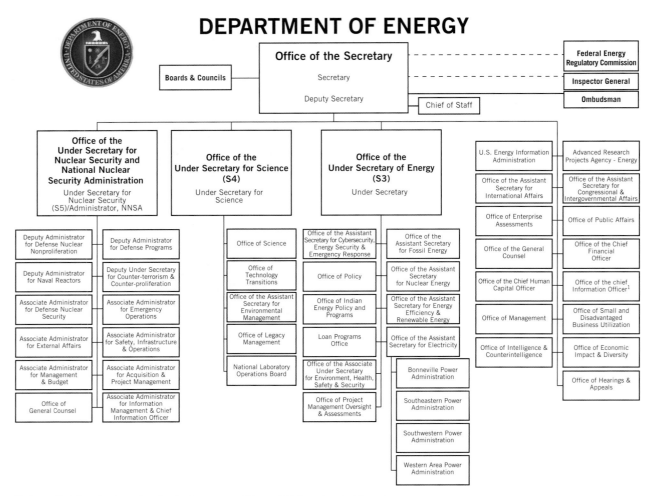

● **Figure 15.2** *Organizational chart for the Department of Energy (US Department of Energy)*

or the pope, or the university chancellor. Every individual along the chain has well-defined superiors and subordinates. Weber noted that the desire to move up the ladder makes most individuals sensitive to their superior's orders. In this way, the efforts of thousands of people can be coordinated.

Figure 15.2 shows the hierarchy of the U.S. Department of Energy (DOE), starting with the cabinet secretary and moving down through elaborate subsets of assistants, deputies, and associate administrators. This chart lists only the top 57 positions, but some 15,000 men and women work in the agency (and another 40,000 or more work under contracts with the DOE). The principle of hierarchy allows leaders to coordinate the work of all their subordinates.

Division of Labor. Bureaucracies divide up complex programs and assign each piece to an individual or a group. Members of the agencies become experts at their own specialized tasks. The hierarchy coordinates all the specialists into a smoothly working operation. For example, the division of labor permits the State Department to have specialists in each region of the globe, each language, and most countries.

Fixed Routines. Rather than making things up as they go along, bureaucrats are expected to follow well-specified codes of conduct called standard operating procedures (SOPs).

Have you ever applied for a passport or unemployment compensation? If you do, you face a sequence of forms, sometimes bewildering details, and multiple visits to different offices. This is bureaucratic routine in action, designed to treat everybody the same way. If you have been stopped for speeding, recall the routine that police officers follow, from requesting your license and registration to checking for outstanding warrants. That's a fixed routine, too, and each step in the SOP has a purpose.

Equal Rules for All. The ideal is always the same in a bureaucracy: The rules apply equally to everyone. In the spoils system, it was all about whom you knew. In contrast, the bureaucratic official is not supposed to care whose daughter you are or what special story you have to tell.

Technical Qualifications. Because bureaucracies operate on the basis of expertise, people get their jobs only on the basis of their qualifications. For example, consider Figure 15.2. On the right of the organizational chart, you will find an Advanced Research Projects Agency (ARPA), which supports research into the origins of the universe. George Washington Plunkitt got his job by rounding up votes for New York's Democratic Party; in contrast, the ARPA staff got their jobs thanks to their scientific expertise.

Hear about bureaucratic pathologies and processes.

Bureaucratic Pathologies

These five characteristics look good on paper. However, bureaucracies often work very differently.

Almost everyone has an annoying bureaucrat story. You may have experienced one in dealing with your university: for example, "You cannot take this course until you take that one"—even though you took one just like it at another school—or, "You can't register until you've paid your tuition"—even though you paid it last week. People who deal with the federal government regularly experience this type of bureaucratic error and are familiar with the annoying chorus: You filed the wrong form, stood in the wrong line, or are forbidden to receive a benefit for which you actually qualify.

Here's a great example: Starting in 2010, eight-year-old Mikey Hicks, an ordinary American boy with no ties to terrorism, was stopped and interrogated every time he and his family boarded a plane. The Transportation Security Authority (TSA) explained that his name was on the agency's no-fly list (because a real suspect had a similar name). Despite his family's complaints, it took the TSA months to remove Mikey from the list. And while the TSA agents were grilling Mikey, a *real* terrorist, Umar Farouk Abdulmutallab, boarded a Northwest Airlines flight and unsuccessfully tried to blow it up. No one asked him any questions, even though two months earlier, his father, a prominent businessperson, had reported that his son was training at an Al Qaeda camp for terrorists in Yemen.

● A threat to national security? Mikey Hicks was subjected to intense questioning every time he flew—thanks to a glitch in the no-fly list. Bureaucratic pathologies include an inability to break routines.

Bureaucratic pathologies:
The problems that tend to develop in bureaucratic systems.

Why do these errors happen? Because every feature of the ideal bureaucracy has its potential downside, known as **bureaucratic pathologies**. Familiar pathologies include the following:

- **Rote.** Some bureaucrats slavishly follow familiar standardized routines despite new developments. The failure to adjust (often accompanied by the excuse of "I'm just doing my job") can lead to problems, even tragedies. When members of an organization get too used to following SOPs, they avoid responsibility—and potential blame—by hiding behind their assigned routines.

- **Imperialism.** Bureaucracies compete just like private companies. They want bigger budgets and better staffs. This status seeking can lead them to grow too big and to engage in time-wasting turf wars.

- **Turf war.** Agencies often find that they are doing overlapping jobs. This replication leads to tensions about who is responsible for what. For example, there are at least 19 intelligence agencies in the federal government. Agencies such as the FBI and CIA view each other as competitors and often refuse to share vital information with the competition.

- **Lack of coordination.** Even agencies skilled at doing their own job may lack mechanisms for cooperating with other agencies. That is because their routines are internal to the agency and do not apply to other organizations. If the agencies are imperialistic or fighting a turf war, the problem can become acute.

- **Clientelism.** Sometimes an agency develops routines that favor some constituents over others. For example, if the Department of Agriculture sends out complicated forms to qualify for loans, they will favor agricultural corporations (which have bookkeepers and secretaries) over small family farms who do not have time to fill in a 50-page forms. The bias may not be intentional, but it is built into the SOPs. And because the most powerful clients—the big farms—don't complain, the routine continues.

Mikey ran into the problem of *rote*. Once his name was on the watch list, the agency kept running through its routine and questioning him. Because the agency would face serious trouble if it crossed a real terrorist off the list, the routine for removing names is slower, with more checkpoints and approvals, than the routine for adding a name. Why did the real terrorist slip through? Here, the problem was a *lack of coordination*, compounded by a *turf war*: different security agencies competing for resources failed to communicate. Umar Farouk Abdulmutallab's father contacted one agency, which neglected to pass the information to another.

In popular culture, the story of bureaucratic pathology often eclipses every other aspect of the subject. This is a mistake. We could not run the military, deliver the mail, operate an airport, process Social Security checks, or predict the weather without bureaucratic agencies. The key question for all governments—for all organizations, including your college or university—is this: How do we produce the benefits of bureaucracy while minimizing the pathologies?

The Democratic Dilemma

Bureaucracies do not fit easily with democracy. Democracy works from the bottom up. Citizens express their opinions about what officials should do. Congress and the presidency are essentially democratic institutions because their authority comes directly from the people (at least, the people who vote).

In contrast, bureaucratic authority comes, not from the people, but from the officials' expertise. The deputy secretary of civilian radioactive waste management in the Energy Department relies on his or her highly specialized knowledge. Security agencies, like the CIA, handle classified information about potential terrorists. NOAA specialists monitor scientific weather data. None of these jobs involves public opinion or popular votes.

The difference between elected office and bureaucratic posts creates a clash of cultures. Democracy flows up from the people. Bureaucracy, when it runs properly, operates on the basis of specialized information, often organized top-down. An enduring challenge for American government is how to manage the tension between these two polarities.

Before considering democratic controls on the bureaucracy, we turn to a more detailed look at what bureaucrats actually do.

Farmers rally in West Fargo, North Dakota, in 2018. Close ties between "Big Ag"—giant agribusiness operations—and the U.S. government arouses complaints: an example of the bureaucratic pathology termed clientelism.

The Bottom Line

» Before the bureaucracy's rise, government jobs were distributed as spoils, or political rewards. Reformers challenged this system and eventually built a national bureaucracy.

» The ideal bureaucracy has five characteristics: hierarchy, division of labor, fixed routines, equal rules for all, and technical expertise.

» Bureaucracies are prone to pathologies: Sticking too closely to a routine, fighting over turf, favoring some clients over others, and refusing to coordinate. These are all exaggerations of the very features that make bureaucracies efficient.

» Because they rely on specialized expertise and information, bureaucracies pose a dilemma for democratic governance which relies on popular opinion.

How Bureaucracies Work

After Congress passes a law or the president issues an executive order, the bureaucracy puts it into effect. Sometimes this work involves routine administrative action: Congress appropriates funds for Social Security checks, and bureaucratic workers at the Social Security Administration issue the checks. Just as often, implementing laws and executive orders requires complicated judgments because inevitably there are gaps in the law. Sometimes Congress sidesteps difficult questions to avoid a conflict or an unpopular decision; sometimes the laws or executive orders are vague because they were written in a hurry or amended at the last minute; and sometimes legislation requires technical details that Congress simply leaves to the bureaucratic experts. In each of these cases, the bureaucracy follows a two-step process of putting a law into practice: rulemaking and implementation.

The process is extremely important. When officials in the Trump Administration tried to introduce changes, they discovered that they could not simply issue a new policy overnight. Instead, each change had to follow a well-organized procedure. Opponents could (and did) go to the courts and blocked any change that missed a step.[15]

Push a program through the bureaucracy.

Rulemaking

Rulemaking showcases classic bureaucratic principles in action: a fixed process with multiple steps always carried out the same way (Figure 15.3). First, the agency studies the law and proposes a "rule" that spells out how the new program will operate; the details must make it clear to the thousands of businesses and individuals exactly what they are required to do. For example, in 2018, the Department of Health and Human Services (HHS)—responding to an executive order by President Trump—proposed reducing prices of pharmaceutical drugs, which are often two to three times higher than the cost of the same drug in other countries.

Cutting drug costs sounds simple enough, right? Not at all, once rule-makers at HHS dug into the details. Would the massive purchasing power of Medicare—which provides care for 57 million Americans aged 65 and over—be leveraged by allowing program administrators to negotiate drug prices with companies? No. Why? This practice has long been forbidden by Congress, thanks to effective lobbying by pharmaceutical companies. Should more generic drugs be brought more quickly to market? Not so easy, owing to elaborate safety rules—not to mention, effective lobbying by large pharmaceutical companies. And so on: the bureaucracy's job is to figure out how to achieve Congress's and the president's goals. Take care not to violate existing laws or rules. And carefully spell out the details.

After the agency has drafted its rule, it sends the proposed rule to the Office of Management and Budget for approval. (Recall from our tour of the White House in the last chapter that the OMB has the power of central clearance—it can say "no" to almost anything.) After the OMB gives its okay, the agency publishes the **proposed rule** in a publication called the *Federal Register*, the daily journal of the federal government. Anybody who is interested can comment.

Who reads the *Federal Register*? In theory, any citizen can read it online or at a library. In practice, most people are unaware it exists, while lobbyists and lawyers pore over it like the latest hot novel. The day we wrote this chapter, for example, the *Federal Register* included proposed rules on air quality (from the Environmental Protection Agency), and a final rule regulating coastal shark harvest limits off the Atlantic coast of the United States (from NOAA).[16] You can be sure that lawyers and lobbyists for manufacturing companies with high pollution emission rates and fishing fleets bombarded the agencies with comments and questions (each comment is also published in the *Federal Register*, usually with a response from the agency). Environmental and consumer groups also join the conversation. The actual details of the proposed rule and the comments are highly technical.

The agency reviews all the public comments and makes changes—a process that can take months or even years—and then hammers out a **final rule**, along with an analysis of the likely impact of the new rule. Back it goes to the OMB, which has 30 days to review the final rule. Then the final rule is published

Proposed rule: A draft of administrative regulations published in the *Federal Register* for the purpose of gathering comments from interested parties.

Final rule: The rule that specifies how a program will actually operate.

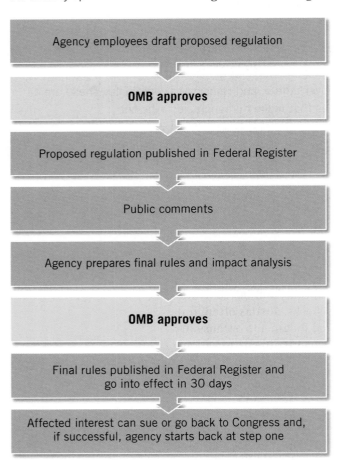

Agency employees draft proposed regulation

OMB approves

Proposed regulation published in Federal Register

Public comments

Agency prepares final rules and impact analysis

OMB approves

Final rules published in Federal Register and go into effect in 30 days

Affected interest can sue or go back to Congress and, if successful, agency starts back at step one

● **Figure 15.3** *Rulemaking in practice. Government rulemaking showcases classic bureaucratic principles in action: a fixed process with multiple steps always carried out in the same way (Office of Management and Budget).*

in the *Federal Register*. Thirty days later, the regulation goes into effect. The final rule is not necessarily the end of the process, however. An individual citizen, group, or corporate firm objecting to the result can sue the agency for misinterpreting Congress's intent. Or it can appeal to its allies in Congress to criticize the rule and push the agency to restart the process.

In practice, lobbyists for the industry negotiate with the agency as proposed and final rules are written. They offer advice or may threaten to sue. Experts in the agency decide when to call the industry's bluff. Consumer groups often jump in as well and try to balance industry views. Once in a while, when a rule taps into a broader controversy, this debate spills over into the public eye. During 2017–2018, the Environmental Protection Agency (EPA) proposed the repeal of a "Clean Power" rule directing states to curb carbon pollution from power plants. Coal producers and power-plant operators originally fought the rule as a direct attack on their livelihood; the proposal to repeal drew fire from environmental groups—and is likely to drag on in the courts for years to come.[17]

● *President Trump, with Department of Health and Human Services Secretary Alex Azar, announces a plan to lower pharmaceutical prices. Many months of HHS rulemaking later, the plan's details remained the subject of much debate.*

View a video about the history and operation of the *Federal Register*.

Each year, all the updated rules published in the *Federal Register*—usually more than 3,000—are published together with a set of permanent administrative rules guiding the bureaucracy's practice and performance. This massive document is known as the *Code of Federal Regulations*.

Next time the White House tweets or announced a new policy, you'll know that that is just the very beginning of the process. What comes next is the whole list we just described: proposed rules, final rules, and quite possibly lawsuits.

Apart from occasional flash points (like the EPA and carbon emissions), rulemaking involves a narrow slice of American life (like shark harvesting) that takes place far from the public eye. Congress gets plenty of media coverage when it considers legislation. But negotiations over rules take place in the shadows, where only the most informed experts understand what is going on. This hidden debate shapes every law, executive order, and public policy. It may be technical, but it involves all of us. Today's proposed rules are about countering climate change and ensuring a steady food supply; tomorrow's could affect student loans and affordable housing. Now you can see the importance of our central question about democracy: How can the public possibly control these battles that occur deep in the bureaucratic leviathan? We will get to that question in the final section of this chapter.

Implementation

After the rules are in place, bureaucracies implement the new policies. The shark fishing fleets have to be inspected, power-plant emissions regulated, and government services such as GI Bill benefits or Veterans Administration medical care delivered to recipients. Who does this work? Mostly "**street-level bureaucrats**": those who interact directly with the public—welfare officers, police, teachers, poultry-plant inspectors, and so on. They implement government policies, by running programs and carrying out oversight.

Street-level bureaucrats: Public officials who deal directly with the public.

Regulating Health Systems

DO WE HAVE TOO MANY REGULATIONS?

Health systems must comply with hundreds of regulatory requirements issued by state and federal bureaucratic agencies. These regulations are designed to ensure patient safety and compliance with a wide expanse of policies. The judiciary and Congress also affect the regulation, providing oversight.

THINK ABOUT IT

Identify three institutions that create regulations for health systems and note which types of regulations they issue. Are you surprised that any of the agencies are involved in healthcare regulation?

Some argue that our health system is too heavily regulated—restricting medical innovation and driving up costs. Do you agree or disagree? Are there areas that should be more or less strictly regulated?

Source: American Hospital Association

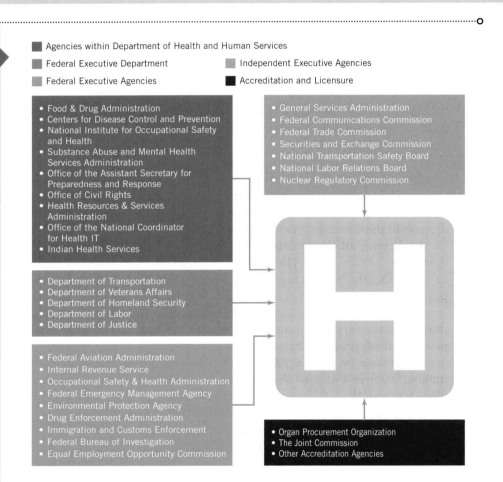

■ Agencies within Department of Health and Human Services
■ Federal Executive Department   ■ Independent Executive Agencies
■ Federal Executive Agencies   ■ Accreditation and Licensure

- Food & Drug Administration
- Centers for Disease Control and Prevention
- National Institute for Occupational Safety and Health
- Substance Abuse and Mental Health Services Administration
- Office of the Assistant Secretary for Preparedness and Response
- Office of Civil Rights
- Health Resources & Services Administration
- Office of the National Coordinator for Health IT
- Indian Health Services

- Department of Transportation
- Department of Veterans Affairs
- Department of Homeland Security
- Department of Labor
- Department of Justice

- Federal Aviation Administration
- Internal Revenue Service
- Occupational Safety & Health Administration
- Federal Emergency Management Agency
- Environmental Protection Agency
- Drug Enforcement Administration
- Immigration and Customs Enforcement
- Federal Bureau of Investigation
- Equal Employment Opportunity Commission

- General Services Administration
- Federal Communications Commission
- Federal Trade Commission
- Securities and Exchange Commission
- National Transportation Safety Board
- National Labor Relations Board
- Nuclear Regulatory Commission

- Organ Procurement Organization
- The Joint Commission
- Other Accreditation Agencies

Implementation is the last step in a long process. The president and/or members of Congress proposed the law; the House and Senate passed it; the courts upheld it; and the bureaucratic agency proposed draft rules, gathered comments, and published final rules in the *Federal Register*. Bureaucrats are active at every stage in the process. For example, they shape proposed programs by suggesting legislative language to allies in Congress and testifying before congressional committees that are considering the law.

Sometimes executive bureaucrats develop close alliances with members of Congress as well as with interest-group lobbyists. A specialist in the EPA might spend years working with "green" members of Congress, along with the environmental groups and industries most affected by the regulations. As another example, the Bureau of Alcohol, Tobacco, Firearms, and Explosives connects frequently with gun makers and members of Congress who care about guns. Some criticize these arrangements as too cozy (recall the iron triangles discussed in Chapter 12). In any case, recognize that the bureaucracy is not walled off from other actors in government. It is part of the process all along the way.

● *A street-level bureaucrat in action. A local official in the Modesto, California, Health Department measures the growth of a young client as part of the Women, Infants, and Children program.*

The bureaucracy affects every aspect of our lives. It inspects the food you eat; monitors the air you breathe; negotiates the trade rules that governed the importation of your T-shirt; regulates seat belts, airbags, and the crash-resistant frame of your car; oversees your student loans; and awards your professors grants to study topics ranging from elections to Emily Dickinson's poems to nanotechnology. Almost everything you do today has been touched, one way or another, by bureaucracies implementing policies that were once proposed rules in the *Federal Register*.

The Bottom Line

» Once a law is passed or an executive order is signed, the program goes to the bureaucracy to be put into effect.

» Bureaucrats propose rules, publish them in the *Federal Register*, gather comments, rewrite the rules, and publish the final version. The law or executive order is now in effect.

» At every step of the process, lawyers and lobbyists interact with the bureaucracy; this interaction engages experts far from the political limelight.

» Bureaucratic officials take part in every step of the political process—from proposing legislation to putting it into effect.

How the Bureaucracy Is Organized

Each presidential administration names the heads of the government bureaucracy— about four thousand people known as political appointees. The Senate approves the highest-ranking twelve hundred or so of these men and women, who include

Civil servants: Members of the permanent executive branch bureaucracy who are employed on the basis of competitive exams and keep their positions regardless of the presidential administration.

BUREAUCRACY BUZZWORDS

Bureaucrat: You need to be more proactive.

Meaning: You should have protected me from myself.

Bureaucrat: We want you to be the executive champion of this project.

Meaning: I want to be able to blame you for my mistakes.

Bureaucrat: We need to syndicate this decision.

Meaning: We need to spread the blame if it backfires.

Bureaucrat: I see you involved your peers in developing your proposal.

Meaning: One person couldn't possibly come up with something this stupid.

Bureaucrat: Our agency is going through a paradigm shift.

Meaning: We have no idea what we've been doing, but in the future we shall do something completely different.

Bureaucrat: Value-added.

Meaning: Expensive.

(Source: H. George Frederickson, *Up the Bureaucracy*).

cabinet secretaries, their assistants and deputies, the ambassadors to countries around the world, and other top figures. Their role: steer their agencies in the direction charted by the president and the voters.

Under these four thousand appointees toil some 2.6 million **civil servants** who work at their jobs regardless of which party occupies the White House. Imagine the tensions when a new political appointee (often a campaign official) arrives eagerly touting the new president's philosophy to an office of career officials. Those long-serving bureaucrats usually have far more expertise than the political appointee who has just been named their boss. The civil servants know that before long (on average, three years), the eager new appointee will move on, to be replaced by another. The civil servants are acutely aware of the rules, regulations, and SOPs that guide their agency. They literally tell their new bosses what they can do; how they should do it; and the many things that they might want to do but that could land them in trouble because they fall outside the rules, clash with another agency's mission, or raise a sore point with a powerful member of Congress.

Over the years, civil servants have built up a vocabulary of their own, often caricatured as "bureaucratese"—the cautious, cover-your-backside language of experts with lifetime positions who are tasked with providing three trillion dollars' worth of federal services every year. H. George Frederickson published a book of humorous "bureaucracy-speak" examples (see Talking Politics). Master these lines, and you will be ready for a summer internship in the executive branch!

The federal government's organizational chart includes four types of agencies: cabinet departments, autonomous bureaus, independent regulatory agencies, and the bureaucracy's service organizations. Let us take a closer look at each.

The Cabinet Departments

President George Washington's cabinet had just four departments: State, Treasury, War (now called Defense), and the Office of the Attorney General (now the Justice Department). Over time, presidents added new departments until the cabinet reached its current size of fifteen. Table 15.1 lists each department, the year it was founded, and total employees. Notice how the military dominates the government's personnel count. The Department of Defense houses some 2.1 million employees, including the men and women in uniform, and manages some 750 facilities that add up to 30 million acres around the world; no other organization in the United States comes close.

Because State and Treasury are the two oldest departments, the secretaries of state and the treasury always sit next to the president in cabinet meetings. The younger the agency, the farther away from the president the secretary sits. (Each position is indicated by a silver plaque on the back of the chair, with the department's founding date.) A similar protocol exists for any formal event—the leaders of the oldest departments enter first, with the secretary of the newest department (currently Homeland Security) bringing up the rear. In the event of a catastrophe, the secretary of state is fourth in line to take over the presidency, followed by each cabinet secretary—again in the order the agencies were founded.

The Challenge of Governing. Nominating cabinet secretaries and other bureaucratic leaders is part of the fanfare of a new administration. The president sings the nominee's praises and the media speculates about fresh policy directions. Then the difficulties begin. Imagine that you are in the secretary's shoes: here are the hurdles you will face.

First, you must go before the Senate for confirmation. In the increasingly partisan Washington environment, any past indiscretion may force you to withdraw. If all goes well, you take office when the president does, on a cold Washington day in late January.

TABLE 15.1 **U.S. Executive Bureaucracies**

DEPARTMENT (WITH YEAR OF FOUNDING)	CURRENT EMPLOYEES (AS OF 2018)
State 1789	73,624*
Treasury 1789	78,734
Defense 1789	749,060 civilians; 1.3 million uniformed military
Justice 1789	111,778
Interior 1849	69,761
Agriculture 1862	73,231
Commerce 1903	35,757
Labor 1913	14,424
Health and Human Services (originally 1953 "Health, Education, and Welfare")	65,866
Housing and Urban Development 1965	7,697
Transportation 1966	53,568
Energy 1977	14,249
Education 1979	3,842
Veterans Affairs 1989	372,127
Homeland Security 2002	193,326
ADDITIONAL FEDERAL AGENCIES	
Social Security Administration	59,680
Environmental Protection Agency	14,172
National Aeronautics and Space Administration	17,581
General Services Administration	11,757
Other independent agencies	55,486
U.S. Postal Service (a semi-independent federal agency since 1971)	503,000
Executive Office of the President (detailed in Chapter 14)	1,869
Total Civilian Federal Service	**2,580,589** (excluding active-duty military)
Estimated number of federal contractors and grantees	**Between 5 and 6 million** (depending on who's counting)

Source: U.S. Office of Personnel Management.
*49,737 foreign service staff overseas, 10,191 U.S. civil servants, and 13,696 foreign service officers

Next, you select your staff—your team is not yet in place. The presidential transition group sends you boxes of résumés. You pick names for your deputies, your assistants, and the leaders of the dozens of offices in your agency; some you know, others the president's advisors recommend, and still others look especially impressive on paper. Now send your selections over to the White House for a thumbs-up. Because White House staffers may have their own favorites, you must negotiate your choices. The FBI examines every nominee's background, which can sometimes take many months. After that, each nominee goes to the Senate for confirmation.

If you are lucky, the White House does not ask a thousand questions, nothing embarrassing turns up in the FBI's detailed check, and no senator objects to the appointment. You might then have your political appointees in place by August.

However, if you get caught in a bottleneck—at the White House, the FBI, or in Congress—it can be a year or more before members of your team are in place. Remember, there are fifteen cabinet departments—in addition to dozens of federal agencies—and all are scrambling to get their people through the neck of the bottle. In September 2001, President George W. Bush did not yet have most of his security team in office when the terrorists attacked September 11, eight months after Inauguration Day. After 500 days in office, the Trump Administration still had not filled 204 of the top 605 posts in the executive branch.[18] As Washington has grown more partisan, the confirmation process has become more difficult. And remember that any senator can put a hold on one of your appointments.

Getting leaders into their offices is just the first challenge. New secretaries also face the more fundamental problem of managing a large bureaucracy that they know very little about. Cabinet secretaries are accomplished individuals, but they are unlikely to have much experience with the many facets of their department. For example, President Trump's first secretary of the Department of Homeland Security (DHS), John Kelly,[19] had previously been a Marine Corps General. Although he was familiar with homeland security issues, Kelly did not know

● President Trump meets with his cabinet. Notice the size of the group – too large for serious policy debates.

COMPARING NATIONS 15.1   Parliamentary Systems

Parliamentary systems—such as those in England, Germany, Japan, or Israel—are different from the U.S. system when it comes to bureaucratic leadership. In all these nations, senior members of the legislature become ministers, the equivalent of cabinet secretaries in the United States. Notice the contrast: Legislative leaders from the majority party also lead the bureaucracy.

Each ministry has two heads. The elected minister drawn from parliament represents the public and sets the policy goals; the other leader is a career civil servant (often called the director general), who provides technical expertise and continuity across the years. Both these positions are highly prestigious—in England, an effective director general of an important ministry may well earn a knighthood.

Some parliamentary systems result in coalition governments. Six parties together form the majority in the government of Israel. The different parties bargain for control of Israel's government ministries—the defense ministry is in the hands of the Yisrael Beiteinu Party, the head of the Kulanu Party directs the ministry of finance, and so on.

In other nations, no one sends in a résumé to become a department head—you have to win an election to parliament and work your way up the party hierarchy. There is no long confirmation process, no hostile congressional committees overseeing the bureaucracy, no checks and balances between the executive and legislative branches. The civil service is extremely prestigious. Successful civil servants can climb to the top of the ministry—rather than always working for a new set of senior appointees rotating in after each presidential election.

In the United States, the Constitution bars members of Congress from taking "any civil office"—to join the bureaucracy or the judiciary, they must resign their House or Senate seat. (Congressman Mike Pompeo, a Kansas Republican, left the House to become CIA Director under President Trump; he subsequently was named Secretary of State.) The founders, as always, insisted on checks and balances.

much about immigration issues, the Coast Guard, or the Animal and Plant Health Inspection Service—all bureaus now under his direction. Almost all secretaries face the same problem. When a new administration comes to town, a huge to-do list of policy goals awaits each new executive.

Explore major agencies within the bureaucracy.

Cabinet Meetings. Fifteen department heads gather around a White House conference room table with the president, vice president, and as many as ten additional senior leaders. Who are those other "senior leaders"? Each president names a set of positions as "cabinet-level"—for example, the CIA Director and the White House chief of staff (more on that role below). Along with the department heads, this group attends cabinet meetings and receives special briefings.

Does the whole group—department secretaries plus additional cabinet-level officials—serve as a president's central advisory team? No. There are too many of them. With twenty-five or more people around the table, plus dozens of staff lining the walls behind them, it is hard to have a serious discussion. Donald Trump convened his full cabinet only nine times during his first year in office.

The Rotating Bureaucracy. The turnover at the top of the U.S. bureaucracy is unique. No other democracy works in this way—nor does any other major institution. No private company, nonprofit organization, or university routinely asks thousands of outsiders to take over for three or so years and then step aside and make way for a new crop of leaders. Yet the political appointees scrambling to catch up are in charge of a huge bureaucratic leviathan. Thousands of civil servants toil away at the agency's tasks, working from one administration to the next even as new agency directors come and go.

Management consultants would run screaming from the room if you suggested setting up a business in this way. We cannot look to the Constitution for justification, because it does not mention cabinet departments, much less an entire bureaucracy. Many political scientists, however, think the bureaucracy works reasonably well. The civil service does its job. And the political leadership, for all the problems we just described, takes over with a definite philosophy, based on a president's central ideas. The Trump team, like the Obama team before them, came to Washington with a distinctive point of view.

Scholars of public policy generally agree that stability is desirable among political appointees during a presidency.[20] President Trump raised concerns when he replaced five cabinet-level officials in his first hundred days—far more than any other administration in history; the six presidents prior to Trump all together replaced only *one* cabinet official during their first hundred days in office.

Pairing a suitable philosophy with skilled political leadership can make a real difference in an agency's management. An example is the Federal Emergency Management Agency (FEMA), which responds to natural disasters. President Bill Clinton named a talented FEMA director, James Lee Witt, who transformed the agency into a decentralized, authority-sharing, proactive outfit. When floods hit the Midwest in 1993, FEMA won applause for its swift, well-organized assistance.

When the George W. Bush administration came to office, FEMA was on its list of target agencies. From a conservative perspective, FEMA had become *too* proactive. The Bush administration restored the old FEMA policies and installed an inexperienced (but politically connected) campaign donor, Michael Brown, as director.

In this case, the changes led to political disaster. In part owing to the restoration of a rules-bound, hierarchical structure, and in part to Brown's inexperience as a leader, FEMA responded feebly to Hurricane Katrina, a massive storm that flooded New Orleans in 2005. The media depicted widespread desperation: more

● *Federal Emergency Management Agency's (FEMA) response to disasters (Hurricane Katrina on left; Maria on right) remains a White House flashpoint. The agency's response to Hurricane Maria's September 2017 devastation in Puerto Rico was widely criticized, recalling the aftermath of Hurricane Katrina in New Orleans a dozen years before.*

than 1,800 people lost their lives in the storms and subsequent flooding—with scant federal response. Director Brown lost his job, and President Bush's popularity ratings tumbled.

President Obama, learning from his predecessors, appointed an experienced, well-regarded FEMA director, W. Craig Fugate, who had directed emergency services under Governor Jeb Bush in Florida. The agency received high marks when another devastating storm, Hurricane Sandy, hit the East Coast in 2012. Along with the value of savvy leadership, the FEMA example illustrates another important point about the federal bureaucracy. Calling for smaller government sounds promising on the campaign trail. However, each nook and cranny of the sprawling government establishment has a job to do; almost all deliver services that people rely on. That responsibility makes cutting government agencies difficult in practice.

The Cabinet and Diversity. Like the bureaucracy they lead, the fifteen secretaries increasingly reflect the American public. Table 15.2 shows the number of women and minority members in the cabinet over time. Until the mid-1960s, just two women

TABLE 15.2 **Demographic Makeup of Presidential Cabinet Department Heads**

PRESIDENT	WOMEN	MINORITIES	CABINET OFFICERS NAMED DURING ADMINISTRATION	YEARS
All presidents to 1963	2	0	—	1789–1963
Johnson	0	1	25	1963–1968
Nixon	0	0	31	1969–1974
Ford	1	1	22	1974–1976
Carter	4	1	22	1977–1980
Reagan	3	2	33	1981–1988
G. H. W. Bush	3	3	21	1989–1992
Clinton	5	10	30	1993–2000
G. W. Bush	6	8	34	2001–2008
Obama	8	10	32	2009–2016
Trump	3	3	18	2017–2019

had served in the cabinet in all of American history—and not a single African American, Latino, or Asian.

The dramatic change that began in the 1970s reflects the social revolution that swept the nation over one generation. During the first 200 years of American history, only three women and two African Americans were appointed as heads of executive departments. Since the 1980s, every president has appointed a diverse set of secretaries that reflects the nation. President Trump has slowed that trend, appointing the most heavily white and male group since the first George Bush.

Other Agencies

Nearly three-quarters of the federal bureaucracy—about 1.9 million civilians—works in the cabinet departments. Three other categories of federal workers each offer a different twist on the bureaucracy.

Executive Agencies. Independent executive agencies have more specific assignments than do the cabinet departments. The Environmental Protection Agency, for example, is entirely focused on one tough job: overseeing the environment. In contrast, the Department of the Interior has responsibilities that include—among many other things—supervising Indian affairs, national parks, geological surveys, oceans and energy, and surface mining.

The more than 30 independent executive agencies perform a wide range of tasks: They land astronauts on the moon (NASA), send Americans around the world to perform service projects (the Peace Corps), gather intelligence about other nations and groups (CIA), manage the banking system (the Federal Reserve), monitor elections (the Federal Election Commission), and investigate violations of civil rights in the workplace (Equal Employment Opportunity Commission).

The U.S. Postal Service became a cabinet agency in 1792. Some 180 years later, in 1971, the post office became an independent agency of the U.S. federal government—operating without direct federal subsidy. The Postal Service has just over 500,000 employees (down from nearly 800,000 in 1999) and 250,000 vehicles; it is the second-largest federal bureaucracy after the Defense Department.

Independent Regulatory Commissions. In the 1880s, farmers and small business complained bitterly that they were at the mercy of the railroads and their arbitrary freight rates. The farmers pleaded for government controls. However, reformers faced a problem. Wealthy, powerful railroad owners dominated the state legislatures and Congress. How could consumers be protected against these "robber barons?" Reformers organized a regulatory agency, the Interstate Commerce Commission (ICC), that would operate separately from Congress and the White House. Reformers hoped that the agency's independence would permit it to regulate industry—free from corrupting lobbyists and politics. That reform set the organizational template for a new kind of agency, independent regulatory commissions.

Independent regulatory commissions (IRCs)—always designed to be independent from the political branches—perform many different jobs: The Federal Election Commission, established in 1975, oversees U.S. electoral practices, for example (Figure 15.4). Today, there are sixteen independent regulatory commissions. Each have the authority to issue regulations, enforce laws, and settle disputes—essentially combining legislative, executive, and judicial powers in one agency. A set of commissioners, nominated by the president and confirmed by the Senate, runs the agency for a fixed term that does not overlap with the president's term—still another way to minimize political influence. The hope, beginning with the ICC, was that modern management methods, rather than politics, would guide regulatory policy.

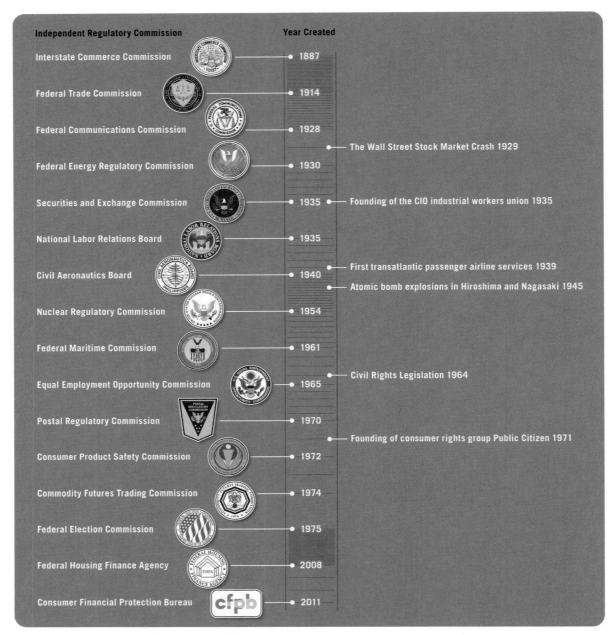

Figure 15.4 *Congress creates independent regulatory commissions in response to stock market failures, the rise of new technologies, or other emerging needs within society.*

You likely recognize the reformers' naiveté: Independent agencies were no less political than any other branch of government. As we saw when we examined rule-making, regulating an industry inevitably involves back-and-forth negotiations between regulators and the industry. Moreover, to understand an industry well enough to monitor its activities, regulators need relevant expertise. Commissioners are frequently drawn from the ranks of the regulated industry. Ironically, the effort to keep the regulatory commissions independent of Congress and the White House has left them more susceptible to industry influence. For decades, critics have charged that the independent regulatory agencies are "captured" or "acquired" by the industry and simply do its bidding.

There is no escaping the politics that pervade the independent regulatory agencies. Still, the "**regulatory capture**" argument is often overstated. Consumer groups also lobby, provide information to, and sue the agencies. Moreover, agency civil servants often work hard to achieve their institution's goals—and express pride in its independent stance.

In the past 30 years, a new generation of reformers has promoted *deregulation*— abolishing these agencies and letting free-market competition protect consumers. The original ICC was dismantled in 1995. The Civil Aeronautics Board, a regulatory commission that protected the airline industry by limiting competition, was abolished in 1985, with good and bad consequences—frequent-flier programs, fewer airlines, and huge fluctuations in fares. Today, business-friendly Republicans have targeted other agencies, especially the Consumer Financial Protection Bureau, created to aid consumers in the wake of the "Great Recession" of 2008–2009.[21]

Deregulation brings us full circle. Once, farmers and small business pleaded for relief from predatory markets. Now, a new generation of reformers offers a solution to problems with the regulatory agencies: return to the markets.

An Army of Their Own. A small support army maintains and services the massive office buildings housing the executive branch. Imagine the job of supplying 2.6 million workers—not to mention hiring, paying, reviewing, promoting, and sometimes firing them. These details require still another type of institution in the American bureaucracy: independent **central service agencies**, most notably the Office of Personnel Management (OPM) and the General Services Administration (GSA).

Do you want to work for the U.S. government? The OPM manages the giant "USAJobs" website, which lists hundreds of thousands of federal bureaucracy job openings each year. Your application will be screened by OPM staff. If you are hired, your employment materials (pay level, vacation time details, and health benefits) will come from them. And when you decide to leave government service, the OPM determines the government pension you have accumulated.

While you are working for the government, the GSA manages all the details of maintenance and supply. Your building just got painted? The GSA did the work—or hired and supervised the company who did it under contract. Do you need a shipment of forest fire–fighting helicopters (for the National Park Service) or a secure smartphone (at the OMB)? The GSA is your one-stop shopping spot.

Private Contractors. The final category of government employees does not work directly for the government. They come from private companies that provide goods and services under contract to the government. **Private contractors** now perform many jobs that once were handled directly by government employees. For example, the military increasingly relies on private firms to provide meals, transportation, security services, and even commando teams. For the first time in American history, there were more private contractors (over 200,000) than uniformed military personnel (about 190,000) in the war zones in both Iraq and Afghanistan. Besides war-related services, private companies provide a full range of government services, spreading to homeland security, international diplomacy, prison management, and garbage collection.

Why contract out government services? Three main reasons: First, private companies, foundations, and nongovernmental organizations often have special skills and resources they can bring to a job. Second, they lobby hard for the business. And third, Americans critical of the bureaucracy often assert that private companies can do a better and cheaper job.

Regulatory capture: The theory that industries dominate the agencies that regulate them.

Central service agencies: The organizations that supply and staff the federal government.

Private contractors: Private companies that contract to provide goods and services for the government.

Private contractors continue to provide security in war zones, including Iraq; here, private guards protect a U.S.–Iraqi diplomatic meeting.

In practice, private contractors sometimes do a better job than the public sector, but at other times they charge more for inferior services. Recognizing that private contracting in government is here to stay, the key to making it work is ensuring that government officials maintain careful oversight of the work that is done for hire.[22]

Executive branch agencies and commissions all face leadership challenges similar to those faced by the cabinet departments. The appointment process is cumbersome and complicated by politics. New appointees scramble to learn the bureaucratic ropes, even as the to-do list piles ever higher—and meanwhile the administrative team takes months or even years to get into place.

How can the nation's agencies operate effectively when their leaders are on the way in and just learning the ropes or are on the way out and operating as lame ducks? For an answer, we need to confront the complicated question of just who is in charge of the American bureaucracy.

The Bottom Line

» The federal bureaucracy includes five different types of agencies. The 15 cabinet departments, forming the largest group, employ roughly 1.9 million civilians.

» The government includes four other types of bureaucracies: executive agencies focus on one type of issue, such as environmental quality; independent regulatory commissions oversee specific industries; central service agencies staff and supply the entire bureaucracy; and private contractors are licensed to provide goods and services for the government. Different types of agencies face different political problems and challenges.

» The president appoints a small number of executives; the rest are members of the permanent civil service. The cabinet has grown far more diverse in the past 25 years.

» The cabinet and other appointed executives provide political direction; the civil servants provide expertise and continuity.

» Among the many challenges to a smoothly functioning system is the time—often more than a year—that it takes a new administration to get its leadership team in place.

Who Controls the Federal Bureaucracy?

Controlling four million civilian bureaucrats and military personnel, and an unknown number of private contractors (one reliable estimate pegs it at 5.3 million),[23] is a daunting leadership responsibility—and a giant management headache. It is also crucial for democracy. Self-rule requires mastering the bureaucracy. But who is in charge?

The People

In a democracy, the federal government must ultimately respond to the people. Most executive departments trumpet something like *"We Serve the People"* on their websites. However, real popular control faces a core problem: Much of what the bureaucracy does is too technical for direct public engagement.

How does the Internal Revenue Service (IRS) compute tax penalties for S corporations that wrongly elect to amortize anticipated losses with write-downs? What is the maximum engineering pendular sway ratio on truss-style bridges? Does the chemical compound bisphenol-A, widely used in plastics, leach into bottled drinking water—and if so, how dangerous is it to public health? Few Americans have the time or knowledge to develop opinions about such matters. We need someone to act on our behalf.

The President

In theory, the president controls the bureaucracy. The Constitution is clear on this issue: "The executive Power shall be vested in a President of the United States of America." The president is the bureaucrat in chief. The form of bureaucratic control that follows from this declaration is known as **overhead democracy**: The people elect presidents who, through their appointees, control the bureaucracy from the top.

In practice, most presidents are frustrated in their efforts to manage the millions of men and women under their command. Harry Truman put it famously when he commented on his successor, General Dwight D. Eisenhower: "He'll sit here and he'll say 'Do this!' and 'Do that!' *And nothing will happen.* Poor Ike, it won't be a bit like the army. He'll find it very frustrating."[24]

When presidents appoint directors of the executive branch, they quickly discover that the bureaucracy has its own preferences, processes, and routines. Before long, many executives begin to see the world through the eyes of their agencies—rather than from the perspective of the White House.

> **Overhead democracy:** A system by which the people elect the president, who, through their appointees, controls the bureaucracy from the top.

When President Richard Nixon, a Republican, came to office, Democrats had run the government for 28 of the previous 36 years, and Nixon believed that many of the career civil servants were simply Democrats waiting for the next liberal administration. "If we don't get rid of these people," Nixon wrote bluntly, "they will sit back on their well-paid asses and wait for the next election to bring back their old bosses."[25] During the Trump Administration, some White House officials voiced a similar concern that a "deep state" of career bureaucrats (and some disloyal political appointees) were thwarting the president's policy goals.

Congress

Although bureaucrats "belong" to the executive branch, the legislative branch wields a

● *Does the public control our federal bureaucracy? This cartoonist suggests otherwise.*

Change versus Stability: Should We Have More Politically Appointed Bureaucrats?

Presidents often complains that "the bureaucracy" is unresponsive to their goals. Career civil servants—hired long before a new administration sweeps into office—owe their loyalty to the department or agency they serve, not to the current president or the appointed head of their bureau. Is this tension a problem?

Yes: "Deep State" Equals Gridlock. Career bureaucrats can be a drag on innovation, which our government desperately needs to keep up with a twenty-first century economy and global political crises. When bureaucrats block the goals of an elected president, they are acting against the popular will. I would vastly increase the proportion of appointed civil servants, following practice in other democratic countries. We should simplify the process for appointing new officials so that each administration can introduce a new team and change the direction of public policy.

No. Leave the Experts in Charge. The complex demands of governing our trillion dollar federal bureaucracy require technical expertise and seasoned experience. Career bureaucrats have been a central feature of the executive branch for well over a century. They are controlled by democratic norms—responding to leaders who are approved by the Senate and appointed by the president. Besides, with all the problems of political gridlock and getting a team into place, the permanent bureaucracy provides stability and is key to the American government's ability to function and adapt.

surprising amount of authority over them. Congress shapes the bureaucracy in four different ways.

- **Funding**. Most important, Congress funds nearly all executive branch programs because it determines the federal budget. If Congress does not like a bureaucratic proposal, or if some agency head falls out of favor with a powerful subcommittee, that program or department may find its budget slashed by congressional appropriators.

- **Oversight**. Congress has formal power to supervise the executive branch, including both White House and federal bureaucratic operations. Policing department and agency actions is normally a routine operation—making sure that funds are properly expended or that programs achieve their stated goals. But Congress can extend its oversight authority into major investigations of executive branch actions. The mere mention of oversight hearings is a major threat to the bureaucracy.

- **Authorization**. Congress often has to reauthorize laws after a specified number of years. Although recent administrations have increasingly relied on executive orders, Congress wields the power to amend programs or even deny their reauthorization.

- **Reorganization**. Finally, Congress can change the structure and nature of executive branch organizations. Currently Congress is considering a White House proposal to shift several programs, such as a revised H1-B visa program for skilled workers, from the Department of Labor to the Department of Education—and possibly even merge the two Departments into one.[26]

These four sources of power add up to extensive congressional influence. Agency heads and cabinet secretaries are often more responsive to Congress—with its power of the purse and oversight authority—than to the president. Bureaucratic leaders regularly lobby Congress for additional funding or authority. They also frequently complain, however, about congressional "micromanagement."

Political scientists view the relationship between Congress and the bureaucracy through **principal-agent theory**. This approach analyzes how a principal (in this case, Congress) hires an agent (the bureaucracy) to do a job. The problem arises when the agent has much more information than the principal. How do you control a bureaucracy when there is "information asymmetry," that is, when "they" know a lot more than "you" do? The answer: Make sure their interests are the same as yours. Many scholars now suggest that although Congress cannot possibly supervise everything the bureaucracy does, even so, the power of its weapons—especially funding and oversight—leads bureaucratic officials, by and large, to conform to congressional wishes. Put differently, the fear of being hauled before a congressional panel and threatened with loss of funding is enough to make bureaucrats worry about congressional intent and desires.

Congressional power also is circumscribed, of course. The power to shape or influence the bureaucracy is still a far cry from the power to command or control it. Presidents and congressional leaders sometimes clash over who controls bureaucratic departments and agencies. Courts also weigh in, striking down regulatory-agency actions, as we saw in the rulemaking discussion earlier. Meanwhile, another powerful set of players—all the interest groups—quietly exert influence as well.

Interest Groups

Interest groups closely engage bureaucrats as they administer the laws. As we saw in Chapter 12, lobbying groups comment extensively on proposed rules. They offer information about the needs and capacity of the affected industry. As bureaucrats finalize the rules and implement the program, they routinely engage industry representatives, whose cooperation may be necessary to make the program work smoothly. Officials in the bureaucracy, trade groups, and consumer alliances often share expertise and interests. Over time, close relations may develop, making lobbyists influential in the day-to-day operations of the executive agencies. Interest groups—often fighting among themselves—have many ways to challenge overzealous regulators: They can go public with complaints, enlist friends in Congress, or sue. The result is another set of influences on bureaucrats in action.

Bureaucratic Autonomy

Partly because they have so many would-be masters, bureaucrats wind up with considerable autonomy in how they do their work. Many civil servants have strong views about their field, whether it is protecting the environment, enforcing civil rights laws, or keeping the homeland safe. They also have an interest in increasing their own autonomy—applying their best judgment to the problems they face.

Some federal bureaucrats themselves call attention to abuses within their department or agency. These happen enough that there is a term for a worker—public or private—who reports corruption or fraud: **whistleblower**. In many cases, permanent civil servants blow the whistle on fraudulent or misbehaving political appointees higher up in the department or agency. In 2017–2018, for example, several whistleblowers detailed abuses of office by EPA Administrator Scott Pruitt,

Principal-agent theory: Details how policymakers (principals) control the actors who work for them (agents)—but who have far more information than they do.

Whistleblower: A federal worker who reports corruption or fraud.

including extravagant travel and security spending and falsifying his official calendar. Pruitt resigned under fire in summer 2018.[27]

This search for autonomy is especially true for government officials who deal directly with the public—the street-level bureaucrats who implement public policy. General policies are formulated in the higher administration, but it is street-level bureaucrats who actually run the programs, constantly using their own judgment. For example, the police officer may write you a speeding ticket—or let you off with a warning.[28]

Consider a more complicated case. The Women, Infants, and Children program (WIC) provides vouchers for meals to low-income families with children. On the national level, Congress debates WIC funding and the administration determines the rules for eligibility. On the local level, street-level bureaucrats constantly make judgment calls about how strictly to apply the rules. For example, one woman makes too much money on paper, but her ex-husband is not paying his child support—does she still qualify? Or another woman was ill and missed the application deadline—do you give her the benefit card allowing her to buy food anyway? Still another family has broken the rules again and again, but if you cut them off from the program, the children will suffer. In all such cases, street-level bureaucrats decide what to do—giving them enormous influence over how to apply the rules. Program beneficiaries quickly learn about the power of the bureaucrats they see again and again.

Moreover, at the street level, every program has its own tone. Some programs (e.g., Social Security) generally treat their beneficiaries with respect; others (e.g., Temporary Assistance for Needy Families) reputedly take a more disciplinary stance.[29]

Democracy Revisited

Many agents—the president, Congress, courts, and interest groups—exert some control over the bureaucracy. Each does so on behalf of others: The White House tries to speak for the national public, Congress for voters in a state or district, courts to defend injured parties or protect the Constitution, and interest groups on behalf of clients who range from a business to the environmental or the civil rights community. Bureaucrats try to maximize their own discretion to do what they think is best. Do all these clashing forces add up to democratic control?

The answer is yes and no. At times, these different forms of democratic control offer a rough kind of popular oversight. Administrations that focus on delivering services can have considerable success; presidents who seek to change the direction of federal policy sometimes succeed; congressional oversight often improves responsiveness. But these levers of democratic control are all blunt instruments. Effectively using them takes hard work and constant attention. In the next section, we examine three reform proposals that might strengthen popular control.

 **The Bottom Line**

» In a democracy, the public must ultimately control the government bureaucracy. The question is how.

» Different actors exert some influence over the bureaucracy: the president (who names the leaders), Congress (through funding and oversight), and interest groups.

» Bureaucrats still operate with considerable autonomy, especially those at the "street level."

Reforming the Bureaucracy

Americans ask a great deal of the bureaucracy, but—as reported at the start of the chapter—we do not like it much. Let us look at the usual criticisms and then explore some solutions.

Critiques

Three major sources of disapproval focus on cost, inertia, and public mistrust.

Cost. Critics complain about the high cost of the bureaucracy and its programs. As a proportion of America's gross domestic product (GDP), however, the cost of the bureaucracy—as well as the number of federal bureaucrats—has remained generally steady over the past 40 years (see Figure 15.5). And although every politician has a story to tell about waste or fraud, most bureaucratic programs have a substantial constituency who rely on the service they provide. The bureaucratic agencies meet real needs, which is one reason elected officials find them difficult to cut. The only president who significantly reduced the number of nonmilitary civil servants in the post–World War II period is Bill Clinton, who slashed the civil service by some 400,000 bureaucrats. Donald Trump has cut the size of individual departments, such as Treasury, but increased others like Interior and Veterans Affairs; the net effect has been little change.

Inertia. American politics and culture are in constant motion. In our restless, innovative nation, the slow, rule-bound, hierarchical bureaucracy never seems to keep up. Many examples illustrate government organizations that are out of touch with a changing nation. Why do NASA flights, such as the space shuttle, always take off from Florida, despite uncertain weather and a growing population potentially endangered by crashes? Because an obscure 1950s rule prohibited the flight of test aircraft west of the Mississippi River. Once bureaucratic routines are set, they are hard to change.

Inertia also comes from clashing political desires. For example, the government is prohibited—again by bureaucratic regulations—from purchasing knives, forks, and spoons from abroad. Employees on State Department business are prohibited from flying aboard non-American airlines. It is often less expensive, however, to buy foreign goods or to fly on international carriers. Why don't bureaucratic

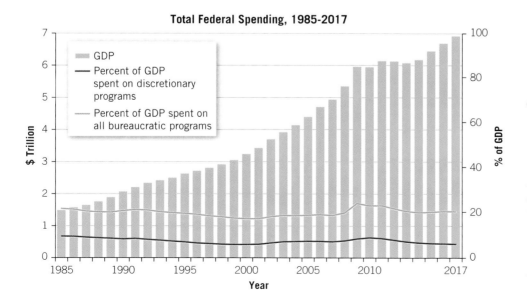

Figure 15.5 *Cost of the federal bureaucracy as a proportion of GDP; federal programs cost slightly less than 30 years ago. The bottom line shows the percentage of the GDP that is discretionary spending (programs that Congress, presidents, and department heads can control); the top line shows the percentage of the GDP that is spent on all federal programs, including those required by law: Social Security, Medicare, and Medicaid are the largest. (Congressional Budget Office)*

rules shift to accommodate this reality? Because multiple political constituencies demand different things. Congress, reflecting many voices, insists on both efficient purchasing policies *and* "buying American."

Clashing rules reflect different goals and values: We want to spread government contracts around the country, ensure social equity, stimulate new kinds of American products and services, and support American producers. These desires can clash with one another—and with the need for lower costs or faster services. Which priority deserves the most weight? The effort to choose among them is what democracy is all about. It is a debate that never ends.

Another, more troubling, problem is the increasing difficulty of recruiting the "best and the brightest" to government service. Individuals tapped for senior positions face the long process—and, often, hardball politics—we have described: Eager appointees linger in limbo for months waiting for a senator to lift their "hold." Then they must generate an extraordinary paper trail to pass security clearance; for example, these busy people must report every trip they took abroad in the last ten years. The media will jump on any past indiscretion. And, after all these hurdles, appointees arrive on the job and discover that civil service pay scales have only inched up since 2010.

Public Mistrust. Politicians from both parties bash the bureaucracy. Republican Ronald Reagan announced that "government is not the solution to our problem" and declared, "It is time to make [bureaucrats] stand by our side, not ride on our back." Democrat Bill Clinton declared, "The era of big government is over."

Fueling public mistrust of bureaucrats are scandals and mistakes, many covered in detail by a 24/7 media mix of headlines, punditry, blogs, and tweets. In an institution as large as the federal bureaucracy, occasional examples of error, corruption, and fraud are inevitable. After all, government officials are human, just as prone to personal flaws and errors as anyone else. But in an environment of constant bureaucracy bashing, the bad news is far more prominently reported than are bureaucratic achievements, which only reinforces the general image of a corrupt, lazy bureaucracy riding "on our backs."

> **Freedom of Information Act (FOIA):** A 1966 law that facilitates full or partial disclosure of government information and documents.

Reforms

The bureaucracy's reputation for being expensive, slow-moving, and scandal-ridden has attracted a long history of reform efforts. Let us consider three popular proposals.

● *Businesswoman turned bureaucrat. Lillian Salerno, who ran a successful healthcare business, joined the Department of Agriculture in 2009 to manage a rural-development program providing some $30 billion annually in grants and low-interest loans to farmers in rural America.*

Open Up the System. The public's faith in government tumbled in the late 1960s and the early 1970s after an unpopular war in Vietnam, civil rights unrest, and President Nixon's shocking behavior during the Watergate scandal. One response was a concerted attempt to make the executive bureaucracy more transparent. Sunshine laws, which require public hearings and citizen input, open up bureaucratic debates to public view. The **Freedom of Information Act** (**FOIA**) extends citizen access to agency and department deliberations. Any individual or news organization may file a FOIA request to see an unreleased government document (the legislation created a new verb, "to FOIA" a document). Today, every federal agency has its own website that tries to explain just what it is doing.

Bureaucratic officials sometimes resist these efforts. Concerns have been raised about the potentially chilling effect on communication by politically motivated FOIA requests: as one headline asked, "Is the Freedom of Information Act Stifling Intellectual Freedom?"[30] Advocates of greater openness push for more access. Many government agencies drag their feet in response to a FOIA request.

Some have genuine security concerns. Others resent the time and effort it takes to ensure transparency. And many simply want to protect themselves from criticism.

Reinventing Government. Efforts to enhance the bureaucracy are as old as the institution itself. During the Clinton administration, Vice President Al Gore ran a sweeping "Reinventing Government" project designed to cut bureaucratic delays, increase efficiency, reduce costs, decentralize management, and empower employees to make decisions. President Trump in summer 2018 announced a major bureaucracy overhaul that he promised would save billions of dollars.[31]

A call for efficiency works, however, only up to a point. Most businesses have a clear and simple goal: maximize returns for investors. In contrast, bureaucratic agencies have many constituencies with multiple goals. For example, if the Department of Agriculture focuses on farmers and helps to maintain price levels, complaints will arise from consumers (high prices), environmentalists (disappearing topsoil), and even foreign governments (protections may violate free trade). Efficiency *sounds* good. However, government officials are called on to juggle many different goals: they have to be fair, responsive, objective, focus on the national interest, attend to international trade rules. Being efficient at one goal can clash with being efficient at another.

Privatization. If the bureaucracy seems slow and inefficient, perhaps private companies can do the job better. One powerful trend in government has been outsourcing public services to private firms. For-profit companies collect garbage, manage prisons, protect the homeland, cook for the troops, and launch commando raids abroad.

The movement for privatizing federal (and many state) programs took flight in the 1970s and received a boost from President Reagan in the 1980s. His administration turned some forty thousand government jobs over to private contractors, for reported savings of more than six hundred million dollars. As we noted previously, some 5.3 million private contractors are working for federal, state, and local governments today.

Private firms often can do a job for less. But the savings are at least partly offset by the need for government supervision. What happens when private managers—worrying about the bottom line and returning money to their investors—cut corners or violate rules?[32]

The benefits of privatization are still debated. Research in this area suggests that *competitive contracting* (requiring more than one bid from outside contractors who want to provide government services) can save money and boost quality. However, the most important calculation, one often overlooked by reformers, is factoring in a way for government officials to supervise the private contractor. Careful oversight is a critical dimension of making privatization work.[33]

● *An employee of the Immigration and Customs Enforcement's Stewart Detention Center in Lumpkin, Georgia, waits for the front gate to be opened. The detention center is operated on contract by the Nashville-based Corrections Corporation of America.*

The Bottom Line

» Critics of the bureaucracy focus on cost, inertia, and public mistrust.

» Solutions include sunshine reforms, reinventing government to make it more constituent friendly, and privatizing some of its functions.

Conclusion: The Real Solution Lies with You

President Kennedy came to office amid a burst of idealism and declared, "Ask not what your country can do for you—ask what you can do for your country." Inspired by the young president, the early civil rights movement, and the general optimism of the era, many college graduates streamed into public service. Today, fewer Americans are attracted to government service: just 6.1 percent of U.S. federal employees are under 30, compared to more than 9 percent in 2010.[34] Can this trend change? What would draw *you* into working for the government?

Wanted: a few good bureaucrats!

The ultimate answer to the problems of bureaucracy, we believe, lies in the interest and commitment of a new generation. We are deeply concerned that men and women like you and your classmates—a well-educated group interested in political science—will bypass government altogether.

What is the problem? Politicians from both parties take shots at the bureaucracy. They freeze pay, downsize departments, and disparage millions of professionals. A closer look suggests that the bureaucracy performs many jobs we need and value, from managing our national finances to predicting the weather to defending the United States. Ultimately, our government—our democracy—is only as good as the bureaucracy that puts public policy into effect. And this brings us back to your generation's commitment to public service, and what public officials can do to foster it.

CHAPTER SUMMARY

Check your understanding of Chapter 15.

● Within the executive branch, the U.S. federal bureaucracy does a vast amount of work in governing the country—and more closely resembles the nation's population than any other segment of our national government. However, Americans express deep ambivalence about our bureaucracy, generally rating it very low in opinion polls.

● The American bureaucracy was established in reaction to the spoils system, dominant between

1828 and 1901. A merit-based hiring system has been in place for more than a century since.

● In theory, all bureaucracies share five characteristics: hierarchy, division of labor, fixed routines, equal rules for all, and technical qualifications.

● Bureaucrats in the United States, as in other countries, perform a wide range of functions—from managing the nation's defense and national economy to organizing and providing food stamps and tax cuts. The bureaucracy is specifically charged with implementing the laws passed by Congress and signed by the president. This typically involves an administrative rulemaking process, as well as actual delivery of services and carrying out of programs.

● Since the 1930s, the federal bureaucracy has grown to nearly four million employees—two-thirds civilians and one-third active-duty military. This growth has occurred despite anti–"big government" sentiment among Americans; helping to overcome this sentiment have been the twin forces of war and enforcing morality.

● Organizing such a sprawling set of cabinet departments and agencies, populated by civil servants and political appointees, is an immense job.

● It is not readily apparent who is in charge of managing the bureaucracy. Many different players have a role, including the public, the president,

Congress, and interest groups. The result of all those masters: bureaucrats have considerable discretion in how they work.

● This freedom can lead to serious tensions between Americans' democratic ideal of representative accountability and an unelected, often-*un*accountable workforce of civil servants.

● Public disapproval of the bureaucracy arises from different complaints. Our executive bureaucracy costs too much, say some critics; others argue that bureaucratic inertia makes it difficult to respond to policy crises. A stream of well-reported scandals influences Americans' perceptions of our bureaucracy, driving up mistrust.

● Reform efforts include enhancing the transparency of bureaucratic practices, reinventing government to improve responsiveness and reduce layers of management, and privatizing government services.

 Need to review key ideas in greater depth? Click here.

KEY TERMS

Bureaucratic pathologies, p. 461	Overhead democracy, p. 477	Regulatory capture, p. 475
Central service agencies, p. 475	Pendleton Civil Service Act, p. 458	Spoils system, p. 458
Civil servants, p. 468	Principal-agent theory, p. 479	Street-level bureaucrats, p. 465
Final rule, p. 464	Private contractors, p. 475	Universalistic politics, p. 458
Freedom of Information Act (FOIA), p. 482	Proposed rule, p. 464	Whistleblower, p. 479

Flashcard review.

STUDY QUESTIONS

1. Is the U.S. federal bureaucracy too large? Do we need four million people working for the government—in addition to several million more hired under federal contracts? If you would like to see a smaller bureaucracy, where do you think we should start cutting workers?

2. Who *should* run the bureaucracy, in your view? Do bureaucrats have too much discretion in how they perform their duties? What are the respective merits of a "street-level" or "top-down" management style? And should presidents (or Congress, or interest groups, etc.) have more authority than they currently wield to exert their will on the bureaucracy?

3. Let's say you have just learned about some unsavory doings in your bureaucratic agency or

department. Do you blow the whistle—that is, report the problem? Or do you keep quiet, knowing your job could be in danger? What factors would affect your decision?

4. Based on what you now know about the U.S. bureaucracy, should we mount a major push for reform? What type(s) of reforms would be most useful? Or are the various agencies and processes, such as rulemaking, of the bureaucracy working pretty well the way they are?

5. Given your expanded knowledge of the bureaucracy, are you more or less likely to be interested in working in an executive office like the Treasury Department or EPA? Does this seem like a promising way to exercise your civic spirit? Why or why not?

16 The Judicial Branch

JUNE WEEKDAY MORNINGS are a good time to visit the Supreme Court's iconic marble steps. Most decisions are announced to the public in that month, as the Court ends its annual term. On June 25 and 26, 2018, the Court issued three major decisions with sweeping implications for American politics and society—each by a 5–4 vote. In *Trump v. Hawaii*, the court ruled that the president's authority to secure the country's borders enabled his controversial ban on travelers from eight majority-Muslim nations. In *National Institute of Family and Life Advocates v. Becerra*, the Court blocked a California law that required religious "crisis pregnancy centers" to inform women about abortions. And, in *Janus v. American Federation of State, County and Municipal Employees*, the Court ruled that workers who do not join unions may not be forced to pay for collective bargaining—a decision that struck down a 40-year precedent and dealt a serious blow to labor unions.[1]

All three cases reshaped vital issues—reflecting the central role the judiciary plays in American politics. During the battle to ratify the Constitution, Alexander Hamilton predicted that the judiciary "will always be the least dangerous" and "the weakest" branch of government, for, he reasoned, it has "no influence" over "the sword" (the president controls the army) or "the purse" (Congress is in charge of the budget).[2] Yet over time, the U.S. judiciary has accumulated sweeping authority. It strikes down laws, rules, and regulations that violate the Constitution—as the courts interpret it.

We have seen the great reach and power of the Supreme Court throughout this book. For example, it struck down hard-won congressional compromises and protected slavery (in *Dred Scott*, 1857); it first permitted segregation (*Plessy v. Ferguson* in 1896) and then rejected it (*Brown v. Board of Education*, 1954); it swept away a network of state laws prohibiting abortion (*Roe v. Wade*, 1973). More recently, the Supreme Court rejected bipartisan efforts to limit money flowing into American elections; struck down sections of the Voting Rights Act that empowered the federal government to monitor election laws in places with a history of racial discrimination; overturned a law that permitted the government to deport immigrants who had committed felonies; and permitted Ohio to purge voter lists of people who had not recently voted.[3] These cases were all the more controversial because each was decided by a single vote—5–4.

● *Union activists protest the Supreme Court ruling in* Janus v. AFSCME, *which held that public employee unions cannot require non-members to pay fees to the union.*

The previous two chapters, on the presidency and on the bureaucracy, asked if and how each still fits into a democratic framework. The question becomes even more pointed for the federal courts. Unelected officials with lifetime appointments wield the power to overrule the long, hard democratic process of forging legislation in both Washington and the states. The founders believed that the more political branches of government—the president and Congress—needed the courts to check them. Has that check now grown too powerful? And too politicized?

Who are we? A nation founded on the world's oldest constitution, which directly or indirectly governs almost every aspect of our collective life. The courts apply the Constitution to the problems we face. Small wonder that the United States long has been a nation of courts, lawyers, and people ready to sue.

We begin with the basics. What does the court system look like? How does it make decisions? How did it amass so much power over American politics, government, and daily lives? Throughout we will ask the same fundamental question: Does the American political system effectively balance the authority of elected officials and lifetime judges? The answer starts with the basic character of the American people: *Who we are?*

Who Are We? A Nation of Laws . . . and Lawyers

The United States relies on courts to resolve more matters than most nations. The result is a deeply legalistic political culture.

Embracing the Law—and Lawsuits

Litigation: The conduct of a lawsuit.

Lawsuits, or **litigation**, are a near-constant feature of American public life. The annual U.S. criminal caseload includes 35 to 40 million cases filed in state courts. Traffic violations add another 55 million cases. Federal courts open about 400,000 new cases a year (notice that federal cases equal about 1% of the volume in state courts). And another three-quarters of a million cases enter bankruptcy courts. Add all of these up, and the United States approaches 100 million legal actions a year. And that is before we get to all the cases heard in specialized federal courts.

Courts are the primary sites for settling both private and public disputes. Advocacy groups, private citizens, and corporations go to court as a "first-strike" option. Litigation is an essential part of the rule-making process (discussed in Chapter 15). Business competition spills into the courts. Most other industrial nations rely more on **mediation** in noncriminal cases; citizens also are more likely to defer to civil servants. In contrast, Americans sue. Only a few other nations—most notably, Great Britain and Denmark—have as many suits per capita as the United States does.

Mediation: A way of resolving disputes without going to court, in which a third party (the mediator) helps two or more sides negotiate a settlement.

Americans are not only a people of litigation but also a people of lawyers, with roughly 1.1 million lawyers (782,200 in active practice). That number has risen fourfold since 1960, six times faster than population growth. The nation now has one lawyer for every 275 people—far outstripping Canada (one in every 450), India (one in every 1,200), France (one in 1,403), and every other nation (see Comparing Nations 16.1). As early as 1835, Alexis de Tocqueville could comment, "There is

The U.S. Judiciary

Original number of Supreme Court justices	**5**
Year in which the number of Supreme Court Justices was set at 9	**1869**
Number of Supreme Court justices appointed, 1882–1910	**18**
Number of Supreme Court justices appointed, 1982–2010	**9**
Average number of years a Supreme Court justice served before retiring from 1790–1954	**16.5**
Average number of years a Supreme Court justice served before retiring from 1970–2018	**26**
Number of Acts of Congress ruled unconstitutional per year from 1800–1900	**0.2 (or 22 in all)**
Number of Acts of Congress ruled unconstitutional per year 1900–1999	**1.3**
Number of Acts of Congress ruled unconstitutional per year 2000–2018	**2.0[4]**
Number of chief justices in American history	**17**
Number since 1953	**4**
Total number of cases heard by Supreme Court, 1987–1988 term	**155**
Total number of cases heard by Supreme Court, 2017–2018 term	**79**
Vacancies on the Supreme Court filled in Obama's eight years	**2**
Vacancies on the Supreme Court filled in the first two years of the Trump presidency	**2**
Estimated number of Americans who served on federal juries in 2016	**44,000**
Estimated number who served on juries in state or local courts	**1.4 million**

How has the character and role of our judicial system changed over time?

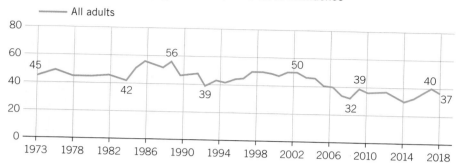

Americans' Confidence in the U.S. Supreme Court
% A great deal/Quite a lot of confidence

● **Figure 16.1** *The Supreme Court gradually declines in public esteem (Gallup, 2018).*

hardly any political question in the United States which does not, sooner or later, turn into a judicial one."[5]

Trust in Courts

Traditionally, lawyers and courts enjoyed high prestige. Tocqueville described early nineteenth century lawyers as democracy's natural aristocrats and noted that the American people trusted them. Not anymore.

Today, law, lawyers, and the legal system all face shrinking reputations. In 2018, only 37 percent of Americans report "a great deal" of confidence in the Supreme Court (see Figure 16.1). Individual cases affect public perception of the courts. The Court stopped the recount of Florida's ballots after the 2000 presidential election in what appeared to be a partisan (5–4) vote. In his dissent to *Bush v. Gore*, Justice Stevens wrote, "Although we may never know with complete certainty the identity of the winner of this year's presidential election, the identity of the loser is perfectly clear. It is the nation's confidence in the judge as an impartial guardian of the rule of law."[6] That was certainly true for Democrats, who again charged the Court with undermining democracy when it struck down a key component of the Voting Rights Act in (2013). Republicans made the same charge when the Court refused to strike down the Affordable Care Act (in 2012) and protected same-sex marriage (in 2015).[7]

In 2016, Justice Scalia died and President Obama nominated Merrick Garland to the Supreme Court. The Republican-controlled Senate refused to hold hearings

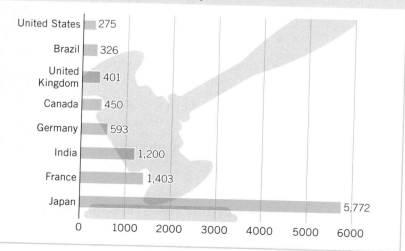

COMPARING NATIONS 16.1 — Number of Lawyers, Per Capita

How many lawyers per capita does each country have? Japan is a society based on consensus and has only 22,000 lawyers in a nation of 127 million people. The United States is at the other extreme, with one lawyer for every 275 citizens.

Country	Number
United States	275
Brazil	326
United Kingdom	401
Canada	450
Germany	593
India	1,200
France	1,403
Japan	5,772

and, a year later, swiftly confirmed Donald Trump's nominee, Neil Gorsuch. Approval rose 15 percent among Republicans and fell 10 percent among Democrats.[8] Smart politics? Or the growing politicization of an institution that was designed to stand above politics?

Even when the judiciary's prestige ebbs, however, it still ranks roughly the same as that of the president (37%) and towers over Congress (just 11% in June 2018).

● *Images of law in popular culture. Here, the cast of* Suits.

Courts in American Culture

Images of law and lawyers run through American culture, with the image alternating between heroism and cynicism. In *To Kill a Mockingbird*, Gregory Peck's Atticus Finch wins the African American community's respect when he passionately defends a black man unjustly accused of rape: "In our courts all men are created equal," he proclaims at the film's climax. "That's no ideal to me. That is a living, working reality." The book and movie's racial idealism reflected the optimism of the early 1960s. Julia Roberts played another legal heroine, the real-life Erin Brockovich, a clerk without any legal training whose indefatigable work led to a major environmental lawsuit against Pacific Gas and Electric for contaminating the water supply of Hinkley, California. A more recent example of movie heroes before the bar: Tom Hanks in *Bridge of Spies* playing real-life lawyer James Donovan, who defended an accused Communist spy then risked his life by arranging a spy exchange with East Germany and Soviet Russia during the Cold War. Images of law as a kind of crusade—for racial justice, environmental protection, or national security—reflect and reinforce images of political idealism.

In American culture, as in politics, the courts are a place where our highest ideals are on display—and where we simultaneously fear that corruption runs rampant. We will return at chapter's end to proposed reforms of the legal system. First, let us explore how that system works in practice.

 **The Bottom Line**

» The United States relies on courts and litigation more than most other nations—a political reality reflected in both its number of lawsuits and its number of lawyers.

» Trust in the Supreme Court has declined in recent years.

» Law continues to play an important role in American popular culture, which portrays it in both idealistic and cynical terms.

Organizing the Judicial Branch

The Constitution offers detailed instruction for Congress (Article 1) and vague rules for the executive branch (Article 2). The judiciary gets the least attention of all. The Constitution vests judicial power in the Supreme Court without specifying the number of justices it should include and empowers Congress to design the rest of our

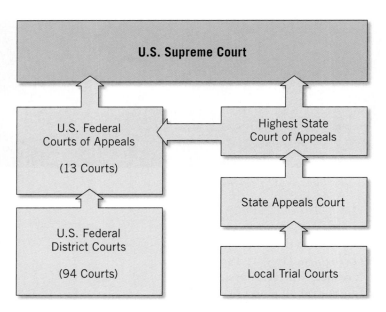

U.S. Supreme Court

U.S. Federal
Courts of Appeals

(13 Courts)

U.S. Federal
District Courts

(94 Courts)

Highest State
Court of Appeals

State Appeals Court

Local Trial Courts

● **Figure 16.2** *Organization of the U.S. federal courts system.*

federal court system. This section examines how the courts are organized. As usual, there is a distinctive look to how Americans run this branch of government.

Divided We Rule

By now you know the story: When Americans see government power, they divide it. Two chambers of Congress, with layers of committees and subcommittees; an executive branch split into departments, agencies, commissions, and White House offices; and a federalist system of national, state, and city officials all cooperating, competing, and overlapping. Court powers also are divided.

Most other nations feature a single unitary system of courts. In contrast, the United States exhibits *judicial federalism*. Both federal and state court systems are further divided into layers; the federal system has three layers as do most states (see Figure 16.2). Lower courts conduct trials, appellate courts hear appeals, and a supreme court in both state and federal systems renders a final verdict. The national Supreme Court is the ultimate arbiter for all cases that involve the Constitution or federal law. Millions of cases are filed each year; around ten thousand appeals reach the Supreme Court, which only accepts and hears about eighty. That leaves a great deal of authority to the lower ranks of the judiciary.

State and Local Courts

Local trial and state appeals courts are the workhorses of the judiciary, handling most of the nontraffic cases in the United States each year. State courts are responsible for all cases that arise under state law; they rule on everything from antitrust disputes to murder cases, from medical malpractice to marijuana possession. Every state organizes its judicial system in its own way—so there is considerable variation around the nation.

The first stop in most cases is a state trial court. Appeals usually are handled in state appellate courts, which typically consist of an appellate court and then a court of final appeal, generally known as the state supreme court. Appeals from the top state courts may be heard by the U.S. Supreme Court. Many landmark cases originate—and sometimes are settled—in state courts. *Roe v. Wade* (which struck down a Texas law banning abortion) and *Bush v. Gore* (halting the recount of disputed presidential ballots in Florida) began in state courts. However, very few of the millions of state cases ever reach a federal judge, as these cases did.

Judicial Selection

Do you think you might like to become a state judge? There are surprisingly few formal criteria for selection. You may not even need a law degree: 22 states and the federal courts require no formal training before judges start hearing cases. Most judges first make their name as lawyers, though many come from government or academic positions. If you plan to lobby a governor to ensure your judicial appointment, make sure you pick the right state: Only 17 states authorize their governor to select judges, and two leave selection to the state legislature. Most states (31) *elect* judges. Judges' terms range across the states, from two to 14 years, and are usually renewable.

The idea of electing judges is controversial. After all, the courts are meant to be above partisan politics, protecting rights and weighing evidence without political pressures. Elections, say the critics, undermine the courts' ability to stand up for the rights of unpopular minorities. Moreover, campaign contributions and campaign promises could lead to bias and even corruption on the state benches. Former Supreme Court justice Sandra Day O'Connor has been an especially vocal critic of electing judges; she calls judicial campaigns "tawdry and embarrassing."[9] Still, the United States is the land of five hundred thousand elected officials. The American ideal—government by the people—leads many states to insist that judges stand before the public.

Federal Courts

Federal courts hear three types of cases. First, they handle crimes that violate federal laws, issues that involve federal treaties, and cases touching on the Constitution. Examples range from the dramatic to the mundane: terrorism, immigration, organized crime, civil rights, patents, insider trading, and flag burning. Second, they decide disputes that spill across state lines—for example, interstate drug trafficking and conflicts between parties in different states (when at least 75 thousand dollars is involved in the dispute). Finally, after state courts have ruled on a case, the parties can appeal to the federal courts—if a federal issue is involved.

District courts: The first level of federal courts, which hear the evidence and make initial rulings.

Most federal cases begin in one of the 94 **district courts**, which together house just under 700 judges. Every state has at least one district court, and the larger

---

What Do YOU Think? | **How Should States Select Their Judges?**

Which of these three approaches to judicial selection in the states seems most persuasive to you?

Let the People Vote. The people are the best guardians of their own welfare. Let them decide who their justices should be. No matter how courts are organized, it is naive to think that politics can be kept out of the equation. Today, 70 percent of the public thinks that justices sometimes let their own political views influence their rulings. Because politics is inevitable, the public should have a direct voice in judicial selection.[10]

Appointment by a Governor. A state governor (with the advice and consent of the state senate) will have valuable information about the candidates and can keep better track of which justice is doing a good job. It also avoids the problems introduced by elections: campaigning, fund-raising, potential corruption, and the temptation to win votes by making promises that could later compromise the court.

Establish Merit Committees. Courts must be above politics. They must defend the rights of minorities and unpopular views. The only way to ensure such fairness is to let impartial commissions select judges. The commission's nominees can then be voted up or down by the legislature.

Unsure. You will probably develop a stronger opinion on this question by the end of the chapter.

Judicial elections: emblem of democracy—or path to corruption?

Circuit courts: The second stage of federal courts, which review the trial record of cases decided in district court to ensure they were settled properly.

states (like California and Texas) have as many as four. District courts determine the facts of the case (did John Smith try to blow up a federal building?), build a record detailing the evidence, and then apply the law to reach a ruling. Cases at this level are heard by a single district judge.

District court judges, like all federal judges, are appointed by the president, subject to the "advice and consent" of the Senate, and hold their office for life. Until recently, the Senate routinely approved nearly all judicial appointments, sometimes with very little scrutiny. In today's hyperpartisan Congress, however, the opposition party generally challenges judicial nominations—slowing them down in the hope that their party will take the presidency and fill the empty seats.

When the Republicans gained the Senate in 2014, they applied the brakes to the Obama Administration's judicial appointments. By 2016, the administration's last year, almost 300 positions were vacant. With the Trump administration in power, Democrats returned the favor and tried to slow down the appointments. By summer 2018, there were 152 vacancies on the federal bench and 88 nominees awaiting confirmation.[11]

Above the 94 district courts are 13 federal appellate courts, known as **circuit courts**. A party that loses in district court can appeal to this next level. Three circuit court judges hear each case, usually to determine whether the district court made the correct ruling. They rule on the basis of the record established on the lower level; there is no jury and no cross-examination. Some 180 judges serve these circuit courts, collectively ruling on nearly 60 thousand cases in a typical year. As with the district courts, the majority of circuit courts are organized geographically (with the exception of two which are organized by issue) and referred to by their number (see Figure 16.3). Appeals from Ohio, for example, go to the Sixth Circuit Court of Appeals in Cincinnati. Some types of cases (like those involving patents or international trade) go directly to a court known as the U.S. Court of Appeals for the Federal Circuit. Like district-court judges, those on circuit courts are nominated by the White House and subject to Senate confirmation.

Sometimes multiple versions of a case reach different district and circuit courts. Rulings on the Trump administration travel ban were handed down in five districts from Hawaii to Massachusetts. On the next level, two circuit courts eventually accepted appeals. The Supreme Court eventually overturned the Ninth Circuit when it ruled in favor of the ban.

Specialized Courts

The federal judiciary also includes a set of specialized courts, each covering a specific subject such as military justice, tax disputes, terrorism, and bankruptcy. These courts' workload rises and falls with larger societal changes: bankruptcy claims, for example, have dropped from more than 1.5 million (during the Great Recession) to about 796,000 in 2017. After 9/11, the FISA court, which rules on federal requests to conduce electronic intelligence saw its caseload (and its prominence) soar.

The president appoints (and the Senate confirms) judges to all of these courts. Unlike other federal judges, however, they do not serve for life. Bankruptcy judges,

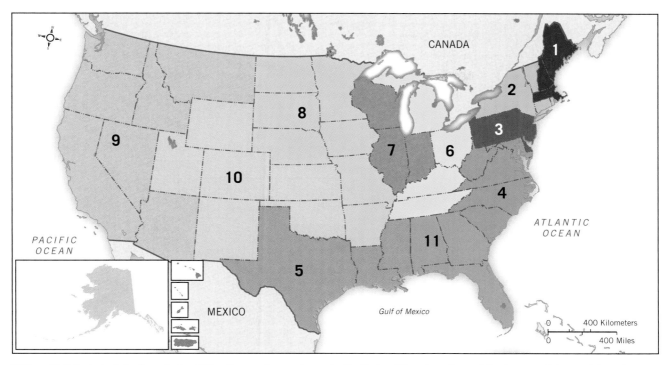

● **Figure 16.3** *The federal circuit courts. In addition, there are two courts, one for Washington, DC, and one for specialized cases, which are not shown here. (Federal Judicial Center)*

for example, serve renewable 14-year terms; federal magistrates, who handle certain types of civil trials, are appointed to renewable eight-year terms.

The U.S. military runs its own separate court system, which addresses breaches of justice by members of the armed forces. These courts became a source of controversy in recent years after President George W. Bush called for military tribunals to try defendants charged with terrorism against the United States, many of whom were being held as enemy combatants in Guantánamo Bay, Abu Ghraib, and other detention centers around the globe. The Obama administration at first suspended the military trials, but after Congress resisted moving the trials to civilian courts, the administration reinstated the tribunals with some changes in their rules. In rare cases, tribunals are permitted under the Constitution. The last large-scale use of military tribunals occurred after World War II, to try Nazi war criminals.[12]

Together, these specialized courts, ranging from bankruptcy to military, constitute something of a "third judiciary" alongside state and federal courts. Periodically, critics advance proposals for a new type of special court, usually to deal with some technical area of law they believe regular citizen juries cannot handle adequately. The latest proposals focus on medical malpractice, for which multimillion-dollar damage suits turn on ambiguous "medical errors." Overall, specialized courts provide a further example of the complexity characterizing the divided, fragmented U.S. judicial branch—as Figure 16.4 vividly demonstrates.

Diversity in the Federal Judiciary

Do federal judges reflect America's population? No. Just below one-third of judges are women, and nearly three-quarters are white. Twelve-and-a-half percent of federal judges are African American (compared to 12.2% of the population), 9.7 percent are Hispanic (compared to 16.3%), 2.9 percent are Asian American (compared to 4.7%), and only one federal judge is Native American. The past six presidents, going back to 1977, each left the federal bench more diverse. The Trump administration,

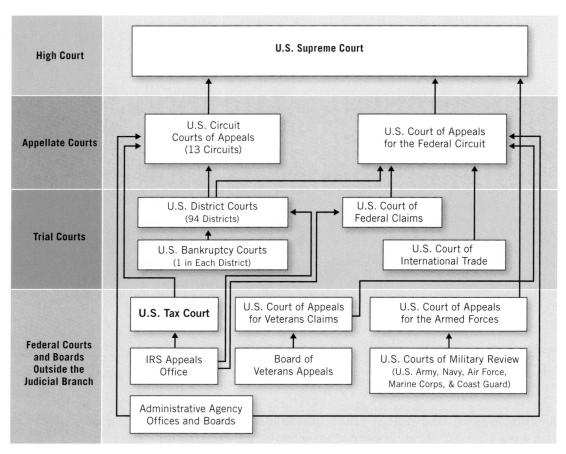

● **Figure 16.4** *Special courts within the federal system. A more detailed snapshot of the federal system illustrates that it is, in reality, far more complicated than the simple tripartite system of district, circuit, and supreme courts.*

in its first 17 months in office, reversed the trend; 90 percent of its nominees were white and 72 percent male (Table 16.1).[13]

Does it make a difference if the judge presiding over a federal case is female or Latino? Supreme Court Justice Sonia Sotomayor suggested that it did, ten years before she was appointed to the court. "I would hope that a wise Latina woman," Sotomayor said, "with the richness of her experience would more often than not reach a better conclusion than a white male who hasn't lived that life." In other

TABLE 16.1 **How Presidents Compare on Racial and Ethnic Diversity of Appointed Judges**

PRESIDENT	JUDGES	WHITE	BLACK	HISPANIC	ASIAN	OTHER	% NONWHITE
Trump	67	60	1	1	5	0	10*
Obama	324	208	58	31	18	0	36
G. W. Bush	324	266	24	30	4	0	18
Clinton	372	282	61	23	5	1	24
Bush	188	169	11	8	0	0	10

*As of September 30, 2018
Source: Pew Research Center

What Do YOU Think? Identity on the Bench

Do you agree with Justice Sotomayor's comment that a person's life experience can deeply inform his or her judgment about politics, culture, and other matters?	**Agree.** Every person inevitably brings his or her life experience to bear in making important decisions, and justices are no different. That's why diversity on the bench is so important.	**Disagree.** Judges should rule on the basis of law. Their background is irrelevant and should not cloud sound legal judgment based on the laws and the facts of a case.

words, personal experience does inform judicial decisions. The comment provided cause for reflection—and also raised controversy. Former House Speaker Newt Gingrich claimed that a white male judge making a similar claim on behalf of white men would be forced to resign.[14]

Does background make a difference? Sometimes. Research suggests that black judges are more likely to vote in favor of affirmative action,[15] more likely to find violations of the Voting Rights Acts,[16] more likely to side with lesbian, gay, bisexual, or transgender claimants, and more likely to accept black defendants' claims of police misconduct.[17] They are also ten percent more likely to be overturned. Likewise, women on the bench rule somewhat differently from male judges in gender related cases. Women are roughly ten percent more likely to find discrimination—as are male judges if they are serving on a panel with a female judge.[18]

 **The Bottom Line**

» State courts handle the vast majority of cases. Nearly all states divide their judiciary into three levels: trial courts, appeals courts, and a state supreme court. A majority of U.S. states elect their judges.

» Federal courts rule on cases involving constitutional questions, federal laws, and federal treaties. They are divided into ninety-four district courts, eleven appeals courts, and the Supreme Court.

» Federal justices are selected by the president and confirmed by the Senate, and they hold their position for life. Party polarization in Congress has created a serious problem of unfilled judgeships.

» Numerous additional federal courts handle everything from bankruptcy to military matters.

The Court's Role

Alexander Hamilton's assurance that the judiciary would play a minor role in American government did not last long. John Marshall, the longest-serving chief justice in U.S. history—he held the office from January 1801 to July 1835—helped establish the U.S. courts as unusually powerful. How did Marshall do it?

● *John Marshall denied Marbury's suit and, in the process, asserted the power of the Supreme Court to strike down acts of Congress when they violated the Constitution.*

How do judges interpret the Constitution?

Judicial review: The Court's authority to determine whether legislative, executive, and state actions violate the Constitution and overrule those that do.

Judicial Review

The breakthrough came in the landmark case of *Marbury v. Madison*, in which Marshall asserted that the Supreme Court has the authority to overrule any act of Congress that violates the Constitution.

The case arose after John Adams lost the 1800 election and, during his final hours as president, made "midnight appointments" that installed his supporters in judicial positions. The new president, Thomas Jefferson, came to office with very different political views and vehemently opposed the last-minute appointments. Jefferson directed his secretary of state, James Madison, to destroy the appointment letters—including one naming William Marbury as justice of the peace for the District of Columbia. The Judiciary Act of 1789, which had established the position, referred some cases (those involving writs of mandamus, or direct orders to government officials) directly to the Supreme Court. Marbury duly petitioned the Court to order Madison to deliver his commission. This action constituted a high-stakes early test of the Court's authority.

Marshall and his fellow justices faced a trap. On the one hand, if the Court ruled in favor of Marbury, the recently elected President Jefferson might very well ignore the Court—and diminish its importance in the new federal government. In fact, neither Jefferson nor Madison, the party being sued, even bothered to show up at the Court for the case. They assumed the Court would rule against them and planned to ignore the decision. Marshall found an ingenious way around Jefferson's defiance and vastly expanded the Court's role in American governance.

Led by Marshall, a unanimous Court ruled that Congress, in drafting the Judiciary Act of 1789, had erred in granting the Supreme Court the direct authority (or "original jurisdiction") to decide the question. The Constitution implied that the Supreme Court should rule on such cases only on appeal from the lower courts. However, the Constitution was silent on what would happen if Congress passed a law that clashed with the Constitution. Marshall filled in the blank with a dramatic move: "It is emphatically the province and duty" of the Court, wrote Marshall, to judge "if a law be in opposition to the Constitution." With that, Marshall established the court system's mighty power of **judicial review**—even though that authority is never mentioned in the Constitution itself.

The Court decided the case by striking down Section 13 of the Judiciary Act of 1789—the section that referred writs of mandamus directly to the Supreme Court. Since Section 13 was the basis of Marbury's petition, the Court ruled that it had no constitutional authority to force the administration to deliver the petition. President Jefferson opposed Marshall's clever move, vigorously denouncing the "despotism" and "oligarchy" by which unelected officials "usurp[ed]" control of the Constitution from elected ones. But what could Jefferson do? In asserting the Court's power, Marshall had sided with the president and denied Marbury his petition. Jefferson had no way to defy a case he had won. By apparently relinquishing power, Marshall permanently strengthened the federal judiciary.[19]

Marshall deftly addressed a basic issue in American government, with profound implications that reverberate to the present day. When there is doubt about what the Constitution holds or implies, the Supreme Court continues to claim that it makes the call.[20]

Activism Versus Restraint

The Supreme Court was slow to wield the power it had asserted. It did not overrule another act of Congress for fifty-four years, until the *Dred Scott* decision struck down the Missouri Compromise and declared that black people were "so far inferior that they had no rights which the white man was bound to respect."[21] That decision brought the issue of slavery to a boil in 1857 and established a pattern: Many of the most intense disputes in American politics wind up decided in court.

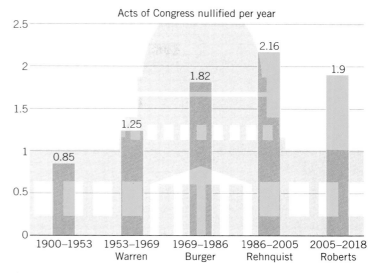

Acts of Congress nullified per year

Figure 16.5 *Acts of Congress Nullified by the Supreme Court. (Journal of Legal Metrics)*

As Figure 16.5 shows, the judiciary has stepped up the pace at which it overrules Congress. In the 150 years following *Marbury*, it struck down just twenty-two federal laws; in the twenty-five years between 1990 and 2018, it struck down fifty-nine, including laws designed to limit flag burning, guns near schoolyards, child pornography, violence against women, barriers to voting, limits on gambling, and same-sex marriage. Today, the Supreme Court is embroiled in many intense debates in addition to the three described at the start of this chapter. May Congress limit campaign contributions? Can the White House regulate emissions from power plants to combat global warming? Are there any limits to the right to bear arms? Does the right of privacy forbid states from banning or curtailing abortions? Each of these questions was removed from the court of public opinion, or the jurisdiction of elected officials, and settled by the Supreme Court—generally by a 5–4 vote.

The Supreme Court also reviews state and local statutes. This power could be wielded with less subtle maneuvering. The Constitution's "supremacy clause" declares that "this Constitution and the laws of the United States . . . shall be the supreme Law of the Land" (Article 6). The Judiciary Act of 1789, which established the federal court system (yes, the same act that created William Marbury's position) granted the Court authority to enforce the supremacy clause and to strike down state laws that clash with the Constitution or with federal statutes. The judiciary has been more active on this level, striking down state actions at about six times the rate it overturns federal laws. Over time, federal courts have declared almost 1,100 state and local laws unconstitutional and ruled that more than another 200 state and local laws were preempted by federal law. Landmark cases overruled state laws that established segregation, outlawed abortion, established school prayer, limited private property rights, or forbade same-sex marriage.

The growing number of rulings that strike down legislation raises an enduring question: How energetic should courts be in reviewing cases? Judicial activists take a vigorous approach to reviewing the other branches of government and believe that the courts must be vigilant in protecting rights. Between the 1950s and the 1970s, liberal activists were in the Supreme Court majority. During this period, the Court struck down segregation, forbade school prayer, and found a right

● *Legal! The court struck down a federal law that banned sports gambling in most states.*

Judicial restraint:
Reluctance to interfere with elected branches, only doing so as a last resort.

Judicial activism: A vigorous or active approach to reviewing the other branches of government.

Common law: A system of law developed by judges in deciding cases over the centuries.

Precedent: Judicial decisions that offer a guide to similar cases in the future.

Civil law: Cases that involve disputes between two parties.

Criminal law: Cases in which someone is charged with breaking the law.

Plaintiff: The party who brings the action in a lawsuit.

to privacy in the penumbra (or shadow) of the Constitution (see Chapters 5 and 6 for a discussion of these cases).

Judicial restraint holds, on the contrary, that the courts should overturn the elected branches of government reluctantly and as a last resort. The terms *activism* and *restraint* are easily politicized. Conservatives bitterly attacked liberal **judicial activism** during the civil-rights era of the 1950s–early 1970s; as the courts turned conservative, however, liberals began to criticize activist judges for being eager to overrule the will of the people's representatives.

The idea of activism recalls our discussion in Chapter 3 about how to read the Constitution. Is it a living and evolving document, as the pragmatists believe? Or should we insist on faithfully reconstructing the original meaning, as originalists think we should do? As we noted in Chapter 3, the difference between these positions is less stark than it might appear. The Constitution can be ambiguous, and a nimble analysis is often required to apply it to a contemporary case—as Marshall illustrated when he first asserted the right of judicial review. Even staunch originalists regularly disagree with one another about the Constitution's meaning and how it applies in any individual case.

The Judicial Process

The judiciary's role goes far beyond weighing constitutionality. Legal cases constantly raise the question of how a law should be applied in a specific dispute. The court's job is to determine legislative intent. We saw this in Chapter 15, in the case of the bureaucratic rule-making process. If lobbyists do not like new regulations for inspecting poultry slaughterhouses, they can go to court and claim that the regulatory agency has mistaken what Congress intended when it authorized those inspections. Ultimately, the court has to rule on what Congress meant to do—perhaps in the distant past. Because lawsuits are a regular feature of policymaking, federal courts stay very busy interpreting the intent of the other branches.

Often there is no legislative record or executive action to settle a case. The American colonists introduced an English system known as **common law**. Common law (also known as *case law*) is a system of law developed by judges in deciding cases over the centuries. Because legal judgments should be consistent from case to case, each time a court settles a case it sets a **precedent** that will guide similar cases in the future. Over the years, the common law offers a rich legal heritage to guide judges in settling disputes. In countries without a common law tradition, such as France, judges may not rule unless there is a statute or regulation to guide them.

American courts handle two different kinds of cases. **Civil law** handles cases between two parties. William Marbury sues James Madison for his commission; a young man sues his Catholic diocese because a priest molested him; a major corporation sues a local pizza chain for borrowing its corporate logo. **Criminal law** involves cases in which someone is charged with doing something prohibited by the government, such as stealing private property or secretly arranging with a competitor to set higher prices (an "antitrust" violation).

The party who complains—Marbury, the man who was molested, or the government coming down on an alleged criminal—is called the **plaintiff**; the party

COMPARING NATIONS 16.2 | Power of the Judiciary

Judges in other advanced democracies rarely exercise anything like the influence that American courts have over government and politics. In Japan, for example, the judiciary is widely viewed as a rubber stamp for executive and legislative decisions, almost never questioning (much less reversing) decisions of the other branches. The United Kingdom goes even further: The doctrine of "parliamentary sovereignty" holds that when Parliament passes a statute, it cannot be overturned in court. Canada abandoned parliamentary sovereignty in 1982 and granted the federal courts fuller judicial review powers; those are only rarely used, however, and the parliament can still overturn the Court's ruling. In Germany, the Supreme Constitutional Court has the power to review all legislation for adherence with the Constitution; it even has the authority to ban a political party (like the Nazi Party) if it moves to deny the rights of others. Yet the German high court does not take cases from lower courts on appeal—its role is solely as a constitutional court. Finally, less democratic nations generally place their power in the executive—their courts do not have the authority to challenge executive decisions. In its extensive authority to reshape public policies and other acts of the executive and legislative branches, the U.S. judiciary stands alone.

---

who is being sued is the **defendant**. In court cases, the plaintiff is listed first and the defendant second; thus, the case is called *Marbury* (the plaintiff) *versus Madison* (the secretary of state who did not deliver the commission). When a party loses in a lower court, it becomes the plaintiff on appeal; that is why you see case titles such as *Trump v. Hawaii* (the 2018 travel ban case) or *Masterpiece Cakeshop v. Colorado Civil Rights Commission* (the court ruled in favor of a bakery that refused to supply cake for a same-sex wedding).

Defendant: The party who is sued in a court case.

Discover how to pursue a case through the court system.

Too Much Power?

Should nine unelected, lifetime appointees wield this much power in a twenty-first-century democracy? Add to that the more than one-hundred circuit- and district-court federal judges, also all appointed to their posts for life: How can we say "the people" rule over the judicial branch?

Both our litigious society and the range of judicial authority—from judicial review to common law—give the courts the power to shape American policy.

In other nations, the elected branches make vital decisions about environmental protection, gun rights, immigration rules, and other urgent questions (see Comparing Nations 16.2). In the United States, courts are major players in resolving these issues . . . and other issues in almost every policy realm.

American courts profoundly shape our politics. Are they the guarantors of American constitutional rights? Or are they an outmoded throwback to an earlier, more elitist age? You can get a better sense in the following sections when we look behind the scenes at the inner workings of the Supreme Court.

. . . Or Still the "Least Dangerous" Branch?

Although the courts are undeniably powerful, every institution faces limits. The courts operate with four restraints.

First, the federal courts have *no electoral base*. Their prestige and mystique are balanced by a lack of democratic authority. This has made some past courts careful about confronting elected officials. For example, the Supreme Court delayed its ruling in *Brown v. Board of Education* (striking down segregated schools) for almost two years while the justices struggled to reach unanimity. Chief Justice Earl Warren felt that such an important case should have the backing of all nine members because a major decision that went against popular opinion could harm the Court's authority and prestige.

Second, courts have relatively *limited resources* compared to other units of government. Senators generally command more than fifty staff members and can call on the Congressional Research Service and the Government Accountability Office: each has hundreds of experts who can study any question a member might raise. In contrast, most federal judges have only two or three clerks—young staffers, usually fresh from law school, with little judicial experience—who serve them for less than a year. Supreme Court justices, whose decisions can shape the course of government for generations, have at most four clerks, who serve for a year or occasionally two.

The courts also command small budgets. The Supreme Court operates on an annual budget of around ninety million dollars a year. The entire federal judiciary—thirteen circuit courts, ninety-four district courts, and the Supreme Court—receives less than seven billion dollars annually. That is about the same budget as that of NOAA, the federal weather service.

Third, courts are by definition *reactive decision makers*. Executive branch agencies or legislators can tackle problems and devise solutions. Courts await disputes; cases must come to them. True, most major issues eventually do wind up before the courts—but, unlike the other branches, the courts do not define the problem or shape the question that is being disputed.

Finally, the courts must rely on other branches for *enforcement*. The Court rules. Other actors—in and out of government—implement the decisions. The Supreme Court could strike down school desegregation; it could not, however, enforce that decision by sending troops to Little Rock or cutting the budgets of schools that refused to comply. In fact, the *Brown* decision was blocked for years by intransigent state and local officials (until civil rights protests finally moved Congress to pass the Civil Rights Act). President Andrew Jackson made this point dramatically. When the Supreme Court struck down a Georgia law, because the state had no "dominion" over the Cherokees, he reputedly said, of the chief justice: "John Marshall has made his decision, now let him enforce it."[22]

 **The Bottom Line**

» Chief Justice John Marshall asserted the court's authority to review acts of Congress to ensure that they fit with the Constitution in *Marbury v. Madison*. The Judiciary Act of 1789 authorized the Court to review state laws.

» At first, the Court rarely struck down acts of Congress, but it began to do so at a quicker pace after the 1970s.

» There are two general approaches to defining the courts' role in government: *activists* believe in a vigorous judiciary that scrutinizes the other branches; judicial *restraint* holds that courts should intervene rarely and reluctantly.

» The vital overarching question regarding the judiciary remains the same one that Chief Justice Marshall and President Jefferson crossed swords over more than two centuries ago: Is the Court acting in ways that are indispensable to democracy? Or is it acting in ways that threaten it?

The Supreme Court and How It Operates

Tucked away at the top of the majestic marble Supreme Court building on East Capitol Street, among all the justices' offices and conference rooms and libraries lined with leather law books, is . . . a small basketball court. Known as the "highest court in the land," the facility is used exclusively by Supreme Court insiders: the justices' clerks, both current and former; a few staff members; and occasionally even one of the justices. We can imagine the basketball court as symbolic of the Supreme Court itself: exclusive, little known, and open to a tiny membership for a lifetime.

Hearing Cases

The Supreme Court is in session for approximately nine months each year, traditionally opening on the first Monday in October. The justices are generally out of public view, except when the Court meets to hear *oral arguments*—the presentation of a case that the Court has agreed to review. Arguments are usually scheduled on Monday, Tuesday, and Wednesday mornings. If you are visiting Washington, DC, on a day when oral arguments are occurring, do attend. These fascinating sessions are free and open to the public, on a first-come, first-served basis. (We recommend that you get to the Court early to wait in line and bring something to read—perhaps this book!)

Supreme Court oral arguments do not resemble the courtroom scenes on TV. Rather than lawyers making dramatic arguments or cross-examining witnesses, the Supreme Court features nine justices as the sole audience: no jury, no witnesses. Any case that the Supreme Court agrees to hear has usually been thoroughly aired by at least one lower court. Normally, cases are heard in one hour, and each side's lawyer—called the "counsel" in Court-speak, regardless of whether it is one lawyer or many—is granted thirty minutes to make his or her best argument. When the Court took up the *Obergefell v. Hodges* same-sex marriage case in 2015, it signaled the importance of the case by scheduling two and a half hours of oral argument; in the Obamacare case, *National Federation of Independent Business v. Sebelius*, it scheduled six hours over three days.

The justices usually interrupt the presenting lawyer almost immediately with questions, some supportive and others combative. They may also deliver mini-speeches of their own; no lawyer ever dares interrupt a Supreme Court justice, even if the lawyer's thirty minutes is slipping away. No photos or video are allowed, so sketches are the most accurate depiction.

Before the hearing, both sides submit written briefs spelling out the details of their argument. Other interested parties may submit their own briefs endorsing the side they favor. The outside contributions are known as ***amicus curiae*** (Latin for "friend of the court") briefs. A creative, well-written *amicus curiae* brief, researchers have found, may well wind up being included in a justice's written opinion on the case.[23]

Are oral arguments important? Perhaps not. Justice Clarence Thomas told one interviewer that they influence his colleagues "in five or ten percent of the cases, maybe, and I'm being generous there." Chief Justice John Roberts once added, "The judges are debating among themselves and just using the lawyers as a blackboard."[24] What matters far more are the written briefs that the counsel submit.

> ***Amicus curiae***: A brief submitted by a person or group who is not a direct party to the case.

Selecting Cases: Formal Requirements

How do the justices decide which cases to hear? Losing parties in lower courts are permitted, depending on the nature of the case, to file a petition with the Supreme Court stating the facts of the case and setting out detailed arguments as to why the

● *The Court hears a case in 2018. The chief justice sits at the center and the seats closest to his are occupied by those justices with the most seniority. From left, Kagan, Alito, Ginsburg, Kennedy (since replaced by Kavanaugh), Roberts, Thomas, Breyer, Sotomayor, and Gorsuch. Only sketches such as this one are permitted in the Supreme Court; no photographs or TV coverage.*

Rule of four: The requirement that at least four Supreme Court judges must agree to hear a case before it comes before the Court.

Listen to oral arguments on the *Fisher v. University of Texas at Austin* affirmative action case.

Listen to oral arguments on the *United States v. Texas* immigration case.

Court should hear it. The petitions are split up among the justices and their clerks; on selected Fridays, the justices meet to choose the cases they will hear. At least four judges have to vote to hear a case for it to make it to the Supreme Court; that requirement is known as the **rule of four**.

When the justices agree to hear a case, the Supreme Court issues a *writ of certiorari* (legal-speak for "to be informed") demanding the official record from the lower court that heard the case. Roughly ten thousand petitions are filed with the Supreme Court each year, and some seventy or eighty are accepted—less than 1 percent. How do cases make it into that elite group? That remains one of the great mysteries of American government. The Court never gives any formal explanation for why it decides to grant certiorari to this case and not that one.

Formally, a case must meet three conditions before it is even eligible for the Supreme Court—or any other court, for these requirements apply at all judicial levels. The case must involve a *legitimate controversy,* that is, an actual dispute between two parties. Supreme Court justices do not deal with hypothetical matters; no federal court offers "advisory opinions" based on something that might someday happen.

Second, the parties bringing a case must have *standing*: They must prove an actual harm (or imminent harm) to receive a hearing. Merely being distressed or concerned about a far-off environmental disaster's effect is not enough to bring a lawsuit, for example; you must prove that the oil spill directly affects your livelihood (or your health or your property).

Finally, if the Court's proceedings will no longer affect the issue at hand, it is considered *moot*—irrelevant—and the case is thrown out. A famous example comes from *Roe v. Wade*, in which a federal district court dismissed the case as moot because the plaintiff, "Jane Roe" (real name: Norma McCorvey), had already delivered her child. The Supreme Court rejected this view, noting that the typical length of legal appeals processes meant that pregnancies would usually conclude too soon for a court decision to be reached.

Selecting Cases: Informal Factors

Thousands of cases each year meet the standards—controversy, standing, and mootness. Informally, we can identify four additional factors that help predict whether a case is more or less likely to be accepted by the Court.

First, the Supreme Court is more inclined to hear a case when two lower courts decide the legal question differently (usually two federal courts, but sometimes federal and state). Different rulings in similar cases require a resolution; hence the Court considered during its 2016–2017 term whether the North Carolina Supreme Court or federal district court was right about allegedly racially biased redistricting practices in the state.

Second, justices are inclined to grant certiorari to cases in which a lower court decision conflicts with an existing Supreme Court ruling. In 1989, the Court ruled in *Penry v. Lynaugh* that a death sentence was sometimes permissible for criminals under the age of eighteen. More than a decade later, the Missouri Supreme Court declared that the death penalty for non-adults was "cruel and unusual punishment," citing a recent Supreme Court ruling that struck down capital punishment for mentally disabled people. The Supreme Court agreed and, in *Roper v. Simmons*, reversed its 1989 decision.

Third, the Supreme Court is more likely to look favorably on cases that have significance beyond the two parties involved. Rarely does a sexual harassment case reach the Supreme Court because this area of law is relatively settled. But when Paula Jones brought such a suit against President Bill Clinton, the Court agreed to hear *Clinton v. Jones* because the case tested the larger question of whether a sitting U.S. president is required to defend himself against a lawsuit while in office. (*Yes*, the Court ruled; it allowed Jones's lawsuit to proceed—and set off a cascade of events that rocked the Clinton presidency and led the House of Representatives to impeach him—although the Senate voted against removing him from office.)

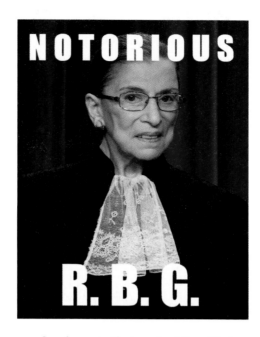

● *Supreme Court Justice Ruth Bader Ginsburg as meme—the notorious R.B.G.—a play on rapper Biggie Smalls, aka The Notorious B.I.G.*

Fourth, the Supreme Court is especially likely to hear a case when the U.S. government is a party. Almost half of the Court's caseload involves the solicitor general, the attorney who represents the Department of Justice before the Supreme Court. Historically, the solicitor general had a "home court advantage" on the Court and usually won cases for its client, the United States Government. Not anymore. President Obama's legal team won just 44% of the time (the worst record in at least a century) and, in the Trump Administration's first year, the administration record was, likewise, 43%.[25]

These criteria increase the odds of making it to the Supreme Court—but even a case that meets all four may be passed over. Again, the Court's decision on whether to grant certiorari to any particular case remains shrouded in mystery.

For the cases that the Court agrees to hear, oral arguments are scheduled (primarily on Monday, Tuesday, and Wednesday mornings) from early October through late April. The Court then issues decisions in all cases that it heard during the session, usually on weekday mornings in May and June. Those days are very exciting—and, for those involved in a case's outcome, very anxious occasions—as we saw with the three cases in June 2018 that began this chapter. No one knows when the Court will hand down a decision in a given case, nor is there a set time period in which the justices must reach a decision. However, the Court generally decides all the cases it has heard during the term before the summer recess begins.

Conference Sessions and Written Decisions

What do the justices do when they are not on the bench hearing oral arguments? There is plenty of work to occupy them. Justices keep busy writing opinions (usually with substantial assistance from their clerks, who prepare drafts and discuss details with their boss), deciding which cases to hear in the future, and reading briefs for upcoming oral arguments. And, most intriguing of all, the justices meet in conference.

Supreme Court conferences, which typically take place on Thursday or Friday afternoons, are closed to everyone except the justices—even their clerks are not allowed in. Justices sit around a conference table; by tradition, the most junior justice sits nearest the door, opening it only to allow a staff member to wheel in carts piled with materials for the next case under consideration. The Supreme Court's most significant collective decisions take place in conference.

Justices discuss the cases they've head, indicate their votes, and the chief justice, if he is in the majority, assigns the job of writing the **majority opinion**; otherwise, the senior member of the majority assigns the job. The majority opinion is the official statement of the Court. Any justice who wishes to can issue a **concurrent opinion** explaining why he or she voted in favor of the majority outcome—different justices come to the same conclusion for different reasons. Justices who disagree about the outcome write a **dissent** indicating why they voted against the majority. Some dissents become celebrated or form the basis for a future judicial shift in thinking.

Though justices are generally publicity averse, they do make public appearances. They typically address law schools or legal conferences. Some justices speak at less formal events, especially after the year's session ends in June. Ruth Bader Ginsburg has become a cultural icon and is the subject of a documentary (*RBG*), a Saturday Night Live parody, a feature film (*On the Basis of Sex*) and a meme, *The Notorious RBG*. The website SCOTUS Map (www.scotusmap.com) tries to track all such appearances, although they are not formally announced by the Court or the individual justices. Whatever the topic, however, all justices maintain a strict norm of not publicly discussing cases before the Court.

Supreme Court Clerks

Supreme Court clerks, usually recent law school graduates, exercise a remarkable amount of influence. They help the justices write opinions and reach decisions, and they initially screen the thousands of certiorari petitions that reach the Court each year.

Though the process is kept strictly secret, the clerks reject many of the petitions, choosing a smaller set of a few hundred potential cases for the justices' consideration. Remember: These cases can shape American government in powerful ways. And a small group of unelected people in their twenties often influence whether a case will reach the Court.

Are you interested in serving as a Supreme Court clerk? It is a tough position to attain: Of the more than one thousand applicants each year, only a tiny handful—less than three dozen—will achieve this post. After completing your law degree (JD), you would generally serve one year in a lower court clerkship for a district court judge or in a state supreme court. During that year, you would apply to a specific Supreme Court justice's chambers, although many aspirants apply to all nine to maximize their chances of being selected. As with other jobs, if you make it through the initial screening, you'll be invited in for an interview, first with the clerks, then with one of the justices. Those interviews are reputedly among the toughest going: former Justice Scalia, for example, subjected his clerkship candidates to a "Scalia grilling" that covered, as one said afterward, "the law: all of it."[26]

Should you receive the congratulatory call, prepare to join one of the most exclusive clubs in American government. Supreme Court clerks who elect to stay in public service often go on to important posts or become professors at top law schools. If you decide instead to go into private practice, you will be a hot commodity: "Court clerk bonuses" to sign with a law firm competing for your talents can be as high as $250,000.

Majority opinion: The official statement of the Supreme Court (or a district court, since they also have multiple justices).

Concurrent opinion: A statement that agrees with the majority opinion.

Dissent: A statement on behalf of the justices who voted in the minority.

Confirmation Battles

In June 2018, Justice Anthony Kennedy announced his retirement. Kennedy had leaned to the right but was, generally, the justice in the middle, between four strong conservatives and four strong liberals. For example, Kennedy wrote a blockbuster opinion in *Obergefell v. Hodges* which guaranteed the right to same-sex marriage (5-4), but also authored *Citizens United v. FEC* which opened the door to campaign spending by corporations (see chapter 10).

The succession battle began immediately. President Trump selected Brett Kavanaugh, a U.S. circuit-court judge who had been a staff member in the George W. Bush White House. Ratings of his prior opinions pegged him as a stalwart conservative. Many court watchers expected the Kavanaugh appointment to tilt the court significantly to the right—ensuring a 5-4 majority, at least until the next retirement. Liberal groups mobilized against the Kavanaugh nomination, but Republicans had the votes and, after four days of hearings, confirmation seemed assured—until an unexpected bombshell.

A psychology professor, Christine Blasey Ford, publicly stated that Kavanaugh had sexually assaulted her at a high-school party thirty-six years earlier. Ford's charges resulted in an additional Senate Judiciary hearing—with Ford and Kavanaugh as the sole witnesses. Kavanaugh, alternately furious and tearful, denied Ford's allegations. After a supplemental FBI investigation, the Senate approved Kavanaugh's confirmation by a 50-48 vote.

Given the lifetime tenure and the immense influence often wielded by the Supreme Court justices, one of the most significant moments on the American political calendar is the appointment of a new justice. Confirmation hearings have become partisan debates engaging a wide range of interest groups and national campaigns—all designed to influence the Senate Judiciary Committee that holds hearings on a nominee and issues a recommendation to the full Senate.

Until recent decades, confirmations were usually uncontroversial. Justice Anthony Kennedy, like most justices before him, was unanimously confirmed. Nomination politics changed dramatically in 1987, when President Ronald Reagan nominated Robert Bork to the Court. Bork certainly seemed qualified: He was a national authority on antitrust law; he had served under President Nixon as solicitor general, representing the U.S. government in cases before the Supreme Court; and he had been acting attorney general and a circuit court judge.

However, Bork was also a no-apologies conservative who would replace Justice Lewis Powell, a moderate "swing vote." Liberal groups mobilized to oppose the nomination; Democratic senators, led by Ted Kennedy, criticized what they called "Robert Bork's America." After twelve days of hearings, the Senate defeated the nomination, 58 to 42. What surprised observers was the swift rise of organized opposition based not on the candidate's qualifications, but on his judicial philosophy. Conservatives coined a new word to describe the phenomenon: *Borking.* They have returned the favor. Every judicial appointment, like

● *Supreme Court nominee Robert Bork testifying at his confirmation hearing. His nomination was a watershed in the politicization of the Court. Before Judge Bork, the major focus was competence; now, the focus is on political perspectives.*

TABLE 16.2 Supreme Court Nominations and Confirmations

Nomination votes have gotten closer over the years. Before the Bork appointment, qualified justices were easily confirmed. Notice that Kennedy, like many justices, before him won confirmation unanimously. As partisanship rose, the court grew politicized, unanimous votes disappeared and the hearings have gotten more contentious. Debates become especially heated when a swing vote—like Justice Kennedy—is up for replacement. It is much easier to replace a liberal with a liberal or a conservative with a conservative.

JUDGE	AGE AT TIME OF APPOINTMENT	APPOINTED BY (PRESIDENT)	SELECTED FROM	YEAR	SENATE VOTE		PUBLIC OPINION	
					YES	NO	YES	NO
Brett Kavanaugh	53	Trump	United States Court of Appeals	2018	50	48	46	45
Neil Gorsuch	49	Trump	United States Court of Appeals	2017	54	45	48	35
Elena Kagan	50	Obama	U.S. Solicitor General	2010	63	37	44	34
Sonia Sotomayor	55	Obama	U.S. Court of Appeals	2009	68	31	56	36
Samuel Alito	55	G. W. Bush	U.S. Court of Appeals	2006	58	42	54	30
John Roberts	50	G. W. Bush	U.S. Court of Appeals	2005	78	22	60	26
Stephen Breyer	55	Clinton	U.S. Court of Appeals	1994	87	9	—	—
Ruth Bader Ginsburg	60	Clinton	U.S. Court of Appeals	1993	96	3	53	14
Clarence Thomas	43	G. H. W. Bush	U.S. Court of Appeals	1991	52	48	58	30
Anthony Kennedy	51	Reagan	U.S. Court of Appeals	1988	97	0	—	—
Robert Bork	43	Reagan	U.S. Court of Appeals	1987	42	58	38	35

Kavanaugh's, now faces a partisan nomination fight: packed hearings, demonstrations (pro and con), intense media coverage, and public opinion polls serving up regular updates on how the nominee fares in the public view, and millions of dollars of ads running back in the states to influence key Senate votes (see Table 16.2).

A single vote makes the difference on a host of issues: the right to privacy and abortion, gun control, the rights of criminals, campaign finance, immigration, health-care reform, the rights of terrorism suspects—and the list goes on. Small wonder that the debates over each new justice get so heated, especially when a nominee's political philosophy differs from his or her predecessor. Donald Trump's surprise presidential victory owed in part to his promise to nominate a conservative to the Court. "The least dangerous branch" was not designed to be in the eye of the political hurricane.

● *The Senate Judiciary Committee grills Brett Kavanaugh before a packed hearing room—and a national audience.*

● *Bork: to turn down a competent nominee for political reasons.*

The Bottom Line

» The Supreme Court generally hears cases on the basis of petitions requesting a review of lower court decisions. Four justices have to vote to hear a case before it becomes part of the 1 percent that comes before the Court.

» To be heard in federal court, a case must meet criteria involving controversy, standing, and mootness. Other factors that make it more likely that the case will be heard include the scope of the question, a clash between lower courts or between a lower court and previous Supreme Court decision, and requests from the solicitor general.

» Cases involve oral arguments, written briefs, and conferences with only the justices present. The chief justice assigns a majority opinion; others write concurring or dissenting opinions for the record.

» Confirmation to the federal bench—and especially to the Supreme Court—was once a polite affair that largely involved questions of competence. Today, confirmations are some of the most politically charged events on the political calendar. This discord raises an important question: How does the charged politics that surrounds the Court affect its own workings—and its standing with the public?

🕤 Judicial Decision Making and Reform

How do judges reach their decisions in a case? Social scientists emphasize four different perspectives.

The Role of Law

In theory, justices decide cases on the basis of the legal facts, as laid out in the documents submitted. They read the law, consider the intent of those who framed the law, and place the case in the context of the Constitution.

According to long-established principle, justices generally abide by the precedents set in previously decided cases. This is known as ***stare decisis*** (literally, "stand by the things decided"). Occasionally the Supreme Court concludes that the

Stare decisis: Deciding cases on the basis of previous rulings or precedents.

precedents were wrongly decided and overrules a past decision: It has reversed itself 236 times—more than it has struck down acts of Congress. Still, legal theory suggests that the Court rules on the facts, guided by precedent. As Chief Justice John Roberts put it at his confirmation hearing, "Judges are like umpires. Umpires don't make the rules; they apply them. . . . My job is to call balls and strikes."[27]

The umpire metaphor is appealing. However, legal cases are very often ambiguous. Applying the Constitution more than two centuries after its passage is rarely simple or straightforward. Political scientists who study Supreme Court decisions have found another perspective with more analytic power.

Ideology and Partisanship

Ideology provides another guide to the judicial mind. Political scientists have generally found that the justices' beliefs are the most powerful predictor of how they will vote, especially on difficult cases. Some studies look at the party identification of the justices, others at their ideology prior to confirmation, and still others at the views of the presidents who appointed them. No matter how ideology is measured, one study after another suggests a very strong relationship between the justices' beliefs and their votes (see Figure 16.6). In brief, we can predict the justices' votes over time with considerable accuracy, based on their political orientation.[28]

Ideology lines up with the judicial philosophy we discussed earlier. *Pragmatists* (who see the Constitution as a living, changing document) will approach cases differently from *originalists* (who believe we must interpret the document's text literally). Likewise, activists may be quicker to strike down acts of Congress, state laws, and court precedents. Conservatives charged liberal justices with being overly

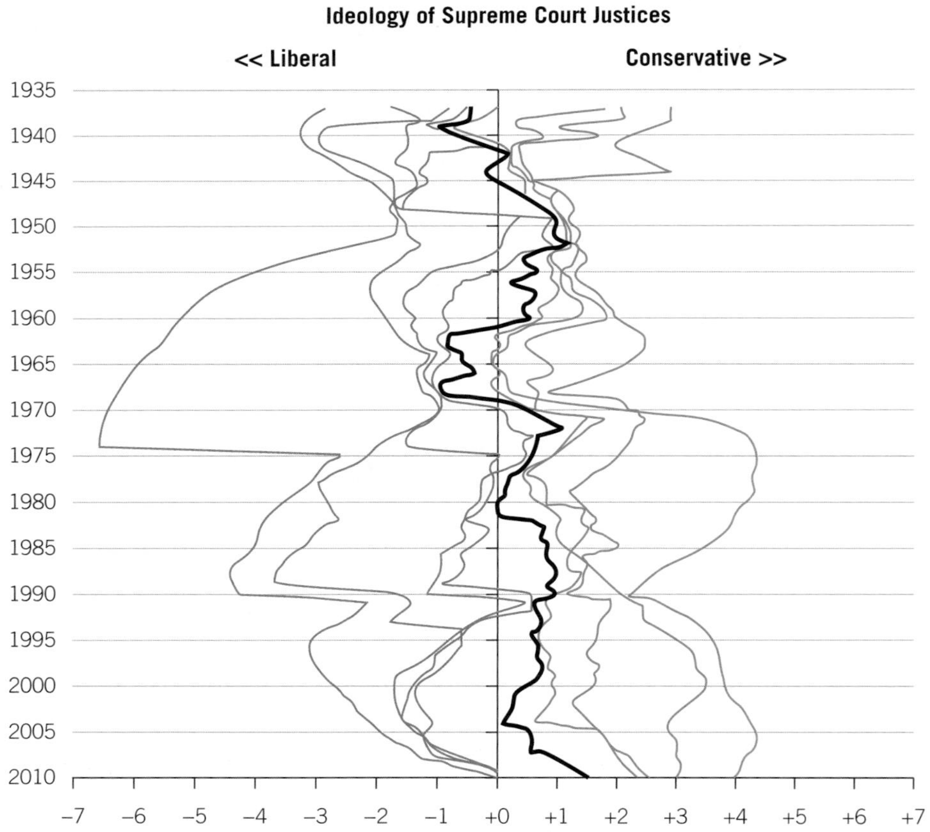

Figure 16.6 *Ideological leanings of the Supreme Court Justices over time. (Nate Silver, FiveThirtyEight)*

activist during the Warren Court (1953–1969); today, liberals repeat the complaint about conservative justices. Ultimately, simple political perspective—liberal versus conservative—is one of the most effective ways of explaining how justices rule.

The public has come to share the scholarly view about how justices decide. In recent polls, a full 75 percent of the public suggested that Supreme Court justices "sometimes let their ideological views influence their decision."[29]

The Court has long broken along the partisan divide: Four members were conservative—and, according to one study, rank among the seven most consistently conservative voters in the past fifty years: Chief Justice Roberts and associate justices Thomas, Alito, and Gorsuch all vote conservative more than 70 percent of the time. Justice Anthony Kennedy tended to vote conservative but provided a swing vote for liberals about one-third of the time. And Associate Justices Ginsburg, Breyer, Sotomayor, and Kagan vote liberal between 60 and 70 percent of the time. In recent years, justices have begun to read their dissenting opinions aloud, a striking step designed to attract public attention to their dissatisfaction, which they often express in strong terms. Keep an eye on Justice Kavanaugh, as many court watchers expect him to provide a fifth strong conservative vote.[30]

The ideological model has its limits and by no means explains all votes. In 2017-18, 39% of the cases were decided unanimously—much lower than the previous year (59% unanimous) or 2013-4 (a record 65%). Ideology does not play a role in many technical cases.

Even so, the idea that the Court often rules on the basis of politics poses a dilemma for our democratic system. The Court is designed to stand above politics, to interpret and explain the rules without partisan consideration. That is the reason justices are selected for life. When they rule on the basis of political ideology—and are widely seen as doing so—they raise a problem for the legitimacy of this powerful institution, precisely as Justice John Paul Stevens warned in *Bush v. Gore*.

Collegiality and Peer Pressure

A third factor shaping Court decisions is *collegiality*, or to put it more bluntly, *peer pressure*. Justices spend a lot of time together, hearing cases and discussing their decisions. They exert some influence on one another. Persuasion is a traditional feature of Court discussions; justices appear to change positions in many cases based on legal arguments and personal appeals of colleagues. They also may change their votes for strategic reasons—trading votes in different cases.[31] The evidence does suggest that past generations engaged in more give-and-take—in the 1950s and 1960s, at least one justice would switch his vote in about half of all cases.[32] Today, justices appear to be more settled in their convictions.

Another angle on the idea of "peer pressure" arises from the larger legal community. A few hundred people—law professors, law students, legal bloggers, congressional members, committee staff for the House and Senate Judiciary Committees, and interest-group activists—make up the attentive audience for most judicial decisions. The audience's judgment about a specific judicial opinion can be laudatory or scathing. Harvard Law professor Frederick Schauer demonstrated that judges—especially Supreme Court justices, the most scrutinized of all judicial figures—seem to notice. Analyzing a large dataset of Court decisions, Schauer found that "judicial reputation" played an important role in explaining why justices moved left or right on an ideological scale during their service on the Court.[33]

Investigate the background of the justices.

How Americans View the Supreme Court

LIBERAL OR CONSERVATIVE?

Americans are divided over their view of the Supreme Court as too liberal, too conservative, or just right. These views are influenced not only by court decisions but by new appointments.

THINK ABOUT IT

How has the public view of the court shifted over time? How have court decisions impacted this view? How have views changed since the appointment of Justice Gorsuch in 2017?

Does the conviction that judges rule on the basis of ideology require us to rethink the way we appoint the justices or how the Court operates? Or is it desirable in our party-polarized age that justices exhibit strong viewpoints as so many politicians and ordinary citizens do today, thereby better representing the public?

Source: Gallup

Major shift in views of Court's ideology
% saying the current Supreme Court is . . .

— Too Conservative — About Right — Too Liberal

Sotomayor nomination

Kagan nomination

Affordable Care Act decision

Gay marriage/ VRA decisions

Hobby Lobby decision

ACA/Gay marriage decisions

Gorsuch nomination

50

28

19

44

29

21

2009 2010 2011 2012 2013 2014 2015 2016 2017 2018

Institutional Concerns

Finally, justices sometimes appear to think about the interests of the Court as an institution. They spend many years on the bench and worry about the standing of the Court—before public opinion, a hostile Congress, or a skeptical executive. We saw a prime example of this kind of thinking in the Court's early years with *Marbury v. Madison*. Marshall was considering the role and standing of his institution as he crafted his complicated opinion. Some recent studies underscore the importance of this perspective.[34]

During much of 2016, with the Court down to eight justices, four members—two liberals and two conservatives—came together and tried to forge a consensus in as many cases as possible. They argued that constant deadlock would diminish the reputation of the Court. Four others (two liberals and two conservatives) responded that it would not help the cause of justice by compromising their judicial philosophies. Which side would you agree with?

 **The Bottom Line**

» Four different perspectives help explain how justices make their decisions.

» First, we should pay attention to their own explanation: They follow precedent and the facts of the case.

» Political scientists are more likely to find that ideology is the best predictor of justices' decisions in the long run. Recently, the public also has taken this view, which poses a dilemma for American governance: An institution designed to be above politics is increasingly seen as essentially political. That perception has helped turn confirmation hearings into volatile battles.

» Two final factors also play a role in judicial decision making: collegiality and institutional protection.

🧑 Nineteen Cases You Should Know

The history of American Court cases includes a long list of famous—and occasionally infamous—decisions. You have already encountered some in our discussion of civil liberties (Chapter 5) and civil rights (Chapter 6). If you take a course in constitutional law (or decide to attend law school), you will study cases by the hundreds. All are part of American *jurisprudence*, or the study of law. Here we list nineteen cases that every student of American government ought to be familiar with, organized chronologically. The ones we have covered elsewhere in this book are briefly described here only to refresh your memory. We have left one place blank in the top twenty. Think about the other cases you have encountered in this and other chapters and join the conversation: Which case would *you* add to our "A list"? Are there any you would subtract?

1. *Marbury v. Madison* (1803)

Without Marshall's momentous decision, we might not have judicial review—or courts so deeply engaged in U.S. government and policymaking. You read about this case earlier in this chapter.

2. *McCulloch v. Maryland* (1819)

James William McCulloch was a clerk at the Baltimore branch of the National Bank of the United States. The state of Maryland levied an annual tax on all banks "not chartered by the state" of Maryland; at the time, the National Bank was the only one. On behalf of the bank, McCulloch refused to pay the Maryland tax and sued. The Maryland Supreme Court ruled against McCulloch, arguing that the Constitution said nothing about establishing a bank—the national bank was unconstitutional in the first place.

Taking a loose interpretation of the Constitution (rather than a strict construction that would have limited Congress to doing only what was explicitly allowed), Chief Justice Marshall upheld the constitutionality of the bank. Marshall argued that Congress had every right to establish a national bank under the Constitution's necessary and proper clause (which authorizes Congress to do anything that is "necessary and proper" for "carrying into execution" the powers it is granted).

Furthermore, declared the Court, Maryland was forbidden to tax the national bank. "The power to tax," declared Marshall for the unanimous majority, "involves the power to destroy."[35] The states had no such power over federal institutions, because the collective American citizenry had established a national government with the Constitution's ratification. The Court's action affirmed the federal government's superiority to state governments in all specific instances named by the Constitution; this decision marked a significant advance toward American nationhood.

3. *Dred Scott v. Sandford* (1857)

As tensions mounted over the spread of slavery into the West, Chief Justice Roger Taney inserted the Supreme Court squarely into the middle of the debate. Writing for a 7–2 Court majority, Taney ruled that Dred Scott, a Missouri slave who was taken to a free state and later back to Missouri, was still a slave. He might have stopped there. Remember, one cannot sue without *standing*, and slaves, by definition, did not have standing.

● Chief Justice Roger Taney, who served on the Court from 1836 to 1864, authored the Dred Scott decision—often described as the worst decision in Court history.

● Dred Scott, a slave, sued for his own freedom and that of his two daughters, arguing that he had been taken to Illinois and the Wisconsin Territory, both free areas. The Court rejected his bid for freedom, 7–2.

The Court, however, went on to rule that Congress did not have the power to prohibit slavery in the territories. Taney continued, in passages that are shocking to read today: blacks, he insisted, were "beings of an inferior order and altogether unfit to associate with the white race." They were not and could never become U.S. citizens. The bottom line: Slavery could not be restricted in any western territory.[36] Many constitutional historians choose *Dred Scott* as the worst Supreme Court decision in American history (for more details, see Chapter 6).

4. *Santa Clara Co. v. Southern Pacific Railroad* (1886)

Santa Clara Co. v. Southern Pacific Railroad was a complex tax case, decided unanimously without much notice—but it reverberates through our politics today. California forbade corporations from deducting their debts from their taxable property. The Court ruled that California had acted improperly because corporations should be treated as persons and afforded the Fourteenth Amendment right of equal protection. The case established a precedent—later expanded—that enhanced the power of corporations. By 1938 Justice Hugo Black would complain that the Fourteenth Amendment had been written "to protect weak and helpless human beings," and not to "remove corporations in any fashion from the control of state governments." A decade later, Justice William O. Douglas added: "The *Santa Clara* case becomes one of the most momentous of all our decisions. . . . Corporations were now armed with constitutional prerogatives." The bottom line: *Santa Clara* set a precedent that, with time, gave corporations all the legal benefits of individual citizens. The legal theory in *Santa Clara* helped inform the Court when it struck down campaign finance laws (in *Citizens United* and other recent cases).[37]

Eighty-five years later, in *Reed v. Reed* (1971), the equal protection clause of the Fourteenth Amendment was unanimously extended to include gender. The court struck down an Idaho law that "preferred males" in naming administrators over estates.

5. *Plessy v. Ferguson* (1896)

The Civil War resulted in freedoms for black Americans, codified in three constitutional amendments (the Thirteenth, Fourteenth, and Fifteenth). After the turbulent period of Reconstruction, the South (followed, if less blatantly, by other sections of the United States) set about reasserting second-class status for African Americans. Across the region, state legislatures passed explicit laws mandating segregated facilities.

One 1890 Louisiana statute, "Law 111," required (among other restrictions) that railroads maintain separate cars for black and white ticketholders. Homer Plessy deliberately challenged the law by refusing to move to the "colored car" on an East Louisiana Railroad train. The case eventually reached the Supreme Court, where Plessy's lawyers argued that the segregation violated his Fourteenth Amendment rights. (Remember that the Fourteenth Amendment guaranteed to all Americans "equal protection under the law.") The Court rejected Plessy's argument and upheld Louisiana's law, cementing the infamous doctrine of "separate but equal" for nearly sixty years (until *Brown v. Board of Education* in 1954). The decision permitted racial segregation, and in the next ten years, the Jim Crow system was put firmly into place with the Supreme Court's blessing.

The sole dissenting justice, John Marshall Harlan (note his first and middle names), wrote a blistering critique of the decision, predicting accurately that *Plessy* "will prove as infamous" as the *Dred Scott* case and insisting that the Constitution was "color blind." After the decision was handed down, Homer Plessy pled guilty to the violation and paid a twenty-five dollar fine (for more details, see Chapter 6).

See a discussion of the *Plessy* case.

● Keith Plessy and Phoebe Ferguson, descendants of the two men named in the famous case, have become friends and formed a foundation to promote innovative ways of studying civil rights. The battle for civil rights is passed on from generation to generation. Now it is in your hands.

6. *Lochner v. New York* (1905)

The rise of mass industry and manufacturing in the late nineteenth century bred strong demands for worker protection. Several states passed laws limiting working hours and banning child labor. New York State's worker protections, passed in 1897, included a "Bakeshop Act" that prohibited anyone from working more than ten hours a day, or sixty hours a week, in a bakery.

Joseph Lochner, a bakery owner in Utica, was fined for requiring employees to exceed the sixty-hour weekly limit. He took his case to court, insisting that the Fourteenth Amendment protected his right to establish free contracts with his workers, independent of state influence.

Two New York courts denied Lochner's appeals. In a 7–2 ruling, the Supreme Court reversed the New York decisions, holding that the Bakeshop Act was an invalid exercise of the state's power. The decision ushered in a thirty-year **Lochner era**, during which courts repeatedly struck down state economic and labor regulations, including minimum wage laws, in the name of individual economic liberty. Governments could not interfere with the private right to contract by introducing worker protections.

In dissent, Justice Oliver Wendell Holmes wrote: "The Fourteenth Amendment does not enact Mr. Herbert Spencer's Social Statics"—that is, society should not operate by survival of the fittest.

7. *Muller v. Oregon* (1908)

Oregon limited the number of hours women could work. Whereas *Lochner* ruled that the state could not regulate men's hours, the Court chose to treat women differently. The Court ruled that "the difference between the sexes does . . . justify a different rule respecting a restriction of the hours of labor." The concern about "healthy mothers" justified state intervention.

Louis Brandeis defended the law with an innovative strategy. He disposed of the legal arguments in two pages and then compiled page after page of data—health statistics, medical evidence, the experience of other nations. From that time forward, this kind of statistical brief, brimming with data, would be known as a "Brandeis brief."

The case is particularly important for gender readings of the law. Yes, women won labor protections, but notice how: The case supported the idea that a woman was different from a man and, more to the point, that her role as child bearer and mother was more important than her role as worker.

8. *Schenck v. United States* (1919)

Charles Schenck, the secretary of the U.S. Socialist Party, printed and distributed leaflets expressing opposition to a U.S. military draft during World War I. Schenck was convicted under the Espionage Act of aiding the enemy during wartime. Insisting that he was exercising his First Amendment free speech rights, Schenck took his appeal to the Supreme Court.

One of the Court's most prolific (and quotable) justices, Oliver Wendell Holmes, Jr., wrote the decision for a 9–0 majority that upheld Schenck's conviction. For the first time, the Court formally marked out boundaries around protected speech: As Holmes wrote, words presenting a "clear and present danger" were legitimate subjects of legislative prohibitions, just like you cannot scream fire in a crowded building. The **clear and present danger** test guided the court for fifty years, until it was rewritten in 1969. Recall that a "test" is a general

Lochner era: A period from 1905 to 1937, during which the Supreme Court struck down laws (e.g., worker protection or minimum wage laws) that were thought to infringe on economic liberty or the right to contract.

● *Lawyer Louis Brandeis, later a Supreme Court justice, relied on social science data to win* Muller v. Oregon. *To this day, we call an argument that emphasizes social science research rather than legal argument a "Brandeis brief."*

Clear and present danger: Court doctrine that permits restrictions of free speech if officials believe that the speech will lead to prohibited action like violence or terrorism.

principle designed to guide future court decisions on a topic (for more details, see Chapter 5).

9. *National Labor Relations Board v. Jones and Laughlin Steel Corporation* (1937)

Jones and Laughlin was the nation's fourth-largest manufacturer of steel—an industry that had very aggressively opposed unionization. The company fired ten workers who tried to launch a union, and was sued by the National Labor Relations Board for violating the Wagner Act of 1935, which protected the right to unionize. The company responded that the Wagner Act violated the Constitution. The lower courts both agreed that precedent was on the company's side.

In a 5–4 decision, Chief Justice Charles Evans Hughes reversed the lower court decisions and held that Congress had the power, under the interstate commerce clause, to regulate the company's treatment of its workers. This decision broadly expanded congressional power to regulate economic matters. It meant that the Court—by a one-vote margin—would accept New Deal legislation. We can understand the enormous scope of this ruling when, three decades later, Congress used its authority over interstate commerce to outlaw segregation in hotels and restaurants (with the Civil Rights Act of 1964, discussed in Chapter 6).

Along with another case, *West Coast Hotel Company v. Parrish* (also decided 5–4 in 1937), the courts now permitted legislatures to regulate relations between business and workers. The cases meant the end of the Lochner era. Today, conservative judicial activists are eager to roll back congressional use of the interstate commerce power. Some even call for a return of the Lochner era.

10. *Korematsu v. U.S.* (1944)

During World War II, an executive order by President Roosevelt forced Japanese Americans out of their homes and into hastily constructed internment camps. Fred Korematsu, a California native, was arrested for defying the order. The Court ruled 6–3 that the need to defend against espionage during wartime justified the order—and its violation of equal protection. The case was one of the first to adopt strict scrutiny of government actions: The Court is primed to strike down any law that singles out a race or ethnicity unless there is a very strong reason for doing so (see Chapter 6 for discussion). In this case, the Court ruled, the government's action met the standards of **strict scrutiny**.

The case was always infamous for its mistreatment of Japanese Americans. It became even more so when legal historian Peter Irons, researching a book about the internment, discovered that the solicitor general had suppressed crucial information. A report from the Office of Naval Intelligence had concluded that there was no evidence that Japanese Americans were disloyal or acting as spies. In 1983, a federal district court in California used the new information to vacate (or void) Korematsu's conviction. To many people, including Fred Korematsu himself, the case stands as an enduring warning. War breeds fear that can threaten civil liberties. Korematsu drew on his own experience to file an *amicus* brief in a case involving the legal rights of enemy combatants held in Guantánamo Bay. The Court formally reversed the precedent of *Korematsu* in 2018—in *Trump v. Hawaii*.

● *Fred Korematsu refused to enter a Japanese internment camp. Today, his lifelong fight on behalf of civil liberties is commemorated by the "Fred Korematsu Day of Civil Liberties and the Constitution."*

Strict scrutiny: A form of judicial review that requires the government to have a "compelling government interest" for any law that singles out race or ethnicity.

11. *Brown v. Board of Education* (1954)

This landmark decision, decided unanimously, declared that segregating schools for black and white children violated the equal protection clause of the Fourteenth

Amendment. As Supreme Court Justice Earl Warren put it, "separate schools are inherently unequal." The decision boosted the civil rights movement and paved the way for an end to legal segregation. It overturned *Plessy v. Ferguson*, described previously (for more details, see Chapter 6).

12. *Mapp v. Ohio* (1961)

Cleveland police received a tip in 1959 that local resident Dollree Mapp was harboring a suspected bombing fugitive, and they swarmed her house without a search warrant. The police found no fugitive—but they did find obscene material, at the time legally forbidden in Ohio. Mapp was arrested and convicted. She appealed. The Supreme Court reversed her conviction and, drawing on the Fourth Amendment (prohibiting unreasonable searches and seizures), devised the "exclusionary rule," stating that illegally obtained evidence cannot be admitted in a criminal trial. The Court extended this federal rule to cover state cases (incorporating part of the Fourth Amendment) and ruled that since the evidence against Mapp was obtained without a search warrant, she could go free. The conservative majority on the Roberts Court recently rolled back the exclusionary rule, and there is some speculation that it may be abolished altogether (for more detail, see Chapter 5).

13. *Gideon v. Wainwright* (1963)

Clarence Gideon, was accused (unjustly, as it eventually was proved) of a minor theft from a Florida pool hall. Lacking funds to hire a defense attorney, Gideon represented himself at his trial—a relatively common practice into the early 1960s. He was swiftly convicted, but he appealed his sentence based on the state's failure to provide him with a competent defense lawyer.

The Supreme Court held that Gideon was wrongly convicted and ordered a new trial. The *Gideon* legacy: Anyone charged with a serious criminal offense has the right to an attorney.[38] Moreover, the state must provide a lawyer to any defendant unable to afford legal counsel. *Gideon* was the first in a series of landmark judicial decisions upholding the rights of defendants in criminal proceedings, including the so-called *Miranda rights* to counsel during police questioning. Recently, the Court has strengthened the right to counsel, holding that it applies to plea bargain cases in which a defendant is offered a deal: plead guilty, avoid a trial, and receive a lighter sentence (for more details, see Chapter 5).

14. *Lemon v. Kurtzman* (1971)

Religion is another constitutionally guaranteed freedom attracting frequent judicial attention. Recall from Chapter 5 that the First Amendment both guarantees the *free exercise* of religion to every person and forbids the *establishment* of religion. It erects what Thomas Jefferson termed a "wall of separation" between church and state.

In *Lemon v. Kurtzman*, described in Chapter 5, the Court created a three-pronged test for judging whether government action violated the First Amendment by "establishing" a religion. The law could not create "excessive government entanglement" in religious affairs; it must not inhibit religious practice; and it must have a secular purpose. Any law that violates any of these tests is unconstitutional.

The Lemon test has come in for a great deal of criticism—especially from more conservative justices—and the Court has been growing more permissive about allowing religious practices. For example, in *Town of Greece v. Galloway* (2014), the court ruled (5–4) that the town's practice of starting its monthly meetings with a prayer did not violate the establishment clause. Despite the new, more permissive orientation, the Court has repeatedly refused to strike down the *Lemon test* (for more detail, see Chapter 5).

15. *Roe v. Wade* (1973)

The *Roe v. Wade* decision, written by Justice Harry Blackmun, struck down a Texas statute outlawing abortion—and expanded the personal right to privacy under the Constitution. The right to privacy, wrote Blackmun, is "fundamental" and "broad enough to encompass a woman's decision whether or not to terminate her pregnancy." The *Roe* decision—since qualified by other cases discussed in Chapter 5—remains one of the great dividing lines in American politics and a "litmus test" for most federal judicial nominations. For years, the Court appears to be divided. Four justices seemed ready to overturn *Roe*, four eager to defend it, and one—Justice Kennedy—in the middle, balancing a woman's right to privacy with a state's interest in limiting abortions. When Justice Kennedy retired, in 2018, the swing vote shifted in a conservative direction with Justice Kavanaugh. Watch carefully to see what the new court lineup decides about this classic case.

16. *U.S. v. Nixon* (1974)

This case revolved around the Watergate break-in and the historic political debate that ensued. President Nixon refused to turn over audiotapes of White House conversations, along with other requested materials, to the special prosecutor investigating Watergate, on the grounds of "executive privilege," a sweeping claim of presidential immunity. In a unanimous 8–0 decision, Chief Justice Warren Burger (appointed by Nixon five years earlier) upheld the doctrine of executive privilege but concluded that presidents could not invoke it in criminal cases to withhold evidence. Nixon acquiesced—and resigned as president a month later.

● *The politics of abortion inflame passions, mobilize demonstrations, and shape American politics. For over 40 years, the judiciary has been the central arena for this conflict.*

Listen to the Supreme Court's oral arguments in *Bush v. Gore* (2000).

17. *Bush v. Gore* (2000)

High drama surrounded a recount of some of Florida's disputed ballots in the 2000 presidential election, stretching well past the November 7 election Date. On December 8, Florida's Supreme Court ordered a manual recount of ballots; George W. Bush's lawyers, fearing this would result in an advantage for Vice President Gore, appealed the decision to the U.S. Supreme Court. The Court, acting with unusual speed because of the urgency of the issue—a presidential election hung in the balance—halted the recount the very next day. Two days later, on December 11, the Court scheduled time to hear from both sides' lawyers. Less than twenty-four hours later, Chief Justice Rehnquist handed down a 5–4 ruling that no constitutionally valid recount could be completed by Florida's December 12 deadline for certifying election results. The long presidential contest of 2000 was over. George Bush won Florida's twenty-five electoral votes and, with them, the presidential election.

18. *National Federation of Independent Business v. Sebelius* (2012)

This blockbuster decision took on two controversial features of the Obama administration health reform law (the Affordable Care Act, or ACA). The ACA required all Americans to buy health insurance or face a fine (paid with their income taxes); it also expanded Medicaid, a joint federal and state program, to cover all Americans under sixty-five who were poor or near poor (the federal government would pay 90 percent of the costs).

Can the federal government require individuals to carry health insurance? Proponents said yes: Congress has the power to regulate interstate commerce (see case number 10, above, *National Labor Relations Board v. Jones and Laughlin Steel Corporation*). Chief Justice Roberts and the four conservative justices ruled that Congress does *not* have the power under interstate commerce to require that people buy health insurance. Then, very dramatically, the chief justice broke with the conservatives and ruled that Congress does have the power to tax—and that the ACA constitutes a tax. The Obama reform was upheld. However, Roberts got Supreme Court–watchers buzzing. Remember, conservatives have long wanted to curtail the congressional use of interstate commerce. Was Roberts handing conservative jurisprudence a victory, perhaps a return to the Lochner era that conservatives have been calling for even while upholding the Obama healthcare law? Time will tell.

In the other part of the case, the Court ruled 7–2 that Congress could not change the rules of the Medicaid program and require states to expand their program. It could only offer the funds and encourage the states to participate. Was this, wondered analysts, a new rollback of the federal government's power over federalism? Again, time will tell. The true scope of a case like this often takes years to reveal itself.

19. *Obergefell v. Hodges* (2015)

John Arthur was dying of ALS and his husband, Jim Obergefell, wanted the death certificate to list him as the surviving spouse. However, Ohio law did not recognize same-sex marriage (the couple had been wed in Maryland) and the state attorney general defended the state ban. In *Obergefell*, a narrowly divided court ruled (5-4) that denying marriage licenses to same-sex couples violated the due process and the equal protection clauses of the Fourteenth Amendment. The ruling, authored by Justice Kennedy, required every state to accord same-sex marriages all the rights and conditions that accompany opposite-sex marriages.

Four different dissenting opinions criticized the majority for stretching the Fourteenth Amendment, for breaking with precedent, and for taking a controversial

What Do YOU Think? | **Name Another Landmark Case**

Why didn't we take our list to a nice round number? To leave room for your choice. Think about the many cases we have already discussed in this book. Then pick one that you would add to the list: What would it be?

Hint: Some cases that are frequently seen as landmarks include *Loving v. Virginia* (which struck down bans on interracial marriage); the *Trump* (immigration) and *Janus* (union dues) cases that opened this chapter; *Citizens United* (striking down campaign finance legislation, discussed in Chapter 10); *Miranda* (the right to remain silent; see Chapter 5); *Tinker* (student free speech; see Chapter 5); or *Bakke* (affirmative action; see Chapter 6); Now it is your turn. Choose a case, add it to the list, and explain why you consider it a landmark.

issue out of the hands of the voters. Again, Justice Kennedy's retirement raises the question of how future decisions might affect this ruling.

The Nineteen Cases—and the Power of the Court

This list illustrates the wide range of questions addressed in U.S. federal courts. There are issues affecting civil rights and liberties (*Dred Scott, Plessy, Korematsu*), federalism and nationhood (*McCulloch, National Federation of Independent Business*), criminal charges (*Mapp, Gideon*), First Amendment freedoms (*Schenck*), business regulation (*Lochner, National Labor Relations Board, National Federation of Independent Business*), elections (*Bush v. Gore*), religion (*Lemon*), gender (*Muller, Roe, Obergefell*), and separated powers (*Nixon*). These cases illustrate the formidable reach of the judiciary in American politics and government.

Many of these cases were very controversial when decided—and some remain disputed today. Such controversy repeatedly raises the question we have asked throughout the chapter: Does the Supreme Court (and do courts in general) overstep democratic boundaries when ruling on such momentous political matters? How deferential should they be to the people's representatives? Each case introduces a different type of judgment call—not just on the substance of the case but on the scope of the Court's authority.

The Bottom Line

» A few judicial decisions become landmark decisions, significantly reshaping American politics and society.

» We have listed nineteen of the most important Supreme Court decisions across more than two centuries. Are there any you would add—or subtract?

Improving the Judiciary

An independent judiciary has deep roots in both our colonial English heritage and the classical liberal tradition (as you saw in Chapter 2). Yet despite its appetite for litigation, the public also expresses concerns about our legal system. Four common criticisms: cost, bias, judicial power, and the dangers of corruption[39]

Criticisms

First, the costs associated with America's litigious society have become a source of widespread discontent, especially among conservatives. Critics estimate that more than five hundred billion dollars is spent annually responding to and adjudicating lawsuits.

Second, the U.S. legal system is sometimes perceived as biased. For example, many minorities, particularly African Americans, have for generations experienced the sting of *racial profiling*, or the use of race by police officers in deciding whom to stop or arrest. Others criticize ideological bias. Declining confidence in our criminal justice system is illustrated in Table 16.3.

The power of the legal system is a third cause of concern. This concern partly owes to our fear of winding up in court, especially as a defendant. The legendary U.S. federal judge Learned Hand wrote in 1926, "As a litigant, I should dread a lawsuit beyond almost anything short of sickness and death."[40] If Judge Hand, after forty-three years as a federal judge, was made anxious by the law's power, imagine how most non-lawyers feel!

Finally, disgust with the perceived corruption of lawyers drives criticism. As we saw in Chapter 12 (Interest Groups), lawyers rank near the bottom of Gallup's annual survey of the honesty and ethical standards of various U.S. professions. As a nation, we have a low opinion of juries as well.

Ideas for Reform: More Resources

One prominent reform proposals would grant the courts more resources. The American judiciary faces a "quiet crisis" in attracting talented judges. One reason is a long-term decline in judges' pay, which has fallen dramatically relative to that of other professionals. In 1969, district court judges earned a substantially higher

TABLE 16.3 Americans' Ranking of Various Public Institutions

Percentage with "a great deal" or "quite a lot" of confidence in the institution		
	2006	2018
Military	73%	74%
Police	58%	59%
Church or organized religion	52%	38%
Medical system	38%	36%
Presidency	33%	37%
U.S. Supreme Court	40%	37%
Public schools	37%	29%
Banks	49%	30%
Organized labor	24%	26%
Criminal justice system	25%	22%
Congress	19%	17%
Source: Gallup		

salary than their academic counterparts at Harvard, the highest-paying law school. Today they make half as much as senior professors—and barely a third as much as law-school deans.

We also have seen that the U.S. court system runs on a very small budget, relative to that of other governing institutions. State courts stagger under the volume of cases—and cope by using strategies like pushing through plea bargains in the vast majority of criminal cases. Public defenders have impossible caseloads. The tensions of underfunding run throughout the court system. Perhaps courts should receive more resources. On the federal level, it may even be worth thinking about developing a research capacity to evaluate the potential impact of court rulings.

Term Limits

Judicial term limits (often proposed as eighteen years) would help address the fear of "unelected judges" overruling the elected branches, for justices would cycle off the Supreme Court with each election.[41] After their term, justices could move to the appellate bench—satisfying the constitutional requirement of lifetime appointment. Judicial term limits may reduce the battles that surround judicial appointments, especially to the Supreme Court. Forty-year-old justices would no longer sit on the bench for three decades or more. It would still keep the Court insulated from political tumult—eighteen years is a long time—while providing for a regular circulation of new judges with fresh perspectives. One version of this proposal would permit the president to nominate a Supreme Court justice (and the Senate to confirm) every two years so that the Court would always balance new ideas and experienced hands. Would you support or oppose such an innovation? What do you think?

Shift Authority to Congress

Some scholars believe Congress should have the authority to modify Court precedents—essentially sharing the power to interpret the Constitution. After taking the oath of office, President Abraham Lincoln argued that American policy could not be "irrevocably fixed by decisions of the Supreme Court" for, if it were, "the people would cease to be their own rulers." Of course, the Court decides the case between the two parties in a suit. But Congress might revise the Court's general policies. In *Federalist 81*, Alexander Hamilton took the same view, suggesting that Congress "may prescribe a new rule for future cases" even if it violates Court precedent. As we have seen, the Court asserted the power to interpret the Constitution. Perhaps that power should now be shared with Congress. What do you think?[42]

 **The Bottom Line**

» The courts face four popular criticisms: cost, bias, power, and corruption.

» One reform proposal: Direct more resources to the judicial branch—in both the state and the federal courts.

» A second often proposed reform: Introduce term limits to the federal bench. Supreme Court justices would serve eighteen years, a time frame permitting each president a judicial nomination every two years.

Conclusion: Democracy and the Courts

Courts wield an unusual amount of influence in the United States—far more than courts in most other nations, and perhaps too much in a modern democratic society. At the same time, there are clear limits to judicial power—from the reactive nature of the judicial process to the courts' reliance on others to implement decisions. Expanding resources and imposing term limits could modernize the courts and enhance their ability to serve American government by doing what they do at their best: faithfully reflecting—and consistently enforcing—the constitutional rules that guide our public life.

Reforms can only go so far. The powerful role of the courts in a democracy will always be vexing for a simple reason: The courts are designed to serve as a check, ultimately, on the majority. The courts, when they are acting properly, stop the people and their representatives from violating the Constitution or from harming minority rights. However, as the steady parade of 5–4 decisions discussed in this chapter indicates, what exactly the Constitution means is often a highly controversial matter. Further, with the benefit of hindsight, we see that the court has interpreted the Constitution in ways that reduce rights in cases like Dred Scott, Plessy, Korematsu, and many others.

As a result, the courts always face a delicate balance between enforcing the Constitution (as a majority on the Court sees it) and deferring to democracy (and the majority of the country).

CHAPTER SUMMARY

Check your understanding of Chapter 16.

● The judiciary has a central place in U.S. government and politics—as well as in our legalistic national culture.

● Americans express uneasiness about their judicial system, despite their faith in the rule of law.

● Compared to other advanced democratic nations, U.S. courts possess a great deal of influence over our politics and government. This owes primarily to the power of judicial review, asserted long ago by Chief Justice John Marshall. Once again, Americans found a way to separate and fragment power—continuing the work begun in the Constitution.

Need to review key ideas in greater depth? Click here.

● Alongside their uncommon influence, courts are hemmed in by restrictions such as limited resources, *stare decisis* requirements, and their lack of an electoral base (at the federal level).

● The judiciary has affected a vast range of areas through its authority to interpret the Constitution, from religion and race to economic regulations and even presidential election outcomes. This impact is evident in a set of landmark cases—each of which has aroused great controversy, leading to renewed calls for limits on judicial activism. The originalist and pragmatist schools of thought have very different views of what constitutes such "activism."

● The Supreme Court marks the pinnacle of judicial—and constitutional—authority in the United States. Its operations, often carried out behind closed doors, are the subject of fascinated speculation: How do nine justices decide? The leading theories: They follow the rule of law, they are guided by their ideology, they are moved by peer pressure, and they are concerned about the institution of the courts.

Given the combination of the power of the courts and Americans' uncertainty about how that power should be wielded, a set of reforms is put forth each year. Two in particular deserve careful attention: the limitation of federal judges' current life terms, and the possibility of rewarding the judiciary's expansive responsibilities with more resources.

KEY TERMS

Flashcard review.

Amicus curiae, p. 503	Dissent, p. 506	Mediation, p. 488
Circuit courts, p. 494	District courts, p. 493	Plaintiff, p. 500
Civil law, p. 500	Judicial activism, p. 500	Precedent, p. 500
Clear and present danger, p. 516	Judicial restraint, p. 500	Rule of four, p. 504
Common law, p. 500	Judicial review, p. 498	*Stare decisis*, p. 509
Concurrent opinion, p. 506	Litigation, p. 488	Strict scrutiny, p. 517
Criminal law, p. 500	Lochner era, p. 516	
Defendant, p. 501	Majority opinion, p. 506	

STUDY QUESTIONS

1. Should the judiciary have less power in American government and politics? If so, how would you propose restraining judicial authority in practice?

2. The Supreme Court is 33 percent female. Other federal courts (district and circuit) have the same proportion. Does that seem too low, given that women make up nearly 52 percent of the population? What about the fact that none of the nine justices is Protestant in a country that is around 51 percent Protestant? Should we care about the religious preferences of Supreme Court justices?

3. Do Supreme Court clerks—and other federal judges' clerks—have too much influence, given their relatively young ages? Should they serve for longer than one year, given the importance of the work they do?

4. Should we mandate more transparency for judicial operations—televise Supreme Court oral arguments, for example, or require that Court conferences be transcribed and publicized? Are there any benefits to the secrecy that characterizes the federal judiciary?

5. Do either of the reforms raised at the end of this chapter appeal to you? Why or why not? Might they be most successful if offered as a package? (Combining term limits, which appeal to critics of judicial activism, with higher judicial pay and more resources for the courts might make term limits palatable to current and future judges.)

6. Should the federal judiciary be the last line of defense in protecting Americans' constitutional rights and liberties? Why or why not? And if not, what other institution or group of people should have this responsibility? Be specific: How would another actor or group protect rights and liberties better than federal judges, and ultimately the Supreme Court, do today?

Go to www.oup.com/us/Morone to find quizzes, flash cards, simulations, tutorials, videos, and other study tools.

17 Public Policymaking and Budgeting

"DRILL, BABY, DRILL!"
The call echoed out across GOP rallies in 2008, as vice-presidential nominee Sarah Palin stirred campaign crowds with promises of American energy independence and lower gas prices. Palin and fellow Republicans promoted drilling in U.S. coastal areas with extensive oil and natural gas deposits. Russia and Middle Eastern countries controlled 80 percent of world oil supply and 70 percent of the gas supply, while the United States claimed only 7 percent of each.[1] Alaskans and others also embraced off-shore drilling because of the number of jobs it would create. Democrats countered that offshore drilling would leach toxic chemicals into pristine waters, decimate marine life, and harm humans as well as other species including the endangered polar bear. Once in office, Democratic President Barack Obama banned all new offshore drilling. Then, in 2018, the Trump Administration reversed the ban and opened up oil and natural-gas drilling in nearly all U.S. coastal waters.[2]

Environmental activists denounced the administration's move and sued to block the new policy. Members of Congress were split, though not necessarily along party lines: House and Senate members from both parties who represented coastal states and districts raised strong objections, in many cases joined by their states' governors. Florida Governor Rick Scott, a close Republican ally of Trump's, received an exception allowing the state's coastal drilling ban to remain, protecting the tourism industry that thrives on the state's inviting shores.

During 2018, thousands of Hondurans, fleeing violent gangs and searching for a way to make a living, wove their way through Central America toward the United States. A group called *Pueblo Sin Fronteras* (people without borders), which advocates for open borders, organized the caravan. President Trump turned images of the caravan into an effective midterm campaign issue, promising to bar undocumented immigrants and refugees alike from crossing into the United States, in order to uphold the rule of law and protect American jobs and security. Democrats slammed the president for stirring up prejudices and driving away those people in greatest need of humanitarian assistance.[3]

Officials in the White House, Congress, statehouses, and courts were not just debating environmental and immigration regulations, but *what*

● *Oil rigs in the wilderness? The Obama administration banned new offshore drilling, a policy that President Trump revoked during his second year in office. Congress, coastal-state governors, and the courts all quickly leapt in: Many actors are involved in American domestic policymaking.*

● Trace the five stages of public policymaking.

● Review the history of U.S. social policy, with attention to "entitlement" programs.

● Assess what counts as good policy, including claims of fairness and economic efficiency.

● Learn how the federal budget process drives much of our domestic policymaking.

● Consider how U.S. policymaking could be reformed.

government should do. In other words, they were making public policy. Exchanges such as these about policy decisions have far-reaching implications, affecting tens of millions of Americans and many more millions around the world. Policy debates also return to this book's familiar chapter-opening question: *Who are we?*

Perhaps Americans are best described in terms of the policies we enact—and those that we reject or abandon. Why do we provide hefty government subsidies to farmers growing corn, dairy, and beef but virtually none to growers of fruits and vegetables? Why do we imprison one in nine young black men? Why do we closely regulate sex but not violence in movies? Why do we control privately owned land to protect spotted owls and flying squirrels? These and thousands of other policy decisions contribute to the kaleidoscopic portrait of who we are.

All the actors introduced in this book—interest groups, Congress, the media, executive branch officials, the courts, the public, and more—come together to create public policy. Here we will look at domestic policymaking, rather than foreign policy, which is the subject of Chapter 18. We will see how government officials craft public policies, with special emphasis on budgeting. In an age of shrinking monetary resources, it is impossible to discuss a policy proposal without considering its costs.

Public Policymaking in Five (Not-So-Easy) Stages

Policies often take the form of laws, but they can also be regulations, presidential executive orders, funding formulas (determining who gets how much), established norms, or action plans. Think of an issue you care about: clean drinking water, infant mortality, or protection against terrorist acts. All of these, as with every political issue addressed by government officials, play out through public policymaking—whether in controlling waterborne pollutants, encouraging prenatal care and mandating safe infant delivery rooms, or devising effective antiterrorism efforts.

Recall the seven basic American political ideas we explored in Chapter 2. For example, consider *limited government* or *self-rule*: Both are at stake whenever we launch new domestic programs that expand federal government authority. At the same time, Americans' sense of *equality* is embedded in a whole range of policies, from affirmative action to welfare rules requiring recipients to find work within a certain time period.

Making domestic policy is an elaborate process, involving five stages. Figure 17.1 displays these stages graphically. We organize our trip through the public policy system by exploring each of these in turn.

1. Agenda Setting

Policymaking does not begin in earnest until public officials recognize that something is a problem worthy of government attention. President Obama, arriving

BY THE NUMBERS

U.S. Public Policy

Number of laws passed, 115th Congress (2017–2018), as of November 15, 2018	**277**
Number of laws passed, 110th Congress (2007–2008)	**460**
Number of laws passed, 80th Congress (1947–1948), labeled the "Do-Nothing Congress" by President Truman	**906**
Average number of new federal regulations introduced each year, George W. Bush Administration	**3,985**
Average number during Barack Obama Administration	**3,640**
Number during first year of Donald Trump Administration	**3,281**
Percentage of proposed federal rules required by the OMB to include a cost-benefit analysis, 2006–2016	**91[4]**
2016 U.S. federal budget deficit	**$548 billion**
2019 federal budget deficit (estimated)	**$1.1 trillion[5]**
Spending on Social Security, Medicare, and Medicaid in 2019 (estimated)	**$2.2 trillion**
Percentage reduction in the national debt if Congress cut all nondefense discretionary spending	**3.6**
Number of U.S. schools offering an accredited program in public policy and administration, 1990	**97[6]**
Number offering such a program in 2018	**211**

How are policymakers' hands constrained by financial obligations established by existing laws and programs?

in office in 2009, identified nuclear power as a promising "clean" alternative to coal and oil. Nuclear power developers began to plan new construction across the United States; they won encouragement in the form of tax incentives and relaxed regulatory restrictions. Then, in 2011, a **focusing event** changed Americans' minds about nuclear power. A massive tidal wave hit a nuclear plant in Fukushima, Japan.

Focusing event: A major happening, often of crisis or disaster proportions, that attracts widespread media attention to an issue.

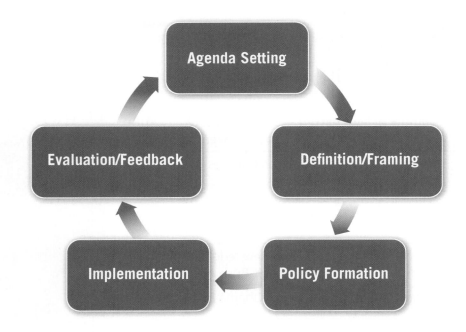

● **Figure 17.1** *The five stages of domestic policymaking.*

Policy agenda: The issues that the media covers, the public considers important, and politicians address. Setting the agenda is the first step in political action.

Safety mechanisms failed, part of the plant melted down, and a radioactive leak affected water, land, and air for miles around. The disaster quickly made nuclear plant safety a high-level agenda item for American policymakers. Government support for new nuclear construction disappeared, and regulators' scrutiny sharpened, halting expansion plans.

Focusing events, such as the Fukushima nuclear meltdown, are critical to shaping **policy agendas**. Those agendas, as we saw in Chapter 9, are typically the source of fierce competition, because the policy system can emphasize only a few priorities at any time. As Table 17.1 shows, the policy agenda changes across the years. "Dissatisfaction with government" is almost always high on the list, but note the big shifts otherwise, in just two years.

Policy agendas are difficult to pin down with any precision at a particular moment, as issues burst suddenly into Americans' collective consciousness . . . and often fade away just as swiftly. This process has only sped up in our social media age. When President Trump announced, in July 2017, a ban on transgender people serving in the military, attention to the issue surged. Polling revealed that most Americans had not previously given the matter any thought.[7] Within a few days, the issue had faded from the news, after top U.S. generals indicated they would essentially ignore the ban. Eight months later, the topic was back on front pages and social-media feeds, after a second Trump announcement—only to disappear again after federal courts blocked the proposed move.

Once an issue hits the agenda, debates erupt about how to describe the topic—moving us to the next stage.

2. Framing

Translating agenda items into proposed policy solution means answering a series of questions. What are the root causes of the problem? How bad a problem *is* this?

TABLE 17.1 **Comparison of Top National Agenda Items, Two Years Apart**

MOST IMPORTANT PROBLEM FACING THE COUNTRY, SUMMER 2016	PERCENTAGE MENTIONING IN 2016	MOST IMPORTANT PROBLEM FACING THE COUNTRY, SUMMER 2018	PERCENTAGE MENTIONING IN 2018
Economy in general	18	Immigration/illegal aliens	22
Dissatisfaction with government	13	Dissatisfaction with government	19
Unemployment/jobs	8	Race relations/racism	7
Immigration/illegal aliens	7	Lack of respect for each other	6
Election reform	6	Unifying the country	6
Budget deficit	5	Economy in general	4
Education	5	Guns/gun control	4
Ethical/moral decline	5	Ethical/moral decline	3
Education	5	Healthcare	3
Source: Gallup			

How should public officials respond, if at all? Most agenda issues involve framing questions such as these (discussed in Chapter 9); the answers are far from obvious, and they can differ greatly depending on who is making the argument.

Consider an example from education policy. Every three years, a representative sample of 15-year-olds from around the world sits for exams in reading, math, and science. When the latest results were released, in 2017, American secondary school students finished well behind their counterparts from many other advanced countries. Poor school performance dominated local and national conversations. Parents, teachers, and businesses anxious to hire well-trained employees in a globally competitive market all agreed: Scores had to improve.

That goal merely placed the issue on the agenda. Then disputes about defining, or framing, the problem began. Was it that American kids were poorly prepared for the tests, compared to children in other countries? Or that many U.S. classrooms were overcrowded, with too few teachers to provide pupils with personalized instruction? Were officials in the Department of Education better positioned to address the problem of mediocre test scores, or should solutions come from the local level, where children attend school?

On and on the discussion rages—retracing familiar paths. Federal officials had no formal say in education policy until the mid-1960s, when Congress established an extensive program of national funding through the Elementary and Secondary Education Act. The U.S. Department of Education was created later still, in 1979. Champions of local control of education have fought to limit federal activity ever since. The Trump Administration's 2018 executive-bureaucracy reorganization plan proposed merging Education with the Labor Department: as one analysis concluded, this would "achieve a holy grail for Republicans: eliminating the Education Department as a standalone agency."[8] Democratic leaders in Congress instead

Focusing event: A nuclear plant in Fukushima, Japan, burns after a partial meltdown following a giant tsunami. The tragedy caused U.S. public approval for nuclear power to plummet, affecting plans to expand American nuclear energy production.

insist that national education officials must reduce inequities in school financing, so that the richest districts in a state, which are able to provide more resources, do not leave school-children in lower-income areas farther behind.

Is education—or, for that matter, any public problem—best addressed on a national or local level? Would progressive solutions reduce inequity or merely amount to federal government "meddling"? Do conservative solutions address inadequate instruction due, some insist, to unionized teachers allowed to remain in classrooms despite poor results, or are they an unjustified assault on public schools? These different ways of "framing" issues, also called *problem definition*, have big consequences: They help determine which policy responses the government considers. As issues are framed and reframed, policy actors translate their preferred solutions into law, propelling policymaking to a third stage.

3. Policy Formation

After a problem reaches the policy agenda and the framing debate settles into one or two primary definitions, proposed solutions must be evaluated—and adopted or discarded. This process of policy formation is again a sprawling, complicated one. Members of Congress and often state and local legislators engage in the myriad activities you studied in Chapter 13: drafting bills, holding hearings, and hammering out compromises in committee meetings and floor debates. Executive branch experts weigh in, all the way up to the president if the issue is sufficiently high profile. Advocacy groups and industry lobbyists swarm around lawmakers; judicial rulings reshape the policy debate; and media experts opine through print, broadcast, the blogosphere, and Twitter.

Analyzing Policy, Ex Ante. Competing ideas, rhetorical displays, deft procedural moves, power plays: These features underpin policy formation in every society, as they have for hundreds of years. Recently, more technical work also has become vital to policy success. Policy analysis involves constructing scientific measures of a proposed policy's costs and benefits ex ante—before it passes and goes into effect. Such assessment efforts are a central feature of contemporary policymaking in the United States and other advanced industrial nations.

Cost effectiveness:
The projected costs of a proposed policy, as revealed by a relatively simple study.

One approach to a proposed policy involves studies of **cost effectiveness**. Here analysts compare several policy alternatives that deliver the same overall benefit to determine which one does so at the *lowest cost*. Imagine that a local government decides to repaint the town hall. Different painting companies bid for the job. Presumably they all provide the same basic service, perhaps with minor differences in paint color or warranty. City officials can compare these similar vendors based on proposed costs and ask which provides the most cost-effective service.

Not many policy decisions are that straightforward, however, especially when they reach the national agenda. In 2018, with gas prices at historic lows, President

Trump recommended a 25-cent per gallon hike in the federal gasoline tax, to pay for a massive infrastructure improvement plan (including improved highway maintenance). For a quarter-century, the national gas tax has remained at 18.4 cents per gallon, after slowly rising over the preceding 60 years from a penny per gallon. To illuminate the likely effects of this policy shift—and to estimate an ideal tax increase—experts performed a **cost-benefit analysis**. This elaborate form of ex ante evaluation is carried out by trained analysts, some of them working in government and others in academia, lobbying firms, or think tanks.

The first step in a cost-benefit analysis is to list all the expected costs of a policy proposal, as well as all the expected benefits. For the gas tax, researchers identified two primary categories of cost and five main areas of benefit. The results are summarized in Table 17.2.

Researchers then "monetize," or assign dollar values to, these costs and benefits, using elaborate mathematical formulas. In the gas tax example, the estimated *costs* of a higher tax are around 75 cents per gallon: 52 cents for the increased price of services (such as higher costs of goods transported by truck) and 23 cents in direct costs to drivers. That is a pretty steep cost for each gallon of gas, but the predicted *benefits* were considerably higher. Adding together the estimated savings yielded a $1.76 benefit per gallon, as Table 17.3 shows.

According to the cost-benefit analysis, national gas taxes could be raised by just over a dollar per gallon ($1.81 in benefits, minus the 78-cent cost). From the perspective of economic effectiveness, society would be better off. Benefits include environmental improvements, public health (fewer accidents, more time saved), and reduced payments for imported oil. One more beneficiary, if the tax passed, would be the federal treasury, which could apply new tax dollars to infrastructure improvement, including transportation funding.

● Should federal officials manage education policy, or leave it to local school districts? Education Secretary Betsy DeVos, with President Trump's backing, seeks to shift federal funding toward "school choice," including support for charter schools and religious instruction.

Cost-benefit analysis: A more complex study of the projected costs and benefits associated with a proposed policy.

TABLE 17.2 Gas Tax Costs/Benefits

GAS TAX COSTS
Direct cost of the tax to drivers (those in rural areas, and with lower incomes, would be hardest hit).
Higher price of services dependent on transportation, such as shipping goods by truck.
GAS TAX BENEFITS
Reduced urban air pollution (thereby improving public health).
Reduced CO_2 emissions (slowing the pace of climate change).
Reduced U.S. dependence on imported oil.
Diminished traffic congestion (saving drivers time).
Reduced traffic accidents (because people drive less or switch to mass transit).

TABLE 17.3 Cost-Benefit Valuation of a Proposed Gas Tax

COSTS OF GAS TAX	VALUE*	BENEFITS OF GAS TAX	VALUE*
Direct cost to drivers	$0.24	Public health (reduced air pollution)	$0.43
Transportation services	$0.54	Climate (reduced CO_2 emissions)	$0.13
		Reduced oil imports	$0.11
		Time saved (less traffic)	$0.58
		Reduced accidents	$0.56
TOTAL	**$0.78**		**$1.81**

Values are estimated per gallon of gas.
Source: Authors' calculation, combining several existing models.

From Cost-Benefit Analysis to Politics. Cost-benefit and other ex ante evaluations are widely used in policymaking, with significant impacts on both legislative votes and judicial decisions. These analyses alone, however, do not determine policy.

President Trump's 2018 proposal to more than double the gas tax, to a total of some 43 cents/gallon, was greeted with headlines such as "Trump's Gas Tax Goes Nowhere in Congress."[9] Some supporters of a tax, such as former Transportation Secretary Ray LaHood, a Republican, saluted Trump's proposal. But especially with gas prices rising as the midterm elections approached, the plan was quietly abandoned. Political considerations regularly overcome even a clearly positive policy analysis.

Policy window: A figurative description of the opportunity—often brief, measured in days or weeks rather than years—to pass a bill in Congress or a state legislature.

If the swirling legislative and executive branch preferences align just right, and the cost-benefit analysis comes out positive, a figurative **policy window** opens.[10] Might a new policy be launched? There is no guarantee of success, especially at the national level. Of the several thousand bills and measures introduced in Congress each year, only two hundred or so make it into the statute books. Policy windows rarely stay open for long. But determined advocates who are organized and savvy about the rules of the policy game can navigate this formation stage and achieve success.

4. Policy Implementation

When a new law makes it onto the books, policymaking passes to the implementation stage. As you read in Chapter 15, this process is not widely understood. During policy formation, televised congressional hearings, White House speeches urging action, and cliffhanger House and Senate floor votes keep the attentive public engaged. Afterward, however, the glare of media attention dims. The implementation of national policies is primarily handled by the executive bureaucracy, which labors mostly out of public view. Does this shift in visibility mean that the work of policy implementation is less politicized? Many American political thinkers and actors have thought so, dating back at least to Woodrow Wilson, who as a political scientist in 1887 described bureaucratic activity as "a technical science." Wilson insisted that "administrative questions are not political questions."[11]

As Wilson learned on becoming president 30 years later, implementing public policy is in fact a highly political event. Implementation involves two main steps: working out the specifics of the law, primarily through the rulemaking process introduced in Chapter 15, and then delivering government services or enforcing new regulations. Both these steps attract intense interest—and, inevitably, political fighting—from the communities most affected by the policy change.

Rulemaking Revisited. Once a law passes and the bureaucracy gets to work, politics is still front and center in this more obscure rulemaking phase. As you will recall from Chapter 15, each aspect of a new law requires a separate rule, and each rule is spelled out in painstaking detail. For example, one part of the Affordable Care Act (or Obamacare) mandates that dependents up to age 26 remain eligible for health insurance through their parents; the previous cutoff age was 18, or 21 for students enrolled in college. In the ACA as written by Congress, this requirement was spelled out in only a couple of sentences. However, the Department of Health and Human Services rule specifying details—who was eligible, under what circumstances, penalties for violation, and so forth—ran to more than 25 single-spaced, tiny-print pages in the *Federal Register*.[12] Each of these rules can impact the cost-benefit analysis of the policy in the long run.

Thumb through the *Federal Register* online.

With such room for maneuvering, complaints abound about politicization by the bureaucracy. Some critics charge that agencies impose rules too quickly to permit proper review by interested parties. These critics include Supreme Court Chief Justice John Roberts, who expressed concern in a 2012 case about a rule that was completed in 22 days—warp speed in a rulemaking process that can take more than a year to finish.[13] Others take exception to the bureaucracy's "political" uses of science. In 2017, 13 federal agencies including the Environmental Protection Agency (EPA) issued a report warning that global warming would increase without significant reductions in burning fossil fuels (in cars and power plants, for example). Then-head of the EPA, Scott Pruitt, criticized the sweeping report as "politicized science," saying "Science is not something that should just be thrown about to try to dictate policy in Washington."[14]

Pruitt's concern, that excessive regulations (here, in the name of slowing global warming) would impede business expansion, is shared by many conservatives. President Trump, soon after arriving in office, announced a "2 for 1" requirement—that every new regulatory action by an executive agency or department had to be accompanied by the *elimination* of two existing rules. A year later, Trump exulted "No president has ever cut so many regulations in their entire term... as we have cut in less than a year."[15] But, as we saw in Chapter 15, thousands of career civil servants and a thicket of existing rules and regulations make significant changes difficult. In fact, rulemaking has proceeded under Trump at a pace not much different from previous presidencies (Figure 17.2).

Remember this key lesson from our discussion of public policy implementation. As with all steps in the policy process, rulemaking involves politics alongside the technical details.

Top-Down Delivery. Once the final rule setting out a policy's details has been issued, it is time to provide the benefits or regulations that the law was designed to produce. As the American national government stepped up its level of domestic policy activity following World War II, delivery of public services was established as a "top-down" process. Confident in the wake of victory, American and British architects of the new science of public policy proclaimed that the executive branch, working from clear goals and strategies, could deliver government services in a coherent, transparent manner. They saw cabinet secretaries and agency heads as firmly in charge of the process. Lower-level bureaucrats and "policy clients" (the

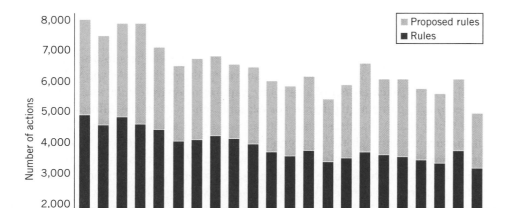

Rules and Proposed Rules in the Federal Register, 1996–2017

● **Figure 17.2** *Rules and proposed rules in the Federal Register. (Federal Register dataset, QuantGov, Jonathan Nelson and Patrick McLaughlin)*

people government was serving) were mainly concerned with *compliance*, or doing what they were told to do.

Many policy planners still promote this top-down model of delivering government benefits and services. It can work when a policy is relatively simple, with clear, well-specified goals that are not difficult to meet. Imagine a national ban on sales of a food product found to be tainted by potentially fatal bacteria, for example. A high-ranking figure, such as the secretary of agriculture or the head of the Food and Drug Administration, issues a public warning. Government inspectors ensure that the dangerous product is removed from grocery shelves, law enforcement officials investigate the cause of the outbreak, and prosecutions may follow. The public's role is simple: avoid the tainted product. The policy aim is clear, as are the lines of authority.

● *Tainted food—and top-down policy response. When the Food and Drug Administration (FDA) receives reports about possibly dangerous food products—like these Goldfish-brand crackers in 2018—the agency, along with the Department of Agriculture, supervises a national top-down recall.*

As you know well by now, the world of politics and policymaking is rarely so straightforward. Most issues involve many interested actors, leading to struggles over jurisdiction. Four different House and Senate committees, in addition to a Justice Department special prosecutor and FBI leadership, investigated Russian interference in the 2016 U.S. presidential election; Congress also passed multiple laws to sanction Russia and protect against future election meddling. Policy goals can be ambiguous or confusing, slowing executive bureaucrats' ability to enact new regulations or hand out services. Our federalist system, described in Chapter 4, does not help matters by creating multiple levels of jurisdiction. Authorities are frequently stymied in their attempts to police pot growers, for example, given all the conflicting local, state, and federal regulations governing medicinal marijuana—especially with

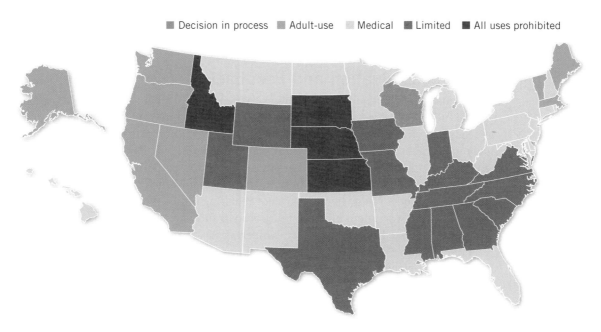

■ Decision in process ■ Adult-use ■ Medical ■ Limited ■ All uses prohibited

● **Figure 17.3** *Marijuana policy in the states, as of fall 2018. A series of conflicting federal (including Congress, executive agencies, and courts) and state policy decisions has left this area a patchwork—illustrating the complexity of policy implementation. (National Cannabis Industry Association)*

several states and Washington, DC, now permitting limited legal marijuana sales (see Figure 17.3).[16]

Bottom-Up Delivery. For complicated policies, "bottom-up" provisions of public services or regulations can be more effective than top-down efforts to command and control outcomes. Bottom-up service delivery starts with street-level bureaucrats, introduced in Chapter 15; recall that these officials work directly with recipients of government benefits. Examples include the social worker who calls on needy families to make sure their food stamps have arrived, the IRS agent who checks to confirm that your charitable claims are all legitimate donations, and the air-traffic controller who brings your flight safely in for landing.

All these policy providers and regulators work directly with the public, and they can exercise discretion in making decisions. Certainly a hierarchy is still in place, with cabinet secretaries and agency heads at the top. But when street-level officials are allowed a measure of autonomy, or input into decision making, government services are often delivered more efficiently and regulations are put in place with less disruption. These street-level actors may even ignore superiors' orders and do what they consider best, based on their experience.

Is this democracy in action—or bureaucracy run amok? Think of residence advisors (RAs) in college and university dormitories. Although vice presidents and deans set official policies for dorm residents, RAs—who are usually students themselves—are directly aware of the needs and concerns of residents on their hall or floor. Academic studies have chronicled how these "street-level" RAs bring their personal experience and knowledge of individual students to improving the implementation of residence-hall rules and benefits.[17] Sometimes this may mean bending university regulations to make sure the residents' needs are served; occasionally, those rules are later revised as a result of an RA's timely suggestion. The same thing happens across the federal bureaucracy: Street-level employees who are directly aware of a policy's effects may change their practices to make sure a program performs effectively.

5. Policy Evaluation and Feedback

Let us imagine that a policy problem has made it onto the agenda and been framed successfully. A solution has been formulated, passed into law, and implemented: The new service is being delivered or the new regulation put in place. Do these accomplishments mean our policymaking story has ended? Not at all. It is still essential to confirm whether a new benefit or regulation actually works.

This is the stage of policy evaluation. Does a school-lunch program need tweaking in practice because its benefits are not reaching many kids? Should we abandon an ineffective government effort to reduce tax fraud and try something else? Policy evaluators analyze how well a policy is meeting its stated goals.

Policymaking proceeds in a context of uncertainty: Even armed with ex ante analyses, no one can be sure how a policy will play out in practice. Therefore, it is essential to evaluate programs after implementation, or ex post, to determine how well they are working and make adjustments. The outcome may include devising yet another new policy to address changes rippling out from one recently put in place.

Ex Post Policy Evaluations. Ideally, evaluators would track every new government benefit or regulation to see how well it works. Because of resource constraints, that does not happen, but many policies are subjected to at least occasional ex post evaluations. These tend to follow a prescribed sequence. An evaluator compares a policy program to the original goals that Congress and executive branch rule-makers had in mind, according to an established set of criteria. The evaluator could be a government agency, an academic or think tank analyst, an interest group, a court-appointed independent authority, or sometimes all of these, as prominent programs often attract multiple evaluations. The evaluator collects and assesses relevant information, using data if available; makes a judgment about program effectiveness; and issues recommendations.[18]

At best, these steps add up to a reasonably objective analysis. If a policy is performing in line with its designers' goals, it should be left alone. If not, a good ex post evaluation will point out how the policy could be altered to improve performance. But rarely is policymaking that straightforward.

When a law is introduced, advocates fight hard to frame it positively, advance the legislation through Congress, and win the president's signature. Many of them remain engaged during the rulemaking process to make sure it is rolled out as they expected. Now imagine an ex post evaluation that suggests the policy is not working well. These supporters probably will not agree that their extensive efforts were in vain. Instead, they may criticize the evaluation for flawed methodology and commission a competing review. Likewise, in the face of a positive evaluation, the opposition—which fought against the new policy all the way from framing to rulemaking—rarely gives up and admits that its criticisms were wrong.

A Case in Point: Gang Violence. The apparently simple evaluator's question—Does the policy work?—is not often answered in a clear, unambiguous way. Take the issue of reducing youth gang violence. Some policymakers have argued for years that a "fight fire with fire" approach is the only sound one: boost police presence, including intrusive stop-and-frisk policies; toughen the penalties for youthful gang involvement; and treat even a first conviction with a long sentence, in harsh prison conditions.

A few years ago, a different idea surfaced in the form of a program called Ceasefire (since renamed "Cure Violence"). The brainchild of David Kennedy, a criminal justice professor, Cure Violence organized "call-ins"—meetings that brought together suspected young gang members with community leaders, ex-gang offenders, religious figures, prosecutors, and police. Organizers offered the youth in attendance counseling, job leads, and an opportunity to talk frankly without fear of reprisal. At the same time, the youth were warned that any hint of violent activity in the future would result in widespread arrests. Not only the offenders but their network of associates would be hauled into court as well.[19]

● Evaluating anti-gang policies. Cure Violence, initially a controversial policy that was widely adopted after ex post evaluations demonstrated some success. Scientific evaluations of the program continue.

Cure Violence has been implemented in dozens of cities, both large ones such as Boston, New York, and Chicago, and smaller places like High Point, North Carolina, and Erie, Pennsylvania. Evaluators have reached mixed conclusions about how well Cure Violence works.[20] By some measures, such as reducing violent crime during the first few weeks after implementation, Cure Violence appears preferable to tough police tactics. By other metrics, the program seems to have made little difference. Rates of youth unemployment in some neighborhoods have hardly changed, nor have longer-term trends in violent crime. Faced with mixed messages, should a mayor invest in Cure Violence in response to the spread of youth gangs? Policy evaluation, like much else in U.S. policymaking, is as much an art as a science.

Policy Feedback. New policies, once implemented, do not just play out in a vacuum. They in turn shape and constrain future policymaking, as a growing body of political science research shows. Scholars term this process *policy feedback*.

A program that distributes benefits will attract loyal supporters who will push for its extension. Lawmakers seeking to reform or cancel the program (perhaps based on an ex post evaluation) can find their efforts thwarted by these grateful recipients. More subtly, as a policy is rolled out, actors of various types will adapt to the policy, making it difficult to change. Bureaucrats get organized to administer a benefit; businesses rework their economic forecasts to account for a new regulatory framework. Political scientist Paul Pierson described these tendencies as **path dependence**: Once a policy is established, possibilities for reform or change are constrained by the "path" it has followed through implementation and service delivery.[21]

A classic example of a policy with powerful feedback effects is Social Security, passed in 1935. By introducing a language of "entitlement," the designers of Social Security achieved far-reaching effects. Senior citizens feel that they have earned their right to receive old-age government benefits. Millions of Americans organize their investment decisions and retirement planning around the path created by Social Security. This makes it virtually untouchable by policymakers.

Path dependence: Social-science term for how policymakers' choices are shaped by institutional "paths" that result from policy choices made in the past.

The Bottom Line

» U.S. policymaking involves five stages. Policies do not proceed neatly from one to the next, but the "stages" idea is a useful way of distinguishing among different actions carried out by policy officials.

» The first of these stages is agenda setting, whereby concerns receiving widespread attention become policy issues.

» A second stage is problem definition and framing, featuring debates about how to describe an issue and which solutions are most viable.

» A third stage is policy formation, a process of legislative and executive activity to develop the policy idea in concrete terms.

» A fourth stage is policy implementation, marked by rulemaking and service delivery.

» A fifth stage includes evaluation and policy feedback, steps that help determine whether a policy works—and that often start the debate all over again.

U.S. Social Policy

Public policy comes in many forms, as the various examples earlier in this chapter attest. *Fiscal policy* has to do with matters of finance, such as monetary supply and taxes; we address fiscal matters later in this chapter when we look at federal budgeting. *Foreign policy* covers topics including wars, defense, diplomacy, and trade agreements; we devote Chapter 18 to those. Most other issues are grouped together as *social policy*, or matters having to do with people's individual or group well-being. Health, housing, education, employment, criminal justice, child welfare, and old age security: all these vital areas make up social policy. Also under this heading are controversial topics such as abortion, same-sex marriage, and recreational drug use.

Compared to industrialized Western European countries, the United States was slow to adopt modern social policies at a national level. Old-age insurance, for example, was provided in Germany as far back as 1883 and in Great Britain in 1911. Yet not until the mid-1930s and Franklin Roosevelt's New Deal was a similar policy (Social Security) established here. Many advanced democracies enacted universal health insurance starting in the 1880s; the United States still does not guarantee healthcare to all its citizens. Americans' embrace of self-help individualist doctrines and its long-standing resistance to "big government," along with a federalist structure that provides a patchwork of benefits through state and local officials, helps explain the distinctive (and slow) growth of social policymaking in the United States.

From colonial days onward, "poor relief" offered support for needy Americans, inspired by both religious tenets and laws inherited from Elizabethan England. Benefits were limited, however—and came with a price. People on relief sometimes faced the loss of their personal property and the right to vote. The able-bodied unemployed were often forced to work or were jailed, although laws varied from state to state. Even with all these conditions, until the Civil War, poor relief was the largest single budget item in most American towns and cities.[22] And the term was still used well into the twentieth century, especially during the Great Depression.

Wars and Social Policy

Wars and their aftermath were the source of most major social policy advances during the first century and a half after the Constitution was ratified. The Revolutionary War inspired the earliest state-level efforts to administer organized benefits. In New York, for example, a "Committee on Superintendence of the Poor" was created to aid people who lost their homes during the fighting. After the Civil War, national government benefits flowed to soldiers and their families. The first old-age pensions were provided to Union Army veterans during the late nineteenth century. Their mothers, widows, and children later received some state support, including monthly welfare payments and regulations on child labor—the sons and daughters of soldiers who died in combat should not be forced to work, the argument went.[23]

● During the Great Depression new federal social policies were created at a rapid clip. Traditional policies, such as "poor relief," were expanded as well in response to social need.

A more recent instance of a war-related policy is the GI Bill, passed in 1944 to reward American troops returning from World War II with a heavily subsidized college education. The bill's designers expected that soldiers themselves would benefit from attending college; a secondary hope was that U.S. labor markets would be able to adjust gradually to millions of newly returned soldiers as universities absorbed many of the veterans.

What policymakers did not expect is that American higher education would be transformed by the GI Bill, as colleges and universities expanded to meet the needs of 4.4 million soldiers turned students—many of them with fewer family resources than the traditionally better-off young men and women who attended U.S. colleges before 1945. Moreover, many GI Bill beneficiaries, political scientist Suzanne Mettler demonstrated, went on to become unusually civic-minded Americans.[24] College attendance continued to grow in subsequent years, aided by a host of new government programs (policy feedback again!) stretching from Pell Grants and low-interest student loans, both established in the 1960s, to the American Opportunity Tax Credit, passed in 2010 and recently extended beyond 2018.

War's domestic equivalent is grave economic hardship, and the Great Depression, starting in 1929, helped lead to more extensive federal social policies, many arising from Franklin Roosevelt's New Deal. Among the numerous social programs run or financed by the U.S. government today, three of the longest lived and most extensive deserve attention here.

Old-Age Insurance: Social Security

Assess current debates on Social Security.

Since its enactment in 1935, Social Security has provided Americans aged 65 and older—provided they have lived in the United States at least five years—with a monthly living stipend. The minimum age was recently raised to 66, and Congress has discussed increasing it by another year or two. Social Security payments vary with income: A worker who retires making $65,000 a year would currently receive around $1,813 per month. The original act also created an unemployment insurance program (more on that later), paid benefits to disabled workers and their families, and offered financial assistance to low-income families with children.

One constant over the years: Social Security's financing comes from a payroll tax on all eligible workers.

The Social Security Act initially excluded a wide range of occupations from the program, primarily limiting benefits (and payroll-tax contributions) to white males. In subsequent years, such jobs as teachers, nurses, domestic helpers, librarians, and agricultural laborers were added to the act's coverage, effectively creating the first universal social policy in American history. Although the program began small—with only 53 thousand beneficiaries in 1937, the first full year of implementation, who together received a little over $1.2 million in benefits—it grew rapidly. In 2018, Social Security paid some $984 billion to more than 63 million workers, supported by payroll taxes from more than 142 million employees. At nearly 5 percent of the nation's **gross domestic product (GDP)**, Social Security is the largest single federal government program.

Gross domestic product (GDP): The value of all the goods and services produced in a nation over a year. For 2019, the U.S. GDP is an estimated $21.4 trillion.

Although the old-age benefits provided by Social Security have helped lift many seniors out of poverty, for decades alarms have been sounded about financially supporting the program. Those concerns deepen today, as the huge baby boomer generation increasingly receives benefits. How urgent is the problem? Many moderates and conservatives argue that Social Security poses a dangerous economic risk as it moves inexorably toward a one trillion dollar annual cost. Many liberals accuse conservatives of exaggerating the threat and argue that relatively small adjustments (increasing the retirement age, raising taxes, limiting benefits) will fix the problem. Once again: a debate over problem definition. However serious the problem, the system is extremely difficult to reform and changes are routinely rejected. Social Security's sacrosanct status has given rise to a colorful metaphor borrowed from electrified train lines: Touch the "third rail" surging with electricity, say railroad workers, and you will receive a fatal shock. Likewise, politicians refer to Social Security as the "third rail of American politics": Propose major changes, and electoral penalties will swiftly follow.

Unemployment Benefits

As the Great Depression stretched into the 1930s, some 34 million Americans (more than a quarter of the 122 million population) lived in households with no full-time wage earner. Across the United States, unemployment rates reached shocking levels, topping out at 80 percent of able-bodied adults in Toledo, Ohio. In 1932, Wisconsin became the first state to provide cash assistance to temporarily jobless residents. Three years later, the Social Security Act included a provision for joint federal–state unemployment benefits, funded like old-age insurance through a payroll tax on employees. States administer the program, with federal oversight and funding assistance.

● *Ida May Fuller, the first recipient (in 1940) of a monthly Social Security check for $22.54.*

During the recent major recession, unemployment levels rose from less than 4 percent in 2008 to above 10 percent in 2009. A federal supplement to laid-off workers extended eligibility for unemployment benefits to 99 weeks, up from the 26 weeks that most states provide. Costs soared accordingly, and Republicans sought to scale back the extra federal assistance. With unemployment rates dropping only slowly, job creation—and the cost of benefits for unemployed workers—was a central issue in the 2010 and 2012 elections. By 2016, unemployment had dropped below 5 percent, and issues such as raising the minimum wage and narrowing the huge gap between richest and poorest Americans moved up the policy agenda.

Health and Disability: Medicare/Medicaid

Explore Medicare/ Medicaid policies in depth.

In the early 1960s, America ranked as the wealthiest nation in the world, but barely half of the nation's seniors had health insurance. Even with Social Security, an estimated third of those over 65 lived in poverty, in significant part because of the cost of healthcare.

Lyndon Johnson, fresh from a landslide election victory in 1964, promoted health insurance coverage for all Americans over 65 as part of his Great Society plan. Critics fought hard against the proposed new social benefit. Johnson's Republican opponent in that election, Arizona senator Barry Goldwater, tapped into a long-lived American vein of disapproval for handouts: "Having given our pensioners their medical care in kind, why not food baskets, why not public housing accommodations, why not vacation resorts, why not a ration of cigarettes for those who smoke and of beer for those who drink?"[25]

After a Democratic landslide in 1964, Congress passed Medicare (in 1965) as an amendment to the Social Security Act. As with old-age and unemployment benefits, Medicare was financed through a payroll tax on employees. And as with

What Do YOU Think?   Should We Reform Social Security and Medicare?

Social Security and Medicare are perhaps the two most fiercely defended U.S. government programs. Some analysts suggest that their continued rapid growth (together, these programs cost more than $1.75 *trillion* in 2019) is outpacing U.S. taxpayers' ability to support them. Concerned policymakers and academics float ideas such as raising the eligibility age for these programs: currently 66, and rising for Social Security to 67 in coming years; further boosting that eligibility age to 68 or even 70 would save tens of billions of dollars—but also delay older Americans' ability to begin drawing these vital benefits.[26] Any hint of a cut in either and senior citizens respond vehemently, as do the House and Senate members who represent them. Are you willing to tackle cutting Social Security and Medicare (and, while you are at it, Medicaid)?

Yes, reform the Social Security and Medicare programs. The budget savings of even minor adjustments— such as raising the eligibility age—would be immense.

No, leave Social Security and Medicare intact. The political fallout would certainly be enormous, but so would the impact on the lives of seniors. Suggesting such reforms could also have long-term political consequences because the opposing party would sound the alarm immediately.

Social Security, the program grew rapidly after it was implemented in 1966. Today, some 55 million Americans receive Medicare benefits; by the late 2020s, the program is expected to serve nearly 80 million people, as the last of the baby boomer generation (born between 1945 and 1964) retire. The program's costs currently exceed $750 billion each year and are projected to grow in coming years to more than $1.5 trillion.

As the battle over Medicare raged in 1965, a companion measure to provide health insurance to disabled and low-income people, dubbed "Medicaid," was passed. Each state was encouraged (but not required) to establish a Medicaid program of its own; Arizona was the last state to sign on, in 1982. Over time, a variety of additional benefits were added to Medicaid, including dental and nursing home coverage. Today Medicaid serves over 72.5 million Americans.

Unlike other large American entitlement programs, Medicaid was established as a "means-tested" program, with benefits provided only to those below a certain income level—which varies by state and whether recipients are children or adults. For a family of three, in Texas the ceiling in 2018 was $3,740; in Washington, DC, it was $45,923. The Affordable Care Act initially included a requirement that all states provide Medicaid funding to everyone whose income is below 133 percent of the **federal poverty line** (nearly $34,000 in 2019, for a family of four). The Supreme Court's historic 2012 decision to uphold the ACA as constitutional, described in Chapter 16, also repudiated the universal Medicare funding requirement. Instead, each state may decide whether it will adopt the standard, which rose to 138 percent in 2018. Thirty-six states have expanded Medicaid.

Figure 17.4 displays costs for the three biggest entitlement programs (Social Security, Medicaid, and Medicare), plus interest on the U.S. federal debt, measured as a percentage of the expected U.S. GDP. Taken together, these **entitlement programs** will require very tough choices about spending on other programs and about increasing tax rates to raise the revenue required to fund them.

Policymakers debate possibilities for "bending the cost curve"—in other words, reducing their drain on the federal budget. On the plus side, the growth of American social policies has greatly reduced the number of people—especially seniors and children, arguably our most vulnerable citizens—living in dire need. Balancing those needs against the budget-busting consequences of continued program growth is among the most important policy challenges facing the country in coming years.

Federal poverty line: The annually specified level of income (separately calculated for individuals and families) below which people are considered to live in poverty, and eligible for certain federal benefits. For 2019, the poverty line is set at $25,100 for a family of four.

Entitlement program: A government benefit program whose recipients are *entitled* by law to receive payments. Social Security, Medicare, and Medicaid are the three largest.

● **Figure 17.4** *Spending on the largest entitlement programs plus interest on the U.S. national debt totals around 14 percent of U.S. GDP. That figure (green line) is projected to sharply increase in coming years; compare defense (blue line) and other spending (gold line), which remain flat relative to GDP.* (Wall Street Journal)

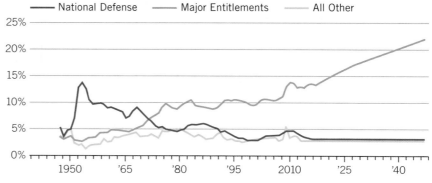

Where the Money Goes
Federal spending as a percentage of GDP, 1947–2047

Note: 2018–2047 projections

Economic Policymaking: Fiscal and Monetary Policy

People judge their governments foremost on their economic performance. Despite scandalous affairs as well as domestic and foreign-policy disappointments, Bill Clinton's presidency is widely considered a success: the economy roared ahead during his time in office. On the other hand, Clinton's predecessor, George H. W. Bush, after the Gulf War (1990–1991) enjoyed the highest popularity rating in modern history. Barely a year later, an economic downturn battered Bush's public opinion ratings and left him a one-term president.

Economic policy is carried out in two primary ways. Government decisions about taxing and spending—generally managed through the budget process described in the following sections—is termed **fiscal policy**. Managing the economy through central banks' control of the money supply, directly affecting unemployment and inflation rates, is known as **monetary policy**. Let us look at each in turn.

Fiscal Policy

Well into the twentieth century, the U.S. government's fiscal policy was described as "laissez-faire," a French term meaning "leave it alone." Most presidents and congressional leaders sought to balance the (relatively small) federal budget, with limited tax or spending authority. That approach changed during wartime, when military needs drove tax collections and spending temporarily much higher.

During the Great Depression, national economic devastation led Franklin Roosevelt and his "brain trust" of policy advisors to more actively manage fiscal policy. Immense New Deal programs were funded through government spending on an unprecedented scale. The resulting budget deficits—federal funds flowing out much faster than tax revenues coming in—reflected a Keynesian approach to national economic policy, named for the influential British and later American economist John Maynard Keynes. Keynes recommended "pump-priming" during economic downturns: pouring government funds into a faltering economy and cutting taxes, giving consumers and businesses enough confidence (and cash) to start spending and hiring again.

Following close on the Depression came World War II, which resulted in a great spike in government spending. At the height of the war in 1943, the federal deficit reached an all-time high of 30 percent of GDP. After the war, American policymakers, brimming with confidence about their ability to manage the economy,

Fiscal policy: Taxing and spending policies carried out by government, generally in an effort to affect national economic development.

Monetary policy: Actions of central banks, which in the United States culminate in the Federal Reserve, designed primarily to maximize employment and moderate inflation.

adopted active taxing and spending policies as a routine national practice. Since then, through conservative and liberal presidents and across Democratic and Republican control of Congress, fiscal policy has continued to serve as a means of securing the general welfare of the American public.

The parties do differ on which fiscal levers to pull. Facing an economic downturn, Democrats are more likely to favor expanded spending—hence the large stimulus package passed early in the Obama presidency, designed to rescue the national economy from the brink of disaster. Republicans generally prefer tax cuts, on the argument that the economy benefits as consumers spend more of the windfall.[27] Hence party leaders, including President Trump, praised the 2017 tax cut as fueling economic growth through 2018.[28]

Though fiscal policymaking may sound straightforward—or even boring, given what can seem like minor technical changes to tax or spending levels—few policy areas are more controversial in practice. In summer 2018, for example, for the second consecutive year a government shutdown loomed, as Congress and the White House debated budget details. "Our budget process is totally broken," lamented Republican Senator Bob Corker (R-Tenn.).[29]

Monetary Policy

Explore the concepts of monetary and fiscal policy.

Following the collapse of the venerable Lehman Brothers investment bank in fall 2008, with other giant financial institutions tottering, the U.S. government leapt into action. Surprisingly, the main actors were not presidents or congressional leaders, but more obscure figures: the Federal Reserve chairman, the treasury secretary, and the chair of the Federal Reserve Bank of New York. And the economic tools they applied had nothing to do with increasing (or cutting) taxes or spending: Instead, the conversation was about liquidity and the national money supply.[30]

These experts were deploying monetary policy in response to the gravest financial crisis in 75 years. By manipulating the national money supply and interest rates, they aimed to increase employment while holding inflation (the rate at which the price of goods and services rises) in check. Such efforts also can impact expectations about economic performance. Although the White House and Congress are the chief institutional architects of fiscal policy, monetary shifts are carried out by central bankers: In the United States, the main actor is the Federal Reserve System, comprising a headquarters in Washington, DC, along with 12 bank branches around the country. The current Federal Reserve (or "Fed," in Washington-speak) director is Jerome Powell.

The Federal Reserve can deploy several tools, such as buying Treasury securities and setting required dollar reserve levels that banks are required to hold, that allow them to influence interest rates. The Fed reduces interest rates to stimulate economic growth, making it easier for businesses to borrow money to expand production and hiring or invest in research and development. Likewise, individuals can borrow at lower interest rates to buy new homes or consumer goods. If, however,

● Though rarely recognized in public, Federal Reserve chair Jerome Powell is a key figure in managing the nation's money supply—a central feature of U.S. economic policy.

economic demand is growing too fast, the Fed raises interest rates to reduce inflationary pressures that raise prices and result in an economic slowdown.

Think of the Federal Reserve as performing an essential balancing act—enabling growth when the economy balks, but slowing things down to ease inflation as the economy heats up. And during crisis times, the Fed and its monetary policy is often the strongest means of sustaining our national economy. Because presidents are judged on economic performance, they often seek to influence Federal Reserve actions—but, like other parts of the bureaucracy, the agency prides itself on independence.

The Bottom Line

» The U.S. government employs both fiscal policy and monetary policy to affect the economy.

» Taxes and spending are the two main levers of fiscal policy. During economic downturns, Republicans prefer to enact tax cuts; Democrats favor spending programs.

» The Federal Reserve is the main architect of monetary policy. By adjusting interest rates and the national supply of money, the Fed works to affect inflation and unemployment.

Economic Policymaking: The Federal Budget Process

"It's a good policy idea, but we don't have the budget to pursue it." That phrase has been repeated countless times in Washington in recent years, as American policymaking has become more oriented around the budget. This bottom-line focus owes primarily to the U.S. **federal budget deficit**—the gap between how much our national government spends and how much we take in through taxes and fees. The deficit for fiscal year 2019, which began October 1, 2018, is projected by the nonpartisan Congressional Budget Office at slightly over $1 trillion dollars, around 4.7 percent of GDP; in 2016, that figure was 2.5 percent (still far short of 2009's record high deficit of $1.3 trillion, or 9.8 percent of GDP).

Federal deficits have, after several years of decline, begun to grow again after the 2017 tax cut. Along with reduced tax revenue, spending is increasing, especially because the most expensive trio of entitlement programs—Social Security, Medicare, and Medicaid—continue to grow rapidly. Together, they now cost an annual $2.2 trillion, half the entire 2019 U.S. budget.

Can the historic deficits projected for coming years be reversed, and is such an effort even desirable? To tackle budget reform, it is essential first to grasp the basics of how national government budgeting works. As we will see, much of American domestic policymaking is organized around our budget process.

Budget politics involves three primary stages, established by a pair of laws: the Budget and Accounting Act of 1921, passed in an age of much smaller American national government; and the Congressional Budget and Impoundment Control Act, passed in 1974 during a time of political turmoil and economic recession. The process begins with the White House (see Figure 17.5).

Federal budget deficit: The gap between revenues received by the national government (primarily through individual income and corporate taxes) and spending on all public programs.

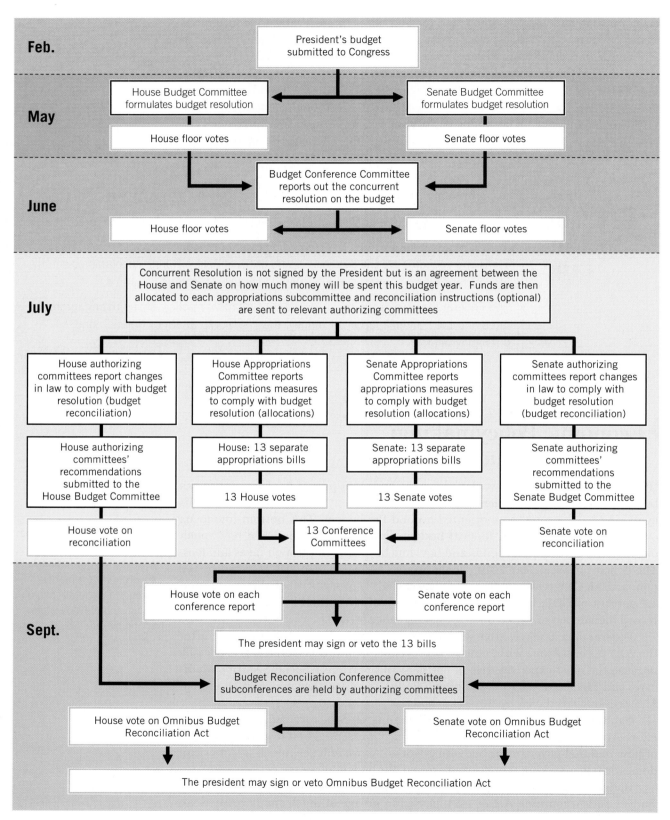

Figure 17.5 *The U.S. federal budget process (House Budget Committee).*

President's Budget Proposal

Since the 1921 Budget and Accounting Act, presidents have been the first movers in federal budgeting. The United States starts its **fiscal year** (**FY**) each October 1, so FY 2019 began October 1, 2018. For each approaching fiscal year, the White House submits to Congress in early February a proposed budget. This document details projected federal spending for thousands of different government programs. The process of assembling that February proposal begins many months earlier in the executive branch, with each cabinet department and federal agency compiling its expected spending totals. The Office of Management and Budget has the massive task of coordinating all these estimates; the Treasury Department chimes in with expected revenue figures. New presidential priorities are included as well.

Unlike in most other countries, the president's budget proposal lacks any statutory authority. Congress is free to ignore it completely, as it did with President Obama's budget proposal in 2016 as well as Donald Trump's two years later (see Comparing Nations 17.1). But the proposal's release by the White House is still a major event. Advocacy groups howl when funding for their pet projects is cut (or not increased enough), and businesses jockey to minimize the costs of new regulations or taxes. Congressional committees with budget responsibilities schedule hearings to question cabinet heads and senior presidential aides, and media organizations compile helpful charts.

Fiscal year (FY): In budget calculations, the "new year" beginning October 1 and ending the following September 30. Organized many decades ago for accounting purposes.

Congressional Budget Resolution

While executive branch analysts feed figures into the White House budget proposal, congressional budget experts create their own blueprint for spending and revenues, known as a **budget resolution**. Congressional budget resolutions are not binding laws, and do not require a presidential signature. Instead, they provide a general "sense of Congress" about budgetary expectations and are meant to guide the committees responsible for finishing the budget during summer and fall.

Budget resolutions are less detailed than the president's several-hundred-page proposal. They set out overarching spending expectations in 19 broad categories, known as "budget functions." Budget committees in both the House and

Budget resolution: A joint House–Senate creation that outlines targets for federal spending, revenue levels, and the resultant budget deficit (or surplus) for the coming fiscal year.

COMPARING NATIONS 17.1 | Budget Policymaking

Nearly all countries grant their chief executive the power to introduce spending bills. The U.S. president merely prepares a budget proposal, however, which Congress largely ignores. The national legislatures of most other countries hold a single, up-or-down binding vote on the executive's budget, with no amendments allowed. None has anything like the elaborate American tangle of budget resolutions, subcommittees, and reconciliation. Chief executives in other countries also have "line-item veto" authority, allowing them to eliminate individual budget items they do not like. Every recent U.S. president has called for

line-item power, with only Bill Clinton managing to persuade Congress to pass it; the Supreme Court struck it down soon afterward. Partly as a result of their centralized and streamlined procedures, few other countries feature a budget deficit as large as America's; however, the U.S. deficit is a smaller portion of all economic activity (a smaller percentage of gross domestic product) than the deficit in several other advanced nations. Many factors feed into the large U.S. deficit, but the size of the deficit inspires innovative thinking about how we might reorganize budget policymaking.

Discover how to
balance the budget.

the Senate, created by the 1974 Congressional Budget and Impoundment Control Act, carry out the bulk of this work. Each committee spends several months assembling a budget resolution, which must pass the full chamber. Senate and House versions are inevitably different, and they must be reconciled in a conference committee. The joint outcome, formally known as a "concurrent budget resolution," is supposed to be approved by April 15 of each year. Owing to partisan differences and other political battles, these resolutions are almost always late. Over the past 40 years, Congress has approved a budget resolution on schedule only six times. In 2018, neither House nor Senate managed to pass a budget resolution at all.

Reign of the Cardinals: Appropriations Committee Action

The two budget committees were created in 1974 to simplify the unwieldy process of creating a budget and funding government programs. Unfortunately, Congress at the time left the old rules in place. As a result, the budget process got more complicated, not less.

A separate step in this process involves the Appropriations Committees in the House and the Senate, which are charged with specifying which departments and programs will get how much money. Recall from Chapter 13 that because of their central role in spending decisions members of Appropriations are informally known on Capitol Hill as "cardinals" after the high-ranking Vatican officials. The cardinals split budget authority into 13 separate jurisdictions (see Table 17.4). Critics complain that these divisions—which date back to 1921, with occasional revisions—make little sense. Some areas are far smaller than others: the District of Columbia appropriation is around $645 million yearly, less than 1/100th of the $700-plus billion for national defense. Others reflect outmoded decisions: Military construction is handled separately from defense, for example.

TABLE 17.4 **Appropriations Subcommittees: Areas of Jurisdiction**

Agriculture; Food and Drug Administration
Departments of Commerce, Justice, and State
Department of Defense
District of Columbia
Energy and Water Development
Foreign Operations
Department of Interior
Departments of Labor, Health and Human Services, and Education
Legislative Branch
Military Construction
Department of Transportation
Department of Treasury; U.S. Postal Service
Department of Housing and Urban Development; Veterans Administration

Each of these 13 areas is assigned to a separate Appropriations subcommittee in the House and Senate. Each subcommittee handles budget planning for all policy areas under its jurisdiction. Some, such as Labor, Health and Human Services, and Education (known informally on the Hill as "Labor-H"), supervise thousands of individual programs. Appropriations' cardinals must remain attentive to the budget resolution blueprint, which is monitored by yet another set of budget "authorizing committees" in each chamber. If spending on all the programs in the Appropriations Committees' jurisdiction exceeds the total specified in the resolution, they must go back and make changes to bring it into line.

After a subcommittee approves its bill with program-by-program spending authorization, the measure must pass the full Appropriations Committee in that chamber. If successful, it heads to the House or Senate floor. Each of the appropriations bills attracts intense attention from House and Senate members, who strive to add amendments funding their favorite programs. If an appropriations bill survives the floor vote in its chamber, a House–Senate conference committee is all but inevitable. This step provides another opportunity for members seeking financial benefits for their district—or lobbyists pushing a client's pet provision—to weigh in. Once the two sides agree in conference, the identical version is voted on in both House and Senate and sent to the president for consideration.

Because they only deal with **discretionary programs**, which require legislative action to explicitly authorize spending, the 13 appropriations bills cover only about a third of all U.S. government spending. Compare the large entitlement programs we read about earlier: Social Security, Medicare, and Medicaid. These are considered *mandatory spending* because they are funded annually, based on a formula, without requiring Congress's reauthorization each year. Thus, a giant chunk of the U.S. federal budget, nearly two trillion dollars, is essentially untouchable. Unless Congress elects to change the spending formula for a program such as Social Security, which would arouse anger from beneficiaries, those funds—with guaranteed annual increases—flow automatically.

Appropriations bills are supposed to be signed by September 1. With the start of the fiscal year looming on October 1, federal agencies and departments have a month to finalize their plans for spending funds and delivering services. As with other deadlines in the budget process, this September 1 marker is far more often missed than hit: 1995 was the last time that all 13 appropriations bills were passed before the new fiscal year.

What happens when one or more bills are not approved? As the new fiscal year approaches, with spending decisions necessary before federal funds can begin flowing, Congress may combine all the outstanding appropriations measures into a single "omnibus" spending bill. This can be thousands of pages long, listing funding for as many as 12 thousand separate programs. It is unlikely that anyone will read every line, especially as this legislation is typically cobbled together with only days or even hours to spare before the September 30 end to the fiscal year.

More often than not in recent years, Congress fails even to pass an omnibus bill, leaving some areas unfunded as the new fiscal year opens. In that case, the president asks Congress to pass a **continuing resolution** (**CR**), which keeps the dollars flowing—usually at the just-ended fiscal year's rate—for a specified period, usually two weeks or a month. In some years, Congress is forced to pass CR after CR. Otherwise, the government officially runs out of spending authority for discretionary programs and shuts down—as almost happened in 2017. President Trump, in his first budget cycle, warned that he would not again tolerate a giant omnibus bill followed by continuing resolutions. Congress clearly got the message, as

Discretionary programs: Non-entitlement program spending, subject to the decision ("discretion") of Congress each year.

Continuing resolution (CR): A congressionally approved act required when no national budget has been passed before the start of a new fiscal year. This extends spending at current levels for a prescribed period of time.

appropriations bills during 2018 moved through the process close to the published schedule.

All big decisions are affected by the budget because every government action has significant financial implications. And because most budget decisions have winners and losers—more money for my program means less for yours—this is one of the most politically charged aspects of policymaking. Who gets what, when, and how? In the United States, we make those decisions in significant part through our budget process.

Budgeting also underscores many of this book's basic lessons about politics and government. Separated powers slow the process by encouraging bargaining, battling, and compromise. The central place of economic efficiency in policymaking is reinforced by a politics organized around budgeting. Cost-benefit calculations are made in monetary terms, after all. Ultimately, budgeting involves the fundamental choices that help define how we Americans see ourselves.

The Bottom Line

» The U.S. budget process, when on schedule, runs from early February through October 1 and encompasses a presidential proposal, a concurrent budget resolution, and appropriations bills.

» In practice, the process rarely runs on time, and various "fixes" like omnibus bills and continuing resolutions have been invented to keep the budget system functioning.

» Although the details can be obscure, budget battles in Washington are almost always among the most dramatic features of U.S. policymaking because of the high stakes that are involved.

Making Good Policy

You now have a handle on how policymaking works, as well as an introduction to economic policies and our largest social programs. Does this system produce desirable outcomes? That is a thorny question; it is by no means clear what counts as a "good" policy, or even how we would decide. But underpinning the heated discussions over U.S. policy—especially social policies—are three basic categories of questions:

- Is the proposed policy *feasible*? Can it attract enough votes in Congress to pass, and will the president sign? And will it stand up to judicial scrutiny, if it winds up in the courts?

- Is the proposed policy *fair*? Is it the right thing to do? Does it correspond to widely held values such as equality and fairness? Or does it benefit one group, perhaps already in a favored position, at the expense of others?

- Is the proposed policy *effective*? Do the expected benefits of the policy outweigh its estimated costs? Are there more *efficient*—faster or cheaper—ways to achieve the desired aims?

Each of these questions leads to extended debates; these issues are rarely re-solved before a policy goes into effect. But most high-profile policy proposals in-spire sustained attention to these three dimensions: political (feasibility), moral (fairness/equity), and economic (effectiveness, usually measured in cost-benefit terms). The first dimension is almost self-evident: A policy counts as politically feasible if it passes Congress and unfeasible if it fails to attract sufficient support. Of course, the next legislative session might result in a different decision. The moral and economic dimensions are where the sharpest contests over "good" domestic policy play out. Let us look at each.

Moral Policies: Justice or Democracy?

Some people—philosophers, regular citizens, politicians—say that the focus of public policy should be creating a *more just society*. In this view, the most important considerations in judging a policy's performance are equality, individual or group rights, and "distributive justice"—attention to a policy's beneficiaries and those who are negatively affected. If millions of Americans lack health insurance, some ad-vocates argue that policymakers must provide it. Policy proposals to reform the healthcare system must keep the uninsured front and center—or so insist those who view public policy through the lens of justice.

Others might agree about the importance of emphasizing justice but throw up their hands at any president's or philosopher's ability to decide what is truly egalitarian or fair. These analysts see the work of policymakers as ensuring dem-ocratic outcomes: give a majority of the people what they want. That goal sounds great in principle, but recall from Chapter 8 that it is difficult to know what any group of Americans, much less the entire populace, wants to achieve. Even if we could measure public opinion more accurately, another vital question arises: Which people should we pay attention to? Yes, there may be too many uninsured in the United States—but 84 percent of the voting public, a large majority, do have health insurance. Some of them are dubious about paying more taxes or changing the healthcare system to help others. The answer eventually involves our essential values. Asking about the right thing to do quickly comes down to that fundamental question we have raised in every chapter: Who are we—as a nation and as a people?

Economically Efficient Policies

Faced with the difficulty of determining the most just policy or the majority opinion, other policy thinkers favor a different approach. Relying on neoclassical economic theory, this view recommends the most efficient system of delivering government services. Utilize an objective assessment, such as a cost-benefit analysis, to iden-tify one policy option as preferable to another: Which provides public goods at the lowest cost? If there is a clear answer, go with that policy.

Better still, these economic theorists say, use our free-enterprise system to maxi-mize efficiency in our slow-moving, polarized policy system. Libertarian thinkers and their followers see markets as the most efficient way of organizing just about any-thing, and they are eager to apply that perspective to policymaking. Citizens should be given choices about the public programs and services they "consume."

To illustrate, again consider the topic of health insurance. Instead of govern-ment support for uninsured people, how about creating a big market for health

Views on Policymaking

DO AMERICANS FEEL THAT U.S. POLICIES ARE BENEFICIAL?

Americans rarely believe that government benefits them, and complain that politicians are self-interested and untrustworthy. In practice, U.S. officials are among the world's least corrupt, as judged by the nonpartisan Transparency International, and provide extensive benefits to people in every income category, from wealthiest (low capital-gains taxes and inheritance taxes) to least well-off (healthcare, food, and income supports).

THINK ABOUT IT

How has trust in government changed over time—and what impact did the terrorist attack of September 11, 2001, have on trust? How do Americans feel about the benefits governments provide?

Can you imagine ways to enhance Americans' trust in our national government? Surely some ways of restoring trust short of national calamity are imaginable; how, for example, might U.S. public officials might do a better job of "marketing" government benefits, including to recipients?

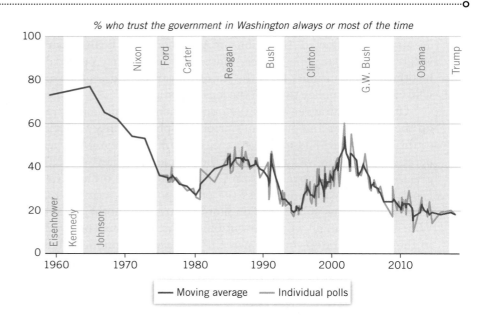

% who trust the government in Washington always or most of the time

Moving average — Individual polls

Perceived benefit from government is very low

Question: "How much would you say that you have personally benefitted from the things that government does?"

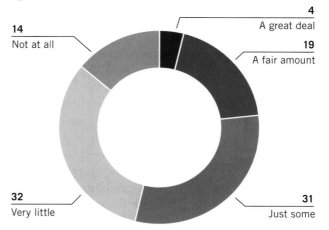

4 — A great deal
19 — A fair amount
14 — Not at all
31 — Just some
32 — Very little

554

insurance and letting Americans' economic preferences drive their decisions? If some want to be cautious about health risks and pay high premiums each month, that is their business. If others figure their chances of getting sick are minimal, there is no need to make them pay for insurance. Recent college graduates, for example, often prefer a regular cash flow to spending funds on the unlikely chance (as they see it) that they will become ill. Why not let them choose for themselves?

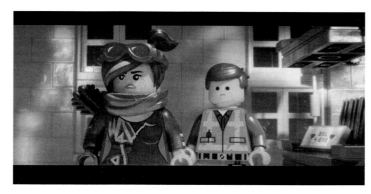

● *Characters from* The Lego Movie 2, *released in 2019. The original* Lego Movie, *featuring an evil "Lord Business" bent on planetary dominance, is among the many onscreen blockbusters that express a clear concern about the power of markets.*

Many advocates of economic efficiency believe in *rational-choice theory*, which considers individual rationality to be the basis for determining what counts as good public policy. People acting rationally will choose to maximize their self-interest; the majority—the largest group sharing an interest—will determine more and less desirable policy choices. Through market-style competitive pressures, as different companies or nonprofit organizations compete to provide services, their cost will come down, saving taxpayers money.

Although in practice Americans combine moral, majoritarian, and economic-efficiency preferences, a belief in markets' guidance has been the dominant view among policymakers, especially conservatives, in recent years. One result is the privatization of public services, discussed in Chapter 15.

Yet the "contracting out" of government functions—turning them over to private firms—is increasingly controversial. Critics of this system have multiplied, even as privatized services have spread across national, state, and local governments. Economic efficiency may be an appealing notion, but its dominance leaves many Americans uneasy. How do we know? Just head to the movies.

Capitalism Goes to the Movies

We know from opinion polls that Americans tend to prefer market-style decisions to "big-government" regulation. You might imagine that those preferences would show up in our most popular movies and books—those drawing the biggest audiences.

Instead, American popular culture displays a deep suspicion of the free-enterprise system. *Avatar*, for example—the largest-grossing film ever—is at heart a morality fable about the dangers of corporate greed, as Earth-based mining companies relentlessly pursue the not-so-subtly named mineral "unobtanium." Another high-earning blockbuster, *Captain America: Civil War*, centers on a team of superheroes refusing to work for the "restrictive capitalist system," as one character dismissively says. Even animated films, aimed primarily at children, tell a similar story. The huge-grossing *Lego Movie* features an ordinary working man turned hero who defeats the evil "Lord Business."

What does popular culture have to do with policymaking? The evident appeal of these works testifies to the different values Americans hold simultaneously. Yes, we are suspicious of big government, but we also question the benefits of big, unregulated markets.

The Bottom Line

» Although everyone wants "good" public policies passed, Americans have a hard time agreeing on what constitutes those.

» Moral arguments about equality and fairness in policymaking have declined in recent years, as attention to economic efficiency as a measure of a policy's worthiness has grown.

» One article of faith among efficiency advocates is that privatizing government programs enables more cost-effective and higher-quality services. But concerns about markets sorting out public policies also are evident. Just take a look at many popular American movies as one indicator.

Reforming U.S. Policymaking

Most would-be reformers of U.S. domestic policymaking and budgeting address specific policies, from protecting against disastrous accidents at nuclear plants to reducing youth violence. Some reformers also work at the *system* level, seeking to alter the procedures or institutions that underlie policymaking.

Systemic Reform

Critics have suggested some systemic reforms that could increase the odds of better policy-production. Term limits for members of Congress (and perhaps other federal officials) would rotate representatives and senators every six years or so, bringing a regular infusion of new blood to Washington. Perhaps the resultant sense of urgency—or the reduced need for campaign funds to run for multiple terms—would improve policymaking. Many political scientists respond that a Congress made up mostly of new and soon-departing members would lack institutional memory and legislative skills. Interest-group lobbyists likely would gain even more sway over policymaking than they already have.

Other calls to streamline the slow-moving process of policy formation range from revising the Senate filibuster and legislative-hold rules, which effectively require 60 votes to advance any policy idea, to requiring Congress to spend five-day workweeks on legislative labors in Washington. As we saw in Chapter 13, most members of the House and Senate fly back home to their district or state every Thursday afternoon, returning to the Capitol the following Tuesday—creating a "workweek" in Washington of less than three days.[31]

Political scientist Paul Light, echoing Alexander Hamilton in the *Federalist Papers*, noted the importance to good policymaking of a "government well executed." He warned that today's federal service, bogged down by lengthy hiring delays and difficulty motivating its workers, is too often a government *ill* executed. Light and fellow executive branch reformers call for a greatly streamlined hiring process, along with financial and other incentives designed to attract the "best and brightest" young Americans to work for the national government.[32]

Ambitious but manageable reforms such as these seem more achievable than a full-system overhaul. In the past decade, Congress has initiated internal reforms, such as an extensive gift ban and other ethics changes. Likewise, the Trump

Administration has proposed a major overhaul of the executive branch, as we saw in Chapter 15.

Policy Entrepreneurs

The term "policy entrepreneur" identifies those who generate new ideas, help move them up policy agendas, translate them into workable proposals, and sometimes help implement them. These entrepreneurs are frequently young, often just out of college. They have not been part of the regular policymaking system long enough to be subject to "groupthink," the tendency to recycle familiar (and sometimes stale) ideas.

What do we know about these innovative individuals? They share some common characteristics. For one, policy entrepreneurs are willing to invest time and resources, often at the risk of their own comfort and financial well-being, in order to achieve policy changes. These innovators also tend to be talented storytellers, able to convey complex policy information through simplified stories and scenarios. Recall from Chapter 8 the importance of powerful narratives in successful policy framing. Third, policy entrepreneurs tend to be connected across the policy system through a network of entrepreneurs, diffusing policy ideas across towns, cities, and states.[33]

Policy entrepreneurs generally share a passion for reform—regardless of age. We began, back in Chapter 1, with a note about the policy entrepreneurs in Parkland High School, pressing for gun control. Another set of policy entrepreneurs, "climate kids," is a group of young Americans, aged nine to 20 who, along with their nonprofit sponsor, Our Children's Trust, filed a lawsuit against the Obama (and later, the Trump) administration; they charged that policymakers in the executive branch had failed to protect the planet from the effects of climate change. As scientists first chronicled in 1979, human activity such as burning fossil fuels was causing warming temperatures, rising sea levels, and increasingly severe storms. The climate kids pointed to sober scientific warnings of the global impact—with dangerously rising temperatures in the American southwest, regular flooding in coastal cities like Miami, and tides wiping out entire nations like the Maldives.[34]

The case, *Juliana v. United States* is winding through the courts. Despite a series of appeals from the Trump Administration, in 2018, the Supreme Court ruled that the case could proceed. Said Kiran Oommen, a Seattle University student who joined the suit, "This is a way we can speak for ourselves and stand up for our future."[35]

Over the years, American government has proved resistant to large-scale changes in individual policy areas—in part because the existing ways of carrying out policy have become institutionalized, reinforcing the status quo. Although this trend can be discouraging to would-be reformers, remember from our discussion of interest groups in Chapter 12 that a great virtue of the U.S. policy system is its remarkable stability. Those who can pursue policies within a context of predictable rules (like "climate kids" using the courts to seek reduced

● *Members of the "Network of Enlightened Women," a group of young conservatives, combine passion for specific causes with engaging symbols—two keys to policy success.*

carbon emissions) may achieve the most long-lasting reforms. That flexible combination also may help explain how America's system of policymaking has endured for so long.

Eight Steps to Successful Policy Reform

Want to change an existing policy or persuade Congress to address a problem you care about? Put on your policy entrepreneur's hat and begin connecting to fellow innovators. Here are eight lessons—distilling much of what you have learned in this book—about how to best advance your policy goals.

It takes Passion. To gain supporters across the decision-making community, it is essential both to have passion and to inspire it in others. Donald Trump's surprising 2016 presidential victory owed much to the passionate support he aroused among his ardent fans.

Act with Speed. As we emphasized earlier, policy windows are typically open only briefly. With the financial system on the brink of failure in 2008, a handful of policymakers swiftly organized a bailout plan that may well have averted a global economic meltdown. Most advocates do not face decisions of that magnitude, but the ability to move quickly to take advantage of favorable contexts is still essential.

Bring a Plan. James Madison is known as the "Father of the Constitution" not because he was the most effective orator or backslapper at the Constitutional Convention. Madison was a shy, quiet man, but he had one vital asset: the Virginia Plan, which he had painstakingly worked out in advance of the convention. He traveled early to Philadelphia and strategically approached other members as they arrived in town. Once the convention opened, it adopted the Virginia Plan as its working document.

Mind the Symbols. Simple, stark words and compelling visual depictions—the American flag, a hungry child, government "death panels"—are essential to successful policy framing. Efforts to reform criminal justice policies continue to feature advocates chanting "Hands Up; Don't Shoot," in homage to the slain Michael Brown—although evidence is unclear whether Brown actually uttered those words before his fatal shooting.

Have a Philosophy. Symbols and stories help convey ideas, but reform must connect to an underlying philosophy to survive the policy process. Franklin Roosevelt articulated his guiding perspective at the height of the Great Depression in 1933, in his first inaugural address as president: "These dark days will be worth all they cost us if they teach us that our true destiny is not to be ministered unto but to minister to ourselves and to our fellow-men."[36] This idea—that government is a source of collective support, helping those down on their luck—was woven through all FDR's subsequent New Deal programs.

Go Public. President Ronald Reagan, faced with a Democratic Congress's opposition to his tax reform proposal, successfully took his case to the American public. Few of us have as prominent a "bully pulpit" as President Reagan did (or his communication skills). But policy reformers who can connect with a wider audience are more likely to see an advance toward law.

Know the Rules. When Lyndon Johnson was inaugurated as a new senator in 1949, he spent his first several weeks quietly at his desk on the Senate floor, following the action but never seeking recognition to speak. Johnson's aides, knowing his famously energetic style, worried that he had become depressed. Eventually Johnson explained brusquely, "I'm learning the rules."[37] LBJ went on to be perhaps the most effective Senate majority leader ever, in part because he knew the rulebook down to every loophole, variation, and exception.

Learn How to Lose. The U.S. system is organized around fragmented power, rather than a unified system that promotes sweeping policy changes. Even the most talented advocate will rack up far more losses than wins in policy battles. To survive to fight another day, it is essential to accept defeat graciously and bounce back.

 **The Bottom Line**

» System-wide policy change is frequently pursued by reformers, but it is very difficult to achieve in a United States that organizes its policymaking around separated powers.

» Policy entrepreneurs, drawn from all walks of life, seek innovative solutions for public policies. The most successful among them tend to develop compelling narratives about their preferred issue, are willing to risk creature comforts to pursue policy change, and develop networks to diffuse and test their ideas.

» Although novel policies are hard to push through to completion, the contest over agenda setting and problem definition is relatively open. As in the business or the nonprofit sector, a persistent entrepreneur can realize rewards.

Conclusion: Policy Matters

As you go about your day today, recognize all the different ways you encounter the policy system. Notice the "USDA Organic" label on your breakfast cereal or yogurt container, along with all those government-mandated nutrition facts. Hopping in your car or on your bike? The cost of any gas you buy, the condition of the roads you travel on, the street signs you navigate by: All are the result of policy decisions, often hard-fought ones. Federal agencies license and manage the electromagnetic spectrum that you use to communicate by smartphone or watch TV, regulate the safety of the gym where you work out, and inspect (plus, moving to the state and local levels, charge tax on) the food you buy. Headed to class? Policy decisions determined the subsidy supporting you and the rates you pay on your student loans—and if you attend a public college or university, they may have some say over the curriculum you study.

These are just a few of the ways in which public policy helps shape your daily experience. As a member of this vast but surprisingly accessible democracy, you have the ability (and now, we hope the enhanced knowledge) to shape those policy decisions in turn. May you find a fulfilling role in the great continuing American experiment: government by the people.

CHAPTER SUMMARY

Check your understanding of Chapter 17.

🔵 Public policymaking inevitably involves choices: Should we reduce the interest rate on student-loan repayments? Launch a manned mission to Mars? Open formerly protected lands to oil and gas drilling? Understanding those choices is the essence of politics and government in America.

🔵 Five stages mark the process of devising domestic policies. These are not a blueprint for action, but most policy achievements pass through all these.

- Agenda *setting* describes the transformation of an idea into a policy issue as public attention expands.

- Once a topic is on the agenda, it must be *defined*—What is this issue about?—and *framed*: How lawmakers and the public talk about an agenda item often determines whether it will move forward.

- A third stage, *policy formation,* involves the legislative and executive activities that translate talk into concrete statutory language.

Need to review key ideas in greater depth? Click here.

- Once a policy has been passed into law, it must be *implemented,* involving rulemaking and then delivery of public services.

- Finally, policies are *evaluated*; once implemented, they create a *feedback* process that affects future policymaking in that area.

🔵 The largest U.S. policy programs, in terms of spending and numbers of people served, are social policies such as Social Security, Medicare, Medicaid, and unemployment insurance. Long-time American resistance to big government helps to explain the slow growth of these and other social policies. That same resistance has encouraged a turn toward privatization—shifting public services to the private sector.

🔵 Heightened attention to fiscal and monetary policy, combined with harder economic times, has elevated the importance of budgeting in American politics and government. The federal budget process is a complicated, slow-moving machine, which rarely meets its key deadlines—largely because the financial stakes are so high.

🔵 Every stakeholder agrees on the importance of good public policies—but controversies will never end about what these are. Some measure "good" policy in moral terms of right and wrong; others prefer clearer metrics such as economic efficiency, utilizing cost-benefit and related analyses.

🔵 Reform-minded groups and individuals seek change, both in the rules of the game (systemic changes) and in specific policy areas. Entrepreneurs who succeed tend to tell memorable stories, sacrifice comfort and resources to advance their policy efforts, and work collaboratively with like-minded reformers. Engaging in the policy process, though it moves slowly and incrementally, can be immensely fulfilling.

KEY TERMS

Flashcard review.

Budget resolution, p. 549

Continuing resolution (CR), p. 551

Cost-benefit analysis, p. 553

Cost effectiveness, p. 532

Discretionary programs, p. 551

Entitlement program, p. 544

Federal budget deficit, p. 547

Federal poverty line, p. 544

Fiscal policy, p. 545

Fiscal year (FY), p. 549

Focusing event, p. 530

Gross domestic product (GDP), p. 542

Monetary policy, p. 545

Path dependence, p. 539

Policy agenda, p. 530

Policy window, p. 534

STUDY QUESTIONS

1. How do items get on the policy agenda?

2. Think of an issue you care about. How is it currently *framed* in national discussions about the issue? Would you frame it differently?

3. Why does policy formation—translating a topic from "good idea" into a bill ready for a congressional vote—typically take so long?

4. What is the difference between an ex ante and ex post policy evaluation? How are both useful in helping shape a government program?

5. Why are our largest entitlement programs—Social Security, Medicare, and Medicaid—so expensive?

6. Given a choice, would you emphasize managing the economy through fiscal policy (taxing and spending) or monetary policy (managed by banks, especially the Federal Reserve)? Defend your choice.

7. Why does Congress have to pass continuing resolutions at the end of most budget years?

8. In your view, how important is balancing the U.S. budget?

9. What are at least two ways to determine whether a policy idea is worth pursuing (in other words, whether it is a good idea)? Do you prefer one approach to others?

10. If you could adopt a major reform to the American policymaking process, what would it be? (You may choose from among options in the last section of this chapter, or propose your own.)

11. What qualities characterize successful policy entrepreneurs?

Go to www.oup.com/us/Morone to find quizzes, flash cards, simulations, tutorials, videos, and other study tools.

18 Foreign Policy

"TRADE WARS ARE GOOD," tweeted President Trump, "and easy to win." Most American leaders, Republicans and Democrats, think just the opposite. For 75 years, the nation's dominant strategy has been to reduce or eliminate barriers to international trade—both to enhance the American economy and to spread prosperity to other nations. Consumers in every country will benefit, went the conventional wisdom, even if most nations (including the United States) sometimes protected some of their industries from international competition by imposing tariffs (taxes) on imports from other countries. Donald Trump broke with that approach and launched an all-out trade war.

Seizing on an obscure 1962 law that permits the president to impose tariffs on imports that "threaten or impair national security," the administration lobbed tariffs on aluminum, steel, washing machines, and solar panels to force other nations to fully open those markets to American goods. Trading partners fired back, imposing tariffs on American products. From farmers exporting soy to Harley Davidson selling choppers, American exporters faced retaliation; they expressed worries about losing market share and upsetting trade agreements delicately negotiated over decades. But the administration pressed firmly on—adamant about forcing China, Europe, Turkey, and even Rwanda to fully open their markets.[1] With the same determination, President Trump renegotiated the North American Trade Agreement between Mexico, Canada, and the United States in order to deliver on his campaign promise to "get a better deal" for U.S. workers.

The political reaction was mixed. For starters, trade wars run counter to bedrock traditional Republican doctrine. Reuters surveyed 80 economists and not a single one thought the American economy would benefit. Most believe that tariffs hurt the nation that imposes them by reducing competition, choking innovation, and raising prices; some feared an international economic crisis if the tariffs stayed in place. Republican leaders in both House and Senate voiced that disapproval—but declined to act. For decades, Congress has been largely deferential to presidents on trade policy and this Congress would not be different.

On the other side, some liberal Democrats cheered. Senator Sherrod Brown (D-OH) embraced the tariffs—and then used them against his Republican opponents who had always supported free trade—to win reelection in 2018.

● *Trade war! Rwanda, a small African nation, found itself in a trade war with the United States when it placed a tax on second hand clothes coming from abroad to protect its own textiles industry.*

The AFL-CIO, a staunchly Democratic organization, also praised the policy. They believe that free trade hurts workers in high income nations. Notice the peculiar line up: Populists on both the left and the right against moderates in the center.

The American public, which generally pays very little attention to foreign policy, began to notice. Large majorities expressed concern over a trade war with China and with other nations.[2] For better or for worse, the Trump tariffs injected a dramatic new approach to American foreign policy (We'll explore the details later in the chapter.)[3]

Foreign policy defines American relations with external nations, groups, and problems. It involves countless decisions, large and small: trade rules with Japan, China, and Uruguay; what to do about nuclear threats from North Korea; whether to intervene in genocide; and when to deploy military force. American foreign policies change the world. They also boomerang back home and change the United States.

Who are we? Foreign policy offers an important answer. What we do around the world broadcasts our values and our interests. Our international policies announce what we stand for as a nation. They also trigger intense arguments. Foreign-policy debates raise a host of important questions: What are America's most fundamental interests? How should the nation pursue them? Should we act alone? Or rely on the web of alliances, partnerships, and relations with nations around the globe?

Foreign policy differs from everything you have read so far. The American political process is usually slow and full of checks and balances. In contrast, foreign policy moves fast, the stakes are high, and the results—triumphs or disasters—are often immediately clear. The president has much wider powers over foreign policy than most other areas. Even so, there are always many different hands involved in shaping foreign policy.

Let's start with the three goals guiding foreign policy: national security, prosperity, and spreading American values. Sometimes, these goals clash with one another. As we describe each, think about which seems most important to you.

American Foreign-Policy Goal No. 1: Security

First, the United States must defend itself. *Security means protecting the nation and its values from external threats.* But what constitutes an external threat? Should policymakers focus on terrorists? North Korea's rising military power? Economic competitors like China? Or perhaps the greatest danger comes from global warming, or limits on natural resources. Different dangers require different strategies.

Military Primacy

Every administration, whether Democratic or Republican, seeks security through a powerful military. The United States spends as much on its armed forces as the other top six nations combined (see Comparing Nations 18.1). Even these numbers understate total military spending: The Department of Homeland Security, intelligence agencies, and the Veterans Administration add more than $200 billion to the total.

A large military comes with a very high price tag. Why spend so much more than other nations? Because U.S. military strategy is based on the theory of

BY THE NUMBERS
Foreign Policy

U.S. military spending as a percentage of all global military spending, 2017	*35*
Percentage spent by China	*13*
Percentage spent by Russia	*3.8*
Percentage of U.S. federal budget spent on defense, 1960	*52*
Percentage spent on defense, 2017	*16*
Rank of the U.S. economy in the world, 2018	*1*
Rank of the Chinese, Japanese, and German economies, respectively	*2, 3, 4*
Total U.S. economic activity, 2017	*$19.3 trillion*
Total combined economic activity of Japan, China, and Germany	*$20.5 trillion*
Rank of the United States, among the top 15 economies, in economic growth in the last five years	*10*
Rank of the United States and Russia and China, respectively, as global arms merchants	*1, 2, 3*

How does the United States economic and military position compare to that of other nations? How has this changed over time?

primacy: Maintain an unrivaled military force that can overwhelm any enemy. Is this expensive doctrine necessary? That depends on how we see the world.

Basis for Primacy: Realism

Two main views of the U.S. role in the world have colored American foreign-policy debates since the 1950s. **Realism** sees the world as dangerous, full of tough rivals competing for advantage. The best way to protect the nation is to maximize military and economic power. Realists see the international system as an anarchy—individual states struggle for dominance in a lawless international arena marked by the survival of the fittest. The only hope for peace and stability: Powerful states assume leadership and establish order.

Primacy: The doctrine asserting that the United States should maintain an unrivaled military.

Realism: A doctrine holding that nation–states seek to amass power to ensure their self-preservation.

COMPARING NATIONS 18.1 | Military Spending Worldwide

The United States spends more than any other nation—by far. *(Stockholm International Peace Research Institute)*

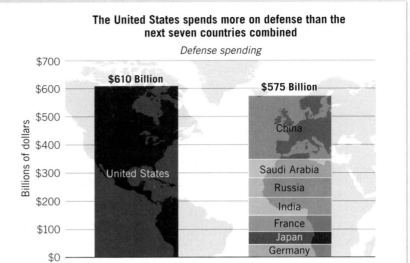

The United States spends more on defense than the next seven countries combined

Defense spending

Billions of dollars

$610 Billion — United States

$575 Billion — China, Saudi Arabia, Russia, India, France, Japan, Germany

$700
$600
$500
$400
$300
$200
$100
$0

As a result, realists emphasize international security threats around the world—terrorists, rivals, and rogue states. In an unstable world, say the realists, the United States must build a powerful military to use as a deterrent—and if necessary to deploy it against threats to American interests.

Realists debate what type of international order is most stable: unipolar (led by one nation), bi-polar (led by two) or multi-polar (with multiple powers). During the cold war, the international order was bi-polar (with the United States and the Soviet Union competing for dominance). The great questions of the present day: What type of international order is emerging? Will it prove stable?

Realism offers a strong perspective that underpins the doctrine of primacy. Yes, it is expensive to maintain such a large army. But today, no other military has the same reach, and none can move as swiftly to respond to trouble around the globe. Realists insist that it is the price of security.

Liberalism: A doctrine that views nation–states as benefiting most from mutual cooperation, aided by international organizations.

A Different View: Liberalism

A very different perspective suggests that, yes, the world can be a dangerous place but the best way for nations to secure peace and prosperity is to work together. **Liberalism** focuses on identifying common goals, building international organizations such as the United Nations, and exchanging cultural ambassadors—from rock stars to football teams. Together nations can create a world that moves beyond self-interest.

Liberal critics of the realist strain in U.S. foreign policy raise an alarming question: Could building such a large military make the United States *less* secure? Liberals identify three potential problems with military primacy.

● *Realists see a world bristling with threats. Here, North Korean troops celebrate their nation's 70th birthday.*

First, they warn of a **security trap**: Using military force often produces a backlash. It humiliates other nations and leaves them more susceptible to anti-American sentiments.[4] When the United States deploys its military, civilians are inevitably killed—some one hundred thousand civilians died during the invasion and occupation of Iraq from 2003 to 2011.[5] Civilian casualties are not America's responsibility alone—but they are sobering.

Security trap: The idea that using military force creates multiple, often unforeseen, problems.

Second, military primacy costs more than half a trillion dollars a year. This is a high economic burden that shifts spending from other priorities. Liberal thinkers argue that mutual engagement with other nations is more likely to foster increased trade and enhances everyone's economic well-being.

Finally, liberal thinkers are joined by conservatives in warning that too much emphasis on military power undermines liberty. As we saw in Chapter 2, Americans long feared that a large army would turn a republic into an empire. That critique evaporated during the Cold War. Facing communists armed with atomic bombs, America could not afford to worry about the problems posed by a standing army. Once communism fell, however, the critics argued that it was time to downsize the military.

Those promoting cuts in military spending face the same problem we have seen in almost every chapter: entrenched institutions. Many local economies depend on military bases, military contractors, or military suppliers. It is always hard to cut any budget.[6]

Soft Power

Packed stadiums around the world shout out the words at Beyoncé or Garth Brooks concerts. To foreign-policy analysts, they are another way to spread American influence. Political scientist Joseph Nye calls it "**soft power**": Use culture and economics to persuade rather than coerce (hard power). Soft power is an important part of liberal foreign policy. The United States is the world's second leading tourist destination (just behind France) with 75.6 million visitors in 2017. American music, movies, and television are everywhere. You see people lined up outside Apple stores (not to mention Starbucks or McDonalds) from Rome to Shanghai. Sharing these cultural experiences forms bonds among people, which create a different type of security.[7]

Soft power: The influence a nation exerts through culture and commerce; a contrast to attempted influence through force.

Of course, some critics push back and accuse the United States of cultural imperialism. However, most administrations rely on "hard" and "soft" power. The sharp question is how to balance the two. What do you think?

Foreign Aid and National Security

The United States is the largest foreign aid donor in the world. Many Americans believe we spend far too much—and from the realist perspective, it is a drain on our economic resources. But there is another way to look at it. The United States devotes about half a percent (about .54%) of the gross national income on humanitarian and development aid—roughly

● Soft power: American lattes are welcome where the army is not. Here, Starbucks in the heart of the Forbidden City, the imperial palace in Beijing, China.

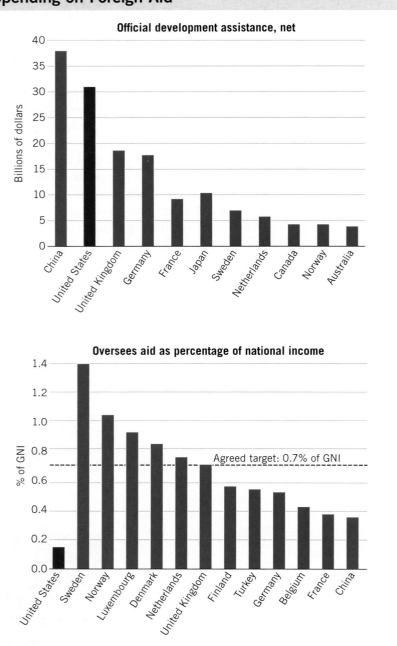

COMPARING NATIONS 18.2 | **Spending on Foreign Aid**

Top: The United States pays more in foreign aid than any other nation. Bottom: Now, look at foreign assistance as a percentage of the gross national income (GNI), or total economy: The United States is low compared to other wealthy nations. In 2005, OECD nations agreed to reach a target of 0.7 percent of their income by 2015. Realists, like Donald Trump, push allies to spend more on military; liberals might respond by asking the United States to hit targets for development assistance. Which would you advise the president to emphasize? (globalissues.org/OECD)

Official development assistance, net

Billions of dollars

China, United States, United Kingdom, Germany, France, Japan, Sweden, Netherlands, Canada, Norway, Australia

Oversees aid as percentage of national income

% of GNI

Agreed target: 0.7% of GNI

United States, Sweden, Norway, Luxembourg, Denmark, Netherlands, United Kingdom, Finland, Turkey, Germany, Belgium, France, China

half as much as China or France (see Comparing Nations 18.2). Is this too much—or too little?[8]

Those with a more liberal view of America's role in the world believe that assisting other nations is an important path to security. It builds goodwill and helps lift nations out of the poverty that breeds extremism. Others counter that financial assistance only makes other nations reliant. Moreover, foreign aid often flies straight into the pockets of the rich and the powerful. The argument goes on, but whatever side you take, remember that foreign aid forms a tiny part of U.S. spending.

> ### The Bottom Line
>
> » The first goal of American foreign policy is security.
>
> » Two leading foreign-policy views, realism and liberalism, differ sharply on how best to ensure security for Americans and allied countries.
>
> » To pursue security, the United States deploys a large military and maintains a policy of primacy—the idea that no military power should rival ours.
>
> » Liberal thinkers emphacize the importance of multinational cooperation, soft (or cultural) power, and foreign aid.

American Foreign-Policy Goal No. 2: Prosperity

The United States is a superpower because of its economy. In the long run, national power always rests not on armies but on economic engines. The second goal of foreign policy: keep that economic engine strong.

Back in 1960 the United States accounted for 40 percent of the world's economic output. No surprise that it was a major international power. Today, American wealth accounts for more than 20 percent of the world's gross domestic product (GDP). That is still the world's largest economy, but some analysts believe the international order is turning multipolar. Growing centers of economic power in Asia and Europe may be challenging U.S. supremacy in the years ahead. The Trump administration's trade war (which opened the chapter) is a direct response to the fear of decline.

Economic Superpower or Nation in Decline?

At first glance, the United States certainly does not look like a country on the skids. The American economy is 45 percent larger than China's, almost four times larger than Japan's, five times larger than Germany's, and larger than 163 other nations *combined* (see Figure 18.1). The American dollar is the international reserve currency—used in foreign trade and investment. And English has become the language of international affairs.

Although the U.S. economy remains by far the largest in the world, China appears to be rapidly catching up. Its economy has been growing twice as fast—vaulting right past Japan and reducing American growth rates to second place. If the current economic trends continue (a very big if), the Chinese economy will surpass America's in the decades ahead. Two other areas with high potential growth could also be potential rivals: the European Union and India.[9]

Another possible risk: The United States buys more from other nations than it sells to them. This imbalance, known as a **trade deficit**, has existed every year since 1975. Is it a problem? Economists differ. Many believe that the United States cannot continue buying more from other nations than it sells to them without eventual economic consequences.

Some critics also worry that the United States is failing to invest in its *infrastructure*—its roads, train tracks, air terminals, and public transportation. Travelers to Asia marvel at the sleek airports and railroads. Does the Chinese

Trade deficit: The deficit arising when a nation imports (or buys) more goods from foreign nations than it exports (or sells) to them.

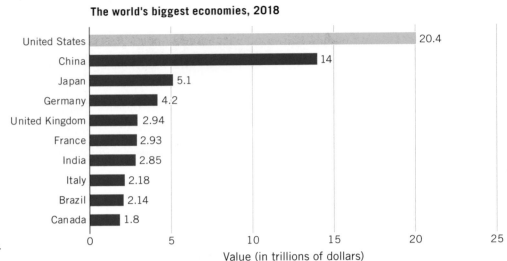

The world's biggest economies, 2018

United States	20.4
China	14
Japan	5.1
Germany	4.2
United Kingdom	2.94
France	2.93
India	2.85
Italy	2.18
Brazil	2.14
Canada	1.8

Value (in trillions of dollars)

● **Figure 18.1** *The United States is still the world's largest economy— though China has been catching up. (International Monetary Fund)*

growth of the past decade mean that authoritarian governments are more efficient at organizing the economy than America's democracy is? Here's an issue where President Trump and the Democrats agree—though their different approaches have, so far, blocked efforts to rebuild American infrastructure.

How do all of these concerns add up? Pessimists worry that other nations, especially China will overtake the United States economically. Optimists disagree. The world's biggest economy can afford to buy more goods and services from around the world. It has been running both trade and budget deficits for almost 50 years, and the financial sky has not fallen. Yes, politicians bicker, but they do not diminish the energy of American inventors. American entrepreneurial genius has powered the information age through Microsoft, Apple, Google, Facebook, Amazon, and the Internet itself. The United States remains an economic powerhouse.[10]

Which is it? A nation in decline? Or an entrepreneurial dynamo setting the pace for the world? You can keep your own score in the years ahead by tracking just one measure of world power: the size of the American economy relative to the rest of the world.

Free Trade

Free trade: Goods and services moving across international boundaries without government interference.

For the past 50 years U.S administrations championed **free trade**—*the idea that goods and services should move across international boundaries without government interference*. Until World War II, most governments tried to protect their own industries by slapping tariffs on foreign goods—special taxes that made foreign competitors more expensive than local products. This kind of favoritism is called **protectionism** because it is designed to protect local industries, like steel and aluminum, from foreign competition.

Protectionism: Efforts to protect local business from foreign competition.

In theory, free trade helps businesses and consumers in every country, because it offers more choices and lower prices. If Detroit can make better cars at a lower price, consumers from Kansas to Kazakhstan should be able to buy them. And because a quarter of all American economic activity involved foreign trade, there is a lot of money on the table.

World Trade Organization (WTO): An international organization that oversees efforts to open markets and promote free trade.

American policy makers pushed for both bilateral trade agreements with individual countries and, more important, multilateral treaties with many nations— the most important resulted in the **World Trade Organization** (**WTO**), which oversees international trade rules. Democratic President Bill Clinton used enormous political capital to push another multilateral agreement, the North American Free Trade Agreement (NAFTA), through Congress in 1994. NAFTA phased out taxes on imports and exports between Canada, Mexico, and the United States. Economists generally agree that NAFTA boosted economic growth in all three countries. However, the costs and benefits are not evenly spread out. Many U.S. companies shifted operations to Mexico leaving hundreds of thousands of workers at least temporarily without jobs. Opposition to free trade deals began to grow. In the last 30 years, presidents have pressed free trade deals; in Congress Democrats generally opposed and Republicans supported them (House Republicans voted for NAFTA, 3–1, House Democrats 3–2 against it).

Then, candidate Donald Trump led the Republicans into a sharp U-turn. He insisted that trade deals like NAFTA must be renegotiated—and then followed through by targeting first Mexico and then Canada. Trump forcefully articulated the backlash against the international trade regime. Why? We will see in the next section.

Examine the concepts of free trade and protectionism.

Challenges to Free Trade

Almost every policy textbook repeats the exact same thing: Free trade makes everyone better off. However, many Americans strongly disagree. Free trade faces four main challenges.

First, critics of free trade charge that it is cheaper to produce goods in nations that pollute, outlaw unions, reject safety standards, and keep wages low. If global agreements are not carefully negotiated, jobs will flow to those nations—leaving American workers and their communities high and dry. Some critics suggest an alternative to free trade: **fair trade**—emphasize worker protections and environmental standards. Fair trade can be built right into trade deals that reduce trade barriers. That way, say proponents, companies in different nations are competing under the same rules.

Second, free markets cause social displacement, at least in the short run. Free trade in agriculture, for example, pushes small farmers in poor nations such as Nigeria off their farms and into the slums of megacities like Lagos. What happens to the Nigerian farmer and his family when they lose their land? What happens to software engineers in Austin, Texas who find their jobs migrating to Bangalore, India? Most nations have not put policies in place to help workers who are displaced by international competition. Even if everyone is better off in the long run, as free trade advocates argue, politics—and individuals—focus on troubles in the short run.

Third, as international markets have expanded to facilitate the huge sums involved in free trade, they have grown volatile. The Greek debt crisis, a Chinese stock market crash, and Turkey's financial troubles all reverberated through the global economy. Liberal economists such as Paul Krugman warn that free markets create a wild ride full of booms, bubbles, and busts.[11]

Fourth, long before President Trump came to office, American leaders championed free trade only until they ran into powerful interests. When government helps American farmers, it violates the rules of free trade that the government itself is championing. However, because few politicians are willing to take on the farm lobby or the rural states, American farm subsidies stay in place despite the different administrations' commitment to free trade.

Today, President Trump has openly embraced protectionism. He charges that the trade deals have been rigged. As the United States pressed for free trade, other nations did not fully reciprocate. The EU charges a 10 percent tariff on American

Fair trade: Trade that emphasizes the inclusion of environmental and labor protections in agreements so that nations do not receive unfair advantages by exploiting workers or harming the environment.

Watch 2016 presidential candidates Bernie Sanders and Donald Trump criticize a free trade agreement, the TPP.

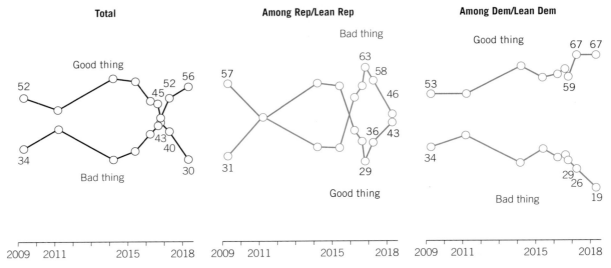

Positive views of free trade agreements rebound to pre-2016 levels
% who say free trade agreements between the U.S. and other countries have generally been a good/bad thing for the U.S.

● **Figure 18.2** *American views of international trade now reflect a Trump effect: Democrats more positive, Republicans more negative. (Pew Research Center)*

cars and trucks, for example, to protect automakers in Italy and France. "All countries that have placed artificial Trade Barriers and Tariffs," tweeted Trump, "remove those Barriers and Tariffs or be met with more than Reciprocity."[12] Quietly left unsaid by all sides was the fact that the United States charges a 25 percent tariff on European pick-up trucks and SUVs.[13]

Almost all experts and most political leaders reject a return to protectionism. They point out that the current system is the result of intricately negotiated agreements in which both sides give and take. Now, however, opposition to those agreements has spread. On the left, critics argue that those deals have hurt workers and the environment; on the right, opponents charge that they have been a source of American economic decline. Polls show a strong Trump effect: Democrats have grown **more** positive about free international trade, Republicans less (see Figure 18.2).

Assess current debates on free trade.

Energy

Foreign policymakers keep a close eye on energy supplies. The United States consumes almost 20 million barrels of oil a day, a fifth of the world total. In the last 30 years, the United States has fought three major wars in the Middle East—which has an estimated 60 percent of the world's oil reserves. However, the energy story is changing rapidly. Natural gas and renewable energy supply 40 percent of the nation's needs and, together, the United States and Canada now produce almost 80 percent of the nation's supply.[14]

Economic Weapons

American officials use economic relations as carrots to reward other nations or as sticks to punish them—for attacking another country, trying to build nuclear weapons, or hacking American elections. Economic sanctions include the following:

- A boycott, or refusing to buy goods or services from a country.

- An economic embargo, or restricting the flow of trade into a country. Sometimes the Navy or the Air Force enforces the embargo.

- Divestment or refusing to invest in another country. Even local governments and private actors can use this strategy.

- Freezing assets, or seizing the bank accounts and other financial assets that foreign nationals have invested here. This strategy targets elites in particular by stripping them of their foreign bank accounts.

- Finally, withholding foreign aid—if the country is receiving any.

Applying these economic sanctions is not easy because it requires building an international coalition. If other countries refuse to go along, the United States may lose a market for its own goods without applying any real pressure. However, being the world's largest economy makes a difference; when the Trump Administration renewed economic sanctions on Iran, overriding Europeans objections, European firms discovered that the United States would punish them for violating the sanctions—few valued their Iran business over their trade with the United States.

One final problem: Economic weapons often hurt ordinary people long before they touch the rich and powerful. When sanctions pinch a nation's economy, it is the poor that go hungry. The wealthy (and the well-connected) have more resources to ride out the hard time.

 **The Bottom Line**

» A second primary goal of foreign policy is to protect prosperity. Economic strength is the ultimate source of power on the world stage.

» Today, the U.S. economy is the largest in the world—but many Americans and allies around the globe wonder: Will the United States maintain its economic strength relative to other nations?

» American economic policy has been guided by the pursuit of free trade—the removal of barriers to international commerce. Resistance has grown to free trade, especially among congressional Democrats. Many support *fair* trade.

» International economic policy also focuses on protecting energy sources and using economic sticks and carrots to influence the behavior of other nations.

Foreign-Policy Goal No. 3: Spreading American Ideals

Most people believe that every nation's foreign-policy goal can be simply described: blunt self-interest. However, explaining American action only in terms of power or prosperity misses something important.

In the very first inaugural address, delivered in 1789, President George Washington declared that the new nation had a special mission: "The sacred fire of liberty and the destiny of the republican model of government are . . . entrusted to the hands of the American people." This, he told his countrymen, might even be liberty's best and final chance. From the very start, Washington and other American leaders believed that the United States had a special role in the world—to champion liberty.[15]

Investigate the economy, military, and politics of other nations.

American leaders often justify foreign-policy action in terms of promoting values such as liberty and democracy. The United States entered World War I, said President Woodrow Wilson, because "the world must be made safe for democracy." America is "privileged to spend its blood," he continued, for "a universal dominion of right." A century later, Secretary of State Hillary Clinton, described her foreign policy in these terms: "upholding universal values and human rights is at the core of what it means to be American. If we . . . let our policies diverge too far from our ideals, our influence will wane."[16]

American Exceptionalism

Again and again, American leaders return to the idea that the United States has a unique duty to spread freedom, democracy, and peace to other nations. The belief that the United States plays a special role in world affairs is known as **American exceptionalism**. This does not mean that Americans ignore their own interests. America's deepest interest, according to this view, lies in promoting the peace, freedom, and democracy that will benefit all people.[17]

● Nineteenth-century artists imagined a spirit of providential destiny that guided America. Here, America flies forward, the star of empire on her forehead with learning and technology in either hand, as Native Americans and wild beasts flee before the irresistible civilization. This painting, by John Gast, was widely copied and reprinted.

American exceptionalism: The view that the United States is unique, marked by a distinct set of ideas such as equality, self-rule, and limited government.

Is the United States really exceptional? Some observers warn that American exceptionalism is a very dangerous myth. It can lead Americans to reduce complicated reality into a simple clash between good and evil. And it can blind American policy makers to other perspectives and interests.[18]

A faith in America's special destiny, whether it is truth or a myth, makes foreign policy more controversial. Political science research suggests that advancing democratic values and economic growth in underdeveloped countries helps everyone. According to the **theory of democratic peace**, nations with legitimate democratic governments do not go to war with each other.[19] Although Republicans have traditionally emphasized a faith in American exceptionalism, President Trump is deeply skeptical of the idea: as a foreign policy realist, he emphasizes national self-interest.

Theory of democratic peace: Theory that strongly democratic nations are less prone to engage in wars with one another.

What Do YOU Think? Is America Exceptional?

Every nation is unique in many ways. But is the United States exceptional in fighting for the great values expressed in its Declaration of Independence?

Yes. The United States is exceptional in that it makes sacrifices to spread values such as freedom and democracy around the world. It does not ignore self-interest but equates it with the spread of liberty and democracy.

No. Americans may like to think that they are acting purely on principle. But, like every other nation, the United States pursues its own self-interest. It is dangerous and misleading to insist that we are helping others when in reality we are helping ourselves.

It depends. Americans pursue their self-interest. They also pursue values such as democracy and rights. Some leaders get the balance right and are cheered around the world. Others are less effective. It depends on the leader and the situation.

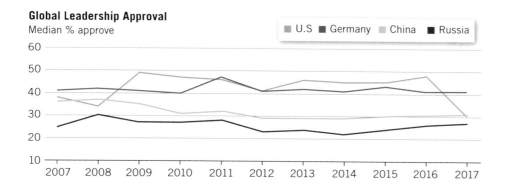

Global Leadership Approval
Median % approve

Legend: ■ U.S ■ Germany ■ China ■ Russia

● **Figure 18.3** *The Trump effect? United States falls from number 1 to number 3 in international approval rankings among four powerful nations. (Gallup)*

The View from Abroad

How do others see the United States? By the end of the Obama years, the United States was viewed far more favorably than other international powers. Now, President Trump's tough positions has caused American approval to crash in many countries—especially Europe, South America, and Canada—falling 50 percent overall and putting the United States behind Germany and China in international esteem (see Figure 18.3). However, a few nations do have confidence in President Trump's policies—most notably, the Philippines, Nigeria, Israel, and Russia.[20]

The debate continues about American values and their meaning for other nations. Even supporters, at home and overseas, fear American society is increasingly unequal, marked by less opportunity and a growing gulf between rich and poor. The United States seems, to many observers, more fixed on hard-knuckle economic competition and amassing great wealth than on a genuine belief that all people are equal.

Nevertheless, more immigrants still crowd into the United States than into any other nation. The numbers are declining (falling 9% from the first quarter of 2017 to 2018) as a result of tougher screening and strong anti-immigrant rhetoric.[21] Still, even in countries that are skeptical of America's intentions, people stand in long lines to sign up for the lottery that will grant a few of them a visa and a green card. People even risk their lives to pursue the American Dream. If the United States is a nation in decline, then why are so many people fighting to move here?

In short, American values have played an important role in guiding American foreign policy. Today, new questions have risen: Are the American values still vital—or are they beginning to fade? Can they inspire people around the world—or do they simply seem like rhetorical cover for American self-interest? And, what will be the long-term effects of the Trump Administration's tough America-First policies?

 **The Bottom Line**

» The United States tries to spread its own values of democracy and freedom—sometimes creating goodwill, at other times a backlash. This is a rare goal for a nation's foreign policy.

» American standing in international polls plummeted after the election of Donald Trump.

» Critics argue that the United States simply uses the language of values to pursue its self-interest. They see even the nation's talk of liberty as little more than a cover for unbridled capitalism and inequality.

Foreign-Policy Perspectives

Every administration develops a foreign-policy strategy by answering three key questions. Should the United States engage the world or withdraw from it? Do we go it alone or work with others? Which foreign-policy goals and values are most important?

Engage the World? Isolationism Versus Intervention

President George Washington warned his countrymen to stay clear of foreign politics: "The great rule of conduct for us, in regard to foreign nations, is . . . to have . . . as little *political* connection as possible." In other words, the United States should limit itself to commerce. We can best promote our values simply by building an ideal society that other nations will admire and want to imitate.[22]

Strategic disengagement: The doctrine that a nation should not interfere in other nations' affairs unless such involvement clearly advances its own interests.

Isolationism: The doctrine that a nation should avoid all foreign-policy commitments and alliances and withdraw from world affairs.

Internationalism: The belief that national interests are best served by actively engaging and working with other nations around the world.

Many Americans hold a version of this view, now known as **strategic disengagement**.[23] While few politicians today embrace all out **isolationism**—avoiding any involvement in other nations' affairs—some argue that the United States will remain strong and secure by limiting its involvement overseas, especially military activity.

Many people believe that the United States traditionally practiced isolationism. This is a myth. Right from the start, the United States exerted its muscle around the world. It battled the French navy in 1798, just ten years after the Constitution went into effect. It fought the Barbary Wars on the north coast of Africa beginning in 1801. (If you are familiar with the Marine Corps anthem, its "shores of Tripoli" refers to the Barbary Wars.) American forces entered Mexico ("the halls of Montezuma") five times between 1836 and 1848 before declaring all-out war. By one count, the military deployed overseas 165 times before World War II.

For all the action, however, the United States maintained only a small standing army until the end of World War II. Then, locked in a Cold War with the Soviet Union, the country built an army ready to deploy anywhere around the globe at a moment's notice. The sheer size and sophistication of its military pushes the United States away from isolationism and toward internationalism.

Indeed, most contemporary foreign-policy analysts opt for **internationalism**. They believe that America's interests are best protected by actively engaging the world. Both the United States and the world would be worse off, they argue, if the United States withdrew into its own borders. Americans must combat terrorism, confront Russian meddling in Syria, fight radical jihadists, protect Asia from an unpredictable North Korea—and the list goes on. This perspective insists that withdrawing from world affairs will allow problems to fester, enemies to multiply, and people to suffer.

● *To the shores of Tripoli. American foreign policy was interventionist right from the beginning. Here, marines lead the charge in Derna, Libya in 1805 during the first Barbary War.*

Go It Alone or Act with Others?

Although the United States was rarely isolationist, through most of its history it acted alone. President Washington broke the alliance with France that had helped win the Revolutionary War, and America did not enter another peacetime alliance for 150 years. Thomas Jefferson sternly warned the country, in his first inaugural address, not to get involved in "entangling alliances." This perspective is known as **unilateralism**—American foreign policy should be independent and self-sufficient. Unilateralists oppose treaties with foreign nations or international organizations, because such agreements, they say, tie America down.

In the half century following World War II, American policy changed. Facing a hostile Soviet Union armed with nuclear weapons and as the newly emerged leader of the Western world, American leaders argued that the United States could no longer afford to go it alone. **Multilateralism** means acting together with other nations to pursue common goals. We cannot solve modern problems by ourselves. Fighting communism during the Cold War required concerted action. Likewise, only international cooperation can defeat terrorism, reverse climate change, secure prosperity, end starvation, stop ethnic killing, resist global pandemics, reduce the international traffic in drugs and sex, and end violence against women. Foreign-policy officials who take an internationalist view are, as you would expect, strong supporters of multilateralism.

Millennial Americans tend to express a clear preference for multilateralism, owing in part to their relatively high level of global engagement: More than three times as many millennials study abroad than did members of "Generation X" 25 years ago.[24] That preference shows up in support for foreign-policy approaches that emphasize cooperation among nations.

One especially pressing issue that cannot be solved through an unilateral, isolationist approach is the spread of nuclear weapons. Five nations openly possess them (the United States, England, France, Russia, and China). Four others are thought to have developed them (India, Pakistan, North Korea, and Israel). A small number of foreign-policy experts argue that the spread of these weapons makes wars less likely, because either side can annihilate the other.[25] Most observers believe the opposite: As nuclear weapons spread to less stable nations, they are more likely to be used and to fall into the hands of extremist groups. In the words of a past U.S. Secretary of Defense under President Bill Clinton, "Today, the danger of . . . a nuclear catastrophe is greater than it was during the Cold War and most people are blissfully unaware of this fact."[26] American foreign policy must work around the globe to avoid this nightmare scenario.

Unilateralism: A doctrine that holds that the United States should act independently of other nations. It should decide what is best for itself—not in coordination with partners and allies.

Multilateralism: A doctrine that emphasizes operating together with other nations to pursue common goals.

● *Diplomatic breakthrough? Or same old pretense? In 2008, North Korea blew up a cooling tower at the Yongbyon nuclear complex to emphasize its commitment to abandoning its nuclear program. Eight years later, having successfully exploded a hydrogen bomb and tested intercontinental missiles that could reach the U.S. mainland, North Korea blew up tunnels at its Punggye-ri nuclear site as show of good faith following President Trump's meeting with North Korean leader Kim Jong Un. North Korea appeared to be quietly continuing its nuclear program.*

What Do YOU Think? Foreign-Policy Perspectives

It is time for you to pick a perspective that ties foreign policy together. Where do your values lie? With which of the following do you most identify?

I am a Wilsonian.	I believe that American foreign policy must rest on American values and work with other nations to secure them.
I am a Hamiltonian.	I believe that the business of America is business.
I am a Jeffersonian.	I prefer to worry about democracy on the home front.
I am a Jacksonian.	I believe that the only criteria for foreign action are American security and American prosperity.
None of these choices seem right.	Feel free to develop a different perspective. You can emphasize some other goal of American foreign policy. Or, simply mix and match from these.

(Source: Adapted from Walter Russell Mead)

President Trump warned North Korea "of fire and fury like the world has never seen" if it continued to threaten others and develop nuclear weapons. He then followed up with an unprecedented initiative: meeting North Korean leader Kim Jong-Un in a summit focused on containing the dangers of a nuclear nightmare. Might the summit lead to a breakthrough peace in Korea? Time will tell.

Today, another threat looms: cyberweapons. Russia, China, and North Korea have turned cyberweapons (developed in the United States) on western nations, threatening power grids, governments, banks, and more. Vulnerable Western nations may find it more effective to cooperate rather than go it alone.[27]

Four Approaches

As you can see, Americans have a lot to balance in making foreign policy—three overarching goals, isolation versus action, and unilateralism versus multilateralism. How do we bring together these goals? Over time, Americans have generally supported four different camps. Each approach emphasizes different foreign-policy goals. Each is named after a famous statesman who helped define it.[28]

Wilsonians believe that American values should be the number one consideration guiding foreign policy. Fighting a war to make the world safe for democracy, as Woodrow Wilson urged America to do during World War I, is the classic Wilsonian move.

Hamiltonians believe that American foreign policy should focus on protecting American prosperity. Named after Alexander Hamilton, the first secretary of the treasury, this approach emphasizes making economic deals that benefit the United States. Hamiltonians favor big business and accept big government. To them, military intervention should always be weighed not against vague values such as freedom or morality, but against hard-headed analysis. Is the action in America's economic interest?

Jeffersonians focus on freedom and democracy at home. Building up a large military and deploying it around the world threatens the American ideals of local and democratic government. Jeffersonians are nervous about the military–industrial complex and its corrosive effect on American freedom. President Thomas Jefferson warned that international alliances would "entangle" the nation in foreign wars and power politics. Modern Jeffersonians firmly believe in *strategic disengagement.*

Jacksonians believe that the United States should simply focus on its own security and well-being. It should worry about itself and let other nations do the same. Jacksonians are skeptical of foreign aid, indifferent to international diplomacy, and slow to support foreign action. However, they put special emphasis on honor. Once the military is deployed, they insist on total victory. Of the four traditions, the Jacksonians are most likely to be chanting, *"USA! USA!"*

 **The Bottom Line**

» Three decisions guide foreign policy: First, policymakers must choose between strategic engagement (only get involved in a global conflict or alliance when it clearly advances the U.S. national interest) or internationalism (engagement with the world).

» Second, policymakers must choose whether to act unilaterally (go it alone) or multilaterally (in alliance with other nations).

» Third, policymakers put it all together with an overall perspective: Wilsonians focus on values, Hamiltonians on economics, Jeffersonians on democracy at home, and Jacksonians on defending American security and well-being.

Who Makes Foreign Policy?

What is misleading about the following newspaper headlines?

- "United States Warns Syria About Attacks on Protesters"
- "South Korea Seeks to Balance Relations with China, United States"
- "Iran Threatens Saudi Arabia"

They all describe nations as if they were *unitary actors,* or individuals with minds of their own. Every chapter in this book has told another story. The United States constructs politics out of many perspectives, interests, institutions, and arguments. So does every other nation. Foreign policy emerges out of negotiation. Several major players have a seat at the table when American foreign policy is made.

Congress

The Constitution carefully balances responsibility for foreign policy between Congress and the president. Congress has the power to declare war, to set the military's budget, and to ratify treaties. These responsibilities worked fine in a slower world. In the early nineteenth century, the Americans defeated the English in the Battle of New Orleans because word had not filtered back across the Atlantic that a peace treaty had already ended the War of 1812.

Today, response time can be measured in minutes rather than weeks or months. As the decision clock sped up, defense—and, more generally, foreign policy—shifted away from Congress to the White House. Congress has not declared war since 1941 despite major wars in Korea (where 36 thousand Americans died), Vietnam (another 58 thousand), the Persian Gulf, the Balkans, Afghanistan, and Iraq. Congress is divided, slow to act, uneasy about taking risks, focused on domestic issues, and always running for reelection. For all these reasons, it has let control of foreign policy slip to the executive branch.

In 1973 Congress tried to reassert some control by passing the **War Powers Act**, which requires presidents to get congressional permission for military action after troops are in the field for no more than 60 days. Presidents often ask Congress for support before they commit troops (see Chapter 14 for details). And when wars drag on and grow unpopular, Congress asserts itself: It holds hearings, rallies opposition, and squeezes the budget.

War Powers Act: Legislation passed in 1973 to increase congressional involvement in undeclared wars. It requires Congress to approve military action undertaken by the president in no more than 60 days.

The Constitution requires the Senate to ratify international treaties with a two-thirds vote—a very high bar in our partisan era. To get around the requirement, presidents sign *executive agreements* with other nations; these have the same legal effect as formal treaties but do not require the two-thirds vote. *Legislative–executive agreements* pass with a simple majority, as any other legislation. A *sole executive agreement* is simply signed by the president without any congressional approval at all.

The Constitution also makes Congress responsible for confirming top foreign-policy appointments. Again, partisan politics has slowed this process in recent years.

In short, Congress has evolved from a partner to a type of check on executive foreign policymaking. The executive branch crafts the policies. It then must win over Congress for funding, legislation, confirmations, and cooperation. In effect, Congress pushes back when presidential policies become unpopular.

The President

The president commands the military, negotiates treaties, rallies Americans during crises, and oversees relations with more than two hundred nations. Each administration defines America's stance toward the world. Presidents and their team decide whether, when, where, and how to intervene around the globe. They balance foreign policy with domestic priorities and political calculations.

Recent administrations have demonstrated the enormous power inherent in the president's foreign-policy role. Ironically, modern presidents have more authority and less experience. Early presidents all had a rich foreign-policy background. Most recent presidents have arrived in the White House with no foreign-policy experience at all (see Table 18.1). Trump's victory came, in part, from a great wave of distrust toward Washington insiders—such as candidate Hillary Clinton.

Although presidents take the lead, they have many partners in conducting international affairs. One key to presidential success is wisely managing the enormous foreign-policy bureaucracy. Each office in the pyramid does a different job and sees the world in its own way.

● *Activists also play a role in American foreign policy. Here, Nadia Murad tells a rapt Senate hearing on the Islamic State: "I was raped and sold and was abused [by IS] but I was lucky." Her mother and six brothers were all killed in one day.*

TABLE 18.1 **Presidents' Foreign-Policy Experience**

The first six presidents had extensive foreign-policy experience. Of the six most recent presidents only one George H. W. Bush had any foreign-policy experience at all.

	SECRETARY OF STATE	OTHER DIPLOMATIC OR CABINET POST	CHIEF U.S. REPRESENTATIVE TO GREAT BRITAIN	CHIEF U.S. REPRESENTATIVE TO OTHER MAJOR POWER	COMMANDED U.S. FORCES IN WAR
FIRST SIX PRESIDENTS					
George Washington					X
John Adams		X	X	X	
Thomas Jefferson	X	X		X	
James Madison	X				
James Monroe	X	X	X	X	
John Quincy Adams	X	X	X	X	
MOST RECENT PRESIDENTS					
Jimmy Carter					
Ronald Reagan					
George H. W. Bush		X		X	
Bill Clinton					
George W. Bush					
Barack Obama					
Donald Trump					

The State Department

The State Department, the very first cabinet agency established under the Constitution, is responsible for managing diplomatic relations with more than two hundred nations. State is responsible for negotiating treaties, distributing foreign assistance, and managing daily contact with other nations.

State Department officers are interested in understanding other nations and cultures. They learn foreign languages, live abroad, and favor diplomatic solutions—usually multilateral ones. The department is sometimes accused of being out of step with majority American opinion, which can favor skeptical disengagement. Critics often have a bit of sarcastic fun with the location of the State Department's headquarters—an area of Washington, DC, known as Foggy Bottom.

This skepticism leads to a serious problem: The State Department is chronically underfunded. Its offices around the world lack key personnel. Many observers (as well as foreign-policy officers talking off the record) worry that the United States is shortchanging its diplomatic efforts by underfunding the State Department. They warn that China is eagerly trying to fill the void left behind by American neglect of statecraft. From this perspective, the United States is ceding the crucial area of diplomacy to rivals like China—which are taking full advantage of American indifference. The Trump Administration, with its tough realist world view, has proven especially skeptical of the diplomats' role. After twenty months in office, the administration still has no ambassador in 78 nations—and has not even nominated ambassadors to 34 countries including Australia, Sweden, Mexico, Ireland, or Chile.[29]

Discover how to negotiate agreements with foreign entities.

The Department of Defense

The Department of Defense (DOD) manages the military. It is the largest organization in government and the largest employer in the United States. The DOD is responsible for over two million military personnel, seven hundred thousand civilian employees, and troops deployed in 177 nations from Turkey to Djibouti. They are all led by the secretary of defense, who is always a civilian. The department is housed in a huge five-sided office building known as the Pentagon.

Not surprising, Defense Department officials see the world very differently than the State Department. The DOD makes military calculations, toting up risks and threats, assets, and strategy. As you can see, when you were talking "government-speak" about the Pentagon and Foggy Bottom, you were sounding a familiar Washington lament about the failure of these two important cabinet offices to coordinate with one another.

Two problems haunt the Defense Department. First, the massive bureaucracy is bound up in red tape and very slow to change.[30] Second, the military is divided by rivalry between the services. The Army, Navy, Air Force, and Marine Corps are all eager to deploy their own tactical assets during military operations. These tensions can create such confusion that, in one notorious case, a Marine involved in the invasion of Grenada had to use a pay phone to report details back to Washington. The Chairman of the Joint Chiefs of Staff, a military figure, is charged on behalf of the president and secretary of defense with coordinating the branches—a tall order, given rivalries among them.

Intelligence

The United States has a large and complicated intelligence community. More than 15 different agencies and offices gather information from around the world. The best known is the Central Intelligence Agency, which is responsible for foreign intelligence. However, the Departments of State, Defense, Energy, and the Treasury all have their own foreign intelligence operations, as do the military branches. The Federal Bureau of Investigation is responsible for domestic intelligence, which often has to be coordinated with information from abroad.

In theory, each intelligence office and agency monitors a different spectrum of threats. In reality, they have overlapping jurisdictions and act as rivals (a familiar theme in the foreign-policy bureaucracy). They are slow to share information or communicate. There is a standard answer to turf wars like the one in the spy community: Create a new agency and charge it with coordinating all the others. In 2004, after hearings into the 9/11 terrorist attacks exposed the chaos, Congress created a director of national intelligence charged with bringing order to American intelligence. Did this mandate impose coordination or simply inject one more voice into the contest? Answer: Both.

The National Security Council

The National Security Council is part of the Executive Office of the President. It brings the most important foreign-policy officers together to advise the president. The council includes the president and the vice president, along with the secretaries of state, defense, and homeland security. It also includes the director of national intelligence, the head of the Joint Chiefs of Staff (the top military officer), and others who the president may name. This is one of the most high-powered groups in a city of high-powered groups. Very different perspectives and personalities come together to hammer out major foreign-policy decisions.

Projections for Economic Growth

WHICH ECONOMIES ARE GROWING THE FASTEST?

The United States has the largest economy but this chart shows what international economists predict for the immediate future.

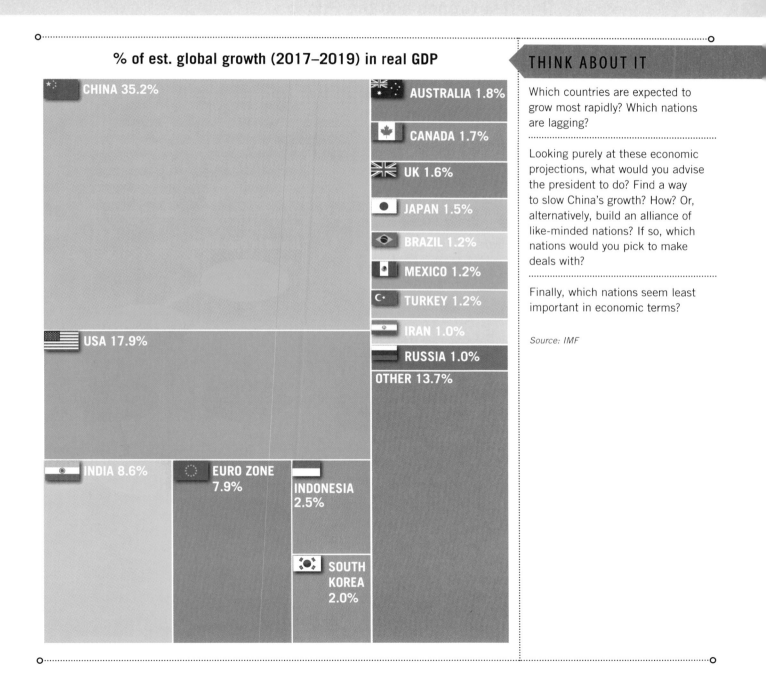

% of est. global growth (2017–2019) in real GDP

CHINA 35.2%

USA 17.9%

INDIA 8.6%

EURO ZONE 7.9%

INDONESIA 2.5%

SOUTH KOREA 2.0%

AUSTRALIA 1.8%

CANADA 1.7%

UK 1.6%

JAPAN 1.5%

BRAZIL 1.2%

MEXICO 1.2%

TURKEY 1.2%

IRAN 1.0%

RUSSIA 1.0%

OTHER 13.7%

THINK ABOUT IT

Which countries are expected to grow most rapidly? Which nations are lagging?

Looking purely at these economic projections, what would you advise the president to do? Find a way to slow China's growth? How? Or, alternatively, build an alliance of like-minded nations? If so, which nations would you pick to make deals with?

Finally, which nations seem least important in economic terms?

Source: IMF

Other Executive Agencies

A great many other bureaus and agencies engage in foreign policy. The president's economic team plays an important role. The Office of the U.S. Trade Representative negotiates trade deals. The Labor Department leads business groups abroad. The Department of Homeland Security brings together a host of agencies ranging from the Coast Guard to the Immigration Service. Each agency and office pushes to define foreign-policy problems. Each seeks to put its own spin on America's approach to the world.

Interest Groups and the Public

Organized groups play an active role in foreign policymaking—far more so than in most other nations. On high-profile issues such as trade agreements, every side mobilizes and lobbies. Some groups focus support for specific countries (see Figure 18.4), while others lobby for specific causes: Human rights groups and Christian organizations that are concerned about religious persecution in other nations are among the most familiar interest groups on Capitol Hill.

Groups are most effective at exerting influence on low-profile issues; cherry growers or health insurance companies can often persuade policymakers to slip favors into a law or regulation. It is much harder to affect high-profile issues because policymakers are usually committed to their positions. In these cases, interest groups assist officials who are already on their side by arming them with information, arguments, and elegant PowerPoint presentations (see Chapter 12).

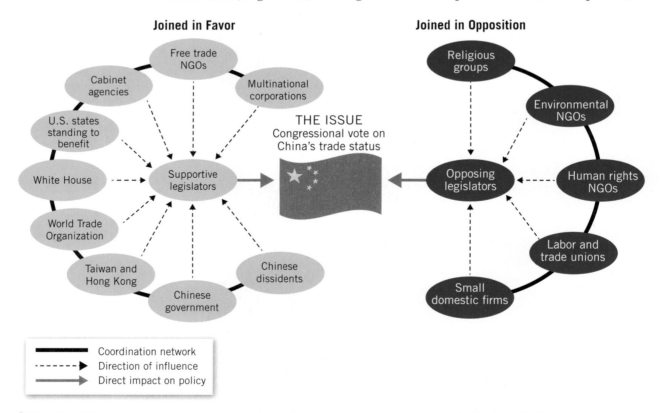

● **Figure 18.4.** *A big vote in Congress brings out the full range of policy influences. Here the line up over a vote taken during the Clinton Administration on whether to renew China's status as a "Most Favored Nation" (originally granted in 1980). Groups fought the renewal on the basis of Chinese policies regarding trade, labor, environment, and religious persecution. The most important actors trying to influence Congress in this case were the government agencies themselves. The Office of the Trade Representative, the State Department, and the White House all effectively rounded up votes. The renewal passed. Note how the complicated trade relationship between these two powers has been a political issue for decades. (Hook)*

Public opinion and the media can also have a powerful impact. The public generally does not pay much attention to foreign policy. Once in a while, however, a foreign-policy issue moves to the forefront of American politics. The media plays it up and the public leaps in with its opinions. The administration—or its opponents—can keep the issue at the top of the newsfeeds. Wars are the most common major events, and they often follow a cycle. At first, the American majority rallies around the flag and throws its support to the president and the troops. The inevitable antiwar demonstrations get scant media attention. Over time, especially if the war bogs down or its purpose grows murky, as in Vietnam or Iraq, the public turns against the action. It becomes a major story. Even small antiwar protests make the news. Congress begins to stir, holding hearings and scrutinizing appropriations. Public outcry, fanned by media coverage, makes unpopular wars difficult to prosecute.

Fragmentation or Success?

The policies produced by these many agencies, offices, legislators, and groups—all pulling and hauling and scrambling for influence—are typical of American government. It is chaotic, messy, unpredictable, open—and often democratic. Yet there is always the foreign-policy difference: At the end of the process, the president can make a decision and break the stalemate—deploy the Navy, issue a warning, embrace one foreign leader and challenge another, sign an executive agreement with one nation, cut off an agreement with another. Strong presidents have considerable leverage. Despite the messy process, U.S. foreign policy has been relatively successful through much of the nation's history. The United States emerged victorious and more powerful than ever from World War I, World War II, and the Cold War.

The great question about the foreign-policy process today is one that we have raised in many other contexts. Does the fragmented, wide-open American policy scramble capture a democratic energy that forces policymakers to see things from many different perspectives? Or does it leave too much power in the hands of the president?

 **The Bottom Line**

» Although we often talk about nations as if they had a single interest, many different individuals and institutions shape foreign policy.

» Congress and the presidents were originally foreign-policy partners. During the Cold War, the checks and balances diminished. Today, the president takes the lead and Congress offers a check.

» The most important executive agencies in foreign policymaking are the State Department, the Defense Department, and the National Security Council.

» Other important foreign-policy influences include intelligence agencies such as the CIA, economic bureaus like the Office of the U.S. Trade Representative, interest groups, corporations, foreign governments, the media, and the public.

» The key question about American foreign policy: Is the messy, fragmented system swirling around the president an effective way to generate new ideas? Or is it too chaotic for the twenty-first century? Or both?

🛈 Adding All of It Up: Grand Strategies in U.S. History

American leaders create an overall framework to meet the challenges of the time. Their **grand strategy** includes everything from a military doctrine to ways of seeing and interpreting the world. The United States has adopted, then moved away, from four different grand strategies over the past century. Once a strategy is in place it can be very difficult to change—until a dramatic event breaks up the old order. Today, many different interests and forces struggle to shape a new grand strategy for our time.

Grand strategy: An overarching vision that defines and guides a nation's foreign policy.

Standing Alone (1918–1939)

World War I was horrific. The fighting bogged down in trenches in eastern France, and hundreds of thousands of men died moving the battle line back and forth a few miles. After Europeans on both sides had bled their armies for three years, the United States entered the war and quickly tipped the balance. At least from the American perspective, the United States led England and France to victory over Germany and Austria.

President Woodrow Wilson championed a new international order after the war. The United States would spread democracy to every nation and join with other countries in a collective security organization called the League of Nations. Wilson's dreams were, he said, "to correct the evil" and to "purify . . . every process of our common life."[31]

Wilson's highly moral and multilateral vision met with furious opposition. Many Americans were scornful of the European leaders who had blundered into the terrible war. Some became isolationists and wanted nothing more to do with international affairs. Many others became unilateralists. They were willing to act abroad, but only on American terms. They would not permit the League of Nations—or any other international organization—to make decisions for the United States. In November 1918, the Republicans won both houses of Congress and, when President Wilson refused to compromise on his multilateral approach, Congress voted down his peace treaty and refused to join the League of Nations.

In the years following World War I, the American grand strategy was simple: The United States would intervene, unilaterally, only when its own interests were threatened. The United States sent ships and troops around the world—to Russia (during and after the Bolshevik Revolution), Mexico, Panama, Turkey, China, and many other places. It almost always acted independently and minded its own interests.

The Cold War (1945–1991)

When World War II began in 1939, many Americans wanted nothing to do with another foreign war. "America first," they said. On December 7, 1941, Japan attacked the naval base at Pearl Harbor, sank 11 ships, and killed 2,400 men. On that day, the era of standing alone ended.

Less than four years later, large swaths of Europe and Asia lay in rubble. A mind-numbing number of people were dead (the chilling estimates vary from 38 to 70 million). When the war ended, in September 1945, the only rival to the United States was the Soviet Union, whose armies occupied the nations of Central Europe. Many observers warned that the Soviets were poised to extend their control. If anyone was going to lead the free world against the Soviet Union, it had to be the United States.

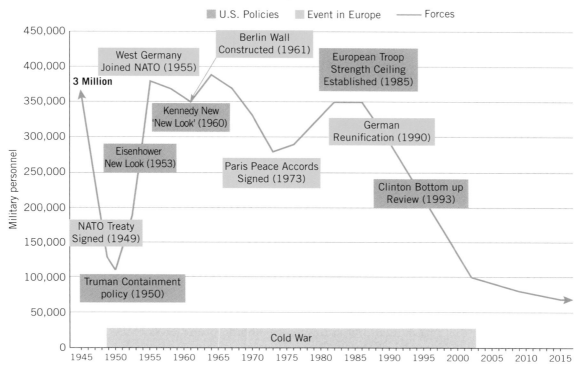

U.S. Forces in Europe (1945–2016) Historical View

Legend: ■ U.S. Policies ■ Event in Europe —— Forces

Y-axis (Military personnel): 0, 50,000, 100,000, 150,000, 200,000, 250,000, 300,000, 350,000, 400,000, 450,000

X-axis: 1945, 1950, 1955, 1960, 1965, 1970, 1975, 1980, 1985, 1990, 1995, 2000, 2005, 2010, 2015

Labels on chart:
- 3 Million
- West Germany Joined NATO (1955)
- Berlin Wall Constructed (1961)
- European Troop Strength Ceiling Established (1985)
- Kennedy New 'New Look' (1960)
- Eisenhower New Look (1953)
- German Reunification (1990)
- Paris Peace Accords Signed (1973)
- NATO Treaty Signed (1949)
- Clinton Bottom up Review (1993)
- Truman Containment policy (1950)
- Cold War

● **Figure 18.5** *U.S. Troop Strength in Europe during the Cold War. For 50 years, the United States, operating with its allies (through the North Atlantic Treaty Organization, or NATO), focused on containing the Soviet Union in its sphere by stationing troops in Europe and elsewhere. (U.S. European Command)*

The Truman administration decided to accept the Soviets' current sphere of influence but to oppose every effort to expand it, a policy known as **containment** (see Figure 18.5). The crucial test came in February 1947. The Democratic administration asked a Republican Congress to pour funds into Greece and Turkey to stop them from turning to communism. Legend has it that the chair of the Foreign Relations Committee, Senator Arthur Vandenberg (R-MI), promised to support Truman but gave him a word of advice about rallying the nation: "You are going to have to scare the hell out of the American people."[32] Truman proceeded to do just this in a famous speech before Congress: Regimes of "terror and oppression," said Truman, exploiting human want and misery" menace the world.[33]

Although the United States retained economic and military primacy, it joined with other nations in **multilateral organizations** dedicated to opposing communism and spreading democracy and capitalism. It broke with its own past to help establish multiple organizations: the United Nations (formed in 1945), the Organization of American States (OAS, 1948), and the North Atlantic Treaty Organization (NATO, 1949). Senator Vandenberg gave the era its famous slogan when he quipped that American party politics "stopped at the water's edge." In other words, Democrats and Republicans would no longer disagree (at least, not too loudly) about international affairs.[34]

All the same, the era posed new and difficult questions for American leaders. Should the United States support brutal dictators if they joined us in fighting communists? Should it resist popular democratic movements if they seemed to tilt toward communism? Where and when should we send troops? Each of these questions eventually escalated into an angry debate. Conservatives defended the fight against "the

Containment: American Cold War strategy designed to stop the spread of communism.

Multilateral organization: An international organization of three or more nations organized around a common goal.

John F. Kennedy's Speech in Berlin— "I am a Berliner"

Ronald Reagan's Speech in Berlin: "Tear down this wall"

See footage of the joyous destruction of the Berlin Wall in 1989

Evil Empire," as some of them dubbed the Soviet Union. Liberals began to charge that an increasingly knee-jerk fight against the fading threat of communism was leading the United States to repress democratic movements around the world.

The debate grew heated. However, with thousands of American and Soviet missiles still threatening a nuclear holocaust, the Cold War framework remained in place—until Soviet communism suddenly collapsed.

The New World Order (1989–2001)

Around the world, people gaped at the incredible television footage in November 1989. Germans were clambering onto the Berlin Wall and ripping it apart. For almost 30 years, the wall—running through Berlin and separating communist Germany from democratic Germany—had been the symbol of the Cold War. Communist guards had shot people trying to leap to freedom. President John Kennedy had looked out at the wall and declared, "All free [people], wherever they may live, are citizens of Berlin." Ronald Reagan had stood on the same spot and challenged the Soviet leader, "Mr. Gorbachev, tear down this wall." Now the East German guards stood awkwardly by, uncertain what to do, as the delirious mob did just that. Within two years, the entire Soviet empire collapsed. The framework that had guided American foreign policy for more than 50 years was suddenly irrelevant. What next?

President George H. W. Bush proclaimed "a new world order." He touted an active, multilateral march toward free markets and democracy. On his right, the neoconservatives began to press for a more muscular foreign policy. The United States should use its unchallenged military strength to make the world more peaceful, democratic, and secure, this group argued. If allies did not want to get on board, they should just get out of our way.

The War on Terror (2001–2009)

The 9/11 attacks killed almost three thousand people. The attacks shut down American institutions from coast to coast—financial markets in New York, Disney World in Florida, the great arch in St. Louis, and air travel across American airspace (for five days). In the stunned aftermath, the George W. Bush administration constructed a formidable new foreign-policy framework. To define the attacks as a crime would have brought in the American justice system. Instead, the administration declared them an act of war and responded with a "war on terror." That choice changed America's role in the world.

The war on terror targeted terrorists, nations that harbored terrorists, and any organizations that assisted terrorists. Opponents soon rose up and charged that a war on terror would become an endless conflict against an amorphous foe and would, in the long run, weaken the United States by undermining its bedrock values—liberty and the rule of law (we discussed this debate in Chapter 5, on civil liberties).

During the Cold War, the United States operated on the theory of *deterrence*: build a

● One of history's turning points: Jubilant Berliners climb the Berlin Wall as communism collapses. Suddenly, American foreign policymakers needed an entirely new grand strategy.

military so overpowering—including nuclear weapons—that other nations will be afraid to attack. Deterrence is aimed at other governments. However, the strategy does not work with extremists who are willing to sacrifice their lives for a cause.

What can be done against such fanatics? President George W. Bush defined the Bush Doctrine—the strategy of **preemptive war**. As the president explained it at West Point, "deterrence—the promise of massive retaliation against nations—means nothing against shadowy terrorist networks with no nation or citizens to defend." The United States, he continued, had to eliminate threats "before they emerge." Our military "must be ready to strike in any dark corner of the globe"—before a nation or group directly threatens us.[35]

We must attack them before they can strike at us. In responding to terrorist threats, the United States launched long and costly wars in Afghanistan and Iraq; it launched air strikes or sent special forces into Libya, Syria, Yemen, Cameroon, and many other hot spots. However, in tackling terrorist threats, conventional means of warfare, such as invading another country, prove less effective than policing measures such as gathering intelligence and punishing criminal behavior.

In the aftermath of the terrorist attacks on 9/11, the administration and Congress created the Homeland Security Act, which set in motion what is sometimes called "the single-largest government reorganization since the creation of the Department of Defense" in 1947.[36] The act created the department of Homeland Security, which has 244,000 employees and 24 subordinate agencies ranging from Immigration and Customs Enforcement (ICE) to the Secret Service protecting the president. Related legislation, the USA Patriot Act gave police and security personnel far more latitude to monitor, search, and detain suspects both abroad and at home.

The War on Terror agencies live on, as part of the national bureaucracy and as voices in foreign policy debates. The Obama administration, however, stopped using the term, "War on Terror," and lowered the rhetorical temperature. Fighting terror—with intelligence, drone strikes, and special forces—remained important but no longer defined the United States role in the world.

Preemptive war: The effort to attack hostile powers before they launch attacks. Highly controversial because it sanctions striking first.

 **The Bottom Line**

» The United States forged four grand strategies in the twentieth century: It stood alone and acted unilaterally (1918–1939), it led the democratic nations in multilateral coalitions during the Cold War (1945–1991), it debated a new world order after the Cold War (1991–2001), and it launched a war on terror (2001–2009).

Conclusion: The Next Grand Strategy

Today, American grand strategy is up for grabs. The Obama administration developed a modest grand strategy with four interlocking components: maintain American military and economic primacy; reduce American military commitments (as the president put it, "don't do stupid shit"); operate through international organizations ("lead from behind," said the president); and pivot toward Asia.[37]

President Trump came to office with a strong "America First" attitude—realist, deeply impatient with international organizations, and ready to reset relations with undemocratic enemies. Time will tell how that strategy develops, how successful it

What Do YOU Think?

Building a New Grand Strategy

The United States is looking for a new grand strategy in international affairs. We need to organize American thinking around a set of ideas—and signal them to the world. What is the most important thing to include?

Emphasize cooperation. The world faces many different kinds of difficulties: Global warming, rogue regimes (like North Korea), terrorism, unfair economic competitors, and the list goes on. The only way to deal with them all is to sit down and negotiate multilateral agreements that enlist many countries in solving problems that no nation, no matter how rich or powerful, can solve alone. No nation will get everything it wants, but working together would be best for everyone.

America First. The United States is the richest and most powerful nation in the world. In pursuit of multilateral agreements, it has permitted other, weaker nations to take advantage. Even if all nations benefit from free trade, the United States has still seen loss of its manufacturing base—a development that hurts the nation and its communities in the long run. Moreover, the world is a dangerous place with many different actors who will respond only to direct threats of force. This will mean scaling back some ambitions—such as global warming—but, even there, we can lead by example.

Mix and Match. A really good doctrine has to be flexible and apply in many kinds of situations. Can you think of a way to combine these two? Or is there some other priority encountered in this chapter—perhaps American values, or Hamiltonian Foreign policy—that you would include in your Grand Strategy?

might be, and how deep its roots will sink. For now, American grand strategy seems up for grabs. The editor of the most widely read foreign-policy journal noted that international policy today was "full of sound and fury, signifying something. Take your pick as to what."[38]

How will it all add up? As you reflect on the options, go back to the goals of American foreign policy. Any grand strategy must successfully protect national security, enhance economic well-being, and reflect American values. As you can see, the national discussion about how best to accomplish these goals points in completely different directions—from going it alone to engaging the world and collaborating with others.

No matter what you would choose, remember the basic truth: The next American foreign-policy strategy will—like all the past ones—reflect American ideals and values. It will answer the same question raised in every chapter of this book, the deepest question of American politics: *Who are we?*

● *Arlington National Cemetery holds the remains of soldiers from every American war. It reminds us that foreign policy reflects America's deepest values and convictions— and often calls for the nation's greatest sacrifices.*

CHAPTER SUMMARY

⬤ Foreign policy explores how the United States engages the world. Ultimately, it raises the deepest question about the nation: Is the United States the richest and most powerful country, ready to lead the world, or is it a declining superpower?

⬤ The three goals of American foreign policy are security, prosperity, and spreading American values. These three goals sometimes conflict.

⬤ The United States spends as much on its military as do other leading powers combined. Primacy suggests that it should act with unparalleled power. The security trap suggests that an effort to achieve and maintain primacy builds resentments and resistance. Soft power leads instead through culture and values.

⬤ The United States is responsible for a fifth of the world economy and more than 50 percent more than its nearest rival, China. However, China's economic growth rate in recent years has been much higher than that of the United States.

⬤ U.S. economic policy had generally revolved around free trade—reducing barriers to trade between nations. Today, free trade meets resistance.

⬤ American policymakers have to make two basic choices: isolationism versus active engagement with the world; unilateralism (going it alone) and multilateralism (working with other nations in organizations and associations);

⬤ Congress originally shared foreign policy with the executive branch, but today prime responsibility has shifted to the executive. However, foreign policy is best understood in light of domestic policy, as the outcome of many agencies and groups pushing for their own interests and advantage.

⬤ Twentieth-century grand strategies included standing alone (1918–1939), primacy in a coalition of anticommunist nations (1946–1989), the search for a new world order (1991–2001), and the war on terror (2001–2009); now it is up for grabs.

⬤ One key question of contemporary foreign policy is whether war makes the United States more secure or whether pursuing security has compromised American values and harmed America's stance in the world.

🔗
Check your understanding of Chapter 18.

🔗
Need to review key ideas in greater depth? Click here.

Flashcard review.

KEY TERMS

American exceptionalism, p. 574
Containment, p. 587
Fair trade, p. 571
Free trade, p. 570
Grand strategy, p. 586
Internationalism, p. 576
Isolationism, p. 576
Liberalism, p. 566

Multilateralism, p. 577
Multilateral organization, p. 587
Preemptive war, p. 589
Primacy, p. 565
Protectionism, p. 570
Realism, p. 565
Security trap, p. 567
Soft power, p. 567

Strategic disengagement, p. 576
Theory of democratic peace, p. 574
Trade deficit, p. 569
Unilateralism, p. 577
War Powers Act, p. 580
World Trade Organization, (WTO) p. 570

STUDY QUESTIONS

1. Name the three foreign-policy goals that the United States pursues. Discuss the relative importance of each goal. If you had to stress one, which would it be?

2. What do you consider the most important threat to American security? Would it be a traditional threat like foreign enemies, or a more common problem such as global warming? Explain your thinking.

3. What is free trade? Describe the difference between free trade and fair trade.

4. Describe "American exceptionalism." Do you consider it a truth, a myth, or something in between? Defend your answer.

5. Define strategic disengagement and internationalism. Pick one perspective and defend it.

6. Define unilateralism and multilateralism. Which position makes more sense to you? Explain why.

7. What do neoconservatives believe? Do you agree or disagree with this perspective?

8. We described four approaches to foreign policy: Wilsonian, Hamiltonian, Jeffersonian, and Jacksonian. Describe each. Defend the one that most appeals to you.

9. What four grand strategies did the United States pursue in the twentieth century? Describe each.

10. If you had to design a grand strategy for today, what would you emphasize?

Go to www.oup.com/us/Morone to find quizzes, flash cards, simulations, tutorials, videos, and other study tools.

APPENDIX I

THE DECLARATION OF INDEPENDENCE

When in the course of human events, it becomes necessary for one people to dissolve the political bands which have connected them with another, and to assume, among the powers of the earth, the separate and equal station to which the Laws of Nature and of Nature's God entitle them, a decent respect to the opinions of mankind requires that they should declare the causes which impel them to the separation.

We hold these truths to be self-evident, that all men are created equal, that they are endowed by their Creator with certain unalienable Rights, that among these are life, liberty and the pursuit of happiness. That to secure these rights, governments are instituted among men, deriving their just powers from the consent of the governed; that whenever any form of government becomes destructive of these ends, it is the right of the people to alter or to abolish it, and to institute new Government, laying its foundation on such principles and organizing its powers in such form, as to them shall seem most likely to effect their safety and happiness. Prudence, indeed, will dictate that Governments long established should not be changed for light and transient causes; and, accordingly, all experience hath shown, that mankind are more disposed to suffer, while evils are sufferable, than to right themselves by abolishing the forms to which they are accustomed. But when a long train of abuses and usurpations, pursuing invariably the same object evinces a design to reduce them under absolute despotism, it is their right, it is their duty, to throw off such government, and to provide new guards for their future security. Such has been the patient sufferance of these colonies; and such is now the necessity which constrains them to alter their former systems of government. The history of the present King of Great Britain is a history of repeated injuries and usurpations, all having in direct object the establishment of an absolute tyranny over these States. To prove this, let facts be submitted to a candid world:

He has refused his assent to laws, the most wholesome and necessary for the public good.

He has forbidden his governors to pass laws of immediate and pressing importance, unless suspended in their operation till his assent should be obtained; and, when so suspended, he has utterly neglected to attend to them.

He has refused to pass other laws for the accommodation of large districts of people, unless those people would relinquish the right of representation in the legislature, a right inestimable to them and formidable to tyrants only.

He has called together legislative bodies at places unusual, uncomfortable, and distant from the depository of their public records, for the sole purpose of fatiguing them into compliance with his measures.

He has dissolved representative houses repeatedly, for opposing with manly firmness his invasions on the rights of the people.

He has refused for a long time, after such dissolutions, to cause others to be elected; whereby the legislative powers, incapable of annihilation, have returned to the People at large for their exercise; the State remaining in the mean time exposed to all the dangers of invasion from without, and convulsions within.

He has endeavored to prevent the population of these States; for that purpose obstructing the laws for naturalization of foreigners; refusing to pass others to encourage their migrations hither, and raising the conditions of new appropriations of lands.

He has obstructed the administration of justice, by refusing his assent to laws for establishing judiciary powers.

He has made judges dependent on his will alone, for the tenure of their offices, and the amount and payment of their salaries.

He has erected a multitude of new offices, and sent hither swarms of officers to harass our people, and eat out their substance.

He has kept among us, in times of peace, standing armies without the consent of our legislatures.

He has affected to render the Military independent of, and superior to, the civil power.

He has combined with others to subject us to a jurisdiction foreign to our constitution and unacknowledged by our laws; giving his assent to their acts of pretended legislation:

For quartering large bodies of armed troops among us;

For protecting them, by a mock trial, from punishment for any murders which they should commit on the inhabitants of these States;

For cutting off our trade with all parts of the world;

For imposing taxes on us without our Consent;

For depriving us, in many cases, of the benefits of Trial by Jury;

For transporting us beyond Seas to be tried for pretended offences;

For abolishing the free System of English Laws in a neighbouring Province, establishing therein an Arbitrary government, and enlarging its Boundaries so as to render it at once an example and fit instrument for introducing the same absolute rule into these colonies;

For taking away our charters, abolishing our most valuable laws, and altering fundamentally the forms of our governments;

For suspending our own legislatures, and declaring themselves invested with power to legislate for us in all cases whatsoever.

He has abdicated government here, by declaring us out of his protection and waging war against us.

He has plundered our seas, ravaged our coasts, burnt our towns, and destroyed the lives of our people.

He is at this time transporting large armies of foreign mercenaries to complete the works of death, desolation and tyranny, already begun with circumstances of cruelty and perfidy scarcely paralleled in the most barbarous ages, and totally unworthy the head of a civilized nation.

He has constrained our fellow citizens taken captive on the high seas to bear arms against their country, to become the executioners of their friends and brethren, or to fall themselves by their hands.

He has excited domestic insurrections amongst us, and has endeavored to bring on the inhabitants of our frontiers, the merciless Indian savages, whose known rule of warfare, is an undistinguished destruction of all ages, sexes and conditions.

In every stage of these oppressions we have petitioned for redress in the most humble terms; our repeated petitions have been answered only by repeated injury. A prince whose character is thus marked by every act which may define a tyrant, is unfit to be the ruler of a free people.

Nor have we been wanting in attentions to our British brethren. We have warned them from time to time of attempts by their legislature to extend an unwarrantable jurisdiction over us. We have reminded them of the circumstances of our emigration and settlement here. We have appealed to their native justice and magnanimity, and we have conjured them by the ties of our common kindred to disavow these usurpations, which, would inevitably interrupt our connections and correspondence. They, too, have been deaf to the voice of justice and of consanguinity. We must, therefore, acquiesce in the necessity, which denounces our separation, and hold them, as we hold the rest of mankind, enemies in war, in peace friends.

We, therefore, the representatives of the United States of America, in general Congress, assembled, appealing to the Supreme Judge of the world for the rectitude of our intentions, do, in the name, and by the authority of the good people of these colonies, solemnly publish and declare, that these united colonies are, and of right ought to be free and independent states; that they are absolved from all allegiance to the British Crown, and that all political connection between them and the state of Great Britain, is and ought to be totally dissolved; and that, as free and independent states, they have full power to levy war, conclude peace, contract alliances, establish commerce, and to do all other acts and things which independent states may of right do. And for the support of this declaration, with a firm reliance on the protection of Divine Providence, we mutually pledge to each other our lives, our fortunes and our sacred honor.

THE CONSTITUTION OF THE UNITED STATES OF AMERICA

We the People of the United States, in Order to form a more perfect Union, establish Justice, insure domestic Tranquility, provide for the common defence, promote the general Welfare, and secure the Blessings of Liberty to ourselves and our Posterity, do ordain and establish this Constitution for the United States of America.

Article I

Section 1

All legislative Powers herein granted shall be vested in a Congress of the United States, which shall consist of a Senate and House of Representatives.

Section 2

The House of Representatives shall be composed of Members chosen every second Year by the People of the several States, and the Electors in each State shall have the Qualifications requisite for Electors of the most numerous Branch of the State Legislature.

No Person shall be a Representative who shall not have attained to the Age of twenty five Years, and been seven Years a Citizen of the United States, and who shall not, when elected, be an Inhabitant of that State in which he shall be chosen.

Representatives [and direct Taxes]* shall be apportioned among the several States [which may be included within this Union, according to their respective Numbers, which shall be determined by adding to the whole Number of free Persons, including those bound to Service for a Term of Years, and excluding Indians not taxed, three fifths of all other Persons].** The actual Enumeration shall be made within three Years after the first Meeting of the Congress of the United States, and within every subsequent Term of ten Years, in such Manner as they shall by Law direct. The Number of Representatives shall not exceed one for every thirty Thousand, but each State shall have at Least one Representative; and until such enumeration shall be made, the State of New Hampshire shall be entitled to choose three, Massachusetts eight, Rhode-Island and Providence Plantations one, Connecticut five, New York six, New Jersey four, Pennsylvania eight, Delaware one, Maryland six, Virginia ten, North Carolina five, South Carolina five, and Georgia three.

When vacancies happen in the Representation from any State, the Executive Authority thereof shall issue Writs of Election to fill such Vacancies.

The House of Representatives shall choose their Speaker and other Officers; and shall have the sole Power of Impeachment.

Section 3

The Senate of the United States shall be composed of two Senators from each State, chosen [by the Legislature thereof]*** for six Years; and each Senator shall have one Vote.

---

*Modified by the Sixteenth Amendment.
**Negated by the Fourteenth Amendment.
***Changed by the Seventeenth Amendment.

Immediately after they shall be assembled in Consequence of the first Election, they shall be divided as equally as may be into three Classes. The Seats of the Senators of the first Class shall be vacated at the Expiration of the second Year, of the second Class at the Expiration of the fourth Year, and of the third Class at the Expiration of the sixth Year, so that one third may be chosen every second Year, [and if Vacancies happen by Resignation, or otherwise, during the Recess of the Legislature of any State, the Executive thereof may make temporary Appointments until the next Meeting of the Legislature, which shall then fill such Vacancies].*

No Person shall be a Senator who shall not have attained to the Age of thirty Years, and been nine Years a Citizen of the United States, and who shall not, when elected, be an Inhabitant of that State for which he shall be chosen.

The Vice President of the United States shall be President of the Senate, but shall have no Vote, unless they be equally divided.

The Senate shall choose their other Officers, and also a President pro tempore, in the Absence of the Vice President, or when he shall exercise the Office of President of the United States.

The Senate shall have the sole Power to try all Impeachments. When sitting for that Purpose, they shall be on Oath or Affirmation. When the President of the United States is tried, the Chief Justice shall preside: And no Person shall be convicted without the Concurrence of two thirds of the Members present.

Judgment in Cases of Impeachment shall not extend further than to removal from Office, and disqualification to hold and enjoy any Office of honor, Trust or Profit under the United States: but the Party convicted shall nevertheless be liable and subject to Indictment, Trial, Judgment and Punishment, according to Law.

Section 4

The Times, Places and Manner of holding Elections for Senators and Representatives, shall be prescribed in each State by the Legislature thereof; but the Congress may at any time by Law make or alter such Regulations, except as to the Places of chusing Senators.

[The Congress shall assemble at least once in every Year, and such Meeting shall be on the first Monday in December, unless they shall by Law appoint a different Day.]**

Section 5

Each House shall be the Judge of the Elections, Returns and Qualifications of its own Members, and a Majority of each shall constitute a Quorum to do Business; but a smaller Number may adjourn from day to day, and may be authorized to compel the Attendance of absent Members, in such Manner, and under such Penalties as each House may provide.

Each House may determine the Rules of its Proceedings, punish its Members for disorderly Behaviour, and, with the Concurrence of two thirds, expel a Member.

Each House shall keep a Journal of its Proceedings, and from time to time publish the same, excepting such Parts as may in their Judgment require Secrecy; and the Yeas and Nays of the Members of either House on any question shall, at the Desire of one fifth of those Present, be entered on the Journal.

Neither House, during the Session of Congress, shall, without the Consent of the other, adjourn for more than three days, nor to any other Place than that in which the two Houses shall be sitting.

---

*Modified by the Seventeenth Amendment.
**Changed to January 3 by the Twentieth Amendment.

Section 6

The Senators and Representatives shall receive a Compensation for their Services, to be ascertained by Law, and paid out of the Treasury of the United States. They shall in all Cases, except Treason, Felony and Breach of the Peace, be privileged from Arrest during their Attendance at the Session of their respective Houses, and in going to and returning from the same; and for any Speech or Debate in either House, they shall not be questioned in any other Place.

No Senator or Representative shall, during the Time for which he was elected, be appointed to any civil Office under the Authority of the United States, which shall have been created, or the Emoluments whereof shall have been increased during such time; and no Person holding any Office under the United States, shall be a Member of either House during his Continuance in Office.

Section 7

All Bills for raising Revenue shall originate in the House of Representatives; but the Senate may propose or concur with Amendments as on other Bills.

Every Bill which shall have passed the House of Representatives and the Senate, shall, before it become a Law, be presented to the President of the United States: If he approve he shall sign it, but if not he shall return it, with his Objections to that House in which it shall have originated, who shall enter the Objections at large on their Journal, and proceed to reconsider it. If after such Reconsideration two thirds of that House shall agree to pass the Bill, it shall be sent, together with the Objections, to the other House, by which it shall likewise be reconsidered, and if approved by two thirds of that House, it shall become a Law. But in all such Cases the Votes of both Houses shall be determined by yeas and Nays, and the Names of the Persons voting for and against the Bill shall be entered on the Journal of each House respectively. If any Bill shall not be returned by the President within ten Days (Sundays excepted) after it shall have been presented to him, the Same shall be a Law, in like Manner as if he had signed it, unless the Congress by their Adjournment prevent its Return, in which Case it shall not be a Law.

Every Order, Resolution, or Vote to which the Concurrence of the Senate and House of Representatives may be necessary (except on a question of Adjournment) shall be presented to the President of the United States; and before the Same shall take Effect, shall be approved by him, or being disapproved by him, shall be re-passed by two thirds of the Senate and House of Representatives, according to the Rules and Limitations prescribed in the Case of a Bill.

Section 8

The Congress shall have Power

To lay and collect Taxes, Duties, Imposts and Excises, to pay the Debts and provide for the common Defence and general Welfare of the United States; but all Duties, Imposts and Excises shall be uniform throughout the United States;

To borrow Money on the credit of the United States;

To regulate Commerce with foreign Nations, and among the several States, and with the Indian Tribes;

To establish an uniform Rule of Naturalization, and uniform Laws on the subject of Bankruptcies throughout the United States;

To coin Money, regulate the Value thereof, and of foreign Coin, and fix the Standard of Weights and Measures;

To provide for the Punishment of counterfeiting the Securities and current Coin of the United States;

To establish Post Offices and post Roads;

To promote the Progress of Science and useful Arts, by securing for limited Times to Authors and Inventors the exclusive Right to their respective Writings and Discoveries;

To constitute Tribunals inferior to the supreme Court;

To define and punish Piracies and Felonies committed on the high Seas, and Offences against the Law of Nations;

To declare War, grant Letters of Marque and Reprisal, and make Rules concerning Captures on Land and Water;

To raise and support Armies, but no Appropriation of Money to that Use shall be for a longer Term than two Years;

To provide and maintain a Navy;

To make Rules for the Government and Regulation of the land and naval Forces;

To provide for calling forth the Militia to execute the Laws of the Union, suppress Insurrections and repel Invasions;

To provide for organizing, arming, and disciplining the Militia, and for governing such Part of them as may be employed in the Service of the United States, reserving to the States respectively, the Appointment of the Officers, and the Authority of training the Militia according to the discipline prescribed by Congress;

To exercise exclusive Legislation in all Cases whatsoever, over such District (not exceeding ten Miles square) as may, by Cession of particular States, and the Acceptance of Congress, become the Seat of the Government of the United States, and to exercise like Authority over all Places purchased by the Consent of the Legislature of the State in which the Same shall be, for the Erection of Forts, Magazines, Arsenals, dock-Yards, and other needful Buildings;—And

To make all Laws which shall be necessary and proper for carrying into Execution the foregoing Powers, and all other Powers vested by this Constitution in the Government of the United States, or in any Department or Officer thereof.

Section 9

The Migration or Importation of such Persons as any of the States now existing shall think proper to admit, shall not be prohibited by the Congress prior to the Year one thousand eight hundred and eight, but a Tax or duty may be imposed on such Importation, not exceeding ten dollars for each Person.

The Privilege of the Writ of Habeas Corpus shall not be suspended, unless when in Cases of Rebellion or Invasion the public Safety may require it.

No Bill of Attainder or ex post facto Law shall be passed.

[No Capitation, or other direct, Tax shall be laid, unless in Proportion to the Census or enumeration herein before directed to be taken.]*

No Tax or Duty shall be laid on Articles exported from any State.

No Preference shall be given by any Regulation of Commerce or Revenue to the Ports of one State over those of another; nor shall Vessels bound to, or from, one State, be obliged to enter, clear, or pay Duties in another.

No Money shall be drawn from the Treasury, but in Consequence of Appropriations made by Law; and a regular Statement and Account of the Receipts and Expenditures of all public Money shall be published from time to time.

No Title of Nobility shall be granted by the United States: And no Person holding any Office of Profit or Trust under them, shall, without the Consent of the Congress, accept of any present, Emolument, Office, or Title, of any kind whatever, from any King, Prince, or foreign State.

---

*Modified by the Sixteenth Amendment.

Section 10

No State shall enter into any Treaty, Alliance, or Confederation; grant Letters of Marque and Reprisal; coin Money; emit Bills of Credit; make any Thing but gold and silver Coin a Tender in Payment of Debts; pass any Bill of Attainder, ex post facto Law, or Law impairing the Obligation of Contracts, or grant any Title of Nobility.

No State shall, without the Consent of the Congress, lay any Imposts or Duties on Imports or Exports, except what may be absolutely necessary for executing it's inspection Laws: and the net Produce of all Duties and Imposts, laid by any State on Imports or Exports, shall be for the Use of the Treasury of the United States; and all such Laws shall be subject to the Revision and Control of the Congress.

No State shall, without the Consent of Congress, lay any Duty of Tonnage, keep Troops, or Ships of War in time of Peace, enter into any Agreement or Compact with another State, or with a foreign Power, or engage in War, unless actually invaded, or in such imminent Danger as will not admit of delay.

Article II

Section 1

The executive Power shall be vested in a President of the United States of America. He shall hold his Office during the Term of four Years, and, together with the Vice President, chosen for the same Term, be elected, as follows:

Each State shall appoint, in such Manner as the Legislature thereof may direct, a Number of Electors, equal to the whole Number of Senators and Representatives to which the State may be entitled in the Congress: but no Senator or Representative, or Person holding an Office of Trust or Profit under the United States, shall be appointed an Elector.

[The Electors shall meet in their respective States, and vote by Ballot for two Persons, of whom one at least shall not be an Inhabitant of the same State with themselves. And they shall make a List of all the Persons voted for, and of the Number of Votes for each; which List they shall sign and certify, and transmit sealed to the Seat of the Government of the United States, directed to the President of the Senate. The President of the Senate shall, in the Presence of the Senate and House of Representatives, open all the Certificates, and the Votes shall then be counted. The Person having the greatest Number of Votes shall be the President, if such Number be a Majority of the whole Number of Electors appointed; and if there be more than one who have such Majority, and have an equal Number of Votes, then the House of Representatives shall immediately choose by Ballot one of them for President; and if no Person have a Majority, then from the five highest on the List the said House shall in like Manner choose the President. But in choosing the President, the Votes shall be taken by States, the Representation from each State having one Vote; a quorum for this purpose shall consist of a Member or Members from two thirds of the States, and a Majority of all the States shall be necessary to a Choice. In every Case, after the Choice of the President, the Person having the greatest Number of Votes of the Electors shall be the Vice President. But if there should remain two or more who have equal Votes, the Senate shall choose from them by Ballot the Vice President.]*

The Congress may determine the Time of choosing the Electors, and the Day on which they shall give their Votes; which Day shall be the same throughout the United States.

No Person except a natural born Citizen, or a Citizen of the United States, at the time of the Adoption of this Constitution, shall be eligible to the Office of

---

*Changed by the Twelfth and Twentieth Amendments.

President; neither shall any Person be eligible to that Office who shall not have attained to the Age of thirty five Years, and been fourteen Years a Resident within the United States.

In Case of the Removal of the President from Office, or of his Death, Resignation, or Inability to discharge the Powers and Duties of the said Office, the Same shall devolve on the Vice President, and the Congress may by Law provide for the Case of Removal, Death, Resignation or Inability, both of the President and Vice President, declaring what Officer shall then act as President, and such Officer shall act accordingly, until the Disability be removed, or a President shall be elected.

The President shall, at stated Times, receive for his Services, a Compensation, which shall neither be increased nor diminished during the Period for which he shall have been elected, and he shall not receive within that Period any other Emolument from the United States, or any of them.

Before he enter on the Execution of his Office, he shall take the following Oath or Affirmation:—"I do solemnly swear (or affirm) that I will faithfully execute the Office of President of the United States, and will to the best of my Ability, preserve, protect and defend the Constitution of the United States."

Section 2

The President shall be Commander in Chief of the Army and Navy of the United States, and of the Militia of the several States, when called into the actual Service of the United States; he may require the Opinion, in writing, of the principal Officer in each of the executive Departments, upon any Subject relating to the Duties of their respective Offices, and he shall have Power to grant Reprieves and Pardons for Offences against the United States, except in Cases of Impeachment.

He shall have Power, by and with the Advice and Consent of the Senate, to make Treaties, provided two thirds of the Senators present concur; and he shall nominate, and by and with the Advice and Consent of the Senate, shall appoint Ambassadors, other public Ministers and Consuls, Judges of the supreme Court, and all other Officers of the United States, whose Appointments are not herein otherwise provided for, and which shall be established by Law: but the Congress may by Law vest the Appointment of such inferior Officers, as they think proper, in the President alone, in the Courts of Law, or in the Heads of Departments.

The President shall have Power to fill up all Vacancies that may happen during the Recess of the Senate, by granting Commissions which shall expire at the End of their next Session.

Section 3

He shall from time to time give to the Congress Information of the State of the Union, and recommend to their Consideration such Measures as he shall judge necessary and expedient; he may, on extraordinary Occasions, convene both Houses, or either of them, and in Case of Disagreement between them, with Respect to the Time of Adjournment, he may adjourn them to such Time as he shall think proper; he shall receive Ambassadors and other public Ministers; he shall take Care that the Laws be faithfully executed, and shall Commission all the Officers of the United States.

Section 4

The President, Vice President and all civil Officers of the United States, shall be removed from Office on Impeachment for, and Conviction of, Treason, Bribery, or other high Crimes and Misdemeanors.

Article III

Section 1

The judicial Power of the United States shall be vested in one supreme Court, and in such inferior Courts as the Congress may from time to time ordain and establish. The Judges, both of the supreme and inferior Courts, shall hold their Offices during good Behaviour, and shall, at stated Times, receive for their Services a Compensation, which shall not be diminished during their Continuance in Office.

Section 2

The judicial Power shall extend to all Cases, in Law and Equity, arising under this Constitution, the Laws of the United States, and Treaties made, or which shall be made, under their Authority;—to all Cases affecting Ambassadors, other public Ministers and Consuls;—to all Cases of admiralty and maritime Jurisdiction;—to Controversies to which the United States shall be a Party;—to Controversies between two or more States;—[between a State and Citizens of another State];—between Citizens of different States;—between Citizens of the same State claiming Lands under Grants of different States, [and between a State,] or the Citizens thereof, [and foreign States, Citizens or Subjects].*

In all Cases affecting Ambassadors, other public Ministers and Consuls, and those in which a State shall be Party, the supreme Court shall have original Jurisdiction. In all the other Cases before mentioned, the supreme Court shall have appellate Jurisdiction, both as to Law and Fact, with such Exceptions, and under such Regulations as the Congress shall make.

The Trial of all Crimes, except in Cases of Impeachment, shall be by Jury; and such Trial shall be held in the State where the said Crimes shall have been committed; but when not committed within any State, the Trial shall be at such Place or Places as the Congress may by Law have directed.

Section 3

Treason against the United States, shall consist only in levying War against them, or in adhering to their Enemies, giving them Aid and Comfort. No Person shall be convicted of Treason unless on the Testimony of two Witnesses to the same overt Act, or on Confession in open Court.

The Congress shall have Power to declare the Punishment of Treason, but no Attainder of Treason shall work Corruption of Blood, or Forfeiture except during the Life of the Person attainted.

Article IV

Section 1

Full Faith and Credit shall be given in each State to the public Acts, Records, and judicial Proceedings of every other State. And the Congress may by general Laws prescribe the Manner in which such Acts, Records and Proceedings shall be proved, and the Effect thereof.

Section 2

The Citizens of each State shall be entitled to all Privileges and Immunities of Citizens in the several States.

---

*Altered by the Twelfth Amendment.

A Person charged in any State with Treason, Felony, or other Crime, who shall flee from Justice, and be found in another State, shall on Demand of the executive Authority of the State from which he fled, be delivered up, to be removed to the State having Jurisdiction of the Crime.

[No Person held to Service or Labour in one State, under the Laws thereof, escaping into another, shall, in Consequence of any Law or Regulation therein, be discharged from such Service or Labour, but shall be delivered up on Claim of the Party to whom such Service or Labour may be due.]*

Section 3

New States may be admitted by the Congress into this Union; but no new State shall be formed or erected within the Jurisdiction of any other State; nor any State be formed by the Junction of two or more States, or Parts of States, without the Consent of the Legislatures of the States concerned as well as of the Congress.

The Congress shall have Power to dispose of and make all needful Rules and Regulations respecting the Territory or other Property belonging to the United States; and nothing in this Constitution shall be so construed as to Prejudice any Claims of the United States, or of any particular State.

Section 4

The United States shall guarantee to every State in this Union a Republican Form of Government, and shall protect each of them against Invasion; and on Application of the Legislature, or of the Executive (when the Legislature cannot be convened), against domestic Violence.

Article V

The Congress, whenever two thirds of both Houses shall deem it necessary, shall propose Amendments to this Constitution, or, on the Application of the Legislatures of two thirds of the several States, shall call a Convention for proposing Amendments, which, in either Case, shall be valid to all Intents and Purposes, as Part of this Constitution, when ratified by the Legislatures of three fourths of the several States, or by Conventions in three fourths thereof, as the one or the other Mode of Ratification may be proposed by the Congress; Provided that no Amendment which may be made prior to the Year One thousand eight hundred and eight shall in any Manner affect the first and fourth Clauses in the Ninth Section of the first Article; and that no State, without its Consent, shall be deprived of its equal Suffrage in the Senate.

Article VI

All Debts contracted and Engagements entered into, before the Adoption of this Constitution, shall be as valid against the United States under this Constitution, as under the Confederation.

This Constitution, and the Laws of the United States which shall be made in Pursuance thereof; and all Treaties made, or which shall be made, under the Authority of the United States, shall be the supreme Law of the Land; and the Judges in every State shall be bound thereby, any Thing in the Constitution or Laws of any State to the Contrary notwithstanding.

The Senators and Representatives before mentioned, and the Members of the several State Legislatures, and all executive and judicial Officers, both of the United

---

*Repealed by the Thirteenth Amendment.

States and of the several States, shall be bound by Oath or Affirmation, to support this Constitution; but no religious Test shall ever be required as a Qualification to any Office or public Trust under the United States.

Article VII

The Ratification of the Conventions of nine States, shall be sufficient for the Establishment of this Constitution between the States so ratifying the Same.

The Word, "the," being interlined between the seventh and eighth Lines of the first Page, the Word "Thirty" being partly written on an Erazure in the fifteenth Line of the first Page, The Words "is tried" being interlined between the thirty second and thirty third Lines of the first Page and the Word "the" being interlined between the forty third and forty fourth Lines of the second Page.

Attest William Jackson Secretary

Done in Convention by the Unanimous Consent of the States present the Seventeenth Day of September in the Year of our Lord one thousand seven hundred and Eighty seven and of the Independence of the United States of America the Twelfth In witness whereof We have hereunto subscribed our Names,

G°. WASHINGTON
Presidt and deputy from Virginia

Delaware
Geo: Read
Gunning Bedford
　jun
John Dickinson
Richard Bassett
Jaco: Broom

Maryland
James McHenry
Dan of St Thos. Jenifer
Danl. Carroll

Virginia
John Blair
James Madison Jr.

North Carolina
Wm. Blount
Richd. Dobbs
　Spaight
Hu Williamson

South Carolina
J. Rutledge
Charles Cotesworth
　Pinckney
Charles Pinckney
Pierce Butler

Georgia
William Few
Abr Baldwin

New Hampshire
John Langdon
Nicholas Gilman

Massachusetts
Nathaniel Gorham
Rufus King

Connecticut
Wm. Saml. Johnson
Roger Sherman

New York
Alexander Hamilton

New Jersey
Wil: Livingston
David Brearley
Wm. Paterson
Jona: Dayton

Pennsylvania
B Franklin
Thomas Mifflin
Robt. Morris
Geo. Clymer
Thos. FitzSimons
Jared Ingersoll
James Wilson
Gouv Morris

Articles

In addition to, and Amendment of the Constitution of the United States of America, proposed by Congress, and ratified by the Legislatures of the several States, pursuant to the fifth Article of the original Constitution.

(The first ten amendments to the U.S. Constitution were ratified December 15, 1791, and form what is known as the "Bill of Rights.")

Amendment I

Congress shall make no law respecting an establishment of religion, or prohibiting the free exercise thereof; or abridging the freedom of speech, or of the press; or the right of the people peaceably to assemble, and to petition the Government for a redress of grievances.

Amendment II

A well regulated Militia, being necessary to the security of a free State, the right of the people to keep and bear Arms, shall not be infringed.

Amendment III

No Soldier shall, in time of peace be quartered in any house, without the consent of the Owner, nor in time of war, but in a manner to be prescribed by law.

Amendment IV

The right of the people to be secure in their persons, houses, papers, and effects, against unreasonable searches and seizures, shall not be violated, and no Warrants shall issue, but upon probable cause, supported by Oath or affirmation, and particularly describing the place to be searched, and the persons or things to be seized.

Amendment V

No person shall be held to answer for a capital, or otherwise infamous crime, unless on a presentment or indictment of a Grand Jury, except in cases arising in the land or naval forces, or in the Militia, when in actual service in time of War or public danger; nor shall any person be subject for the same offence to be twice put in jeopardy of life or limb; nor shall be compelled in any criminal case to be a witness against himself, nor be deprived of life, liberty, or property, without due process of law; nor shall private property be taken for public use, without just compensation.

Amendment VI

In all criminal prosecutions, the accused shall enjoy the right to a speedy and public trial, by an impartial jury of the State and district wherein the crime shall have been committed, which district shall have been previously ascertained by law, and to be informed of the nature and cause of the accusation; to be confronted with the witnesses against him; to have compulsory process for obtaining witnesses in his favor, and to have the Assistance of Counsel for his defence.

Amendment VII

In Suits at common law, where the value in controversy shall exceed twenty dollars, the right of trial by jury shall be preserved, and no fact tried by a jury, shall be otherwise re-examined in any Court of the United States, than according to the rules of the common law.

Amendment VIII

Excessive bail shall not be required, nor excessive fines imposed, nor cruel and unusual punishments inflicted.

Amendment IX

The enumeration in the Constitution, of certain rights, shall not be construed to deny or disparage others retained by the people.

Amendment X

The powers not delegated to the United States by the Constitution, nor prohibited by it to the States, are reserved to the States respectively, or to the people.

Amendment XI

Passed by Congress March 4, 1794. Ratified February 7, 1795.

Note: Article III, Section 2, of the Constitution was modified by Amendment XI.

The Judicial power of the United States shall not be construed to extend to any suit in law or equity, commenced or prosecuted against one of the United States by Citizens of another State, or by Citizens or Subjects of any Foreign State.

Amendment XII

Passed by Congress December 9, 1803. Ratified June 15, 1804.

Note: A portion of Article II, Section 1, of the Constitution was superseded by the Twelfth Amendment.

The Electors shall meet in their respective states and vote by ballot for President and Vice-President, one of whom, at least, shall not be an inhabitant of the same state with themselves; they shall name in their ballots the person voted for as President, and in distinct ballots the person voted for as Vice-President, and they shall make distinct lists of all persons voted for as President, and of all persons voted for as Vice-President, and of the number of votes for each, which lists they shall sign and certify, and transmit sealed to the seat of the government of the United States, directed to the President of the Senate;—the President of the Senate shall, in the presence of the Senate and House of Representatives, open all the certificates and the votes shall then be counted;—The person having the greatest number of votes for President, shall be the President, if such number be a majority of the whole number of Electors appointed; and if no person have such majority, then from the persons having the highest numbers not exceeding three on the list of those voted for as President, the House of Representatives shall choose immediately, by ballot, the President. But in choosing the President, the votes shall be taken by states, the representation from each state having one vote; a quorum for this purpose shall consist of a member or members from two-thirds of the states, and a majority of all the states shall be necessary to a choice. [And if the House of Representatives shall not choose a President whenever the right of choice shall devolve upon them, before the fourth day of March next following, then the Vice-President shall act as President, as in case of the death or other constitutional disability of the President.—]* The person having the greatest number of votes as Vice-President, shall be the Vice-President, if such number be a majority of the whole number of Electors appointed, and if no person have a majority, then from the two highest numbers on the list, the Senate shall choose the Vice-President; a quorum for the purpose shall consist of two-thirds of the whole number of Senators, and a majority of the whole number shall be necessary to a choice. But no person constitutionally ineligible to the office of President shall be eligible to that of Vice-President of the United States.

---

*Superseded by Section 3 of the Twentieth Amendment.

Amendment XIII

Passed by Congress January 31, 1865. Ratified December 6, 1865.

   Note: A portion of Article IV, Section 2, of the Constitution was superseded by the Thirteenth Amendment.

Section 1

Neither slavery nor involuntary servitude, except as a punishment for crime whereof the party shall have been duly convicted, shall exist within the United States, or any place subject to their jurisdiction.

Section 2

Congress shall have power to enforce this article by appropriate legislation.

Amendment XIV

Passed by Congress June 13, 1866. Ratified July 9, 1868.

   Note: Article I, Section 2, of the Constitution was modified by Section 2 of the Fourteenth Amendment.

Section 1

All persons born or naturalized in the United States, and subject to the jurisdiction thereof, are citizens of the United States and of the State wherein they reside. No State shall make or enforce any law which shall abridge the privileges or immunities of citizens of the United States; nor shall any State deprive any person of life, liberty, or property, without due process of law; nor deny to any person within its jurisdiction the equal protection of the laws.

Section 2

Representatives shall be apportioned among the several States according to their respective numbers, counting the whole number of persons in each State, excluding Indians not taxed. But when the right to vote at any election for the choice of electors for President and Vice-President of the United States, Representatives in Congress, the Executive and Judicial officers of a State, or the members of the Legislature thereof, is denied to any of the male inhabitants of such State, being twenty-one years of age,* and citizens of the United States, or in any way abridged, except for participation in rebellion, or other crime, the basis of representation therein shall be reduced in the proportion which the number of such male citizens shall bear to the whole number of male citizens twenty-one years of age in such State.

Section 3

No person shall be a Senator or Representative in Congress, or elector of President and Vice-President, or hold any office, civil or military, under the United States, or under any State, who, having previously taken an oath, as a member of Congress, or as an officer of the United States, or as a member of any State legislature, or as an executive or judicial officer of any State, to support the Constitution of the United States, shall have engaged in insurrection or rebellion against the same, or given aid or comfort to the enemies thereof. But Congress may by a vote of two-thirds of each House, remove such disability.

*Changed by Section 1 of the Twenty-sixth Amendment.

Section 4

The validity of the public debt of the United States, authorized by law, including debts incurred for payment of pensions and bounties for services in suppressing insurrection or rebellion, shall not be questioned. But neither the United States nor any State shall assume or pay any debt or obligation incurred in aid of insurrection or rebellion against the United States, or any claim for the loss or emancipation of any slave; but all such debts, obligations and claims shall be held illegal and void.

Section 5

The Congress shall have the power to enforce, by appropriate legislation, the provisions of this article.

Amendment XV

Passed by Congress February 26, 1869. Ratified February 3, 1870.

Section 1

The right of citizens of the United States to vote shall not be denied or abridged by the United States or by any State on account of race, color, or previous condition of servitude.

Section 2

The Congress shall have the power to enforce this article by appropriate legislation.

Amendment XVI

Passed by Congress July 2, 1909. Ratified February 3, 1913.

Note: Article I, Section 9, of the Constitution was modified by Amendment XVI.

The Congress shall have power to lay and collect taxes on incomes, from whatever source derived, without apportionment among the several States, and without regard to any census or enumeration.

Amendment XVII

Passed by Congress May 13, 1912. Ratified April 8, 1913.

Note: Article I, Section 3, of the Constitution was modified by the Seventeenth Amendment.

The Senate of the United States shall be composed of two Senators from each State, elected by the people thereof, for six years; and each Senator shall have one vote. The electors in each State shall have the qualifications requisite for electors of the most numerous branch of the State legislatures.

When vacancies happen in the representation of any State in the Senate, the executive authority of such State shall issue writs of election to fill such vacancies: Provided, That the legislature of any State may empower the executive thereof to make temporary appointments until the people fill the vacancies by election as the legislature may direct.

This amendment shall not be so construed as to affect the election or term of any Senator chosen before it becomes valid as part of the Constitution.

Amendment XVIII

Passed by Congress December 18, 1917. Ratified January 16, 1919. Repealed by Amendment XXI.

Section 1

After one year from the ratification of this article the manufacture, sale, or transportation of intoxicating liquors within, the importation thereof into, or the exportation thereof from the United States and all territory subject to the jurisdiction thereof for beverage purposes is hereby prohibited.

Section 2

The Congress and the several States shall have concurrent power to enforce this article by appropriate legislation.

Section 3

This article shall be inoperative unless it shall have been ratified as an amendment to the Constitution by the legislatures of the several States, as provided in the Constitution, within seven years from the date of the submission hereof to the States by the Congress.

Amendment XIX

Passed by Congress June 4, 1919. Ratified August 18, 1920.

The right of citizens of the United States to vote shall not be denied or abridged by the United States or by any State on account of sex.

Congress shall have power to enforce this article by appropriate legislation.

Amendment XX

Passed by Congress March 2, 1932. Ratified January 23, 1933.

Note: Article I, Section 4, of the Constitution was modified by Section 2 of this amendment. In addition, a portion of the Twelfth Amendment was superseded by Section 3.

Section 1

The terms of the President and the Vice President shall end at noon on the 20th day of January, and the terms of Senators and Representatives at noon on the 3d day of January, of the years in which such terms would have ended if this article had not been ratified; and the terms of their successors shall then begin.

Section 2

The Congress shall assemble at least once in every year, and such meeting shall begin at noon on the 3d day of January, unless they shall by law appoint a different day.

Section 3

If, at the time fixed for the beginning of the term of the President, the President elect shall have died, the Vice President elect shall become President. If a President shall not have been chosen before the time fixed for the beginning of his term, or if the President elect shall have failed to qualify, then the Vice President elect shall act as President until a President shall have qualified; and the Congress may by law provide for the case wherein neither a President elect nor a Vice President shall have qualified, declaring who shall then act as President, or the manner in which one who is to act shall be selected, and such person shall act accordingly until a President or Vice President shall have qualified.

Section 4

The Congress may by law provide for the case of the death of any of the persons from whom the House of Representatives may choose a President whenever the right of choice shall have devolved upon them, and for the case of the death of any of the persons from whom the Senate may choose a Vice President whenever the right of choice shall have devolved upon them.

Section 5

Sections 1 and 2 shall take effect on the 15th day of October following the ratification of this article.

Section 6

This article shall be inoperative unless it shall have been ratified as an amendment to the Constitution by the legislatures of three-fourths of the several States within seven years from the date of its submission.

Amendment XXI

Passed by Congress February 20, 1933. Ratified December 5, 1933.

Section 1

The eighteenth article of amendment to the Constitution of the United States is hereby repealed.

Section 2

The transportation or importation into any State, Territory, or Possession of the United States for delivery or use therein of intoxicating liquors, in violation of the laws thereof, is hereby prohibited.

Section 3

This article shall be inoperative unless it shall have been ratified as an amendment to the Constitution by conventions in the several States, as provided in the Constitution, within seven years from the date of the submission hereof to the States by the Congress.

Amendment XXII

Passed by Congress March 21, 1947. Ratified February 27, 1951.

Section 1

No person shall be elected to the office of the President more than twice, and no person who has held the office of President, or acted as President, for more than two years of a term to which some other person was elected President shall be elected to the office of President more than once. But this Article shall not apply to any person holding the office of President when this Article was proposed by Congress, and shall not prevent any person who may be holding the office of President, or acting as President, during the term within which this Article becomes operative from holding the office of President or acting as President during the remainder of such term.

Section 2

This article shall be inoperative unless it shall have been ratified as an amendment to the Constitution by the legislatures of three-fourths of the several States within seven years from the date of its submission to the States by the Congress.

Amendment XXIII

Passed by Congress June 16, 1960. Ratified March 29, 1961.

Section 1

The District constituting the seat of Government of the United States shall appoint in such manner as Congress may direct:

A number of electors of President and Vice President equal to the whole number of Senators and Representatives in Congress to which the District would be entitled if it were a State, but in no event more than the least populous State; they shall be in addition to those appointed by the States, but they shall be considered, for the purposes of the election of President and Vice President, to be electors appointed by a State; and they shall meet in the District and perform such duties as provided by the twelfth article of amendment.

Section 2

The Congress shall have power to enforce this article by appropriate legislation.

Amendment XXIV

Passed by Congress August 27, 1962. Ratified January 23, 1964.

Section 1

The right of citizens of the United States to vote in any primary or other election for President or Vice President, for electors for President or Vice President, or for Senator or Representative in Congress, shall not be denied or abridged by the United States or any State by reason of failure to pay poll tax or other tax.

Section 2

The Congress shall have power to enforce this article by appropriate legislation.

Amendment XXV

Passed by Congress July 6, 1965. Ratified February 10, 1967.
    Note: Article II, Section 1, of the Constitution was affected by the Twenty-Fifth Amendment.

Section 1

In case of the removal of the President from office or of his death or resignation, the Vice President shall become President.

Section 2

Whenever there is a vacancy in the office of the Vice President, the President shall nominate a Vice President who shall take office upon confirmation by a majority vote of both Houses of Congress.

Section 3

Whenever the President transmits to the President pro tempore of the Senate and the Speaker of the House of Representatives his written declaration that he is unable to discharge the powers and duties of his office, and until he transmits to them a written declaration to the contrary, such powers and duties shall be discharged by the Vice President as Acting President.

Section 4

Whenever the Vice President and a majority of either the principal officers of the executive departments or of such other body as Congress may by law provide, transmit to the President pro tempore of the Senate and the Speaker of the House of Representatives their written declaration that the President is unable to discharge the powers and duties of his office, the Vice President shall immediately assume the powers and duties of the office as Acting President.

Thereafter, when the President transmits to the President pro tempore of the Senate and the Speaker of the House of Representatives his written declaration that no inability exists, he shall resume the powers and duties of his office unless the Vice President and a majority of either the principal officers of the executive department or of such other body as Congress may by law provide, transmit within four days to the President pro tempore of the Senate and the Speaker of the House of Representatives their written declaration that the President is unable to discharge the powers and duties of his office. Thereupon Congress shall decide the issue, assembling within forty-eight hours for that purpose if not in session. If the Congress, within twenty-one days after receipt of the latter written declaration, or, if Congress is not in session, within twenty-one days after Congress is required to assemble, determines by two-thirds vote of both Houses that the President is unable to discharge the powers and duties of his office, the Vice President shall continue to discharge the same as Acting President; otherwise, the President shall resume the powers and duties of his office.

Amendment XXVI

Passed by Congress March 23, 1971. Ratified July 1, 1971.

Note: Amendment XIV, Section 2, of the Constitution was modified by Section 1 of the Twenty-Sixth Amendment.

Section 1

The right of citizens of the United States, who are eighteen years of age or older, to vote shall not be denied or abridged by the United States or by any State on account of age.

Section 2

The Congress shall have power to enforce this article by appropriate legislation.

Amendment XXVII

Originally proposed Sept. 25, 1789. Ratified May 7, 1992.

No law, varying the compensation for the services of the Senators and Representatives, shall take effect, until an election of representatives shall have intervened.

APPENDIX III

THE FEDERALIST PAPERS

By Alexander Hamilton, James Madison, John Jay

The debate over ratifying the Constitution in 1787-8 was very close, especially in New York. To persuade the people of the state, Hamilton, Madison, and Jay wrote eighty-five newspaper essays arguing for ratification. Three of the most influential, reproduced here, are Federalist Papers 1, 10, and 51.

FEDERALIST No. 1
General Introduction
For the Independent Journal. Saturday, October 27, 1787

HAMILTON
To the People of the State of New York:

AFTER an unequivocal experience of the inefficacy of the subsisting federal government, you are called upon to deliberate on a new Constitution for the United States of America. The subject speaks its own importance; comprehending in its consequences nothing less than the existence of the UNION, the safety and welfare of the parts of which it is composed, the fate of an empire in many respects the most interesting in the world. It has been frequently remarked that it seems to have been reserved to the people of this country, by their conduct and example, to decide the important question, whether societies of men are really capable or not of establishing good government from reflection and choice, or whether they are forever destined to depend for their political constitutions on accident and force. If there be any truth in the remark, the crisis at which we are arrived may with propriety be regarded as the era in which that decision is to be made; and a wrong election of the part we shall act may, in this view, deserve to be considered as the general misfortune of mankind.

This idea will add the inducements of philanthropy to those of patriotism, to heighten the solicitude which all considerate and good men must feel for the event. Happy will it be if our choice should be directed by a judicious estimate of our true interests, unperplexed and unbiased by considerations not connected with the public good. But this is a thing more ardently to be wished than seriously to be expected. The plan offered to our deliberations affects too many particular interests, innovates upon too many local institutions, not to involve in its discussion a variety of objects foreign to its merits, and of views, passions and prejudices little favorable to the discovery of truth.

Among the most formidable of the obstacles which the new Constitution will have to encounter may readily be distinguished the obvious interest of a certain class of men in every State to resist all changes which may hazard a diminution of the power, emolument, and consequence of the offices they hold under the State establishments; and the perverted ambition of another class of men, who will either hope to aggrandize themselves by the confusions of their country, or will flatter themselves with fairer prospects of elevation from the subdivision of the empire into several partial confederacies than from its union under one government.

It is not, however, my design to dwell upon observations of this nature. I am well aware that it would be disingenuous to resolve indiscriminately the opposition of any set of men (merely because their situations might subject them to suspicion) into interested or ambitious views. Candor will oblige us to admit that even such men may be actuated by upright intentions; and it cannot be doubted that much of the opposition which has made its appearance, or may hereafter make its appearance, will spring from sources, blameless at least, if not respectable—the honest errors of minds led astray by preconceived jealousies and fears. So numerous indeed and so powerful are the causes which serve to give a false bias to the judgment, that we, upon many occasions, see wise and good men on the wrong as well as on the right side of questions of the first magnitude to society. This circumstance, if duly attended to, would furnish a lesson of moderation to those who are ever so much persuaded of their being in the right in any controversy. And a further reason for caution, in this respect, might be drawn from the reflection that we are not always sure that those who advocate the truth are influenced by purer principles than their antagonists. Ambition, avarice, personal animosity, party opposition, and many other motives not more laudable than these, are apt to operate as well upon those who support as those who oppose the right side of a question. Were there not even these inducements to moderation, nothing could be more ill-judged than that intolerant spirit which has, at all times, characterized political parties. For in politics, as in religion, it is equally absurd to aim at making proselytes by fire and sword. Heresies in either can rarely be cured by persecution.

And yet, however just these sentiments will be allowed to be, we have already sufficient indications that it will happen in this as in all former cases of great national discussion. A torrent of angry and malignant passions will be let loose. To judge from the conduct of the opposite parties, we shall be led to conclude that they will mutually hope to evince the justness of their opinions, and to increase the number of their converts by the loudness of their declamations and the bitterness of their invectives. An enlightened zeal for the energy and efficiency of government will be stigmatized as the offspring of a temper fond of despotic power and hostile to the principles of liberty. An over-scrupulous jealousy of danger to the rights of the people, which is more commonly the fault of the head than of the heart, will be represented as mere pretense and artifice, the stale bait for popularity at the expense of the public good. It will be forgotten, on the one hand, that jealousy is the usual concomitant of love, and that the noble enthusiasm of liberty is apt to be infected with a spirit of narrow and illiberal distrust. On the other hand, it will be equally forgotten that the vigor of government is essential to the security of liberty; that, in the contemplation of a sound and well-informed judgment, their interest can never be separated; and that a dangerous ambition more often lurks behind the specious mask of zeal for the rights of the people than under the forbidden appearance of zeal for the firmness and efficiency of government. History will teach us that the former has been found a much more certain road to the introduction of despotism than the latter, and that of those men who have overturned the liberties of republics, the greatest number have begun their career by paying an obsequious court to the people; commencing demagogues, and ending tyrants.

In the course of the preceding observations, I have had an eye, my fellow-citizens, to putting you upon your guard against all attempts, from whatever quarter, to influence your decision in a matter of the utmost moment to your welfare, by any impressions other than those which may result from the evidence of truth. You will, no doubt, at the same time, have collected from the general scope of them, that they proceed from a source not unfriendly to the new Constitution. Yes, my countrymen, I own to you that, after having given it an attentive consideration, I am clearly of opinion it is your interest to adopt it. I am convinced that this is the safest course for your liberty, your dignity, and your happiness. I affect not reserves which I do not feel. I will not amuse you with an appearance of deliberation when I have decided. I frankly acknowledge to you my convictions, and I will freely lay before you the reasons on which they are founded. The consciousness of good intentions disdains ambiguity. I shall not, however, multiply professions on this head. My motives must remain in the depository of my own breast. My arguments will be open to all, and may be judged of by all. They shall at least be offered in a spirit which will not disgrace the cause of truth.

I propose, in a series of papers, to discuss the following interesting particulars:

THE UTILITY OF THE UNION TO YOUR POLITICAL PROSPERITY—THE INSUFFICIENCY OF THE PRESENT CONFEDERATION TO PRESERVE THAT UNION—THE NECESSITY OF A GOVERNMENT AT LEAST EQUALLY ENERGETIC WITH THE ONE PROPOSED, TO THE ATTAINMENT OF THIS OBJECT—THE CONFORMITY OF THE PROPOSED CONSTITUTION TO THE TRUE PRINCIPLES OF REPUBLICAN GOVERNMENT—ITS ANALOGY TO YOUR OWN STATE CONSTITUTION—and lastly, THE ADDITIONAL SECURITY WHICH ITS ADOPTION WILL AFFORD TO THE PRESERVATION OF THAT SPECIES OF GOVERNMENT, TO LIBERTY, AND TO PROPERTY.

In the progress of this discussion I shall endeavor to give a satisfactory answer to all the objections which shall have made their appearance, that may seem to have any claim to your attention.

It may perhaps be thought superfluous to offer arguments to prove the utility of the UNION, a point, no doubt, deeply engraved on the hearts of the great body of the people in every State, and one, which it may be imagined, has no adversaries. But the fact is, that we already hear it whispered in the private circles of those who oppose the new Constitution, that the thirteen States are of too great extent for any general system, and that we must of necessity resort to separate confederacies of distinct portions of the whole. This doctrine will, in all probability, be gradually propagated, till it has votaries enough to countenance an open avowal of it. For nothing can be more evident, to those who are able to take an enlarged view of the subject, than the alternative of an adoption of the new Constitution or a dismemberment of the Union. It will therefore be of use to begin by examining the advantages of that Union, the certain evils, and the probable dangers, to which every State will be exposed from its dissolution. This shall accordingly constitute the subject of my next address.

PUBLIUS

FEDERALIST No. 10
The Same Subject Continued (The Union as a Safeguard Against Domestic Faction and Insurrection)
From the Daily Advertiser. Thursday, November 22, 1787.

MADISON
To the People of the State of New York:

AMONG the numerous advantages promised by a well constructed Union, none deserves to be more accurately developed than its tendency to break and control the violence of faction. The friend of popular governments never finds himself so much alarmed for their character and fate, as when he contemplates their propensity to this dangerous vice. He will not fail, therefore, to set a due value on any plan which, without violating the principles to which he is attached, provides a proper cure for it. The instability, injustice, and confusion introduced into the public councils, have, in truth, been the mortal diseases under which popular governments have everywhere perished; as they continue to be the favorite and fruitful topics from which the

adversaries to liberty derive their most specious declamations. The valuable improvements made by the American constitutions on the popular models, both ancient and modern, cannot certainly be too much admired; but it would be an unwarrantable partiality, to contend that they have as effectually obviated the danger on this side, as was wished and expected. Complaints are everywhere heard from our most considerate and virtuous citizens, equally the friends of public and private faith, and of public and personal liberty, that our governments are too unstable, that the public good is disregarded in the conflicts of rival parties, and that measures are too often decided, not according to the rules of justice and the rights of the minor party, but by the superior force of an interested and overbearing majority. However anxiously we may wish that these complaints had no foundation, the evidence, of known facts will not permit us to deny that they are in some degree true. It will be found, indeed, on a candid review of our situation, that some of the distresses under which we labor have been erroneously charged on the operation of our governments; but it will be found, at the same time, that other causes will not alone account for many of our heaviest misfortunes; and, particularly, for that prevailing and increasing distrust of public engagements, and alarm for private rights, which are echoed from one end of the continent to the other. These must be chiefly, if not wholly, effects of the unsteadiness and injustice with which a factious spirit has tainted our public administrations.

By a faction, I understand a number of citizens, whether amounting to a majority or a minority of the whole, who are united and actuated by some common impulse of passion, or of interest, adversed to the rights of other citizens, or to the permanent and aggregate interests of the community.

There are two methods of curing the mischiefs of faction: the one, by removing its causes; the other, by controlling its effects.

There are again two methods of removing the causes of faction: the one, by destroying the liberty which is essential to its existence; the other, by giving to every citizen the same opinions, the same passions, and the same interests.

It could never be more truly said than of the first remedy, that it was worse than the disease.

Liberty is to faction what air is to fire, an aliment without which it instantly expires. But it could not be less folly to abolish liberty, which is essential to political life, because it nourishes faction, than it would be to wish the annihilation of air, which is essential to animal life, because it imparts to fire its destructive agency.

The second expedient is as impracticable as the first would be unwise. As long as the reason of man continues fallible, and he is at liberty to exercise it, different opinions will be formed. As long as the connection subsists between his reason and his self-love, his opinions and his passions will have a reciprocal influence on each other; and the former will be objects to which the latter will attach themselves. The diversity in the faculties of men, from which the rights of property originate, is not less an insuperable obstacle to a uniformity of interests. The protection of these faculties is the first object of government. From the protection of different and unequal faculties of acquiring property, the possession of different degrees and kinds of property immediately results; and from the influence of these on the sentiments and views of the respective proprietors, ensues a division of the society into different interests and parties.

The latent causes of faction are thus sown in the nature of man; and we see them everywhere brought into different degrees of activity, according to the different circumstances of civil society. A zeal for different opinions concerning religion, concerning government, and many other points, as well of speculation as of practice; an attachment to different leaders ambitiously contending for pre-eminence and power; or to persons of other descriptions whose fortunes have been interesting to the human passions, have, in turn, divided mankind into parties, inflamed them with mutual animosity, and rendered them much more disposed to vex and oppress each other than to co-operate for their common good. So strong is this propensity of mankind to fall into mutual animosities, that where no substantial occasion presents itself, the most frivolous and fanciful distinctions have been sufficient to kindle their unfriendly passions and excite their most violent conflicts. But the most common and durable source of factions has been the various and unequal distribution of property. Those who hold and those who are without property have

ever formed distinct interests in society. Those who are creditors, and those who are debtors, fall under a like discrimination. A landed interest, a manufacturing interest, a mercantile interest, a moneyed interest, with many lesser interests, grow up of necessity in civilized nations, and divide them into different classes, actuated by different sentiments and views. The regulation of these various and interfering interests forms the principal task of modern legislation, and involves the spirit of party and faction in the necessary and ordinary operations of the government.

No man is allowed to be a judge in his own cause, because his interest would certainly bias his judgment, and, not improbably, corrupt his integrity. With equal, nay with greater reason, a body of men are unfit to be both judges and parties at the same time; yet what are many of the most important acts of legislation, but so many judicial determinations, not indeed concerning the rights of single persons, but concerning the rights of large bodies of citizens? And what are the different classes of legislators but advocates and parties to the causes which they determine? Is a law proposed concerning private debts? It is a question to which the creditors are parties on one side and the debtors on the other. Justice ought to hold the balance between them. Yet the parties are, and must be, themselves the judges; and the most numerous party, or, in other words, the most powerful faction must be expected to prevail. Shall domestic manufactures be encouraged, and in what degree, by restrictions on foreign manufactures? are questions which would be differently decided by the landed and the manufacturing classes, and probably by neither with a sole regard to justice and the public good. The apportionment of taxes on the various descriptions of property is an act which seems to require the most exact impartiality; yet there is, perhaps, no legislative act in which greater opportunity and temptation are given to a predominant party to trample on the rules of justice. Every shilling with which they overburden the inferior number, is a shilling saved to their own pockets.

It is in vain to say that enlightened statesmen will be able to adjust these clashing interests, and render them all subservient to the public good. Enlightened statesmen will not always be at the helm. Nor, in many cases, can such an adjustment be made at all without taking into view indirect and remote considerations, which will rarely prevail over the immediate interest which one party may find in disregarding the rights of another or the good of the whole.

The inference to which we are brought is, that the CAUSES of faction cannot be removed, and that relief is only to be sought in the means of controlling its EFFECTS.

If a faction consists of less than a majority, relief is supplied by the republican principle, which enables the majority to defeat its sinister views by regular vote. It may clog the administration, it may convulse the society; but it will be unable to execute and mask its violence under the forms of the Constitution. When a majority is included in a faction, the form of popular government, on the other hand, enables it to sacrifice to its ruling passion or interest both the public good and the rights of other citizens. To secure the public good and private rights against the danger of such a faction, and at the same time to preserve the spirit and the form of popular government, is then the great object to which our inquiries are directed. Let me add that it is the great desideratum by which this form of government can be rescued from the opprobrium under which it has so long labored, and be recommended to the esteem and adoption of mankind.

By what means is this object attainable? Evidently by one of two only. Either the existence of the same passion or interest in a majority at the same time must be prevented, or the majority, having such coexistent passion or interest, must be rendered, by their number and local situation, unable to concert and carry into effect schemes of oppression. If the impulse and the opportunity be suffered to coincide, we well know that neither moral nor religious motives can be relied on as an adequate control. They are not found to be such on the injustice and violence of individuals, and lose their efficacy in proportion to the number combined together, that is, in proportion as their efficacy becomes needful.

From this view of the subject it may be concluded that a pure democracy, by which I mean a society consisting of a small number of citizens, who assemble and administer the government in person, can admit of no cure for the mischiefs of faction. A common passion or interest will, in almost every case, be felt by a majority of the whole; a communication and concert result from the form of government itself; and there is nothing to check the inducements to sacrifice the weaker party or an obnoxious individual. Hence it is that such democracies have ever been spectacles of turbulence and contention; have ever been found incompatible with personal security or the rights of property; and have in general been as short in their lives as they have been violent in their deaths. Theoretic politicians, who have patronized this species of government, have erroneously supposed that by reducing mankind to a perfect equality in their political rights, they would, at the same time, be perfectly equalized and assimilated in their possessions, their opinions, and their passions.

A republic, by which I mean a government in which the scheme of representation takes place, opens a different prospect, and promises the cure for which we are seeking. Let us examine the points in which it varies from pure democracy, and we shall comprehend both the nature of the cure and the efficacy which it must derive from the Union.

The two great points of difference between a democracy and a republic are: first, the delegation of the government, in the latter, to a small number of citizens elected by the rest; secondly, the greater number of citizens, and greater sphere of country, over which the latter may be extended.

The effect of the first difference is, on the one hand, to refine and enlarge the public views, by passing them through the medium of a chosen body of citizens, whose wisdom may best discern the true interest of their country, and whose patriotism and love of justice will be least likely to sacrifice it to temporary or partial considerations. Under such a regulation, it may well happen that the public voice, pronounced by the representatives of the people, will be more consonant to the public good than if pronounced by the people themselves, convened for the purpose. On the other hand, the effect may be inverted. Men of factious tempers, of local prejudices, or of sinister designs, may, by intrigue, by corruption, or by other means, first obtain the suffrages, and then betray the interests, of the people. The question resulting is, whether small or extensive republics are more favorable to the election of proper guardians of the public weal; and it is clearly decided in favor of the latter by two obvious considerations:

In the first place, it is to be remarked that, however small the republic may be, the representatives must be raised to a certain number, in order to guard against the cabals of a few; and that, however large it may be, they must be limited to a certain number, in order to guard against the confusion of a multitude. Hence, the number of representatives in the two cases not being in proportion to that of the two constituents, and being proportionally greater in the small republic, it follows that, if the proportion of fit characters be not less in the large than in the small republic, the former will present a greater option, and consequently a greater probability of a fit choice.

In the next place, as each representative will be chosen by a greater number of citizens in the large than in the small republic, it will be more difficult for unworthy candidates to practice with success the vicious arts by which elections are too often carried; and the suffrages of the people being more free, will be more likely to centre in men who possess the most attractive merit and the most diffusive and established characters.

It must be confessed that in this, as in most other cases, there is a mean, on both sides of which inconveniences will be found to lie. By enlarging too much the number of electors, you render the representatives too little acquainted with all their local circumstances and lesser interests; as by reducing it too much, you render him unduly attached to these, and too little fit to comprehend and pursue great and national objects. The federal Constitution forms a happy combination in this respect; the great and aggregate interests being referred to the national, the local and particular to the State legislatures.

The other point of difference is, the greater number of citizens and extent of territory which may be brought within the compass of republican than of democratic government; and it is this circumstance principally which renders factious combinations less to be dreaded in the former than in the latter. The smaller the society, the fewer probably will be the distinct parties and interests composing it; the fewer the distinct parties and interests, the more frequently will a majority be found of the same party; and the smaller the number of individuals composing a majority, and the smaller the compass within which they are placed, the more easily will they concert and execute their plans of oppression. Extend the sphere, and you take in a greater variety of parties and interests; you make it less probable that a majority of the whole will have a common motive to invade the rights of other citizens; or if such a common motive exists, it will be more difficult for all who feel it to discover their own strength, and to act in unison with each other. Besides other impediments, it may be remarked that, where there is a consciousness of unjust or dishonorable purposes, communication is always checked by distrust in proportion to the number whose concurrence is necessary.

Hence, it clearly appears, that the same advantage which a republic has over a democracy, in controlling the effects of faction, is enjoyed by a large over a small republic,—is enjoyed by the Union over the States composing it. Does the advantage consist in the substitution of representatives whose enlightened views and virtuous sentiments render them superior to local prejudices and schemes of injustice? It will not be denied that the representation of the Union will be most likely to possess these requisite endowments. Does it consist in the greater security afforded by a greater variety of parties, against the event of any one party being able to outnumber and oppress the rest? In an equal degree does the increased variety of parties comprised within the Union, increase this security. Does it, in fine, consist in the greater obstacles opposed to the concert and accomplishment of the secret wishes of an unjust and interested majority? Here, again, the extent of the Union gives it the most palpable advantage.

The influence of factious leaders may kindle a flame within their particular States, but will be unable to spread a general conflagration through the other States. A religious sect may degenerate into a political faction in a part of the Confederacy; but the variety of sects dispersed over the entire face of it must secure the national councils against any danger from that source. A rage for paper money, for an abolition of debts, for an equal division of property, or for any other improper or wicked project, will be less apt to pervade the whole body of the Union than a particular member of it; in the same proportion as such a malady is more likely to taint a particular county or district, than an entire State.

In the extent and proper structure of the Union, therefore, we behold a republican remedy for the diseases most incident to republican government. And according to the degree of pleasure and pride we feel in being republicans, ought to be our zeal in cherishing the spirit and supporting the character of Federalists.

PUBLIUS

FEDERALIST No. 51
The Structure of the Government Must Furnish the Proper Checks and Balances Between the Different Departments.
For the Independent Journal. Wednesday, February 6, 1788.

MADISON
To the People of the State of New York:

TO WHAT expedient, then, shall we finally resort, for maintaining in practice the necessary partition of power among the several departments, as laid down in the Constitution? The only answer that can be given is, that as all these exterior provisions are found to be inadequate, the defect must be supplied, by so contriving the interior structure of the government as that its several constituent parts may, by their mutual relations, be the means of keeping each other in their proper places. Without presuming to undertake a full development of this important idea, I will hazard a few general observations, which may perhaps place it in a clearer light, and enable us to form a more correct judgment of the principles and structure of the government planned by the convention.

In order to lay a due foundation for that separate and distinct exercise of the different powers of government, which to a certain extent is admitted on all hands to be essential to the preservation of liberty, it is evident that each department should have a will of its own; and consequently should be so constituted that the members of each should have as little agency as possible in the appointment of the members of the others. Were this principle rigorously adhered to, it would require that all the appointments for the supreme executive, legislative, and judiciary magistracies should be drawn from the same fountain of authority, the people, through channels having no communication whatever with one another. Perhaps such a plan of constructing the several departments would be less difficult in practice than it may in contemplation appear. Some difficulties, however, and some additional expense would attend the execution of it. Some deviations, therefore, from the principle must be admitted. In the constitution of the judiciary department in particular, it might be inexpedient to insist rigorously on the principle: first, because peculiar qualifications being essential in the members, the primary consideration ought to be to select that mode of choice which best secures these qualifications; secondly, because the permanent tenure by which the appointments are held in that department, must soon destroy all sense of dependence on the authority conferring them.

It is equally evident, that the members of each department should be as little dependent as possible on those of the others, for the emoluments annexed to their offices. Were the executive magistrate, or the judges, not independent of the legislature in this particular, their independence in every other would be merely nominal.

But the great security against a gradual concentration of the several powers in the same department, consists in giving to those who administer each department the necessary constitutional means and personal motives to resist encroachments of the others. The provision for defense must in this, as in all other cases, be made commensurate to the danger of attack. Ambition must be made to counteract ambition. The interest of the man must be connected with the constitutional rights of the place. It may be a reflection on human nature, that such devices should be necessary to control the abuses of government. But what is government itself, but the greatest of all reflections on human nature? If men were angels, no government would be necessary. If angels were to govern men, neither external nor internal controls on government would be necessary. In framing a government which is to be administered by men over men, the great difficulty lies in this: you must first enable the government to control the governed; and in the next place oblige it to control itself. A dependence on the people is, no doubt, the primary control on the government; but experience has taught mankind the necessity of auxiliary precautions.

This policy of supplying, by opposite and rival interests, the defect of better motives, might be traced through the whole system of human affairs, private as well as public. We see it particularly displayed in all the subordinate distributions of power, where the constant aim is to divide and arrange the several offices in such a manner as that each may be a check on the other—that the private interest of every individual may be a sentinel over the public rights. These inventions of prudence cannot be less requisite in the distribution of the supreme powers of the State.

But it is not possible to give to each department an equal power of self-defense. In republican government, the legislative authority necessarily predominates. The remedy for this inconveniency is to divide the legislature into different branches; and to render them, by different modes of election and different principles of action, as little connected with each other as the nature of their common functions and their common dependence on the society will admit. It may even be necessary to guard against dangerous encroachments by still further precautions. As the weight of the legislative authority requires that it should be thus divided, the weakness of the executive may require, on the other hand, that it should be fortified. An absolute negative on the legislature appears, at first view, to be the natural defense with which the executive magistrate should be armed. But perhaps it would be neither altogether safe nor alone sufficient. On ordinary occasions it might not be exerted with the requisite firmness, and on extraordinary occasions it might be perfidiously abused. May not this defect of an absolute negative be supplied by some qualified connection between this weaker department and the weaker branch of the stronger department, by which the latter may be led to support the constitutional rights of the former, without being too much detached from the rights of its own department?

If the principles on which these observations are founded be just, as I persuade myself they are, and they be applied as a criterion to the several State constitutions, and to the federal Constitution it will be found that if the latter does not perfectly correspond with them, the former are infinitely less able to bear such a test.

There are, moreover, two considerations particularly applicable to the federal system of America, which place that system in a very interesting point of view.

First. In a single republic, all the power surrendered by the people is submitted to the administration of a single government; and the usurpations are guarded against by a division of the government into distinct and separate departments. In the compound republic of America, the power surrendered by the people is first divided between two distinct governments, and then the portion allotted to each subdivided among distinct and separate departments. Hence a double security arises to the rights of the people. The different governments will control each other, at the same time that each will be controlled by itself.

Second. It is of great importance in a republic not only to guard the society against the oppression of its rulers, but to guard one part of the society against the injustice of the other part. Different interests necessarily exist in different classes of citizens. If a majority be united by a common interest, the rights of the minority will be insecure. There are but two methods of providing against this evil: the one by creating a will in the community independent of the majority—that is, of the society itself; the other, by comprehending in the society so many separate descriptions of citizens as will render an unjust combination of a majority of the whole very improbable, if not impracticable. The first method prevails in all governments possessing an hereditary or self-appointed authority. This, at best, is but a precarious security; because a power independent of the society may as well espouse the unjust views of the major, as the rightful interests of the minor party, and may possibly be turned against both parties. The second method will be exemplified in the federal republic of the United States. Whilst all authority in it will be derived from and dependent on the society, the society itself will be broken into so many parts, interests, and classes of citizens, that the rights of individuals, or of the minority, will be in little danger from interested combinations of the majority. In a free government the security for civil rights must be the same as that for religious rights. It consists in the one case in the multiplicity of interests, and in the other in the multiplicity of sects. The degree of security in both cases will depend on the number of interests and sects; and this may be presumed to depend on the extent of country and number of people comprehended under the same government. This view of the subject must particularly recommend a proper federal system to all the sincere and considerate friends of republican government, since it shows that in exact proportion as the territory of the Union may be formed into more circumscribed Confederacies, or States, oppressive combinations of a majority will be facilitated: the best security, under the republican forms, for the rights of every class of citizens, will be diminished: and consequently the stability and independence of some member of the government, the only other security, must be proportionately increased. Justice is the end of government. It is the end of civil society. It ever has been and ever will be pursued until it be obtained, or until liberty be lost in the pursuit. In a society under the forms of which the stronger faction can readily unite and oppress the weaker, anarchy may as truly be said to reign as in a state of nature, where the weaker individual is not secured against the violence of the stronger; and as, in the latter state, even the stronger individuals are prompted, by the uncertainty of their condition, to submit to a government which may protect the weak as well as themselves; so, in the former state, will the more powerful factions or parties be gradually induced, by a like motive, to wish for a government which will protect all parties, the weaker as well as the more powerful. It can be little doubted that if the State of Rhode Island was separated from the Confederacy and left to itself, the insecurity of rights under the popular form of government within such narrow limits would be displayed by such reiterated oppressions of factious majorities that some power altogether independent of the people would soon be called for by the voice of the very factions whose misrule had proved the necessity of it. In the extended republic of the United States, and among the great variety of interests, parties, and sects which it embraces, a coalition of a majority of the whole society could seldom take place on any other principles than those of justice and the general good; whilst there being thus less danger to a minor from the will of a major party, there must be less pretext, also, to provide for the security of the former, by introducing into the government a will not dependent on the latter, or, in other words, a will independent of the society itself. It is no less certain than it is important, notwithstanding the contrary opinions which have been entertained, that the larger the society, provided it lie within a practical sphere, the more duly capable it will be of self-government. And happily for the REPUBLICAN CAUSE, the practicable sphere may be carried to a very great extent, by a judicious modification and mixture of the FEDERAL PRINCIPLE.

PUBLIUS

Glossary

116th Congress: The Congress elected in November 2018, meeting in 2019–2020. The first Congress met in 1789–1790. Each Congress is elected for two years and numbered consecutively.

527 groups: Organizations that raise and spend unlimited amounts for "issue advocacy."

1963 March on Washington: A massive rally for civil rights that included Martin Luther King's "I Have a Dream" speech.

Abolition: A nineteenth-century movement demanding an immediate and unconditional end to slavery.

Accommodation: The principle that government does not violate the establishment clause as long as it does not confer an advantage to some religions over others. (See "strict separation.")

Advocacy explosion: A vast and relatively swift increase in interest groups active in Washington, DC, beginning in the mid-1960s.

Affirmative action: Direct steps to recruit members of previously underrepresented groups into schools and jobs.

American exceptionalism: The view that the United States is uniquely characterized by a distinct set of ideas such as equality, self-rule, and limited government.

Amicus curiae: A brief submitted by a person or group who is not a direct party to the case.

Approval rating: A measure of public support for a political figure or institution.

Astroturf lobbying: An attempt by interest groups to simulate widespread public engagement on an issue.

Bandwagon effect: When people join a cause because it seems popular or support a candidate who is leading in the polls.

Base voters: Party members who tend to vote loyally for their party's candidates in most elections.

Bicameral: Having two legislative houses or chambers—such as the House and the Senate.

Bill of Rights: The first ten amendments to the Constitution, listing the rights guaranteed to every citizen.

Black power: A slogan that emphasized pride in black heritage and the construction of black institutions to nurture black interests. It often implied racial separation in reaction to white racism.

Block grants: National government funding provided to state and local governments with relatively few restrictions or requirements on spending; programs to block grants introduced a trade-off for state officials: more authority, fewer funds.

Boomerang effect: The discrepancy between candidates' high poll ratings and election performance, caused by supporters' assumption that an easy win means they need not turn out.

Brown v. Board of Education: The landmark Supreme Court case that struck down segregated schools as unconstitutional.

Budget resolution: A joint House–Senate creation that outlines targets for federal spending, revenue levels, and the resultant budget deficit (or surplus) for the coming fiscal year.

Bundling: A form of fundraising in which an individual persuades others to donate large amounts that are then delivered together to a candidate or campaign.

Bureaucratic pathologies: The problems that tend to develop in bureaucratic systems.

Call list: A long list of potential donors who candidates must phone.

Candidate-centered elections: A system in which individual candidates decide run, raise their own money, and design their own strategy—as opposed to party systems, in which political parties play these roles.

Caucus: A local meeting of voters to select candidates to represent a political party in a general election or to choose delegates who select candidates at a convention.

Central clearance: The OMB's authority to review and "clear" (or approve) anything a member of the administration says or does in public.

Central service agencies: The organizations that supply and staff the federal government.

Checks and balances: The principle that each branch of government has the authority to block the other branches, making it more difficult for any one branch or individual to exercise too much power. This system makes passing legislation far more difficult in the United States than in most other democracies.

Chicanismo: A defiant movement expressing pride in Latino origins and culture in the face of discrimination.

Chief of staff: The individual responsible for managing the president's office.

Circuit courts: The second stage of federal courts, which review the trial record of cases decided in district court to ensure they were settled properly.

Civic voluntarism: Citizen participation in public life without government incentives or coercion (speaking at a town meeting vs. paying taxes, for example).

Civil disobedience: Protesting laws one considers unjust by refusing to obey them—and accepting the punishment.

Civil law: Cases that involve disputes between two parties.

Civil liberties: The limits on government that allow people to freely exercise their rights.

Civil rights: The freedom to participate in the full life of the community—to vote, use public facilities, and exercise equal economic opportunity.

Civil Rights Act of 1964: Landmark legislation that forbade discrimination on the basis of race, sex, religion, or national origin.

Civil servants: Members of the permanent executive branch bureaucracy who are employed on the basis of competitive exams and keep their positions regardless of the presidential administration.

Class action: A lawsuit filed on behalf of an entire category of individuals, such as all public housing residents in a state or all female managers in a large company.

Classical republicanism: A democratic ideal, based in ancient Greece and Rome that calls on citizens to participate in public affairs, seek the public interest, shun private gain, and defer to natural leaders.

Clear and present danger: Court doctrine that permits restrictions of free speech if officials believe that the speech will lead to prohibited action such as violence or terrorism.

Clicktivism: Democratic engagement in an online age: point your mouse or scan a QR code, click, and you have donated funds, "liked" a candidate, or (in some states) even cast your vote.

Closed primary: A vote cast by party members to select candidates to represent the party in the general election.

Cloture vote: The Senate's only approved method for halting a filibuster or lifting a legislative hold. If sixty senators—three-fifths of the body, changed in 1975 from the original two-thirds—vote for cloture, the measure can proceed to a vote.

Commerce clause: The Constitutional declaration (in Article 1, Section 8) empowering Congress to regulate commerce with foreign nations, between states, and with Indian tribes.

Committee hearing: A way for committees to gather information and gauge members' support as legislative policymaking gets underway. Hearings usually feature witnesses who submit testimony, make an oral presentation, and answer questions from members of Congress.

Committee markup session: A gathering of a full committee to draft the final version of a bill before the committee votes on it.

Common law: A system of law developed by judges in deciding cases over the centuries.

Compact: A mutual agreement that provides for joint action to achieve defined goals.

Compromise of 1850: A complicated compromise over slavery that permitted territories to vote on whether they would be slave or free and permitted California to enter the Union as a free

state. It also included a strict—and hugely controversial—fugitive slave law forcing Northerners to return black men and women into bondage.

Concurrent opinion: A statement that agrees with the majority opinion.

Concurrent powers: Governmental authority shared by national and state governments, such as the power to tax residents.

Confederation: A group of independent states or nations that yield some of their powers to a national government, although each state retains a degree of sovereign authority.

Conference committee: A special House–Senate committee that must reconcile the differences between House and Senate versions of the same bill.

Congressional caucus: A group of House or Senate members who convene regularly to discuss common interests; they may share political outlook, race, gender, or geography.

Conservatives: Americans who believe in reduced government spending, personal responsibility, traditional moral values, secure borders, and a strong national defense. Also known as right or right-wing.

Consolidation: The process whereby a media company grows, acquires other companies, and threatens to dominate the market.

Constitution: A statement of fundamental principles that governs a nation or an organization.

Containment: American Cold War strategy designed to stop the spread of communism.

Continuing resolution (CR): A congressionally approved act required when no national budget has been passed before the start of a new fiscal year. This extends spending at current levels for a prescribed period of time.

Cooperative federalism: Also called marble cake federalism, a system of mingled governing authority, with functions overlapping across national and state governments.

Cost-benefit analysis: A more complex study of the projected costs and benefits associated with a proposed policy.

Cost effectiveness: The projected costs of a proposed policy, as revealed by a relatively simple study.

Covenant: A compact invoking religious or moral authority.

Criminal law: Cases in which someone is charged with breaking the law.

Cycle of nonparticipation: Resistance by political parties to mobilizing disengaged Americans to vote—because their lack of involvement makes their allegiance to one or the other party suspect.

De facto discrimination: More subtle forms of discrimination that exist without a legal basis.

Defendant: The party who is sued in a court case.

De jure discrimination: Discrimination established by laws.

Delegated powers: Powers that Congress passes on to the president.

Delegate representation: Representatives follow the expressed wishes of the voters.

Democracy: A form of government in which the people hold power, either by acting directly or through elected representatives.

Demographic group: People sharing specific characteristics such as age, ethnicity/race, religion, or country of origin.

Devolution: The transfer of authority from the national to the state or local government level.

Diffusion: The spreading of policy ideas from one city or state to others; a process typical of U.S. federalism.

Din: Shorthand for the sheer volume of information and noise generated by online sources; can be a disincentive to participate politically.

Direct action: Participating outside of normal political and social channels through civil disobedience, demonstrations, and even riots.

Discretionary programs: Non-entitlement program spending, subject to the decision ("discretion") of Congress each year.

Disproportionate impact: The effect some policies have of discriminating, even if discrimination is not consciously intended.

Dissent: A statement on behalf of the justices who voted in the minority.

District courts: The first level of federal courts, which actually try the cases.

Each decision is based not on a statute but on previous judicial decisions.

Divided government: Periods during which at least one house of Congress is controlled by a party different from the one occupying the White House.

Domestic dependent nation: Special status that grants local sovereignty to tribal nations but does not grant them full sovereignty equivalent to that enjoyed by independent nations.

Double jeopardy: The principle that an individual cannot be tried twice for the same offense.

Dred Scott v. Sandford: A landmark Supreme Court decision holding that black men could not be citizens under the Constitution of the United States. It created a national uproar.

Dual federalism: Also called layer cake federalism, the clear division of governing authority between national and state governments.

Earmark: A legislative item, usually included in spending ("appropriations") bills, that directs Congress to fund a particular item in one House member's district or a senator's state.

Economic equality: A situation in which there are small differences in wealth among citizens.

Electoral activities: Public engagement in the form of voting, running for office, volunteering in a campaign, or otherwise participating in elections.

Electoral bounce: The spike in the polls that follows an event such as a party's national convention.

Electoral College: The system established by the Constitution to elect the president; each state has a group of electors (equal in size to that of its congressional delegation in the House and the Senate); the public in each state votes for electors, who then vote for president.

Emancipation Proclamation: An executive order issued by President Abraham Lincoln that declared the slaves in all rebel states to be free.

Entitlement program: A government benefit program whose recipients are *entitled* by law to receive payments. Social Security, Medicare, and Medicaid are the three largest.

Equal Employment Opportunity Commission (EEOC): Federal law enforcement agency charged with monitoring compliance with the Civil Rights Act.

Equality: All citizens enjoy the same privileges, status, and rights before the laws.

Equal opportunity: The idea that every American has the same chance to influence politics and achieve economic success.

Equal outcome: The idea that citizens should have roughly equal economic circumstances.

Equal protection of the laws: The landmark phrase in the Fourteenth Amendment that requires equal treatment for all citizens.

Equal Rights Amendment (ERA): An amendment, originally drafted by Alice Paul in 1923, passed by Congress in 1972, and ratified by thirty-five states, that declared: "Equality of rights . . . shall not be denied or abridged . . . on account of sex."

Establishment clause: The First Amendment principle that government may not establish an official religion.

Exclusionary rule: The ruling that evidence obtained in an illegal search may not be introduced in a trial.

Executive agreement: An international agreement made by the president that does not require the approval of the Senate.

Executive Office of the President (EOP): The agencies that help the president manage daily activities.

Executive order: A presidential declaration, with the force of law, that issues instructions to the executive branch without any requirement for congressional action or approval.

Executive privilege: Power claimed by the president to resist requests for authority by Congress, the courts, or the public. Not mentioned in the Constitution but based on the separation of powers.

Expressed powers: Powers the Constitution explicitly grants to the president.

Expressive benefits: Values or deeply held beliefs that inspire individuals to join a public interest group.

Fairness doctrine: Regulation that required media outlets to devote equal time to opposite perspectives.

Fair trade: Trade that emphasizes the inclusion of environmental and labor protections in agreements so that nations do not receive unfair advantages by exploiting workers or harming the environment.

Fake news: The deliberate spread of falsehood or misinformation—often a charge made by politicians facing unfavorable stories.

Federal budget deficit: The gap between revenues received by the national government (primarily through individual income and corporate taxes) and spending on all public programs.

Federalism: Power divided between national and state government. Each has its own sovereignty (independent authority) and its own duties.

Federal poverty line: The annually specified level of income (separately calculated for individuals and families) below which people are considered to live in poverty, and eligible for certain federal benefits. For 2019, the poverty line is set at $25,100 for a family of four.

Federal Regulation of Lobbying Act: The initial U.S. statute spelling out requirements on lobbyists active in Congress, which was passed in 1946.

Fighting words: Expressions inherently likely to provoke violent reactions and not necessarily protected by the First Amendment.

Filibuster: Rule unique to the U.S. Senate that allows any senator to hold the floor indefinitely and thereby delay a vote on a bill to which he or she objects. Ended only when sixty senators vote for cloture.

Final rule: The rule that specifies how a program will actually operate.

First Continental Congress: A convention of delegates from twelve of the thirteen colonies that met in 1774.

Fiscal policy: Taxing and spending policies carried out by government, generally in an effort to affect national economic development.

Fiscal year (FY): In budget calculations, the "new year" beginning October 1 and ending the following September 30. Organized many decades ago for accounting purposes.

Floor: The full chamber, either in the House of Representatives or the Senate. A bill "goes to the floor" for the final debate and vote, usually after approval by one or more committees.

Focusing event: A major happening, often of crisis or disaster proportions, that attracts widespread media attention to an issue.

Framing: The way an issue is defined; every issue has many possible frames, each with a slightly different tilt in describing the problem and highlighting solutions.

Framing effects: The way the wording of a polling question influences a respondent

Freedom: The ability to pursue one's own desires without interference from others.

Freedom of Information Act (FOIA): A 1966 law that facilitates full or partial disclosure of government information and documents.

Freedom Riders: Black and white activists who rode buses together to protest segregation on interstate bus lines.

Free exercise clause: The First Amendment principle that government may not interfere in religious practice.

Free rider problem: A barrier to group or collective action arising because people who do not participate still reap the benefits.

Free trade: Goods and services moving across international boundaries without government interference.

Full faith and credit clause: The constitutional requirement (in Article 4, Section 1) that each state recognizes and upholds laws passed by any other state.

Gerrymander: Redraw an election district in a way that gives the advantage to one party.

Gift ban: A regulation that eliminates (or sharply reduces the permitted dollar amount of) gifts from interest groups to lawmakers.

Going public: Directly addressing the public to win support for oneself or one's ideas.

Grand jury: A jury that does not decide on guilt or innocence but only on whether there is enough evidence for the case to go to trial.

Grand Old Party (GOP): Longstanding nickname for the Republican Party; ironically, bestowed early in the party's history, in the 1870s.

Grand strategy: An overarching vision that defines and guides a nation's foreign policy.

Grants-in-aid: National government funding provided to state and local governments, along with specific instructions about how the funds may be used.

Great Migration: The vast movement of African Americans from the rural South to the urban North between 1910 and the 1960s.

Gross domestic product (GDP): The value of all the goods and services produced in a nation over a year. For 2019, the U.S. GDP is an estimated $21.4 trillion.

Groupthink: The tendency among a small group of decision makers to converge on a shared set of views; can limit creative thinking or solutions to policy problems.

Hate speech: Hostile statements based on someone's personal characteristics, such as race, ethnicity, religion, or sexual orientation.

Hyperpluralism: The collective effect of the vast number of interest groups in slowing the process of American democratic policymaking.

Imperial presidency: A characterization of the American presidency that suggests it is demonstrating imperial traits, and that the republic is morphing into an empire.

Incorporation: The process by which the Supreme Court declares that a right in the Bill of Rights also applies to state governments.

Incumbency advantage: The tendency for members of Congress to win reelection in overwhelming numbers.

Indentured servant: A colonial American settler contracted to work for a fixed period (usually three to seven years) in exchange for food, shelter, and transportation to the New World.

Individualism: The idea that individuals, not the society, are responsible for their own well-being.

Information shortcuts: Cues about candidates and policies drawn from everyday life.

Infotainment: The blurred line between news and entertainment.

Inherent powers: Powers that, although neither specified or implied by the Constitution are necessary for the President or Congress to fulfil their duties.

Inherent powers of the presidency: Powers assumed by presidents, often during a crisis, on the basis of the constitutional phrase "The executive power shall be vested in the president."

Initiative: A process in which citizens propose new laws or amendments to the state constitution.

Institutions: The organizations, norms, and rules that structure government and public action.

Interest group: An organization whose goal is to influence government.

Intergovernmental lobbying: Attempts by officials in one part of the government to influence their counterparts in another branch, or at a different (state or local) level.

Internationalism: The belief that national interests are best served by actively engaging and working with other nations around the world.

Iron triangle: The cozy relationship in one issue area among interest-group lobbyists, congressional staffers, and executive branch agencies.

Isolationism: The doctrine that a nation should avoid all foreign-policy commitments and alliances and withdraw from world affairs.

Issue advocacy: Organized effort to advance (or block) a proposed public policy change.

Issue campaign: A concerted effort by interest groups to arouse popular support or opposition for a policy issue.

Issue network: Shifting alliances of public and private interest groups, lawmakers, and other stakeholders all focused on the same policy area.

Jim Crow: The system of racial segregation in the U.S. South that lasted from 1890 to 1965, and that was often violently enforced.

Judicial activism: A vigorous or active approach to reviewing the other branches of government.

Judicial restraint: Reluctance to interfere with elected branches, only doing so as a last resort.

Judicial review: The Court's authority to determine whether legislative, executive, and state actions violate the Constitution and overrule those that do.

Judicial rules: Hard-and-fast boundaries between what is lawful and what is not.

Judicial standards: Guiding principles that help governments make judgment calls.

K Street: A major street in downtown Washington, DC, that is home to the headquarters for many lobbying firms and advocacy groups—and thus synonymous with interest-group lobbying.

Legislative hold: An informal way for a senator to object to a bill or other measure reaching the Senate floor. The action effectively halts Senate proceedings on that issue, sometimes for weeks or longer.

Liberalism: A doctrine that views nation–states as benefiting most from mutual cooperation, aided by international organizations.

Liberals: Americans who value cultural diversity, government programs for the needy, public intervention in the economy, and individuals' right to a lifestyle based on their own social and moral positions. Also known as left or left-wing.

Likely voters: Persons identified as probable voters in an upcoming election. Often preferred by polling organizations, but difficult to specify with great accuracy.

Literacy test: A requirement that voters exhibit an ability to read; in reality, a way to restrict black suffrage.

Litigation: The conduct of a lawsuit.

Lobbying coalition: A collection of lobbyists working on related topics or a specific legislative proposal.

Lobbyist: A person who contacts government officials on behalf of a particular cause or issue.

Lochner era: A period from 1905 to 1937, during which the Supreme Court struck down laws (e.g., worker protection or minimum wage laws) that were thought to infringe on economic liberty or the right to contract.

Loud signal: Media stories with very broad coverage and an unambiguous message.

Majority opinion: The official statement of the Supreme Court (or district courts, since they also have multiple justices).

Mandate: Political authority claimed by an election winner as reflecting the approval of the people.

Margin of sampling error: The degree of inaccuracy in any poll, arising from the fact that surveys involve a sample of respondents from a population, rather than every member.

Mass media: Information and entertainment for broad popular audiences including newspapers, magazines, radio, and television.

Material benefits: Items distributed by public interest groups as incentives to sign up or remain a member.

Median: A statistical term for the number in the middle or the case that has an equal number of examples above and below it.

Mediation: A way of resolving disputes without going to court, in which a third party (the mediator) helps two or more sides negotiate a settlement.

Mercantilism: An economic theory according to which government controls foreign trade to maintain prosperity and security.

Midterm elections: National elections held between presidential elections, involving all seats in the House of Representatives, one-third of those in the Senate, 36 governorships, and other positions.

Midterm loss: The president's party loses Congressional seats during the midterm elections. This has occurred in most midterm elections.

Millennials: Americans born between 1983 and 2001. Though very large (some 80 million people) and diverse, millennials tend to share certain characteristics, including political outlook.

Miller test: Three-part test for judging whether a work is obscene (if it has all three, the work loses First Amendment protection).

Miranda warnings: A set of rights that police officers are required to inform suspects of, including the right to remain silent.

Missouri Compromise: An agreement to open southern territories west of the Mississippi to slavery while closing northern territories to slavery.

Monetary policy: Actions of central banks, which in the United States culminate in the Federal Reserve, designed primarily to maximize employment and moderate inflation.

Motor voter law: Passed in 1993, this act enables prospective voters to register when they receive their driver's license.

Multilateralism: A doctrine that emphasizes operating together with other nations to pursue common goals.

Multilateral organization: An international organization of three or more nations organized around a common goal.

Name recognition: An advantage possessed by a well-known political figure, a political celebrity.

National Association for the Advancement of Colored People (NAACP): A civil rights organization formed in 1909 and dedicated to racial equality.

National Organization for Women (NOW): An organization formed in 1966 to take action for women's equality.

Necessary and proper clause: The constitutional declaration (in Article 1, Section 8) that defines Congress's constitutional authority to exercise the "necessary and proper" powers to carry out its designated functions.

Negative campaigning: Running for office by attacking the opponent.

Negative liberty: Freedom from constraints or the interference of others.

New Deal: Broad series of economic programs and reforms introduced between 1933 and 1936 and associated with the Franklin Roosevelt administration.

New federalism: A version of cooperative federalism, but with stronger emphasis on state and local government activity versus national government.

New Jersey Plan: Put forward at the Constitutional Convention by the small states, this plan left most government authority with the state governments.

The New Jim Crow: The idea that mass incarceration of African Americans has the sweeping effects of Jim Crow discrimination laws. The term is the title of a book by Michelle Alexander.

New media: On-demand access to information through digital devices that increasingly feature interactive participation with content.

Nonattitudes: The lack of a stable perspective in response to opinion surveys; answers to questions may be self-contradictory or may display no ideological consistency.

Nonpartisan election: An election in which candidates run as individuals, without any party affiliation. Many towns and cities feature nonpartisan elections.

Open primary: a vote cast by any eligible voter to select candidates to represent the party in the general election.

Open seat: A seat in Congress without an incumbent running for reelection.

Opinion poll: Systematic study of a defined population, analyzing a representative sample's views to draw inferences about the larger public's views. Also termed *survey research*.

Originalism: A principle of legal interpretation that relies on the original meaning of those who wrote the Constitution.

Overhead democracy: A system by which the people elect the president, who, through their appointees, controls the bureaucracy from the top.

Override: The process by which Congress can overcome a presidential veto with a two-thirds vote in both chambers.

Paradox of voting: For most individuals, the cost of voting (acquiring necessary information, traveling to polling site, and waiting in line) outweighs the apparent benefits. Economic theory would predict very low voter turnout, given this analysis.

Partisanship: Taking the side of a party or espousing a viewpoint that reflects a political party's principles or position on an issue.

Party boss: The senior figure in a party machine.

Party caucus: A meeting of all House or Senate members of one or the other main party, usually to discuss political and policy strategies.

Party identification: Strong attachment to one political party, often established at an early age.

Party in government: The portion of a political party's organization that comprises elected officials and candidates for office.

Party in the electorate: The largest (and least organized) component of a political party, drawn from the public at large: registered members and regular supporters.

Party machine: A hierarchical arrangement of party workers, often organized in an urban area to help integrate immigrants and minority groups into the political system. Most active in the late nineteenth and early twentieth centuries.

Party organization: The portion of a political party that includes activists, state/local leaders, and affiliated professionals such as fundraisers and public relations experts.

Party platform: The written statement of a party's core convictions and issue priorities. Generally revised every four years, in time for the national party convention.

Party system: The broad organization of U.S. politics comprising the two main parties, the coalition of supporters backing each, the positions they take on major issues, and each party's electoral achievements.

Path dependence: Social-science term for how policymakers' choices are shaped by institutional "paths" that result from policy choices made in the past.

Pendleton Civil Service Act: The law that shifted American government toward a merit-based public service.

Personal presidency: The idea that the president has a personal link to the public. Made initially possible by twentieth century media.

Plaintiff: The party who brings the action in a lawsuit.

Plessy v. Ferguson: An 1896 Supreme Court case that permitted racial segregation.

Pluralism: An open, participatory style of government in which many different interests are represented.

Policy agenda: The issues that the media covers, the public considers important, and politicians address. Setting the agenda is the first step in political action.

Policy window: A figurative description of the opportunity—often brief, measured in days or weeks rather than years—to pass a bill in Congress or a state legislature.

Political action committee (PAC): An organization of at least fifty people, affiliated with an interest group that is permitted to make contributions to candidates for federal office.

Political appointees: Top officials in the executive agencies, appointed by the president.

Political culture: The orientation of citizens of a state toward politics.

Political elites: Individuals who control significant wealth, status, power, or visibility and consequently have significant influence over public debates.

Political equality: All citizens have the same political rights and opportunities.

Political mobilization: Efforts to encourage people to engage in the public sphere: to vote for a particular candidate (or donate money, work on the campaign, etc.) or to get involved in specific issues.

Political order: The set of institutions, interests, and ideas that shape a political era. Great presidents reconstruct the framework, launching a new order.

Political party: a group that shares political principles and is organized to win elections and hold power.

Political socialization: Education about how the government works and which policies one should support; provided by parents, peers, schools, parties, and other national institutions.

Political voice: Exercising one's public rights, often through speaking out in protest or in favor of some policy change.

Positive liberty: The ability—and provision of basic necessities—to pursue one's goals.

Power elite theory: The view that a small handful of wealthy, influential Americans exercises extensive control over government decisions.

Pragmatism: A principle of legal interpretation based on the idea that the Constitution evolves and that interpretations of the Constitution must be framed in the context of contemporary realities.

Precedent: A judicial decision that offers a guide to similar cases in the future.

Preemption: The invalidation of a U.S. state law that conflicts with federal law.

Preemptive war: The effort to attack hostile powers before they launch attacks. Highly controversial because it sanctions striking first.

President pro tempore: Majority party senator with the longest Senate service.

Primacy: The doctrine asserting that the United States should maintain an unrivaled military.

Priming: Affecting public perceptions of political leaders, candidates, or issues by reporting on topics in ways that either enhance or diminish support.

Principal-agent theory: Details how policymakers (principals) control the actors who work for them (agents)—but who have far more information than they do.

Prior restraint: Legal effort to stop speech before it occurs.

Private contractors: Private companies that contract to provide goods and services for the government.

Progressive federalism: Approach that gives state officials considerable leeway in achieving national programs and goals.

Proportional representation: The allocation of votes or delegates on the basis of the percentage of the vote received; contrasts with the winner-take-all system.

Proposed rule: A draft of administrative regulations published in the *Federal Register* for the purpose of gathering comments from interested parties.

Protectionism: Efforts to protect local business from foreign competition.

Public ownership: A situation in which media outlets are run by the government and paid for by tax dollars.

Public–private partnership: A government program or service provided through the joint efforts of private sector actors (usually businesses) and public officials.

Public watchdog: Media coverage that alerts the public when a problem arises in politics or society.

Push poll: A form of negative campaigning that masquerades as a regular opinion survey. They usually feature unflattering information about an opponent.

Quasi-suspect category: A legal standard that requires governments to have an important state purpose for any legislation that singles out sex or gender. This is not as strong as the suspect category, which requires strict scrutiny.

Racial profiling: A law enforcement practice of singling out people on the basis of physical features such as race or ethnicity.

Random sample: A sample in which everyone in the population (sampling frame) has an equal probability of being selected.

Rational-choice theory: An approach to political behavior that views individuals as rational, decisive actors who know their political interests and seek to act on them.

Realism: A doctrine holding that nation–states seek to amass power to ensure their self-preservation.

Reapportionment: Reorganization of the boundaries of House districts, a process that follows the results of the U.S. census, taken every ten years. District lines are redrawn to ensure rough equality in the number of constituents represented by each House member.

Reconstruction: The failed effort, pursued by Northerners and Southerners, to rebuild the South and establish racial equality after the Civil War.

Referendum: An election in which citizens vote directly on an issue.

Reframing the issue: To redefine the popular perception of an issue.

Regulatory capture: The theory that industries dominate the agencies that regulate them.

Republic: A government in which citizens rule indirectly and make government decisions through their elected representatives.

Reserved powers: The constitutional guarantee (in the Tenth Amendment) that the states retain government authority not explicitly granted to the national government.

Response bias: The tendency of poll respondents to misstate their views frequently to avoid "shameful" opinions that might appear sexist or racist.

Reverse lobbying: Attempts by government officials to influence interest groups on behalf of their preferred policies.

Revolving door: The tendency of many Washington lobbyists to move from government work (e.g., as a Congressional or White House advisor) to lobbying and back again.

Roll-call vote: A congressional vote in which each member's vote is recorded, either by roll call (Senate) or electronically (House).

Rule of four: The requirement that at least four Supreme Court judges must agree to hear a case before it comes before the Court.

Safe district: a district consisting of voters who have historically voted for one party over the other by a large majority.

Sampling frame: A designated group of people from whom a set of poll respondents is randomly selected.

School busing: An effort to integrate public schools by mixing students from different neighborhoods.

Second Continental Congress: A convention of delegates from the thirteen colonies that became the acting national government for the duration of the Revolutionary War.

Section 504: An obscure provision in an obscure rehabilitation act that required all institutions that received federal funds to accommodate people with disabilities.

Security trap: The idea that using military force creates multiple, often unforeseen, problems.

Selective incorporation: The extension of protections from the Bill of Rights to the state governments, one liberty at a time.

Self-rule: The idea that legitimate government flows from the people.

Seneca Falls Convention: The first convention dedicated to women's rights, held in July 1848 in Seneca Falls, NY.

Signing statements: Written presidential declarations commenting on the bill that is being signed into law—often including criticism of one or more provisions.

Social capital: Relations between people that build closer ties of trust and civic engagement, yielding productive benefits for the larger society.

Social democracy: the idea that government policy should ensure that all are comfortably cared for within the context of a capitalist economy.

Social equality: All individuals enjoy the same status in society.

Soft power: The influence a nation exerts through culture and commerce; a contrast to attempted Solidarity benefits: The feeling of shared commitment and purpose experienced by individuals who join a public interest group.

Solidarity benefits: The feeling of shared commitment and purpose experienced by individuals who join a public interest group.

Sound bite: A short audio clip; often refers to a brief excerpt from a politician's speech.

Speaker of the House: The chief administrative officer in the House of Representatives.

Special interest: A pejorative term, often used to designate an interest group whose aims or issue preferences one does not share.

Split-ticket voter: Votes for at least one candidate from each party, dividing his or her ballot between the two (or more) parties.

Spoils system: A system in which government jobs are given out as political favors.

Stare decisis: Deciding cases on the basis of previous rulings or precedents.

Straight-ticket voter: Votes for the same party for all offices on a ballot.

Strategic disengagement: The doctrine that a nation should not interfere in other nations' affairs unless such involvement clearly advances its own interests.

Street-level bureaucrats: Public officials who deal directly with the public.

Strict scrutiny: The standard by which courts judge any legislation that singles out race or ethnicity.

Strict separation: The strict principles articulated in the Lemon test for judging whether a law establishes a religion. (See "accommodation.")

Sunshine laws: Laws that permit the public to watch policymakers in action and to access the records of the proceedings.

Supermajority: An amount higher than a simple majority (50% plus one)—typically, three-fifths or two-thirds of the voters.

Super PACs: Organizations that raise and spend unlimited amounts of money to promote a candidate or publicize a cause. However, they may not directly contribute to a candidate or coordinate with a campaign.

Super Tuesday: The date on the presidential primary calendar when multiple states hold primaries and caucuses.

Supremacy clause: The constitutional declaration (in Article 6, Section 2) that the national government's authority prevails over any conflicting state or local government's claims, provided the power is granted to the federal government.

Symbolic expression: An act, rather than actual speech, used to demonstrate a point of view.

Telecommunications Act of 1996: A major overhaul of communications law that opened the door to far more competition by permitting companies to own outlets in multiple media markets such as radio, television, and magazines, and removing or reducing limits on how many outlets one company can own.

Theory of democratic peace: Theory that strongly democratic nations are less prone to engage in wars with one another.

Time, place, and manner clause: The constitutional clause that delegates control of elections to the state governments.

Trade association: An organized group representing individuals and businesses that belong to the same industry.

Trade deficit: The deficit arising when a nation imports (or buys) more goods from foreign nations than it exports (or sells) to them.

Traditional participation: Engaging in political activities through the formal channels of government and society.

Trustee representation: Representatives do what they regard as being in the best interest of their constituents—even if constituents do not agree.

Unanimous consent: A Senate requirement, applied to most of that body's business, that all senators agree before an action can proceed.

Underdog effect: Sympathy for a candidate behind in the polls, contributing to a higher-than-predicted vote total—and sometimes a surprise election victory.

Unfunded mandate: An obligation imposed on state or local government officials by federal legislation without sufficient federal funding support to cover the costs.

Unicameral: Having a single legislative house or chamber.

Unilateralism: A doctrine that holds that the United States should act independently of other nations. It should decide what is best for itself—not in coordination with partners and allies.

Unitary executive theory: The idea that the Constitution puts the president in charge of executing the laws and that therefore no other branch may limit presidential discretion over executive matters.

Unitary government: A national polity governed as a single unit, with the central government exercising all or most political authority.

Universalistic politics: A government run according to transparent rules, impartially applied.

United Farm Workers (UFW): An influential union representing migrant farm workers in the west.

USA Patriot Act: Legislation that sought to enhance national security, passed in the aftermath of the September 11, 2001, terrorist attacks.

Veto: The constitutional procedure by which a president can prevent enactment of legislation passed by Congress.

Veto power: The presidential power to block an act of Congress by refusing to sign—and returning it to Congress with objections.

Virginia Plan: Madison's plan, embraced by the Constitutional Convention delegates from larger states; this plan strengthened the national government relative to state governments.

Voice vote: A congressional vote in which the presiding officer asks those for and against to say "yea" or "nay," respectively, and announces the result. No record is kept of House or Senate members voting on each side.

Voter turnout: A measure of which proportion of eligible voters actually cast a legitimate ballot in a given election.

War Powers Act: Legislation passed in 1973 to increase congressional involvement in undeclared wars. It requires Congress to approve military action undertaken by the president in no more than 60 days.

Watergate scandal: A failed effort in 1972 by Republican operatives to break into Democratic Party headquarters in the Watergate office complex in Washington, DC. President Nixon tried to cover up the event—eventually causing him to resign from the presidency.

Whistleblower: A federal worker who reports corruption or fraud.

Winner-take-all: The candidate receiving a simple majority (or, among multiple candidates, a plurality) receives all electoral votes or primary delegates. Sometimes called "first-past-the-post."

World Trade Organization (WTO): An international organization that oversees efforts to open markets and promote free trade.

Notes

Chapter 1 The Spirit of American Politics

1. RealClear Politics, "Congressional Job Approval," https://www.realclear-politics.com/epolls/other/congressional_job_approval-903.html.
2. Dred Scott v. Sandford, 60 U.S. (19 How) 393 (1857).
3. For a classic statement of this view, see G. William Domhoff, *Who Rules America Now* (New York: McGraw Hill, 2006); for a recent book, warning about dynastic wealth, see Thomas Piketty, *Capital in the Twenty-First Century*, trans. Arthur Goldhammer (Cambridge, MA: Harvard University Press, 2017). Data from "Forbes Releases 36th Annual Forbes 400 Ranking of the Richest Americans," *Forbes Magazine 2017*, October 17, 2017, https://www.forbes.com/sites/forbespr/2017/10/17/forbes-releases-36th-annual-forbes-400-ranking-of-the-richest-americans/2/#9757dfd44aff.
4. Harold D. Lasswell, *Politics: Who Gets What, When, and How*, rev. ed. (New York: Smith Books, 1990).
5. Roger Sherman, quoted in James Madison, *Notes of Debates in the Federal Convention*, ed. Adrienne Koch (New York: Norton, 1987), p. 39.
6. Philip Tetlock, *Expert Political Judgment: How Good Is It? How Can We Know?* (Princeton, NJ: Princeton University Press, 2005).
7. Ronald Reagan: "Inaugural Address," January 20, 1981. Online by Gerhard Peters and John T. Woolley, *The American Presidency Project*. http://www.presidency.ucsb.edu/ws/?pid=43130.
8. Alexis de Tocqueville, a young French aristocrat, spent nine months traveling around the United States in 1831–1832 and published a book on his observations, *Democracy in America*. It is one of our favorite books on America and on democracy. Many of his observations remain fresh today; no matter where you are on the political spectrum, you will find insights to challenge your views. For a vital book on civic engagement, see Robert Putnam, *Bowling Alone* (New York: Simon & Schuster, 2000).
9. Pew Research Center, "Public Trust in Government: 1958–2017," May 3, 2017, http://www.people-press.org/2017/05/03/public-trust-in-government-1958-2017/.
10. Michael Lind, *Land of Promise: An Economic History of the United States* (New York: HarperCollins, 2012), 205.
11. Pew Research Center, "Government Gets Lower Ratings for Handling Health Care, Environment, Disaster Response," December 14, 2017
12. For an analysis of the federal budget, see Anna Malinovskaya and Louise Sheiner, "The Hutchins Center Explains: Federal Budget Basics," Brookings, May 23, 2017, https://www.brookings.edu/blog/up-front/2016/06/01/the-hutchins-center-explains-federal-budget-basics/.
13. Organisation for Economic Co-operation and Development, OECD. "STAT, Revenue Statistics—Comparative Tables," https://stats.oecd.org/Index.aspx?DataSetCode=REV.
14. Suzanne Mettler, *The Submerged State* (Chicago: University of Chicago Press, 2011); Christopher Howard, *The Hidden Welfare State* (Princeton, NJ: Princeton University Press, 1997); Jacob Hacker, *The Divided Welfare State* (New York: Cambridge University Press, 2002).
15. Kate Zernicke, "The Hidden Subsidy that Helps Pay for Health Insurance," *The New York Times*, July 7, 2017, https://www.nytimes.com/2017/07/07/health/health-insurance-tax-deduction.html.
16. David Blumenthal and James Morone, *The Heart of Power: Health and Politics in the Oval Office* (Berkeley: University of California Press, 2009), chap. 3.
17. Abigail Geiger, "About Six-in-Ten Americans Support Marijuana Legalization," Pew Research Center, January 5, 2018, http://pewrsr.ch/2F1u1cm.
18. Keith Humphreys, "Young People Are Committing Much Less Crime. Older People Are Still Behaving as Badly as Before," *Washington Post*, Sept. 7, 2016, http://wapo.st/2FRNCwA; Bradley Depew, "Learn about Millennials and Charity: The Generation That Wants Real Change, Not Platitudes ," *The Balance*, May 29, 2017, http://bit.ly/2dWCoZV; Malcolm Harris, *Kids These Days: Human Capital and the Making of Millennials* (Boston: Little, Brown, 2017).

Chapter 2 The Ideas That Shape America

1. John Gramlich, "How Countries Around the World View Democracy, Military Rule and Other Political Systems," Pew Research Center, October 30, 2017, http://www.pewresearch.org/fact-tank/2017/10/30/global-views-political-systems/.
2. Rasmussen Reports, "Americans Want Christmas, More Religion in Schools," December 15, 2015, http://www.rasmussenreports.com/public_content/lifestyle/holidays/december_2015/americans_want_christmas_more_religion_in_schools.
3. Simon Schama, *Rough Crossings: Britain, the Slaves, and the American Revolution* (New York: Harper-Collins, 2006).
4. The classic statement comes from Isaiah Berlin, "Two Concepts of Liberty," reprinted in *Liberty*, ed. Henry Hardy (Oxford: Oxford University Press, 2002), 166–217.
5. Samuel Huntington, *American Politics: The Promise of Disharmony* (Cambridge, MA: Harvard University Press, 1981).
6. Samuel Huntington, *American Politics: The Promise of Disharmony*, rev. ed. (Cambridge, MA: Harvard University Press, 1983); Rogers Smith, *Civic Ideals: Conflicting Visions of Citizenship in U.S. History* (New Haven, CT: Yale University Press, 1997).
7. Quoted in James A. Morone, *The Democratic Wish: Popular Participation and the Limits of American Government* (New Haven, CT: Yale University Press, 1998), 54.
8. Thomas Jefferson, "Response to the Citizens of Albemarle," February 12, 1790; First Inaugural Address, March 4, 1801. Jefferson's first inaugural address offers the best summary of what we now call Jeffersonian democracy.

9. James Madison, *Federalist* no. 10. The quote is from Roger Sherman, recorded in "Madison's Notes of Debates," in *The Federal Convention and the Formation of the Union*, ed. Winston Solberg (Indianapolis, IN: Bobbs Merrill, 1958), 84–85.

10. Michael Kammen, *People of Paradox* (New York: Knopf, 1972), 31.

11. Alexis de Tocqueville, *Democracy in America*, trans. George Lawrence (Garden City, NY: Doubleday, 1969), 1:60, 89; James Bryce, *The American Commonwealth* (London: Macmillan, 1888), 3:267.

12. Steven Levitsky and Daniel Ziblatt, *How Democracies Die* (New York: Crown Books, 2018).

13. John Kingdon, *America the Unusual* (New York: St. Martin's Press, 1999), 1.

14. Hilary Silver, "Social Exclusion and Social Solidarity: Three Paradigms. *International Labour Review,* Vol 133 (1994): 531-578

15. Martin Luther King Jr., Speech given at Ohio Northern University, January 11, 1968, http://www.onu.edu/node/28513.

16. Milton Friedman, *Capitalism and Freedom* (Chicago: University of Chicago Press, 1962).

17. The original statement of this theory is by Louis Hartz, *The Liberal Tradition in America* (New York: Harcourt, Brace, and World, 1955).

18. See Noel Ignatiev, *How the Irish Became White*, 2nd ed. (New York: Routledge, 2009).

19. Franklin quotes taken from *Poor Richard's Almanac*, see http://www.ushistory.org/franklin/quotable/.

20. James Truslow Adams, *The Epic of America* (New York: Taylor and Francis, 1938), xx.

21. Quoted in Jennifer Hochschild, *Facing Up to the American Dream* (Princeton, NJ: Princeton University Press, 1995), vi, 18.

22. Gordon Wood, *The Radicalism of the American Revolution* (New York: Knopf, 1992), 369.

23. Bureau of Labor Statistics, "Measuring Wage Inequality in and Across U.S. Metropolitan Areas, 2003–13," *Monthly Labor Review* (September 2015): 1.

24. Timothy Noah, *The Great Divergence: America's Growing Inequality Crisis and What We Can Do About It* (New York: Bloomsbury, 2012).

25. Roosevelt quoted in James Morone, *Hellfire Nation* (New Haven, CT: Yale University Press, 2004), 347. Tom Krattenmaker, *The Evangelicals You Don't Know: Introducing the Next Generation of Christians* (Roman and Littlefield, 2013).

26. Johnson quoted in Morone, *Hellfire Nation*, 427.

27. Robert Sattelmeyer, "'When He Became My Enemy': Emerson and Thoreau, 1848–49," *New England Quarterly* 62, no. 2 (1989): 188–89.

28. Pew Research Center, "Political Typology Reveals Deep Fissures on the Right and Left," October 24, 2017, http://pewrsr.ch/2zzfX6p.

29. Harvard Kennedy School Institute of Politics, "Survey of Young Americans' Attitudes toward Politics and Public Service 34th Edition, October 31–November 10, 2017," November 2017, http://iop.harvard.edu/sites/default/files/content/docs/171128_Harvard%20IOP_Fall%202017%20Topline.pdf. (The survey is conducted every two years.)

30. Tocqueville, *Democracy in America*, 1:9.

31. Hugh Brogan, *Alexis de Tocqueville: A Life* (New Haven, CT: Yale University Press, 2007), 352.

32. Tocqueville, *Democracy in America*, 2:558.

33. George Gao, "15 Striking Findings from 2015," December 22, 2015, http://www.pewresearch.org/fact-tank/2015/12/22/15-striking-findings-from-2015/.

34. John Winthrop, "A Model of Christian Charity" (Sermon delivered aboard the *Arbella*, 1630), Collections of the Massachusetts Historical Society, Boston, 1838, 3rd series, 7:31–48.

35. Gallup.com, "Religion," http://www.gallup.com/poll/1690/religion.aspx.

36. See Putnam and David Campbell, *American Grace: How Religion Divides and Unites Us* (New York: Simon & Schuster, 2010); David Masci, "Why Millennials Are Less Religious than Older Americans," Pew Research Center, January 8, 2016, http://www.pewresearch.org/fact-tank/2016/01/08/qa-why-millennials-are-less-religious-than-older-americans/.

37. Eileen W. Lindner, ed., *Yearbook of American & Canadian Churches* (Washington, DC: National Council of Churches, 2013).

38. Pew Research Center, Religion and Public Life Project, "Religious Landscape Study," http://religions.pewforum.org/.

39. Samantha A. Maldonado, "Will Millennials Return to Religion?," *Publishers Weekly*, Feb. 28, 2018, http://bit.ly/2FXjArh.

40. Thomas Jefferson, "Letter to the Danbury (Connecticut) Baptists," Library of Congress collection, www.loc.gov/loc/lcib/9806/danpost.html.

41. Clifford Geertz, *The Interpretation of Cultures* (New York: Basic Books, 1973).

42. James A Morone, "Is There an American Political Culture?," in James Morone, ed., *The Devils We Know: Us and Them in America's Raucous Political Culture* (Lawrence: Univ. of Kansas Press, 2014): 1–30

43. Madison, *Federalist* no. 10.

Chapter 3 The Constitution

1. Edmund Burke, "Speech to the Bristol Electors," in *Representation*, ed. Hannah Pitkin (New York: Atherton Press, 1969), 175–76.

2. See James A Morone, *The Democratic Wish* (New Haven: Yale University Press, 1998), chap. 1.

3. Robert Middlekauff, *The Glorious Cause* (New York: Oxford University Press, 1982), 74.

4. Bernard Bailyn, David Brion Davis, David Herbert Donald, John Thomas, Robert Wiebe, and Gordon Wood, *The Great Republic: A History of the American People* (Boston: Little, Brown, 1977), 256.

5. Middlekauff, *Glorious Cause*, 223–28, quotation on 226.

6. David Hackett Fischer, *Liberty and Freedom: A Visual History of America's Founding Ideas* (New York: Oxford University Press, 2005), 95–96.

7. See David Hackett Fischer, *Washington's Crossing* (New York: Oxford University Press, 2004), 384–85.

8. Gordon Wood, *The Creation of the American Republic* (Chapel Hill: University of North Carolina Press, 1969), 404.

9. Rogan Kersh, *Dreams of a More Perfect Union* (Ithaca, NY: Cornell University Press, 2001), 60-67.

10. Quoted in Gordon Wood, *Empire of Liberty* (New York: Oxford University Press, 2009), 14.

11. George Washington, Circular Letter of Farewell to the Army, June 8, 1873.

12. Richard Beeman, *Plain, Honest Men: The Making of the American Constitution* (New York: Random House, 2009), 3–7, 12.

13. Leonard Richards, *Shays's Rebellion: The American Revolution's Final*

Battle (Philadelphia: University of Pennsylvania Press, 2002).

14. Beeman, *Plain, Honest Men*, 84.

15. James Madison, "Madison's Notes of Debates," in *The Federal Convention and the Formation of the Union*, ed. Winston Solberg (Indianapolis: Bobbs Merrill, 1958), 84–85.

16. Madison, "Madison's Notes," 81.

17. Madison, "Madison's Notes," 81.

18. Madison, "Madison's Notes," 122 (quotes); also see David Brian Robertson, *The Constitution and America's Destiny* (New York: Cambridge University Press, 2005), 139.

19. Luther Martin, "Letter on the Federal Convention of 1787," American Constitution Society, http://www.constitution.org/je/lumarltr.htm.

20. Robertson, *Constitution and America's Destiny*, 140.

21. Francis Fukuyama, "American Political Dysfunction," *The American Interest,* November/December 2011. https://bit.ly/2MQLxTS

22. Max Farrand, ed., *The Records of the Federal Convention of 1787*, rev. ed. (New Haven: Yale University Press, 1966), 3:179.

23. Beeman, *Plain, Honest Men*, 335. On slavery in early America, see also Wendy Warren, *New England Bound* (New York: Norton, 2016).

24. Beeman, *Plain, Honest Men*, 333.

25. Madison, "Madison's Notes," 344.

26 Ford in *Congressional Record,* 116 (1970), p. 11913.

27. *United States v. Windsor,* 570 U.S. 744 (2013) struck down key portions of the Defense of Marriage Act; *Obergefell v Hodges* 576_____ (2015), guaranteed the right of same-sex couples to marry.

28. Herbert Storing, *What the Anti-Federalists Were For: The Political Writings of the Opponents of the Constitution* (Chicago: University of Chicago Press, 1981).

29. Lilliana Mason, *Uncivil Agreement: How Politics Became Our Identity* (Chicago: Univ. of Chicago Press, 2018). Yascha Mounk, McPolitics: "Once, all politics was local. Now all politics is national. Can we survive the shift?" *The New Yorker.* July 2, 2018: 59-63

30. Gordon Wood, *Radicalism of the American Revolution*.

31. Thomas Jefferson, "Letter to Samuel Kercheval, July 12, 1816," in *The Works of Thomas Jefferson*, ed. Paul Leicester Ford (New York: Putnam's Sons, 1905), 12:13–14.

32. Robert Dahl, *How Democratic Is the American Constitution?*, 2nd ed. (New Haven, CT: Yale University Press, 2003).

Chapter 4 Federalism and Nationalism

1. Peter Haden, "West Palm Beach Declares Itself 'Welcoming City' For Immigrants," WLRN, March 28, 2017, http://wlrn.org/post/west-palm-beach-declares-itself-welcoming-city-immigrants.

2. Christina Littlefield, "Sanctuary Cities: How Kathryn Steinle's Death Intensified the Immigration Debate," *Los Angeles Times,* July 24, 2015, http://www.latimes.com/local/california/la-me-immigration-sanctuary-kathryn-steinle-20150723-htmlstory.html.

3. David Goodhart, *The Road to Somewhere: The New Tribes Shaping British Politics* (London: Penguin UK, 2017).

4. U.S. Census, American Fact Finder, 2012: https://www.census.gov/newsroom/releases/archives/governments/cb12-161.html.

5. Annual Survey of Public Employment & Payroll Summary Report: 2013: https://www2.census.gov/govs/apes/2013_summary_report.pdf.

6. Gallup, "Americans Are Still More Trusting in Local over State Government," September 19, 2016, http://news.gallup.com/poll/195656/americans-trusting-local-state-government.aspx; Pew Research Center, "Public Trust in Government: 1958–2017, Dec. 14, 2017, http://www.people-press.org/2017/12/14/public-trust-in-government-1958-2017/.

7. David Brian Robertson, *Federalism and the Making of America* (New York: Routledge, 2012).

8. From Justice Brandeis's dissenting opinion in *New State Ice Co. v. Liebmann*, 285 U.S. 262, 311 (1932).

9. William Berry, Richard Fording, and Russell Hanson, "Reassessing the Race to the Bottom in State Welfare Policy," *Journal of Politics* 65, no. 2 (2003): 327–49. A study that reviews both diffusion and "race to the bottom" ideas is Martino Maggetti and Fabrizio Gilardi, "Problems (and Solutions) in the Measurement of Policy Diffusion Mechanisms," *Journal of Public Policy* 36, no. 1 (2016): 87–107, http://dx.doi.org/10.1017/S0143814X1400035X.

10. James Morone, *Hellfire Nation: The Politics of Sin in American History* (New Haven, CT: Yale University Press, 2003): part 3.

11. Dirksen quoted in Richard P. Nathan, "Updating Theories of American Federalism," in *Intergovernmental Management for the Twenty-First Century*, ed. Timothy Conlan and Paul Posner (Washington, DC: Brookings Institution Press, 2008), 15.

12. Heather K. Gerken, "Progressive Federalism: A User's Guide," *Democracy Journal* 44 (2017).

13. Timothy Conlan and Pual Posner, "American Federalism in an Era of Partisan Polarization: The Intergovernmental Paradox of Obama's New Federalism," *Publius*: *The Journal of Federalism* Vol. 46, no. 3 (2016): 281–307.

14. Quoted in Robert Dreyfuss, "Grover Norquist: 'Field Marshal' of the Bush Plan," *The Nation,* May 14, 2001.

15. See James A. Morone and David Blumenthal, "The Arc of History Bends toward Coverage: Health Policy at a Crossroads. *Health Affairs* Vol 37 no.3 (2018): 351, https://www.healthaffairs.org/doi/abs/10.1377/hlthaff.2017.1312.

16. *McCulloch v. Maryland*, 17 U.S. 316 (1819).

17. Robert Taylor, Mary-Jo Kline, and Greg L. Lint, eds., *Papers of John Adams* (Cambridge, MA: Harvard University Press, 1980), 3:141.

18. David Waldstreicher, *"In the Midst of Perpetual Fetes": The Making of American Nationalism, 1776–1820* (Chapel Hill: University of North Carolina Press, 1997).

19. John R. Hibbing and Elizabeth Theiss-Morse, *Stealth Democracy: Americans' Beliefs About How Government Should Work* (New York: Cambridge University Press, 2002).

20. National Center for Education Statistics (NCES), "Fast Facts: Expenditures: How Much Money Does the United States Spend on Public Elementary and Secondary Schools?," https://nces.ed.gov/fastfacts/display.asp?id=66.

21. Tocqueville, *Democracy in America*, 1:115n (see chap. 2, n. 8). For a modern perspective, see Anthony M. Pellegrino, Kristen Zenkov, Melissa A. Gallagher, and Liz Long, "Picturing New Notions of Civic Engagement in the U.S.: Youth-Facilitated, Visually-Based Explorations of the Prospections of Our Least Franchised and Most Diverse Citizens," in *Youth Voices, Public Spaces, and Civic Engagement,* ed. Stuart Greene, Kevin J. Burke, and Maria K. McKenna (New York: Routledge, 2016), 25–49.

Chapter 5 Civil Liberties

1. Allison Stranger, "Understanding the Angry Mob that Gave Me a Concussion," *New York Times*, March 13, 2017; Brian Miller, "Supreme Court Rules Professional Speech is Covered by First Amendment," *Forbes* (June 26, 2018), https://bit.ly/2xeiyns.

2. *Matal v. Tam*, 582 U.S. ____ (2017).

3. *Schenck v. United States* (249 U.S. 47, 1919)

4. The cases referred to in the paragraph: *Virginia v. Black* 538 US 343 (2003); *Brown v. Entertainment Merchants Association*, 564 U.S. 786 (2011); *Brandenburg v. Ohio*, 395 U.S. 444 (1969).

5. Gallup, "Death Penalty," (2017), http://news.gallup.com/poll/1606/death-penalty.aspx.

6. Death Penalty Information Center, "States with and without the Death Penalty," https://deathpenaltyinfo.org/states-and-without-death-penalty.

7. Shawn Francis Peters, *Judging Jehovah's Witnesses: Religious Persecution and the Dawn of the Rights Revolution* (Lawrence: University Press of Kansas, 2000).

8. The two cases are *Minersville School District v. Gobitis*, 310 U.S. 586 (1940); *West Virginia State Board of Education v. Barnette*, 319 U.S. 624 (1943).

9. Tocqueville, *Democracy in America*, 252 (see chap. 2, note 9).

10. *Barron v. Baltimore*, 32 U.S. 243 (1833).

11. The *Slaughter-House Cases*, 83 U.S. 36 (1873).

12. *Palko v. Connecticut*, 302 U.S. 319 (1937).

13. If you're interested in reading more on any of the cases we discuss, see Corey Brettschneider, ed., *Constitutional Law and American Democracy: Cases and Readings* (New York: Wolters Kluwer, 2012).

14. *Whole Woman's Health v. Hellerstedt*, 579 U.S.__ (2016).

15. Thomas Jefferson, "Letter to the Danbury Baptist Association," January 1, 1802, https://www.loc.gov/loc/lcib/9806/danpre.html.

16. *Everson v. Board of Education*, 330 U.S. 1 (1947).

17. *Engel v. Vitale*, 370 U.S. 421 (1962).

18. *Lamb's Chapel v. Center Moriches Union Free School District*, 508 U.S. 384 (1993).

19. Perry Grossman and Mark Joseph Stern, "Goodbye, Establishment Clause," *Slate*, June 27, 2017.

20. In *Good News Club v. Milford Central School*, 533 U.S. 98 (2001), the Court ruled 6–3 in favor of the club.

21. *Employment Division, Department of Human Resources of Oregon v. Smith*, 494 U.S. 872 (1990).

22. The decision that explicitly adopted a preferred position for free speech was *Brandenburg v. Ohio*, 395 U.S. 444 (1969), discussed later in this section.

23. John Stuart Mill, *On Liberty* (New York: Penguin Classics, 1982), 103. Oliver Wendell Holmes expressed a powerful faith in the marketplace of ideas in his dissent in *Abrams v. United States*, 250 U.S 616 (1919).

24. Cornell Law School, Cornell Center on the Death Penalty Worldwide project, www.deathpenalty-worldwide.org.

25. *Gitlow v. New York*, 268 U.S. 652 (1925). Gitlow, the socialist author of a left-wing manifesto, was convicted, but in the process the courts incorporated free speech.

26. *Brandenburg v. Ohio*, 395 U.S. 444 (1969). For a fine discussion, see Harold Sullivan, *Civil Rights and Liberties* (Upper Saddle River, NJ: Pearson Prentice Hall, 2005), chap. 2.

27. See Rebecca Barrett-Fox, *God Hates: Westboro Baptist Church, American Nationalism, and the Religious Right* (Lawrence: University of Kansas Press, 2016).

28. Posner cited in Patricia J. Williams, "ISIS Is Changing Our Attitude Toward Free Speech, but Not Guns," *The Nation*, February 4, 2016, http://bit.ly/29VHnYd.

29. *Virginia v. Black*, 538 U.S. 343 (2003).

30. *Virginia v. Black*, 538 U.S. 343 (2003).

31. *Texas v. Johnson*, 109 S. Ct. 2544 (1989).

32. Corey Brettschneider, *When the State Speaks, What Should it Say?* (Princeton: Princeton University Press, 2012).

33. *Chaplinsky v. New Hampshire*, 315 U.S. 568 (1942).

34. *Tinker v. Des Moines Independent Community School District*, 393 U.S. 503 (1969).

35. *Bethel School District No. 403 v. Fraser*, 478 U.S. 675 (1986); *Hazelwood School District v. Kuhlmeier*, 484 U.S. 260 (1988).

36. *New York Times Company v. United States*, 403 U.S. 713 (1971).

37. Bob Egelko, "S.F. Judge Dissolves His Wikileaks Injunction," *San Francisco Chronicle*, March 1, 2008, http://www.sfgate.com/bayarea/article/S-F-judge-dissolves-his-Wikileaks-injunction-3226168.php.

38. *United States v. Stevens*, 130 U.S.C. 1577 (2010).

39. Catharine MacKinnon, "Pornography, Civil Rights, and Speech," in *Constitutional Law and American Democracy*, ed. Corey Brettschneider (New York: Wolters Kluwer, 2011), see note 10, 661–70.

40. *Ashcroft v. Free Speech Coalition* (00–795) 535 U.S. 234 (2002) struck down the first statute; *United States v. Williams*, 553 U.S. 285 (2008) upheld the second.

41. Michael M. Grynbaum, "Trump Renews Pledge to "Take a Strong Look" at Libel Laws," *New York Times*, January 11, 2018, B3.

42. Seth Lipsky, *The Citizen's Constitution: An Animated Guide* (New York: Basic Books, 2009), 222.

43. German Lopez, Ryan Mark, and Soo Oh, "After Sandy Hook We Said Never Again," *Vox*, May 18, 2018, https://www.vox.com/a/mass-shootings-sandy-hook.

44. Joseph Story, *Commentaries on the Constitution of the United States* (Boston: Hilliard, Gray, 1833), 3:746.

45. Charlton Heston quoted in "Charlton Heston Rips Media," *Chicago Tribune*, September 12, 1997. *District of Columbia v. Heller*, 554 U.S. 570 (2008).

46. Associated Press, "After Parkland massacre, only two states passed meaningful gun control. Florida was one of them," *Tampa Bay Times*, September 27, 2018, www.tampabay.com/florida-politics/buzz/2018/09/27/after-parkland-massacre-only-two-states-passed-meaningful-gun-control-florida-was-one-of-them/.

47. Bruce A. Arrigo and Austin Acheson, "Concealed Carry Bans and the American College Campus: A Law, Social Sciences, and Policy Perspective," *Contemporary Justice Review* 19, no. 1 (2016): 120–41, http://dx.doi.org/10.1080/10282580.2015.1101688; Adam Nagourney and Erik Eckholm, "2nd Amendment Does Not Guarantee Right to Carry Concealed Weapons, Court Rules," *New York Times*, June 9, 2016, http://www.nytimes.com/2016/06/10/us/second-amendment-concealed-carry.html?_r=0.

48. *Olmstead v. United States*, 277 U.S. 438 (1928).

49. *United States v. Leon*, 468 U.S. 897 (1984).

50. *Herring v. United States*, 555 U.S. 135 (2009).

51. *Kentucky v. King*, 131 U.S. 865 (2011); *Utah v. Strief*, 579 U.S. ____, 136 S. Ct. 2056.

52. Linda Monk, *The Words We Live By: Your Annotated Guide to the*

Constitution (New York: Hyperion, 2003), 165.

53. *Dickerson v. United States*, 530 U.S. 428 (2000).

54. *Illinois v. Perkins*, 496 U.S. 292 (1990); *New York v. Quarles*, 467 U.S. 649 (1984); *Harris v. New York*, 401 U.S. 222 (1970).

55. Anthony Lewis, *Gideon's Trumpet* (New York: Vintage, 1989).

56. *Missouri v. Frye*, 132 U.S. 55 (2012); Emily Yoffe, "Innocence Is Irrelevant: This Is the Age of the Plea Bargain." *The Atlantic Monthly*, September 2017.

57. U.S. Department of Justice, "Access to Justice," http://www.justice.gov/atj/file/788166/download.

58. "New Study Reveals 'Profound and Dramatic Understaffing' of Rhode Island Public Defender System," National Association of Criminal Defense Lawyers website, November 16, 2017, https://www.nacdl.org/Rhode-Island-Project-Release/.

59. The Death Penalty Information Center has put together a useful clearing house of data, https://deathpenaltyinfo.org/race-death-row-inmates-executed-1976?scid=5&did=184.

60. For a list of executions by state and region since 1976, see https://deathpenaltyinfo.org/number-executions-state-and-region-1976.

61. For an updated list of inmates whose crimes have been exonerated by Innocence Project efforts, see http://www.innocenceproject.org/free-innocent/improve-the-law/fact-sheets/dna-exonerations-nationwide.

62. *Kennedy v. Louisiana*, 554 U.S. 407 (2008); *Atkins v. Virginia*, 536 U.S. 304 (2002); *Roper v. Simmons*, 543 U.S. 551 (2005); *Baez v. Rees*, 271 S. W. 3d. 207 affirmed (2007).

63. Adam Goldman, Jia Lynn Yang, and John Muyskens, "The Islamic State's Suspected Inroads into America," *Washington Post*, updated June 25, 2016, https://www.washingtonpost.com/graphics/national/isis-suspects/.

64. Charlie Savage, Eileen Sullivan, and Nicholas Fandos, "House Extends Surveillance Law Rejecting Privacy Safeguards," *New York Times*, January 12, 2018, A1.

Chapter 6 The Struggle for Civil Rights

1. "Unite the Right Torch Rally Ends in Violence at the Rotunda," *The Roanoke Times*, August 11, 2017, https://bit.ly/2tWfPxB.

2. Dominique Mosbergen, "Neo-Nazi Site Daily Stormer Praises Trump's Charlottesville Reaction: 'He Loves Us All,'" HuffPost, August 13, 2017, https://bit.ly/2u1IeCd.

3. Samuel Huntington, *American Politics: The Promise of Disharmony* (Cambridge, MA: Harvard University Press, 1981).

4. Smith, *Civic Ideals* (see chap. 2, note 3).

5. African American Mayors Association, ourmayors.org.

6. Jessica L. Semega, Kayla R. Fontenot, and Melissa A. Kollar, "Income and Poverty in the United States, 2016" (U.S. Census Report P60-269, September 2017), Table 3.

7. Pew Research Center, http://www.pewsocialtrends.org/2017/05/18/1-trends-and-patterns-in-intermarriage/.

8. Gallup: http://bit.ly/2FxklGv.

9. *Pierce v. Society of Sisters*, 268 U.S. 510 (1925); *Romer v. Evans*, 517 U.S. 620 (1996).

10. W. E. B. DuBois, *The Souls of Black Folk* (New York: New American Library, 1982), 220.

11. Garry Wills, *Lincoln at Gettysburg* (New York: Simon & Schuster, 1992).

12. C. Vann Woodward, *The Burden of Southern History*, 3rd ed. (Baton Rouge: University of Louisiana Press, 1993), 72.

13. The Civil Rights Cases, 109 U.S. 3 (1883).

14. Richard Valelly, *The Two Reconstructions* (Chicago: University of Chicago Press, 2004), 2.

15. *Plessy v. Ferguson*, 163 U.S. 537 (1896); *Williams v. Mississippi*, 170 U.S. 213 (1898).

16. Jessie Parkhurst Guzman, *The Negro Yearbook* (Tuskegee, AL: Tuskegee Institute, 1947).

17. Peggy Pascoe, *What Comes Naturally: Miscegenation Law and the Making of Race in America* (New York: Oxford University Press, 2008).

18. Daniel P. Franklin, *Politics and Film: The Political Culture of Film in the United States* (Lanham, MD: Rowman and Littlefield, 2006).

19. *Smith v. Allright*, 21 U.S. 649 (1944).

20. *Morgan v. Virginia*, 328 U.S. 373 (1946); *Sweatt v. Painter*, 339 U.S. 629 (1950); *McLaurin v. Oklahoma*, 339 U.S. 637 (1950).

21. *Brown v. Board of Education*, 347 U.S. 483 (1954).

22. Taylor Branch, *Parting the Waters* (New York: Simon & Schuster, 1988), 203.

23. See Raymond Arsenault, *Freedom Riders: 1961 and the Struggle for Racial Justice* (New York: Oxford, 2006).

24. *Heart of Atlanta Motel Inc. v. United States*, 379 U.S. 241 (1964); *Katzenbach v. McClung*, 379 U.S. 294 (1964).

25. *Griggs v. Duke Power Co.*, 401 U.S. 424 (1971).

26. *Sheet Metal Workers v. EEOC*, 478 U.S. 421 (1986).

27. *Adarand Construction v. Peña*, 515 U.S. 299 (1995).

28. Jon Marcus, "Why Men Are the New College Minority," *The Atlantic*, August 8, 2017, https://bit.ly/2vIEuXY.

29. *University of California v. Bakke*, 438 U.S. 265 (1978); *Fisher v. University of Texasat Austin et al.*, 579 U.S. 14–981 (2016); Laura Jarrett and Claire Foran, "Trump Administration Reverses Obama-Era Guidance on Use of Race in College Admissions," CNN (July 3, 2018), at https://cnn.it/2m0udAE.

30. Abby Kelly Foster, quoted in Morone, *Hellfire Nation*, 166 (see chap. 2, note 22).

31. Cecilia Hyunjung Mo, "The Consequences of Explicit and Implicit Gender Attitudes and Candidate Quality in the Calculation of Voters," *Political Behavior* 37, no. 2 (2015): 357–95.

32. Center for Women and American Politics, Eagleton Institute of Politics, Rutgers University, "Women in State Legislatures 2018," http://www.cawp.rutgers.edu/women-state-legislature-2018.

33. Donald Critchlow, *Phyllis Schlafly and Grassroots Conservatism* (Princeton, NJ: Princeton University Press, 2005), chap. 9.

34. Francine D. Blau and Lawrence M. Kahn, "The Gender Wage Gap: Extent, Trends, and Explanations," *IZA Discussion Paper* 9656 (January 2016), http://ftp.iza.org/dp9656.pdf.

35. Sheryl Gay Stolberg, "Obama Signs Equal Pay Legislation," *New York Times*, January 1, 2009.

36. *Wal-Mart Stores Inc. v. Dukes*, 603 F. 3d 571, reversed (2011).

37. Jena McGregor, "The Number of Women CEOs in the Fortune %00 is at an all-time high – of 32. The Washington Post. June 7, 2017. https://www.washingtonpost.com/news/on-leadership/wp/2017/06/07/the-number-of-women-ceos-in-the-fortune-500-is-at-an-all-time-high-of-32/?utm_term=.6899e3495391

38. Honorable Henry Cabot Lodge, "Lynch Law and Unrestricted Immigration," *North American Review* 152 (1891): 602–12.

39. Seung Min Kim and Matthew Nussbaum, "White House Doesn't Deny Trump's Shithole Integration Remark," *Politico*, January 12, 2018, accessed April 11, 2018, https://www .politico.eu/article/donald-trump-white-house-doesnt-deny-trumps-shithole-immigration-remark/.

40. On immigration history, see Rogers Smith, *Civic Ideals* (New Haven: Yale University Press, 1997); Daniel Tichenor, *Dividing Lines: The Politics of Immigration Control in America*(Princeton: Princeton University Press, 2002); on Shithole countries, Julie Hirshfield Davis, Sheryl Stolberg, and T. Kaplan, "Trump Alarms Lawmakers with Disparaging Words for Haiti and Africa," *New York Times*, January 11, 2018, https://www.nytimes .com/2018/01/11/us/politics/trump-shithole-countries.html; on polls, Poll-ingReport.com, "CBS News Poll," June 14–17, 2018, http://www .pollingreport.com/immigration.htm.

41. John Burnett, "Arrests for Illegal Border Crossings Hit 46 Year Low. December" *National Public Radio*. December 5, 2017. https://www.npr .org/2017/12/05/568546381/arrests-for-illegal-border-crossings-hit-46-year-low; Department of Homeland Security, Office of Immigration Statistics, "2015 Annual Update" (August 31, 2015), https://www.dhs .gov/immigration-data-statistics.

42. The Stanford Open Policing Project 2017, "Findings: The Results of Our Nationwide Analysis of Traffic Stops and Searches," https://openpolicing.stanford.edu/ findings/.

43. For updates on Hispanic inequality, see David Grusky, Tomás Jiménez, Doug Massey, and Beth Mattingly, "Hispanic Poverty and Inequality," Stanford Center on Poverty & Inequality, http://inequality.stanford.edu/ cpi-research/area/hispanic-trends.

44. Jens Manuel Krogstad, "After Decades of GOP support, Cubans Shifting Toward Democratic Party," Pew Research Center, June 24, 2014, http://www.pewresearch.org/ fact-tank/2014/06/24/after-decades-of-gop-support-cubans-shifting-toward-the-democratic-party/.

45. Heather Silber Mohamed, "Can Protests Make Latinos 'American'? Identity, Immigration Politics, and the 2006 Marches," *American Politics Research* 41, no. 2 (2013): 298–327.

46. U.S. Census Bureau data, released June 23, 2016, http://www.census.gov/ newsroom/press-releases/2016/cb16-107.html.

47. Smith, *Civic Ideals*, 361.

48. "Discrimination in America: Experiences and Views of Asian Americans," NPR, Harvard Chan School of Public Health, and the Robert Wood Johnson Foundation, November 2017, https://www.npr.org/ assets/news/2017/12/discrimination-poll-asian-americans.pdf. Charlotte Brooks, *Alien Neighbors, Foreign Friends: Asian Americans, Housing and the Transformation of Urban California* (Chicago: University of Chicago Press, 2009), 194; Cindy I-Fen Cheng, *Citizens of Asian America: Democracy and Race during the Cold War* (New York: New York University Press, 2013).

49. Kristina Campbell, "The 'New Selma' and the Old Selma: Arizona, Alabama, and the Immigration Civil Rights Movement in the Twenty-First Century," *Journal of American Ethnic History* 35, no. 3 (Spring 2016); Anemona Hartocollis, "Does Harvard Admissions Discriminate?" New York Times, Oct. 15, 2018, https://nyti. ms/2yj4UjE.

50. Pekka Hämäläinen, *The Comanche Empire* (New Haven, CT: Yale University Press, 2008).

51. *Washington v. United States*, 584 U.S. ___ (2018).

52. *California v. Cabazon Band of Mission Indians*, 480 U.S. 202 (1987).

53. Pew Research Center, "Changing Attitudes on Gay Marriage," June 26, 2017, http://www.pewforum.org/ fact-sheet/changing-attitudes-on-gay-marriage/.

54. Trevor G. Gates and Margery C. Saunders, "Executive Orders for Human Rights: The Case of Obama's LGBT Nondiscrimination Order," *International Journal of Discrimination and the Law* 16, no. 1 (2016).

55. Alan Feur, "Justice Department Says Rights Law Does not Protect Gays," *New York Times*. July 27, 2017; Alan Feuer and Benjamin Weiser,"Civil Rights Act Protects Gay Workers, Court Rules," *New York Times*, February 26 2018, p. AI.

56. See Jaime M. Grant, et al., *Injustice at Every Turn: A Report of the National Transgender Discrimination Survey* (Washington, DC: National Center for Transgender Equality and National Gay and Lesbian Task Force, 2011), 2.

57. Steve Harrison, "Charlotte City Council Approves LGBT Protections in 7–4 Vote," *Charlotte Observer*, February 22, 2016, http://www .charlotteobserver.com/news/politics-government/article61786967.html.

58. For a defense of the North Carolina legislation and cautions about LGTBTQX rights, see Peter Shuck, "A Bathroom of One's Own?" *New York Times*, May 18, 2016; Jane Clark, "The True Trauma Trigger that the North Carolina Bathroom Bill Is Designed to Prevent, *National Review*, March 30, 2016; Michael Lipka, "Americans Are Divided Over Which Bathrooms Transgender People Should Use," Pew Research Center, October 3, 2016, http://www .pewresearch.org/fact-tank/2016/10/ 03/americans-are-divided-over-which-public-bathrooms-trans-gender-people-should-use/; Jason Hanna, Madison Park, and Eliott C. McLaughlin, "North Carolina Repeals Bathroom Bill,"*CNN Politics*, March 30, 2017, https://www.cnn.com/ 2017/03/30/politics/north-caro-lina-hb2-agreement/index.html.

59. Emery P. Dalesio and Jonathan Drew, "'Bathroom Bill' to Cost North Carolina $3.76B," *AP News*, March 30, 2017, https://www.apnews.com/ e6c7a15d2e16452c8dcbc2756fd67b44.

60. Associated Press, "Miami Catholic School Teacher Says She Was Fired for Being Gay," February 12, 2018, https:// www.nbcnews.com/feature/nbc-out/ miami-catholic-school-teacher-says-she-was-fired-being-gay-n847116.

61. *Shelby County v. Holder*, 557 U.S. 193 (2013); *Abbot v Perez*, 17 – 586 (2018).

62. Marina Sheriff, "Testimony: Public Hearings on the Rockefeller Drug Laws, Special Housing Units, and Transitional Services for Inmates," *New York Civil Liberties Union*, May 4, 2001, https://www.nyclu.org/ en/publications/testimony-public-hearings-rockefeller-drug-laws-special-housing-units-and-transitional.

Chapter 7 Public Opinion

1. Maureen Dowd, "Don't Harsh Our Mellow, Dude," *New York Times*, June 4, 2014, A23.

2. Tom Hiddlestone, "Colorado Topped $1 Billion in Legal Marijuana Sales. *Fortune*, December 13, 2016, http://fortune.com/2016/12/13/colo-rado-billion-legal-marijuana-sales/.

3. Hannah Fingerhut, "Support Steady for Same-Sex Marriage and Acceptance of Homosexuality," Pew Research Center, May 12, 2016, http:// pewrsr.ch/2ajmvN7; a 2016 update from Gallup: "In Depth: Topics A to Z: Marriage," http://bit.ly/1iiDKeI.

4. Coral Davenport and Eric Lipton, "How G.O.P. Leaders Came to View Climate Change as Fake Science," *New*

York Times, June 3, 2017, p. A1; Cary Funk and Brian Kennedy, "The Politics of Climate," Pew Research Center, October 4, 2016, http://www.pewinternet.org/2016/10/04/the-politics-of-climate/. For a good overview, see Justin Fox, "97 Percent Consensus on Climate Change? It's Complicated," *Bloomberg View*, June 15, 2017, https://bloom.bg/2takmKz.

5. "History of Opinion Polling," *NOW with Bill Moyers on PBS*, June 6, 2002, http://www.pbs.org/now/politics/polling.html.

6. Haven Insights (blog), "Just 37% of Americans Can Name Their Representative," by Nick Freiling, posted May 31, 2017, http://www.haveninsights.com/just-37-percent-name-representative/.

7. Pew Research Center, "Chapter 2: Generations and Issues," March 7, 2014, http://www.pewsocialtrends.org/2014/03/07/chapter-2-generations-and-issues/.

8. Why? Because older people vote and politicians are very unlikely to withdraw benefits from highly mobilized voters. Republicans are unlikely to threaten the program because seniors are their most staunch supporters—and are focused on protecting social security; Democrats are not likely to because they consider it an important program. In short, the political support for Social Security is very strong. Despite forty years of repeating that the program will soon collapse (despite no real evidence for that claim) the program enjoys robust support from both parties.

9. Michael Jackman, ed., *Crown's Book of Political Quotations* (New York: Crown Books, 1982), 181.

10. Mark Losey, "Why I Am a Democrat," DemocraticUnderground.com, accessed July 24, 2011, http://bit.ly/oHsB2C.

11. Orrin Hatch, "Why I Am a Republican," *Ripon Forum* 41, no. 6 (2008): 8.

12. Scott Jaschik, "Professors and Politics: What the Research Says," *Inside Higher Education*, February 27, 2017, http://bit.ly/2mm2igq; Christopher Ingraham, "The Dramatic Shift Among College Professors That's Hurting Student's Education," *The Washington Post*, January 11, 2016, https://www.washingtonpost.com/news/wonk/wp/2016/01/11/the-dramatic-shift-among-college-professors-thats-hurting-students-education/.

13. Shanto Iyengar and Sean J Westwood, "Fear and Loathing across Party Lines," *American Journal of Political Science* 59, no 3 (July 2015): 690–707.

14. Drew DeSilver, "Partisan Polarization, in Congress and Among Public, Is Greater than Ever," Pew Research Center, July 17, 2013, http://www.pewresearch.org/fact-tank/2013/07/17/partisan-polarization-in-congress-and-among-public-is-greater-than-ever/.

15. Nolan McCarthy, Keith Poole and Howard Rosenthal, *Polarized America: The Dance of Ideology and unequal Riches.* (Cambridge, MA: MIT Press, 2016). For a summary of the older debate about polarization between elites versus polarization of the base, see Morris Fiorina with Samuel Abrams and Jeremy Pope, *Culture War?: The Myth of a Polarized America* (Pearson, 2010); Alan Abramowitz and Kyle Sanders, "Is Polarization a Myth," *The Journal of Politics* 70, no 2 (April 2008): 542–55.

16. See Katherine J. Cramer, *The Politics of Resentment: Rural Consciousness in Wisconsin and the Rise of Scott Walker* (Chicago: University of Chicago Press, 2016); David K. Jones, "Health Reform in the South: Re-Tracing Robert F. Kennedy's Steps in Mississippi and Kentucky," *World Medical & Health Policy* 9, no. 2 (2017). For a skeptical view of Frank's book, see Larry Bartels, "What's the Matter with What's the Matter with Kansas," (paper, American Political Science Association, Washington, DC, September 2005), https://www.thenation.com/wp-content/uploads/2015/04/kansas.pdf.

17. Andrew Gelman, Red State, Blue State, Rich State, Poor State: Why Americans Vote the Way They Do (Princeton: Princeton University Press, 2009).

18. John Zaller, *The Nature and Origins of Mass Opinion* (New York: Cambridge University Press, 1992).

19. Bruce Drake, "More Americans Say U.S. Failed to Achieve Its Goals in Iraq," Pew Research Center, June 12, 2014, http://pewrsr.ch/1lsN29q.

20. Steven Shepard, "Trump's Challenge: A Wall of Public Skepticism on Afghanistan War," *Politico*, August 21, 2017, http://politi.co/2szdFWo.

21. A good overview is in Spencer Kimball, "2016 Presidential Statewide Polling—A Substandard Performance: A Proposal and Application for Evaluating Preelection Poll Accuracy," *American Behavioral Scientist*, October 12, 2017, https://doi.org/10.1177/0002764217735622.

22. Nate Cohn, "Political Calculus: A 2016 Review: Why Key State Polls Were Wrong About Trump," *New York Times* , June 1, 2017, A12.

23. Jonathon P. Schuldt, Sungjong Roh, and Norbert Schwarz, "Questionnaire Design Effects in Climate Change Surveys," *Annals of the American Academy of Political and Social Science* 658, no. 1 (2015): 71.

24. Jon Coupal, "Pernicious Push Polls Pervert Politics, *Orange County Register*. May 19, 2018. https://www.ocregister.com/2018/05/19/pernicious-push-polls-pervert-politics/

25. Scott Keeter and Kyley McGeeney, "Pew Research Will Call More Cellphones in 2015," Pew Research Center, January 7, 2015, http://www.pewresearch.org/fact-tank/2015/01/07/pew-research-will-call-more-cellphones-in-2015/.

26. Thomas Patterson, "News Coverage of the 2016 General Election: How the Press Failed the Voters," Shorenstein Center on Media, Politics, and Public Policy, Harvard Kennedy School, December 7, 2016, Figure 6, https://shorensteincenter.org/wp-content/uploads/2016/12/2016-General-Election-News-Coverage-1.pdf?x78124.

27. Philip Bump, "The polling miss that defines 2018 might not be the one from 2016. It may be the one from 2017," *Washington Post*, November 7, 2018, www.washingtonpost.com/politics/2018/11/05/polling-miss-that-defines-might-not-be-one-it-may-be-one/?utm_term=.711dc6aa612d

28. See, e.g., Laura Reston, "Trump and the Bandwagon Effect," *New Republic*, April 26, 2016, http://bit.ly/2aOONgP.

29. Todd Rogers and Don A. Moore, "The Motivating Power of Under-Confidence: 'The Race Is Close but We're Losing'" (paper, HKS Working Paper No. RWP14–047, October 1, 2014).

30. David O. Sears, "An Ignorant and Easily Duped Electorate?," *Perspectives on Politics* 15, no.1 (2017): 137–41.

31. Walter Lippmann, *Public Opinion* (New York: Harcourt, Brace, 1922). On the movement to govern through technical expertise, see Morone, *The Democratic Wish*, chap. 3 (see chap. 2, note 4).

32. Annenberg Public Policy Center, "Americans Are Poorly Informed About Basic Constitutional Provisions," September 12, 2017, http://bit.ly/2wZZzvD.

33. Ilya Somin, *Democracy and Political Ignorance*, 2nd ed. (Stanford, CA: Stanford University Press, 2016).

34. Angus Campbell, Philip E. Converse, Warren E. Miller, and Donald E. Stokes, *The American Voter* (New York: Wiley, 1960).

35. Jennifer L. Hochschild and Katherine Levine Einstein, *Do Facts Matter? Information and Misinformation in American Politics* (Norman: University of Oklahoma Press, 2015); Arthur Lupia, *Uninformed: Why People Seem to Know So Little About Politics and What We Can Do About It* (New York: Oxford University Press); Rick Shenkman, *Just How Stupid Are We? Facing the Truth About the American Voter* (New York: Basic Books, 2008).

36. Christopher H. Achen and Larry M. Bartels, *Democracy for Realists: Why Elections Do Not Produce Responsive Government (Princeton: Princeton University Press, 2016).* Milton Lodge and Charles Taber, *The Rationalizing Voter* (Cambridge: Cambridge University Press, 2013).

37. The classic statement of this position comes from the dean of public opinion research, V. O. Key, *Public Opinion and American Democracy* (New York: Knopf, 1967); Benjamin I. Page and Robert Y. Shapiro, *The Rational Public: Fifty Years of Trends in Americans' Policy Preferences* (Chicago: University of Chicago Press, 1992).

38. "The Support for the Keystone Pipeline," Rasmussen Reports, http://www.rasmussenreports.com/public_content/politics/current_events/environment_energy/support_down_for_keystone_pipeline.

39. James Surowiecki, *The Wisdom of Crowds* (New York: Doubleday, 2004), xii.

40. Jon Marino, "The US Is Still Angry at Wall Street, and It May Be Hurting Recruiting," *CNBC News, Finance*, June 9, 2016, http://cnb.cx/1tel2h4.

41. John F. Harris, *The Survivor: Bill Clinton in the White House* (New York: Random House, 2005), 331.

42. Lawrence R. Jacobs and Robert Y. Shapiro, *Politicians Don't Pander: Political Manipulation and the Loss of Democratic Responsiveness* (Chicago: University of Chicago Press, 2000).

43. Barry Schwartz, *The Paradox of Choice: Why More Is Less* (New York: Harper Perennial, 2004).

Chapter 8 Political Participation

1. Mary Jordan and Scott Clement, "Rallying Nation: In Reaction to Trump, Millions of Americans Are Joining Protests and Getting Political," *Washington Post*, April 6, 2018.

2. Jose Pagliery, "Suspect in Congressional Shooting Was Sanders Supporter, Strongly Anti-Trump," *CNN Investigates*, June 15, 2017, https://cnn.it/2swlrhb.

3. Peter Beinart, "The Rise of the Violent Left," *The Atlantic*, September 2017, https://www.theatlantic.com/magazine/archive/2017/09/the-rise-of-the-violent-left/534192/.

4. Max Halupka, "The Legitimization of Clicktivism," *Australian Journal of Political Science* 53:1 (2018), 130-41.

5. Rebecca Blood, *We've Got Blog: How Weblogs Are Changing Our Culture* (Cambridge MA: Perseus Publishing, 2002).

6. Authors' compilation.

7. Pew Research Center, "Public Trust in Government: 1958–2017," December 14, 2017, http://www.people-press.org/2017/12/14/public-trust-in-government-1958-2017/.

8. Case Foundation, *Millennial Impact Report 2016* (Washington, DC: Case Foundation, 2016).

9. Harvard IOP poll, Spring 2018, https://bit.ly/2JCBHEu.

10. OpenSecrets.org, "Donor Demographics," 2016 campaign cycle, https://bit.ly/2e3aVJe.

11. Tocqueville, *Democracy in America*, 1:189–95 (see chap. 2, note 3).

12. Anna Isaac, "The 10 Most Generous Nations in the World. *The Guardian*. Nov 10, 2015. https://www.theguardian.com/voluntary-sector-network/gallery/2015/nov/10/the-10-most-generous-nations-in-the-world-in-pictures

13. Jacob Pramuk, "A Record Number of Women Are Running for the House this Year," *CNBC*, April 6, 2018, https://cnb.cx/2GYwgkz.

14. Peter Augustine Lawler, "Days of Apathy," *American Enterprise Review* (November 1, 1997): 22–24.

15. https://www.nytimes.com/2017/01/19/opinion/voting-should-be-mandatory.html

16. Gallup, "2016 Global Civic Engagement Report," September 19, 2016, https://bit.ly/2rTtQKm.

17. Open Secrets, "Donor Demographics," OpenSecrets.org: Center for Responsive Politics, November 13, 2018, https://www.opensecrets.org/overview/donordemographics.php.

18. Jens Manuel Krogstad and Mark Hugo Lopez, "Black Voter Turnout Fell in 2016, Even as a Record Number of Americans Cast Ballots," Pew Research Center, May 12, 2017, http://www.pewresearch.org/fact-tank/2017/05/12/black-voter-turnout-fell-in-2016-even-as-a-record-number-of-americans-cast-ballots/.

19. See, e.g., Rob Griffin, Ruy Teixeira, and John Halpin, "Voter Trends in 2016," Center for American Progress, November 1, 2017, https://ampr.gs/2s79roN; Jennifer C. Lee and Samuel Kye, "Racialized Assimilation of Asian Americans," *Annual Review of Sociology* 42 (July 2016): 253–73.

20. Donald P. Green and Alan S. Gerber, *Get Out the Vote: How to Increase Voter Turnout*, 3rd ed. (Washington, DC: Brookings Institution Press, 2015).

21. Rogan Kersh, Michael Lamb, and Cameron Silverglate, *Trust, Leadership, and Social Capital Among Millennials*, (City, Publisher, forthcoming 2019).

22. Mark Guarino, "How Organic Farming and YouTube Are Taming the Wilds of Detroit," *The Washington Post*, November 14, 2015, https://www.washingtonpost.com/national/how-organic-farming-and-youtube-are-taming-the-wilds-of-detroit/2015/11/14/c8f8df26-71da-11e5-8d93-0af317ed58c9_story.html.

23. Aaron C. Weinschenk and Christopher T. Dawes, "The Relationship Between Genes, Personality Traits, and Political Interest," *Political Research Quarterly* 70, no. 3 (2017); James H. Fowler, Laura A. Baker, and Christopher T. Dawes, "Genetic Variation in Political Participation," *American Political Science Review* 102, no. 2 (2008): 233–48.

24. Doug McAdam and Karina Kloos, *Deeply Divided: Racial Politics and Social Movements in Post War America* (New York: Oxford University Press, 2014).

25. Joe Soss, *Unwanted Claims* (Ann Arbor: University of Michigan, 2002).

26. Doug McAdam, *Political Process and the Development of Black Insurgency, 1930–1970*, 2nd ed. (Chicago: University of Chicago Press, 1999).

27. Sidney Verba and Norman Nie, *Voice and Equality* (Chicago: University of Chicago, 1972).

28. Hanes Walton, Jr., Robert C. Smith, and Sherri L. Wallace, *American Politics and the African American Quest for Universal Freedom* (New York: Routledge, 2017), esp. 77–79.

29. See Pew Research, "The Generation Gap in American Politics" (March 1, 2018), https://pewrsr.ch/2GTWX6k.

30. Gary C. Jacobson, "The Triumph of Polarized Partisanship in 2016: Donald

Trump's Improbable Victory." *Political Science Quarterly* 132, no. 1 (2017): 9–41.

31. John Kenneth Galbraith, *The Culture of Contentment* (New York: Mariner Books, 1993).

32. Theda Skocpol, "Voice and Inequality: The Transformation of American Civic Democracy," *Perspectives on Politics* 2, no. 1 (2004): 14.

33. Yascha Mounk, "Can Liberal Democracy Survive Social Media?," *New York Review of Books* (April 30, 2018), https://bit.ly/2r9Hclz.

34. See Matthew Hindman, *The Myth of Digital Democracy* (Princeton, NJ: Princeton University Press, 2009).

35. See, e.g., Cass R. Sunstein, *#Republic: Divided Democracy in the Age of Social Media* (Princeton, NJ: Princeton University Press, 2018).

36. Frank Konkel, "Pentagon Thwarts 36 Million Email Breach Attempts Daily," *NextGov* (blog), January 11, 2018, https://bit.ly/2kcWcfg.

37. See Saul Levmore and Martha C. Nussbaum, eds., *The Offensive Internet* (Cambridge, MA: Harvard University Press, 2010). See, for falsehoods, Rhodri Marsden, "Websites Can Create Outrageous Lies Just for Clicks," *Independent*, July 9, 2015, http://www.independent.co.uk/news/science/websites-can-create-outrageous-lies-just-for-clicks-but-why-and-how-is-this-legal-10379088.html.

38. Michael Grunwald, "How Obama Is Using the Science of Change," *Time*, April 2, 2009.

39. Pew Research Center, "Wide Gender Gap, Growing Educational Divide in Voters' Party Identification" (March 20, 2018), https://pewrsr.ch/2DIaDzc.

40. Pew Charitable Trusts, *Millennials in Adulthood: Detached from Institutions, Networked with Friends* (Washington, DC: Pew Research Center, 2014): 7.

41. Cathy J. Cohen, Matthew Fowler, Vladimir E. Medenica, and Jon C. Rogowski, "Who Belongs? Millennial Attitudes on Immigration," GenForward, January 2018, https://bit.ly/2EGm4fq.

Chapter 9 Media, Technology, and Government

1. Properly speaking, *media* is the plural of *medium*—usually defined as the way we convey something. We use the term *media*—meaning mass communication—as a singular noun in keeping with the way the language is evolving.

2. Nicholas Trübner, *Biographical Guide to American Literature* (London: Trübner & Co., 1859), xciii.

3. William A. Palmer, ed., *Hazell's Annual* (London, 1908): 579

4. Suzanne Kirchoff, "The U.S. Newspaper Industry in Transition," Congressional Research Service Report, September 9, 2010, https://fas.org/sgp/crs/misc/R40700.pdf.

5. Kristen Bialik and Katerina Eva Matsa, "Key Trends in Social and Digital News Media," Pew Research Center, October 4, 2017, https://pewrsr.ch/2fK9az3.

6. Pew Research Center, "News Use Across Social Media Platforms 2018," Sept. 2018. https://pewrsr.ch/2Qee8VE.

7. Pew Research Center, "Digital News Fact Sheet," June 6, 2018, updated June 19, 2018, http://www.journalism.org/fact-sheet/digital-news/.

8. Nassim Nicholas Taleb, *Black Swan: The Impact of the Highly Improbable* (New York: Random House, 2010).

9. Mark Remillard, "Trump Tweets Fake Video of Himself Attacking CNN Logo," *ABC News (kcrg.com)*, July 2, 2017, https://bit.ly/2ME6PEQ.

10. Shanto Iyengar and Donald R. Kinder, *News that Matters: Television and Public Opinion,* 2nd ed. (Chicago: University of Chicago Press, 2010).

11. Norbert J. Michel, "It's Time to Just Kill the Volcker Rule," *Fortune*, June 4, 2018, https://for.tn/2sHNrOi; Matthew Yglesias, "Republicans Are Sowing the Seeds of the Next Financial Crisis," *Vox*, May 31, 2018, https://bit.ly/2JoNybV.

12. Emily Flitter and Daniel Rappeport, "Bankers Hate the Volcker Rule. Now, It Could Be Watered Down," *New York Times*, May 21, 2018, https://nyti.ms/2LmlIuX.

13. David Bach and Daniel J. Blake, "Frame or Get Framed," *California Management Review* 58, no. 3 (2016).

14. Reliable historical counts of U.S. newspapers appear in the Inter-University Consortium for Political and Social Research's "United States Newspaper Panel," https://bit.ly/2JpIcxK (accessed June 2018).

15. American Society of Newspaper Editors, "2015 Census" (Columbia, MO, 2015), http://asne.org/content.asp?contentid=415 (accessed June 2018). Updated figures for U.S. newspaper circulation appear regularly in Pew Research Center's "Journalism & Media" analyses, see http://www.pewresearch.org/topics/state-of-the-news-media/.

16. Lpinto, "NPR Media Bias Update," *Allsides*, (blog) December 13, 2017, https://www.allsides.com/blog/npr-media-bias-update.

17. Samuel Kernell and Laurie L. Rice, "Cable and Partisan Polarization of the President's Audience," *Presidential Studies Quarterly* 41, no. 3 (2011), 693–711.

18. Erik Wemple, "President Trump Is in Constant Contact with Sean Hannity. How Long until He Turns on Him?" *Washington Post*, May 14, 2018, https://wapo.st/2sS8X3V. The *New York Times* described a "symbiotic relationship" between the president and Fox News: see Matthew Haag, "Former Fox News Analyst Calls Network a 'Destructive Propaganda Machine,'" *New York Times*, June 7, 2018, https://nyti.ms/2JtFVOl.

19. "Excerpts from Trump's Interview with *The Times*," *New York Times*, December 28, 2017, https://nyti.ms/2lfHeWH.

20. Markus Prior, "News v. Entertainment: How Increasing Media Choice Widens Gaps in Political Knowledge and Turnout," *American Journal of Political Science* 49, no. 3 (2005): 577–92.

21. Doris A. Graber and Johanna Dunaway, *Mass Media and American Politics*, 10th ed. (Washington, DC: CQ Press, 2017): 171.

22. See, e.g., Michael A. DeVito, "From Editors to Algorithms," *Digital Journalism* 5, no. 6 (2017).

23. Brian McNair, *Fake News: Falsehood, Fabrication, and Fantasy in Journalism* (New York: Routledge, 2017).

24. David M.J. Lazer et. al., "The Science of Fake News," *Science* 359, no. 6380 (2018): 1094–96, https://doi: 10.1126/science.aao2998.

25. Jeffrey M. Jones and Zacc Ritter, "Americans See More News Bias, Most Can't Name Neutral Source," Gallup/Knight Foundation, January 17, 2018, https://bit.ly/2mMUfam.

26. "Brat/Melvin MSNBC Interview," *YouTube*, July 15, 2017, https://bit.ly/2l8oLLD.

27. Nik DeCosta-Klipa, "Harvard Study Both Confirms and Refutes Bernie Sanders' Complaints about the Media," *Boston.com*, June 14, 2016, https://bit.ly/2JuILXg.

28. Chris Cillizza, "Just 7 Percent of Journalists Are Republicans. That's Far Fewer Than Even a Decade Ago," *Washington Post*, May 6, 2014, https://wapo.st/2tiFwXO.

29. Jack Shafer and Tucker Doherty, "The Media Bubble Is Worse Than You Think," *Politico Magazine* 4, no. 3 (May/June 2017): 17–20.

30. See the summary in S. Robert Lichter, "Theories of Media Bias," in *The Oxford Handbook of Political Communication*, eds. Kate Kenski and Kathleen Hall Jamieson (New York, Oxford University Press, 2017). Chap. 29.

31. Martin Gilens and Craig Hertzman, "Corporate Ownership and News Bias: Newspaper Coverage of the 1996 Telecommunications Act," *Journal of Politics* 62, no. 2 (2000): 369–86; Graham Beattie, Ruben Durante, Brian Knight, and Ananya Sen, "Advertising Spending and Media Bias: Evidence from News Coverage of Car Safety Recalls." NBER Working Paper No. 23940 (October 2017).

32. "Zell speaking on *Last Week Tonight with John Oliver*," YouTube, August 7, 2016, https://bit.ly/2M6SK1M.

33. See, for example, Isaac Chotiner, "Did the Press Create Donald Trump?" *Slate*, March 22, 2016, http://slate.me/22u0KjM.

34. Elaine Tyler May, *Fortress America: How We Embraced Fear and Abandoned Democracy* (New York: Basic Books, 2017).

35. Jones, "Americans See," (2018).

36. Figures from *Statistia*, "Leading TV Broadcasters in the United Kingdom in 2017 by Audience Share," June 2018, https://bit.ly/2MolRyp.

37. "Silvio Berlusconi: Italy's Perpetual Power Broker," *BBC News*, March 5, 2018, https://www.bbc.com/news/world-europe-11981754.

38. Andrei Markovits, *Uncouth Nation: Why Europeans Dislike America* (Princeton, NJ: Princeton University Press, 2007).

39. Michael Jetter, "The Effect of Media Attention on Terrorism," *Journal of Public Economics* 153 (2017): 53–48.

40. Paul Mozur, "China Presses Its Internet Censorship Efforts across the Globe," *New York Times*, March 3, 2018, https://nyti.ms/2HXlbOm.

41. Michael Wines and Sharon LaFraniere, "In Baring Facts of Train Crash, Blogs Erode China Censorship," *New York Times*, July 29, 2011.

42. Iyengar, *News that Matters: Television and Public Opinion*, 1st ed. (1989).

Chapter 10 Campaigns and Elections

1. For the conventional political science wisdom that Trump (and Sanders almost) shattered: Marty Cohen, David Karol, Hans Noel, and John Zaller, *The Party Decides: Presidential Nominations Before and After Reform* (Chicago: University of Chicago Press, 2008).

2. Ben Schreckinger, "16 Insults that Redefined Acceptable Political Rhetoric," *Politico*, November 6, 2016, https://www.politico.com/story/2016/11/2016-election-best-insults-230794.

3. John Sides and Lynn Vavreck, *The Gamble: Choice and Chance in the 2012 Presidential Election* (Princeton, NJ: Princeton University Press, 2013); William J. Feltus, Kenneth M. Goldstein, and Matthew Dallek, *Inside Campaigns: Elections Through the Eyes of Political Professionals* (New York: CQ Press, 2017), esp. chap. 2, "Political Math: How Campaigns Matter."

4. Christopher H. Achen and Larry Bartels, *Democracy for Realists: Why Elections Do Not Produce Responsive Government* (Princeton, NJ: Princeton University Press, 2016).

5. Pew Research Center, "Most Americans Want to Limit Campaign Spending," May 2018, https://pewrsr.ch/2IppJ2Z

6. David Shribman, "In Canada, the Lean Season," *Boston Globe*, May 23, 1997, A3.

7. Christopher Ingraham, "About 100 Million People Couldn't Be Bothered to Vote This Year," wonkblog, *Washington Post*, November 12, 2016, https://www.washingtonpost.com/news/wonk/wp/2016/11/12/about-100-million-people-couldnt-be-bothered-to-vote-this-year/?utm_term=.1078b6dbe1a8; Alexander Keyssar, *The Right to Vote* (New York: Basic Books, 2000).

8. *Citizens United v. Federal Election Commission*, 558 U.S. 310 (2010); *McCutcheon v. Federal Election Commission*, 572 U.S. ____ (2014).

9. "Election Overview: 2018 Data," Open Secrets: Center for Responsive Government, https://www.opensecrets.org/overview/index.php?display=T&type=A&cycle=2018; "Election Overview: 2016 Data," Open Secrets: Center for Responsive Government, https://www.opensecrets.org/overview/index.php?display=T&type=A&cycle=2016.

10. "Incumbent Advantage," Open Secrets: Center for Responsive Government, https://www.opensecrets.org/overview/incumbs.php.

11. James Holman, "Mick Mulvaney's confession highlights the corrosive role of money in politcs. *The Washington Post*. April 25, 2018. https://www.washingtonpost.com/news/powerpost/paloma/daily-202/2018/04/25/daily-202-mick-mulvaney-s-confession-highlights-the-corrosive-influence-of-money-in-politics/5adfea2230fb043711926869/?utm_term=.e333789d4b43

12. Richard L. Hansen, "Lobbying, Rent-Seeking, and the Constitution," *Stanford Law Review* 64, no. 1 (2012): 191–253; Richard L. Hall and Frank Wayman, "Buying Time: Moneyed Interests and the Mobilization of Bias in Congressional Committees," *American Political Science Review* 84, no. 3 (1990): 797–820; Anthony Fowler, Haritz Garro, and Jörg Spenkuch, "When Corporations Donate to Candidates, Are they Buying Influence?," *Kellogg Insight*, September 5, 2017, https://insight.kellogg.northwestern.edu/author/haritz-garro.

13. Editorial, "How Super PACs Run Campaigns, *New York Times*, April 27, 2015, A18.

14. Donald Trump with Tony Schwartz, *The Art of the Deal* (New York: Ballantine Books, 1987) p. 176.

15. John Sides, Michael Tesler, and Lynn Vavreck, *Identity Crisis: The 2016 Presidential Campaign and the Battle for the Meaning of America* (Princeton, NJ: Princeton University Press, 2018).

16. Political scientists have documented how Russia also has been meddling in former Soviet Union states since 1991, and in Western European countries since 2014—with little success. See Jonathan Masters, *Russia, Trump, and the 2016 U.S. Election*, Council on Foreign Relations, February 26, 2018, https://www.cfr.org/backgrounder/russia-trump-and-2016-us-election.

17. Lucan Ahmad Way and Adam Casey, "Russia Has Been Meddling in Foreign Elections for Decades. Has It Made a Difference?," *Washington Post*, January 8, 2018, https://www.washingtonpost.com/news/monkey-cage/wp/2018/01/05/russia-has-been-meddling-in-foreign-elections-for-decades-has-it-made-a-difference/?noredirect=on&utm_term=.65abad657362

18. John Sides, *Identity Crisis* (2018); Matt Barreto, Tyler Rey, and Bryan Wilcox Archuleta, "Survey Methodology and the Latina/o Vote," *Aztlan: A Journal of Chicano Studies* 42, no. 2 (Fall 2017): 211–27.

19. Molly O'Toole and Dan De Luce, "The 2016 Election Turned the Politics of Foreign Policy on Its Head: Clinton Is the Hawk this Year, Trump the Isolationist," *Foreign Policy*, November 2, 2016, https://foreignpolicy.com/2016/11/02/the-2016-election-turned-the-politics-of-foreign-policy-on-its-head/.

20. Samuel L. Popkin, *The Candidate: What It Takes to Win—and Hold—the White House* (New York: Oxford University Press, 2012); Ashley Parker and David E. Sanger, "Donald Trump Calls on Russia to Find Hillary Clinton's Missing Emails," *New York Times*, July 27, 2016, https://www.nytimes.com/2016/07/28/us/politics/donald-trump-russia-clinton-emails.html.

21. Stephen Anslobehere, Jonathan Rodden and James M. Snyder, "The Strength of Issues: Using Multiple Measures to Gauge Preference Stability, Ideological Constraint, and Issue Voting," *American Political Science Review* 102, no. 2 (2008): 215–32

22. Mark Halperin and John Heilemann, *Double Down: Game Change 2012* (New York, Penguin Press): 177–96.

23. "US Election: The Team Shaping Donald Trump's Campaign," *BBC News*, August 19, 2016, https://www.bbc.com/news/election-us-2016-37108732.

24. Stanley Feldman and Melissa Herrmann, "CBS News Exit Polls: How Donald Trump Won the U.S. Presidency," *CBS News*, November 9, 2016, https://www.cbsnews.com/news/cbs-news-exit-polls-how-donald-trump-won-the-us-presidency/.

25. National Constitution Center Staff, "A Recent Voting History of the 15 Battleground States," *Constitution Daily*, November 2, 2016, https://constitutioncenter.org/blog/voting-history-of-the-15-battleground-states/; Larry J. Sabato, Kyle Kondik, and Geoffrey Skelley, "The Electoral College: The Only Thing That Matters," *Center for Politics*, March 31, 2016, http://www.centerforpolitics.org/crystalball/articles/the-only-thing-that-matters/.

26. Wendell Cox, "America's Most Urban State," *Newgeography*, March 8, 2016, http://www.newgeography.com/content/005187-america-s-most-urban-states; Emily Schultheis and Julia Boccagno, "Trump v. Clinton: What the Popular Vote in Each State Shows," *CBS News*, December 19, 2016, https://www.cbsnews.com/news/trump-v-clinton-what-the-popular-vote-in-each-state-shows-electoral-college/.

27. For the classic analysis of the bystanders, see E. E. Schattschneider, *The Semisovereign People* (New York: Holt, Reinhardt, and Wilson, 1960).

28. For a good picture of the divide, see Katherine J. Cramer, *The Politics of Resentment* (Chicago: University of Chicago Press, 2016); Adrienne LaFrance, "Three Decades of Donald Trump Film and TV Cameos," *The Atlantic*, December 21, 2015, http://www.theatlantic.com/entertainment/archive/2015/12/three-decades-of-donald-trump-film-and-tv-cameos/421257/.

29. Robert Mickey, Steven Levitsky, and Lucan Ahmad Way, "Is America Still Safe for Democracy? Why the United States Is in Danger of Backsliding," *Foreign Affairs*, May/June 2017, 20–29, https://www.foreignaffairs.com/articles/united-states/2017-04-17/america-still-safe-democracy.

29a. Gary Langer and Benjamin Siu, "Election 2018 exit poll analysis: Voter turnout soars, Democrats take back the House, ABC News projects" *ABC News*, November 7, 2018, https://abcnews.go.com/Politics/election-2018-exit-poll-analysis-56-percent-country/story?id=59006586; and Jens Manuel Krogstad and Mark Hugo Lopez, "Hillary Clinton won Latino vote but fell below 2012 support for Obama," *Pew Research Center*, November 29, 2016, http://www.pewresearch.org/fact-tank/2016/11/29/hillary-clinton-wins-latino-vote-but-falls-below-2012-support-for-obama/.

30. "Cost of Election," Open Secrets: Center for Responsive Government, https://www.opensecrets.org/overview/cost.php.

31. David Hawkings, "Wealth of Congress: Richer than Ever, but Mostly at the Very Top, *Roll Call*, February 27, 2018, https://www.rollcall.com/news/hawkings/congress-richer-ever-mostly-top.

32. Peter Applebome, "Personal Cost for 2 Senate Bids: $100 million," *New York Times*, November 3, 2012, A16.

33. Nathan Burroughs, "The 'Money Primary' and Political Inequality in Congressional Elections," SSRN Working Paper, 2013, http://dx.doi.org/10.2139/ssrn.2251978.

34. On the Frelinghuysen family and other American "dynasties," see Stephen Hess, *America's Political Dynasties: From Adams to Clinton*, 2nd ed. (Washington, DC: Brookings Institution Press, 2016).

35. Jennifer L. Lawless and Richard L. Fox, *It Takes a Candidate: Why Women Don't Run for Office* (New York: Cambridge University Press, 2005).

36. Richard F. Fenno, Jr., *Home Style: House Members in their Districts* (New York: Longman Classics, 2002).

37. Ibid.

38. *Shaw v. Reno*, 509 U.S. 630 (1993).

39. Nina Totenberg, "Divided Court Upholds Nearly All of Texas GOP Redistricting Plan," *NPR.org*, June 25, 2018, https://www.npr.org/2018/06/25/623327469/divided-supreme-court-upholds-nearly-all-of-texas-gop-redistricting-plan; Michael Wines and Richard Fausset, "North Carolina is Ordered to Redraw Its Gerrymandered Congressional Map. Again. *New York Times*. August 27, 2018. https://www.nytimes.com/2018/08/27/us/north-carolina-congressional-districts.html.

40. See David C. W. Parker, *The Power of Money in Congressional Campaigns* (Norman: University of Oklahoma Press, 2008).

41. For the classic account of candidate-centered politics, see Martin P. Wattenberg, *The Rise of Candidate-Centered Politics: Presidential Elections of the 1980s* (Cambridge, MA: Harvard University Press, 1991).

42. Gerald M. Pomper, *Voters, Elections and Parties: The Practice of Democratic Theory* (Piscataway, NJ: Transaction, 1988), 104. See also Sean J. Miller, "Why Technology Can't Replace Old-Fashioned Politicking," *Campaigns & Elections*, April 19, 2012, https://www.campaignsandelections.com/campaign-insider/why-technology-can-t-replace-old-fashioned-politicking.

43. Richard Lau, Lee Sigleman, and Ivy Brown Rovner, "The Effects of Negative Political Campaigns: A Meta-Analytic Reassessment," *Journal of Politics* 69, no. 4 (November, 2007): 1176–1209; Erika Franklin Fowler, Michael Franz, and Travis Ridout, *Political Advertising in the United States* (New York: Westview, 2016).

44. Clayton D. Peoples, "Campaign Finance and Policymaking: PACs, Campaign Contributions, and Interest Group Influence in Congress," *Sociology Compass* 7, no. 11 (2013): 900–13,doi:10.1111/soc4.12079.

45. Craig Volden and Alan Wiseman, *Legislative Effectiveness in the United States Congress: The Lawmakers* (New York: Cambridge University Press, 2014).

Chapter 11 Political Parties

1. Machtley story reported by the congressman to one of the authors.

2. Pew Research Center, "Think Environmental Laws and Regulations Should Be Stricter," April 18, 2007, http://pewrsr.ch/2bCNp4U.

3.   Pew Research Center, "Political Partisanship and Animosity in 2016," June 22, 2016, http://pewrsr.ch/28WYkmr; Coral Davenport, "Climate Change Divide Bursts to Forefront of Presidential Campaign," *New York Times,* August 1, 2016, http://nyti.ms/2af8L2W; Hannah Fingerhut, "Why Do People Belong to a Party? Negative Views of the Opposing Party Are a Major Factor," Pew Research Center, March 29, 2018, https://pewrsr.ch/2J5d4Qs.

4.   Christopher Hare and Keith T. Poole, "The Polarization of Contemporary American Politics," *Polity* 46 (2014): 411–29; Nolan McCarty, Keith Poole, and Howard Rosenthal, *Polarized America: The Dance of Ideology and Unequal Riches,* 2nd ed. (Cambridge MA: MIT Press, 2016).

5.   Thomas Jefferson to Francis Hopkinson, Paris, March 13, 1789, National Archive, http://founders.archives.gov/documents/Jefferson/01-14-02-0402. For Washington's text and an informed commentary, see Matthew Spalding and Patrick J. Garrity, *A Sacred Union of Citizens: George Washington's Farewell Address and the American Character* (Lanham, MD: Rowman & Littlefield, 1998).

6.   Congressman David Cicillini (D-RI), remarks at Brown University, Providence, RI, June 9, 2015.

7.   Bruce Keith, David Magleby, Candice Nelson, Elizabeth A. Orr, Mark C. Westlye, and Raymond E. Wolfinger, *The Myth of the Independent Voter* (Berkeley: University of California Press, 1992).

8.   Rachel Weiner, "The Fix: Black Voters Turned Out at Higher Rate than White Voters in 2012 and 2008," *Washington Post,* April 29, 2013, https://www.washingtonpost.com/news/the-fix/wp/2013/04/29/black-turnout-was-higher-than-white-turnout-in-2012-and-2008/?utm_term=.e7e2866b9144.

9.   John H. Aldrich, *Why Parties? The Origin and Transformation of Political Parties in America* (Chicago: University of Chicago Press, 1995).

10.   See especially Teresa Amato, *Grand Illusion: The Myth of Voter Choice in a Two-Party Tyranny* (New York: New Press, 2009).

11.   The Libertarian Party and Green Party websites: https://www.lp.org/elected-officials-2/, http://www.gp.org/officeholders.

12.   J. David Gillespie, *Challengers to Duopoly: Why Third Parties Matter in Two-Party American Politics* (Columbia: University of South Carolina Press, 2012).

13.   R. Kent Newmyer, *Supreme Court Justice Joseph Story: Statesman of the Old Republic* (Chapel Hill: University of North Carolina Press, 1985), 158.

14.   For a picture of the spoils system, see James A Morone, *The Democratic Wish: Private Power and American Democracy* (New Haven, CT: Yale University Press, 1998), chap 2.

15.   Daniel Walker Howe, *What Hath God Wrought: The Transformation of America, 1815–1848* (New York: Oxford University Press, 2007).

16.   A good summary of this and related views is in Mark E. Neely, Jr., *The Union Divided: Party Conflict in the Civil War North* (Cambridge, MA: Harvard University Press, 2002).

17.   You can read all about Prohibition in Morone, *Hellfire Nation,* chapters 9 and 10 (see chap. 2, note 22).

18.   President William Jefferson Clinton, State of the Union Address, January 23, 1996, Washington DC, https://clinton2.nara.gov/WH/New/other/sotu.html (the era of big government is over); President Barack Hussein Obama, Inaugural Address, January 20, 2009, Washington DC, http://bit.ly/1VG1k9q (promising to end programs that do not work).

19.   See Katherine Tate, *Concordance: Black Lawmaking in the U.S. Congress from Carter to Obama* (Ann Arbor: University of Michigan Press, 2014).

20.   Sides, *Identity Crisis* (2018), (see chap. 10, note 17).

21.   Alan S. Gerber, Gregory A. Huber, David Doherty, Conor M. Dowling, and Shang E. Ha, "Personality and Political Attitudes: Relationships Across Issue Domains and Political Contexts," *American Political Science Review* 104, no. 1 (2010): 111–33, http://dx.doi.org/10.1017/S0003055410000031.

22.   Party identification averages monthly results from Gallup, "Party Affiliations," January–June 2018, https://news.gallup.com/poll/15370/party-affiliation.aspx.

23.   See Mark Z. Barabak, "Why the Rise of the Independent Voter Is a Political Myth," *Los Angeles Times,* March 1, 2018, https://lat.ms/2NNMD39; see also, Samantha Smith, "5 Facts about America's Political Independents," Pew Research Center, July 5, 2016, http://www.pewresearch.org/fact-tank/2016/07/05/5-facts-about-americas-political-independents/.

24.   Frank D. Bean, "Changing Ethnic and Racial Diversity in the United States," *Population and Development Review* 42, no. 1 (2016): 135–42, 10.1111/j.1728-4457.2016.00113.x.; Rob Griffin, Ruy Teixeira, and William H. Frey, "America's Electoral Future," *Brookings,* April 19, 2018, https://www.brookings.edu/research/americas-electoral-future_2018/; Dante Chinni, "Demographic Shifts Show 2020 Presidential Race Could Be Close," *NBC News,* April 22, 2018, https://www.nbcnews.com/politics/first-read/demographic-shifts-show-2020-presidential-race-could-be-close-n868146.

25.   Barbara Norrander, "The Nature of Crossover Voters," in *Routledge Handbook of Primary Elections,* ed. Robert G. Boatright (New York: Routledge, 2018), chap. 6.

26.   Marjorie Randon Hershey, *Party Politics in America,* 17th ed. (New York: Routledge, 2017), 108.

27.   "Government, Regulation, and the Social Safety Net," Pew Research Center, October 5, 2017, http://www.people-press.org/2017/10/05/2-government-regulation-and-the-social-safety-net/; "When Americans Say They Believe in God, What Do They Mean?," Pew Research Center, April 25, 2018, https://pewrsr.ch/2vFmEqu.

28.   Greg Sargent, "A GOP's Remarkable Admission about Trump and Mueller," *The Washington Post,* March 21, 2018; Joseph Lowndes, "White Populism and the Transformation of the Silent Majority," *The Forum* 14, no. 1 (April 2016): 25–37, 10.1515/for-2016-0004. For the limits of Trumpism in the Republican Party, see Eric Levitz, "Trump Has Not Transformed the Republican Party—Yet," *New York,* June 14, 2018, http://nymag.com/daily/intelligencer/2018/06/trump-has-not-transformed-the-republican-party-yet.html.

29.   Henry Olsen, "What Happened to the Libertarian Movement, *National Review,* November 20, 2017, https://www.nationalreview.com/2017/11/libertarian-conservatives-influence-republican-party-shrinking/.

30.   Bradley Thompson, *Neo Conservatism: An Obituary for an Idea* (New York: Taylor & Francis, 2010).

31.   Lydia Saad, "Conservative Lead in U.S. Ideology Down to Single Digits," Gallup, January 11, 2018, https://news.gallup.com/poll/225074/conservative-lead-ideology-down-single-digits.aspx.

32.   See James Feigenbaum, Alexander Hertel-Fernandez, and Vanessa Williamson, "Demobilizing Democrats

and Labor Unions: Political Effects of Right to Work Laws," *Brookings Institute*, October 4, 2017, https://businessinnovation.berkeley.edu/wp-content/uploads/2017/10/rtw-laws-manuscript_oct2017.pdf; Nate Silver, "The Effects of Union Membership on Democratic Voting, *The New York Times*, February 26, 2011, https://fivethirtyeight.blogs.nytimes.com/2011/02/26/the-effects-of-union-membership-on-democratic-voting/.

33. David S. Broder, *The Party's Over: The Failure of Politics in America* (New York: Harper & Row, 1972); Martin P. Wattenberg, *The Decline of American Political Parties, 1952–1980* (Cambridge, MA: Harvard University Press, 1985).

34. Frances Lee, *Beyond Ideology: Politics, Principles, and Partisanship in the U.S. Senate* (Chicago: University of Chicago Press, 2009).

35. On rising party polarization and possible responses, see the essays in Nathaniel Persily, ed., *Solutions to Political Polarization in America* (New York: Cambridge University Press, 2015).

36. See Alan I. Abramowitz, *The Great Alignment: Race, Party Transformation, and the Rise of Donald Trump* (New Haven, CT: Yale University Press, 2018) for the view that the public is divided. Donald Kinder and Nathan Kalmoe, *Neither Liberal Nor Conservative: Ideological Innocence in the American Public* (Chicago: University of Chicago Press, 1918).

37. Nancy Roman, "Bitter Fruits of Partisanship," *Baltimore Sun*, October 19, 2005.

38. David R. Mayhew, *Divided We Govern: Party Control, Investigations, and Lawmaking, 1946–2002*, 2nd ed. (New Haven, CT: Yale University Press, 2005).

39. See Thomas E. Mann and Norman J. Ornstein, *It's Even Worse than It Was: How the American's Constitutional System Collided with the New Politics of Extremism*, 2nd ed. (New York: Basic Books, 2016); Alan I. Abramowitz, *The Disappearing Center: Engaged Citizens, Polarization and American Democracy* (New Haven, CT: Yale University Press, 2010).

40. On the benefits that proportional representation could bring to the United States, see generally Douglas J. Amy, *Real Choices/New Voices: How Proportional Representation Elections Could Revitalize American Democracy* (New York: Columbia University Press, 2002).

41. The term *core commitments* and an extended argument on behalf of stronger parties is in Russell Muirhead, *The Promise of Party in a Polarized Age* (Cambridge, MA: Harvard University Press, 2014).

Chapter 12 Interest Groups

1. Jeffrey M. Berry and Clyde Wilcox, *The Interest Group Society*, 6th ed. (New York: Routledge, 2018).

2. National Rifle Association website, https://home.nra.org/about-the-nra/.

3. Professor James Thurber, American University.

4. "Lobbying Database 1998–2018," Open Secrets: Center for Responsive Politics, https://www.opensecrets.org/lobby/

5. "Annual Lobbying on Health," Open Secrets: Center for Responsive Politics, https://www.opensecrets.org/lobby/indus.php?id=H&year=2017.

6. Office of Management & Budget, U.S. Federal Budget, 2019.

7. "Year to Date Summary," Open Secrets: Center for Responsive Politics, https://www.opensecrets.org/lobby/incdec.php.

8. Carolyn M. Proctor, "Here's What D.C. Region's Top Trade Group CEOs Get Paid," *Washington Business Journal*, October 18, 2017, https://www.bizjournals.com/washington/news/2017/10/18/heres-what-d-c-regions-top-trade-group-ceos-get.html.

9. For more on how AARP (and other membership groups) wield influence, see Peter Murray, "The Secret of Scale," *Stanford Social Innovation Review* (Fall 2013), http://ssir.org/articles/entry/the_secret_of_scale.

10. Liza Gross, "Smoke Screen," *The Verge*, November 16, 2017, https://www.theverge.com/2017/11/16/16658358/vape-lobby-vaping-health-risks-nicotine-big-tobacco-marketing; Fergus Mason, "The Big Vape Lobby Strikes Again," *Vaping Post*, June 8, 2018, https://www.vapingpost.com/2017/11/28/the-big-vape-lobby-strikes-again/; and "About Us," CASAA website, http://www.casaa.org/gallery-with-sidebar/, accessed June 20, 2018.

11. Charles M. Cameron, Cody Gray, Jonathan P. Kastellec, and Jee-Kwang Park, "From Genteel Pluralism to Hyper-Pluralism: Interest Groups and Supreme Court Nominations, 1930–2017," SSRN Working Paper, 2018, https://ssrn.com/abstract=3087987.

12. Alan Shipman, June Edmunds, and Bryan S. Turner, *The New Power Elite: Inequality, Politics, and Greed* (New York: Anthem Press, 2018).

13. Kay Lehman Schlozman, Sidney Verba, and Henry Brady, *The Unheavenly Chorus: Unequal Political Voice and the Broken Promise of American Democracy* (Princeton, NJ: Princeton University Press, 2012), chap. 1; Schattschneider, *The Semisovereign People* (1960), 35, (see chap. 10, note 30).

14. Professional Association of Therapeutic Horsemanship: professionals who provide equine therapy to children and adults.

15. See https://www.wearestillin.com; as of summer 2018, more than 2,800 groups and leaders had signed on to this effort.

16. Jeffrey H. Birnbaum, *The Lobbyists: How Influence Peddlers Work Their Way in Washington* (New York: Times Books, 1993), 8.

17. Raymond A. Bauer, Ithiel de Sola Pool, and Lewis Anthony Dexter, *American Business and Public Policy* (2d ed., New Brunswick, NJ: Transaction Press, 1968): 34.

18. Rogan Kersh, "Ten Myths About Health Lobbyists," in *Health Politics and Policy*, 5th ed., ed. James A. Morone and Daniel C. Ehlke (Stamford, CT: Cengage, 2014).

19. Cindy Skrzycki, "GOP's Young Lions Are Now in the Lobbying Catbird Seat," *Washington Post*, December 23, 1994; Brennan Hoban, "Millennials Are on the Frontlines of Political and Cultural Change in America," *Brookings* 2018, https://www.brookings.edu/blog/brookings-now/2018/02/02/millennials-are-on-the-frontlines-of-political-and-cultural-change-in-america/; "The Millennial Generation: A Demographic Bridge to America's Diverse Future—Part 2," Brookings Institute, YouTube panel, https://www.youtube.com/watch?v=5KD74kH8iJ8&t=577s.

20. Myron A. Mehlman, "Benzene, A Multi-Organ Carcinogen," *European Journal of Oncology* 13, no. 1 (2008), 7–19; Union of Concerned Scientists, "Fossil Fuel Companies Distorted the Science About the Dangers of Benzene," October 24, 2017, https://bit.ly/2lMZSp6.

21. Drew Lindsay and Peter Olsen-Phillips, "Tax Bill Targets Million-Dollar Club of Nonprofit Executives," *Chronicle of Philanthropy*, November 6, 2017, 1, https://www.philanthropy.com/article/Tax-Bill-Targets/241681.

22. Fraser Nelson, David W. Brady, and Alana Conner Snibbe, "Learn to Love

Lobbying," *Stanford Social Innovation Review* 5, no. 2 (Spring 2007): 57.

23. Catherine Boudreau, "How Congress Killed Efforts to Slash Subsidies For Wealthy Farmers," *Politico*, Aug. 20, 2018, https://politi.co/2MEPkHw.

24. Mark Peterson, "Congress in the 1990s: From Iron Triangles to Policy Networks," in *The Politics of Health Care Reform*, ed. James Morone and Gary Belkin (Durham, NC: Duke University Press, 1994), 108, 127.

25. Timothy M. LaPira and Herschel F. Thomas, *Revolving Door Lobbying* (Lawrence: University Press of Kansas, 2017).

26. Paul F. Boller, Jr., *Congressional Anecdotes* (New York: Oxford University Press, 1991), 122.

27. James Thurber estimate cited in Lee Fang, "Michael Cohen and the Felony Overtaking Washington," *New York Times*, June 18, 2018, https://nyti.ms/2JVNvBf.

28. On the shift to lobbying states, see Dante Chinni, "With Gridlock in Washington, Lobbyists Turn to State-houses," *Wall Street Journal*, January 16, 2016. The Internet Association's "50-State Government Affairs program" is described on the Association's website, https://bit.ly/2ymRWnz.

29. Eric R. Hansen, Caroline Carlson, and Virginia Gray, "Interest Group Density and Policy Change in the States" (working paper, Department of Political Science, University of North Carolina, Chapel Hill, 2018), https://unc.live/2I38bWf.

30. See Lee Fang, "Where Have All the Lobbyists Gone?" *The Nation*, March 17, 2014.

31. On e-commerce and regulation see Efraim Turban et al., "E-Commerce: Regulatory, Ethical, and Social Environments," in *Electronic Commerce 2018*, ed. Turban et al.(New York: Springer, 2018).

32. One book-length study of interest groups concludes that "the connection between money and influence is subtle." Thomas Holyoke, *Interest Groups and Lobbying: Pursuing Political Interests in America* (Boulder, CO: Westview Press, 2014), 251.

33. Isaac Arnsdorf, "Trump Lobbying Ban Weakens Obama Rules," *Politico*, January 28, 2017, https://politi.co/2tlQgVB.

34. Sharon LaFreniere, "Judge Orders Manafort Jailed Before Trial," *New York Times*, June 15, 2018, p. A1.

35. Bok quoted in Ronald J. Hrebenar and Clive S. Thomas, "American Interest Group Politics in the 21st Century" (paper, Western Political Science Association, Vancouver, Canada, March 20, 2009).

36. Ronnie Greene, "Bush Blasts 'Swarms of Lobbyists' But Once Registered as One," *Associated Press*, July 23, 2015, http://apne.ws/1VUcMhZ.

37. Poul A. Nielsen and Donald P. Moynihan, "How Do Politicians Attribute Bureaucratic Responsibility for Performance? Negativity Bias and Interest Group Advocacy," *Journal of Public Administration Research and Theory* 27, no. 2 (2017): 269–83.

38. See Lee Drutman, *The Business of America is Lobbying* (New York: Oxford University Press, 2015).

39. Theda Skocpol and Vanessa Williamson, *The Tea Party and the Remaking of Republican Conservatism* (New York: Oxford University Press, 2012), 100–101.

40. For a good recent study of citizen groups' influence, in this case on behalf of uninsured Americans, see Timothy Callaghan and Lawrence W. Jacobs, "Interest Group Conflict Over Medicaid Expansion," *American Journal of Public Health* 106, no. 2 (2016).

41. On voter turnout: Daniel E. Bergan, Alan S. Gerber, Donald P. Green, and Costas Panagopoulos, "Grassroots Mobilization and Voter Turnout in 2004," *Public Opinion Quarterly* 69, no. 5 (2005): 760–77. On social-media connections: Cass R. Sunstein, *#republic: Divided Democracy in the Age of Social Media* (Princeton, NJ: Princeton University Press, 2017): chap. 11.

42. Lee Drutman and Christine Mahoney, "On the Advantages of a Well-Constructed Lobbying System: Toward a More Democratic, Modern Lobbying Process," *Interest Groups & Advocacy* 6, no. 3 (2017): 290–310.

Chapter 13 Congress

1. Ed O'Keefe, "The House Has Voted 54 Times in Four Years on Obamacare," *Washington Post*, March 21, 2014, A18.

2. Quoted in Sheryl Gay Stolberg and Nicholas Fandos, "As Gridlock Deepens in Congress, Only Gloom Is Bipartisan," *New York Times*, January 27, 2018, A1; see also Thomas E. Mann and Norman J. Ornstein, *The Broken Branch: How Congress Is Failing America and How to Get It Back On Track* (New York: Oxford University Press, 2006).

3. Robert A. Caro, *Master of the Senate: The Years of Lyndon Johnson* (New York: Knopf, 2002), 52.

4. This and following figure at "Congress and the Public," Gallup, https://news.gallup.com/poll/1600/congress-public.aspx.

5. This and previous figure available at Congress.gov.

6. For a different view of Andrew Johnson, as an important President who, sadly, formulated the arguments for white supremacy, see Jeffrey Tulis and Nicole Mellow, *Legacies of Losing in American Politics* (Chicago: University of Chicago Press, 2018) Chapter 3. Robert A. Caro, *Master of the Senate: The Years of Lyndon Johnson* (New York: Knopf, 2002), 52.

7. For more along this line, see Mark Twain and Charles Dudley Warner, *The Gilded Age* (New York: Oxford University Press, 1996).

8. Frank Bruni, "An Obama Nominee's Crushed Hopes," *New York Times*, June 6, 2016, http://nyti.ms/2aC1OIG. On the rising use of filibusters and holds more generally, see Gregory Koger, "Partisanship, Filibustering, and Reform in the Senate," in *Party and Procedure in the United States Congress*, 2nd ed., ed. Jacob R. Straus and Matthew E. Glassman (Lanham, MD: Rowman & Littlefield, 2016), chap. 10.

9. Caro, *Master of the Senate*, 9.

10. Sean Theriault, *The Gingrich Senators: The Roots of Partisan Warfare in Congress* (New York: Oxford University Press, 2013).

11. Trump has called several times for the filibuster to end. See, e.g., Chad Pergram, "Trump Amplifying Calls to Ditch the Filibuster as Midterms Near," *Fox News*, July 3, 2018, https://fxn.ws/2NBN8gM.

12. Jane Mansbridge, "Rethinking Representation," *American Political Science Review* 97, no. 4 (2003): 515–28.

13. A thoughtful treatment is in Daniele Caramani, "Will vs. Reason: The Populist and Technocratic Forms of Political Representation," *American Political Science Review* 111, no.1 (2017): 54–67.

14. Lawrence R. Jacobs and Robert Y. Shapiro, *Politicians Don't Pander: Political Manipulation and the Loss of Democratic Responsiveness* (Chicago: University of Chicago Press, 2000).

15. David R. Mayhew, *Congress: The Electoral Connection*, 2d ed. (New Haven, CT: Yale University Press, 2004).

16. Ibid. See also Jamie L. Carson and Jeffery A. Jenkins, "Examining the Electoral Connection Across Time," *Annual Review of Political Science* 14, no. 1 (2011).

17. Nora Kelly, "Are Members of Congress Overpaid?" *The Atlantic*, June 2, 2016, http://theatln.tc/28NLSaE.

18. David E. Price, "Congressional–Executive Balance in an Era of Congressional Dysfunction," *PS: Political*

Science & Politics 49, no. 3 (2016): 485–86, http://dx.doi.org/10.1017/S1049096516000755.

19. Carl Bernstein, *A Woman in Charge: The Life of Hillary Rodham Clinton* (New York: Knopf, 2007), 546–47.

20. Linda Greenhouse, "David E. Price; Professor in Congress Is Doing Homework on Theory and Reality," *New York Times*, February 11, 1988.

21. Political scientists also find roll-call votes compelling, in part as a handy data source (hundreds of votes each session, each with a clear yes/no alternative). Despite years of roll-call analyses and associated theories, we are not very good at predicting vote outcomes. Whips and other nose-counters in Congress perform better than academic models.

22. Gail Russell Chaddock, "In Congress, All Roads Lead to a Conference Room," *Christian Science Monitor*, August 4, 2003, https://bit.ly/2LjGv66.

23. Sarah A. Binder, "Where Have All the Conference Committees Gone?," *Brookings Institution*, December 21, 2011, https://www.brookings.edu/opinions/where-have-all-the-conference-committees-gone/.

24. Public Policy Polling, "Congress Losing Out to Zombies, Wall Street, and . . . Hipsters," October 8, 2013, accessed August 1, 2014, http://www.publicpolicypolling.com/main/2013/10/congress-losing-out-to-zombies-wall-street-andhipsters.html.

25. Juliet Eilperin, *Fight Club Politics: How Partisanship Is Poisoning the House of Representatives* (Lanham, MD: Rowman & Littlefield, 2007), 13.

26. Barbara Sinclair, *Unorthodox Lawmaking: New Legislative Processes in the U.S. Congress*, 3rd ed. (Washington, DC: CQ Press, 2007), 71.

27. Eilperin, *Fight Club (2007)*; Mann, *Broken Branch (2006)*; Ken Buck with Bill Blankschaen, *Drain the Swamp: How Washington Corruption Is Worse than You Think* (Washington, DC: Regnery Publishing, 2017).

28. Danielle M. Thomsen, *Opting Out of Congress: Partisan Polarization and the Decline of Moderate Candidates* (New York: Cambridge University Press, 2017); Jacob S. Hacker and Paul Pierson, *Off Center: The Republican Revolution and the Erosion of American Democracy* (New Haven, CT: Yale University Press, 2006).

29. See, e.g., Patricia A. Kirkland and Justin H. Phillips, "Is Divided Government a Cause of Legislative Delay?" *Quarterly Journal of Political Science* 13, no. 2 (2018), 173–206.

30. David R. Mayhew, *Divided We Govern: Party Control, Lawmaking, and Investigations, 1946–2002*, 2nd ed. (New Haven, CT: Yale University Press, 2005); Keith Krehbiel, *Pivotal Politics: A Theory of U.S. Lawmaking* (Chicago: University of Chicago Press, 1998).

31. David Parker and Matthew Dull, "Divided We Quarrel: The Politics of Congressional Investigations, 1947–2004," *Legislative Studies Quarterly* 34 (2009): 319–45; John J. Coleman, "Unified Government, Divided Government, and Party Responsiveness," *The American Political Science Review* 93, no. 4 (December, 1999): 821–35.

32. Mann, *It's Even Worse Than It Looks*, 110. See also Sarah Binder, *Stalemate: Causes and Consequences of Legislative Gridlock* (Washington, DC: Brookings Institution Press, 2003).

33. John R. Hibbing and Elizabeth Theiss-Morse, *Stealth Democracy: Americans' Beliefs About How Government Should Work* (New York: Cambridge University Press, 2002).

Chapter 14 The Presidency

1. Joseph Ellis, *His Excellency: George Washington* (New York: Random House, 2004), 194–95.

2. See Corey Brettschneider, *The Oath and the Office: A Guide to the Constitution for Future Presidents* (New York: Norton, 2018).

3. The Editorial Board, "Bigoted and Feckless, the Travel Ban Is Pure Trump," opinion, *New York Times*, June 27, 2018, A12, https://www.nytimes.com/2018/06/26/opinion/trump-travel-ban-supreme-court.html.

4. See e.g., Julia Glum, "Some Republicans Still Think Obama Was Born in Kenya," *Newsweek*, July 30, 2018; [reporting that 51% believed the so-called birther theory] "Trump Supporters Think Obama Is a Muslim Born in Another Country," *Public Policy Polling*, September, 2015, https://www.publicpolicypolling.com/wp-content/uploads/2017/09/PPP_Release_National_90115.pdf. For discussion, see Michael Tesler, *Post Racial or Most Racial: Race and Politics in the Obama Era* (Chicago: University of Chicago Press, 2016), pp. 65–68.

5. George Edwards, *Why the Electoral College Is Bad for America* (New Haven, CT: Yale University Press, 2011).

6. For a classic treatment of presidential power, see Richard Neustadt, *Presidential Power and the Modern Presidents: The Politics of Leadership from Roosevelt to Reagan* (New York: Free Press, 1990).

7. Paul Harris, Kamal Ahmed, and Martin Bright, "Seeing Eye to Eye," *Observer*, November 16, 2003, 1; David Nakamura and Carol D. Leonnig, "Five Myths About Presidential Travel," *Washington Post*, January 23, 2015, http://wapo.st/1SxP5qa; Alexander Ma, "750 Hotel Rooms, a Personal Chef, and the Nuclear Football: Here's Everything Trump Is Bringing on His 4-Day UK Trip," *Business Insider*, July 12, 2018, http://www.businessinsider.com/trump-uk-trip-what-us-president-is-reportedly-bringing-on-4-day-trip-2018-7.

8. Stephen Skowronek, "The Conservative Insurgency and Presidential Power: A Developmental Perspective on the Unitary Executive" *Harvard Law Review* 122 (June 2009): 2070–103; Steven Calabresi and Kevin Rhodes, "The Structural Constitution: Unitary Executive, Plural Judiciary," *Harvard Law Review* 105 (April 1992): 1153–1216.

9. Frances Fukuyama, *Political Order and Political Decay* (New York: Farrar, Straus, & Giroux, 2015); Arthur Schlesinger, *The Imperial Presidency* (New York: Houghton Mifflin, 1973); Andrew Rudalevige, *The New Imperial Presidency: Renewing Presidential Power after Watergate* (Ann Arbor: University of Michigan, 2005).

10. Kirk Scharfenberg, "Now It Can Be Told: The Story Behind Campaign '82's Favorite Insult," *Boston Globe*, November 6, 1982.

11. Tocqueville, *Democracy in America*, p. 126 (see chap. 2, note 11).

12. Eric Talbot Jensen, "Future War and the War Powers Resolution," *Emory International Law Review* 499 (2014–2015), https://heinonline.org/HOL/LandingPage?handle=hein.journals/emint29&div=20&id=&page=.

13. Francis Biddle, *In Brief Authority* (New York: Doubleday, 1962), 219.

14. For a description of this episode, taken from White House telephone tapes, see David Blumenthal and James Morone, *The Heart of Power: Health and Politics in the Oval Office* (Berkeley: University of California Press, 2009), 142.

15. Dan Bilefsky and Catherine Porter, "Trump's 'Bully' Attack' on

Trudeau Outrages Canadians, *New York Times*, June 10, 2018, A5; Tom Newton Dunn, "Trump's Brexit Blast," *The Sun*, July 13, 2018; Christina Maza, "Donald Trump Threw Starburst at Angela Merkel, Said 'Don't Say I Never Give You Anything,'" *Newsweek*, June 20, 2018, https://www .newsweek.com/donald-trump-threw-starburst-candies-angela-merkel-dont-say-i-never-give-you-987178.

16. "Donald Trump tells Nato allies to spend 4% of GDP on defense – US president suggests doubling 2% spending target," *The Guardian*. June 11, 2018. https://www.theguardian .com/world/2018/jul/11/donald-trump-tells-nato-allies-to-spend-4-of-gdp-on-defence

17. Michael Birnbaum, "As Trump Hammers NATO Allies on Defense Spending, Military Planners Worry About His '2 Percent' Obsession," *Washington Post*, July 10, 2018; Julie Hirschfeld Davis, "Trump Presses NATO on Military Spending, but Signs Its Criticism of Russia," *New York Times*, July 11, 2018.

18. Louis Jacobson, "Has President Trump Signed More Bills than Anyone? No. (His count ranks last)," *Politifact*, December 29, 2017.

19. Leonard White, *The Federalists* (New York: Macmillan, 1942).

20. Kenneth Mayer, *With the Stroke of a Pen: Executive Orders and Presidential Power* (Princeton, NJ: Princeton University Press, 2001)

21. William Howell, Saul Jackman, and Jon Rogowski, *The Wartime President: Executive Influence and the Nationalizing Politics of Threat* (Chicago: University of Chicago Press, 2013).

22. For a description of Roosevelt's approach, see James Morone, *The Democratic Wish* (New Haven, CT: Yale University Press, 1998), 131.

23. Memo from Pat Caddell to "Governor Carter," December 21, 1976, Carter Library; see also Blumenthal, *Heart of Power*, 249.

24. Richard Neustadt, *Presidential Power and the Modern Presidents*, rev. ed. (New York: Free Press, 1991), chap. 3.

25. Martha Joynt Kumar, *Managing the President's Message: The White House Communications Operation* (Baltimore: Johns Hopkins University Press, 2010).

26. Samuel Kernell, *Going Public* (Washington, DC: CQ Press, 2007).

27. Lawrence R. Jacobs and Robert Y. Shapiro, *Politicians Don't Pander: Political Manipulation and the Loss of Democratic Responsiveness* (Chicago: University of Chicago Press, 2000).

28. George Edwards, *On Deaf Ears: The Limits of the Bully Pulpit* (New Haven, CT: Yale University Press, 2003).

29. Barbara Hinckley, *Follow the Leader: Opinion Polls and the Modern President* (New York: Basic Books, 1992).

30. Harry Truman, *Where the Buck Stops*, ed. Margaret Truman (New York: Warner Books, 1989) 371–2; Marc Landy and Sidney Milkis, *Presidential Greatness* (Lawrence: University Press of Kansas, 2001).

31. Stephen Skowronek, *The Politics Presidents Make: Leadership from John Adams to Bill Clinton* (Cambridge, MA: Harvard University Press, 1997).

32. Peggy Noonan, *When Character Was King* (New York: Penguin Books, 2001), 242–43, 245–49.

33. Blumenthal, *Heart of Power*, 293.

34. On personality theories, see Michael Nelson, "The Psychological Presidency," in *The Presidency and the Political System*, 10th ed. (Washington, DC: CQ Press, 2013), 167–90.

35. Mortality data from Robert E. Gilbert, *The Mortal Presidency: Illness and Anguish in the White House* (New York: Fordham University Press, 1998), 4–5.

36. Rose McDermott, *Presidential Leadership, Illness, and Decision Making* (New York: Cambridge University Press, 2008).

37. Quoted in Jody C. Baumgartner, "The Second Best Choice? Vice-Presidential Candidates in the Modern Era," in *White House Studies Compendium*, ed. Anthony J. Eksterowicz and Glenn P. Hastedt (New York: Nova Science Publishers, 2008), 158.

38. Quoted in Elliot A. Rosen, "'Not Worth a Pitcher of Warm Piss': John Nance Garner as Vice President," in *At the President's Side: The Vice Presidency in the Twentieth Century*, ed. Timothy Walch (Columbia: University of Missouri Press, 2007), 45.

39. Stephen E. Ambrose, *Eisenhower: Soldier and President* (New York: Simon & Schuster, 1990), 564.

40. Joel Goldstein, *The White House Vice Presidency: The Path to Significance, Mondale to Biden* (Lawrence: University Press of Kansas, 2016).

41. Richard J. Ellis, *The Development of the American Presidency* (New York: Routledge, 2012), 284.

42. Joseph Califano, *Governing America: An Insider's Report from the White House and the Cabinet* (New York: Simon & Schuster, 1981), 431; personal interview with the authors, June 15, 2006.

43. For a fine description, see Matthew Dickinson, "The Executive Office of the President: The Paradox of Politicization," in *The Executive Branch*, ed. Joel Aberbach and Mark Peterson (New York: Oxford University Press, 2005), 135–73.

44. Johnson, quoted in Blumenthal, *Heart of Power*, 8.

45. For a marvelous case study of "massaging the numbers," see Robert Saldin, *How Bad Policy Makes Good Politics* (New York: Oxford University Press, 2017).

46. See the excellent treatment in Lauren A. Wright, *On Behalf of the President: Presidential Spouses and White House Communications Strategy Today* (Santa Barbara, CA: Praeger, 2016).

47. Julie Azari and Jennifer Smith, "Unwritten Rules: Informal Institutions in Established Democracies," *Perspectives on Politics* 10, no. 1 (March 2012): 37–55; Brendan Nyhan, "Norms Matter," *Politico*, September/October 2017, https:// www.politico.com/magazine/ story/2017/09/05/why-norms-matter-politics-trump-215535.

48. Tocqueville, *Democracy in America* (1966) p. 122 (see chap. 2, note 11).

Chapter 15 Bureaucracy

1. Missouri Department of Health and Senior Services, *Health in Rural Missouri: Biennial Report, 2016–2017*, October 2017, https:// bit.ly/2KI9NGf.

2. "Rural America Comes to HRSA," Health Resources Services Administration, accessed March 2018, https:// bit.ly/2noP6py.

3. HealthData: USA, comparison of past/present county data for seven primary Bootheel counties, https:// datausa.io/profile/geo/mississippi-county-mo/.

4. "Public Troubled by 'Deep State,'" Monmouth University Polling Institute, March 19, 2018, https://bit.ly/2pvHOlF.

5. Cruz quoted in Stuart Shapiro, "Government Bureaucrats Are People Too," *The Hill*, November 12, 2015, https://bit.ly/1Sm9Khg; President Barack Obama, First Inaugural Address (see chap. 11, note 18).

6. Megan Brenan and Steve Ander, "Republicans Push Government Agency Ratings Up, But Not FBI," *Gallup*, January 2, 2018, https://bit.ly/2uq2fCN.

7. "Branches of the U.S. Government," USA.gov, https://www.usa.gov/independent-agencies.

8. Paul C. Light, *The True Size of Government* (Washington, DC: Volker Alliance, 2017).

9. William Riordan, *Plunkitt of Tammany Hall: A Series of Very Plain Talks on Very Practical Politics* (New York: Penguin, 1995).

10. What inspired the term *bureaucracy*? The word comes from France where, beginning in the 19th century, executive offices were termed *bureaus*. French officials governed ("-cracy") through these rule-based organizations rather than the whims of a king or ruling family. Though Americans are more apt to use words like *agency* (Central Intelligence Agency) or *department* (Treasury Department), we have a few bureaus as well—the best-known our FBI, the Federal **Bureau** of Investigation.

11. James Sparrow, *Warfare State: World War II Americans and the Age of Big Government* (New York: Oxford University Press, 2012).

12. **S**ee Daniel Carpenter, *The Forging of Bureaucratic Autonomy: Reputations, Networks, and Policy Innovation in Executive Agencies* (Princeton, NJ: Princeton University Press, 2001); Morone, *Hellfire Nation* (see chap. 2, note 22).

13. Erika Lee, "The Chinese Exclusion Example: Race, Immigration, and American Gatekeeping, 1882-1924," *Journal of American Ethnic History* 21, no. 3 (2002): 36–62.

14. Max Weber, "Bureaucracy," in *From Max Weber: Essays in Sociology*, ed. H. H. Gerth and C. Wright Mills (New York: Oxford University Press, 1946), 196–98.

15. Jonathan Adler, "Hostile Environment: Trump's EPA is Having a Hard Time in Federal Court," *National Review*, October 15, 2018, 18-20.

16. *Federal Register*, July 18, 2018, https://bit.ly/2Lx9LSO.

17. Lisa Friedman and Brad Plumer, "EPA Announces Repeal of Major Obama-Era Carbon Rule," *New York Times*, October 10, 2017, A1.

18. Joseph Schoen, "After 500 days, hundreds of white house jobs remain unfilled by the Trump Administration." *CNBC.* June 4, 2018. https://www.cnbc.com/2018/06/04/after-500-days-dozens-of-white-house-jobs-remain-unfilled.html

19. Kelly left DHS after six months to become White House Chief of Staff.

20. See, for example, Laurence J. O'Toole, Jr. and Kenneth J. Meier, "Plus ça Change: Public Management, Personnel Stability, and Organizational Performance." *Journal of Public Administration Research and Theory* 13, no.1 (2003): 43–64; Alexander Bolton, John M. De Figueiredo, and David Lewis, "Elections, Ideology, and Turnover in the U.S. Federal Government," *Academy of Management Proceedings* 2018 no. 1 (2018).

21. Chris Arnold, "Trump Administration's Latest Strike on CFPB: Budget Cuts," *NPR*, February 18, 2018, https://www.npr.org/2018/02/18/586493309/trump-administrations-latest-strike-on-cfpb-budget-cuts.

22. Bert A. Rockman, "The Melting Down of Government: A Multidecade Perspective," Governance 30, no. 1 (2017): 29–35; Allison Stanger, *One Nation Under Contract: The Outsourcing of American Power and the Future of Foreign Policy* (New Haven, CT: Yale University Press, 2011).

23. Light, "The True Size of Government" (2017).

24. Truman quoted in Richard Neustadt, *Presidential Power* (New York: Free Press, 1990), 10.

25. Richard Nixon, *RN: Memoirs of Richard Nixon* (New York: Simon & Schuster, 1990), 352.

26. Glenn Thrush and Erica L. Green, "Trump to Propose Government Reorganization, Targeting Safety Net Programs," *New York Times*, June 21, 2018, A17.

27. Anthony Adragna, Alex Guillén, and Emily Holden, "Pruitt Resigns Amid Torrent of Ethics Woes," *Politico*, July 5, 2018, https://bit.ly/2uDAeHV.

28. Michael Lipsky, *Street-Level Bureaucracy: Dilemmas of the Individual in Public Services* (New York: Russell Sage Foundation, 1980).

29. Joe Soss, *Unwanted Claims: The Politics of Participation in the U.S. Welfare System* (Ann Arbor: University of Michigan Press, 2000).

30. Emily Willingham, "Is the Freedom of Information Act Stifling Intellectual Freedom?" *Forbes*, November 21, 2015, https://bit.ly/2mzCbAE.

31. Al Gore, *Common Sense Government: Works Better and Costs Less* (New York: Random House, 1995); White House, "President Donald J. Trump Is Reforming the Federal Government, Making it More Efficient, Effective, and Accountable," news release, June 21, 2018, https://bit.ly/2yvBAZL.

32. A good summary of privatization—including discussion of a $1 trillion public–private Trump Administration infrastructure plan—is in Reed Karaim, "Privatizing Government Services," *CQ Researcher* 27, no. 43 (December 2017), https://bit.ly/2A4Wa3M.

33. John Goodman and Gary Loveman, "Does Privatization Serve the Public Interest? *Harvard Business Review*. November-December, 1991. https://hbr.org/1991/11/does-privatization-serve-the-public-interest

34. "Data, Analysis, & Documentation: Full-Time Permanent Age Distributions," opm.gov, September 2017, https://bit.ly/2OWow3S.

Chapter 16 The Judicial Branch

1. The cases are *Trump v. Hawaii*; *National Institute of Family and Life Advocates v. Becerra*; and *Janus v. American Federation of State, County and Municipal Employees*.

2. Alexander Hamilton, *Federalist* no. 78.

3. The cases are, respectively: *Citizens United* followed by *McCutcheon v. Federal Election Commission* (on money in elections); *Shelby County v. Holder* (striking down key sections of the voting rights act); *Sessions v. Dimaya* (deporting felon), *Husted v. A. Philip Randolph Institute* (Ohio purge).

4. Congressional Research Service, *The Constitution: Analysis and Interpretation,* prepared for the U.S. Senate, Document No.1129, August 26, 2017, https://www.govinfo.gov/content/pkg/GPO-CONAN-2017/pdf/GPO-CONAN-2017-11.pdf data for 1789–2017; SCOTUSblog http://www.scotusblog.com/case-files/terms/ot2017/ for data on 2017–2018 term.

5. Tocqueville, *Democracy in America*, 1:270 (see chap. 2, note 11).

6. *Bush v. Gore*, 531 U.S. 98 (2000).

7. Jeffrey M. Jones, "Republicans' Approval of the Supreme Court Sinks to 18%," *Gallup Politics*, July 16, 2015, http://www.gallup.com/poll/184160/republicans-approval-supreme-court-sinks.aspx?g_source=Supreme%20Court&g_medium=search&g_campaign=tiles.

8. Justin McCarthy, "GOP Approval of Supreme Court Surges, Democrats' Slides," Gallup, September 28, 2017, https://news.gallup.com/poll/219974/gop-approval-supreme-court-surges-democrats-slides.aspx.

9. John Schwartz, "Effort Begun to End Voting for Judges," *New York Times*, December 23, 2009.

10. The 70% figure from "Negative Views of Supreme Court at Record High," Pew Research Center, July 29, 2015, http://www.people-press .org/2015/07/29/negative-views-of-supreme-court-at-record-high-driven-by-republican-dissatisfaction/.

11. "Current Judicial Vacancies: Judges and Judgeships," The United States Courts, last updated September 10, 2018, http://www.uscourts.gov/judges-judgeships/judicial-vacancies/current-judicial-vacancies.

12. In *Boumediene v. Bush* [553 US 723 (2008)] the Supreme Court ruled that prisoners head in Guantánamo have habeas corpus rights and cannot be held without charges; in *Hamdan v. United States* [696 F.3d 1238 (D.C. Cir. 2012)] the court ruled that military commission trials do not conform to U.S. law.

13. Barry J. McMillion, "U.S. Circuit and District Court Judges: Profile of Select Characteristics," *Congressional Research Service*, August 1, 2017, https://www.fas.org/sgp/crs/misc/R43426.pdf; Rorie Soberg and Eric N. Waltenburg, "Trump's Presidency Marks the First Time in 24 Years that the Federal Bench Is Less Diverse," June 11, 2018, *The Conversation*, https://theconversation.com/trumps-presidency-marks-the-first-time-in-24-years-that-the-federal-bench-is-becoming-less-diverse-97663.

14. Charlie Savage, "A Judge's View of Judging Is on the Record," *New York Times*, May 14, 2009.

15. Jonathan Kastellec, Racial Diversity and Judicial Influence on Appellate Courts, *American Journal of Political Science* **57**, no. 1(2013): 167–83.

16. Adam Cox and Thomas Miles, Thomas, "Judging the Voting Rights Act." Columbia Law Review, 108 (2008), University of Chicago Law & Economics, Olin Working Paper No. 337; University of Chicago, Public Law Working Paper No. 159, Second Annual Conference on Empirical Legal Studies Paper, Available at SSRN: https://ssrn .com/abstract=977271.

17. Nancy Scherer, "Blacks on the Bench," *Political Science Quarterly* 119, no. 4 (2004/2005): 655–75.

18. S. Welsh, M. Combs, and J. Gruhl, "Do Black Judges Make a Difference?," *American Journal of Political Science* 32, 1 (1988): 125–36; Christine Boyd, Lee Epstein, and Andrew Martin, "Untangling the Causal Effects of Sex on Judging," *American Journal of Political Science* 54, no. 2 (April 2010): 389–411).

19. Thomas Jefferson, "Letter to Justice Spencer Roane on the Limits of Judicial Review," in *Writings* (New York: Library of America, 1984), 1425–28.

20. See, e.g., Robert G. McCloskey and Sanford Levinson, *The American Supreme Court*, 6th ed. (Chicago: University of Chicago Press, 2016), esp. 302–12.

21. *Dred Scott v. Sandford*, 60 U.S. 393 (1857).

22. The case was *Worcester v. Georgia*, 31 U.S. (6 Pet.) 515 (1832).

23. Paul M. Collins Jr., Pamela C. Corley, and Jesse Hamner, "The Influence of Amicus Curiae Briefs on U.S. Supreme Court Opinion Content," *Law and Society Review* 49, no. 4 (December 2015), 917–44, 10.1111/lasr.12166.

24. Adam Liptak, "Are Oral Arguments Worth Arguing About?" *New York Times: Sunday Review*, May 6, 2012.

25. Lee Epstein and Eric Posner, "The Decline of Supreme Court Deference to the President," *University of Pennsylvania Law Review* 166, no. 4 (March 2018): 829–60.

26. Randee Fenner, "Clerking at the Supreme Court," *Stanford Lawyer* 77 (Fall 2007): 7–9.

27. Senate Hrg. 109–158, Hearing Before the Committee on the Judiciary, United States Senate One Hundred Ninth Congress (September 12, 2005), http://bit.ly/2aLRGSW.

28. See, e.g., Kevin Buckler and Elizabeth L. Gilmore, "Originalism, Pragmatic Conservatism, and Living Document Judicial Philosophies: Explaining Variation in U.S. Supreme Court Votes in Criminal Procedure Cases for the 1994–2004 Terms of Court," *American Journal of Criminal Justice* 42, published electronically July 28, 2016, http://bit.ly/2aUoirR; see also Jeffrey Segal, Lee Epstein, Charles Cameron, and Harold Spaeth, "Ideological Values and the Votes of U.S. Supreme Court Justices Revisited," *The Journal of Politics* 57, no. 3 (August, 1995): 812–23.

29. "Negative Views of Supreme Court at Record High." Pew Research Center. July 29, 2015. http://www.people-press.org/2015/07/29/negative-views-of-supreme-court-at-record-high-driven-by-republican-dissatisfaction/. In 2012, A Kaiser Family Foundation poll found that 75% of the public "sometimes lets their own ideological vies influence decisions; only 17% thought decisions were based on legal analysis. https://www.kff.org/health-reform/poll-finding/kaiser-health-tracking-poll-january-2012/

30. Adam Liptak, "In a Polarized Court, Getting the Last Word," *New York Times*, March 8, 2010; for data on justices' voting patterns and other details, see Lee Epstein, Jeffrey A. Segal, Harold J. Spaeth, and Thomas G. Walker, *Supreme Court Compendium*, 6th ed. (Washington, DC: CQ Press, 2015).

31. Jeffrey R. Lax and Kelly Rader, "Bargaining Power in the Supreme Court: Evidence from Opinion Assignment and Vote Switching," *Journal of Politics* 77, no. 3 (2015): 648–63.

32. Saul Brenner, "Fluidity on the Supreme Court, 1956–1967," *American Journal of Political Science* 90, no. 56 (1996): 90–107.

33. Frederick Schauer, "Incentives, Reputation, and the Inglorious Determinants of Judicial Behavior," *University of Cincinnati Law Review* 68, no. 3 (2000): 615–36.

34. Thomas Keck, "Party, Policy, or Duty: Why Does the Supreme Court Invalidate Federal Statutes?" *American Political Science Review* 101, no. 2 (May 2007): 321ff.

35. *McCulloch v. Maryland*, 17 U.S. (4 Wheat.) 316 (1819).

36. *Dred Scott v. Sandford*, 60 U.S. 393 (1857).

37. Justice Black in *Connecticut General Life Insurance Co. v. Johnson*, 303 U.S. 77 (1938); William O. Douglas, "Stare Decisis," *Columbia Law Review* 49, no. 6 (1949): 735–58.

38. What constitutes a serious crime? In *Duncan v. Louisiana* (1968) the court ruled that they were defined by the potential penalty—more than $500 in fines or six months in prison.

39. A good political science survey of the Supreme Court's declining public approval is in James L. Gibson and Michael J. Nelson, "Changes in Institutional Support for the U.S. Supreme Court," *Public Opinion Quarterly* 80, no. 3 (2016).

40. Learned Hand, "The Deficiencies of Trials to Reach the Heart of the Matter," *Lectures on Legal Topics* 3 (1926): 89, 105.

41. Steven G. Calabresi and James Lindgren, "Term Limits for the Supreme Court: Life Tenure Reconsidered," *Harvard Journal of Law & Public Policy* 29, no. 3 (2009): 769–877.

42. Abraham Lincoln, First Inaugural Address, March 4, 1861; Roy Basler, ed., *The Collected Works of Abraham Lincoln*, Vol. IV (New Brunswick, NJ:

Rutgers Univ. Press, 1953): 262–71, quoted at 268.; Alexander Hamilton, *Federalist* No. 78; this argument is developed in Ryan Emenaker, "Repairing the Judicial Void: Modifying the Rights-Rescinding Court," PhD dissertation, Political Science Department, Brown University, Providence, RI.

Chapter 17 Public Policymaking and Budgeting

1. Jude Clemente, "U.S. Energy Security Begins at Home," Forbes, April 16, 2018, https://www.forbes.com/sites/judeclemente/2018/04/15/u-s-energy-security-begins-at-home/.
2. Lisa Friedman, "Trump Moves to Open Nearly All Offshore Wates to Drilling," *New York Times*, January 4, 2018, https://nyti.ms/2lU0SXW.
3. Aaron Hegarty, "Timeline: Immigrant children separated from families at the border," *USA Today*, June 27, 2018, www.usatoday.com/story/news/2018/06/27/immigrant-children-family-separation-border-timeline/734014002/; Ben Gittleson, "Amid pressure from Trump, Mexico says it's dealing with migrant 'caravan'," *ABC News*, April 3, 2018, abcnews.go.com/International/amid-pressure-trump-mexico-dealing-migrant-caravan/story?id=54197928.
4. Office of Management and Budget, "2017 Draft Report to Congress on the Benefits and Costs of Federal Regulations and Agency Compliance with the Unfunded Mandates Reform Act," *Federal Register*, March 5, 2018, https://www.federalregister.gov/documents/2018/03/05/2018-04383/draft-2017-report-to-congress-on-the-benefits-and-costs-of-federal-regulation-and-agency-compliance.
5. All federal budget estimates in this chapter are from Congressional Budget Office, "The Budget and Economic Outlook, 2018 to 2028," April 2018, https://bit.ly/2GKR1kH.
6. "Data Report," National Association of Schools of Public Affairs & Administration, http://www.naspaa.org/DataCenter/index.asp.
7. Aaron Belkin, "Here Today, Gone Tomorrow: Why the US Military's Transgender Ban Unraveled So Quickly," *Palm Center Blueprints for Sound Public Policy*, June 2016, https://bit.ly/2LW4I2G.
8. Libby Nelson, "Donald Trump's Plan to (Sort of) Eliminate the Education Department, Briefly Explained,"

Vox, June 21, 2018, https://bit.ly/2yu1jSi.
9. Ari Natter and Mark Niquette, "Trump's Gas Tax Goes Nowhere in Congress," *Bloomberg News*, February 25, 2018, https://bloom.bg/2ol63l4.
10. Deborah Stone, *Policy Paradox: The Art of Political Decision Making*, 3rd ed. (New York: Norton, 2011).
11. Woodrow Wilson, "The Study of Administration," *Political Science Quarterly* 2, no. 2 (1887): 197–222.
12. Rogan Kersh, "Health Reform: The Politics of Implementation," *Journal of Health Politics, Policy, and Law* 36, no. 3 (2011): 613–23.
13. Lawrence Hurley and John McArdle, "Supreme Court Puts Spotlight on Speed of Rulemaking," *Environment & Energy News*, December 4, 2012, http://www.eenews.net/stories/1059973307.
14. Emily Holden, "Pruitt: EPA Will Review 'Politicized' Climate Science Report," *Politico*, August 11, 2017, https://politi.co/2vhIjT5.
15. Linda Qiu, "Claims on Rules That Could Use a Little Regulation," *New York Times*, February 24, 2018, A17.
16. Rebecca L. Haffajee, Robert J. MacCoun, and Michelle M. Mello, "Behind Schedule—Reconciling State and Federal Marijuana Policy," *New England Journal of Medicine* 379 (2018): 501–504, DOI: 10.1056/NEJMp1804408.
17. Emil Robert Mackey, *Street-Level Bureaucrats and the Shaping of University Housing Policy* (Fayetteville: University of Arkansas Press, 2008).
18. On this sequence, see Mark Bovens, Paul't Hart, and Sanneke Kuipers, "The Politics of Policy Evaluation," in *Oxford Handbook of Public Policy*, ed. Michael Moran, Martin Rein, and Robert E. Goodin (New York: Oxford University Press, 2008), 320.
19. Anthony A. Braga, David M. Kennedy, Elin J. Waring, and Anne Morrison Piehl, "Problem-Oriented Policing, Deterrence, and Youth Violence: An Evaluation of Boston's Operation Ceasefire," *Journal of Research in Crime and Delinquency* 38, no. 3 (2001): 195–225.
20. Magdalena Cerda, Melissa Tracy, and Katherine M. Keyes, "Reducing Urban Violence," *Epidemiology* 29, no. 1 (2018): 142–50.
21. Paul Pierson, "When Effect Becomes Cause: Policy Feedback and Political Change," *World Politics* 45, no. 4 (1993): 595–628; for a recent overview of policy feedback and path dependence, see Joe Soss and Donald P. Moynihan, "Policy Feedback and

the Politics of Administration," *Public Administration Review* 74, no. 3 (May/June 2014): 320–32.
22. Walter I. Trattner, *From Poor Law to Welfare State: A History of Social Welfare in America*, 6th ed. (New York: Free Press, 1998).
23. Theda Skocpol, *Protecting Soldiers and Mothers* (Cambridge: Harvard University Press, 1995).
24. Suzanne Mettler, *Soldiers to Citizens: The G.I. Bill and the Making of the Greatest Generation* (New York: Oxford University Press, 2005).
25. American Medical Association, "Goldwater–Johnson: Remarks," *Washington News* 189, no. 3 (July 20, 1964): 3.
26. Pamela Herd, Melissa Favreault, Madonna Harrington Meyer, and Timothy M. Smeeding, "A Targeted Minimum Benefit Plan: A New Proposal to Reduce Poverty among Older Social Security Recipients," *RSF: The Russell Sage Foundation Journal of the Social Sciences* 4, no. 2 (February 2018): 74–90.
27. A good contrast of Republican and Democratic views of fiscal policy, especially of tax cuts, is in Alexander Hertel-Fernandez and Theda Skocpol, "Congress Makes Tax Policy," in *Congress and Policy Making in the 21st Century*, ed. Jeffrey A. Jenkins and Eric M. Patashnik (New York: Cambridge University Press, 2016), 137–61.
28. Ken Thomas and Darlene Superville, "Trump in Ohio Praises Tax Cuts for Growing Economy," *PBS News Hour*, February 5, 2018, https://to.pbs.org/2shj9oL.
29. Burgess Everett and Sarah Ferris, "Coming Soon: The Fiscal Cliff to End All Fiscal Cliffs," *Politico*, May 8, 2017, https://politi.co/2ncc17s.
30. For a good insider's recap of the crisis and monetary policy responses, see Timothy F. Geithner, *Stress Test: Reflections on Financial Crises* (New York: Random House, 2014), 258–387.
31. Casey Burgat and Charles Hunt, "Are Long Weekends Reducing Congress' Productivity?" *R Street Shorts* 42, July 27, 2017, https://www.rstreet.org/2017/07/27/are-long-weekends-reducing-congress-productivity-2/.
32. Paul Light, *A Government Ill Executed: The Decline of the Federal Service and How to Reverse It* (Cambridge, MA: Harvard University Press, 2008).
33. On policy entrepreneurship, see Lynn Ross, *Policy Entrepreneurship: A Guide to Shaping and*

Understanding Policy (WCashington, DC: Brookings Institution Press, 2016).

34. Kathy Scott, Can Climate Kids take on governments and win? CNN. July 24, 2018. https://www.cnn .com/2018/07/24/health/youth-climate-march/index.html

35. James Conca, "Children Change the Climate in the U.S. Supreme Court," *Forbes*, August 3, 2018, https://bit.ly/2vLfI7U; Oommen quoted in Laura Parker, "'Biggest Case on the Planet' Pits Kids vs. Climate Change," *National Geographic*, March 27, 2017, https://bit.ly/2zKdL0b.

36. President Franklin Delano Roosevelt, First Inaugural Address, March 4, 1933, http://avalon.law.yale. edu/20th_century/froos1.asp.

37. Robert Caro, *Master of the Senate* (New York: Knopf, 2002), 151–53.

Chapter 18 Foreign Policy

1. Yuwa Hedrick-Wong, "China's Japanese Lesson for Fighting Trump's Trade War," *Forbes*, August 5, 2018; Bob Bryan, "There's No End in Sight for Trump's Trade War with China, Because 'Both Sides Are More Inclined to Elevate Tension than Blink,'" *Business Insider*, August 6, 2018, https://www.businessinsider.com/ trump-china-trade-war-tariffs-no-end-2018-8; "The Trade War Is On: Timeline of How We Got Here and What's Next," *Bloomberg News*, July 6, 2018, https://www.bloomberg.com/ news/articles/2018-07-06/the-trade-war-is-on-timeline-of-how-we-got-here-and-what-s-next.

2. Shrutee Sarkar, "Economists United: Trump Tariffs Won't Help the Economy," *Reuters*, March 13, 2018, https://www.reuters.com/article/ us-usa-economy-poll-economists-united-trump-tariffs-wont-help-the-economy-idUSKCN1GQ02G; "Most Americans Concerned About U.S.–China Trade War," *Rasmussen Reports*, July 16, 2018, http://www .rasmussenreports.com/public_ content/business/general_business/ july_2018/most_americans_concerned_ about_u_s_china_trade_war; "NBC News/*Wall Street Journal* Poll Conducted by Hart Research Associates (D) and Public Opinion Strategies (R), July 15–18, 2018. *N* = 900 Registered Voters Nationwide. Margin of error ffl 3.3," *PollingReport.com*, http://www .pollingreport.com/trade.htm.

3. Michael Birnman, "'Dear America, Appreciate Your Allies. After All, You Don't Have that Many,' E.U. Leader Warns Trump," *Washington Post*, July 10, 2018, https://www.washingtonpost.com/ news/worldviews/wp/2018/07/10/ dear-america-appreciate-your-allies-after-all-you-dont-have-that-many-e-u-leader-warns-trump/?utm_term= .cc67e39d3540; For Trump Tweet, see "Jamie Ehrlich, "Trump Tweaks EU Before Landing in Brussels," *CNN Politics*, July 10, 2018, https://www.cnn .com/2018/07/10/politics/tusk-european-council-nato-trump/index.html.

4. John Ikenberry, "The Security Trap," *Democracy: A Journal of Ideas* 1, no. 2 (Fall 2006), https://democracyjournal.org/magazine/2/ the-security-trap/.

5. See, John Tirman, *The Death of Others: The Faith of Civilians in America's Wars* (New York: Oxford University Press, 2012); Philip Bump, 15 Years After the Iraq War Began, the Death Toll Is Still Murky, *Washington Post*, March 20, 2018, https://www .washingtonpost.com/news/politics/ wp/2018/03/20/15-years-after-it-began-the-death-toll-from-the-iraq-war-is-still-murky/?utm_term= .e6344da7cb80; For an analysis of civilian casualty estimates, see the MIT Center for International Studies, "Iraq: The Human Cost," http://web .mit.edu/humancostiraq/.

6. Paul Pierson, "Increasing Returns, Path Dependence, and the Study of Politics," *American Political Science Review* 94, no. 2 (June, 2000): 251–67.

7. Joseph Nye, *Soft Power: The Means to Success in World Politics* (New York: Public Affairs Books, 2004).

8. This figure excludes military aid. See James McBride, "How Does the US Spend its Foreign Aid?" *Council on Foreign Relations*. https://www.cfr.org/backgrounder/ how-does-us-spend-its-foreign-aid

9. Rob Smith, "The World's Biggest Economies in 2018," *World Economic Forum*, April 18, 2018, https://www .weforum.org/agenda/2018/04/the-worlds-biggest-economies-in-2018/.

10. See Charles Mayer, *Among Empires: American Ascendancy and Its Predecessors* (Cambridge, MA: Harvard University Press, 2007).

11. Paul Krugman, "How Did Economists Get It So Wrong?," *New York Times Magazine*, September 2, 2009.

12. Javier E. David, "Trump Issues Challenge to Trading Partners: Bring Down Barriers or Face 'Reciprocity,'" June 24, 2018, *CNBC*, https:// www.cnbc.com/2018/06/24/trump-challenges-trading-partners-on-trade-barriers.html.

13. Doron Levin, "Want to Sink Detroit Automakers? Make a Trade Deal that Weakens U.S. Tariff Protecting Pickups, *Forbes*, March 27, 2018, https://www.forbes.com/ sites/doronlevin/2018/03/27/ want-to-sink-detroit-automakers-make-a-trade-deal-that-weakens-tariff-protecting-pickups/.

14. See the detailed analysis of energy sources in "The United States Is Projected to Become a Net Energy Exporter in Most AEO2018 Cases," U.S Energy Information Administration, February 2, 2018, https://www .eia.gov/todayinenergy/detail .php?id=34912.

15. George Washington, "First Inaugural Address, in the City of New York," April 30, 1789, http://www.bartleby. com/124/pres13.html; see also, Alexander Hamilton, *Federalist* no. 1.

16. President Woodrow Wilson, "Joint Address to Congress Leading to Declaration of War Against Germany (1917)," April 2, 1917, https://www .ourdocuments.gov/doc_large_image .php?doc=61; Hillary Clinton, *Hard Choices* (New York: Simon & Schuster, 2014), p. 566.

17. On foreign policy and American exceptionalism, see Kalevi Holsti, *Kalevi Holsti: A Pioneer in International Relations Theory, Foreign Policy, Analysis, History of International Order, and Security Studies* (New York: Springer, 2016), chap. 8.

18. For an introduction to American exceptionalism, see Martin Lipsett, *American Exceptionalism: A Double Edged Sword* (New York: Norton, 1996); Godfrey Hodgson, *The Myth of American Exceptionalism* (New Haven: Yale University Press, 2010)

19. For a recent summary of "democratic peace" debates in political science, see Alex Weisiger and Erik Gartzke, "Debating the Democratic Peace in the International System," *International Organization* 60 (2016), http://dx.doi.org/10.1093/isq/sqw022.

20. Richard Wike, Bruce, Stokes, Jacob Poushter, and Janell Fetterolf, "Worldwide, Few Confident in Trump or His Policies," Pew Research Center, June 26, 2017, http://www.pewglobal .org/2017/06/26/worldwide-few-confident-in-trump-or-his-policies/.

21. "Legal Immigration and Adjustment of Status Report Fiscal Year 2018, Quarter 1," Homeland Security, July 12, 2018, https://www.dhs.gov/ immigration-statistics/ special-reports/legal-immigration.

22. George Washington, Farewell Address: To the People of the United

States, September 19, 1796, http:// avalon.law.yale.edu/18th_century/ washing.asp.

23. A thoughtful summary appears in Richard Falk, "An Unlikely AMEXIT: Pivoting Away from the Middle East: The Case for Disengagement," *Global Justice in the 21st Century* (blog), July 14, 2016, http://bit.ly/2a8JoEz.

24. Philip Lohaus, "The Foreign Policy Message Millennials Need," *U.S. News & World Report*, April 13, 2016, http://bit.ly/29nm2Wn.

25. Ken Waltz, "Why Iran Should Get the Bomb," *Foreign Affairs*, July/August 2012; John Mearsheimer, "Here We Go Again," opinion, *New York Times*, May 17, 1998, http://www.nytimes.com/1998/05/17/opinion/here-we-go-again.html.

26. ²⁶William J Perry, "The Risk of Nuclear Catastrophe is Greater than During the Cold War, *HuffPost*, January 20, 2016, https://www.huffingtonpost.com/william-jperry/nuclear-catastrophe-risk_b_9019558.html

27. David Sanger, *The Perfect Weapon: War, Sabotage and Fear in the Cyber Age* (New York: Crown, 2018); Brian Naylor, "Russia Hacked U.S. Power Grid—So What Will the Trump Administration Do About It?" *NPR*, March 23, 2018, https://www.npr.org/2018/03/23/596044821/russia-hacked-u-s-power-grid-so-what-will-the-trump-administration-

do-about-it?t=1533679209110; Kate O'Flaherty, "Cyber Warfare: The Threat From Nation States," *Forbes*, May 3, 2018, https://www.forbes.com/sites/kateoflahertyuk/2018/05/03/cyber-warfare-the-threat-from-nation-states/#1e4d145c1c78; "Russian Government Cyber Activity Targeting Energy and Other Critical Infrastructure Sectors," Alert (TA18–074A), US Computer Emergency Readiness Team, March 15, 2018; "Joint US–UK Statement on Malicious Cyber Activity Carried Out by Russian Government," National Cyber Security Centre, April 16, 2018, https://www.ncsc.gov.uk/news/joint-us-uk-statement-malicious-cyber-activity-carried-out-russian-government.

28. These categories are adopted from Walter Russell Mead, *Special Providence: American Foreign Policy and How It Changed the World* (New York: Routledge, 2001).

29. "Tracker: Current U.S Ambassadors." *American Foreign Service Association*. September 13, 2018. http://www.afsa.org/list-ambassadorial-appointments

30. David Barno and Nora Bensahel, "Six Ways to Fix the Army's Culture," *War on the Rocks,* September 6, 2016, https://warontherocks.com/2016/09/six-ways-to-fix-the-armys-culture/.

31. Woodrow Wilson, "First Inaugural Address," March 4, 1913, http://www.pbs.org/wgbh/

americanexperience/features/primary-resources/tr-woodrow/.

32. Robert Mann, *A Grand Delusion: America's Descent into Vietnam* (New York: Basic Books, 2002), 24.

33. President Harry Truman, "The Truman Doctrine: Address Before a Joint Session of Congress," March 12, 1947, Washington DC.

34. Arthur Vandenberg, *American Foreign Policy, January 10, 1945 (in the Senate),* http://www.senate.gov/artandhistory/history/resources/pdf/VandenbergSpeech.pdf.

35. President George W. Bush, Graduation Address, United States Military Academy, June 1, 2002, https://georgewbush-whitehouse.archives.gov/news/releases/2002/06/20020601-3.html.

36. "Celebrating the History of ICE," Department of Homeland Security, December 7, 2017, https://www.ice.gov/features/history.

37. Hal Brands, "Breaking Down Obama's Grand Strategy," *The National Interest*, June 23, 2014; both Obama quotes are cited here: https://dukespace.lib.duke.edu/dspace/bitstream/handle/10161/8917/Breaking%20Down%20Obama%27s%20Grand%20Strategy%20_%20The%20National%20Interest.pdf?sequence=1.

38. Gideon Rose, "Which World Are We Living in Now," *Foreign Affairs* 97, no. 4 (July/August 2018): 8.

Credits

Photos

About the Authors

p. xviii: Gabby Salazar; p. xviii: WFU/Ken Bennett

Chapter 1

P. 2: Chip Somodevilla/Getty Images; p. 4: Bettman/Getty Images, Pat Benic/dpa picture alliance/Alamy Stock Photo; p. 6 RHONA WISE/AFP/Getty Images; p. 8: Jacob Byk/The Wyoming Tribune Eagle via AP; p. 9: MATTES René/hemis.fr via Getty Images; p. 10: AP Photo/Suzanne Plunkett; p. 11: pixelheadphoto/iStock.com, Jim West/Alamy Stock Photo, Huntington Beach Police Department via AP; p. 13: © Tribune Content Agency, LLC. All Rights Reserved. Reprinted with permission.; p. 16: bauhaus1000/Getty Images.

Chapter 2

p. 22: Courtesy of the U.S. Air Force. Photo by Staff Sergeant Aaron D. Allmon II.; p. 25: Bettman/Getty Images; p. 26: Universal History Archive/Getty Images; p. 30: REUTERS/Jason Redmond; p. 35: AP Photo/David J. Phillip; p. 38: Win McNamee/Getty Images, Justin Sullivan/Getty Images; p. 39: MPI/Stringer/Getty Images; p. 46: Danny Johnston/ASSOCIATED PRESS, Ian West/PA Archive/PA Images; p. 51: DOONESBURY © 2011 G. B. Trudeau. Reprinted with permission of ADREWS MCMEEL SYNDICATION. All rights reserved.; p. 52: AP Photo/Josh Boak.

Chapter 3

p. 56: Hank Walker/The LIFE Picture Collection/Getty Images; p. 60: Library of Congress Prints and Photographs Division, LC-USZC4-7155; p. 61: *Twenty Brave Men*, a National Guard Heritage Painting by Jackson Walker, courtesy the National Guard Bureau.; p. 64: Image copyright © The Metropolitan Museum of Art. Image source: Art Resource, NY; p. 68: National Archives and Records Administration NAID 532935; p. 69: "Regulators" Artwork by Bryant White - www.whitehistoricart.com; p. 71: VCG Wilson/Corbis via Getty Images; p. 72: George Caleb Bingham, *The County Election*, 1852; p. 75: © Louis Glanzman; p. 80: Original Photographers: McPherson and Oliver; p. 87: SuperStock/Getty Images; p. 89: Sara Krulwich/The New York Times/Redux; p. 91: FatCamera/Getty Images.

Chapter 4

p. 98: REUTERS/Lucas Jackson TPX IMAGES OF THE DAY; p. 103: Michael Beiriger/Alamy Stock Photo; p. 109: Copyright © Chad Crowe.; p. 111: Bettman/Getty Images; p. 113: A 1949 Herblock Cartoon, © The Herb Block Foundation.; p. 115: ROB KERR/AFP/Getty Images; p. 116: Nick Anderson Editorial Cartoon used with the permission of Nick Anderson, the Washington Post Writers Group and the Cartoonist Group. All rights reserved.; p. 119: Andrew Harrer/Bloomberg via Getty Images; p. 122: Mitchell Leff/Getty Images.

Chapter 5

p. 124: Suzi Pratt/FilmMagic/Getty Images; p. 128: Nathan Benn/Corbis via Getty Image, Bettman/Getty Images; p. 131: © Steve Gates; p. 134: AP Photo/David J. Phillip; p. 135: AP Photo/Harry Cabluck, AP Photo/Harry Cabluck; p. 136: AP Photo/Javier Galeano; p. 140: AP Photo/Alaric Lambert; p. 141: Brendan Hickey/Wikimedia Commons; p. 142: Mark Peterson/Redux, AP Photo/Texas Department of Motor Vehicles; p. 143: Clay Good/Zuma Press; p. 144: Niko Tavernise/20th Century Fox; p. 146: Antonio de Moraes Barros Filho/WireImage/Getty Images; p. 147: REUTERS/Jason Miczek; p. 152: Bettman/Getty Images; p. 156: Gina Ferazzi / Los Angeles Times via Getty Images.

Chapter 6

p. 160: Chip Somodevilla/Getty Images; p. 164: Bettman/Getty Images; p. 165: Paula Bronstein/Getty Images; p. 171: Library of Congress, Prints & Photographs Division, Visual Materials from the NAACP Records [LC-USZ62-116927]; p. 172: Bettman/Getty Images, Bettman/Getty Images; p. 173: AP Photo/File; p. 176: The Soiling of Old Glory, StanelyFormanPhotos.com; p. 177: AP Photo/Jacquelyn Martin; p. 180: © Aaron Doster-USA TODAY Sports; p. 184: Photo by Adam Jones, PhD/Wikimedia Commons; p. 188: AP Photo/Matt Rourke; p. 189: Fotosearch/Stringer/Getty Images; p. 191: Frontier Forts; p. 192: Hannah Foslien/Getty Images.

Chapter 7

p. 202: REUTERS/Robert Galbraith/File photo; p. 206: AP Photo/Julio Cortez; p. 209: Photo by Paul Drinkwater/NBCUniversal via Getty Images; p. 213: Copyright © 2006 Jake Fuller; p. 219: iStock.com/mamado; p. 220: AP Photo/Charlotte Observer, Diedra Laird; p. 222: Douglas Graham/Roll Call/Getty Images.

Chapter 8

p. 226: AP Photo/Chris O'Meara; p. 228: Via @Alyssa_Milano on Twitter; p. 230: Jessica McGowan/Getty Images; p. 231: AP Photo/The Brownsville Herald, Brad Doherty; p. 237: AP Photo/Files; p. 238: Salwan Georges/For the Washington Post via Getty Images, Photo by Timothy Hiatt/Getty Images; p. 240: via YouTube; p. 244: AP Photo/Pablo Martinez Monsivais; p. 248: via NBC News.

(w/c on paper), Waterhouse, C.H. (fl.1812) / Private Collection / Peter Newark Historical Pictures / Bridgeman Images; p. 577: AP Photo/Xinhua, Gao Haorong, Korea Pool/Yonhap via AP, File; p. 580: Mark Wilson/Getty Images; p. 588: dpa/picture-alliance/dpa/AP Images; p. 590: KAREN BLEIER/ AFP/Getty Images.

Figures

Chapter 1
p. 12: Created by OUP based on data from Pew; p. 13: Created by OUP based on data from usgovernmentspending.com; p. 14: Created by OUP based on data from the OECD; p. 17: Created by OUP using data from the U.S. Census Bureau.

Chapter 2
p. 29: Source: NYConstitution.org, a project of the Howard Samuels New York Policy Center, Inc.; p. 37: Inglehart, R., C. Haerpfer, A. Moreno, C. Welzel, K. Kizilova, J. Diez-Medrano, M. Lagos, P. Norris, E. Ponarin & B. Puranen et al. (eds.). 2014. World Values Survey: Round Six - Country-Pooled Datafile Version: http://www.worldvaluessurvey.org/WVSDocumentationWV6.jsp. Madrid: JD Systems Institute.; p. 42: Created by OUP based on data from Robert Frank, Falling Behind. University of California Press, 2007., Created by OUP based on data from Elizabeth Sawhill and John Morton, Economic Mobility: Is the American Dream Alive and Well? Economic Mobility Project, Pew Charitable Trusts; Larry Bartells, Unequal Democracy (Princeton, NJ: Princeton University Press/ Russell Sage Foundation, 2008),; p. 43: Created by OUP using data from the Pew Research Center Global Attitudes Project. American Exceptionalism Subsides: The American-Western European Values Gap, November 17, 2011; updated February 29, 2012.; p. 49: Created by OUP based on data from the Pew Research Center.

Chapter 3
p. 62: Map by Miklos Pinther in *Atlas of Great Lakes Indian History*, edited by Helen Hornbeck Tanner. Copyright © 1987 by the University of Oklahoma Press, Norman. Reprinted by permission of the publisher.; Map by Miklos Pinther in *Atlas of Great Lakes Indian History*, edited by Helen Hornbeck Tanner. Copyright © 1987 by the University of Oklahoma Press, Norman. Reprinted by permission of the publisher.

Chapter 4
p. 102: Created by OUP using data from Gallup; p. 104: Created by OUP based on data from The Kaiser Family Foundation; p. 106: © Copyright 2018 athenahealth, Inc. All Rights Reserved.

Chapter 7
p. 204: Created by OUP based on data from the Pew Research Center; p. 207: Created by OUP based on data from the Pew Research Center; p. 210: Created by OUP based on data from the Pew Research Center; p. 212: Created by OUP based on data from the Pew Research Center; p. 214: Created by OUP based on data from the Pew Research Center; p. 215: Created by OUP based on data from the MEER Research Center.

Chapter 8
p. 234: Created by OUP based on data from the U.S. Census Bureau, Current Population Survey; p. 235: Created by OUP based on data from the Pew Research Center; p. 236: Copyright © 2018 The Human Rights Campaign. All Rights Reserved; p. 242-243: Pew Research Center; p. 245: Pew Research Center.

Chapter 9
P. 261: Pew Research Center

Chapter 15
P. 457: Source: Office of Personnel Management; U.S. Census.; p. 460: Source: US Department of Energy; p. 464: The Office of Management and Budget; p. 466: American Hospital Association; p. 474: Provided by authors, created by OUP.

Chapter 16
P. 490: Source: Gallup; p. 510: Created by OUP, data from Five Thirty Eight; p. 512: Created by OUP, data from Gallup.

Index

Note: Page references followed by a *t* indicate table; *f* indicate figure.